Fromme

Provence & the Riviera

Here's what the critics say about Frommer's:

"Amazingly easy to use. Very portable, very complete."
—Booklist

♦

"The only mainstream guide to list specific prices. The Walter Cronkite of guidebooks—with all that implies."
—Travel & Leisure

♦

"Complete, concise, and filled with useful information."
—New York Daily News

♦

"Hotel information is close to encyclopedic."
—Des Moines Sunday Register

♦

"Detailed, accurate and easy-to-read information for all price ranges."
—Glamour Magazine

Other Great Guides for Your Trip:

Frommer's France

Frommer's Born to Shop France

Frommer's Europe

Frommer's Europe from $60 a Day

Frommer's Gay & Lesbian Europe

Frommer's Europe's Greatest Driving Tours

Frommer's®

2nd
Edition

Provence & the Riviera

by Darwin Porter & Danforth Prince

IDG Books Worldwide, Inc.
An International Data Group company
Foster City, CA • Chicago, IL • Indianapolis, In • New York, NY

ABOUT THE AUTHORS

France and its southern tier are "second home" to **Darwin Porter,** a native of North Carolina, and **Danforth Prince,** who lived in France throughout most of his 20s. Darwin, who has worked in television advertising and as a bureau chief for the *Miami Herald* and who hopes someday to create a perfect bouillabaisse, wrote the original version of *Frommer's France.* Dan, who began his association with Darwin in 1982, worked for the Paris bureau of the *New York Times* between renovations of a historic building in the Loire Valley and bicycle trips through Provence and the Camargue. Both writers know southern France well, as they've made countless trips there, for both work and R&R.

IDG BOOKS WORLDWIDE, INC.

An International Data Group Company
919 E. Hillsdale Blvd.
Suite 400
Foster City, CA 91404

Find us online at **www.frommers.com**

ISBN 0-02-863087-4
ISSN 1094-7647

Editor: Ron Boudreau
Production Editor: Robyn Burnett
Photo Editor: Richard Fox
Design by Michele Laseau
Staff Cartographer: Roberta Stockwell
Additional cartography: Raffaele DeGenarro
Page creation by Sean Monkhouse, Natalie Evans, Ellen Considine, Carl Pierce
Front cover photo: A field of lavender, near Grasse

SPECIAL SALES

For general information on IDG Books Worldwide's books in the U.S., please call our Consumer Service department at 800/762-2979. For reseller information, including discounts, bulk sales, customized editions, and premium sales, please call our Reseller Customer Service department at 800/434-3422.

Manufactured in the United States of America

5 4 3 2 1

Contents

4   Provence   111

**5   The Western Riviera: From St-Tropez to
        Cannes to Cap d'Antibes   206**

6   The Eastern Riviera: From Biot to Monaco to Menton 267

Appendix: The South of France in Depth   343

Index   361

List of Maps

An Invitation to the Reader

In researching this book, we discovered many wonderful places—hotels, restaurants, shops, and more. We're sure you'll find others. Please tell us about them, so we can share the information with your fellow travelers in upcoming editions. If you were disappointed with a recommendation, we'd love to know that, too. Please write to:

Frommer's Provence & the Riviera, 2nd Edition
IDG Travel
1633 Broadway
New York, NY 10019

An Additional Note

Please be advised that travel information is subject to change at any time—and this is especially true of prices. We therefore suggest that you write or call ahead for confirmation when making your travel plans. The authors, editors, and publisher cannot be held responsible for the experiences of readers while traveling. Your safety is important to us, however, so we encourage you to stay alert and be aware of your surroundings. Keep a close eye on cameras, purses, and wallets, all favorite targets of thieves and pickpockets.

What the Symbols Mean

✪ Frommer's Favorites

Our favorite places and experiences—outstanding for quality, value, or both.

The following abbreviations are used for credit cards:

AE	American Express	EC	EuroCard
CB	Carte Blanche	JCB	Japan Credit Bank
DC	Diners Club	MC	MasterCard
ER	enRoute	V	Visa

Find Frommer's Online

Arthur Frommer's Budget Travel Online (**www.frommers.com**) offers more than 6,000 pages of up-to-the-minute travel information—including the latest bargains and candid, personal articles updated daily by Arthur Frommer himself. No other Web site offers such comprehensive and timely coverage of the world of travel.

The Best of Provence & the Riviera

Provence is one of the world's most evocative regions—both the western area, known as Provence, whose landscapes and magical light have seduced innumerable artists, and the eastern coastal area, known as the Riviera, whose beach resorts have seduced innumerable hedonists. Provence and the Riviera are beautiful, diverse, and culturally rich, offering everything from fabulous beaches to amazing art museums to white-hot nightlife to a distinctive cuisine that blends the best of the mountains and the sea.

As you're heading to the south of France to luxuriate in life along the sunny and sexy Mediterranean—not to exhaust yourself making difficult decisions—we've searched out the best deals and once-in-a-lifetime experiences for this book. What follows in this chapter is our roster of the best of the best, the kind of discoveries we'd share with our closest friends.

1 The Best Travel Experiences

- **Dining and Drinking Provence Style:** Many people flock to the south of France specifically to enjoy *cuisine Provençale,* a Mediterranean mix of bold flavors with an emphasis on garlic, olive oil, and aromatic local herbs like thyme and basil. The world's greatest bouillabaisse is made here, especially in Marseille; Provençal lamb is among the best in France; and the vegetables (such as asparagus, eggplant, tomatoes, and artichokes) will make you realize that this is France's market garden. The regional wines, though not equaling those of Bordeaux and Burgundy, are the perfect accompaniment, ranging from the warm, full-bodied Châteauneuf-du-Pape to the rare, choice Bellet, produced on Nice's hill slopes. See chapter 3.
- **Partying in the Land of Festivals:** Provence is called the Land of Festivals with good reason: It hosts some 500 with an astonishing 4,000 events. Of course, the ultimate example is the you-won't-believe-it-until-you've-seen-it Cannes Film Festival in May. July and August are the busiest months, as Aix-en-Provence, Toulon, and Nice host jazz festivals and Nîmes and Arles stage theater and dance performances. On May 16, St-Tropez's riotous *bravades* honor the saint in theory but are really just an excuse for revelry. Many festivals have deep roots in Provençal folklore, honoring the bounty of earth and sea: the wine harvest in numerous villages, the rice harvest in Languedoc's Camargue, and the apple

harvest in Peyruis. Everything seems to end in a feast where the wine and pastis flow. Contact any tourist office for the free booklet *Provence—Terre de Festivals*. See chapter 2.

- **Breaking the Bank at Monte Carlo:** Few other casinos can match the excitement generated at the Monte Carlo Casino. The world's wealthy flocked to Monaco when the casino was opened by Charles Garnier in 1878. But since 1891 much of the non-wealthy world has followed—even those who can't afford losses. During a 3-day gambling spree that year, an American, Charles Deville Wells, turned $400 into $40,000, an astonishing amount back then. His feat was immortalized in the song "The Man Who Broke the Bank at Monte Carlo." Even if you do no more today than play the slot machines, a visit to this casino will be a highlight of your trip, as you bask amid the extravagant decor and under the gilded rococo ceilings. (Some not as lucky as Wells have leaped to their deaths from the casino windows or the "Suicide Terrace.") See chapter 6.

- **Sunning and Swimming on the Riviera Beaches:** There are greater beaches but none more fabled, overcrowded though they are. Most of them are sandy, except those stretching from Antibes to the Italian frontier, including Nice's. These are shingled (covered with coarse gravel), but that doesn't stop the world from flocking to them. A beach mattress fits just fine on the shingles, and there are umbrellas to rent when you want to escape the relentless sun. Along the Riviera, topless is almost universally accepted. Legend has it that it began with Brigitte Bardot, who pulled off her bra and said, "Let's wake up sleepy St-Trop." There are also nudist beaches, notably at Cap d'Agde and Port Cros. If you decide not to go topless or bottomless, you can still wear your most daring bikini or thong. Also see "The Best Beaches," below.

- **Following in the Footsteps of the Great Artists:** Modern art wasn't born in Provence, but artists from all over came here to paint its "glaring festive light." The good news is that most of them left behind fabulous legacies. Perhaps it all began when Monet arrived with Renoir in 1883. In time, they were followed by a host of others, including Bonnard, who took a villa in St-Tropez. Van Gogh arrived in Arles in 1888, and Gauguin showed up a few months later. Even the Fauves sought out this region, notably Matisse, whose masterpiece is his chapel at Vence. Not long afterward, Picasso arrived at Antibes. Deeply jealous of Picasso and Matisse, Chagall moved to Vence and was later infuriated that the street on which he lived was renamed avenue Henri-Matisse. He got over it and lived and painted on the Riviera until he died at 97.

- **Spending a Day in St-Rémy-de-Provence:** Our favorite town in Provence is St-Rémy. We're not alone in our enthusiasm, for we've spotted Princess Caroline here several times. Long before us, St-Rémy was known to Nostradamus, who was born here. Gertrude Stein and Alice B. Toklas liked to come down for tranquil visits. Tragically, van Gogh spent his last year near here in an asylum; his "cell" was later occupied by an interned German during World War I—Albert Schweitzer. To wander St-Rémy's streets is to recapture Provence's essence, especially its Vieille Ville (old town). After exploring its alleys, pause on one of its immaculate leafy squares. Then go in search of an art gallery or two and perhaps reward yourself with a painting and a memory. See chapter 4.

- **Having Fun Day and Night:** If nothing else, the Riviera is about the art of entertainment, both high and low. The Côte d'Azur offers not only beaches and race cars and yachts but also fêtes and festivals and even bullfights, real Spanish-style ones where the animals are killed, in the old Roman arenas at Arles and

The Regions of France

Nîmes. Glittering casinos are seemingly everywhere—Monte Carlo, Cannes, Cassis, and Beaulieu, to name a few. Many cities have elegant restaurants and opera houses with resident companies. But mainly the Riviera offers white-hot nightclubs and dance clubs for all sexes and sexual orientations, especially in Cannes, Nice, Monte Carlo, and St-Tropez. See chapters 5 and 6.

- **Absorbing a Unique Lifestyle:** Provence and Languedoc share a uniquely Mediterranean lifestyle. Compared to the rest of France, the air here is drier, the sun beats down more strongly, and the light beloved by so many painters appears clearer. Nothing could be more typical than a game of boules played under shade trees on a hot afternoon in a Provençal village. This is a place that respects time-honored crafts; Picasso might have arrived here a painter, but he left a potter. And nothing is finer in life than to be invited into a Provençal kitchen—the heart of family life—and smell the aroma of herbs and wines cooking with the catch of the day. To walk in the gardens, filled with vegetables, flowers, and fruit trees, is reason enough to visit. Attend a harvest, not just grapes, but perhaps linden blossoms. The dramatic landscape somehow seems at its most romantic when hit with the dreaded mistral winds blowing north from Africa. Discovering this land of ingrained traditions and making it your own is one of the great rewards of all European travel, especially if you go in the best months: May and September.

2 The Best Romantic Getaways

- **Les Baux** (Provence): Les Baux stands in a spectacular position on a promontory of sheer rock ravines. In the distance across the plain you can view the Val d'Enfer (Valley of Hell). After a turbulent history, the town today is one of the great escapes for the savvy French who can gaze from their windows on the thousands of olive trees (many planted by the Greeks) that produce the best oil in France. A pocket of posh, it has some of the country's grandest inns and finest cuisine. The most notable is **L'Oustau de Beaumanière,** Maussanel-les-Alpilles (☎ **04-90-54-33-07**)—after you and your loved one sample the ravioli with truffles, you'll understand why. See chapter 4.
- **Iles d'Hyères** (Provence): If an off-the-record weekend is what you have in mind, there's no better spot than what was known during the Renaissance as the "Iles d'Or," because of the golden glow of the island rocks in the sun. This string of enchanting little islands is 24 miles east-southeast of the port of Toulon. The largest and westernmost island is Ile de Porquerolles, thickly covered with heather, eucalyptus, and exotic shrubs. Ile de Port-Cros is hilly and mysterious, with spring-fed lush vegetation. The best spot for a romantic retreat is on this island—**Le Manoir** (☎ **04-94-05-90-53**), an 18th-century colonial-style mansion set in a park. See chapter 4.
- **Mougins** (Western Riviera): Only 5 miles north of Cannes, the once-fortified town of Mougins is a thousand years old, but never in its history has it been so popular as a place to enjoy the good life. Picasso, who could afford to live anywhere, chose a place nearby, Notre-Dame-de-Vie, to spend his last years. The wonderful old town is known for its cuisine, and Roger Vergé reigns supreme at his elegant **Le Moulin de Mougins** (☎ **04-93-75-78-24**). However, you can live for less at more secluded and less publicized oases. See chapter 5.
- **Peillon** (Eastern Riviera): Of all the "perched" villages (*villages perchés*) along the Côte d'Azur, this fortified medieval town on a craggy mountaintop, 12 miles northeast of Nice, is our favorite. It stands 1,000 feet above the Mediterranean. Peillon is the least spoiled of the perched villages and still boasts its medieval look, with covered alleys and extremely narrow streets. Tour buses avoid the place, but artists and writers flock there (we once spotted Françoise Sagan) to escape the mad carnival of the Riviera. For a cozy hideaway with your significant other, try the **Auberge de la Madone** (☎ **04-93-79-91-17**). Dinner for two on the terrace set among olive trees is the best way to start a romantic evening. See chapter 6.
- **Roquebrune and Cap-Martin** (Eastern Riviera): Along the Grande Corniche, Roquebrune is one of the most charming of the Côte d'Azur's villages, and its satellite resort of Cap-Martin occupies a lovely wooded peninsula. Between Monaco and Menton, these two have long been romantic retreats. The best choice for hiding away with that certain someone is the **Vista Palace,** Grande Corniche (☎ **800/223-6800** in the U.S., or 04-92-10-40-00), a modern luxury hotel clinging giddily to a cliffside over Monte Carlo. See chapter 6.

3 The Most Dramatic Countryside Drives

- **From Carcassonne to Albi** (Languedoc-Roussillon): From the walled city of Carcassonne, D118 takes you north into the Montagne Noire (Black Mountains), which are both arid and lush in parts, marking the southeastern extension of the Massif Central. You can spend a full day here exploring the Parc Régional du Haut-Languedoc, crowned by the 3,700-foot Pic de Noire. You can base yourself in the old wool town of Mazamet and have lunch here before continuing northwest on N112 to Castres with its Goya Museum. Then you can continue exploring the surrounding area or head for Albi, 25 miles away, the hometown of Toulouse-Lautrec. See chapter 3.

- **From St-Rémy-de-Provence to Eygalières** (Provence): A 40-mile drive northeast of Arles takes you into some of the most dramatic and forlorn countryside in Provence, even to the Val d'Enfer (Valley of Hell). At the beginning of the tour, you pass Roman monuments before climbing into the hills with their distant views of the Parc Naturel Régional de la Camargue and Mont Ventoux. The tour, also takes you to Les Baux, the most dramatically situated town in Provence and today a gourmet citadel. After many turns and twists, you eventually reach the ancient village of Eygalières, with its medieval castle and church. See chapter 4.

- **Along the Ours Peak Road** (Western Riviera): The best driving tour in the area starts in St-Raphaël and lasts for only 35 miles, but because the terrain is so rough and torturous, allow at least 3 hours. The views are among the most dramatic along the Côte d'Azur, as you traverse a backdrop of the red porphyry slopes of Rastel d'Agay. Along the way you'll go through the passes of Evèque and Lentisques. Eventually, hairpin bends in the road lead to the summit of Ours Peak (Pic de l'Ours) at 1,627 feet, and you're rewarded with a superb panorama. See chapter 5.

- **From Vence to Grasse** (Western and Eastern Riviera): After calling on the Matisse chapel in Vence, you can take D2210 through some of the most luxuriant countryside along the French Riviera, with views of the Gorges du Loup, and stop over in the artisans' village of Tourrettes-sur-Loup, where the main street is filled with the ateliers of craftspeople. As you continue, follow the signs to Point-du-Loup and you'll be rewarded with a panorama of waterfalls, and will later pass fields of flowers that eventually will lead you to the perfume center of Grasse. See chapter 6.

- **From Nice to Mont Chauve** (Eastern Riviera): The hilltops surrounding Nice have long been known for their colorful villages and rural scenery. In our view, the best countryside and the best panoramas unfold by driving to Mont Chauve (Bald Mountain) across a circuit that traverses 33 miles. You can stop at several villages along the way, including Aspremont and Tourette-Levens. You'll even pass the Gorges du Gabres, with its sheer walls of limestone, before reaching the enchanting village of Falicon. Eventually you'll come to Mont Chauve. Allow at least 30 minutes to hike to the summit. See chapter 6.

4 The Best Beaches

- **La Côte Vermeille** (Languedoc-Roussillon): In contrast to the eastern Riviera's pebbly beaches, the Côte Vermeille is filled with sand stretching toward Spain's Costa Brava. The best place for fun in the sun is the 6-mile beach between the resorts of Leucate-Plage and Le Barcarès in the Pyrénées-Orientales district. The "Vermilion Coast" takes its name from the red-clay soil studded with the ubiquitous olive groves. Henri Matisse was so taken with the light on this coast that he painted it. See chapter 3.

- **Beaches of Ile de Porquerolles** (Provence): These beaches lie 15 minutes by ferry from the Giens peninsula east of Toulon. One of the Iles d'Hyères (see "The Best Romantic Getaways," above), Porquerolles is only 5 miles long and some 1½ miles across and enjoys national-park status. Its beaches, along the northern coast facing the mainland, get 275 days of sunshine annually. There are several white-sand beaches; the best are Plage d'Argent, Plage de la Courtade, and Plage de Notre-Dame. See chapter 4.

- **Plage de Tahiti** (St-Tropez, Western Riviera): And God created woman and man and all the other critters found on this sizzling sandy beach outside St-Tropez. Tahiti is France's most infamous beach, mainly because of all the topless or bottomless action going on. Ever since the days of Brigitte Bardot, this beach has been a favorite of movie stars. It's very cruisy, very animated, with a French non-chalance about nudity. If you bother to wear a bikini, it should be only the most daring. See chapter 5.

- **Plage Port Grimaud** (St-Tropez, Western Riviera): This long golden-sand beach is set against the backdrop of the urban architect François Spoerry's *cité lacustre,* facing St-Tropez. Spoerry created this 247-acre marine village inspired by an ancient fishing village—"the most magnificent fake since Disneyland." The world has since flocked to Port Grimaud and its beach, including homeowners like Joan Collins, who comes here to hide from the paparazzi. Some of the Riviera's most expensive yachts are tied up in the harbor. This beach isn't as decadent as those at St-Trop, but it does pick up the "overflow" on the see-and-be-seen circuit. See chapter 5.

- **The Beaches at Cannes** (Western Riviera): From the Palais des Festivals and west to Mandelieu, the beach at Cannes has real sand, not pebbles as at Nice. This beach resort offers a movable feast of high-fashion swimsuits. Ever since the 1920s, the word on the beach here has been: "Menton's dowdy. Monte's brass. Nice is rowdy. Cannes is class!" Along the fabled promenade, La Croisette, the white sands are littered with sunbeds and parasols rented at the beach concessions. The beach is actually divided into 32 sections, our favorites being Plages Gazagnaire, Le Zénith, and Waikiki. Some of the beaches are privately run, but the best public beach is in front of the Palais des Festivals. See chapter 5.

- **Monte-Carlo Beach** (at the Monaco border, Eastern Riviera): This beach, once frequented by Princess Grace, is actually on French soil. Of all the Riviera's beaches, this is the most fashionable, even though its sands are imported. The property adjoins the ultra-chic **Monte-Carlo Beach Hotel,** 22 av. Princesse-Grace (☎ **04-93-28-66-66**). The great months to be here are July and August, when you never know who's likely to be sharing the sands with you—perhaps Luciano Pavarotti or Claudia Schiffer. The main topic on the beach? Both legal and funny money. See chapter 6.

5 The Best Offbeat Experiences

- **Spending a Night in Aigues-Mortes** (Languedoc-Roussillon): St. Louis sailed from this port to fight in the Crusades to the east. He died in Tunis in 1270, but his successor, Philip III, held this port, the only stretch of the Mediterranean in French hands at the time. Great walls were built around the town, and ships all the way from Antioch used to anchor here. But beginning around the mid-14th century, Aigues-Mortes began to live up to its name of "dead waters," as the harbor filled with silt and the waters receded. Today it sits marooned in time and space right in the muck of the advancing Rhône delta. Nothing along the coast is as evocative of the Middle Ages as this town, where you can walk along its walls and slumber in one of its inns. See chapter 3.

- **Checking In and Stripping Down** (Cap d'Agde, Languedoc-Roussillon): Except in foul weather, it's compulsory to walk around nude in the holiday town on the outskirts of Cap d'Agde. You'll have to check your apparel at the gate. Along the Languedoc coast, between the Rhône delta and Béziers, Cap d'Agde was constructed like a pastiche of a local fishing village, similar to Port Grimaud near St-Tropez. At its outskirts is a town with supermarkets, nightclubs, a casino, and rooms for 20,000 bodies—nude bodies. See chapter 3.

- **Exploring Les Calanques** (between Marseille and Cassis, Provence): At the old fishing port of Cassis, with its white cliffs and beaches that were a favorite of Fauve painters, you can rent a boat and explore the Calanques, small fjords along the rugged coast. Covered with gorse and heather, the white cliffs form a backdrop for this adventure. By car from Cassis you can drive to the creek of Port Miou, with its rock quarries. To reach the Port Pin and En Vau creeks farther west, you must travel on foot (trails are well signposted). You can, however, take one of the boat excursions that leave regularly from Cassis. If you go on your own (not on the boat) you can take a picnic and spend the day skinny-dipping in these cool crystal waters. See chapter 4.

- **Searching for the Unknown Masterpiece of Edith Wharton** (Hyères, Provence): *The Age of Innocence* was Miss Wharton's best-known masterpiece, but her relatively unknown masterpiece, *La Solitude,* stands in Hyères, the oldest of all Côte d'Azur resorts. Over the years the resort attracted everybody from Napoléon to Queen Victoria before falling out of fashion. Miss Wharton fell in love with Hyères and stayed there to create 28 terraced acres of gardens that you can visit today. See chapter 4.

6 The Best Small Towns

- **Cordes-sur-Ciel** (Languedoc-Roussillon): Perched like an eagle's nest on a hilltop, Cordes is an arts-and-crafts town, its ancient houses on narrow streets filled with artisans plying their trades. Once fabled in France for the brilliance of its silks, today it's a sleepy town 15½ miles northwest of Albi, the city of Toulouse-Lautrec. Ideally, you should visit Cordes as a side trip from Albi, but you may become enchanted with the place, as did François Mitterrand and Albert Camus before you, and decide to stop over in this town of a hundred Gothic arches. See chapter 3.

- **Uzès** (Provence): It's with good reason that this town of lofty towers and narrow streets was selected for the location of Jean-Paul Rappeneau's *Cyrano de Bergerac,* starring Gérard Depardieu. Uzès is a gem, a bit of a time capsule. Racine once lived here and was inspired by the town to write his only comedy, *Les Plaideurs.* André Gide also found a home in this "dream of the Middle Ages." Once Louis XIII called Uzès "the premier duchy of France." You can see why by staying at the stately 18th-century Château d'Arpaillargues. See chapter 4.

- **Gordes** (Provence): One of the best known of Provence's hill villages, Gordes, east of Avignon, is deservedly called *le plus beau village de France.* Today an escape for in-the-know Parisians, it's a town of silk painters, weavers, and potters. The setting is bucolic, between the Coulon valley and the Vaucluse plateau. Houses built of golden stone rise to the Renaissance château crowning the top. The late artist, Victor Vasarély, lived here in a fortified château that has been turned into a museum displaying much of his work. See chapter 4.

- **Roussillon** (Provence): Northeast of Gordes, Roussillon stands on a hilltop in the heart of "ocher country," where the earth is a bright red (*roussillon* means "russet"). This ancient village boasts houses in every shade of burnt orange, dusty pink, and russet red—they take on a particular brilliance at sunset. Roussillon, however, is no longer the sleepy village described in Laurence Wylie's 1961 *Village in the Vaucluse.* Artists, writers, and trendy Parisians have discovered its charms, and today many use it as their second home. See chapter 4.

- **Roquebrune** (Eastern Riviera): This medieval hill village southwest of Menton is the finest along the Côte d'Azur. It has been extensively restored, and not even the souvenir shops can spoil its charm. Steep stairways and alleys lead up to its feudal castle crowning the village. But before heading here, take in rue Moncollet, flanked by houses from the Middle Ages. This castle, dating from the 10th century, is the oldest in France—in fact, it's the only Carolingian castle left standing. See chapter 6.

7 The Best Châteaux & Palaces

- **Château d'If** (off Marseille, Provence): One of France's most notorious fortresses, this was the famous state prison whose mysterious guest was the Man in the Iron Mask. Alexandre Dumas père's *Count of Monte Cristo* made the legend famous around the world. It doesn't really matter that the story was apocryphal: People flock here because they believe it, just as they go to Verona to see where Romeo and Juliet lived and loved and died. The château was built by François I in 1524 as part of the defenses of Marseille. To reach it, you take a boat in the harbor to the islet 2 miles offshore. See chapter 4.

- **Palais des Papes** (Avignon, Provence): This was the seat of Avignon's brief golden age as the capital of Christendom. From 1352 to 1377, seven popes—all French—ruled here, a period called "the Babylonian Captivity." And they lived with pomp and circumstance, knowing "fleshly weaknesses." The Italian poet Petrarch denounced the palace as "the shame of mankind, a sink of vice." Even after Gregory XI was persuaded to return to Rome, some cardinals remained, electing their own pope or "anti-pope," who was finally expelled by force in 1403. See chapter 4.

- **Château de La Napoule** (La Napoule, Western Riviera): The Riviera's most eccentric château is also the most fascinating. This great medieval castle was purchased in 1917 by American sculptor Henry Clews, heir to a banking fortune. He lived, worked, and was buried here in 1937. In this castle, Crews created his own grotesque menagerie—scorpions, pelicans, gnomes, monkeys, lizards, whatever came to his tortured mind. His view of feminism? A distorted suffragette depicted in his *Cat Woman.* He likened himself to Don Quixote. See chapter 5.

- **Palais du Prince** (Monte Carlo, Monaco, Western Riviera): The world has known greater palaces, but this Italianate one on The Rock houses the man who presides over the tiny but incredibly rich principality of Monaco, Europe's second-smallest state. As head of the House of Grimaldi, Prince Rainier III (alas, without his Princess Grace) sits on the throne, wondering if his heir apparent, Prince Albert, now in his 40s, will ever get married and produce an heir. (Without a male heir, Monaco will revert back to France.) When the prince is here, a flag will be flying and you can watch the changing of the guard. The throne room is decorated with paintings by Holbein, Brueghel, and others, and in one wing of the palace is a museum devoted to souvenirs of Napoléon. See chapter 6.

- **Villa Kerylos** (Beaulieu, Eastern Riviera): This villa is a faithful reconstruction of an ancient Greek palace, built between 1902 and 1908 by the archaeologist Théodore Reinach. Reinach, a bit of an eccentric, lived here for 20 years, preferring to take baths and eat and dress with his male friends (who pretended to be Athenian citizens), while segregating the women to separate suites. Designated a historic monument of France, with its white, yellow, and lavender Italian marble and its ivory and bronze copies of vases and mosaics, Kérylos is a visual knockout. The parties that went on here are legendary. See chapter 6.

8 The Best Museums

- **Musée Toulouse-Lautrec** (Albi, Languedoc-Roussillon): This museum displays the world's greatest collection from this crippled genius, who immortalized cancan dancers, cafe demimonde, and prostitutes. In the brooding 13th-century Palais de la Berbie in the artist's hometown, the "red city" of Albi, this museum takes you into the special but tortured world of Toulouse-Lautrec. Particularly memorable are the posters that marked the beginning of an entirely new art form. When he died, his family donated the works remaining in his studio. See chapter 3.

- **Musée Picasso** (Antibes, Western Riviera): After the bleak war years in Paris, Picasso returned to the Mediterranean in 1945. He didn't have a studio, so the curator of this museum offered him space. Picasso labored here for several months—it was one of his most creative periods. At the end of his stay, he astonished the curator by leaving his entire output on permanent loan to the museum, along with some 200 ceramics he produced at Vallauris. This museum reveals Picasso in an exuberant mood, as evoked by his fauns and goats in cubist style, his still lifes of sea urchins, and his masterful *Ulysses et ses Sirènes*. A much-reproduced photograph displayed here shows him holding a sunshade for his lover, Françoise Gilot. See chapter 5.

- **Musée Ile-de-France** (St-Jean-Cap-Ferrat, Eastern Riviera): Baronne Ephrussi de Rothschild left a treasure trove of art and artifacts to the Institut de France on her death in 1934. The Villa Ephrussi, the 1912 palace that contains these pieces, reveals what a woman with unlimited wealth and highly eclectic tastes can collect. It's all here: paintings by Carpaccio and other masters of the Venetian Renaissance; canvases by Sisley, Renoir, and Monet; Ming vases; Dresden porcelain; and more. An eccentric, she named her house after the ocean liner *Ile de France* and insisted that her 35 gardeners dress as sailors. The baronne lived here for only 3 years before moving to Monaco. See chapter 6.

- **Musée des Beaux-Arts** (Nice, Eastern Riviera): In the former home of the Ukrainian Princess Kotchubey, the collection comes as an unexpected delight, with not only many belle époque paintings but also modern works, including an impressive number by Sisley, Braque, Degas, and Monet, plus Picasso ceramics. There's whimsy too, especially the sugar-sweet canvases by Jules Chéret, who died in Nice in 1932. Well represented also are the Van Loo family, a clan of Dutch descent whose members worked in Nice. The gallery of sculptors honors Rude, Rodin, and J. B. Carpeaux. See chapter 6.

- **Fondation Maeght** (St-Paul-de-Vence, Eastern Riviera): One of Europe's greatest modern-art museums, this foundation is remarkable for both its setting and its art. Built in 1964, the avant-garde building boasts a touch of fantasy, topped by two inverted domes. The colorful canvases radiate with the joy of life. All your favorites are likely to be here: Bonnard, Braque, Soulages, Chagall, Kandinsky, and more. Stunningly designed is a terraced garden that's a setting for Calder murals, Hepworth sculptures, and the fanciful fountains and colorful mosaics of Miró. A courtyard is peopled with Giacometti figures that look like gigantic emaciated chessmen. See chapter 6.

- **Musée National Fernand-Léger** (Biot, Eastern Riviera): Ridiculed as a Tubist, Léger survived many of his most outspoken critics and went on to win great fame. This museum was built by Léger's widow, Nadia, after his death in 1955, and it became one of the first in France dedicated to a single artist. It owns some 300 of Léger's highly original works. You wander into a dazzling array of robot-like figures, girders, machines, cogs, and cubes. The museum allows you to witness how he changed over the years, dabbling first in impressionism, as shown by his 1905 *Portrait de l'oncle.* Our favorite here—and one of our favorite artworks along the Riviera—is Léger's *Mona Lisa,* contemplating a set of keys with a wide-mouthed fish dangling at an angle over her head. See chapter 6.

9 The Best Cathedrals & Churches

- **Basilique St-Sernin** (Toulouse, Languedoc-Roussillon): Consecrated in 1096, this is the largest and finest Romanesque church extant. It was built to honor the memory of a Gaulish martyr, St. Sernin, and was for a long time a major stop on the pilgrimage route to Santiago de Compostela in Spain. The octagonal bell tower is particularly evocative, with five levels of twin brick arches. Unusual for a Romanesque church, St-Sernin has five naves. The crypt, where the saint is buried, is a treasure trove of ecclesiastical artifacts, some from the days of Charlemagne. See chapter 3.
- **Cathédrale St-Jean** (Perpignan, Languedoc-Roussillon): In 1324, Sancho of Aragón began this cathedral, but the consecration didn't come until its completion in 1509. Despite the different builders and architects over the decades, it emerged as one of Languedoc's most evocative cathedrals. The bell tower contains a great bell that dates from the 1400s (it's held in a wrought-iron cage from the 1700s). The single nave is typical of church construction in the Middle Ages, and is enhanced by the altarpieces of the north chapels and the high altar, the work of the 1400s and the 1500s. See chapter 3.
- **Cathédrale St-Just** (Narbonne, Languedoc-Roussillon): Though construction on this cathedral, begun in 1272, was never completed, it's an enduring landmark. Construction had to be halted 82 years later to prevent breaching the city's ancient ramparts to make room for the nave. In High Gothic style, the vaulting in the choir soars to 130 feet. Battlements and loopholes crown the towering arches of the apse. The cathedral's greatest treasure is the evocative *Tapestry of the Creation,* woven in silk and gold thread. See chapter 3.
- **Cathédrale Notre-Dame** (Avignon, Provence): Next to the Palais des Papes, this was a luminous Romanesque structure before baroque artists took over. It was partially reconstructed from the 14th to the 17th century. In 1859, it was topped by a tall gilded statue of the Virgin, which earned it harsh criticism from many architectural critics. The cathedral houses the tombs of two popes, John XXII and Benedict XII. You'd think this cathedral would be more impressive because of its role in papal history, but it appears that far more time and money went into the construction of the papal palace. Nevertheless, the cathedral reigned during the heyday of Avignon. See chapter 4.

- **Basilique St-Victor** (Marseille, Provence): This is one of France's most ancient churches, first built in the 5th century by St. Cassianus to honor St. Victor, a 3rd-century martyr. The saint's church was destroyed by the Saracens, except for the crypt. In the 11th and 12th centuries, a fortified Gothic church was erected. In the crypt are both pagan and early Christian sarcophagi; those depicting the convening of the Apostles and the Companions of St. Maurice are justly renowned. See chapter 4.

10 The Best Vineyards

Southern France is home to thousands of vineyards, many of which are somewhat anonymous agrarian bureaucracies known as *cooperatives*. Employees at these cooperatives tend to be less enthusiastic about showing off their product than those who work at true vineyards, where the person pouring your *dégustation des vins* might be the son or daughter of one of the owners. At least in southern France, don't assume that just because the word *Château* appears in the name that there'll be a magnificent historic residence associated with the property. In some cases, the crenellated battlement you're looking for might be nothing more than a feudal ruin.

We selected the vineyards below because of the emotional involvement of their (private) owners, their degree of prestige, and in many cases, their architectural interest.

- **Château de Simone,** 13590 Meyreuil (☎ **04-42-66-92-58**): Simone is less than a mile north of Aix-en-Provence (take N7 toward Nice, then follow the signs to Trois Sautets). Its 40 acres of vineyards surround a small 18th-century palace that might have been transported unchanged from *La Belle du bois dormant.* You can't visit the interior, but you can buy vintages 3 years old or older for less than 100F ($17). The minimum purchase is six bottles of red, white, or rosé. Advance notification is important.

- **Château de Virant,** R.D. 10, 13680 Lançon-de-Provence (☎ **04-90-42-44-47**): Set 14 miles east of Aix-en-Provence and named after a nearby rock whose ruined feudal fortress is barely standing, this property produces Appellation d'Origine Contrôlée–designated Coteaux d'Aix-en-Provence as well as a translucent brand of olive oil from fruit grown on 40 of the vineyard's 200 acres. The English-speaking Cheylan family showcase a labyrinth of cellars dating from 1630 and 1890. Tours, tastings, and sales can all be arranged. Advance notification is wise.

- **Château de Calissane,** R.D. 10, 13680 Lançon-de-Provence (☎ **04-90-42-63-03**): On the premises is a substantial 18th-century château, a white-stone house sporting very old terra-cotta tiles and a sense of the ancien régime. Even older is the Gallo-Roman *oppidum Constantine,* a sprawling ruined fortress that you can visit if you obtain a special pass from the sales staff. Set amid the vineyards, it evokes old Provence. The white, rosé, and red Coteaux d'Aix-en-Provence and the two grades of olive oil produced by this property's 110 acres of vineyards and olive groves are sold in an outbuilding. Advance reservations are vital.

- **Château de Fonscolombe** (☎ **04-42-61-89-62**) and **Château de LaCoste** (☎ **04-42-61-89-98**), 13610 Le Puy Ste-Réparade: These vineyards are adjacent to each other, 12½ miles north of Aix-en-Provence. Fonscolombe controls 400 acres of vineyards, has an exterior-only view of an 18th-century manor house and its garden, and offers tours of a modern facility that's of interest to wine-industry professionals. LaCoste is smaller and less state-of-the-art, but offers an exterior view of a stone-sided villa that was built for a cardinal during the reign of the popes in Avignon. You can buy their red, white, and rosé wines. Advance notification is needed.

- **Château de Coussin,** R.N. 7, 13530 Trets (☎ **04-42-29-26-32**): This property, 10 miles east of Aix-en-Provence, is centered around a 16th-century manor whose stone facade bears geometric reliefs associated with Renaissance-era construction in Provence. The 600 acres of vineyards scattered over three neighboring regions have been owned by the same family for nearly a century. You can visit the château's interior (it even contains a vaulted cloister) only by special request, but the overview of the wine-making industry as shown within its bottling facility is worth the trip.

  On adjacent properties, two amiable competitors also offer wine tours to those who phone in advance: **Château de Grand'Boise,** 13530 Trets (☎ **04-42-29-22-95**), whose venerable château you can admire from the outside; and **Mas Cadenet Negrel,** 13530 Trets (☎ **04-42-29-51-59**), where a substantial Provençal farmhouse is the centerpiece for modern wine-making equipment that has produced many well-respected vintages.

11 The Best Luxury Hotels

- **Hôtel du Cap–Eden Roc** (Cap d'Antibes, Western Riviera; ☎ **04-93-61-39-01**): Looming large in F. Scott Fitzgerald's *Tender Is the Night,* this is the most stylish of the Côte's luxury palaces, standing at the tip of the Cap d'Antibes peninsula in its own 22-acre manicured garden. The hotel reflects the opulence of a bygone era and has catered to the rich and famous since it opened in 1870. Everybody has shown up here: from Haile Selassie to Betty Grable, from George Bernard Shaw to John F. Kennedy, from John Travolta to Madonna. See chapter 5.
- **Hôtel Carlton Intercontinental** (Cannes, Western Riviera; ☎ **800/327-0200** in the U.S., or 04-93-06-40-06): A World War II Allied commander issued orders to bombers to avoid hitting the Carlton "because it's such a good hotel." The 1912 hotel survived the attack and today is at its most frenzied during the annual film festival. Taste and subtlety aren't what the Carlton is about—it's all glitter, glitterati, and glamour, the most splendid of the area's architectural "wedding cakes." The white-turreted doyenne presides over La Croisette like some permanent sand castle. See chapter 5.
- **Grand Hôtel du Cap-Ferrat** (St-Jean-Cap-Ferrat, Eastern Riviera; ☎ **04-93-76-50-50**): The Grand Hôtel, built in 1908, competes with the Hôtel du Cap–Eden Roc as the Riviera's most opulent. Set in a well-manicured 14-acre garden, it was once a winter haven for royalty. It was totally refurbished in 1990. This pocket of posh has it all, including a private beach club with a heated seawater pool and a Michelin-starred restaurant utilizing market-fresh ingredients. See chapter 6.
- **Hostellerie du Château de la Chèvre d'Or** (Eze, Eastern Riviera; ☎ **04-93-10-66-66**): In striking contrast to the palaces above, this gem of an inn lies in a medieval village 1,300 feet above sea level. Following in the footsteps of former guests like Roger Moore and Elizabeth Taylor, you can stay in this artistically converted medieval château. All its elegant rooms open onto vistas of the Mediterranean. Everything here has a refreshingly rustic appeal rather than false glitter. As the paparazzi catch you sipping a champagne cocktail by the pool, you'll know you've achieved Côte d'Azur chic. See chapter 6.
- **Hôtel de Paris** (Monte Carlo, Monaco, Eastern Riviera; ☎ **92-16-30-00**): The 19th-century aristocracy flocked here, and though the hotel isn't quite that fashionable anymore, it's still going strong. Onassis, Sinatra, and Churchill long ago checked out, but today's movers and shakers still pull up in limousines with tons

of luggage. This luxury palace boasts two Michelin-starred restaurants, the more celebrated of which is Le Louis XV, offering the sublime specialties of Alain Ducasse. Le Grill boasts Ligurian-Niçois cooking, a retractable roof, and a wraparound view of the sea. See chapter 6.

- **Hôtel Négresco** (Nice, Eastern Riviera; ☎ **04-93-16-64-00**): An aging Lillie Langtry sitting alone in the lobby, her once-great beauty camouflaged by a black veil, is but one of the many memories of this nostalgic favorite. Self-made millionaires and wannabes rub shoulders at this 1906 landmark. We could write a book about the Négresco, but here we'll give only two interesting facts: The carpet in the lobby is the largest ever made by the Savonnerie factory (the cost was about one-tenth the cost of the hotel), and the main chandelier was commissioned from Baccarat by Tsar Nicholas II. See chapter 6.

12 The Best Hotel Bargains

- **Hôtel des Croisades** (Aigues-Mortes, Languedoc-Roussillon; ☎ **04-66-53-67-85**): Set within the medieval ramparts of this ancient city, a former private home from the late 19th century has been successfully converted to receive paying guests. Prices are still like those charged 30 years ago. You don't get grand luxury here, but you are assured of comfort and hospitality. See chapter 3.
- **Hôtel du Palais** (Montpellier; Languedoc-Roussillon; ☎ **04-67-60-47-38**): In the old town, in a labyrinth of narrow streets, this hotel dates from the late 18th century but has been successfully modernized to receive guests today at prices that are within the range of most travelers' budgets. The rooms are cozily arranged, and the hotel has a special French charm. It's one of the most historic hotels in town, and the bedrooms are relatively large, ideal for a short or even a long visit. See chapter 3.
- **Hôtel Renaissance** (Castres, Languedoc-Roussillon; ☎ **05-63-59-30-42**): In the quaint town of Castres, with its celebrated Goya Museum, 26 miles south of Albi, this hotel is a good introduction to the bargains awaiting you in provincial France. Built in the 1600s as a courthouse, it was long ago converted from a dilapidated site into a hotel of discretion and charm—all at an affordable price, even if you opt for a suite. Some rooms have exposed timbers, and you'll sleep in grand but rustic comfort. See chapter 3.
- **Hôtel du Donjon** (Carcassonne, Languedoc-Roussillon; ☎ **800/528-1234** in the U.S. and Canada, or 04-68-71-08-80): Built into the solid bulwarks of Carcassonne, one of France's most perfectly preserved medieval towns, is this small-scale hotel whose well-appointed furnishings provide a vivid contrast to the crude stone shell that contains them. A stay here truly allows you personal contact with a site that provoked bloody battles between medieval armies. See chapter 3.
- **La Réserve** (Albi, Languedoc-Roussillon; ☎ **05-63-60-80-80**): La Réserve's design approximates a *mas provençal,* the kind of severely dignified farmhouse usually surrounded by scrublands, vineyards, olive groves, and cypresses. It's less expensive than many of the luxurious hideaways along the nearby Côte d'Azur and has the added benefit of lying just outside the center of one of our favorite fortified sites in Europe, the medieval town of Albi. See chapter 3.
- **Hôtel Danieli** (Avignon, Provence; ☎ **04-90-86-46-82**): Built during the reign of Napoléon, this 29-room gem is classified a historic monument. Small and informal, it has Italian flair but Provençal furnishings. The tile floors, chiseled stone, and baronial stone staircase add style in a town where too many budget hotels are bleak. See chapter 4.

- **Hôtel d'Arlatan** (Arles, Provence; ☎ 04-90-93-56-66): At reasonable rates, you can stay in one of Provence's most charming cities at the former residence of the comtes d'Arlatan de Beaumont, built in the 15th century on the ruins of an old palace. Near the historic place du Forum, this small hotel has been run by the same family since 1920. The rooms are furnished with Provençal antiques, and the antique tapestries are grace notes. The best rooms overlook the garden. See chapter 4.
- **Hôtel Clair Logis** (St-Jean-Cap-Ferrat, Eastern Riviera; ☎ 04-93-76-04-57): The real estate surrounding this converted 19th-century villa is among Europe's most expensive; nonetheless, the hotel manages to keep its prices under levels that really hurt. If you opt for one of the pleasant rooms (each named after a flower that thrives in the 2-acre garden), you'll be among prestigious predecessors: Even General de Gaulle, who knew the value of a *centime* and *sou,* selected it for his retreats. See chapter 6.

13 The Best Luxury Restaurants

- **La Barbacane** (Carcassonne, Languedoc-Roussillon; ☎ 04-68-25-03-34): Christophe Turquier may not be as famous as the Riviera legends, but he's on his way. He has brought to his cuisine (based on seasonal ingredients) a refinement rarely known in this walled medieval town, where cuisine is often based on great-grandmother's recipes. He's daring and imaginative with many dishes, though some of his platters would've pleased Escoffier. Opt for his more experimental food, including green ravioli perfumed with seiche, a species of octopus. See chapter 3.
- **Jardin des Sens** (Montpellier, Languedoc-Roussillon; ☎ 04-67-79-63-38): Twins Laurent and Jacques Pourcel have set off a culinary storm in Montpellier. Michelin has bestowed two stars on them, the same rating it gives to Ducasse at his Monaco citadel. Postnouvelle reigns supreme, and both men know how to take the bounty of Languedoc and turn it into meals sublime in flavor and texture. Though inspired by other chefs, they now feel free to let their imaginations roam. The results are often stunning, like the fricassée of langoustines and lamb sweetbreads. See chapter 3.
- **Christian Etienne** (Avignon, Provence; ☎ 04-90-86-16-50): In a house as old as the nearby papal palace, Etienne reigns as Avignon's culinary star. A chef of imagination and discretion, he has a magical hand, reinterpreting and improving French cuisine. He keeps a short menu so that he can give special care and attention to each dish. His menu is often themed—one might be devoted to the tomato. Save room for his chocolate/pine-nut cake, something of a local legend. See chapter 4.
- **L'Oustau de Beaumanière** (Les Baux, Provence; ☎ 04-90-54-33-07): This Relais & Châteaux occupies an old Provençal farmhouse. Founded in 1945 by the late Raymond Thuilier, the hotel's restaurant was once touted as France's greatest. It may long ago have lost that lofty position, but it continues to tantalize today's palates. Thuilier's heirs carry on admirably as they reinvent and reinterpret some of the great Provençal recipes. At the foot of a cliff, you dine in Renaissance charm, enjoying often flawless meals from the bounty of Provence. See chapter 4.
- **Le Louis XV** (Monte Carlo, Monaco; ☎ 92-16-30-01): A few years ago, Michelin lowered Alain Ducasse's rating here from three stars to two, but this regal restaurant is finer than ever and won back that third star in 1999. Ducasse divides his time between here and his eponymous three-star restaurant in Paris. That makes him the world's only six-star chef! The kitchen specializes in the

ultimate blending of the flavors of Liguria with the tastes and aromas of Provence and Tuscany. Yes, Ducasse dares grace the local macaroni gratin with truffles. See chapter 6.

- **Chantecler** (Nice, Eastern Riviera; ☎ 04-93-16-64-00): The most prestigious restaurant in Nice, and the most intensely cultivated, Chantecler is currently in the hands of Alain Llorca, who's attracting the area's demanding gourmets and gourmands. You dine in a monument to turn-of-the-century extravagance, and the menu is attuned to the seasons and to quality ingredients. A true taste of the country is evident in the fresh asparagus, black truffles, sun-dried tomatoes, and beignets of fresh vegetables—all deftly handled by a chef on the rise. See chapter 6.

14 The Best Deals on Dining

- **Chez Michel Sarran** (Toulouse; Languedoc-Roussillon; ☎ 05-61-12-32-32), is stylish and consistently praised, yet offers great dining value. Even the prime minister of France has praised the place. The cuisine brings out the best of the flavors of southwest France, and you can feast on such dishes as grilled snapper with caramelized tomatoes or grilled foie gras served with a duckmeat bouillon. See chapter 3.
- **Le Bistro Latin** (Aix-en-Provence, Provence; ☎ 04-42-38-22-88): The economic virtue of this Provençal restaurant lies in its fixed-price menus, whose composition is something of an art form. The prices are low, the flavors are sensational, and hints of Italian zest pop up frequently in such dishes as risotto with scampi. See chapter 4.
- **L'Echalotte** (St-Tropez, Western Riviera; ☎ 04-94-54-83-26): A reasonably priced restaurant in St-Tropez sounds like a contradiction, but this one is the most affordable and charming. Though the dining room is simple, it offers a tiny garden as a grace note. Post-moderne never made it here, for the cuisine is solidly bourgeois—the chefs serve recipes presumably taught them by their mothers. Many of southwestern France's classic dishes appear, like magret of duckling. But the true Côte devotee will opt for fresh fish, especially the delectable sea bass in a salt crust. See chapter 5.
- **Le Monaco** (Cannes, Western Riviera; ☎ 04-93-38-37-76): Restaurant tabs on La Croisette often resemble the annual budget of an Ivory Coast country. But believe it or not, pricey Cannes has working people who have to eat, and they often go to Le Monaco, a blue-collar eatery with great food served bistro style. You eat as the locals do, devouring couscous, roast rabbit with mustard sauce, and even grilled sardines. It's hearty and robust fare and completely affordable. See chapter 5.
- **Le Safari** (Nice, Eastern Riviera; ☎ 04-93-80-18-44): This ever-popular, ever-crowded brasserie overlooking the cours Saleya market soaks up every ray of Riviera sun. Dressed in jeans, waiters hurry back and forth, serving the habitués and visitors alike on the sprawling terrace. This place makes one of the best salade Niçoise concoctions in town, as well as a drop-dead spring lamb roasted in a wood-fired oven. See chapter 6.

15 The Best Shopping Bets

- **Caves de l'Hôtel de France** (Auch, Languedoc-Roussillon; ☎ 05-62-61-71-71): Southwestern France is fabled for its Armagnac brandies produced in the foothills of the Pyrénées since 1422, making them older than cognac. The best selection of this fire water, representing the output of some 100 distilleries, is found in this off-the-beaten-path shop. See chapter 3.

- **Centre Sant-Vicens** (Perpignan, Languedoc-Roussillon; ☎ **04-68-50-02-18**): This region of France is next door to Catalonia, whose capital is Barcelona. Catalan style, as long ago evoked by Antoni Gaudí, is modern and up-to-date here—at affordable prices. Textiles, pottery, and furnishings in forceful geometric patterns are displayed at this showcase. See chapter 3.
- **Véronique Pichon** (Avignon, Provence; ☎ **04-90-85-89-00**): This is the best outlet for a reasonably priced porcelain manufacturer who has been turning out quality wares since the 18th century. Decorative urns, statues, lamps, and tableware—all manufactured in the nearby town of Uzès—reveal fine craftsmanship. Shipping can be arranged virtually anywhere. See chapter 4.
- **Les Indiens de Nîmes** (Avignon, Provence; ☎ **04-90-86-32-05**): Provence has long been celebrated for its fabrics, and one of the best, most original, and affordable selections is found here. Open since the early 1980s, this outlet went back into the attic to rediscover old Provençal fabrics and to duplicate them in a wide assortment. The fabric is sold by the meter and can be shaped into everything from clothing to tableware. See chapter 4.
- **Les Olivades Factory Store** (St-Etienne-du-Grès, Provence; ☎ **04-90-49-19-19**): About 7½ miles north of Arles on the road leading to Tarascon, this store features the region's most fully stocked showroom of art objects and fabrics inspired by the traditions of Provence. You'll find fabrics, dresses, shirts for both men and women, table linen, and fabric by the yard. Part of the Olivades chain, this store has the widest selection and the best prices. See chapter 4.
- **Santons Fouque** (Aix-en-Provence, Provence; ☎ **04-42-26-33-38**): Collectors from all over Europe and North America purchase *santons* (figures of saints) in Provence. You'll find the best ones here, cast in terra-cotta, finished by hand, and decorated with an oil-based paint. The figures are from models made in the 1700s. See chapter 4.
- **Shopping for *Brocante*** (Provence): *Brocante*—items sold in French flea markets—is sold all over Provence, but the little village of Isle-sur-la-Sorgue, 14 miles east of Avignon, has long been known as the best center. The market takes place on Saturday and Sunday mornings. Few customers come away without a purchase of some sort.
- **Verrerie de Biot** (Biot, Eastern Riviera; ☎ **04-93-65-03-00**): Biot has long been known for its unique pottery, *verre rustique*. Since the 1940s artisan glassmakers here have been creating this bubble-flecked glass in brilliant colors like cobalt and emerald. They're collector's items but sold at affordable prices on home turf. The Verrerie de Biot is the oldest, most famous, and most frequently visited outlet. A half-dozen others are within a short distance of the town. If you arrive at this shop on any day except Sunday, you can actually see the glassmakers creating this unique product. See chapter 6.

Planning Your Trip to the South of France

In the pages that follow, we've compiled everything you need to know about the practical details of planning your trip: what documents you'll need, how to use French currency, how to find the best airfare, when to go, and more.

1 The Regions in Brief

LANGUEDOC-ROUSSILLON

Languedoc may be a less popular destination than Provence, but it's compelling all the same and is also less frenetic and more affordable. Much of its landscape, cuisine, and lifestyle is similar to that of its neighbor, Provence. **Roussillon** is the rock-strewn arid French answer to ancient Catalonia, just across the Spanish border, linked more to Barcelona than to Paris. The **Camargue** is the name given to the steaming marshy delta formed by two arms of the Rhône River. Rich in bird life, it's famous for its flat expanses of tough grasses and for such fortified medieval sites as **Aigues-Mortes.** Also appealing are **Toulouse,** the bustling pink capital of Languedoc; and the "red city" of **Albi,** birthplace of Toulouse-Lautrec. **Carcassonne,** a marvelously preserved walled city with fortifications begun around A.D. 500, is the region's highlight.

PROVENCE

This legendary region flanks the Alps and the Italian border along its eastern end and incorporates a host of sites that have long been frequented by the rich and reclusive. It's a land of gnarled olive trees, cypresses, umbrella pines, almond groves, lavender fields, and countless vineyards. The western section is more like Italy, its Mediterranean neighbor, than like France. Premier destinations are **Aix-en-Provence,** associated with Cézanne; **Arles,** "the soul of Provence," captured so brilliantly by van Gogh; **Avignon,** once the capital of Christendom during the 14th-century; and **Marseille,** a port city established by the ancient Phoenicians (in some ways more North African than French). Special Provence gems are the small villages, like **Les Baux, Gordes,** and **St-Rémy-de-Provence,** birthplace of Nostradamus.

THE CÔTE D'AZUR (FRENCH RIVIERA)

The strip of glittering coastal towns along Provence's southern edge is known as the Azure Coast. Long a playground of the rich and famous, the Riviera has become hideously overbuilt and spoiled by tourism. Even so, the names of its resorts still ring with excitement and evoke glamour: **Cannes, St-Tropez, Cap d'Antibes, St-Jean-Cap-Ferrat.** July and August are the most crowded times, but spring and fall can be a delight. **Nice** is the most affordable base for exploring the area. The principality of **Monaco,** the fabled piece of the Côte d'Azur, occupies less than a square mile. Don't expect sandy beaches—most are rocky. Topless bathing is common, especially in St-Tropez. Glitterati and eccentrics have always been attracted to this narrow strip of real estate, but so have dozens of artists and their patrons, who have left behind a landscape of world-class galleries and art museums.

2 Visitor Information

REGIONAL INFORMATION

Your best source of information before you go is the **French Government Tourist Office,** which can be reached at the following addresses:

In the **United States,** at 444 Madison Ave., 16th Floor, New York, NY 10022 (☎ 212/838-7800); 676 N. Michigan Ave., Suite 3360, Chicago, IL 60611-2819 (☎ 312/751-7800); or 9454 Wilshire Blvd., Suite 715, Beverly Hills, CA 90212-2967 (☎ 310/271-6665). To request information, you can also try the general info phone number ☎ 410/286-8310.

In **Canada,** contact the **Maison de la France/French Government Tourist Office,** 1981 av. McGill College, Suite 490, Montréal, H3A 2W9 (☎ 514/288-4264).

In the **United Kingdom,** contact the **Maison de la France/French Government Tourist Office,** 178 Piccadilly, London, W1V 0AL (☎ 0891/244-123; fax 020/7493-6594).

In **Ireland,** call the **Maison de la France/French Government Tourist Office,** 10 Suffolk St., Dublin 2, Ireland (☎ 01/679-0813).

In **Australia,** contact the **French Tourist Bureau,** 6 Perth Ave., Xarralumia, NSW 2000, Australia (☎ 02/6216-0100).

In **New Zealand,** there's no representative, so you can contact the Consular Section of the **French Embassy,** 1 Willeston St., Wellington (☎ 64/4-4720-200).

In **South Africa,** the **French Government Tourist Office** is in a suburb of Johannesburg. Call ☎ 011/880-8062 for information.

INFORMATION ON MONACO

Information on travel to Monaco is available from the **Monaco Government Tourist and Convention Bureau,** 565 Fifth Ave., 23rd Floor, New York, NY 10017 (☎ 020/7286-3330; fax 020/7286-9890). Most of its facilities (along with its consulate) are in New York at the above address.

In **London,** the office is at 3/18 Chelsea Garden Market, The Chambers, Chelsea Harbour, London SW10 OXF (☎ 020/7352-9962; fax 020/7352-2103).

Document requirements for travel to Monaco are exactly the same as those for travel to France, and there are virtually no border patrols or passport formalities at the Monégasque frontier.

INFORMATION ON THE WEB

- Official Web site: **www.francetourism.com**
- French Government Tourist Office: **www.fgtousa.org**
- Maison de la France: **www.franceguide.com**
- Beyond the French Riviera: **www.beyond.fr**
- Provence Touristic Guide: **www.provence.guideweb.com**

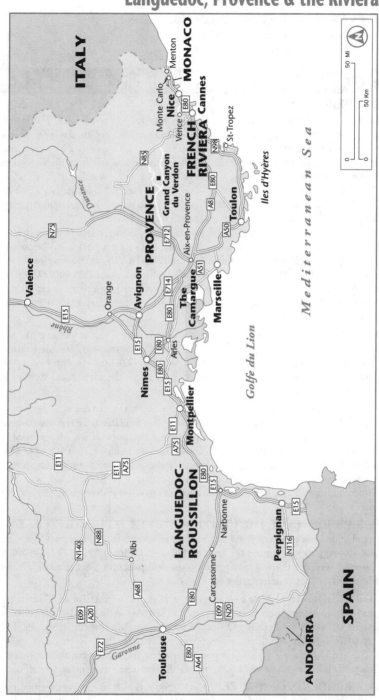

ITALY

MONACO
Menton
Monte Carlo
Nice
Vence
Cannes
St-Tropez
FRENCH RIVIERA
Grand Canyon
du Verdon
Aix-en-Provence
Toulon
Iles d'Hyères
PROVENCE
Avignon
Orange
The Camargue
Marseille
Valence
Arles
Nîmes
Montpellier
Mediterranean Sea
Golfe du Lion
LANGUEDOC-
ROUSSILLON
Narbonne
Perpignan
Albi
Carcassonne
Toulouse
ANDORRA
SPAIN

Rhône
Durance
Garonne

N85 E712 E714 E80 E15 N75 A8 E80 A50 N98 A51 E80 E15 E11 A75 E11 A75 E80 E15 E15 N116 N140 N88 A68 E09 A20 E72 E80 A64 E09 N20

50 Mi
50 Km

- Relais & Châteaux: **www.integra.fr/relaischateaux**
- FranceScape: **www.france.com/francescape**
- WebMuseum: **www.sunsite.unc.edu/wm**

3 Entry Requirements & Customs Regulations

DOCUMENTS

FOR U.S. RESIDENTS   Only a passport is required to enter France. The French government does not require visas for **U.S. citizens** unless they are staying in France for more than 90 days. For longer stays, U.S. visitors must apply for a long-term visa, residence card, or temporary-stay visa. Applications are available from the **Consulate Section of the French Embassy,** 4101 Reservoir Rd. NW, Washington, DC 20007 (☎ 202/944-6000), or from the visa section of the French Consulate at 10 E. 74th St., New York, NY 10021 (☎ 212/606-3689). Visas are required for students planning to study in France even if the stay is for less than 90 days.

For information about applying for a passport, contact a major post office to obtain an application (also downloadable from the Internet sites listed below), or contact **National Passport Agency** (☎ 202/647-0518). To find your regional passport office, call the **National Passport Information Center** (☎ 900/225-5674; http://travel.state.gov). Be warned that obtaining or renewing a passport can take up to 3 weeks. Passports are valid for 10 years. A first-time passport costs $60; a renewal $40.

FOR RESIDENTS OF AUSTRALIA   Australians need a visa as well as a passport to enter France. Visas are available from the **French Consulate,** Consulate General, 31 Market St., 26th Floor, Sydney, NSW 2000 (☎ 02/9261-5931). Apply for a passport at your local post office or passport office, or search the government Web site at **www.dfat.gov.au/passports/**.

FOR CANADIAN RESIDENTS   Canadian residents must have a valid passport to enter France, but no visa is required. Applications are available at 28 regional passport offices, at most travel agencies, or from the central **Passport Office, Department of Foreign Affairs and International Trade,** Ottawa, Ont. K1A 0G3 (☎ 800/567-6868; www.dfait-maeci.gc.ca/passport). Processing takes 5 to 10 days if you apply in person, or about 3 weeks by mail. Passports are valid for 5 years and cost $60. Children under 16 may be included on a parent's passport if they are traveling with a parent.

FOR RESIDENTS OF THE UNITED KINGDOM   As a member of the European Union, only an identity card is needed for travel in other EU countries. For a regular 10-year passport, contact the **London Passport Office** at ☎ 020/7271-3000 or search its Web site at **www.open.gov.uk/ukpass/ukpass.htm**. Passports cost £21 for adults and £11 for children under 16.

FOR RESIDENTS OF IRELAND   Irish citizens, as members of an EU country, need only an identity card to enter France. You can also apply for a 10-year passport, costing IR£45, at the **Passport Office,** Setanta Centre, Molesworth Street, Dublin 2 (☎ 01/671-1633; www.irlgov.ie/iveagh/foreignaffairs/services). Those under age 18 and over 65 must apply for a 3-year passport, costing IR£10. You can also apply at 1A South Mall, Cork (☎ 021/272-525) or over the counter at most main post offices.

FOR RESIDENTS OF NEW ZEALAND   You can pick up a passport application at any travel agency or Link Centre. For more info, contact the **Passport Office,** P.O. Box 805, Wellington (☎ 0800/225-050). Passports for adults cost NZ$80 and for those under 16, NZ$40. A visa is also required for New Zealand residents.

FOR RESIDENTS OF SOUTH AFRICA   South Africans also need visas as well as a passport to enter France. They're available from the **French Consulate,** 2 Dean St. (next to Queen Victoria St.), Cape Town 8001 (☎ **021/23-15-75;** fax 021/24-84-70).

CUSTOMS

WHAT YOU CAN BRING INTO FRANCE   Customs restrictions for visitors entering France differ for citizens of the European Union and for citizens of non-EU countries. Non-EU nationals can bring in duty-free 200 cigarettes, 100 cigarillos, 50 cigars, or 250 grams of smoking tobacco. You can also bring in 2 liters of wine and 1 liter of alcohol over 22 proof and 2 liters of wine 22 proof or under, 50 grams of perfume, a quarter liter of eau de toilette, 500 grams of coffee, and 200 grams of tea. Visitors 15 and over can bring in other goods totaling 300F ($51); for those 14 and under, the limit is 150F ($25.50). (Customs officials tend to be lenient about general merchandise, realizing that the limits are unrealistically low.)

Visitors from European Union (EU) countries can bring in 300 cigarettes or 150 cigarillos or 75 cigars or 400 grams of smoking tobacco. You can also bring in 2 liters of wine and either 1 liter of alcohol over 38.80 proof or 2 liters of wine under 38.80 proof, 75 grams of perfume, ⅜ liter of eau de toilette, 1,000 grams of coffee, and 80 grams of tea. Visitors 15 and over can bring in 2,400F ($408) of merchandise duty-free; those 14 and under can bring in 620F ($105.40) worth.

WHAT YOU CAN BRING HOME   Returning **U.S. citizens** who have been away for 48 hours or more are allowed to bring back, once every 30 days, $400 worth of merchandise duty-free. You'll be charged a flat rate of 10% duty on the next $1,000 worth of purchases. Be sure to have your receipts handy. On gifts, the duty-free limit is $100. You cannot bring fresh foodstuffs into the United States; tinned foods, however, are allowed. For more information, contact the **U.S. Customs Service,** 1301 Constitution Ave. (P.O. Box 7407), Washington, DC 20044 (☎ **202/927-6724**), and request the free pamphlet *Know Before You Go.* It's also available on the Web at **www. customs.ustreas.gov/travel/kbygo.htm**.

Citizens of the U.K. who are returning from a European Union country will go through a separate Customs Exit (called the "Blue Exit") especially for EU travelers. In essence, there is no limit on what you can bring back as long as the items are for personal use (this includes gifts), and you have already paid the necessary duty and tax. However, Customs law sets out guidance levels. If you bring in more than these levels, you may be asked to prove that the goods are for your own use. Guidance levels on such goods are 800 cigarettes, 200 cigars, 1kg smoking tobacco, 10 liters of spirits, 90 liters of wine and 110 liters of beer. For more information, contact **HM Customs & Excise,** Passenger Enquiry Point, 2nd Floor Wayfarer House, Great South West Road, Feltham, Middlesex, TW14 8NP (☎ **020/8910-3744;** from outside the U.K. 44/ 181-910-3744), or consult their Web site at **www.open.gov.uk**.

For a clear summary of **Canadian** rules, write for the booklet *I Declare,* issued by **Revenue Canada,** 2265 St. Laurent Blvd., Ottawa K1G 4KE (☎ **613/993-0534**). Canada allows its citizens a $500 exemption, once a year after an absence of 7 days or more. You can bring back duty-free 200 cigarettes, 2.2 pounds of tobacco, 40 imperial ounces of liquor, and 50 cigars. In addition, you're allowed to mail gifts to Canada from abroad at the rate of Can$60 a day, provided they're unsolicited (write on the package "Unsolicited gift, under $60 value"). All valuables should be declared on the Y-38 form before departure from Canada, including serial numbers of such items as expensive foreign cameras.

The duty-free allowance in **Australia** is A$400 or, for those under 18, A$200. Personal property mailed back from England should be marked "Australian goods returned" to avoid payment of duty. Upon returning to Australia, citizens can bring in 250 cigarettes or 250 grams of loose tobacco, and 1,125ml of alcohol. If you are returning with valuable goods you already own, such as foreign-made cameras, you should file form B263. A helpful brochure, available from Australian consulates or Customs offices, is *Know Before You Go.* For more information, contact **Australian Customs Services,** GPO Box 8, Sydney NSW 2001 (☎ **02/9213-2000**).

The duty-free allowance for **New Zealand** is NZ$700. Citizens over 17 can bring in 200 cigarettes, or 50 cigars, or 250 grams of tobacco (or a mixture of all three if their combined weight doesn't exceed 250 grams); plus 4.5 liters of wine and beer, or 1.125 liters of liquor. Most questions are answered in a free pamphlet available at New Zealand consulates and Customs offices: *New Zealand Customs Guide for Travellers, Notice no. 4.* For more information, contact **New Zealand Customs,** 50 Anzac Ave., P.O. Box 29, Auckland (☎ **09/359-6655**).

4 Money

France is one of the world's most expensive destinations. But, to compensate, it often offers top-value food and lodging. Part of the problem is the value-added tax (VAT—called TVA in France), which tacks between 6% and 33% onto everything.

It's expensive to rent and drive a car in France (gasoline is costly, too), and flying within France costs more than flying within the United States. Train travel is relatively inexpensive, however, especially if you purchase a rail pass. Inflation has stayed at 2% during the late 1990s.

THE FRENCH FRANC

The basic unit of French currency is the **franc (F),** which consists of 100 centimes. Coins are issued in units of 5, 10, 20, and 50 centimes, plus 1, 2, 5, and 10 francs. Notes are denominated in 20, 50, 100, 200, 500, and 1,000 francs. The new 200F note honors Gustave Eiffel on the front.

All banks are equipped for foreign exchange, and you'll find exchange offices at the airports and airline terminals. Banks are open Monday through Friday from 9am to noon and 2 to 4pm. Major bank branches also open their exchange departments on Saturday from 9am to noon.

When converting your home currency into francs, be aware that rates may vary. Your hotel will offer the worst rate. In general, banks offer the best, but even they charge a commission, often $3, depending on the transaction. Whenever you can, stick to the big banks of France, like Crédit Lyonnais, which usually offer the best rates and charge the least commission. Always make sure you have enough francs for *le weekend.*

If you need a check denominated in French francs before your trip (for example, to pay a deposit on a hotel room), contact **Ruesch International** (☎ **800/424-2923**). Ruesch performs a wide variety of conversion-related services, usually for $3 per transaction. You can also inquire at a local bank.

THE EURO

The **euro,** the new single European currency, became the official currency of France and 10 other countries on January 1, 1999, but not in the form of cash. (There are still no euro banknotes or coins in circulation—payment in euros can only be made by check, credit card, or some other bank-related system.)

The French Franc, the U.S. Dollar, the British Pound & the Euro

FF	US$	UK£	Euro	FF	US$	UK£	Euro
1	0.17	0.11	0.15	75.00	12.75	8.25	11.25
2	0.34	0.22	0.30	100.00	17.00	11.00	15.00
3	0.51	0.33	0.45	125.00	21.25	13.75	18.75
4	0.68	0.44	0.60	150.00	25.50	16.50	22.50
5	0.85	0.55	0.75	175.00	29.75	19.25	26.25
6	1.02	0.66	0.90	200.00	34.00	22.00	30.00
7	1.19	0.77	1.05	225.00	38.25	24.75	33.75
8	1.36	0.88	1.20	250.00	42.50	27.50	37.50
9	1.53	0.99	1.35	275.00	46.75	30.25	41.25
10	1.70	1.10	1.50	300.00	51.00	33.00	45.00
15	2.55	1.65	2.25	350.00	59.50	38.50	52.50
20	3.40	2.20	3.00	400.00	68.00	44.00	60.00
25	4.25	2.75	3.75	500.00	85.00	55.00	75.00
50	8.50	5.50	7.50	1000.00	170.00	110.00	150.00

The French franc will remain the only currency in France for cash transactions until December 21, 2001, when more and more businesses will start posting their prices in euros alongside those in French francs, which will continue to exist for a while longer. Over a maximum 6-month transition period, French franc banknotes and coins will be withdrawn from circulation.

The symbol of the euro is a stylized **E,** which actually looks like an uppercase C with a horizontal double bar through the middle (€); its official abbreviation is EUR.

Although at this time, very few, if any, French hotel and restaurant bills are actually paid in euros, there will be an increasing emphasis on the new pan-European currency during the lifetime of this edition. As a rough guideline, subject to change, of course, the euro equaled approximately $1.17 U.S. and approximately 6.60 French francs at press time.

ATMS

ATMs are linked to a national network that most likely includes your bank at home. **Cirrus** (☎ 800/424-7787; www.mastercard.com/atm/) and **Plus** (☎ 800/843-7587; www.visa.com/atms) are the two most popular networks; check the back of your ATM card to see which network your bank belongs to. Use the 800 numbers to locate ATMs in your destination. Also ask your bank whether you will need a new PIN. Cirrus is linked to **Crédit Lyonnais, Banque Nationale de Paris, Ceile de France,** and **Société Generale.** Plus is linked to **Société Generale, Banque National de Paris, Carte Bleue Group,** and **Crédit Lyonnais.**

TRAVELER'S CHECKS

Traveler's checks, though they have become less important since the advent of the ATM, still offer security to many travelers. If they are lost or stolen and you have a record of their serial numbers, they are easily replaced.

American Express offers traveler's checks in denominations of $10, $20, $50, $100, $500, and $1,000. You'll pay a service charge ranging from 1 to 4%. You can also get American Express traveler's checks over the phone by calling ☎ **800/221-7282;** by using this number, Amex gold and platinum cardholders are exempt from the fee. AAA members can obtain checks without a fee at most AAA offices.

Visa offers traveler's checks at Citibank locations and at other banks nationwide. The service charge ranges between 1.5 and 2%; checks come in denominations of $20, $50, $100, $500, and $1,000. **MasterCard** also offers traveler's checks. Call ☎ **800/ 223-9920** for a location near you.

CREDIT CARDS

Credit cards are a safe way to carry money and also provide a convenient record of all your expenses. You can also withdraw cash advances from your credit cards at any bank (though you'll start paying hefty interest on the advance the moment you receive the cash, and you won't receive frequent-flyer miles on an airline credit card). At most banks, you don't even need to go to a teller; you can get a cash advance at the ATM if you know your PIN. (If you've forgotten your PIN or didn't even know you had one, call the phone number on the back of your credit card and ask the bank to send it to you. It usually takes 5 to 7 business days.)

Almost every credit card company has an emergency 800 number that you can call if your wallet or purse is stolen. They may be able to wire you a cash advance off your credit card immediately, and in many places can deliver an emergency credit card in a day or two. Citicorp Visa's U.S. emergency number is ☎ **800/336-8472.** American Express cardholders and traveler's check holders should call ☎ **800/ 221-7282** for all money emergencies. MasterCard holders should call ☎ **800/ 307-7309.**

5 When to Go

In terms of weather, the most idyllic months for visiting the south of France are May and June. Though the sun is intense, it's not uncomfortable. Coastal waters have warmed up by then, so swimming is possible, and all the resorts have come alive after a winter slumber but aren't yet overrun. The flowers and herbs in the countryside are at their peak, and driving conditions are ideal. In June, it remains light until around 10:30pm.

The most overcrowded times—also the hottest, in more ways than one—are July and August, when seemingly half of Paris shows up in the briefest of bikinis. Reservations are difficult to make, discos are blasting, and space is tight on the popular beaches. The worst traffic jams on the coast occur all the way from St-Tropez to Menton.

Aside from May and June, our favorite time is September and even early October, when the sun is still hot, at least during the day, and the great hordes have headed back north. This is also a good time for seeing the art museums along the Côte d'Azur and the cultural attractions in Avignon and other Provençal cities.

In November, the weather is often pleasant, especially at midday, though some of the restaurants and inns you'll want to visit might take a sudden vacation. It's the month that many chefs and hoteliers elect to go on their own vacations after a summer of hard work.

Winter hasn't been the fashionable season since the 1930s. In the early days of tourism, when Queen Victoria came to visit, all the fashionable people showed up in winter, deserting the Côte by April. Today it's just the reverse. However, winter on the Riviera is being rediscovered, and many visitors (particularly retired people or those with leisure time) elect to visit then. If you don't mind the absence of sunbathing and beach life, this could be a good time to show up. However, some resorts, like St-Tropez, become ghost towns when the cold weather comes, though Cannes, Nice, Monaco, and Menton remain active year-round.

WEATHER

The Mediterranean coast has the driest climate in France. Most rain falls in spring and autumn. Summers are comfortably dry—beneficial to humans but deadly to much of the vegetation, which (unless it's irrigated) often dries and burns up in the parched months.

Provence dreads *le mistral* (a cold, violent wind from the French and Swiss Alps that roars south down the Rhône Valley). It most often blows in winter, sometimes for a few days, but sometimes for up to 2 weeks.

For up-to-the-minute **weather forecasts,** dial ☎ **900/WEATHER** in the United States (95¢ per minute). This report comes from the cable TV station Weather Channel. The 24-hour service reports on conditions in Provence and the Riviera.

HOLIDAYS *(JOURS FERIÉS)*

In France, holidays are known as *jours feriés.* Shops and many businesses (banks and some museums and restaurants) close on holidays, but hotels and emergency services remain open.

The main holidays—a mix of secular and religious—include New Year's Day (Jan 1), Easter Sunday and Monday (early April), Labor Day (May 1), V-E Day in Europe (May 8), Whit Monday (mid May), Ascension Thursday (40 days after Easter), Bastille Day (July 14), Assumption of the Blessed Virgin (Aug 15), All Saints' Day (Nov 1), Armistice Day (Nov 11), and Christmas (Dec 25).

Provence Calendar of Events

January
- **Monte Carlo Motor Rally.** The world's most venerable car race. For more information, call ☎ **92-16-61-66.** Usually mid-January.

February
- **Fête de la Chandeleur (Candlemas),** Basilique St-Victor, Marseille. A celebration in honor of the arrival in Marseille of the three Marys. A procession brings the Black Virgin up from the crypt of the abbey. For more information, call ☎ **04-91-13-89-00.** Early February.
- ✪ **Carnival of Nice.** Float processions, parades, confetti battles, boat races, street music and food, masked balls, and fireworks are part of this ancient celebration. The climax follows a 113-year-old tradition in which King Carnival is burned in effigy, an event preceded by Les Batailles des Fleurs (Battles of the Flowers), during which members of opposing teams pelt one another with flowers. Come with proof of a hotel reservation. For information or reservations, contact the **Nice Convention and Visitors Bureau,** 1 esplanade Kennedy (BP 4079), 06302 Nice CEDEX 4 (☎ **04-92-14-48-00;** fax 04-92-14-48-03). Mid-February to early March.

April
- **Féria Pascale (Easter Bullfighting Festival),** Arles. This is a major bullfighting event that includes not only appearances by the greatest matadors but also *abrivados* and *bodegas* (wine stalls). For more information, call ☎ **04-90-18-41-20.** Easter.
- **Festival des Musiques d'Aujourd'hui (Festival of Contemporary Music),** Marseille. This festival presents the works of very young French and European composers in music and dance. For more information, call Experimental Music Groups of Marseille at ☎ **04-91-39-29-00.** April 29 to May 12.

May

- **La Fête des Gardians (Camargue Cowboys' Festival),** Arles. This event features a procession of Camargue cowboys through the streets of town. Activities feature various games involving bulls, including Courses Camarguaises, in which competitors have to snatch a rosette from between the horns of a bull. For information, call ☎ **04-90-18-41-20.** Early May.
- ✪ **Cannes Film Festival.** Movie madness transforms this city into the kingdom of the media-related deal, with daily melodramas acted out in cafes, on sidewalks, and in hotel lobbies. Great for voyeurs. Reserve early and make a deposit. Getting a table on the Carlton terrace is even more difficult than procuring a room. Admission to some of the prestigious films is by invitation only. There are box-office tickets for the less important films, which play 24 hours. For information, contact the Direction du Festival International du Film, 99 bd. Malesherbes, 75008 Paris (☎ **01-45-61-66-00;** fax 01-42-66-68-85). Two weeks before the festival, the event's administration moves en masse to the Palais des Festivals, esplanade Georges-Pompidou, 06400 Cannes (☎ **04-93-39-01-01**). Early to mid-May.
- **Fête de la Transhumance (Move to Summer Grazing),** St-Rémy. This event celebrates the now-abandoned custom of shepherds presenting their flocks to the public before moving them to higher ground for summer. In this mock event, the flocks move off as if really going up to the mountains. For more information, call ☎ **04-90-92-05-22.** Mid- to late May.
- **Monaco Grand Prix.** Hundreds of cars race through the narrow streets and winding corniche roads in a surreal blend of high-tech machinery and medieval architecture. For more information, call ☎ **01-42-96-12-23.** May 13 to 16.
- **Le Pélerinage des Gitans (Gypsies' Pilgrimage),** Stes-Maries-de-la-Mer. This festival is in memory of the two Marys for whom the town is named (Mary, the mother of James the lesser, and Mary Salome, the mother of James the greater and John). A model boat containing statues of the saints and a statue of St. Sarah, patron saint of Gypsies, is taken to the seashore and blessed by the bishop. For more information, call ☎ **04-90-97-82-55.** Last week of May.

June

- **Festival de la St-Eloi (St. Eloi Festival),** Maussane-les-Alpilles. For this festival, wagons are decorated and raced in the Carreto Ramado, followed by mass, a procession in traditional dress, and a benediction. Special events are held and local produce and handcrafts sold. For more information, call ☎ **04-90-54-52-04.** Mid-June.
- **Festival Aix en Musique ("Aix in Music" Festival),** Aix-en-Provence. Concerts of classical music and choral singing are held in historic buildings, such as the Cloisters of the Cathédrale St-Sauveur and the Hôtel Maynier d'Oppède. For more information, call ☎ **04-42-21-69-69.** Throughout June.
- **Festival d'Expression Provençale (Festival of Provençal Language),** Abbaye St-Michel de Frigolet, Tarascon. At this festival, homage is paid to the region's language with works by Provençal writers that are acted in French and Provençal. For more information, call ☎ **04-90-95-50-77.** Late June to early July.
- **Fête de la Tarasque,** Tarascon. The town relives St. Martha's victory over the dragon known as the Tarasque, which was believed to live in the Rhône in the lst century. There's a procession of horsemen, an archery competition, historical events, a medieval tournament, a Tarasque procession, Novilladas (young bull-fighters), and an orchestral concert with fireworks. For more information, call ☎ **04-90-91-03-52.** Late June.

- **Feu de la St-Jean (St. John's Fire),** Fontvieille. This event features folk troupes and Camargue cowboys who gather in front of the Château de Montauban. For more information, call ☎ 04-90-54-67-49. June 24.
- **La Fête des Pêcheurs (Fishermen's Festival),** Cassis. The local "Prud'hommes" (members of the elected industrial tribunal) walk in procession wearing traditional dress, and a mass is held in honor of St. Peter, followed by a benediction. For more information, call ☎ 04-42-01-71-17. Late June.
- **Reconstitution Historique (Historical Pageant),** Salon-de-Provence. This pageant held in honor of Nostradamus includes a cast of 700 in historical costume and is followed by a son-et-lumière at the Château d'Empéri. For more information, call ☎ 04-90-56-77-92. Late June to early July.

July

- **St-Guilhem Music Season,** St-Guilhem le Désert, Languedoc. This festival of baroque organ and choral music is held in a medieval monastery. For information, call ☎ 04-67-63-14-99. July to early August.
- **Festival International d'Art Lyrique et de Musique d'Aix (Aix International Festival of Opera and Music),** Palais de l'Archévêche and Cathédrale St-Sauveur, Aix-en-Provence. This highly prestigious festival presents operas, particularly of Mozart, as well as concerts and recitals. For more information, call ☎ 04-42-17-34-34. Throughout July.
- ✪ **Bastille Day.** Celebrating the birth of modern-day France, the festivities in the south reach their peak in Nice with street fairs, pageants, fireworks, and feasts. The day begins with a parade down promenade des Anglais and ends with fireworks in the Vieille Ville. No matter where you are, by the end of the day you'll hear Piaf warbling "La Foule" (The Crowd), the song that celebrated her passion for the stranger she met and later lost in a crowd on Bastille Day. Similar celebrations also take place in Cannes, Arles, Aix, Marseille, and Avignon. July 14.
- **Nuit Taurine (Nocturnal Bull Festival),** St-Rémy-de-Provence. At this festival, the focus is on the age-old allure of bulls and their primeval appeal to roaring crowds. *Abrivados* involve bulls in the town square as "chaperoned" by trained herders on horseback; *encierros* highlight a Pamplona-style stampeding of bulls through the streets. Music from local guitarists and flaming torches add drama. For more information, call ☎ 04-90-92-05-22. Mid-July.
- ✪ **Grand Parade du Jazz (Nice Jazz Festival).** This is the biggest, flashiest, and most prestigious jazz festival in Europe, with world-class entertainers. Concerts begin in early afternoon and go on until late at night (sometimes all night in the clubs) on the Arènes de Cimiez, a hill above the city. Reserve hotel rooms way in advance. For information, contact the Grand Parade du Jazz, c/o the Cultural Affairs Department of the city of Nice (☎ 04-93-92-82-82; fax 04-93-92-82-85). Mid-July.
- ✪ **Festival d'Aix-en-Provence.** This musical event par excellence features everything from Gregorian chant to melodies composed on computerized synthesizers. The audience sits on the sloping lawns of the 14th-century papal palace for operas and concertos. Local recitals are performed in the medieval cloister of the Cathédrale St-Sauveur. Make advance hotel reservations and take a written confirmation with you when you arrive. Expect heat, crowds, and traffic. For more information, contact the Festival International d'Art Lyrique et de Musique, Palais de l'Ancien Archévêche, 13100 Aix-en-Provence (☎ 04-42-17-34-34; fax 04-42-63-13-74). Mid- to late July.
- **Les Chorégies d'Orange,** Orange. One of southern France's most important lyric festivals presents oratorios and choral works by master performers whose voices are

---

Tickets to the Avignon Festival

Global Tickets/Edwards and Edwards can order tickets to many of the musical or theatrical events at the Avignon festival, as well as other cultural events throughout France; contact them at 1270 Ave. of the Americas, Suite 2414, New York, NY 10020 (☎ **800/ 223-6108**).

---

amplified by the ancient acoustics of France's best-preserved Roman amphitheater. For more information, call ☎ **04-90-34-24-24.** Mid-July to early August.

✪ **Festival d'Avignon.** One of France's most prestigious theater events, this world-class festival has a reputation for exposing new talent to critical acclaim. The focus is usually on avant-garde works in theater, dance, and music by groups from around the world. Mime, too. Make hotel reservations early. For information, call ☎ **04-90-82-65-11** or fax 04-90-82-95-03. **Edwards and Edwards** can order tickets to virtually any of the musical or theatrical events at the Avignon festival, as well as other cultural events throughout France. Its address is 1270 Ave. of the Americas, Suite 2414, New York, NY 10020 (☎ **800/ 223-6108**). Mid- to late July.

• **Festival de Marseille Méditerranée.** This festival features concerts and recitals of music and song from the entire Mediterranean region. Theater and dance are also presented, along with special exhibitions in the city's main museums. For more information, call ☎ **04-91-99-00-20** or fax 04-91-99-00-22. Second 2 weeks in July.

• **Fête de la St-Eloi (Feast of St. Eloi),** Gémenos. Some hundred draft horses draw a procession of traditional flower-decked wagons. Folk troupes also perform. For more information, call ☎ **04-42-32-18-44.** Late July.

August

• **Fêtes Daudet (Daudet Festival),** Fontvieille. At this festival, mass said in Provençal is held in the Avenue of Pine Trees. There's folk dancing outside Daudet's mill and a torchlight procession through the streets of town to the mill. For more information, call ☎ **04-90-54-67-49.** Mid-August.

• **Féria de St-Rémy (Bullfights),** St-Rémy-de-Provence. This event features a 4-day celebration of bulls with *abrivado* and *encierro* (see the Nuit Taurine entry above), branding, and Portuguese bull fighting (matadors on horseback). For more information, call ☎ **04-90-92-05-22.** Mid-August.

September

• **Fête des Olives (Olive Festival),** Mouriès. A mass is held in honor of the green olives. There's a procession of groups in traditional costume, an olive tasting, and sales of regional produce. For more information, call ☎ **04-90-47-56-58.** Mid-September.

• **Féria des Prémices du Riz (Rice Harvest Festival),** Arles. Bullfights are held in the amphitheater with leading matadors, and a procession of floats makes its way along boulevard des Lices; there are also traditional events with cowboys and women in regional costume. For more information, call ☎ **04-90-18-41-20.** Mid-September.

• **Journée de l'Olivier en Provence (Day Celebrating the Olive in Provence),** Salon-de-Provence. This event is attended by producers of olive oil, Marseille soap, olive-wood articles, booksellers, and pottery and earthenware makers. Special events are held in the history center. For more information, call ☎ **04-90-56-27-60.** Late September.

- **Perpignan Jazz Festival.** Musicians from everywhere jam in what many visitors consider Languedoc's most appealing season. For more information, call ☎ **04-68-66-30-30.** Late September.

November

- **Marché aux Santons,** Tarascon. Craftspersons from throughout Provence congregate in this medieval village to sell their *santons* (carved representations of saints). For more information, call ☎ **04-90-91-22-96** or fax 04-90-91-03-52. Four days in late November. This event is supplemented, sometimes with the same sellers, who move to the **Foire aux Santons** in Marseille, held between November 27 and December 31. For more information, call ☎ **04-91-13-89-00** or fax 04-91-13-89-20.

December

- **Fête des Bergers (Shepherds Festival),** Istres. This festival features a procession of herds on their way to winter pastures. There are cowboys, a Carreto Ramado, a blessing of the horses, an all-night Provençal party with shepherds and Provençal storytellers, and folk troupes. For more information, call ☎ **04-42-55-51-15.** First 2 weeks in December.
- **Foire de Noël,** Mougins. Hundreds of merchants, selling all manner of Christmas ornaments and gifts, descend on Mougins in Provence, to herald in the Christmas spirit. December 11 and 12.
- **Midnight Mass,** Fontvieille. A traditional midnight mass, including the *pastrage* ceremony, the presentation of a new-born lamb. There's a procession of folk troupes, Camargue cowboys, and women in traditional costume from Daudet's mill to the church, followed by the presentation of the lamb. For more information, call ☎ **04-90-54-67-49.** December 24.
- **Noël Provençal (Provençal Christmas),** Eglise St-Vincent, Les Baux. The procession of shepherds is followed by a traditional midnight mass, including the *pastrage* ceremony, traditional songs, and performance of a nativity play. For more information, call ☎ **04-90-54-40-20.** December 24.
- **Fête de St-Sylvestre (New Year's Eve),** nationwide. Along the Riviera, it's most boisterously celebrated in Nice's Vieille Ville around place Garibaldi. At midnight, the city explodes. Strangers kiss strangers, and place Masséna and promenade des Anglais become virtual pedestrian malls. December 31.

6 The Active Vacation Planner

Provence and the Côte d'Azur are especially well organized for visitors looking for sports pursuits. Most clubs will accept temporary members, and activities are wide-ranging, from biking through the countryside to golfing on the pine-fringed fairways of Provence to swinging a tennis racquet close to Mediterranean waters. If you like your activities offbeat, you can even go barging along the lowlands of the Camargue.

Of course, if you want to go really local, you'll take up *boules* and its local variant, *pétanque.* The game is relatively simple to learn—any local can teach you—and it's played with small metal balls on earth courts in every dusty village square.

BARGING

Before the advent of the railways, many of the crops, building supplies, raw materials, and other products were barged through a series of rivers, canals, and estuaries. Many of these are still graced with their old-fashioned locks and pumps, allowing shallow-draft barges easy passage through idyllic countryside.

The **Crown Blue Line,** c/o Fenwick & Lang, 100 W. Harisson, Suite 350, Seattle, WA 98119 (☎ **800/243-6244**), acts as a clearinghouse for the chartering of at least 400 cruise craft with shallow drafts that can navigate the locks and channels of the waterways. You choose from among 27 kinds of boats, each suitable for between two and about a dozen passengers. Rentals can be arranged with a staff or without. Plan on cruising no more than 5 hours a day, spending the rest the time exploring the countryside, perhaps on bicycle. A 7-day rental ranges from $1,500 to $5,000, depending on the vessel's capacity and the season.

With **Kemwel's Premier Selections,** 106 Calvert St., Harrison, NY 10528 (☎ **800/234-4000** or 914/835-5555; fax 914/835-5449), you'll discover the secret corners of France as you wind your way along waterways on board a luxury hotel barge. Enjoy fine wines and cuisine, bicycling, walking, and exploring. Its fleet can accommodate individuals as well as groups and offers a wide array of cruising in the south of France. Inclusive fares per person for 3 nights (double occupancy) begin at $1,410, with 6 nights beginning at $2,615.

Le Boat, 105 Franklin Turnpike, Suite 204-B, Ramsey, NJ 07446 (☎ **800/992-0291** or 201/236-2333), focuses on regions of France not covered by many other barge operators. The company's pair of barges are luxury craft of a size and shape that fit through the relatively narrow canals and locks of the Camargue, Languedoc, and Provence. Each 6-night tour accommodates no more than 10 passengers in five cabins outfitted with mahogany and brass, plus meals prepared by a Cordon Bleu chef. Prices depend on many factors and are highly variable, but call for information.

BICYCLING

A well-recommended company, since 1979, is the California-based **Backroads,** 801 Cedar St., Berkeley, CA 94710 (☎ **800/462-2848** or 510/527-1555; fax 510/527-1444). Its well-organized tours of Provence last between 6 and 8 days and include stays in everything from Relais & Châteaux hotels to campgrounds where staff members prepare meals featuring local cuisine. All tours include an accompanying vehicle that provides liquid refreshments and assists in the event of breakdowns. A 6-day tour costs $2,498 per person, increasing to $3,098 for 8 days.

Holland Bicycling Tours, Inc., P.O. Box 6485, Thousand Oaks, CA 91359 (☎ **800/852-3258;** fax 805/495-8601), is the North American representative of a Dutch-based company that leads a 10-day tour through Provence, past Roman ruins, van Gogh's sunflowers, and fields pungent with lavender, thyme, and basil. The trip begins in Avignon and concludes with a 2-day stay near Gordes, a charming town with vaulted passageways. The price is $1,850 per person. Occupants of single rooms pay a supplement of $325.

Bridges Tours, 2855 Capital Dr., Eugene, OR 97403 (☎ **800/461-6760**), offers several regional biking and walking tours. All tours feature groups of eight, escorts, van support, and stays at inns and small hotels, costing $250 or $300 per person per day.

Châteaux Bike Tours, P.O. Box 5706, Denver, CO 80217 (☎ **800/678-2453**), promotes luxury tours of France with small groups, van support, two guides, and stays in châteaux. Tours (usually for 5 to 18 people) range from 5 to 9 days and cost $2,500 to $3,000 per person, double occupancy.

FISHING

The Mediterranean provides a variety of fish and fishing methods. You can line fish from the rocks along the coast or from small boats known as *pointu.* Local fishers often take visitors along when fishing in the sea for tuna. The rivers provide sea trout, speckled trout, and silver eel, and the sandy shores of the Camargue offer the *tellina* or sunset shell, which are small shellfish. For more information on regulations and access to fishing areas, contact the **Comité Régional PACA de la Fédération des Pêcheurs en Mer** (☎ **04-91-72-63-96**).

GOLFING

The area around Bouches-du-Rhône has many fine golf courses, with seven 18-hole courses, five 9-hole courses, and several practice courses in the Provence area. A few of the 18-hole courses **are Golf de la Salette,** impasse des Vaudrans, 13011 Marseille (☎ **04-91-27-12-16**); and **Golf de l'Ecole de l'Air,** Base Aérienne 701, 13300 Salon-de-Provence (☎ **04-90-53-90-90**). One of the finest courses is **Golf de Valcros,** La Londe-Les Maures, 23 miles east of Toulouse off N98 (it's signposted). Call ☎ **04-94-66-81-02** for more information.

Golf **International, Inc.,** 275 Madison Ave., New York, NY 10016 (☎ **800/ 833-1389** or 212/986-9176; fax 212/986-3720), offers the Golfing Epicurean package: a week-long trip based in the historic hilltop village of Mougins, a 10-minute drive from Cannes. Mougins is the golfing capital of the south of France and provides a wealth of fine dining opportunities. As part of this package, you spend 6 nights at the four-star Les Mas Candille, a 200-year-old converted farmhouse in the village. The price includes golf on four of the best courses in the area: Royal Mougins, Cannes-Mougins, Valbonne, and Cannes-Mandelieu. Also included is a car rental with collision-damage waiver insurance and unlimited mileage. The cost is $1,895. You can request a copy of Golf International's *Complete Golfing Vacation Guide* by calling the number above.

For more information on the options available, contact the **Fédération Française de Golf,** 69 av. Victor-Hugo, 75116 Paris (☎ **01-44-17-63-00**).

HIKING

The Bouches-du-Rhône area is a walker's heaven, whether you enjoy a stroll or a strenuous long-distance hike or even mountain climbing. Walking challenges include the wetlands of the Camargue, the semi-arid desert of La Crau, and the mountainous hills to the wild rocky inlets of Les Calanques. Long-distance hiking paths, **Sentiers de Grande Randonnée (GRs),** join the area's major places of interest. GR6 starts in Tarascon, runs along the foot of the Lubéron Hills, and crosses the Alpilles Hills. GR9 goes down the Lubéron, passes Mont Ste-Victoire, and ends in Ste-Baume. GR98 is an alternative path linking Ste-Baume with Les Calanques and ends in Marseille. GR51 links Marseille and Arles via La Crau. GR99A links GR9 to the highlands of the Var départment.

Spring and autumn are the best for hiking, as many of the paths are closed in summer because of forest fires. Be sure to check with the départment before you begin your walk. For information, call the **Comité Départmental de Randonnée Pédestre** (Bouches-du-Rhône Hiking Committee), M. Busti, 24 av. du Prado-Immeuble B, Bureau 401, 13008 Marseille (☎ **04-91-81-12-08**), or **Comité Départmental Mont-Alp-Escalade** (Bouches-du-Rhône Mountaineering & Climbing Committee), Daniel Gorgeon, 5 impasse du Figuier, 13114 Puyloubier (☎ **04-42-66-35-05**).

The **Adventure Center,** 1311 63rd St., Suite 200, Emeryville, CA 94608 (☎ **800/ 227-8747**), sponsors 8-day hiking/camping trips in Provence, beginning and ending in Nice. The cost of an outing, exclusive of airfare and other travel-related expenses, is $595 to $630 per person, $95 of which is a local fee added in France. Included are 4 nights of campground accommodations. Eight evening meals are provided; the other seven are usually purchased in Provençal restaurants along the way. Campers are also expected to purchase three lunches. The company offers 16 trips per year, and though dates may vary, these include departures in May to September.

Another company known for its adventure trips is **Mountain Travel Sobek,** 6420 Fairmount Ave., El Cerrito, CA 94530 (☎ **800/227-2384**), which offers a tour package in summer. Trip dates vary, but are offered four times a year between June and September. The "Pleasures of Provence" ranges from $2,390 to $2,590 per person (travel not included), which covers a 6-day, 57-mile trek with accommodations provided in mostly luxury hotels. The fee also includes five dinners at fine restaurants and six breakfasts. Starting in Vaison-la-Romaine, the hike encompasses the immediate environs of the lower Alpilles, St-Rémy, Les Baux, and Arles.

HORSEBACK RIDING

One of the best ways to see the wildlife, salt swamps, and marshlands of the Camargue or the wooded hills around Alpilles, Ste-Baume, and Mont Ste-Victoire is on horseback. For more information, contact the **Délégation Nationale des Sports Equestres** (National Equestrian Sports Board), Centre Equestre Les Décanis, chemin Collavery, 13760 St-Cannat (☎ **04-42-57-35-42**), or the **Association Camarguaise de Tourisme Equestre** (Camargue Equestrian Tourism Association), Centre de Ginès-Pont de Gau, 13460 Stes-Maries-de-la-Mer (☎ **04-90-97- 86-32**).

A clearinghouse for at least eight French stables is **Equitour FITS (Fun in the Saddle),** P.O. Box 807, Dubois, WY 82513 (☎ **800/545-0019** or 307/455-3363). It can arrange 9-day cross-country treks through Provence and the Camargue regions, with prices starting from $1,690 per person.

7 Gourmet Tours & Language Schools

GOURMET TOURS

Cuisine International, P.O. Box 25228, Dallas, TX 75225 (☎ **214/373-1161**), offers a week-long culinary experience in Provence. Accommodations are in hotels and private homes, such as the one overlooking a lake in Provence that houses the school. Classes are arranged to allow time for sightseeing, and meals are eaten in restaurants and private homes. Rates are inclusive, except for airfare: The price is $1,800 to $2,800. A tour by **European Culinary Adventures,** 5 Ledgewood Way, no. 6, Peabody, MA 01960 (☎ **800/852-2625**), touts culinary vacations during which you stay in an 18th-century farmhouse (also the school) between Bordeaux and Toulouse. The price of a 7-day/6-night tour is $1,895 to $2,850 per person, including lodging, cooking classes, most meals, touring, and local transportation. In addition, four people can charter an 85-foot barge for a week of cooking, dining, and touring.

Endless Beginnings Tours, 12650 Sabre Springs Pkwy., Suite 207, San Diego, CA 92128 (☎ **800/822-7855**), specializes in food and wine tours, garden and villa visits, and art programs. Small groups of 10 to 15 travel with knowledgeable guides. Accommodations are in four-star hotels and occasionally in charming three-star lodgings. The 16-day tour of Provence and the Côte d'Azur (beginning and ending in Nice) is from $4,500 per person, double occupancy.

LANGUAGE SCHOOLS

A clearinghouse for information on French-language schools is **Lingua Service Worldwide,** 211 E. 43rd St., Suite 1303, New York, NY 10017 (☎ **800/394-LEARN** or 212/867-1225; fax 212/983-2590). Its programs cover Antibes, Aix-en-Provence, Avignon, Cannes, Juan-les-Pins, Montpellier, and Nice. Courses can be both long- or short-term, the latter with 20 lessons per week. They range from $425 to $993 for 2 weeks, depending on the city, the school, and the accommodations.

The **National Registration Center for Studies Abroad (NRCSA),** 823 N. 2nd St., Milwaukee, WI 53201 (☎ **414/278-0631**), has a $2 catalog of schools in France, including the International House in Nice and Provence Langues and CELA (Centre d'études Linguistiques d'Avignon) in Avignon. It'll register you at the school of your choice, arrange for room and board, and make your airline reservations—all for no extra fee. Ask for a free copy of its newsletter. Prices vary greatly depending on the university and the course length, from $1,171 to $34,158. A 2-week program in Nice, for example, costs from $875 to $1,215.

8 Health & Insurance

STAYING HEALTHY

If you need a doctor away from home, your hotel will locate one for you. You might want to consider **medical travel insurance** (see below). In many cases, however, your existing health plan will provide all the coverage you need (though if you belong to an HMO, you should check to see whether you are fully covered when away from home). The **International Association for Medical Assistance to Travelers (IAMAT)** (☎ **716/754-4883** or 416/652-0137; www.sentex.net/~iamat) offers tips on travel and health concerns and lists many local English-speaking doctors. Remember that **Medicare** covers only U.S. citizens traveling in Mexico and Canada.

If you suffer from chronic illness like epilepsy, diabetes, or heart problems, wear a **Medic Alert Identification Tag** (☎ 800/825-3785; www.commedicalert.org), which will give doctors access to your records through Medic Alert's 24-hour hot line. Membership is $35, plus a $15 annual fee. Carry written prescriptions in generic, not brand-name form, since brands available in France may differ from those at home.

INSURANCE

There are three kinds of travel insurance: trip cancellation, medical, and lost-luggage coverage. **Trip cancellation insurance** is a good idea if you have paid a large portion of your vacation expenses up front. The other two types of insurance, however, don't make sense for most travelers. Rule number one: Check your existing policies before you buy any additional coverage.

The differences between travel assistance and insurance are often blurred, but in general the former offers on-the-spot assistance and 24-hour hot lines (mostly oriented toward medical problems), while the latter reimburses you for travel problems (medical, travel, or otherwise) after you have filed the paperwork. The coverage you should consider will depend on how much protection you already have. Some credit- and charge-card companies may insure you against travel accidents if you buy plane, train, or bus tickets with their cards. Some credit cards (American Express and certain gold and platinum Visa and MasterCards, for example) offer automatic flight insurance against death or dismemberment.

If you do require additional insurance, try one of the companies listed below. For example, if you need only trip-cancellation insurance, don't purchase coverage for lost or stolen property. Your homeowner's insurance should cover stolen luggage.

Among the reputable issuers of travel insurance are:

- **Access America,** 6600 W. Broad St., Richmond, VA 23230 (☎ **800/ 284-8300**)
- **Travel Guard International,** 1145 Clark St., Stevens Point, WI 54481 (☎ **800/ 826-1300**)
- **Travel Insured International, Inc.,** P.O. Box 280568, East Hartford, CT 06128 (☎ **800/243-3174**)
- **Columbus Travel Insurance,** 279 High St., Croydon CR0 1QH (☎ **0171/ 375-0011** in London; www2.columbusdirect.com/columbusdirect)

- **International SOS Assistance,** P.O. Box 11568, Philadelphia, PA 11916 (☎ **800/523-8930** or 215/244-1500), strictly an assistance company
- **Travelex Insurance Services,** P.O. Box 9408, Garden City, NY 11530-9408 (☎ **800/228-9792**)
- **MEDEX International,** P.O. Box 5375, Timonium, MD 21094-5375 (☎ **888/ MEDEX-00** or 410/453-6300; fax 410/453-6301; www.medexassist.com)
- **Travel Assistance International** (Worldwide Assistance Services, Inc.), 1133 15th St. NW, Suite 400, Washington, DC 20005 (☎ **800/821-2828** or 202/828-5894; fax 202/828-5896)

For information on car renter's insurance, see "By Car" under "Getting Around the South of France," later in this chapter.

9 Tips for Travelers with Special Needs

FOR TRAVELERS WITH DISABILITIES

Facilities for travelers with disabilities are above average in Europe, and nearly all modern hotels in the south of France now provide rooms designed for persons with disabilities. However, older hotels (unless they've been renovated) may not have such important features as elevators, special toilet facilities, or ramps for wheelchair access.

The new high-speed **TGV trains** are wheelchair accessible; older trains have special compartments for wheelchair boarding. Guide dogs ride free. Be aware that some older stations don't have escalators or elevators.

There are agencies in the United States and France that can provide advance-planning information and can save you a lot of frustration.

The **Association des Paralysés de France,** 17 bd. Auguste-Blanqui, 75013 Paris (☎ **01-40-78-69-00**), is a privately funded organization that provides wheelchair-bound individuals with documentation, moral support, and travel ideas. In addition to the central Paris office, it maintains an office in each of the 90 *départements* of France and can help you find accessible hotels, transportation, sightseeing, house rentals, and (in some cases) companionship for paralyzed or partially paralyzed travelers. It's not, however, a travel agency.

A World of Options, a 658-page book of resources for disabled travelers, covers everything from biking trips to scuba outfitters. It costs $35 ($30 for members) and is available from **Mobility International USA,** P.O. Box 10767, Eugene, OR 97440 (☎ **541/343-1284,** voice and TDD; www.miusa.org). Annual membership for Mobility International is $35, which includes their quarterly newsletter, *Over the Rainbow.* In addition, **Twin Peaks Press,** P.O. Box 129, Vancouver, WA 98666 (☎ **360/694-2462**), publishes travel-related books for people with disabilities.

The **Moss Rehab Hospital** (☎ **215/456-9600**) has been providing friendly and helpful phone advice and referrals to disabled travelers for years through its **Travel Information Service** (☎ **215/456-9603;** www.mossresourcenet.org).

You can join **The Society for the Advancement of Travel for the Handicapped (SATH),** 347 Fifth Ave. Suite 610, New York, NY 10016 (☎ **212/447-7284;** fax 212/725-8253; www.sath.org) for $45 annually, $30 for seniors and students, to gain access to their vast network of connections in the travel industry. They provide information sheets on travel destinations, and referrals to tour operators that specialize in traveling with disabilities. Their quarterly magazine, *Open World for Disability and Mature Travel,* is full of good information and resources. A year's subscription is $13 ($21 outside the US).

Travelers with disabilities may also want to consider joining a tour that caters specifically to them. One of the best operators is **Flying Wheels Travel,** 143 West Bridge (P.O. Box 382), Owatonna, MN 55060 (☎ **800/535-6790**). They offer various escorted tours and cruises, with an emphasis on sports, as well as private tours in minivans with lifts. Other reputable specialized tour operators include **Access Adventures** (☎ **716/889-9096**), which offers sports-related vacations; **Accessible Journeys** (☎ **800/TINGLES** or 610/521-0339), for slow walkers and wheelchair travelers; **The Guided Tour, Inc.** (☎ **215/782-1370**); **Wilderness Inquiry** (☎ **800/728-0719** or 612/379-3858); and **Directions Unlimited** (☎ **800/533-5343**).

You can obtain a copy of *Air Transportation of Handicapped Persons* by writing to Free Advisory Circular No. AC12032, Distribution Unit, U.S. Department of Transportation, Publications Division, M-4332, Washington, DC 20590.

Vision-impaired travelers should contact the **American Foundation for the Blind,** 11 Penn Plaza, Suite 300, New York, NY 10001 (☎ **800/232-5463**), for information on traveling with seeing-eye dogs.

In the United Kingdom, **RADAR (Royal Association for Disability and Rehabilitation),** Unit 12, City Forum, 250 City Rd., London EC1V 8AF (☎ **0171/250-3222**), publishes holiday "fact packs" (three in all), which sell for £2 each or £5 for a set of all three. The first one provides general information, including planning and booking a holiday, insurance, finances, and useful organization and holiday providers. The second outlines transport and equipment, transportation available when going abroad, and equipment for rent. The third deals with specialized accommodations.

Another good resource is the **Holiday Care Service,** 2nd floor, Imperial Building, Victoria Road, Horley, Surrey RH6 7PZ, UK (☎ **01293/774-535;** fax 01293/784-647), a national charity that advises on accessible accommodations for elderly and persons with disabilities. Once a member, you can receive a newsletter and access to a free reservations network for hotels throughout Britain and, to a lesser degree, Europe and the rest of the world.

FOR GAY & LESBIAN TRAVELERS

Before going to France, both lesbians and gay men might want to pick up a copy of Frommer's brand-new *Gay & Lesbian Europe.*

The **International Gay & Lesbian Travel Association (IGLTA)** (☎ **800/448-8550** or 954/776-2626; fax 954/776-3303; www.iglta.org) links travelers with the appropriate gay-friendly service organization or tour specialist. With around 1,200 members, it offers quarterly newsletters, marketing mailings, and a membership directory that's updated quarterly. Membership is open to individuals for $150 yearly, plus a $100 administration fee for new members. Members are kept informed of gay and gay-friendly hoteliers, tour operators, and airline and cruise-line representatives. Contact the IGLTA for a list of its member agencies, who will be tied into IGLTA's information resources.

Gay and lesbian travel agencies include **Family Abroad** (☎ **800/999-5500** or 212/459-1800; gay and lesbian); **Above and Beyond Tours** (☎ **800/397-2681;** mainly gay men); and **Yellowbrick Road** (☎ **800/642-2488;** gay and lesbian).

There are also two good, biannual English-language gay guidebooks, both focused on gay men but including information for lesbians as well. You can get the *Spartacus International Gay Guide* or *Odysseus* from most gay and lesbian book stores, or order them from **Giovanni's Room** (☎ **215/923-2960**) or **A Different Light Bookstore** (☎ **800/343-4002** or 212/989-4850). Both lesbians and gays might want to pick up a copy of *Gay Travel A to Z* ($16). **The Ferrari Guides** (www.q-net.com) is yet another very good series of gay and lesbian guidebooks.

Out and About, 8 W. 19th St. no. 401, New York, NY 10011 (☎ **800/929-2268** or 212/645-6922) offers guidebooks and a monthly newsletter packed with good information on the global gay and lesbian scene. A year's subscription to the newsletter costs $49. *Our World,* 1104 North Nova Rd., Suite 251, Daytona Beach, FL 32117 (☎ **904/441-5367**), is a slicker monthly magazine promoting and highlighting travel bargains and opportunities. Annual subscription rates are $35 in the U.S., $45 outside the U.S.

FOR SENIOR TRAVELERS

Many discounts are available in France for seniors—men and women who've reached the "third age," as the French say. For more information, contact the French Government Tourist Office (see section 2 in this chapter).

At any rail station in the country, seniors (men and women 60 and older—with proof of age) can obtain a **La Carte Senior.** The pass goes for 285F ($48.45) and is good for a 50% discount on unlimited rail travel throughout a year.

There are some restrictions on the carte—for example, you can't use it between 3pm Sunday and noon Monday and from noon Friday to noon Saturday. The carte also delivers reduced prices on certain regional bus lines, as well as half-price admission at state-owned museums.

The French domestic airline **Air Inter Europe** honors "third agers" by offering a 25% to 50% reduction on its regular nonexcursion tariffs. Restrictions do apply, however. Also, discounts of around 10% are offered to passengers 62 or over on selected Air France flights. These include some flights between Paris and Nice, as well as many international flights, including some on the Concorde.

Don't be shy about asking for discounts, but always carry some kind of identification that shows your date of birth. Many hotels offer seniors discounts. In most cities, people over the age of 60 qualify for reduced admission to theaters, museums, and other attractions, and discounted fares on public transportation.

The **American Association of Retired Persons (AARP),** 601 E St. NW, Washington, DC 20049 (☎ **800/424-3410** or 202/434-2277), offers members a wide range of special benefits.

The **National Council of Senior Citizens,** 8403 Colesville Rd., Suite 1200, Silver Spring, MD 20910 (☎ **301/578-8800**), a nonprofit organization, offers a newsletter six times a year (partly devoted to travel tips) and discounts on hotel and auto rentals; annual dues are $13 per person or couple.

Mature Outlook, P.O. Box 9390, Des Moines, IA 50306 (☎ **800/336-6330**), began as a travel organization for people over 50, though it now caters to people of all ages. Members receive discounts on hotels and receive a bimonthly magazine. Annual membership is $19.95.

Golden Companions, P.O. Box 5249, Reno, NV 89513 (☎ **702/324-2227**), helps travelers 45-plus find compatible companions through a personal voice-mail service. Contact them for more information.

The Mature Traveler, a monthly 12-page newsletter on senior citizen travel, is a valuable resource. It is available by subscription ($30 a year) from GEM Publishing Group, Box 50400, Reno, NV 89513-0400. GEM also publishes *The Book of Deals,* a collection of more than 1,000 senior discounts on airlines, lodging, tours, and attractions around the country; it's available for $9.95 by calling ☎ **800/460-6676.** Another helpful publication is *101 Tips for the Mature Traveler,* available from Grand Circle Travel, 347 Congress St., Suite 3A, Boston, MA 02210 (☎ **800/ 221-2610** or 617/350-7500; fax 617/346-6700).

Grand Circle Travel is one of the hundreds of travel agencies specializing in vacations for seniors (347 Congress St., Suite 3A, Boston, MA 02210 (☎ **800/221-2610** or 617/350-7500). Many of these packages, however, are of the tour-bus variety. **SAGA International Holidays,** 222 Berkeley St., Boston, MA 02116 (☎ **800/343-0273**), offers inclusive tours and cruises for those 50 and older. SAGA also sponsors the more substantial **"Road Scholar Tours"** (☎ **800/621-2151**), which are fun-loving but with an educational bent.

If you want something more than the average vacation or guided tour, try **Elderhostel,** 75 Federal St., Boston, MA 02110-1941 (☎ **877/426-8056;** www.elderhostel.org) or the University of New Hampshire's **Interhostel** (☎ **800/733-9753**), both variations on the same theme: educational travel for senior citizens. On these escorted tours, the days are packed with seminars, lectures, and field trips, and sightseeing is led by academic experts.

Elderhostel arranges study programs for persons 55 and over (and a spouse or companion of any age) in the U.S. and in 77 countries around the world. Most courses last about 3 weeks and many include airfare, accommodations in student dormitories or modest inns, meals, and tuition. Write or call for a free catalog, which lists upcoming courses and destinations. **Interhostel** takes travelers 50 and over (with companions over 40), and offers 2- and 3-week trips, mostly international. The courses in both these programs are ungraded, involve no homework, and often focus on the liberal arts.

Although all the **specialty books** on the market are U.S.-focused, three do provide good general advice and contacts for the savvy senior traveler. Thumb through *The 50+ Traveler's Guidebook* (St. Martin's Press), *The Seasoned Traveler* (Country Roads Press), or *Unbelievably Good Deals and Great Adventures That You Absolutely Can't Get Unless You're Over 50* (Contemporary Books). Also check out your newsstand for the quarterly magazine *Travel 50 & Beyond.*

FOR FAMILIES

Several books on the market offer tips to help you travel with kids. Most concentrate on the U.S., but two, *Family Travel* (Lanier Publishing International) and *How to Take Great Trips with Your Kids* (The Harvard Common Press), are full of good general advice that can apply to travel anywhere. Another reliable tome, with a worldwide focus, is *Adventuring with Children* (Foghorn Press).

Family Travel Times is published six times a year by TWYCH (Travel with Your Children; ☎ **888/822-4388** or 212/477-5524), and includes a weekly call-in service for subscribers. Subscriptions are $40 a year for quarterly editions. A free publication list and a sample issue are available by calling or sending a request to the above address.

Families Welcome!, 92 N. Main, Ashland, OR 97520 (☎ **800/326-0724** or 541/482-6121), a travel company specializing in worry-free vacations for families, offers "City Kids" packages to certain European destinations, including France.

The University of New Hampshire runs **Familyhostel** (☎ **800/733-9753**), an intergenerational alternative to standard guided tours. You live on a European college campus for the 2- or 3-week program, attend lectures and seminars, go on lots of field trips, and do all the sightseeing—all of it guided by a team of experts and academics. It's designed for children (ages 8 to 15), parents, and grandparents.

FOR STUDENTS

The best resource for students is the **Council on International Educational Exchange,** or CIEE. They can set you up with an ID card (see below), and their travel branch, **Council Travel Service** (☎ **800/226-8624;** www.ciee.com), is the biggest student travel agency operation in the world. It can get you discounts on plane tickets, rail passes, and the like. Ask them for a list of CTS offices in major cities so you can keep the discounts flowing (and aid lines open) as you travel.

From CIEE you can obtain the student traveler's best friend, the $18 **International Student Identity Card (ISIC).** It's the only officially acceptable form of student identification, good for cut rates on rail passes, plane tickets, and other discounts. It also provides you with basic health and life insurance and a 24-hour help line. If you're no longer a student but are still under 26, you can get a GO 25 card from the same people, which will get you the insurance and some of the discounts (but not student admission prices in museums).

In Canada, **Travel CUTS,** 200 Ronson St., Ste. 320, Toronto, ONT M9W 5Z9 (☎ **800/667-2887** or 416/614-2887; www.travelcuts.com), offers similar services. **Campus Travel,** 52 Grosvenor Gardens, London SW1W 0AG (☎ **0171/730-3402;** www.campustravel.co.uk), opposite Victoria Station, is Britain's leading specialist in student and youth travel.

FOR SINGLE TRAVELERS

Many people prefer traveling alone except for the relatively steep cost of booking single rooms. **Travel Companion** (☎ **516/454-0880**) is one of the nation's oldest roommate finders for single travelers. Register with them and find a trustworthy travel mate who will split the cost of the room with you and be around as little, or as often, as you like during the day.

Several tour organizers cater to solo travelers as well. **Experience Plus** (☎ **800/ 685-4565;** fax 907/484-8489) offers an interesting selection of single-only trips. **Travel Buddies** (☎ **800/998-9099** or 604/533-2483) runs single-friendly tours with no singles supplement. **The Single Gourmet Club,** 133 E. 58th St., New York, NY 10022 (☎ **212/980-8788;** fax 212/980-3138), is an international social, dining, and travel club for singles, with offices in 21 cities in the U.S. and Canada, and one in London.

You may also want to research the **Outdoor Singles Network,** P.O. Box 781, Haines, AK 99827. It offers an established quarterly newsletter (since 1989) for outdoor-loving singles ages 19 to 90; a 1-year subscription costs $45, and your own personal ad is printed free in the next issue. Current issues are $15. Write for free information or check out the group's Web site at **www.kcd.com/bearstar/osn.html**.

10 Getting to the South of France from North America

BY PLANE

Most airlines divide their year roughly into seasonal slots, with the lowest fares between November 1 and March 13. Shoulder season, between the high and low seasons, is only slightly more expensive and includes mid-March to mid-June and all of October. These can be ideal times to visit southern France.

THE MAJOR U.S. CARRIERS   All major airlines fly to Paris from the U.S. cities listed below. Once you fly into Orly or Charles de Gaulle, you must take **Air France** or **Air Inter** (☎ **800/237-2747;** www.airfrance.com), a division of Air France, to reach your destination in Languedoc, Provence, or the Riviera. From Orly and Charles de Gaulle, there are 20 flights per day to Marseille and to Nice, 16 to Toulouse, and four Monday to Friday and two Saturday and Sunday to Avignon.

American Airlines (☎ **800/433-7300;** www.americanair.com) offers daily flights to Paris from Dallas/Fort Worth, Chicago, Miami, Boston, and New York. **Delta Airlines** (☎ **800/241-4141;** www.delta-air.com) flies to Paris from the southeastern

———————————————

If you've bought this book you're obviously headed to the south of France, but your flight will be routed through Paris. In rare instances, the flight will merely stop in Paris and then continue on to Marseille or Nice. Most frequently, you will have to change planes in Paris. However, Delta offers one flight per day direct from New York to Nice.

Flying time to Paris from New York is about 7 hours; from Chicago, 9 hours; from Los Angeles, 11 hours; from Atlanta, 8 hours; from Miami, 8½ hours; and from Washington, D.C., 7½ hours.

———————————————————————————————————————

United States or the Midwest. From cities like New Orleans, Phoenix, Columbia (S.C.), and Nashville, Delta flies to Atlanta, connecting every evening with a nonstop flight to Paris. Delta also operates daily nonstop flights from both Cincinnati and New York. All these flights depart late enough in the day to permit transfers from much of Delta's vast North American network. Note that Delta is the only airline offering non-stop service from New York to Nice.

Continental Airlines (☎ 800/231-0856; www.flycontinental.com) provides non-stop flights to Paris from Newark and Houston. Flights from Newark depart daily, while flights from Houston depart four to seven times a week, depending on the season. **US Airways** (☎ 800/428-4322) offers daily nonstop service from Philadelphia to Paris.

TWA (☎ 800/221-2000; www.twa.com) operates daily nonstop service to Paris from New York. In summer, several flights a week from Boston and Washington, D.C., go through New York; several times a week there are nonstop flights from St. Louis; and three times a week there are flights from Los Angeles, connecting in St. Louis or New York. In winter, flights from Los Angeles and Washington are suspended, and flights from St. Louis are direct, with brief touchdowns in New York or Boston en route.

THE FRENCH NATIONAL CARRIER   Air France (☎ 800/237-2747) was formed from a merger combining three of France's largest airlines. The conglomerate offers routes that, until the merger, were maintained separately by Air France, UTA (Union des Transports Aériens), and France's internal domestic airline, Air Inter (now Air Inter Europe).

The airline offers daily or several-times-a-week flights between Paris and such North American cities as Newark; Washington, D.C.; Miami; Atlanta; Boston; Cincinnati; Chicago; New York; Houston; San Francisco; Los Angeles; Montréal; Toronto; Mexico City; and Los Angeles. Flights to Paris from Los Angeles originate in Papeete, French Polynesia.

THE MAJOR CANADIAN CARRIER   Canadians usually choose the **Air Canada** (☎ 800/776-3000 in the U.S. and Canada; www.aircanada.ca) flights to Paris from Toronto and Montréal that depart every evening. Two of Air Canada's flights from Toronto are shared with Air France and feature Air France aircraft.

FLYING FOR LESS: TIPS FOR GETTING THE BEST AIRFARES

Passengers within the same airplane cabin are rarely paying the same fare. Travelers who need to purchase tickets at the last minute or change their itinerary at a moment's notice pay the premium rate or full fare. Passengers who book long in advance, who don't mind staying over Saturday night, or who are willing to travel on a Tuesday, Wednesday, or Thursday after 7pm, will pay a fraction of the full fare. On most flights,

Cyber Deals for Net Surfers

It's possible to get some great deals on airfare, hotels, and car rentals via the Internet. Grab your mouse and surf before you take off—you could save a bundle on your trip. The Web sites highlighted below are worth checking out, especially since all services are free. Always check the lowest published fare, however, before you shop for flights online.

Arthur Frommer's Budget Travel Online (www.frommers.com)   Home of the Encyclopedia of Travel and *Arthur Frommer's Budget Travel* magazine and daily newsletter, this site offers detailed information on 200 cities and islands around the world, and up-to-the-minute ways to save dramatically on flights, hotels, car reservations, and cruises. Book an entire vacation online and research your destination before you leave. Consult the message board to set up "hospitality exchanges" in other countries, to talk with other travelers who have visited a hotel you're considering, or to direct travel questions to Arthur Frommer himself. The newsletter is updated daily to keep you abreast of the latest-breaking ways to save, to publicize new hot spots and best buys, and to present veteran readers with fresh, ever-changing approaches to travel.

Microsoft Expedia (www.expedia.com)   The best part of this multipurpose travel site is the "Fare Tracker": You fill out a form on the screen indicating that you're interested in cheap flights from your hometown, and, once a week, they'll e-mail you the best airfare deals on up to three destinations. The site's "Travel Agent" will steer you to bargains on hotels and car rentals, and with the help of hotel and airline seat pinpointers, you can book everything right on line. This site is even useful once you're booked. Before you depart, log on to Expedia for maps and up-to-date travel information, including weather reports and foreign exchange rates.

Travelocity (www.travelocity.com)   This is one of the best travel sites out there, especially for finding cheap airfare. In addition to its "Personal Fare Watcher," which notifies you via e-mail of the lowest airfares for up to five different

even the shortest hops, the full fare is close to $1,000 or more, but a 7-day or 14-day advance purchase ticket can be closer to $200 to $300. Here are a few other easy ways to save.

1. Periodically, airlines lower prices on their most popular routes. Check your newspaper for advertised discounts or call the airlines directly and ask if any **promotional rates** or special fares are available. You'll almost never see a sale during the peak summer vacation months of July and August, or during the Thanksgiving or Christmas seasons; but in periods of low-volume travel, you should pay no more than $400 for a cross-country flight. If your schedule is flexible, ask if you can secure a cheaper fare by staying an extra day or by flying midweek. (Many airlines won't volunteer this information.) If you already hold a ticket when a sale breaks, it may even pay to exchange your ticket, which usually incurs a $50 to $75 charge.

   Note, however, that the lowest-priced fares are often nonrefundable, require advance purchase of 1 to 3 weeks and a certain length of stay, and carry penalties for changing dates of travel.

destinations, Travelocity will track the three lowest fares for any routes on any dates in minutes. You can book a flight right then and there, and if you need a rental car or hotel, Travelocity will find you the best deal via the SABRE computer reservations system (another huge travel agent database). Click on "Last Minute Deals" for the latest travel bargains, including a link to "H.O.T. Coupons" (www.hotcoupons.com), where you can print out electronic coupons for travel in the U.S. and Canada.

The Trip (www.trip.com)   This site is really geared toward the business traveler, but vacationers-to-be can also use The Trip's exceptionally powerful fare-finding engine, which will e-mail you every week with the best city-to-city airfare deals for as many as 10 routes. The Trip uses the Internet Travel Network, another reputable travel agent database, to book hotels and restaurants.

E-Savers Programs   Several major airlines offer a free e-mail service known as E-Savers, via which they'll send you their best bargain airfares on a regular basis. Here's how it works: Once a week (usually Wednesday), or whenever a sale fare comes up, subscribers receive a list of discounted flights to and from various destinations, both international and domestic. Here's the catch: These fares are usually available only if you leave the very next Saturday (or sometimes Friday night) and return on the following Monday or Tuesday. It's really a service for the spontaneously inclined and travelers looking for a quick getaway. But the fares are cheap, so it's worth taking a look. If you have a preference for certain airlines (in other words, the ones you fly most frequently), sign up with them first.

Smarter Living (www.smarterliving.com)   If the thought of all that surfing and comparison shopping gives you a headache, then head right for Smarter Living. Sign up for their newsletter service, and every week you'll get a customized e-mail summarizing the discount fares available from your departure city. Smarter Living tracks more than 15 different airlines, so it's a worthwhile time-saver.

2. **Consolidators,** also known as bucket shops, are a good place to find low fares. Consolidators buy seats in bulk from the airlines and then sell them back to the public at prices below even the airlines' discounted rates. Their small boxed ads usually run in the Sunday travel section at the bottom of the page. Before you pay a consolidator, however, ask for a record locator number and confirm your seat with the airline itself. Be prepared to book your ticket with a different consolidator—there are many to choose from—if the airline can't confirm your reservation. Also be aware that bucket shop tickets are usually nonrefundable or rigged with stiff cancellation penalties, often as high as 50% to 75% of the ticket price.

Council Travel (☎ 800/226-8624; www.counciltravel.com) and **STA Travel** (☎ 800/781-4040; www.sta.travel.com) cater especially to young travelers, but their bargain-basement prices are available to people of all ages. **Travel Bargains** (☎ 800/AIR-FARE; www.1800airfare.com) was formerly owned by TWA but now offers the deepest discounts on many other airlines, with a 4-day advance purchase. Other reliable consolidators include **1-800-FLY-CHEAP** (www. 1800flycheap.com); **TFI Tours International** (☎ 800-745-8000 or 212/

736-1140), which serves as a clearinghouse for unused seats; or "rebaters" such as **Travel Avenue** (☎ 800/333-3335 or 312/876-1116) and the **Smart Traveller** (☎ **800/448-3338** in the U.S. or 305/448-3338; www.smarttraveller@juno.com), which rebate part of their commissions to you.

3. Book a seat on a **charter flight.** Discounted fares have pared the number available, but they can still be found. Most charter operators advertise and sell their seats through travel agents, thus making these local professionals your best source of information about available flights. Before deciding to take a charter flight, however, check the restrictions on the ticket: You may be asked to purchase a tour package, to pay in advance, to be amenable if the day of departure is changed, to pay a service charge, to fly on an airline you're not familiar with (this usually is not the case), and to pay harsh penalties if you cancel. If the charter doesn't fill up, it may be canceled up to 10 days before departure. Summer charters fill up more quickly than others and are almost sure to fly, but if you decide on a charter flight, seriously consider cancellation and baggage insurance.

4. Look into **courier flights.** Companies that hire couriers use your luggage allowance for their business baggage; in return, you get a deeply discounted ticket. Flights are often offered at the last minute, and you may have to arrange a pretrip interview to make sure you're right for the job. **Now Voyager,** open Monday to Friday from 10am to 5:30pm and Saturday from noon to 4:30pm (☎ **212/431-1616**), flies from New York. Now Voyager also offers noncourier discounted fares, so call the company even if you don't want to fly as a courier.

5. Join a travel club such as **Moment's Notice** (☎ **718/234-6295**) or **Sears Discount Travel Club** (☎ **800/433-9383,** or 800/255-1487 to join), which supplies unsold tickets at discounted prices. You pay an annual membership fee to get the club's hot-line number. Of course, you're limited to what's available, so you have to be flexible.

11 Getting to the South of France from Paris

BY PLANE
From Paris, if you're heading for the French Riviera, your connecting flight will probably land you in Nice's international airport, Aéroport Nice–Côte d'Azur. There are also airports at Avignon, Marseille, Montpellier, Nîmes, and Toulouse. If you have already been traveling in France before heading for the south, you can opt for Air France's **Euro-Flyer Pass,** a series of identically priced coupons for travel along intra-European air routes. If these coupons are purchased simultaneously with transatlantic passage to France from North America, they'll cost between $99 and $120 each, depending on the season. Call **Air France** at ☎ **800/237-2747** in the U.S. for information before you go.

BY TRAIN
With some 50 cities in France, including Marseille and Nice, linked by the world's fastest trains, you can reach the south of France by a trip of just a few hours. With 24,000 miles of track and about 3,000 stations, **SNCF (French National Railroads)** is fabled throughout the world for its on-time performance. You can travel first- or second class by day as well as in couchette or sleeper by night. Many trains carry dining facilities, which range from cafeteria-style meals to formal dinners. There's excellent and fast service from Paris's Gare de Lyon to Marseille via Avignon. Passengers take the TGV (Train à Grande Vitesse). The TGV zips from Paris to Marseille in 5 hours, to Avignon in 4 hours, and to Nice in 7 hours.

INFORMATION   If you plan much travel on European railroads, get the latest copy of the *Thomas Cook European Timetable of Railroads.* This comprehensive 500-plus-page book documents all Europe's mainline passenger rail services with detail and accuracy. It's available exclusively in North America from the **Forsyth Travel Library,** P.O. Box 480800, Kansas City, MO 64148 (☎ **800/367-7984**), at a cost of $27.95 (plus $4.95 priority airmail postage to the U.S. and US$6.95 for shipments to Canada).

In the United States: For more information and to purchase rail passes (see below) before you leave, contact **Rail Europe** at 226–230 Westchester Ave., White Plains, NY 10604 (☎ **800/848-7245;** fax 914/682-3712).

In Canada: Rail Europe offices are at 2087 Dundas St. East, Suite 105, Mississauga, ON L4X 1M2 (☎ **800/361-7245** or 905/602-4195; fax 905/602-4198).

In London: SNCF maintains offices at French Railways, 179 Piccadilly, London W1V OBA (☎ **0345/48-49-50;** fax 020/7491-9956).

In Paris: For train information or to make reservations, call **SNCF** at ☎ **08-36-35-35-35.** You are charged at the rate of 3F (50¢) per minute to use this service. You can also go to any local travel agency, of course, and book tickets. A simpler way to book tickets is to take advantage of the *Billetterie* or ticket machines in every train station. If you know your PIN, you can use credit cards such as American Express, MasterCard, and Visa to purchase your ticket.

FRENCH RAIL PASSES   Working cooperatively with SNCF, Air Inter Europe, and Avis, Rail Europe offers three flexible cost-saving rail passes that can reduce travel costs considerably, especially if you're heading somewhere else in France either before or after you explore the south.

The **France Railpass** provides unlimited rail transport throughout France for 3 days within 1 month, costing $205 in first class and $175 in second. You can purchase up to 6 more days for an extra $30 per person per day. Costs are even more reasonable for two adults traveling together: $328 per person for first class and $280 for second. Children 4 to 11 travel for half price; 3 and under ride free.

The **France Rail 'n Drive Pass,** available only in North America, combines good value on both rail travel and Avis car rentals and is best used in conjunction with arriving at a major rail depot, then striking out to explore the countryside by car. It includes the rail pass above, along with unlimited mileage on a car rental. Costs are lowest when two or more adults travel together. You can use it during 5 nonconsecutive days in 1 month, and it includes 3 days of travel on the train and 2 days' use of a rental car. If rental of the least expensive car is combined with first-class rail travel, the price is $204 per person; if rental of the least expensive car is combined with second-class travel, the price is $187 per person. Cars can be upgraded for a supplemental fee. The above prices apply to two people traveling together; solo travelers pay from $289 for first class and $255 for second.

EURAILPASSES   For years, many in-the-know travelers have been taking advantage of one of Europe's greatest travel bargains: the **Eurailpass,** which permits unlimited first-class rail travel in any country in Western Europe except the British Isles (good in Ireland). Passes are for periods as short as 15 days or as long as 3 months and are strictly nontransferable.

The pass is sold only in North America. A Eurailpass for 15 days is $554; it's $718 for 21 days, $890 for 1 month, $1,260 for 2 months, and $1,558 for 3 months. Children 3 and under travel free providing they don't occupy a seat (otherwise they're charged half fare); children 4 to 11 are charged half fare. If you're under 26, you can purchase a **Eurail Youth Pass,** entitling you to unlimited second-class travel for $388 for 15 days, $499 for 21 days, $623 for 1 month, $882 for 2 months, and $1,089 for 3 months.

Seat reservations are required on some trains. Many of the trains have couchettes (sleeping cars), which cost extra. Obviously, the 2- or 3-month traveler gets the greatest economic advantages; the Eurailpass is ideal for such extensive trips—you can visit all of France's major sights, from Normandy to the Alps.

If you'll be traveling for 14 days to 1 month, you have to estimate rail distance before determining if such a pass is to your benefit. To obtain full advantage of the ticket for 15 days or a month, you'd have to spend a great deal of time on the train. Eurailpass holders are entitled to considerable reductions on certain buses and ferries as well.

Travel agents in all towns and railway agents in such major cities as New York, Montréal, and Los Angeles sell all these tickets. A Eurailpass is available at the North American offices of CIT Travel Service, the French National Railroads, the German Federal Railroads, and the Swiss Federal Railways.

The **Eurail Flexipass** allows you to visit Europe with more flexibility. It's valid in first class and offers the same privileges as the Eurailpass. However, it provides a number of individual travel days that you can use over a much longer period of consecutive days. That makes it possible to stay in one city and yet not lose a single day of travel. There are two passes: 10 days of travel in 2 months for $654 and 15 days of travel in 2 months for $862.

With many of the same qualifications and restrictions as the previously described Flexipass is a **Eurail Youth Flexipass.** Sold only to travelers under 26, it allows 10 days of travel within 2 months for $458, and 15 days of travel within 2 months for $599.

12 Getting to the South of France from the United Kingdom

BY PLANE

If you're in the United Kingdom and don't want to go to Paris before flying to the south of France, you'll find a number of flights directly to the Nice-Côte d'Azur Airport and the Marseille-Provence airport. Daily flights are offered by **British Airways** (☎ 0345/222-111; www.british-airways.com), **Air France** (☎ 020/8742-6600), and **British Midland** ☎ (0345/554-554).

The newspapers are always full of classified ads touting "slashed" fares from London to other parts of the world. Another good source is *Time Out* magazine. London's *Evening Standard* maintains a daily travel section, and the Sunday editions of virtually every newspaper in Britain run many ads. Though competition is fierce, a well-recommended company that consolidates bulk ticket purchases and passes the savings on to you is **Trailfinders** (☎ 020/7938-3999 in London). It offers access to tickets on such carriers as British Airways, KLM, and SAS.

BY TRAIN

From the United Kingdom, most passengers arrive in Paris before going the rest of the way by train to Provence. Passengers can take the TGV (Train à Grande Vitesse) from the Gare de Lyon. The TGV zips from Paris to Marseille in 5 hours, to Avignon in 4 hours, and to Nice in 7 hours.

Rail passes as well as individual train tickets are available at most travel agents or at **BritRail Travel International** (☎ 020/7928-5151), Victoria Station, London SW1B

1JY. In London, an especially convenient place to buy rail tickets to virtually anywhere is **Wasteels Ltd.,** opposite Platform 2 in Victoria Station, London SW1V 1JY (☎ 020/7834-6744). It provides railway-related services and information on the pros and cons of various types of fares and rail passes; its staff will probably spend more than the usual amount of time with you while planning your itinerary. Depending on circumstances, Wasteels sometimes charges a £5 fee, but for the information provided the fee might be worth it.

BY FERRY

Service aboard ferryboats and hydrofoils operates day and night, in all seasons, with the exception of last-minute cancellations during particularly fierce storms. Many Channel crossings are carefully timed to coincide with the arrival/departure of major trains (especially those between London and Paris). Trains unload passengers and their luggage only a short walk from the piers. Most ferries carry cars, trucks, and massive amounts of freight, but some hydrofoils take passengers only. The major routes include at least 12 trips a day between Dover or Folkestone and Calais or Boulogne. Hovercraft and hydrofoils make the trip from Dover to Calais, the shortest distance across the Channel, in just 40 minutes during good weather, whereas the slower-moving ferries might take several hours, depending on weather conditions and tides. If you're bringing a car, it's important to make reservations, as space below decks is usually crowded. Timetables can vary depending on weather conditions and many other factors.

   P&O Stena Lines (☎ 800/677-8585 for reservations in the U.S. and Canada, or 01301/212-121 in England) operates car and passenger ferries between Portsmouth, England, and Cherbourg, France (three departures a day; 4¼ hours each way during daylight hours, 7 hours each way at night); and between Portsmouth and Le Havre, France (three a day; 5½ hours each way). A typical fare from Dover to Calais is £24 ($39.60) one way for adults and £12 ($19.80) one-way for children.

   The shortest route across the Channel is between Calais and Dover. **Hoverspeed** operates at least 12 hovercraft crossings daily; the trip takes 35 minutes. It also runs a SeaCat (a catamaran propelled by jet engines) that takes slightly longer to make the crossing between Boulogne and Folkestone; the SeaCats depart about four times a day on the 55-minute voyage. For reservations and information, call Hoverspeed (☎ **800/677-8585** for reservations in the U.S. and Canada or 08705/240-241 in Britain). Typical one-way fares are £25 ($41.25) per person.

   If you plan to transport a rental car between England and France, check in advance with the rental company about license and insurance requirements and additional drop-off charges. And be alert that many car-rental companies, for insurance reasons, forbid transport of one their vehicles over the water between England and France. Transport of a car each way begins at £75 ($123.75).

BY THE CHANNEL TUNNEL (CHUNNEL)

There is twice-daily passenger service between London and both Paris and Brussels on the *Eurostar Express.* The 31-mile journey between Great Britain and France takes 35 minutes, though the actual time spent in the Chunnel is only 19 minutes.

   Rail Europe (☎ 800/94-CHUNNEL) sells tickets for the Eurostar direct train service between London and Paris or Brussels. A round-trip fare between London and Paris, for example, is $278 to $298 in first class and $150 to $278 in second. But you can cut costs to $140 with a second-class 15-day nonrefundable advance-purchase round-trip ticket. In Britain, make reservations for *Eurostar* at ☎ **0990/300-003;** in Paris, call ☎ **01-44-51-06-02;** and in the United States call ☎ **800/387-6782.**

The Chunnel's *Le Shuttle* accommodates passenger cars, charter buses, taxis, and motorcycles under the English Channel from Folkestone, England, to Calais, France. It operates 24 hours a day year-round, running every 15 minutes during peak travel times and at least once an hour at night. You can buy tickets at the toll booth. With *Le Shuttle,* gone are weather-related delays, seasickness, and the need for advance reservations.

Before boarding *Le Shuttle,* motorists stop at a toll booth and pass through Immigration for both countries at one time. Travel time between the English and French highway systems is about 1 hour. Stores selling duty-free goods, restaurants, and service stations are available to travelers on both sides of the Channel. A bilingual staff is on hand to assist travelers at both the French and the British terminals.

13 Package Tours & Escorted Tours

For package tours that offer adventure and activity, see "The Active Vacation Planner," earlier in this chapter. For other types of tours, see "Gourmet Tours & Language Schools," also earlier in this chapter.

Before you start your search for the lowest airfare, you may want to consider booking your flight as part of a travel package such as an escorted tour or a package tour. What you lose in adventure, you'll gain in time and money saved when you book accommodations, and maybe even food and entertainment, along with your flight.

PACKAGE TOURS

Package tours are not the same thing as escorted tours. They are simply a way to buy airfare and accommodations at the same time. For popular destinations like the South of France, they are a smart way to go, because they save you a lot of money. In many cases, a package that includes airfare, hotel, and transportation to and from the airport will cost you less than just the hotel alone would have, had you booked it yourself. That's because packages are sold in bulk to tour operators—who resell them to the public at a cost that drastically undercuts standard rates.

Packages, however, vary widely. Some offer a better class of hotel than others. Some offer the same hotels for lower prices. Some offer flights on scheduled airlines, while others book charters. In some packages, your choice of accommodations and travel days may be limited. Some packages let you choose between escorted vacations and independent vacations; others will allow you to add on just a few excursions or escorted day trips (also at lower prices than you could locate on your own) without booking an entirely escorted tour. Each destination usually has one or two packagers that are usually cheaper than the rest because they buy in even greater bulk. If you spend the time to shop around, you will save in the long run.

FINDING A PACKAGE DEAL The best place to start your search is the travel section of your local Sunday newspaper. Also check the ads in the back of national travel magazines like *Travel & Leisure, National Geographic Traveler,* and *Condé Nast Traveler.*

American Express Vacations (☎ 800/241-1700; www.leisureweb.com) is an option. Check out its **Last Minute Travel Bargains** site, offered in conjunction with **Continental Airlines** (www6.americanexpress.com/travel/lastminutetravel/default.asp), with deeply discounted vacations packages and reduced airline fares that differ from the E-savers bargains that Continental e-mails weekly to subscribers.

Another good resource is the airlines themselves, which often package their flights together with accommodations. Fly-by-night packagers are uncommon, but they do exist; when you buy your package through the airline, however, you can be pretty sure that the company will still be in business when your departure date arrives. Among the airline packagers, your options include **American Airlines FlyAway Vacations** (☎ **800/321-2121**) and **Delta Dream Vacations** (☎ **800/872-7786**).

The biggest hotel chains, casinos, and resorts also offer package deals. If you already know where you want to stay, call the resort itself and ask if they can offer land/air packages.

The French Experience, 370 Lexington Ave., New York, NY 10017 (☎ **212/986-1115;** fax 212/986-3808), offers prearranged package tours lasting 6 or 7 days in Languedoc, in Provence, and on the Riviera. Stops are arranged in hotels and hostelleries in Provence and on the Riviera and in private homes that might be a farmhouse or a small castle or manor house in Languedoc. Figure on a 7-night stay at Avignon costing in the range of $183 to $240 per person per night. A car and breakfast are included plus one dinner based on a 7-night booking.

Trafalgar Tours, 11 E. 26th St., New York, NY 10010 (☎ **800/854-0103**), offers cost-conscious packages with lodgings in unpretentious hotels. Its "Best of France" is a 14-day trip starting and ending in Paris, with stops on the Riviera and in Lourdes, Nice, Monaco, and others. Most meals and twin-bed accommodations in first-class hotels are part of the package, which is $1,525 per person for the land package only. Call your travel agent for more information (Trafalgar takes calls only from agents).

For top-of-the-line travel, try **Travcoa,** P.O. Box 2360, Newport Beach, CA 92658 (☎ **800/992-2003**). All its tours are fully escorted, with stays in four-star hotels and three à la carte meals a day. The 19-day "Exotic France" begins and ends in Paris and circles the country going down the west coast, then up the east side back to Paris while visiting numerous historic sites; prices begin at $9,495 per person, double occupancy.

ESCORTED TOURS

Packaged travel may not be the option for you. If you like to plan your coordinates in advance, however, many package options will enable you to do just that—and save you money in the process.

Escorted tours spell out your costs up front; they allow you to relax and take in the sights while a bus driver fights traffic for you and someone takes care of your luggage and hotel reservations. They take you to the maximum number of sights in the minimum amount of time with the least amount of hassle. If you do choose an escorted tour, you should ask a few simple questions before you buy:

1. What is the **cancellation policy?** Do they require a deposit? Can they cancel the trip if they don't get enough people? Do you get a refund if they cancel? If you cancel? How late can you cancel if you are unable to go? When do you pay in full?

2. How busy is the **schedule?** How much sightseeing do they plan each day? Do they allow ample time for relaxing by the pool, shopping, or wandering?

3. What is the **size** of the group? The smaller the group, the more flexible the itinerary, and the less time you'll spend waiting for people to get on and off the bus. Tour operators may be evasive about this, because they may not know the exact size of the group until everybody has made their reservations; but they should be able to give you a rough estimate. Some tours have a minimum group size and may cancel the tour if they don't book enough people.

4. What is included in the **price?** Don't assume anything. You may have to pay for transportation to and from the airport. A box lunch may be included in an excursion, but drinks might cost extra. Beer might be included, but wine might not. Can you opt out of certain activities, or does the bus leave once a day, with no exceptions? Are all your meals planned in advance? Can you choose your entree at dinner, or does everybody get the same chicken cutlet?

Note: If you choose an escorted tour, think about purchasing travel insurance from an independent agency, especially if the tour operator asks you to pay up front. See the section on Insurance above. One final caveat: Since escorted tour prices are based on double occupancy, the single traveler is usually penalized.

14 Getting Around the South of France

The most charming Provençal villages and best country hotels always seem to lie away from the main cities and train stations. You'll find that renting a car is usually the best way to travel once you get to the south of France, especially if you plan to explore in depth and not stick to the standard route along the coast.

Driving time in Europe is largely a matter of conjecture, urgency, and how much sightseeing you do along the way. The driving time from Marseille to Paris is a matter of national pride, and tall tales abound about how rapidly the French can do it. With the accelerator pressed to the floor, you might conceivably make it in 7 hours, but we always make a 2-day journey of it.

If you're not driving, you'll find that the south of France has one of the most reliable bus and rail transportation systems in Europe. Trains connect all the major cities and towns, such as Nice and Avignon. Where the train leaves off, you can most often rely on the trusty local bus service.

BY CAR

Renting a car in France is easy. You'll need to present a passport, a valid driver's license, and a valid credit card. You'll also have to meet the minimum age requirement of the company. For their least expensive cars, this is 21 at Hertz, 23 at Avis, and 25 at Budget. (More expensive cars might require that you be at least 25.) While it isn't obligatory, some car companies, especially the smaller ones, sometimes ask for an International Driver's License.

The best deal is usually a weekly rental with unlimited mileage. All car-rental bills in France are subject to a whopping 20.6% government tax, among the highest in Europe. And while the rental company usually won't mind if you drive your car across the French border—into, say, Italy or Spain—it's often expressly forbidden to transport your car on any ferryboat, especially across the Channel to England.

Unless it's already factored into the rental agreement, an optional collision-damage waiver (CDW) carries an extra charge of 110F to 125F ($18.70 to $21.25) per day for the least expensive cars. Buying this will usually eliminate all but $250 of your responsibility in the event of accidental damage to the car. Because most newcomers aren't familiar with local driving customs and conditions, we highly recommend that you buy the CDW, though certain credit/charge-card issuers will compensate you for any accident-related liability to a rented car if their card was used for the original rental contract. At some of the companies, the CDW won't protect you against the theft of a car, so if this is the case, ask about buying extra theft protection. This cost is around 45F ($7.65) extra per day.

At all four of the big car-rental companies, the least expensive car will probably be a Ford Fiesta, a Nissan Micra, a Renault Clio, a Peugeot 106, a VW Polo, a Fiat Punto, or an Opel Corsa, usually with manual transmission, no air-conditioning, and few frills. Depending on the company and the season, prices may range from $212 to $251 per week, with unlimited mileage (but not tax or CDW) included. Discounts are sometimes granted for rentals of 2 weeks or more. Automatic transmission is regarded as a luxury in Europe, so if you want it you'll have to pay dearly. All agencies allow you to prepay your rental in U.S. dollars, though the benefits of prepayment vary from case to case and company to company, depending on what's included as part of the proposed prepayment.

Budget (☎ 800/472-3325 in the U.S. and Canada) has numerous locations in southern France, including those in **Avignon** at the airport (☎ 04-90-27-94-95) and at 2 av. de Montclair-Gare (☎ 04-90-27-94-95); in **Marseille** at the airport (☎ 04-42-14-24-55), at 40 bd. de Plombières (☎ 04-91-64-40-03), and at Première Avenue No. 23 (☎ 04-42-10-03-10); in **Montpellier** at the airport (☎ 04-67-20-07-34) and at 4 rue J.-Ferry, Immeuble Le Regent (☎ 04-67-92-69-00); in Nice at the airport (☎ 04-93-21-36-50) and at 23 rue de Belgique, opposite the rail station (☎ 04-93-16-24-16); and in **Toulouse** at the airport (☎ 05-61-71-85-80) and at 49 rue Bayard (☎ 05-61-63-18-18).

For rentals of more than 7 days, in most cases cars can be picked up in one French city and dropped off in another, but there are additional charges. Still, Budget's rates are among the most competitive, and its cars are well maintained.

Hertz (☎ 800/654-3001 in the U.S. and Canada) is also well represented, with offices in **Avignon** at the airport (☎ 04-90-84-19-50) and at 2 Av. Montclair (☎ 04-90-82-37-67); in **Marseille** at the airport (☎ 04-42-14-32-70) and at 16 bd. Charles-Nedeler (☎ 04-91-14-04-24); in **Montpellier** at De Frejorgnes (☎ 04-67-20-04-64) and at Parking des Gares (☎ 04-67-58-65-18); in **Nice** at the airport (☎ 04-93-21-36-72) and at 12 av. de Suède (☎ 04-93-87-11-87); and in **Toulouse** at the airport (☎ 05-61-30-00-26) and at the rail station (☎ 05-62-73-39-47). When making inquiries, be sure to ask about promotional discounts.

Avis (☎ 800/331-2112 in the U.S. and Canada) has offices in **Avignon** at the airport (☎ 04-90-87-17-75) and at 160 bis av. Pierre-Senmard (☎ 04-90-87-17-75); in **Marseille** at the airport (☎ 04-42-14-21-67) and at 267 bd. National (☎ 04-91-50-70-11); in **Montpellier** at the airport (☎ 04-67-20-14-95) and at 900 av. des Prés d'Arènes (☎ 04-67-92-51-92); in **Nice** at the airport (☎ 04-93-21-36-33) and at place Massena, 2 av. des Phocéens (☎ 04-93-80-63-52); and in **Toulouse** at the airport (☎ 05-61-30-04-94) and at the train station (☎ 05-93-87-90-11).

National (☎ 800/227-3876 in the U.S. and Canada) is represented in France by Europcar, with locations in **Avignon** at 27–29 av. St-Ruf (☎ 04-90-85-96-47) and at the train station, 2A av. Montclair (☎ 04-90-84-01-48); in **Marseille** at the airport (☎ 04-42-14-24-90) and at the St-Charles train station, 96 blvd. Rabatau (☎ 04-91-83-05-05); in **Montpellier** at the airport (☎ 04-67-15-13-47); in **Nice** at the airport (☎ 04-93-21-42-53); and in **Toulouse** at the airport (☎ 05-61-30-00-01). You can rent a car on the spot at any of these offices, but lower rates are available by making advance reservations from North America.

GASOLINE   Known in France as *essence,* gas is extraordinarily expensive for those used to North American prices. All but the least expensive cars usually require an octane rating that the French classify as *essence super,* the most expensive variety. At press time, essence super sold for about 6 to 7F ($1 to $1.20) per liter, which works out to around 24.50F ($4.15) per U.S. gallon. (Certain smaller engines might get by on *essence ordinaire,* which costs a fraction less than super, but be warned that these are increasingly rare, if they ever appear at all.) Depending on your car, you'll need either leaded *(avec plomb)* or unleaded *(sans plomb),* which costs just a fraction (about 25 centimes per liter) less than the version with lead. Depending on the capacity of your tank, filling a medium-size car will cost between $45 and $65.

Beware of the mixture of gasoline and oil sold in certain rural communities called *mélange* or *gasoil;* this mixture is for very old two-cycle engines.

Note: Sometimes you can drive for miles in rural France without encountering a gas station, so don't let your tank get dangerously low.

DRIVING RULES Everyone in the car, in both front and back seats, must wear seat belts. Children 11 and under must ride in the back seat. Drivers are supposed to yield to the car on their right, except where signs indicate otherwise, as at traffic circles. If you violate the speed limit, expect a big fine. Those limits are about 130 kilometers per hour (80 m.p.h.) on expressways, about 100 kilometers per hour (60 m.p.h.) on major national highways, and 90 kilometers per hour (56 m.p.h.) on small country roads. In towns, don't exceed 60 kilometers per hour (37 m.p.h.).

MAPS & ASSISTANCE Michelin publishes a series of yellow maps for regions of France that are quite good: Look for Languedoc-Roussillon (no. 240), Provence and the Côte d'Azur (no. 245), Rhône-Alpes (no. 244), or Vallée du Rhône (no. 246). Big travel-book stores in North America carry these maps, and they're commonly available in France (at lower prices). One useful feature of the Michelin map is its designations of alternative *routes de dégagement,* which let you skirt big cities and avoid traffic-clogged highways. Most tourist offices offer free maps of their city or town.

A breakdown is called *une panne* in France, and it's just as frustrating here as anywhere else. Call the police at ☎ **17** anywhere in France, and they'll put you in touch with the nearest garage. Most local garages have towing services. If your breakdown should occur on an expressway, find the nearest roadside emergency phone box, pick up the phone, and put a call through. You'll immediately be connected to the nearest breakdown-service facility.

SAVING MONEY ON A RENTAL CAR Car rental rates vary even more than airline fares. The price you pay will depend on the size of the car, where and when you pick it up and drop it off, the length of the rental period, where and how far you drive it, whether you purchase insurance, and a host of other factors. A few key questions could save you hundreds of dollars:

- Are weekend rates lower than weekday rates? Ask if the rate is the same for pickup Friday morning, for instance, as it is for Thursday night.
- Is a weekly rate cheaper than the daily rate? If you need to keep the car for 4 days, it may be cheaper to keep it for 5, even if you don't need it that long.
- Does the agency assess a drop-off charge if you do not return the car to the same location where you picked it up? Is it cheaper to pick up the car at the airport compared to a downtown location?
- Are special promotional rates available? If you see an advertised price in your local newspaper, be sure to ask for that specific rate; otherwise, you may be charged the standard cost. The terms change constantly.
- Are discounts available for members of AARP, AAA, frequent-flyer programs, or trade unions? If you belong to any of these organizations, you are probably entitled to discounts of up to 30%.
- How much tax will be added to the rental bill? Local tax? State use tax?
- What is the cost of adding an additional driver's name to the contract?
- How many free miles are included in the price? Free mileage is often negotiable, depending on the length of your rental.
- How much does the rental company charge to refill your gas tank if you return with the tank less than full? Though most rental companies claim these prices are "competitive," fuel is almost always cheaper in town. Try to allow enough time to refuel the car yourself before returning it.

Some companies offer "refueling packages," in which you pay for an entire tank of gas up front. The price is usually fairly competitive with local gas prices, but you don't get credit for any gas remaining in the tank. If a stop at a gas station on the way to the airport will make you miss your plane, then by all means take advantage of the fuel purchase option. Otherwise, skip it.

DEMYSTIFYING RENTER'S INSURANCE   Before you drive off in a rental car, be sure you're insured. Hasty assumptions about your personal auto insurance or a rental agency's additional coverage could end up costing you tens of thousands of dollars—even if you are involved in an accident that was clearly the fault of another driver.

If you already hold a **private auto insurance** policy, you are most likely covered in the United States for loss of or damage to a rental car, and liability in case of injury to any other party involved in an accident. Coverage probably doesn't extend outside the U.S., however. Be sure to find out whether you are covered in the area you are visiting, whether your policy extends to all persons who will be driving the rental car, how much liability is covered in case an outside party is injured in an accident, and whether the type of vehicle you are renting is included under your contract. (Rental trucks, sports utility vehicles, and luxury vehicles such as the Jaguar may not be covered.)

Most **major credit cards** provide some degree of coverage as well—provided they were used to pay for the rental. Terms vary widely, however, so be sure to call your credit-card company directly before you rent.

If you are **uninsured or driving abroad,** your credit card provides primary coverage as long as you decline the rental agency's insurance. This means that the credit card will cover damage or theft of a rental car for the full cost of the vehicle. (In a few states, however, theft is not covered; ask specifically about state law where you will be renting and driving.) If you already have insurance, your credit card will provide secondary coverage—which basically covers your deductible.

Credit cards **will not cover liability,** or the cost of injury to an outside party and/or damage to an outside party's vehicle. If you do not hold an insurance policy, or if you are driving outside the U.S., you may seriously want to consider purchasing additional liability insurance from your rental company. Be sure to check the terms, however: some rental agencies cover liability only if the renter is not at fault; even then, the rental company's obligation varies from state to state.

Bear in mind that each credit-card company has its own peculiarities. Most American Express Optima cards, for instance, do not provide any insurance. American Express does not cover vehicles valued at over $50,000 when new, luxury vehicles such as the Porsche, or vehicles built on a truck chassis. MasterCard does not provide coverage for loss, theft, or fire damage, and it covers collision only if the rental period does not exceed 15 days. Call your own credit-card company for details.

The basic insurance coverage offered by most car-rental companies, known as the **Loss/Damage Waiver (LDW)** or **Collision Damage Waiver (CDW),** can cost as much as $20/day. It usually covers the full value of the vehicle with no deductible if an outside party causes an accident or other damage to the rental car. In all states but California, you will probably be covered in case of theft as well. Liability coverage varies according to the company policy and state law, but the minimum is usually at least $15,000. If you are at fault in an accident, however, you will be covered for the full replacement value of the car but not for liability. Some states allow you to buy additional liability coverage for such cases. Most rental companies will require a police report in order to process any claims you file, but your private insurer will not be notified of the accident.

PACKAGE DEALS   Many packages are available that include airfare, accommodations, and a rental car with unlimited mileage. Compare these prices with the cost of booking airline tickets and renting a car separately to see if these offers are good deals.

ARRANGING CAR RENTALS ON THE WEB Internet resources can make comparison shopping easier. **Microsoft Expedia** (www.expedia.com) and **Travelocity** (www.travelocity.com) help you compare prices and locate car rental bargains from various companies nationwide. They will even make your reservation for you once you've found the best deal.

BY TRAIN

Rail services between the large cities of Languedoc-Roussillon and Provence and the French Riviera are excellent. If you don't have a car, you can tour all the major hot spots by train. Of course, with a car you can also explore the hidden villages, such as the little Riviera hill towns, but for short visits with only major stopovers on your itinerary, such as Nice and Avignon, the train should suffice. Service is fast and frequent.

The major train hub for Languedoc is the city of **Toulouse** in southwestern France, which has frequent service from Paris and Lyon. Toulouse is also linked to Marseilles by 11 trains running every day. **Montpellier** is another major transportation hub for the Languedoc-Roussillon area. Eight high-speed TGVs arrive daily from Paris, taking just 4½ hours. Montpellier also has good rail connections to **Avignon.** The ancient city of **Nîmes,** one of the most visited in the area, also is a major transportation rail terminus, a stop on the rail link between Bordeaux and Marseille.

Marseille, the largest city in the south of France, has rail connections with all major towns on the Riviera as well as with the rest of France. Twelve high-speed TGVs arrive from Paris daily (trip time: 4¾ hours).

The major rail transportation hub along the French Riviera is **Nice,** although Cannes also enjoys good train connections. Nice and Monaco are linked by frequent service, and in summer about 10 trains per day connect Nice with the rapid TGV train from Paris to Marseille. In winter, the schedule is curtailed depending on demand.

The most visited Riviera destination in the east, **Monaco,** also has excellent rail links along the Riviera.

BY BUS

While the trains are faster and more efficient if you are traveling between major cities, both the towns and villages of Languedoc and Provence, including the French Riviera, are linked by frequent bus service. If you are not driving, you can use the network of buses that link the villages and hamlets with each other and the major cities to get off the beaten path.

Historic towns like Castres and Albi (of Toulouse-Lautrec fame) can be reached by bus from Toulouse; St-Paul-de-Vence from Nice; and Grasse, the perfume center, from Cannes.

Plan to take advantage of the bus services from Monday to Saturday when they run frequently; there are very few buses running on Sunday.

BY PLANE

With the convenience of the train and bus service in the south of France, flying is not particularly attractive. Not only are domestic flights within France more expensive and less convenient than their counterparts in North America, but in recent years the increasingly rigid designation of Paris as the centerpiece for the country's hub-and-spoke system has rendered short-term air transfers between such provincial cities as Toulouse and Nice unfeasible. Very often, passengers between such cities are routed on connecting flights through Paris. A coach class flight from Toulouse to Nice, depending on restrictions, ranges between $132 and $234 each way, while a coach fare from Paris to Nice costs between $125 and $207.

While Air France's **Euro-Flyer Pass,** described in section 11 above (for information, call Air France at **800/237-2747**), is especially attractive for long-haul flights from, say, Paris to Marseille, or from Paris to Nice, it isn't very appealing for short-haul flights between southern French cities—if you must transfer through Paris, you'll use up two (rather than one) of your coupons.

15 Tips on Accommodations

French hotels are rated by stars: from four-star luxury and four-star deluxe (no five stars) down through three star (first class), two star (good-quality "tourist" hotel), and one star (budget). In some of the lower categories, the rooms may not have private baths; instead, many have what the French call a *cabinet de toilette* (hot and cold running water and a bidet), whereas others have only sinks. In such hotels, bathrooms are down the hall. Nearly all hotels in France have central heating, but in some cases you might wish the owners would turn it up a little on a cold night.

Most hotel rates quoted in France are for double occupancy, since most rooms are doubles; if you're traveling solo, be sure to ask about rates for a single. Some of these rooms contain twin beds, but most have double beds, suitable for one or two.

RELAIS & CHÂTEAUX

Now known worldwide, this organization of deluxe and first-class hostelries began in France for visitors seeking the ultimate in hotel living and dining, most often in a traditional atmosphere. Relais & Châteaux establishments (numbering about 150 in France) are former castles, abbeys, manor houses, and town houses that have been converted into hostelries or inns and elegant hotels. All have a limited number of rooms, so reservations are imperative. Sometimes these owner-run establishments have pools and tennis courts. The Relais part of the organization refers to inns called relais, meaning "posthouse." These tend to be less luxurious than the châteaux, but they're often quite charming. Top-quality restaurants are *relais gourmands*. Throughout this guide, we've listed our favorite Relais & Châteaux, but there are many more.

For an illustrated catalog of these establishments, send $8 to **Relais & Châteaux,** 11 E. 44th St., Suite 704, New York, NY 10017 (for information and reservations of individual Relais & Châteaux, call ☎ **212/856-0115;** fax 800/860-4930 or 212/867-4968). Check out its Internet Web site at **www.integra.fr/relaischateaux**.

BED-&-BREAKFASTS

Called *gîtes-chambres d'hôte* in France, these accommodations may be one or several bedrooms on a farm or in a village home. Many of them offer one main meal of the day as well (lunch or dinner).

There are at least 6,000 of these accommodations listed with **La Maison des Gîtes de France et du Tourisme Vert,** 59 rue St-Lazare, 75009 Paris (☎ **01-49-70-75-75**). Sometimes these B&Bs aren't as simple as you might think: Instead of a bare-bones farm room, you might be housed in a mansion deep in the French countryside.

In the United States, a good source for this type of accommodation is **The French Experience,** 370 Lexington Ave., New York, NY 10017 (☎ **212/986-1115;** fax 212/986-3808). It also rents furnished houses for as short a period as 1 week.

CONDOS, VILLAS, HOUSES & APARTMENTS

If you can stay for at least a week, the local French Tourist Board might help you obtain a list of real-estate agencies that represent this type of rental. One of the best groups of real-estate agents is the **Fédération Nationale des Agents Immobiliers,** 129 rue du Faubourg St-Honoré, 75008 Paris (☎ **01-44-20-77-00**).

In the United States, **At Home Abroad,** 405 E. 56th St., Apt. 6H, New York, NY 10022-2466 (☎ **212/421-9165;** fax 212/752-1591), specializes in villas on the French Riviera, as well as places in the Provençal hill towns. Rentals usually are for 2 weeks. For a $25 registration fee (applicable to any rental), it will send you photographs of the properties and a newsletter.

A worthwhile competitor is **Vacances en Campagne,** British Travel International, P.O. Box 299, Elkton, VA (☎ **800/327-6097;** fax 540/298-2347). Its $4 directory contains information on more than 700 potential rentals across Europe, including the south of France.

Barclay International Group, 150 E. 52nd St., New York, NY 10022 (☎ **800/ 845-6636** or 212/832-3777), can give you access to about 3,000 apartments and villas throughout Languedoc, Provence, and the Riviera, ranging from modest modern units to those among the most stylish. Units rent from 1 night up to 6 months; all have color TVs and kitchenettes, and many have concierge staffs and lobby-level security. The least-expensive units cost $75 to $111 per night, double occupancy. Incremental discounts are granted for a stay of 1 week or 3 weeks. Rentals must be prepaid in U.S. dollars or by a major U.S. credit or charge card.

If after reading Peter Mayles's *A Year in Provence* and *Toujours Provence* you want to follow in his footsteps, at least for a week or two, you can contact **Provence West Ltd.,** P.O. Box 2105, Evergreen, CO 80437 (☎ **303/674-6942;** fax 303/674-8773; e-mail: www.provencewest.com). This outfit specializes in *gîtes* (rural cottages), many in Provence and Languedoc. It advises travelers about rental possibilities and processes the reservation with French *gîte* offices. Its owner, Lida Posson, has visited some 100 properties in France and can offer personal advice. She also publishes a quarterly journal and newsletter, *Window on France—An Insider's View of French Country Life.*

Hometours International, Inc., P.O. Box 11503, Knoxville, TN 37939 (☎ **800/ 367-4668** or 423/690-8484), offers beautiful Riviera villas, all with pools, at reasonable rates.

HOTEL ASSOCIATIONS

For budget travelers, **Hometours International, Inc.** (see above) offers a prepaid voucher program for the Campanile hotels, a chain of about 350 two-star family-run hotels throughout France. Rates begin as low as $90 per night double. This is an excellent alternative to B&B hotels because all chain members provide a buffet breakfast for only 35F ($5.95) per person. B&B catalogs for $9 or apartment brochures for free are available from the address above.

Others wanting to trim costs might want to check out the **Mercure** chain, an organization of simple but clean and modern hotels offering attractive values throughout France. Even at the peak of the tourist season, a room at a Mercure in Provence rents for $105 to $177 per night. For more information on Mercure hotels and a copy of a 100-page directory, call **RESINTER** at ☎ **800/221-4542** in the United States.

Formule 1 hotels are bare bones and basic though clean and safe, offering rooms for up to three at around $30 per night. Built from prefabricated units, these air-conditioned, soundproof hotels are shipped to a site and assembled. (Formule 1, a member of the French hotel giant Accor, also owns the Motel 6 chain in the United States, to which Formule 1 bears a resemblance.)

While you can make a reservation at any member of the Accor group through the RESINTER number above, the chain finds that the low cost of Formule 1 makes it unprofitable and impractical to pre-reserve (from the States) rooms in the Formule chain. So, you'll have to reserve your Formule 1 room on arrival in France. Be warned that Formule 1 properties have almost none of the Gallic charm for which some country inns are famous, but you can save money by planning your itinerary at Formule 1 properties. For a directory, contact **Formule 1/ETAP Hotels,** 6–8 rue du Bois Bernard, 91021 Evry CEDEX (☎ **01-69-36-75-00**).

Other worthwhile economy bets, sometimes with a bit more charm, are the hotels and restaurants belonging to the **Fédération Nationale des Logis de France,** 83 av. d'Italie, 75013 Paris (☎ **01-45-84-70-00**). This is a marketing association of 3,828 hotels, usually simple country inns especially convenient for motorists, most rated one or two stars. The association publishes an annual directory. Copies are available for $23.95 from the **French Government Tourist Office,** 444 Madison Ave., 16th Floor, New York, NY 10022 (☎ **212/838-7800**), and also from stores specializing in travel publications, including **Rand-McNally,** 150 East 52nd St., New York, NY 10022 (☎ **212/758-7488**), where virtually any travel guide currently in print, as well as a rich assortment of maps to virtually everywhere, either is stocked or can be ordered.

TIPS FOR SAVING ON YOUR HOTEL ROOM   The rack rate is the maximum rate that a hotel charges for a room. It's the rate you'd get if you walked in off the street and asked for a room for the night. Hardly anybody pays these prices, however, and there are many ways around them.

- **Don't be afraid to bargain.** Get in the habit of asking for a lower price than the first one quoted. Most rack rates include commissions of 10% to 25% or more for travel agents, which many hotels will cut if you make your own reservations and haggle a bit. Always ask politely whether a less expensive room is available than the first one mentioned, or whether any special rates apply to you. You may qualify for corporate, student, military, senior citizen, or other discounts. Be sure to mention membership in AAA, AARP, frequent flyer programs, or trade unions, which may entitle you to special deals as well.
- **Rely on a qualified professional.** Certain hotels give travel agents discounts in exchange for steering business their way, so if you're shy about bargaining, an agent may be better equipped to negotiate discounts for you.
- **Dial direct.** When booking a room in a chain hotel, call the hotel's local line, as well as the toll-free number, and see where you get the best deal. A hotel makes nothing on a room that stays empty. The clerk who runs the place is more likely to know about vacancies and will often grant deep discounts in order to fill up.
- **Remember the law of supply and demand.** Resort hotels are most crowded and therefore most expensive on weekends, so discounts are usually available for mid-week stays. To the contrary, business hotels in downtown locations are busiest during the week; expect discounts over the weekend. Avoid high-season stays whenever you can: Planning your vacation just a week before or after official peak season can mean big savings.
- **Look into group or long-stay discounts.** If you come as part of a large group, you should be able to negotiate a bargain, since the hotel can then guarantee occupancy in a number of rooms. Likewise, when you're planning a long stay in town (usually from 5 days to a week) you'll qualify for a discount. As a general rule, you will receive 1 night free after a 7-night stay.
- **Avoid excess charges.** When you book a room, ask whether the hotel charges for parking. Most hotels have free, available space, but many urban or beachfront hotels don't. Also, find out before you dial whether your hotel imposes a surcharge on local or long-distance calls. A pay phone, however inconvenient, may save you money.

Museum Passes

The **Carte Musée Côte d'Azur** gives you entry to more than 60 museums and other attractions along the Riviera. A 3-day pass costs 70F ($12) and a 7-day pass 140F ($25). For details call ☎ **04-93-13-17-51**, or e-mail **cmca.nice@hol.fr**.

Nice, Marseille, Nîmes, and Toulouse are part of a cultural program offered by 13 French cities. The **Culture/Ville** 3-day pass costs 50F ($10). It features a guided or audio tour in each city included and entrance to one museum or one monument. Ask at the cities' tourist offices or contact the French Government Tourist Office in the U.S. at ☎ **900/990-0040** (50¢ per minute) for the *Cities in France* brochure.

- **Consider a suite.** If you are traveling with your family or another couple, you can pack more people into a suite (which usually comes with a sofa bed), and thereby reduce your per-person rate. Remember that some places charge for extra guests, some don't.
- **Book an efficiency.** A room with a kitchenette allows you to grocery-shop and eat some meals in. Especially during long stays with families, you're bound to save money on food this way.
- **Investigate reservation services.** These outfits usually work as consolidators, buying up or reserving rooms in bulk, and then dealing them out to customers at a profit. They do garner special deals that range from 10% to 50% off; but remember, these discounts apply to rack rates, inflated prices that people rarely end up paying. You're probably better off dealing directly with a hotel, but if you don't like bargaining, this is certainly a viable option. Most of them offer online reservation services as well. Here are a few of the more reputable providers:

Accommodations Express (☎ **800/950-4685;** www.accommodationsxpress.com); **Hotel Reservations Network** (☎ **800/96HOTEL;** www.180096HOTEL.com); **Quikbook** (☎ **800/789-9887,** includes fax-on-demand service; www.quikbook.com); and **Room Exchange** (☎ **800/846-7000** in the U.S., 800/486-7000 in Canada).

At the inexpensive end, **Hostelling International/American Youth Hostels,** 733 15th St. NW, Suite 840, Washington, DC 20005 (☎ **800/444-6111** or 202/783-6161), offers a directory of low-cost accommodations around the country.

On the Net, try booking your hotel through **Arthur Frommer's Budget Travel Online** (www.frommers.com), and save up to 50% on the cost of your room. **Microsoft Expedia** (www.expedia.com) features a "Travel Agent" that will also direct you to affordable lodgings.

Fast Facts: The South of France

Auto Club An organization designed to help motorists navigate their way through breakdowns and motoring problems is **Club Automobile de Provence,** 149 bd. Rabatau, 13010 Marseille (☎ **04-91-78-83-00**).

Business Hours Business hours here are erratic, as befits a nation of individualists. Most **banks** are open Monday to Friday from 9:30am to 4:30pm. Many, particularly in smaller towns or villages, take a lunch break at varying times. Hours are usually posted on the door. Most **museums** close 1 day a week (often Tuesday), and they're generally closed on national holidays. Usual hours are

9:30am to 5pm. Some museums, particularly the smaller and less-staffed ones, close for lunch from noon to 2pm. Most French museums are open on Saturday; many are closed Sunday morning but open Sunday afternoon. Again, refer to the individual museum listings.

Generally, **offices** are open Monday to Friday from 9am to 5pm, but always call first. In larger cities, **stores** are open from 9 or 9:30am (often 10am) to 6 or 7pm without a break for lunch. Some shops, particularly those operated by foreigners, open at 8am and close at 8 or 9pm. In some small stores, the lunch break can last 3 hours, beginning at 1pm.

Drugstores   In France they are called *pharmacie*. Pharmacies take turns staying open at night and on Sunday; the local Commissariat de Police will tell you the location of the nearest one.

Electricity   In general, expect 200 volts, 50 cycles, though you'll encounter 110 and 115 volts in some older establishments. Adapters are needed to fit sockets. Many hotels have two-pin (in some cases, three-pin) sockets for electric razors. It's best to ask your hotel concierge before plugging in any appliance.

Embassies/Consulates   All embassies are in Paris. The Embassy of **Australia** is at 4 rue Jean-Rey, 75015 Paris (☎ 01-40-59-33-00; Métro: Bir-Hakeim), open Monday to Friday from 9am to 1pm and 2:30 to 5pm. The Embassy of **Canada** is at 35 av. Montaigne, 75008 Paris (☎ 01-44-43-29-00; Métro: Franklin-D.-Roosevelt), open Monday to Friday from 9am to noon and 2 to 5pm; the Canadian Consulate is at the same address. The Embassy of the **United Kingdom** is at 35 rue du Faubourg St-Honoré, 75383 Paris CEDEX 08 (☎ 01-44-51-31-00; Métro: Concorde), open Monday to Friday from 9:30am to 1pm and 2:30 to 6pm; the U.K. consulate, 16 rue d'Anjou, 75008 Paris (☎ 01-44-51-31-00), is open Monday to Friday from 9:30am to 12:30pm and 2:30 to 5pm. The Embassy of **New Zealand** is at 7 ter rue Léonard-de-Vinci, 75116 Paris (☎ 01-45-00-24-11; Métro: Victor-Hugo), open Monday to Friday from 9am to 1pm and 2 to 5:30pm; summer hours are Monday to Thursday 8:30am to 1pm and 2 to 5:30pm and Friday 8:30am to 2pm. The Embassy of the **United States** is at 2 av. Gabriel, 75008 Paris (☎ 01-43-12-22-22; Métro: Concorde), open Monday to Friday from 9am to 6pm. Passports are issued at its consulate at 2 rue St-Florentin (☎ 01-43-12-22-22; Métro: Concorde). Getting a passport replaced costs about $65. In addition to its embassy and consulate in Paris, the United States maintains a consulate at 12 bd. Paul-Peytral, 13286 Marseille (☎ 04-91-54-92-00). The Embassy of **Ireland** is at 12 ave. Foch, 16e, 75116 Paris (☎ 01-44-17-67-00; Métro: Argentine). Hours are Monday to Friday 9:30am to noon. The Embassy of **South Africa** is at 59 quai d'Orsay (☎ 01-53-59-23-23; Métro: Invalides). Hours are Monday to Friday 8:45 to 11am.

Emergencies   In an emergency while at a hotel, contact the front desk to summon an ambulance or do whatever is necessary. But for something like a stolen wallet, go to the police station in person. Otherwise, you can get help anywhere in France by calling ☎ 17 for the **police** or ☎ 18 for the **fire** department (*pompiers*). For roadside emergencies, see "Getting Around the South of France," earlier in this chapter.

Legal Aid   The French government advises foreigners to consult their embassy or consulate (see above) in case of an arrest or similar problem. The staff can

How to Get Your VAT Refund

French sales tax, or **VAT (value-added tax)**, is now a hefty 20.6%, but you can get most of that back if you spend 1,200F ($216) or more at any participating retailer. The name of the refund is *détaxe,* meaning exactly what it says. You never really get the full 20.6% back, but you can come close.

After you spend the required minimum amount, ask for your détaxe papers; fill out the forms before you arrive at the airport and allow at least half an hour for standing in line. All refunds are processed at the final point of departure from the EU, so if you're going to another EU country, apply for the refund there.

Mark the paperwork to request that your refund be applied to your credit card so you aren't stuck with a check in francs that you can't cash. Even if you made the purchase in cash, you can still get the refund put on a credit card. This ensures the best rate of exchange. While some airports will give you the refund in cash, you'll lose money unless you take the cash in French francs.

If you're considering a major purchase, especially one that falls between 1,200 to 2,000F ($204 to $340), ask the store policy before you get too involved—or be willing to waive your right to the refund.

generally offer advice as to how you can obtain help locally, and can furnish you with a list of local attorneys. If you are arrested for illegal possession of drugs, the U.S. embassy and consular officials cannot interfere with the French judicial system. A consulate can advise you only of your rights.

Mail   Most post offices in France are open Monday to Friday from 8am to 7pm and Saturday from 8am to noon. Allow 5 to 8 days to send or receive mail from your home. Airmail letters to North America cost 4.30F (75¢) for 20 grams or 7.90F ($1.35) for 40 grams. Letters to the U.K. cost 2.80F (50¢) for up to 20 grams. An airmail postcard to North America or Europe (outside France) costs 4.30F (75¢).

You can exchange money at post offices. Many hotels sell stamps, as do local post offices and cafes displaying a red "tabac" sign outside.

Newspapers/Magazines   Most major cities carry copies of the *International Herald Tribune, USA Today,* and usually a major London paper or two. Nearly all big-city newsstands also sell copies of *Time* and *Newsweek.* The leading French newspapers are *Le Monde, Le Figaro,* and *La Libération.* The major French newsmagazines are *L'Express, Le Point,* and *Le Nouvel Observateur.*

Police   Call ☎ **17** anywhere in France.

Rest Rooms   If you're in dire need, duck into a cafe or brasserie. It's customary to make some small purchase if you do so. France still has many "hole-in-the-ground" toilets, so be forewarned.

Safety   Those intending to visit the south of France, especially the Riviera, should exercise extreme caution—robberies and muggings here are commonplace. It's best to check your baggage into a hotel and then go sightseeing instead of leaving it unguarded in the trunk of a car, which can easily be broken into. Marseille is among the most dangerous cities.

Taxes   *Watch it:* You could get burned. As a member of the European Union, France routinely imposes a value-added tax (VAT) on many goods and services.

The standard VAT on merchandise is 20.6%. Refunds are made for the tax on certain goods, but not on services. The minimum purchase is 1,200F ($204) for nationals or residents of countries outside the EU. See the box for more details.

Telephone   You'll find public **phone booths** in cafes, restaurants, post offices, airports, and train stations and occasionally on the streets. Pay phones accept coins of ½F, 1F, 2F, and 5F; the minimum charge is 1F (15¢). Pick up the receiver, insert the coin(s), and dial when you hear the tone, pushing the button when there's an answer.

The French also use a *télécarte,* a phone debit card, which you can purchase at rail stations, post offices, and other places. Sold in two versions, it allows you to use either 50 or 120 charge units (depending on the card) by inserting the card into the slot of most public phones. Depending on the type of card you buy, they cost 41F to 98F ($6.95 to $16.65).

If possible, avoid making calls from your hotel, as some French establishments double or triple the charges.

When you're calling **long distance** within France, pick up the receiver, wait for the dial tone, and then dial the 10-digit number of the person or place you're calling. To make an **international call** from France to anywhere in the world, dial 00 (double zero, the French international access code), wait for the dial tone, then dial the country code (1 for the United States and Canada), the area or city code, and the local number you want to reach. To reach an **AT&T operator** from within France, for assistance in placing collect or credit-card calls back to North America or whatever, dial ☎ **00-CALL-ATT.** For **information,** dial ☎ **12.**

When calling from outside France, dial the international access code for your country, the country code for France (**33**), and then the last nine digits of the number, dropping the 0 (zero) from the area code.

Time   The French equivalent of daylight saving time lasts from around April to September, which puts it 1 hour ahead of French winter time. Depending on the time of year, France is 6 or 7 hours ahead of U.S. eastern standard time.

Tipping   All bills, as required by law, are supposed to say *service compris,* which means that the tip has been included. Here are some general guidelines: For **hotel staff,** tip 6F to 10F ($1 to $1.70) for every item of baggage the porter carries on arrival and departure, and 10F ($1.70) per day for the chambermaid. You're not obligated to tip the concierge (hall porter), doorperson, or anyone else—unless you use his or her services. In cafes, **waiter** service is usually included. For **porters,** there's no real need to tip extra after their bill is presented, unless they've performed some special service. Tip **taxi drivers** 10% to 15% of the amount on the meter. In theaters and restaurants, give **cloakroom attendants** at least 5F (85¢) per item. Give **rest-room attendants** about 2F (40¢) in nightclubs and such places. Give **cinema and theater ushers** about 2F (35¢). Tip the **hairdresser** about 15%, and don't forget to tip the person who gives you a shampoo or a manicure 10F ($1.70). For **guides** for group visits to sights, 5F to 10F (85¢ to $1.70) per person is a reasonable tip.

3 Languedoc-Roussillon & the Camargue

Languedoc, one of southern France's great old provinces, is a loosely defined area encompassing such cities as Nîmes, Toulouse, and Carcassonne. It's one of France's leading wine-producing areas and is fabled for its art treasures.

The coast of Languedoc—from Montpellier to the Spanish frontier—might be called France's "second Mediterranean," first place naturally going to the Côte d'Azur. A land of ancient cities and a generous sea, it's less spoiled than the Côte d'Azur. An almost-continuous strip of sand stretches west from the Rhône and curves snakelike toward the Pyrénées. Back in the days of de Gaulle, the government began an ambitious project to develop the Languedoc-Roussillon coastline that has been a booming success, as the miles of sun-baking bodies in July and August testify.

Ancient **Roussillon** is a small region of greater Languedoc, forming the Pyrénées Orientales *département*. This is the French Catalonia, inspired more by Barcelona in neighboring Spain than by remote Paris. Over its long and colorful history it has known many rulers. Legally part of the French kingdom until 1258, it was surrendered to James I of Aragón, and until 1344 it was part of the ephemeral kingdom of Majorca, with Perpignan as the capital. By 1463, Roussillon was annexed to France again. Then Ferdinand of Aragón won it back, but by 1659 France had it once again. In spite of some local sentiment for reunion with the Catalans of Spain, France still firmly controls the land.

The Camargue is a marshy delta between two arms of the Rhône. South of Arles is cattle country. Strong wild black bulls are bred here for the arenas of Arles and Nîmes. They are herded by *gardiens,* French cowboys, who wear wide-brimmed black hats and ride amazingly graceful small white horses, said to have been brought here by the Saracens. The whitewashed houses, plaited-straw roofs, pink flamingos that inhabit the muddy marshes, vast plains, endless stretches of sandbars—all this qualifies as "exotic" France.

EXPLORING THE REGION BY CAR

Here's how to link together the best of the region if you are driving a car.

Days 1–2 Begin in **Toulouse,** the ancient capital of Languedoc and France's fourth-largest city. On the second day here, consider a detour to **Auch,** 43 miles west along N124, for a meal at the **Hôtel de France.** If the idea of spending time in a major urban center like

Toulouse doesn't appeal to you, consider spending only a night, skipping Auch, and proceeding with the rest of this tour.

Day 3   From Toulouse, drive northeast on N88 and D922 for 43 miles to **Cordes,** a medieval village perched on a rocky hilltop. After your visit, drive southeast on D600 to **Albi,** site of the fortified Eglise Ste-Cecilia, that once saw one of the bloodiest religious massacres in French history. Spend the night here.

Day 4   Drive south for 25 miles on N112 for a visit to the brooding medieval city of **Castres.** Then continue 40 miles south on D112 and D118 for a tour of a spectacular fortified site, **Carcassonne,** where you'll stay the night.

Day 5   The day's final destination is **Perpignan,** but rather than reaching it via high-speed superhighways, we prefer to drive south and then west along D118 and D117. Spend the afternoon exploring Perpignan, but retire early with the expectation of some complicated driving (and serious sunbathing) tomorrow.

Day 6   Your day's final destination is Collioure, but en route we recommend a mountain detour to the hamlet of **Céret.** Reach Céret from Perpignan by driving south—toward Spain—along A9, then exiting after about 12 miles and driving west for 4 miles along D115. Céret is well suited to a quiet hour or two in the sun, and you may decide to dine at **La Terrasse au Soleil,** route de Fontfrède, a hideaway once favored by Salvador Dalí.

After your meal, drive east along D618 for 20 miles to the seaside hamlet of **Collioure.** Shaped like a half moon and flanked by a fortified château, it resembles St-Tropez before the tourist invasion. It was favored by artists during the Fauve period of early modern art. Spend the night here near what's the most charming village on the Côte Vermeille.

Day 7   This is your day to beach hop. Stop for a swim or a snack wherever the view inspires you, but keep moving with your final destination in mind: **Narbonne,** 50 miles north of Collioure. Even though A9 can get you there most efficiently, we suggest that you at least begin the day by driving north on the narrow coastal road, admiring the string of fast-developing beach resorts. If traffic is dense, you can detour inland 7 miles, then continue along A9. Spend the night in Narbonne.

Day 8   Now you can explore the **Camargue,** a grass-covered wetland. Your first destination is canal-sided **Sète,** 50 miles northeast of Narbonne. Drive along A9, then detour through Agde along N112. Follow N112 east to Sète, which is built on a network of canals. Its golden age was in the 19th century, when it became the principal link to France's North African colonies; a ferry still departs daily for Algeria. Many visitors are fascinated by its architecture, a somewhat bizarre combination of Second Empire and art deco. Try to stop for a meal at the **Restaurant La Rotonde,** in Le Grand Hôtel, 17 quai de Tassigny (☎ **04-67-74-86-14**); closed for lunch on Saturday and during 1 week in January.

From Sète, drive the coastal road off to the northeast. Your route will follow a string of connected barrier islands and lead you through wetlands favored by waterfowl to the heart of the Camargue. The crown jewel of the district is **Aigues-Mortes,** where you'll stay overnight.

Day 9   Backtrack westward 20 miles on D62 for a view of the ancient Roman town of **Montpellier.** Know in advance that despite the town's *charme méridionale,* traffic is going to be dense. Tour the town, then drive 31 miles northeast along A9 to visit **Nîmes,** where you'll spend the night.

1 Toulouse

438 miles (704.89km) SW of Paris, 152 miles (244.62km) SE of Bordeaux, 60 miles (96.56km)
W of Carcassonne

The old capital of Languedoc and France's fourth-largest city, Toulouse (known as La
Ville Rose) today is cosmopolitan in flavor. The major city of the southwest, it's the
gateway to the Pyrénées. Toulouse may be a city with a distinguished historical past,
but it is also a city of the future, and the high-tech center of the aerospace industry in
France. It is home to two huge aircraft makers—Airbus and Aérospatiale, and the
National Center for Space Research has been headquartered here for more than 3
decades. The first regularly scheduled airline flights from France took off from the
local airport in the 1920s. Today long-range passenger planes of the Airbus consortium, the most important rivals in the world to Boeing, are assembled in a gargantuan
hangar in the suburb of Colombiers. In 1997, Toulouse launched an air and space
museum (see the entry below for La Cité de Espace). Also making the city tick is its
extraordinarily high population of students: some 100,000 in all, out of a population
of 600,000.

An ancient city, filled with gardens and squares, it has a stormy history. It has played
many roles—once it was the capital of the Visigoths and later the center of the comtes
de Toulouse. The city has 20 historic pipe organs, more than any other city in France,
and hosts an annual international organ festival.

ESSENTIALS

GETTING THERE   The **Toulouse-Blagnac airport** lies in the northwestern suburbs, 7 miles from the city center; call ☎ **05-61-42-44-00** for flight information.
Some nine high-speed TGV trains per day arrive from Paris (trip time: 5 hrs.), eight
from Bordeaux (trip time: 2¼ hrs.), and 11 from Marseille (trip time: 4½ hrs.). For **rail
information** and schedules, call ☎ **08-36-35-35-35.**

The drive to Toulouse from Paris is a lengthy one. From Paris, take A10 south to
Bordeaux, connecting to A62 to Toulouse. The Canal du Midi links many of the
region's cities with Toulouse by waterway.

VISITOR INFORMATION   The **Office de Tourisme** is in the Donjon du Capitole, rue Lafayette near the Town Hall (☎ **05-61-11-02-22**).

SEEING THE SIGHTS

✪ **Basilique St-Sernin.** 13 place St-Sernin. ☎ **05-61-21-80-45.** Admission free to church,
10F ($1.70) to crypt. Church: July–Sept daily 9am–6:30pm, Oct–June daily 9am–noon and
2–6pm. Crypt: Mon–Sat 9am–noon and 2–6pm, Sun noon–6pm.

The city's major monument, consecrated in 1096, is the largest and finest
Romanesque church extant in Europe. An outstanding feature is the Porte Miègeville,
opening onto the south aisle and decorated with 12th-century sculptures. The door to
the south transept is the Porte des Comtes, with capitals depicting the story of Lazarus.
Nearby are the tombs of the comtes de Toulouse. Entering by the main west door, you
can see the double side aisles that give the church five naves, an unusual feature in
Romanesque architecture. An upper cloister forms a passageway around the interior.
Look for the Romanesque capitals surmounting the columns.

In the axis of the basilica, 11th-century bas-reliefs depict *Christ in His Majesty.* The
ambulatory leads to the crypt (ask the custodian for permission to enter), containing
the relics of 128 saints, plus a thorn said to be from the Crown of Thorns. In the

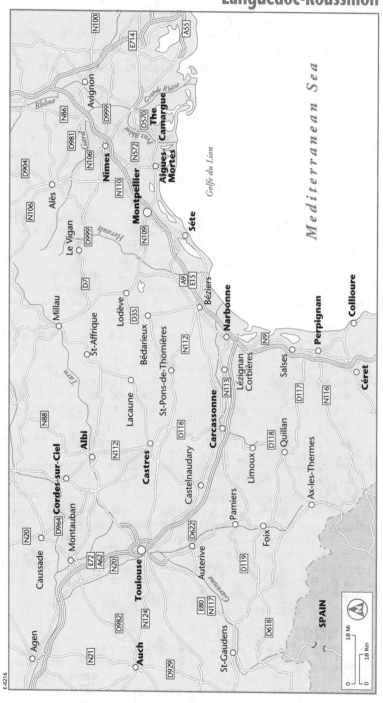

ambulatory, the old baroque retables and shrine have been reset; the relics here are those of the Apostles and the first bishops of Toulouse. You are asked to refrain from purely touristic visits during Sunday-morning masses.

Musée des Augustins. 21 rue de Metz. ☎ **05-61-22-21-82.** Admission 12F ($2.05) adults, free children 11 and under. Wed 10am–9pm, Thurs–Mon 10am–6pm.

Originally conceived as a convent, its 14th-century cloisters contain the world's largest and most valuable collection of Romanesque capitals. The sculptures and carvings are magnificent, and there are some fine examples of early Christian sarcophagi. On the upper floors is a large painting collection, with works by Toulouse-Lautrec, Gérard, Delacroix, and Ingres. The museum also contains several portraits by Antoine Rivalz, a major local artist.

Fondation Bemberg. Place d'Assézat, rue de Metz. ☎ **05-61-12-06-89.** Admission 30F ($5.10). Tues, Wed, and Fri–Sun 10am–6pm; Thurs 10am–9pm.

Opened in 1995, it quickly became one of the city's most important museums. Housed in the Assézat mansion, a magnificent structure that's a sightseeing attraction in its own right (see below), the museum offers an overview of five centuries of European art. The nucleus of the collection represents the lifelong work of George Bemberg, collector extraordinaire, who donated 331 works. The largest bequest was 28 paintings by Pierre Bonnard, including his *Moulin Rouge*. Bemberg also donated works by Pissarro, Matisse *(Vue d'Antibes)*, and Monet, plus the Fauves. The foundation also owns Canaletto's much-reproduced *Vue de Mestre*.

Cathédrale St-Etienne. Place St-Etienne, at the eastern end of rue de Metz. ☎ **05-61-52-03-82.** Admission free. Daily 7:30am–7pm.

This is the city's other major ecclesiastical building. Because of the centuries required to build it (it was designed and constructed between the 11th and the 17th century), some critics scorn it for its mishmash of styles, yet it nonetheless conveys a solemn dignity. The rectangular bell tower is from the 16th century. It has a unique ogival nave to which a Gothic choir has been added.

La Cité de Espace. av. Jean-Gonord (at Exit 17 of the East Peripheral Highway). ☎ **05-62-71-48-71.** Admission 69.40F ($11.80) adults, 48.20F ($8.20) children 6 to 17, under 6 free, 58.50F ($9.95) seniors over 60. Family tickets (2 adults and 2 children) 192.60F ($32.75). Tues–Sun 9:30am–6pm (closes 7pm Sat and Sun). Line 19 bus, Sat and Sun only.

This is the place to go to learn about space exploration and how it's done. Some half a million visitors a year come here to learn what it's like to program the launch of a satellite into orbit or how satellites are maneuvered in space. You learn, for example, how easy it is to lose a satellite in space by putting on a burst of speed at the wrong point during a launch. Life-size structural models abound, including a model of an astronaut riding an exercise bike in zero gravity. On the grounds outside you can walk through the Mir orbital station constructed by the Russians. The place is both a teaching tool and a lot of fun to visit. The top floor focuses on exploration of the universe, with close-ups from flybys of the moons of Jupiter.

MORE SIGHTS

The Gothic brick **Eglise des Jacobins,** parvis des Jacobins, is in Old Toulouse, west of place du Capitole along rue Lakanal (☎ **05-61-22-21-92**). The convent, daring in its architecture, has been restored and forms the largest extant monastery complex in France. It's open daily throughout the year from 10am to 6pm. Entrance to most of the complex is free, but a visit to the cloisters is 10F ($1.70) per person.

Toulouse

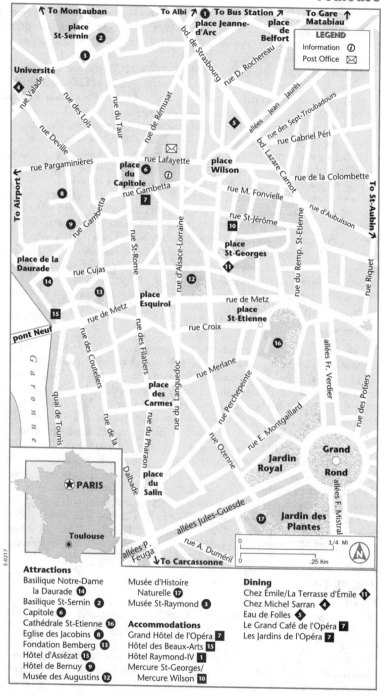

LEGEND
Information ⓘ
Post Office ✉

★ PARIS

Toulouse

E-0217

Attractions
Basilique Notre-Dame
  la Daurade 🄬
Basilique St-Sernin ❷
Capitole ❻
Cathédrale St-Etienne 🄰
Eglise des Jacobins ❽
Fondation Bemberg 🄭
Hôtel d'Assézat 🄭
Hôtel de Bernuy ❾
Musée des Augustins 🄬

Musée d'Histoire
  Naturelle 🄱
Musée St-Raymond ❸

Accommodations
Grand Hôtel de l'Opéra 7
Hôtel des Beaux-Arts 🄯
Hôtel Raymond-IV ❶
Mercure St-Georges/
  Mercure Wilson 🄰

Dining
Chez Émile/La Terrasse d'Émile 🄫
Chez Michel Sarran ❹
Eau de Folles ❺
Le Grand Café de l'Opéra 7
Les Jardins de l'Opéra 7

65

Small, charming, and dating mostly from the 18th century, the **Basilique Notre-Dame La Daurade** is at 7 quai de la Daurade (☎ **05-61-21-38-32**); its name derives from the gilding that covers some of its partially baroque exterior. It's open daily from 8am to 7pm. Admission is free.

The **Capitole,** place du Capitole (☎ **05-61-22-29-22**), is an outstanding achievement in civic architecture, and one of the most potent symbols of Toulouse itself. Built in 1753, it houses the **Hôtel de Ville** (city hall), plus the **Théâtre du Capitole** (☎ **05-61-22-80-22**), where concerts, ballets, and operas are presented. Renovated in 1996, the theater is outfitted in an Italian-inspired 18th-century style in shades of scarlet and gold. In the Hotel de Ville, the only area that can be visited is the richly ornate **Salle des Illustres,** where you can see portraits of personalities who influenced the politics or culture of the city. Entrance is free. The Capitole complex is open Monday to Friday 9am to noon and 2 to 5pm; Saturday 9am to noon.

The city has a number of fine old mansions, most of them dating from the Renaissance when Toulouse was one of the richest cities in Europe. The finest is the **Hôtel d'Assézat,** on rue de Metz. Built in 1555, it has an unaltered 16th-century courtyard. It houses the Académie des Jeux-Floraux (Academy of the Floral Games), whose purpose is to uphold the highest literary traditions of the region. Since 1323 it has presented to poets awards of flowers made of wrought metal. It's also the headquarters of the above-mentioned Fondation Bemberg.

After all that sightseeing, head for the oval **place Wilson,** a showcase 19th-century square sheltering fashionable cafes.

SHOPPING

The streets to attack during your shopping frenzy include **rue St-Rome** and **rue d'Alsace-Lorraine,** both of which are especially rich in clothing and housewares. This town has a great shopping mall, **Centre Commercial St-Georges,** rue du Rempart St-Etienne, where you can fill your suitcases with all kinds of glittery loot. But for upscale clothing boutiques, head for rue **Croix-Baragnon** and **rue des Arts,** and the **rue St-Antoine du T** (yes, that's right). The pearly gates of antiques heaven can be found on **rue Fermat.** More downmarket antiques are sprawled out each Sunday from 8am to noon during the weekly **flea market** that's conducted adjacent to the Basilique St-Sernin. In addition to that, there's a once-a-month sale of knickknacks *(brocante)* on the first weekend (Friday, Saturday, and Sunday from 8am to 1pm) of every month. Here, the contents of attics that have been undisturbed since the invasion of Normandy are disgorged, with trash and possible treasures as well, into the light of day.

In addition, **Olivier Desforges,** 3 place St-Georges (☎ **05-61-12-07-00**), sells the most exotic and luxurious linens, and **Violettes & Pastels,** 10 rue St-Pantaléon (☎ **05-61-22-14-22**), offers everything imaginable connected with violets, from violet-scented perfume to silk scarves patterned with the dainty purple flower.

WHERE TO STAY
EXPENSIVE

✪ **Grand Hôtel de l'Opéra.** 1 place du Capitole, 31000 Toulouse. ☎ **05-61-21-82-66.** Fax 05-61-23-41-04. 49 units. A/C TV TEL. 720F–1,050F ($122.40–$178.50) double; 1,300F ($221) suite. AE, DC, MC, V. Métro: Capitole. Parking 75F ($12.75).

The owners of this opulent hotel have won several prestigious awards for transforming a 17th-century building (once a convent) into a sophisticated new address. The public rooms contain early 19th-century antiques, with Napoleonic-inspired tenting over the bars. Some guest rooms have urn-shaped balustrades overlooking formal squares, and all have high ceilings and modern amenities. Bedrooms are spacious and stylish with private safes, most often with ample sitting areas and good desk space. The beds are elegantly attired in tasteful fabrics, fine mattresses, and soft pillows. Bathrooms come with combination tub and shower, hair dryer, scales, robes, deluxe toiletries, and thick towels. A radical restoration of the upper floors following fire damage was completed in 1998. The hotel also runs the town's most prestigious restaurant (see "Where to Dine," below), plus a brasserie.

MODERATE

Hôtel des Beaux-Arts. 1 place du pont-Neuf, 31000 Toulouse. ☎ **05-61-23-40-50.** Fax 05-61-22-02-27. www.internetclub.fr/hotel-des-beauxarts/acceui/htm. E-mail: hba@ internetclub.fr. 20 units. A/C MINIBAR TV TEL. 480F–980F ($81.60–$166.60) double. AE, DC, MC, V. Parking 70F ($11.90).

Occupying a dignified pink-brick villa built 250 years ago on the banks of the Garonne, this charming hotel is in the heart of town. Despite the historic facade, the well-equipped, soundproofed rooms are modern, refined, and comfortable. Each contains a quality mattress and some form of original modern art. Bathrooms are compact and efficiently organized with adequate shelf space, often with both tub and shower. Breakfast is the only meal served.

Mercure St-Georges. Rue St.-Jérome (place Occitaine), 31000 Toulouse. ☎ **05-61-23-11-77.** Fax 05-61-23-19-38. 170 units. A/C MINIBAR TV TEL. 660F ($112.20) double. AE, DC, MC, V. Parking 80F ($13.60). Métro: Capitole.

Just a few paces from the Mercure Wilson (the two share staff and management) this seven-story hotel is a less historic twin of the older and cozier-looking hotel. Decor is rigidly standardized—bedrooms are identical, comfortably modern, with first-rate mattresses. Bathrooms are compact and tidily maintained, with adequate shelf space and a shower stall or a tub-and-shower combination. Renovations here were made less recently than those in the Mercure Wilson. On the premises is a restaurant serving specialties of Toulouse, with a special emphasis on a locally produced wine, Le Fronton. Business travelers here are the prime clientele.

Mercure Wilson. 7 rue Labéda, 31000 Toulouse. ☎ **05-61-21-21-75.** Fax 05-61-22-77-64. 93 units. A/C MINIBAR TV TEL. 680F ($115.60) double. AE, DC, MC, V. Parking 60F ($10.20). Métro: Capitole.

This is the more appealing of the two Mercure hotels that stand almost adjacent to each other in the heart of Toulouse's historic central zone. Originally built as a hotel around 1850, it's constructed of the distinctive pink-toned bricks cherished by local preservationists. In 1999, Mercure radically upgraded the hotel's interior, transforming it into one of the most up-to-date middle-bracket places in town. Most bedrooms are medium in size, and in spite of their chain format, furnishings are agreeable, with comfortable mattresses and fine linens. Bathrooms have shower stalls or tub-and-shower combinations, along with adequate shelf space and a rack of medium-size towels. There's no restaurant on the premises, but room service is available between 7am and 10pm, and meals are served in the form of well-composed platters. Guests can easily migrate a few steps to the premises of the Mercure St-Georges (see above). Amenities include radios, alarm clocks, and private safe-deposit boxes.

Novotel Toulouse Centre. 5 place Alfonse-Jourdain, 31000 Toulouse. ☎ **05-61-21-74-74.** Fax 05-61-22-81-22. 131 units. A/C MINIBAR TV TEL. 560F ($95.20) double, 800F ($136) suite. AE, DC, MC, V. Parking 35F ($5.95). Bus: 1 or 2.

Set in the most verdant part of Toulouse's center, this modern and efficient hotel is a few paces from the city's Japanese gardens. The Matabiau train station is within a 5-minute walk, and the nerve center of the old city, place St-Sernin, is less than half a mile away. All rooms are alike, each with a single bed (which can be converted into a couch), a double bed, a long writing desk, and a fully equipped bathroom. In spite of the chain-style format, this is one of the best Novotel hotels, with larger than usual bedrooms, and quality mattresses on the beds. Bathrooms are roomy and have shower-and-tub combinations. A grill restaurant serves regional and French dishes daily from 6am to midnight, meals beginning at 170F ($28.90). There's also an international bar, usually filled with businesspeople.

INEXPENSIVE

Hôtel Raymond-IV. 16 rue Raymond-IV, 31000 Toulouse. ☎ **05-61-62-89-41.** Fax 05-61-62-38-01. 38 units. MINIBAR TV TEL. 210F–600F ($35.70–$102) double. AE, DC, MC, V. Parking 25F ($4.25). Métro: Jean-Jaurès or Capitole.

On a quiet street close to the town center and the train station, this antique building contains pleasantly decorated rooms with bland but comfortable furniture and restful mattresses. Bathrooms are small and tiled and come with either tub or shower (sometimes a combination), plus a rack of good-size towels. The location means that you're within walking distance of the historic quarter with its theaters, shops, and nightclubs. Although breakfast is the only meal served, the English-speaking staff will direct you to nearby restaurants.

WHERE TO DINE
EXPENSIVE

✪ **Chez Michel Sarran.** 21 bd. Armand du Portal. ☎ **05-61-12-32-32.** Reservations recommended. Main courses 120F–175F ($20.40–$29.75). Set-price lunch or dinner 240F ($40.80). AE, MC, V. Mon–Fri noon–2pm and 7:30–10pm. Métro: Capitole. FRENCH.

The most stylish and consistently praised restaurant in Toulouse occupies two beige-and-salmon dining rooms in the heart of town, on two separate floors of a building near the Novotel Centre; one dignified and contemporary-looking dining room is upholstered with beige-toned linen from the Provençal upholsterer Soleiado. You'll enjoy the well-cultivated cuisine of rising star Michel Sarran. Your order might be taken by his wife, Françoise, who will suggest something from the very fresh, very creative array of dishes that have attracted diners as diverse as the Prime Minister of France and show-biz types like Sophie Marceau and Gilbert Becaud. Food seems designed to bring out the savors of southern and southwestern France, and is usually permeated with the pungency of fresh herbs and seafood. Examples include a platter of stuffed seasonal vegetables served with an anchovy-flavored mayonnaise and ratatouille; a salad of braised crayfish with crabmeat and a tapenade of olives; a creamy soup of white beans, lard, and foie gras; grilled snapper with caramelized tomatoes and sweet Basque tomatoes stuffed with anchovies; grilled sea wolf "à la plancha" with a summer ragout of sea cucumbers; and grilled foie gras in a duckmeat bouillon with sage and parmesan. And dessert might be ravioli stuffed with creamed oranges and served with an aspic of sweet white Gaillac wine.

✪ **Le Pastel.** 237 route de St-Simon. ☎ **05-62-87-84-30.** Reservations required. Main courses 130F–250F ($22.10–$42.50); set-price lunches 155F–215F ($26.35–$36.55); set-price dinner 370F ($62.90). AE, DC, MC, V. Tues–Sat noon–4pm and 8–9:30pm. Métro: Basso-Cambo.

One of Toulouse's most luxurious and appealing restaurants occupies a stone-sided manor house built around 1850 that is today the domain of Paris-trained chef and entrepreneur Gérard Garrigues. The setting is as restful as the cuisine is superb: Terraces ringed with flowers, and a pair of dining rooms whose walls are accented with paintings by local artists (the works are for sale) contribute to the feeling of reflective calm and well-being. Menu items change about every 2 weeks, a policy that's tactfully explained by the mistress of the dining room, Marie-Noelle Garrigues.

During our visit, the menu featured such game dishes as partridge cooked "in the Russian style," in a terrine with foie gras and puffy pastry, and sealed in with its own juices; filet of line-caught sea bass prepared in a minestrone of shellfish; caramelized turnips served as a "tarte tatin" and topped with pan-seared foie gras; and pigeon stuffed with pine nuts and dried fruit, served on a bed of braised cabbage. Wine choices are as comprehensive and sophisticated as anything else you're likely to find in Toulouse.

✪ **Les Jardins de l'Opéra.** In the Grand Hôtel de l'Opéra, 1 place du Capitole. ☎ **05-61-23-07-76.** Reservations required. Main courses 165F–280F ($28.05–$47.60); fixed-price lunch 200F ($34); fixed-price menus 295F–540F ($50.15–$91.80). AE, DC, MC, V. Mon–Sat noon–2pm and 8–10pm. Closed Jan 1–4 and Aug 3–26. Métro: Capitole. FRENCH.

The entrance to the city's best restaurant is in the 18th-century Florentine courtyard of the Grand Hôtel. The dining area is a series of intimate salons, several of which face a winter garden and a reflecting pool. You'll be greeted by the gracious Maryse Toulousy, whose husband, Dominique, prepares what critics have called the perfect combination of modern and old French cuisine. The outstanding menu listings are likely to include a salad of scallops and purple artichokes; tournedos of rabbit and fresh foie gras with a pepper sauce; strips of duckling with tarragon-flavored butter sauce; crayfish served in a mushroom-enriched puff pastry; and leg of lamb stuffed with exotic mushrooms, braised in saffron. His *vice versa de poivron rouge et calmar* is a tour de force. Calamari is stuffed with roasted red peppers in a red pepper sauce, and roasted red peppers are stuffed with calamari and flavored with squid ink. Desserts feature a sophisticated array of soufflés and tarts, some of which must be ordered at the beginning of the meal. A particularly luscious dessert—you can order it spontaneously, depending on how much appetite you have left at the end of the meal—is roasted figs stuffed with vanilla ice cream, drenched with Banyuls wine.

MODERATE

Chez Emile/La Terrasse D'Emile. 13 place St-Georges. ☎ **05-61-21-05-56.** Reservations recommended. Main courses 88F–139F ($14.95–$23.65); fixed-price menus 99F–165F ($16.85–$28.05) at lunch, 225F–250F ($38.25–$42.50) at dinner. AE, DC, MC, V. Tues–Sat noon–2pm and 7–10:30pm (also Mon 7–10:30pm in summer). Métro: Capitole or Esquirol. TOULOUSIEN.

In an old-fashioned house on one of the most beautiful squares of Toulouse, this restaurant offers the specialties of chef François Ferrier. In winter meals are served one floor above street level in a cozy enclave overlooking the square; in summer, the venue moves to the street-level dining room and the flower-filled terrace. Menu choices include cassoulet toulousain, magret de canard (duck) traditional style, a medley of Catalonian fish, and parillade of grilled fish with a pungently aromatic cold sauce of sweet peppers and olive oil. The wine *carte* is filled with intriguing surprises.

Le Grand Café de l'Opéra. In the Grand Hôtel de l'Opéra, 1 place du Capitole. ☎ **05-61-21-37-03.** Reservations recommended. Main courses 90F–150F ($15.30–$25.50). Fixed-price lunch 130F ($22.10). AE, DC, MC, V. Daily 9am–midnight. Closed Aug 1–15. Métro: Capitole. FRENCH.

Le Grand Café, in the most prestigious hotel in the city, evokes memories of the old Brasserie Lipp in Paris. It is warmly decorated with rich cove moldings, lots of burnished hardwood, shimmering glass, and cut flowers. Fresh shellfish is featured. Other specialties include calf's head ravigotte, steak tartare, "butterfly oysters," and an array of *plats du jour,* based on traditional brasserie cuisine. Seasonal ingredients are used "with respect," in the words of one food critic.

INEXPENSIVE

Eau de Folles. 14 Allée du President Roosevelt. ☎ **05-61-23-45-50.** Reservations recommended. Set-price menu 139F ($23.65). AE, DC, MC, V. Tues–Fri noon–1pm and 8–10pm. Métro: Capitole. FRENCH.

A relative newcomer to the restaurant scene in Toulouse, its low prices and the variety of its menu promise to make this a long-term contender. Within a mostly white, *fin-de-siècle* setting that includes lots of mirrors, you'll be offered a fixed-price menu with a choice of 10 starters, 10 main courses, and 10 desserts. Menu items vary according to the inspiration of the chef, the availability of fresh ingredients, and whatever happens to be in stock on the day of your visit. You might begin with a marinade of fish, followed with strips of duck meat with green pepper sauce, and end it all with a homemade pastry such as a *tarte tatin*. Everything is very simple, served within a cramped but convivial setting.

WHERE TO STAY & DINE NEARBY

Hôtel de Diane. 3 route de St-Simon, 31100 St-Simon. ☎ **05-61-07-59-52.** Fax 05-61-86-38-94. 22 units, 13 bungalows. MINIBAR TV TEL. 390F ($66.30) double; 450F ($76.50) bungalow. AE, DC, MC, V. Take D23 to exit 27, 5 miles east from Toulouse. Free parking.

This hotel/restaurant surrounded by a 5-acre park is the most tranquil retreat in the area. In a turn-of-the-century villa with comfortable, not particularly opulent rooms, it appeals to people who want to be away from the traffic and congestion of the inner city. Bedrooms are of a standard motel size, but each comes with a quality mattress and fine linen on the comfortable beds. Bathrooms are not large but there's adequate space to spread out your stuff. The bungalow-style units are built side by side in a row facing the park; none have kitchens, but each has a private terrace, and private parking. The rustic atmosphere befits this getaway, where there's a private pool and groves of pines and venerable hardwoods. The restaurant, Saint-Simon, offers a choice of meals in the garden or the Louis XV-style dining room. The fixed-price menus at 105F to 190F ($17.85 to $32.30) offer the best value. The restaurant serves lunch Monday to Friday and dinner Monday to Saturday until 9:30pm. In spite of the attentive service and gracious welcome, the food is somewhat uneven, sometimes delicious, other times less so. The bordeaux, however, is divine.

TOULOUSE AFTER DARK

The theater, dance, and opera in Toulouse is often on a par with that found in Paris. The best way to stay on top of the city's arts scene is to pick up a copy of the free monthly magazine *Toulouse Culture* from the Office de Tourisme.

One of the city's most notable theaters is the **Théâtre du Capitole,** place du Capitole (☎ **05-61-23-21-35**), which offers opera, operetta, and works from the classical French repertoire. The **Théâtre de la Digue,** 3 rue de la Digue (☎ **05-61-42-97-79**), presents ballet and works by local theater companies; and the **Halle aux Grains,** place Dupuy (☎ **05-61-63-18-65**), is the venue for many pop and classical concerts. Another contender is the **Théâtre Garonne,** 1 av. du Château d'Eau (☎ **05-61-42-33-99**), offering everything from works by Molière to 20th-century existentialist dramas.

The liveliest squares to wander after dark are place du Capitole, place St-Georges, place St-Pierre, and just off rue St-Rome and rue des Filatiers.

For bars and pubs, check out the Latin flair of **La Tantina de Bourgos,** 27 rue de la Garonette (☎ **05-61-55-59-29**), popular as a student scene; and the rowdier **Chez Tonton,** 16 place St-Pierre (☎ **05-61-21-86-54**), with its *après*-match frolicking atmosphere, complete with the winning team boozing it up. To keep the party going, try out the rock club **Le Bikini,** route de Lacroix-Falgarde (☎ **05-61-55-00-29**), that has occasional live concerts and an endless supply of hot bods, and a clientele that doesn't usually exceed age 25.

A couple of out-of-the-ordinary entertainment venues are the **Cave Poésie,** 71 rue du Taur (☎ **05-61-23-62-00**), where you can see a full range of one-acts, stand-up comics, poetry readings, small concerts—you name it; and the disco/restaurant **L'Ubu,** 16 rue St-Rome (☎ **05-61-23-26-75**), where the stars come out to eat, dance, and be seen.

Mostly heterosexual audiences migrate to **Disco La Strada,** 4 rue Gabrielle Peri (☎ **05-61-62-56-31**), which begins to get animated every Wednesday to Saturday after 11pm. A vaguely Iberian-looking establishment, **Bar La Bodega Bodega,** 1 rue Gabrielle Peri (☎ **05-61-63-03-63**), features recorded music and a scene that's more hip and fashionable than at many of its competitors; many friends seem to meet here spontaneously over drinks.

As you first enter **Le New Shanghai,** 12 rue de la Pomme (☎ **05-61-23-37-80**), you notice that this is a man's dance domain playing the latest in techno; then, venturing farther inside, you'll discover that it gives way to a darker, sexy cruise-bar environment with lots of hot men on the prowl. Plan on paying 50F to 80F ($8.50 to $13.60) to get in. Gay women appreciate **Le B. Machine,** 37 place des Carmes (☎ **05-61-55-57-59**), the most popular women's bar in town, which plays recorded music but doesn't have a dance floor.

2 Auch

451 miles (725.81km) SW of Paris, 126 miles (202.78km) SE of Bordeaux, 40 miles (64.37km) W of Toulouse

The lively market town of Auch is on the west bank of the Gers in the heart of the ancient Duchy of Gascony, of which it was once the capital.

ESSENTIALS

GETTING THERE   Five to 10 SNCF trains or buses per day run between Toulouse and Auch (trip time: 1½ hrs.), at a one-way fare of 75F ($12.75). Six to 13 SNCF buses arrive in Auch daily from Agen. The trip takes 1½ hours and costs 60F ($10.20) one-way. For more **information and schedules,** call ☎ **08-36-35-35-35.** If you're driving to Auch, take N124 west from Toulouse.

VISITOR INFORMATION   The **Office de Tourisme** is at 1 rue Dessoles (☎ **05-62-05-22-89**).

EXPLORING THE TOWN

The town is divided into an upper and a lower quarter, connected by several flights of steps. In the old part of town, the narrow streets, called *pousterles,* center on **place Salinis,** from which there's a good view of the Pyrénées. Branching off from here, the **Escalier Monumental** leads down to the Le Gers river, a descent of 232 steps.

On the north of the square is the **Cathédrale Ste-Marie,** place de la Cathédrale (☎ **05-62-05-72-71**). Built between the 15th and the 17th century, this is one of the handsomest Gothic churches in the south of France. It has 113 Renaissance choir stalls made of carved oak, and a custodian will let you in for 8F ($1.35). The stained-glass windows, also from the Renaissance, are impressive. Its 17th-century organ was one of the finest in the world at the time of Louis XIV. The cathedral is open daily from 8:30am to noon and 2 to 6pm (from 9:30am to noon and 2 to 5pm in winter).

Next to the cathedral stands the 18th-century **archbishop's palace** with a 14th-century bell tower, the **Tour d'Armagnac,** which was once a prison. The tower and palace are not open to the public.

Most of the shops and boutiques are along **rue Dessoles** and **avenue Alsace.** You'll find everything from confectionery shops to clothing stores. Also consider visiting the ✪ **Caves de l'Hôtel de France,** rue d'Etigny (☎ **05-62-61-71-71**), for a bottle or two of Armagnac. It has the best selection of this fire water, with more than 100 distilleries represented.

WHERE TO STAY

Hôtel de France (Restaurant Gourmand du Terroir/Brasserie Le Neuvième). Place de la Libération, 32003 Auch CEDEX. ☎ **05-62-61-71-84.** Fax 05-62-61-71-81. 29 units. A/C MINIBAR TV TEL. 365F–800F ($62.05–$136) double; 1,000F–1,750F ($170–$297.50) suite. AE, DC, MC, V. Parking 35F ($5.95).

This establishment is a lot different, and so less appealing, than it was during its glamorous heyday in the 1970s. Built around the much-modernized 16th-century core of an old inn, it offers comfortable, conservative rooms that come in various shapes and sizes and are furnished with French provincial pieces—some looking a bit dowdy. You get a comfortable night's sleep here on fine mattresses and good linens. Bathrooms are small but have tidy maintenance along with aging but still functioning plumbing.

The restaurant somewhat slavishly follows many of the culinary trends established by its since-departed founder, André Daguin. Today, with kitchens directed by Roland Garreau, its cuisine is "innovative within traditional boundaries." The more glamorous of the hotel's two restaurants includes the **Restaurant Gourmand du Terroir,** where set menus cost from 170F to 506F ($28.90 to $86), and main courses cost from 150F to 220F ($25.50 to $37.40). Menu choices include an assortment of preparations of foie gras from Gascony, brochette of oysters with foie gras, a duo of magret de canard (duck) cooked in a rock-salt shell and served with a medley of vegetables, and stuffed pigeon roasted with spiced honey. Desserts include a platter of four chocolate dishes, and café au café, a presentation of mousses and pastries unified by their coffee content. Over the years we've had some of our most memorable meals here, yet there have also been disappointments, particularly since the staff is simply not as hip or as alert as is needed to sustain the high expectations associated with a visit here.

You might actually be happier within the hotel's less pretentious and much less expensive **Brasserie Le Neuvième,** where set menus represent good value at 79F to 100F ($13.45 to $17). Both places are open for business daily from noon to 2pm, and from 7:30 to 10pm.

Le Relais de Gascogne. 5 av. de la Marne, 32000 Auch. ☎ **05-62-05-26-81.** Fax 05-62-63-30-22. 28 units. A/C TV TEL. 278F–299F ($47.25–$50.85) double. MC, V. Closed Dec 25–Jan 10. Parking 35F ($5.95).

This hotel, the second choice in town, offers economical accommodations and meals. The rooms were modernized in the 1990s, and are comfortably furnished with firm mattresses and fine linen on the beds, most often doubles or twins. Bathrooms are small, compact, and neatly organized, containing adequate shelf space and a shower stall. The food is often quite good, especially the salad of duck breast, foie gras of duck, and hearty cassoulet. This place, though small, remains a stronghold of Gascon gastronomy. Fixed-price menus run 87F to 158F ($14.80 to $26.85).

WHERE TO DINE

Most people still head for the Hôtel de France (see above), if only for the memories. But gone are the days when this was one of the great restaurants in the south of France.

Le Daroles. Place de la Liberation. ☎ **05-62-05-00-51.** Reservations not necessary. Set-price lunches 69F–175F ($11.75–$29.75); set-price dinners 99F–175F ($16.85–$29.75). DC, MC, V. Daily noon–2:30pm and 7:30–11pm. AE, DC, MC, V. FRENCH.

Despite its much, much lower prices, this Parisian-style brasserie attracts many of the former clients of the Hotel de France. Within an old-timey setting that includes mirrors, polished copper, mahogany paneling, and leather banquettes, you can enjoy a bustling, no-nonsense cuisine. Examples are grilled sole in butter sauce; scallops with herb and wine sauce; sauerkraut; foie gras; and pepper steak.

3 Cordes-sur-Ciel

421 miles (677.53km) SW of Paris, 15½ miles (24.94km) NW of Albi

This site is remarkable—it's like an eagle's nest on a hilltop, above the Cérou valley. In days gone by, many celebrities, such as Jean-Paul Sartre and Albert Camus, considered this town a favorite hideaway.

The name Cordes is derived from the textile and leather industries that thrived here during the 13th and 14th centuries. Artisans working with linen and leather prospered, and the town also became known throughout France for its brilliantly colored silks. In the 16th century, however, plagues and religious wars reduced the city to a minor role. A brief renaissance occurred in the 19th century, when automatic weaving machines were introduced.

Today Cordes is an arts-and-crafts city, and many of the ancient houses on the narrow streets contain artisans plying their skills—blacksmiths, enamelers, graphic artists, weavers, engravers, sculptors, and painters. You park outside, then go under an arch leading to the old town.

ESSENTIALS

GETTING THERE   The nearest train station is in Vindrac, 2 miles from Cordes. There you will have to rent a bicycle or take a taxi the remaining distance. For **rail information** and schedules, call ☎ **08-36-35-35-35.**

VISITOR INFORMATION   The **Office de Tourisme** is in the Maison Fonpeyrouse, Grand'Rue Raymond VII (☎ **05-63-56-00-52**).

EXPLORING THE TOWN

Often called "the city of a hundred Gothic arches," Cordes contains numerous **old houses** built of pink sandstone. Many of the doors and windows are fashioned of pointed (broken) arches that still retain their 13th- and 14th-century grace. Some of the best-preserved line **Grand'Rue,** also called **"rue Droite."**

The **Musée d'Art et d'Histoire le Portail-Peint (Musée Charles-Portal),** Grand'Rue Haute (no phone), is named after the archivist of the Tarn region who was also an avid historian of Cordes. It is in a medieval house whose foundations date from the Gallo-Roman era. It contains everyday artifacts of the textile industry of long ago, farming measures, samples of local embroidery, a reconstructed peasant home interior, and other medieval memorabilia. Official visiting hours are limited to the busiest seasons: In July and August, it's open daily from 11am to noon and 3 to 6pm. April to June and September and October it's officially open only on Sunday and public holidays from 3 to 6pm. If you happen to arrive when the museum is closed, ask someone at the tourist office (see above) to accompany you for your visit (if they're not busy, they often will). Barring that, try to make an appointment for a visit later in the day. Admission is 15F ($2.55) for adults and 7F ($1.20) for children. There's no phone within this museum, and definitely no full-time staff to answer even if they had a phone, so for information, contact the Tourist Office.

The **Maison du Grand-Fauconnier (House of the Falcon Master)** is named for the falcons carved into the stonework of the wall. A grandly proportioned staircase in the building leads to the **Musée Yves-Brayer,** Grande'Rue (☎ **05-63-56-00-40**). Yves Brayer came to Cordes in 1940 and became one of its most ardent civic boosters. After watching Cordes fall gradually into decay, he renewed interest in its restoration. The museum contains minor artifacts relating to the town's history; the most interesting exhibits are rather fanciful scale models of the town itself. The museum is open for prolonged hours only during July and August, when it's open Wednesday to Monday from 10am to noon and from 2 to 6pm. The rest of the year, it's open the same hours, but only on Saturday and Sunday. Admission costs 15F ($2.55) for adults and 2F (35¢) for children 11 and under.

The **Eglise St-Michel,** Grande'Rue, dates from the 13th century, but many alterations have been made since. From the top of the tower you can view the surrounding area. Much of the lateral design of the side chapels probably comes from the cathedral at Albi. Before being shipped here, the organ (dating from 1830) was in Notre-Dame de Paris. Visiting hours are erratic. If the church is closed, ask at the *tabac* (tobacco shop) across from the front entrance or call the tourist office to make an appointment.

WHERE TO STAY & DINE

Hostellerie du Parc. Les Cabannes, 81170 Cordes. ☎ **05-63-56-02-59.** Fax 05-63-56-18-03. Reservations recommended. Main courses 75F–110F ($12.75–$18.70); fixed-price lunches 90F–300F ($15.30–$51); fixed-price dinners 160F–300F ($27.20–$51). AE, MC, V. Mon–Sat noon–2pm and 7–10pm, Sun noon–2pm. Closed Mon Nov–Mar. Take route de St-Antonin (D600) for about 1 mile west from the town center. FRENCH.

This century-old stone house offers generous meals in a wooded garden or paneled dining room. The specialties include homemade foie gras, duckling, *poularde* (chicken) occitaine, rabbit with cabbage leaves, and calf's sweetbreads with morels. Specialties of the house are unusual and in many cases, charming, featuring such dishes as pâté of pheasant garnished with foie gras; a ballotine of guinea fowl served with sweetbreads; and a confit of roasted rabbit with pink garlic from the nearby town of Lautrec.

The hotel offers 17 simply furnished rooms; a double costs 290F to 380F ($49.30 to $64.60). There's an outdoor pool, and lessons in French cuisine are offered by the chef.

✪ **Maison du Grand Ecuyer.** Rue Voltaire, 81170 Cordes. ☎ **05-63-53-79-50.** Fax 05-63-53-79-51. Reservations required. Main courses 150F–210F ($25.50–$35.70); fixed-price menus 170F–440F ($28.90–$74.80). AE, DC, MC, V. July–Aug, daily noon–2pm and 7–9:30pm; Easter–June and Sept–Oct 14, Tues 7–9:30pm, Wed–Sun noon–2pm and 7–9:30pm. Closed Oct 15–Easter. FRENCH.

The 15th-century hunting lodge of Raymond VII, comte de Toulouse, that contains this restaurant is classified as a national historic treasure. It's perched near the top of the steep rock that's the site of the village of Cordes. Despite its glamour and undeniable charm, it remains intimate and unstuffy. Chef Yves Thuriès prepares specialties that have made his restaurant an almost mandatory stop; these include three confits of lobster, red mullet salad with fondue of vegetables, and noisette of lamb in chicory sauce. The dessert selection is about the grandest in this part of France. If you want to enjoy the same meal President Mitterrand was served, it can be reproduced for 340F ($57.80); the menu that duplicates the food offered Elizabeth II costs 360F ($61.20); while the grandest replication of all is the 440F ($74.80) menu dished up for the emperor of Japan.

The hotel contains 12 rooms and one suite, all with antiques and an undeniable sense of the Middle Ages blended discreetly with modern comforts. Doubles cost 450F to 850F ($76.50 to $144.50); the suite is 1,200F ($204). The room honoring a former guest, Albert Camus, has a four-poster bed and a fireplace.

4 Albi

433 miles (696.85km) SW of Paris, 47 miles (75.64km) NE of Toulouse

The "red city" of Albi straddles both banks of the Tarn River. The cathedral and the bridges spanning the river are made of brick, as are most of the town's buildings, earning Albi its title—in the rosy glow of a setting sun, Albi often looks as if it were in flames, a spectacular sight.

The town is the birthplace of Toulouse-Lautrec, and contains an important museum of his works. The town's history has been stormy. The fortified cathedral that broods over the medieval center is a reminder of the bloody struggle between the Roman Catholic Church and the Cathars, a religious group the Church considered heretical. They were also called Albigenses after the town, which was an important center of their movement.

ESSENTIALS

GETTING THERE   Fifteen trains per day (one every 90 minutes) link Toulouse with Albi (trip time: 1 hr.); the fare is from 70F ($11.90) one-way. There's also a direct Paris-Albi night train. For **rail information** and schedules, call ☎ 08-36-35-35-35. Motorists from Paris can take R.N. 20 via Cahors and Caussade; from Bordeaux, take the autoroute des Deux Mers (A-62) and exit at Montauban. If you're driving from Toulouse, take N88 going northeast.

VISITOR INFORMATION   The **Office de Tourisme** is in the Palais de la Serbie, place Ste-Cécile (☎ 05-63-49-48-80).

SEEING THE SIGHTS

Note that the **Musée St-Raymond,** place St-Sernin (☎ 05-61-22-21-85), with its fine collection of Roman busts, will be closed for renovations throughout the life of this edition.

Cathédrale Ste-Cécile. Near place du Vigan. ☎ **05-63-49-48-80.** Admission to the cathedral 5F (85¢); to the treasury 20F ($3.40). Daily June–Oct 9am–7pm, Nov–May 9am–noon and 2:30–6pm.

Fortified with ramparts and parapets, this cathedral was built in 1282 by the lord bishop during the Albigensian Crusade, waged by the Church against the Cathars and the comte de Toulouse. The church contains frescoes and paintings; exceptional is the 16th-century rood screen with its unique polychromatic statues from the Old and New Testaments.

Opposite the north side of the cathedral is the **Palais de la Berbie** (Archbishop's Palace), another fortified structure dating from the late 13th century.

IN THE FOOTSTEPS OF TOULOUSE-LAUTREC

Although he spent most of his life in Paris, Toulouse-Lautrec is closely connected with Albi. He was born in Albi in the **Hôtel Bosc;** it's still a private home and cannot be toured, but there's a plaque on the wall of the building at 14 rue Toulouse-Lautrec in the historic town core.

You can visit the family's **Château de Bosc,** Camjac, 12800 Naucelle, 29 miles from Toulouse. It was built in 1180 and renovated in the 1400s. The present owner, Mlle de Céleran, and her team welcome visitors interested in Toulouse-Lautrec, but it's best to call ahead, as tours are guided. It is usually open daily from 9am to 7pm. Admission is 35F ($5.95) for adults, 20F ($3.40) for children 8 to 14, and free for children 7 and under.

✪ **Musée Toulouse-Lautrec.** ☎ **05-63-49-48-70.** Admission 24F ($4.10) adults, 12F ($2.05) children. Apr–Sept, daily 9am–noon and 2–6pm; Oct–Mar, Wed–Mon 10am–noon and 2–5pm.

This is the world's most important collection of the artist's paintings—more than 600 specimens. His family bequeathed the works remaining in his studio. Toulouse-Lautrec was born at Albi on November 24, 1864, into a much-intermarried family of aristocrats whose ancestors can be traced back to Charlemagne. He was the only surviving child in a family probably genetically prone to pycnodysostosis, a form of dwarfism, and skeletal disorders. Despite his physical shortcomings, no one can debate the titanic dimensions of Toulouse-Lautrec's art. He is best known for his paintings, posters, and sketches of characters in music halls and circuses. The museum also owns paintings by Degas, Bonnard, Matisse, Utrillo, and Rouault.

WHERE TO STAY

Hostellerie St-Antoine. 17 rue St-Antoine, 81000 Albi. ☎ **05-63-54-04-04.** Fax 05-63-47-10-47. www.chatotel.com. E-mail: st-antoine@ilink.fr. 44 units. A/C MINIBAR TV TEL. 620F–880F ($105.40–$149.60) double; 1,080F ($183.60) suite. AE, DC, MC, V. Parking 30F ($5.10).

This 250-year-old hotel has been owned by the same family for five generations; today it's managed by Jacques and Jean-François Rieux. Their great-grandfather was a friend of Toulouse-Lautrec, who gave him several paintings, sketches, and prints. Some of these can be seen in the lounge, which opens onto a rear garden. The rooms have been delightfully decorated, with a sophisticated use of color, good reproductions, and occasional antiques. Bedrooms are generally spacious, furnished with French provincial pieces, including quality mattresses and fine linens. Bathrooms are well equipped with good-size towels and hair dryers. Even if you're not spending the night, consider dining here: The Rieux culinary tradition is in the hands of chef Laurent Dodé, who produces a traditional yet creative cuisine; of course, everything tastes better washed down with Gallac wines. Specific menu items include breast of chicken prepared with sherry sauce; fried lamb chops served with a confit of garlic; and dessert crèpes flambéed with Grand Marnier.

Hôtel Chiffre. 50 rue Séré-de-Rivières, 81000 Albi. ☎ **05-63-48-58-48.** Fax 05-63-47-20-61. 36 units. TV TEL. 360F–420F ($61.20–$71.40) double. AE, DC, MC, V. Parking 25F ($4.25).

This well-managed hotel in the city center was originally built as lodgings for passengers on the mail coaches that hauled letters and people across the landscape of southern France.

Despite frequent renovations, the original porch that once sheltered carriages from rain and sun as they pulled up to unload their passengers has been preserved. Today, bedrooms are outfitted with an artful kind of coziness, usually with upholstered walls in floral patterns, sometimes with views of the quiet inner courtyard. About half contain air conditioning. Most rooms are medium in size and beds have first-rate mattresses. The compact bathrooms, each with a shower and tub, are tiled and well maintained. The hotel restaurant, Bateau Ivre, is popular among locals because of the good value of the set menus; they range in price from 135F to 350F ($22.95 to $59.50). One is especially interesting: Named after Toulouse-Lautrec, it's composed of dishes he himself often used to prepare for his dinner parties. The recipes were compiled after his death by his friends, and include radishes stuffed with braised foie gras, supreme of sandre, and ducklings from the nearby town of Lautrec roasted with garlic. The menu is priced at 190F ($32.30).

Hôtel George V. 29 av. Maréchal-Joffre, 81000 Albi. ☎ **05-63-54-24-16.** Fax 05-63-49-90-78. www.ilink.fr/hotel.georgev. E-mail: hotel.georgev@ilink.fr. 9 units. TV TEL. 180F–250F ($30.60–$42.50) double. AE, MC, V. Free parking.

This hotel offers a dignified kind of charm, and a Spartan, pleasingly old-fashioned setting at prices that are fair and reasonable. It was built around 1900, and is about a quarter-mile from the center. Bedrooms are high-ceilinged and generally spacious, with efficient, serviceable furniture and excellent beds. They are simply decorated, in some cases with a bit of whimsy. Bathrooms are small but contain adequate shelf space, medium-sized towels, and showers and tubs. Breakfast is the only meal served.

✪ La Réserve. Rte. de Cordes à Fonvialane, 81000 Albi. ☎ **05-63-60-80-80.** Fax 05-63-47-63-60. 28 units. MINIBAR TV TEL. 650F–1,100F ($110.50–$187) double; 1,100F–1,500F ($187–$255) suite. AE, DC, MC, V. Closed Nov–Apr. From the center of town, follow the signs to Carmaux-Rodez until you cross the Tarn, then follow the signs to Cordes; the hotel is adjacent to the main road to Cordes.

This country-club villa, 1¼ miles from Albi, is managed by the Rieux family, who also run the Hostellerie St-Antoine. It's in Mediterranean style, with tennis courts, a pool, and a fine garden in which you can dine. The rooms, have charm and style, and contain imaginative decorations (but avoid those rooms over the kitchen); upper-story rooms have sun terraces and French doors. All have comfortable mattresses and fine linens, plus well-equipped bathrooms with showers, good-size towels, and tidy maintenance. In the restaurant, specialties are *pâté de grives* (thrush), *carré d'agneau aux cèpes* (lamb with flap mushrooms), and filet of beef with béarnaise sauce. Even if you're not a guest, consider a visit. The wine *carte* is rich in bordeaux and the prices per bottle are reasonable.

WHERE TO DINE

La Réserve (see "Where to Stay," above) boasts a wonderful restaurant.

Jardin des Quatre Saisons. 19 bd. de Strasbourg. ☎ **05-63-60-77-76.** Reservations recommended. Fixed-price menus 145F–230F ($24.65–$39.10), main courses 95F–120F ($16.15–$20.40). AE, DC, MC, V. Tues–Sun 12:30–3pm and Tues–Sat 7:30–10pm. FRENCH.

The best food in Albi is served by Georges Bermond, who believes that menus, like life, should change with the seasons—and that's how the restaurant got its name. The setting is a modern, deceptively simple pair of dining rooms where the lighting has been subtly arranged to make everyone look as attractive as possible. Service is always competent and polite. Menu items have been fine-tuned, and include delicious versions of a fricassée of snails garnished with strips of the famous hams produced in the nearby hamlet of Lacaune; ravioli stuffed with pulverized shrimp and served with a truffled cream sauce; and a gratinée of mussels in a compote of fish. Most delectable of all—an excuse for returning a second time—is a pot-au-feu of the sea that contains three or four species of fish garnished with a crayfish-flavored cream sauce. The wine *carte* is the finest in Albi.

Le Lautrec. 13 rue Toulouse-Lautrec. ☎ **05-63-54-86-55.** Reservations recommended. Main courses 60F–105F ($10.20–$17.85); set-price menus 68F ($11.55) lunch Tues–Fri, otherwise 90F–230F ($15.30–$39.10). DC, MC, V. Tues–Sun noon–2pm and Tues–Sat 7–9:30pm. FRENCH.

Part of its charm derives from its associations with Toulouse-Lautrec—it lies across the street from his birthplace, and it's decorated with copies of his paintings. Also appealing is the rich patina of its interior brickwork. The skillfully prepared food items include a salad of fried scallops that come with rose oil and essence of shrimp; sweetbreads with morels; roasted rack of lamb marinated in a brewed infusion of Provençal thyme. Most unusual of all is a medieval recipe for breast of duck "à Hippocrace" wherein cinnamon, rosewater, and honey are used.

5 Castres

452 miles (727.42km) SW of Paris, 26 miles (41.84km) S of Albi

Built on the bank of the Agout River, Castres is the point of origin for trips to the Sidobre, the mountains of Lacaune, and the Black Mountains. Today the wool industry, whose origins go back to the 14th century, has made Castres one of France's two most important wool-producing areas. The town was formerly a Roman military installation. A Benedictine monastery was founded here in the 9th century, and the town fell under the comtes d'Albi in the 10th century. During the 16th-century wars of religion it was Protestant.

ESSENTIALS

GETTING THERE   From Toulouse, 8 trains arrive per day (trip time: 1 hr.); one-way fare is 75F ($12.75). From Albi, there are 7 trains via St-Sulpice (trip time: 2 hrs.); fares are 78F ($13.25) one-way. For **rail information** and schedules, call ☎ 08-36-35-35-35. In addition, about a half-dozen buses arrive in town from Albi every day, at the **Gare Routière,** on the avenue Charles de Gaulle (☎ 05-63-35-37-31). One-way fares from Albi begin at 30F ($5.10) each for the 30-minute ride. Castres is located on N126 east from Toulouse and along N112 south from Albi.

VISITOR INFORMATION   The **Office de Tourisme** is at 3 rue Milhau-Ducommun (☎ 05-63-62-63-62). During July and August, guided walking tours of the city's historic district depart daily from the tourist office at 10am and 4pm. The tours last 75 minutes, and cost 20F ($3.40) for adults and 10F ($1.70) for children under 16.

THE TOP ATTRACTIONS

✪ **Musée Goya.** In the Jardin de l'Evêché. ☎ **05-63-71-59-27.** Admission: Sept–June, 15F ($2.55) adults, 8F ($1.35) children; July–Aug, 25F ($4.25) adults, 13F ($2.20) children. July–Aug, daily 9am–noon and 2–5pm and Sun 10am–noon and 2–6pm; Apr–June and Sept, Tues–Sat and Sun same hours; Oct–Mar same days and hours, but closes at 5pm.

The museum is in the town hall, an archbishop's palace designed by Mansart in 1669. The paintings of Francisco Goya y Lucientes were donated to the town in 1894 by Pierre Briguiboul, son of the Castres-born artist Marcel Briguiboul. *Les Caprices*, created in 1799 after the illness that left Goya deaf, fills nearly an entire room. A satire on Spanish society, the work is composed of symbolic images of demons and monsters. The museum collection also includes 16th-century tapestries and Spanish paintings from the 15th to the 20th century.

Le Centre National et Musée Jean-Jaurès. 2 place Pélisson. ☎ **05-63-72-01-01.** Admission 10F ($1.70) adults, 5F (85¢) students, free for children under 14. Hours are the same as Museum Goya's (see above).

This museum is dedicated to the workers' movements of the late 19th and early 20th centuries. Its collection contains printed material from the various Socialist movements in France during that period as well as paintings, sculptures, films, and slides. See, in particular, an issue of *L'Aurore* containing Zola's famous *"J'accuse"* article about the Dreyfus case.

Eglise St-Benoît. Place du 8-Mai-1945. ☎ **05-63-59-05-19.** Admission free. Mon–Sat 9am–noon and 2–6:30pm, Sun 2–4pm. Closed on Sun Oct–May for religious services.

The town's most visible and important church is Castres's outstanding example of French baroque architecture. The architect Caillau began construction of the church in 1677, on the site of a 9th-century Benedictine abbey. The baroque structure was never completed according to its original plans. The painting at the church's far end, above the altar, was executed by Gabriel Briard in the 18th century.

WHERE TO STAY

Hôtel de l'Europe. 5 rue Victor-Hugo, 81100 Castres. ☎ **05-63-59-00-33.** Fax 05-63-59-21-38. 35 units. MINIBAR TV TEL. 290F ($49.30) double. MC, V. Free parking on street.

The most charming thing about this hotel are the bedrooms that, in most cases, are capped with ceiling beams and ringed with pinkish-gray masonry from the building's original 18th-century construction. All have views over the oldest part of the historic town, are outfitted with comfortable mattresses, and have cramped but cozy bathrooms with good-sized towels. An in-house restaurant serves a cold buffet every day at lunch, priced at 49F ($8.35) per person; evening meals have set-price menus that cost from 69F ($11.75). Don't expect glamour—what you get is unpretentious, solid comfort at a price that's affordable.

✪ **Hôtel Renaissance.** 17 rue Victor-Hugo, 81100 Castres. ☎ **05-63-59-30-42.** Fax 05-63-72-11-57. 20 units. TV TEL. 350F–410F ($59.50–$69.70) double; 520F–660F ($88.40–$112.20) suite. AE, DC, MC, V.

The Renaissance is the best hotel in Castres. It was built in the 17th century as the courthouse. In 1993, the colorful but run-down hotel was discreetly restored. Today you'll see a severely dignified building composed, depending on which part you look at, of *colombages*-style half-timbering, with a mixture of chiseled stone blocks and bricks. Some rooms have exposed timbers; all are clean and comfortable, evoking the crafts of yesteryear. Each has good beds and tile bathrooms equipped with hair dryers. Simple platters can be prepared if you wish to eat in your room, but a recently completed restaurant and bar, Le Montaigne, provides other options. Fixed-price menus are available for 95F to 250F ($16.15 to $42.50).

WHERE TO DINE

In addition to those below, another worthy choice is **Le Victoria,** 24 place du 8-Mai-1945 (☎ **05-63-59-14-68**), where meals cost 110F to 250F ($18.70 to $42.50). A superb French cuisine is served, with regional products used whenever available.

Brasserie des Jacobins. 1 place Jean-Jaurès. ☎ **05-63-59-01-44.** Reservations recommended. Main courses 40F–90F ($6.80–$15.30). AE, MC, V. Daily noon–2:15pm and 7–10:30pm. FRENCH/PROVENÇAL.

A likely bet for solid, well-seasoned, and conservative French and Provençal cuisine is this simple modern brasserie where the menu hasn't changed in many years, and where most of the clients are local residents. Menu items include blanquettes of veal, cassoulets, and caramelized filets of pork with Provençal herbs. Decor is rustic, service is cordial, and many visitors find it especially suitable for a simple noontime meal.

La Mandragore. 1 rue Malpas. ☎ **05-63-59-51-27.** Reservations recommended. Main courses 80F–130F ($13.60–$22.10); fixed-price menus 75F ($12.75) with wine, served at lunch and dinner; and 90F–240F ($15.30–$40.80). AE, MC, V. Mon 7–10pm, Tues–Sat noon–2pm and 7–10pm. LANGUEDOCIEN.

On an easily overlooked narrow street, this restaurant occupies a small section of one of the many wings of the medieval château-fort of Castres. The decor is consciously simple, perhaps as an appropriate foil for the stone walls and overhead beams. Sophie Belaut (in the dining room) and Jean-Claude Belaut (in the kitchen) prepare a regional cuisine that's among the best in town, served with charm and tact. It might include artichokes with foie gras and truffle-flavored vinaigrette, roast pigeon stuffed with foie gras and served with gâteau of potatoes and flap mushrooms, filet of tuna with sweet peppers and cured ham, and magret of duckling with truffle oil and braised leeks.

6 Carcassonne

495 miles (796.63km) SW of Paris, 57 miles (91.73km) SE of Toulouse, 65 miles (104.61km) S of Albi

Evoking bold knights, fair damsels, and troubadours, the greatest fortress city of Europe rises against a background of the snow-capped Pyrénées. Floodlit at night, it captures a fairy-tale magic, but back in its heyday in the Middle Ages it was the target of assault by battering rams, grapnels, a mobile tower (inspired by the Trojan horse), catapults, flaming arrows, and the mangonel.

The city that was used as a backdrop for the 1991 movie *Robin Hood, Prince of Thieves,* is overrun with hordes of visitors and tacky gift shops. The elusive charm of Carcassone comes out in the evening, when day-trippers depart and floodlights bathe the ancient monuments.

ESSENTIALS

GETTING THERE   Carcassonne is a major stop for trains between Toulouse and destinations south and east. About 24 trains from Toulouse arrive daily (trip time: 50 mins.); a one-way fare is 80F ($13.60). From Monpellier there are 14 trains per day (trip time: 2 hrs.); a one-way fare is 140F ($23.80). There are 12 trains per day from Nîmes (trip time: 2½ hrs.); one-way fare is 150F ($25.50). For **rail information** and schedules, call ☎ 08-36-35-35-35. If you're driving, Carcassone lies on A61 south of Toulouse.

VISITOR INFORMATION   The **Office de Tourisme** is at 15 bd. Camille-Pelletan (☎ 04-68-10-24-30) and in the medieval town at Porte Narbonnaise (☎ 04-68-10-24-36).

SPECIAL EVENTS   The town sparkles with real pizzazz during its major summer festivals. The month of July is devoted to the **Festival de Carcassonne,** when the city is filled with classical concerts, dance, opera, and original theater. Tickets range from 125F to 300F ($21.25 to $51) and can be purchased by calling ☎ 04-68-77-74-18. Most of the cultural and theatrical events are presented in the **Grand Theatre de la Cité,** an angular-looking theater set behind the Basilique St-Nazaire. For more information, contact either the Grand Theatre (see above) or the **Theatre Municipal** (☎ 04-68-25-33-13).

On the night of **Bastille Day** one of the best fireworks displays in all of France lights up the skies. *L'Embrasement de la Cité* begins every July 14 at 10:30pm.

Spectacles Médiévaux is an event that re-creates medieval jousting, medieval music, and plays that celebrate the Middle Ages during a 2-week period every year in mid-August. You can get more information about these events by contacting either the tourist office or the local history council, **Carcassonne Terre d'Histoire,** chemin de Serres (☎ 04-68-47-97-97).

EXPLORING LA CITE

Carcassonne consists of two towns: **La Bastide St-Louis** (also known as **La Ville Basse,** or Lower City), and the older, more evocative medieval **Cité.** The former has

A Scenic Side Trip

After a visit to the walled city of Carcassonne, take D118 for 30 miles north to the **Montagne Noire (Black Mountains).** Arid on the southern slopes but wooded and lush on the northern rim, they mark the southeastern extension of the Massif Central. Towering over the region is the 3,700-foot Pic de Noire, around which is the **Parc Régional du Haut Languedoc,** studded with panoramic scenery and tranquil lakes. The area is crisscrossed with narrow unmarked roads leading to one scenic vista after another. It's easy to get lost—but if you have the time, that's part of the fun.

For more specific guidance within the park, you can visit the town of **Mazamet,** 30 miles north of Carcassonne. Here the **Office de Tourisme,** rue des Casernes (☎ **05-63-61-27-07**), can provide maps and outline some of the best trails for exploring. Mazamet also makes a good lunch stop. The most elegant choice for dining there is **Le Métairie Neuve** (☎ **05-63-61-23-31**), a hotel 1 mile from the center at Boul-du-Point-de-Larn (reached via D54). Here you'll find the area's best selection of regional dishes, with a menu that changes frequently, based on what's seasonal. Meals range from 95F to 120F ($16.15 to $20.40). If you'd like to anchor for a day, the hotel rents 14 rooms furnished in a traditional French style at 460F ($78.20) for a double.

After exploring the beauty of the park, you can continue northwest on N112 to Castres on the banks of the Agout River (see "Castres," above). From Castres a detour east on D622 will take you to **Sidobre** to see its bizarre rock formations. The Agout and Durenque Rivers have cut deep gorges into the earth here, and the area is filled with giant granite quarries. These great boulders have been given names such as Rock of the Three Cheeses and Rock of the Goose.

little interest, but the latter is a major attraction, the goal of many a pilgrim. The fortifications of La Cité consist of a double line of **ramparts,** with inner and outer walls. The inner rampart was built by the Visigoths in the 5th century. Clovis, king of the Franks, attacked in 506 but failed. The Saracens overcame the city in 728, and held it until 752, when Pepin the Short (father of Charlemagne) drove them out. During a long siege by Charlemagne, when the populace of the walled city was starving and near surrender, Dame Carcas came up with an idea. According to legend, she gathered up the last remaining bit of grain, fed it to a sow, then tossed the pig over the ramparts. It's said to have burst, scattering the grain. The Franks concluded that Carcassonne must have unlimited food supplies and ended their siege.

Carcassonne's walls were further fortified by the vicomtes de Trencavel in the 12th century and by Louis IX and Philip the Bold in the 13th century. However, by the mid–17th century its importance as a strategic frontier fort ended and the ramparts were left to decay. In the 19th century the builders of the Lower Town began to remove the stone for use in new construction. But a revival of interest in the Middle Ages led the government to order Viollet-le-Duc (who restored Notre-Dame in Paris) to repair and, where necessary, rebuild the walls. Reconstruction continued until very recently.

Walks along the outer ramparts are free, and are possible year-round without restriction. Walks along the inner ramparts, however, are possible only as part of guided tours. Hour-long tours depart at 10-minute intervals in summer, daily between 9am and 7:30pm, and at 30-minute intervals in winter, daily between 9am and 5pm. Three of these per day in summer, and one per day in winter, are conducted in English. The cost is 35F ($5.95) for adults and 23F ($3.90) for persons aged 12 to 26; children 11 and under are free. For information call the **Caisse National des Monuments Historique** at ☎ **04-68-11-70-77.**

A small populace still resides within the walls. The **Basilique St-Nazaire,** La Cité (☎ **04-68-25-27-65),** dates from the 11th to the 14th century, and contains some beautiful stained-glass windows and a pair of rose medallions. The nave is in the Romanesque style, but the choir and transept are Gothic. The organ, one of the oldest in southwestern France, is 16th century. Note the well-preserved tomb of Bishop Radulph, dating from 1266. The cathedral is open daily: in July and August from 9am to 7pm, and off-season from 9:30am to noon and 2 to 5:30pm. Mass is celebrated on Sunday at 11am. Admission is free.

Musée des Memoires du Moyen Age, Immeuble du Pont-Levis, Chemin des Anglais (☎ **04-68-71-08-65),** is set within the stone bulwarks that used to contain the drawbridge. This museum documents the traumatic battles, sieges, and feuds that marked life in Carcassonne during the Middle Ages. You'll be shown a video depicting a thousand years of medieval life in the town, and exhibitions that showcase the values and lifestyles of long ago. Entrance is 25F ($4.25) for adults or 15F ($2.55) for children and students. It is open mid-September to mid-June daily 10am to 6pm; from mid-June to mid-September daily 10am to 8pm.

SHOPPING

Carcassone, more than other French cities, is really two distinct shopping towns in one—the walled medieval city and the modern lower city. The whole of the medieval city is chock full of tiny stores and boutiques selling mostly gift items, antiques, and local arts and crafts. In the modern city, the major streets for shopping are **rue Clemenceau** and **rue de Verdun,** particularly if you're in the market for clothing. On the third Saturday of every month at the portail Jacobin, in the modern town center, a **flea market** sets up from 8am to 6pm.

Stores worth visiting are the **Caveau des Vins,** tour du Tréseau (☎ **04-68-25-29-38),** where you'll find a wide selection of regional wines ranging from simple table wines to those awarded the distinction of Appellation d'Origine Controlée; **Antiquités "Le St-Georges,"** 36 rue Victor-Hugo (☎ **04-68-47-52-66),** which specializes in antique scientific instruments and furniture from the 17th to the 19th century; and **Dominique Sarraute,** 15 rue Porte-d'Aude (☎ **04-68-72-42-90),** for antique firearms.

WHERE TO STAY
IN THE CITÉ

✪ **Cité.** Place de l'Eglise, 11000 Carcassonne. ☎ **04-68-25-03-34.** Fax 04-68-71-50-15. www.orient-expresshotels.com. 61 units. A/C MINIBAR TV TEL. 1,000F–1,900F ($170–$323) double; 2,500F–3,200F ($425–$544) suite. AE, DC, MC, V. Parking 80F ($13.60).

Originally a palace for whatever bishop or well-placed prelate happened to be in control at the time, this historically important site has thrived as the most desirable hotel in town since it was built in 1909. Massively and luxuriously renovated, it's built into the walls of the old city, adjoining the cathedral. The hotel has been acquired by the luxury-minded Orient-Express Hotel group and grandly fluffed up to the tune of $3 million. You enter a long Gothic corridor/gallery leading to the lounge. Many rooms open onto the ramparts and the garden and feature antiques or reproductions. All have comfortable mattresses and plenty of thick towels, and a few rooms boast brass beds and four-posters. Unit 33 is the only one with a balcony, opening onto views of Carcassonne. Modern equipment has been discreetly installed, as well as a heated pool.

The hotel is renowned for its restaurant, La Barbacane, which is recommended separately below.

Hôtel des Remparts. 3–5 place du Grand-Puits, 11000 Carcassonne. ☎ **04-68-71-27-72.** Fax 04-68-72-73-26. 18 units. TEL. 330F ($56.10) double. MC, V. Parking 20F ($3.40).

An abbey in the 12th century, this building at the edge of a stone square in the town center was converted into a charming hotel in 1983 after major repairs to the masonry and roof. The rooms contain no-frills furniture and acceptably comfortable mattresses. Most were renovated, or at least repainted, in the late 1990s. Bathrooms are small and compact, but efficiently organized with adequate shelf space. The owners are proud of the massive stone staircase that twists around itself. Make reservations at least a couple of months ahead if you plan to stay here during summer.

AT THE ENTRANCE TO THE CITÉ

✪ **Hôtel du Donjon.** 2 rue du Comte-Roger, 11000 Carcassonne. ☎ **800/528-1234** in the U.S. and Canada, or 04-68-71-08-80. Fax 04-68-25-06-60. E-mail: hotel.donjon.best. western@wanadoo.fr. 37 units. A/C MINIBAR TV TEL. 395F–500F ($67.15–$85) double; 760F–860F ($129.20–$146.20) suite. AE, DC, MC, V. Parking 26F ($4.40).

This little hotel is big on charm and the best value in the moderate range. Built in the style of the old Cité, it has a honey-colored stone exterior with iron bars on the windows. The interior is a jewel, reflecting the sophistication of the owner, Christine Pujol. Elaborate Louis XIII-style furniture graces the reception lounges. A newer wing contains additional rooms in a medieval architectural style, and the older rooms have been renewed. Furnishings are in a severe style consistent with the look of the nearby medieval ramparts. Mattresses are comfortable, and bathrooms have adequate towels and hair dryers. The hotel also runs a restaurant nearby, the Brasserie Le Donjon. In summer the garden is the perfect breakfast spot.

BASTIDE ST-LOUIS

Grand Hôtel Terminus. 2 av. du Maréchal-Joffre, 11001 Carcassonne. ☎ **04-68-25-25-00.** Fax 04-68-72-53-09. 110 units. TEL. 295F–340F ($50.15–$57.80) double, 650F ($110.50) suite. AE, DC, MC, V. Parking 40F ($6.80). Bus: 4. Closed Dec–Feb.

Built in 1914, with frequent renovations ever since, this old-style, very grand hotel functioned as the Nazi local headquarters between 1941 and 1943. Bedrooms are high-ceilinged, comfortable, and rather charmingly old-fashioned, thanks to the presence of most of the original furnishings as well as art deco pieces added during the 1920s and 1930s. Rooms come in many shapes and sizes, some quite spacious, others a bit cramped. The furnishings are comfortable, especially the inviting beds, most often doubles or twins. Bathrooms are tiled, with tub-and-shower combinations. The hotel lies in the heart of *la Ville Basse*, adjacent to the railway station and the Canal du Midi, about 2 miles from the medieval Cité. On the premises is a hardworking management team staffed by members of the same family. A simple brasserie-style restaurant, where not particularly elaborate meals priced from 70F to 140F ($11.90 to $23.80), are served in a no-nonsense setting, is attuned to serving large numbers of people in relatively short amounts of time.

Hôtel du Pont-Vieux. 32 rue Trivalle, 11000 Carcassonne. ☎ **04-68-25-24-99.** Fax 04-68-47-62-71. 19 units. TV TEL. 310F–376F ($52.70–$63.90) double; 360F–475F ($61.20–$80.75) triple. Rates include breakfast. AE, DC, V. Closed Jan 15–31. Parking 30F ($5.10).

One of the best and most reasonably priced hotels in Carcassonne, this rustic boarding house lies at the foot of the Cité. Completely restored without losing its provincial French charm, it's cozy and inviting, from the elegantly furnished lounge to the quiet reading room. The medium-sized rooms have traditional furnishings and double-glazed windows to cut down on noise. Beds, most often twins or doubles, have quality mattresses and fine linens. Each has a fully fitted bath, with hair dryers and good-sized towels, and maintenance is state of the art. An indoor garden provides a retreat from the crowds.

STAYING NEARBY

✪ **Domaine d'Auriac.** Rte. St-Hilaire, 11000 Carcassonne. ☎ **04-68-25-72-22.** Fax 04-68-47-35-54. 26 units. A/C MINIBAR TV TEL. 600F–1,700F ($102–$289) double. AE, DC, MC, V. Closed Feb 15–Mar 2 and Nov 15–Dec 7. Take D104 about 2 miles from Carcassonne. Free parking.

A premier place for food and lodging is this Relais & Châteaux moss-covered 19th-century manor house, boasting gardens with reflecting pools and flowered terraces. The individually decorated rooms have a certain photo-magazine glamour; some are in an older building with high ceilings, others have a more modern decor. Renovations are ongoing. Mattresses and bath amenities are top-of-the-line. Bernard Rigaudis sets a grand table in his lovely dining room. In summer, meals are served beside the pool on the terraces. Afterward you might work off lunch on the tennis courts or golf course. The menu changes about five or six times yearly but might include truffles and purple artichokes with essences of pears and olives. Meals cost around 225F ($38.25) for the minimalist and around 450F ($76.50) for the gourmand. The restaurant is open daily from 12:30 to 2pm and 7:30 to 9:15pm, and reservations are required.

WHERE TO DINE

Au Jardin de la Tour. 11 rue Porte-d'Aude. ☎ **04-68-25-71-24.** Reservations recommended in summer. Main courses 60F–140F ($10.20–$23.80), 80F–100F ($13.60–$17) at dinner. MC, V. Daily noon–2pm and 8–10pm. Closed Mon Nov–Easter. FRENCH.

Part of the charm of this restaurant derives from the location of its verdant garden adjacent to the western foundation of the château, providing a green space that's very much appreciated in the midst of the city's closely built-up medieval core. The building dates from the early 1800s, although wide-ranging renovations have brought it up to date. The decor features rustic finds from local antique fairs. You can order from a large selection of salads, filet of beef with morels, cassoulet, terrines of foie gras, and all kinds of grilled fish. The cookery is consistently good, relying on fresh ingredients deftly handled by a talented kitchen staff.

✪ **La Barbacane.** In the Hôtel de la Cité, place de l'Eglise. ☎ **04-68-25-03-34.** Reservations recommended. Main courses 175F–320F ($29.75–$54.40); fixed-price menus 380F–550F ($64.60–$93.50). AE, DC, MC, V. Daily 7:30–10pm. Closed Sun in Nov, Dec, and Mar. FRENCH.

Named after the medieval neighborhood (La Barbacane) where it sits, this restaurant enjoys equal billing with the celebrated hotel that contains it. Its soothing-looking dining room, with walls upholstered in fabric with gold fleur-de-lis on a cerulean blue background, features the cuisine of the noted chef Franck Putelat. Menu items are based on seasonal ingredients, with just enough zest. Examples are green ravioli perfumed with *seiche* (a species of octopus) in its own ink; crisp-fried cod with black olives; saltwater crayfish with strips of Bayonne ham; leg of hare stuffed with foie gras; a fraîcheur of Breton lobster with artichoke hearts and caviar; and organically fed free-range chicken stuffed with truffles. A particularly succulent dessert is chestnut parfait with malt-flavored cream sauce and date-flavored ice cream.

Le Languedoc. 32 allée d'Léna. ☎ **04-68-25-22-17.** Reservations recommended. Fixed-price menus 130F–250F ($22.10–$42.50); main courses 100F–130F ($17–$22.10). AE, DC, V.

Tues–Sat noon–2pm and 7:30–9:30pm (till 10pm June–Sept), Sun noon–2pm. Closed Dec 20–Jan 20. FRENCH.

Acclaimed chef Didier Faugeras, assisted in the dining room by his wife, Isabelle, is the creative force behind the cuisine served here. (Along with Didier's semi-retired father, Laurent, they also own the Hotel Montségur, just across the street.) The high-ceilinged century-old dining room has a warm Languedoc atmosphere, with rough plaster walls, ceiling beams, and an open brick fireplace, a proper setting for their culinary repertoire. The specialty is *cassoulet au confit de canard* (the famous casserole made with duck cooked in its own fat), celebrated here since the early 1960s. The *pièce de résistance* is tournedos Rossini, with foie-gras truffles and madeira sauce. A smooth dessert is flambéed crêpes Languedoc. In summer you can dine on a pleasant patio or in the air-conditioned restaurant.

DINING NEARBY

✪ **Château Saint-Martin.** Montredon. ☎ **04-68-71-09-53.** Reservations required. Main courses 85F–145F ($14.45–$24.65). Set menus 160F–285F ($27.20–$48.45). AE, DC, MC, V. Thurs–Tues noon–1:45pm and 7:15–9:45pm. Lies 2½ miles northeast of La Cité. Follow the signs pointing to Stade Albert Domec.

One of the most successful chefs in Languedoc operates out of this historic 16th-century château at Amontredon, 2½ miles northeast of Carcassonne. Ringed by a wooded park, the restaurant is graced with the superb cuisine of co-owners Jean-Claude and Jacqueline Rodriguez. Dine inside or on the outdoor terrace. Menu items that have proven successful include turbot with a fondue of baby vegetables, sea bass with a mousseline of scallops, sole in tarragon, and a richly flavored *confit d'oie carcassonnaise* (goose meat delicately cooked in its own fat and kept in earthenware pots). Two other specialties include a *cassoulet languedocienne* and a *boullinade nouvelloise,* a bouillabaisse (complete with rouille and aïoli) made with scallops, sole, and turbot (but definitely *not* a *rascasse* or hogfish). The site is composed of a 12th-century tower and entrance, and a 16th-century main core with the original ceiling beams and pale yellow walls, which has the grand dignity of a château.

CARCASSONNE AFTER DARK

Carcassonne nightlife is centered along the rue **Omer-Sarraut** (in La Bastide) and the **place Marcou** (in La Cité). One of these, **La Bulle,** 115 rue Barbacane (☎ **04-68-72-47-70**), explodes with techno and rock dance tunes for an under-30 crowd, and keeps the energy pumping and the place hopping till 4am. The cover charge, depending on the night of the week, ranges from 50F to 80F ($8.50 to $13.60). Another enduringly popular disco, 2½ miles southwest of town, is **Le Black Bottom,** route de Limoux (☎ **04-68-47-37-11**), which rocks and rolls to every conceivable kind of dance music every Thursday to Saturday beginning at 11:30pm. Entrance costs 80F ($13.60).

7 Perpignan

562 miles (904.45km) SW of Paris, 229 miles (368.54km) NW of Marseille, 40 miles (64.37km) S of Narbonne

At Perpignan you may think you've crossed the border into Spain, for it was once Catalonia's second city after Barcelona. Even earlier it was the capital of the kingdom of Majorca. But when the Roussillon—the French part of Catalonia—was finally partitioned off, Perpignan became permanently French by the Treaty of the Pyrénées in 1659. However, Catalán is still spoken here, especially among the country people.

Legend has it that Perpignan derives its name from Père Pinya, a plowman who followed the Tèt River down the mountain to the site of the town today, where he cultivated the fertile soil while the river kept its promise to water the fields.

Today Perpignan is content to rest on its former glory, its residents—some 110,000 in all—enjoying the closeness of the Côte Catalane and the mountains to their north. The pace is decidedly relaxed. You'll have time to smell the flowers that grow here in great abundance.

This is one of the sunniest places in France, but summer afternoons in July and August can be a cauldron. That's when many of the locals take the 6-mile ride to the beach to cool off. There's a young, vibrant scene here, especially along the quays of the Basse River, site of impromptu nighttime concerts, beer drinking, and the devouring of endless tapas, a tradition inherited from nearby Barcelona.

Our favorite time for this area is the grape harvest in September after temperatures have dropped. If you visit then, you may want to drive through the Rivesaltes district bordering the city to the west and north.

ESSENTIALS

GETTING THERE   Four trains per day arrive from Paris (trip time: 6 to 10 hrs.); TGV passengers transfer to a local train in Monpellier to reach Perpignan. At least 15 trains per day arrive from Nice (trip time: 6 hrs.). For **rail information** and schedules, call ☎ **08-36-35-35-35.** From the French Riviera, motorists can continue west along A9 to Perpignan.

VISITOR INFORMATION   The **Office Municipal du Tourisme** is within the Palais des Congrès, place Armand-Lanoux (☎ **04-68-66-30-30**).

SPECIAL EVENTS   In midsummer the city explodes with **Les Estivales,** a 3-week festival of music, expositions, and theater. For information, call ☎ **04-68-35-01-77.**

From August 28th to September 12, the **Festivale Internationale de Photo-Journalisme** (also referred to as **Le Visa pour l'Image**) takes place. This is one of the most important events of the photo-journalism industry, established in the late 1980s. The area's historic sites host photo-journalistic expositions from around the world. Entrance to all expositions is free, and prizes are awarded by an international committee for the best of the art form.

SEEING THE SIGHTS

A worthwhile way to cover the main attractions in the town's historic core is a **3-hour guided walking tour,** offered only between mid-June and mid-September, at hours that change every day according to demand. The tours depart from the sidewalk in front of the tourist office, and are priced at 25F ($4.25), regardless of age. For more information, contact the tourist office (see above). The tour leader may or may not be able to add English-language commentary to his/her dialogue.

✪ **Cathédrale St-Jean.** Place Gambetta/rue de l'Horloge. ☎ **04-68-51-33-72.** Admission free. Daily 8–11:30am and 3–6pm.

The cathedral dates from the 14th and 15th centuries and has an admirable nave and interesting 17th-century retables. Leaving via the south door, you'll find on the left a chapel with the *Devout Christ,* a magnificent wood carving depicting Jesus contorted with pain and suffering—his head, crowned with thorns, drooping on his chest.

The Castillet/Musée des Arts et Traditions Populaires Catalans. Place de Verdun. ☎ **04-68-35-42-05.** Admission 25F ($4.25) adults, 15F ($2.55) students and children 17 and under. Mid-June to mid-Sept, Wed–Mon 9:30am–7pm; mid-Sept to mid-June, 9am–6pm.

The **Castillet** is one of the chief sights of Perpignan. The machicolated and crenellated redbrick building from the 14th century is a combination gateway and fortress. It houses the museum, also known as La Casa Païral, which contains exhibitions of Catalán regional artifacts and folkloric items, including typical dress. Part of the charm of the Castillet derives from its bulky-looking tower, which you can climb for a good view of the town.

Palais des Rois de Majorque. Rue des Archers. ☎ **04-68-34-48-29.** Admission 20F ($3.40) adults, 10F ($1.70) students, free for children 7 and under. June–Sept, daily 10am–6pm; Oct–May daily 9am–5pm. Guided tours Mon–Sat (in French only) 4 times a day, 20F ($3.40); hours vary with demand.

At the top of the town, the Spanish citadel encloses the Palace of the Kings of Majorca. A structure from the 13th and 14th centuries, built around a court encircled by arcades, it has been restored by the government. You can see the old throne room with its large fireplaces and a square tower with a double gallery; from the tower there's a fine view of the Pyrénées.

A MAJOR HISTORIC SITE NEARBY

✪ **Château de Salses.** ☎ **04-68-38-60-13.** Admission 39F ($6.65) adults, 21F ($3.55) students and those under 16. Daily: July–Aug, 9:30am–7pm; June and Sept, 9:30am–6:30pm; Apr, May, and Oct, 9:30am–12:30pm and 2–6pm; Nov–Mar 10am–noon and 2–5pm.

This important historic site is in the hamlet of Salses, 15½ miles north of the city center. Since the days of the Romans, this fort has guarded the main road linking Spain and France. Ferdinand of Aragón erected a fort here in 1497 to protect the northern frontier of his kingdom. Even today, Salses marks the language-barrier point between Catalonia in Spain and Languedoc in France. This Spanish-style fort, designed by Ferdinand himself, is a curious example of an Iberian structure in France. In the 17th century it was modified by Vauban to look more like a château. After many changes of ownership, Salses fell to the forces of Louis XIII in September 1642, and its Spanish garrison left forever. Less than 2 decades later Roussillon was incorporated into France. There's a small-scale gift shop dispensing film and cold drinks on the premises.

SHOPPING

With its inviting storefronts and pedestrian streets, Perpignan is a good town for shopping. Catalán is the style indigenous to the area, and it's reflected in textiles and pottery in strong geometric patterns and sturdily structured furniture. For one of the best selections of Catalán pottery, furniture, carpets, and even a small inventory of antiques, visit the ✪ **Centre Sant-Vicens,** rue Sant-Vicens (☎ **04-68-50-02-18**), site of about a dozen independent merchants. You'll find it 2½ miles south of the town center, following the signs pointing to Enne and Collioures. In the town center, **La Maison Quinta,** 3 rue des Grands-des-Fabriques (☎ **04-68-34-41-62**), offers Catalán-inspired items for home decorating.

WHERE TO STAY

Hôtel de la Loge. 1 rue des Fabriques-Nabot, 66000 Perpignan. ☎ **04-68-34-41-02.** Fax 04-68-34-25-13. www.vitrinezi.com. E-mail: laloge@vitrine21.com. 22 units. MINIBAR TV TEL. 285F–360F ($48.45–$61.20) double. AE, DC, MC, V. Parking 50F ($8.50).

This beguiling little place dates from the 16th century but has been renovated into a modern three-star hotel. It's located right in the heart of town, near Loge de Mer, the town hall, from which it takes its name, and the Castillet. The cozy rooms are attractively furnished, all with good-quality mattresses and a sense of warmth and hospitality. The tiled bathrooms are small but well organized, with adequate shelf space, hair dryers, and medium-sized towels. Many are air-conditioned.

✪ **La Villa Duflot.** 109 av. Victor-Dalbiez, 66000 Perpignan. ☎ **04-68-56-67-67.** Fax 04-68-56-54-05. www.little-france.com/villa.duflot. 24 units. A/C MINIBAR TV TEL. 590F–790F ($100.30–$134.30) double. Half board 530F–630F ($90.10–$107.10) per person double occupancy. AE, DC, MC, V.

When this hotel opened, one local mayor proclaimed, "Now we have some class in Perpignan." While it's the area's greatest hotel, its prices are reasonable for the luxury offered. Tranquillity, style, and refinement reign supreme. Located in a suburb, La Villa Duflot is a Mediterranean-style dwelling surrounded by a 3-acre park of pine, palm, and eucalyptus. The hotel has an appealing, almost family touch to it and isn't the least bit intimidating. You can sunbathe in the gardens surrounding the pool and order drinks at any hour at the outside bar. The good-sized guest rooms are situated around a patio planted with century-old olive trees. All are spacious and soundproof, with solid marble baths and art deco interiors. They were renovated in the late 1990s with emphasis on upgrading the mattresses and bathroom accessories. Most bathrooms have a tub-and-shower combination, and each comes with a hair dryer and a rack of thick towels. The chef is a whiz, and the cuisine is reason enough to stay here. Surely you'll agree after sampling his lasagne made with fresh duck liver and asparagus, grilled red mullet in anchovy butter, or (most definitely) roast lamb with a tapenade of eggplant and caviar.

WHERE TO DINE

Côté Théâtre. 7 rue du Théâtre. ☎ **04-68-34-60-00.** Reservations recommended. Main courses 70F–120F ($11.90–$20.40). Set-price menus 148F ($25.15; available only at lunch Mon–Fri). Otherwise 230F–330F ($39.10–$56.10). AE, DC, MC, V. Tues–Sat noon–2pm and Mon–Sat 7:30–10:30pm. Closed: 2 weeks in late July to early Aug. MEDITERRANEAN.

This restaurant is housed within a severely dignified stone building. It was constructed in the 15th century as the home of the Catholic Inquisition's grand inquisitor. It attracts a quietly conservative crowd who dine beneath an elaborately crafted wooden ceiling that is designated a historic monument in its own right. The cuisine is traditional, earthy, and completely unafraid of strong, even gutsy flavors and old-fashioned traditions. Menu items include calamari or octopus salad with herbs and vinaigrette; braised sea scallops with shallots; a variety of different fish hauled from local waters, sometimes prepared with flap mushrooms; and deboned and stuffed pig's foot prepared in the old-fashioned way.

La Villa Duflot. 109 ave. Victor Dalbiez, 66000 Perpignan. ☎ **04-68-56-67-67.** Fax 04-68-56-54-05. Reservations required. Main courses 100F–120F ($17–$20.40). Set-menu only Sat–Sun 200F ($34). Daily noon–2:30pm and 8–11pm. AE, MC, V. Take N9 from the town center leading to the autoroute, exiting at Perpignan Sud (South) heading toward Argeles.

Slightly removed from the city center, this *restaurant avec chambres* is the most tranquil oasis in the area. Built in the 1970s, the Mediterranean-style villa stands in its own tree-dotted park, with a swimming pool and a reflecting pool. André Duflot, the owner, employs top-notch chefs who turn out dish after dish with remarkable skill and professionalism. Try, for example, a salad of warm squid or a platter of fresh anchovies marinated in vinegar. Sample the excellent foie gras of duckling. Two new specialties include gratin of lobster and a succulent magret of duckling with figs. The dessert sensation is fresh peaches in Banyuls wine. On the premises is an American bar.

Upstairs, bedrooms are fitted in a 1930s art deco style, each with TV, phone, and a good mattress, plus a small, compact, and tiled bathroom fitted with shower stalls and a set of thick towels. Rooms range from 590F to 790F ($100.30 to $134.30) in a double, with suites going for 1,050F ($178.50).

Le Bistrot Gourmand. 40 rue de la Fusterie. ☎ **04-68-51-21-14.** Reservations recommended. Main courses 60F–92F ($10.20–$15.65); set-price lunch 65F ($11.05); set-price dinners 85F–115F ($14.45–$19.55). V. FRENCH/CATALONIAN.

Set in the heart of Perpignan's oldest neighborhood, this informal and charming bistro serves excellent cuisine to a clientele that tends to congregate in greater numbers at lunch than at dinner, partly because of the noon meal's good value, partly because it's a lunch favorite of local workers and shop owners. Menu items include mussels in cream sauce; salmon steak with a leek-flavored cream sauce; medaillons of sea bass with a sweet white wine sauce; filet of beef drenched in a heady Banyuls wine. One particular dish that's not to be missed if you crave strong Mediterranean flavors is an *anchoiade* (a paste of grilled anchovies) served with a medley of grilled Languedocien red peppers.

PERPIGNAN AFTER DARK

Spanish and Catalán influences permeate the town even at night, with an emphasis on tapas and late-night promenades. The streets that radiate outward from **place de la Loge** contain a higher concentration of bars and nightclubs than any other part of town. For a traditional Catalán-style bar with a hip staff, visit **Le Festival,** 40 place Rigaud (☎ **04-68-34-31-60**), a hot spot for tantalizing tapas and heady sangría. The bars in the center of town, such as the **Républic Café,** 2 place de la République (☎ **04-68-51-11-64**), have a vivacious and stimulating student scene and offer live music. Two discos in the town center are **Club le Napoli,** 3 place de Catalogne (☎ **04-68-35-55-88**); and **Le Privée,** place Arago (☎ **04-68-34-46-05**). Both open their doors sometime around 11pm, and play highly danceable music until at least 4am. The town's most visible gay and lesbian hangout, featuring both a bar and a disco, is **Le Tapis Volé,** 3 rue Honoré Daumier (☎ **04-68-63-90-79**), about a half-mile north of the town center.

During summer, the nearby resort complex of **Canet-Plage,** 7½ miles east of Perpignan's historic core, contains a beachfront strip of seasonal bars and dance clubs that come and go with the tides and with midsummer tourism.

8 Collioure

577 miles (928.59km) SW of Paris, 17 miles (27.36km) SE of Perpignan

You may recognize this port and its sailboats from the Fauve paintings of Lhote and Derain. It's said to resemble St-Tropez before it was spoiled. In the past it attracted Matisse, Picasso, and Dalí. Collioure is the most authentic and alluring port of Roussillon, a gem with a vivid Spanish/Catalán image and flavor. Some visitors believe it's the most charming village on the Côte Vermeille.

ESSENTIALS

GETTING THERE   Collioure has frequent train and bus connections, especially from Perpignan. For **rail information** and schedules, call ☎ **08-36-35-35-35.** Buses pull into town at the **Gare Routière,** in the Parking de la Poste, avenue de la République (☎ **04-68-35-29-02**). If you're driving, go along the coastal road (R.N. 114) leading to the Spanish border.

VISITOR INFORMATION   The **Office de Tourisme** is on place du 18-Juin (☎ **04-68-82-15-47**).

SPECIAL EVENTS   The annual **Salon des Antiquaires** takes place on a 3-day weekend around November 1. Antiques dealers from throughout southern France set up shop for wholesalers and retailers. For more information, contact the tourist office.

EXPLORING THE TOWN

The town's sloping, narrow streets, charming semifortified church, antique lighthouse, and eerily introverted culture make it worth an afternoon stopover. This is the ideal small-town antidote to the condo-choked Riviera, and out of season, things around here are relatively calm.

The two curving ports are separated from each other by the heavy masonry of the 13th-century **Château Royal,** place du 8-Mai-1945 (☎ **04-68-82-06-43**). The château, now a museum of painting and folkloric artifacts, is open daily: June to September from 10am to 6pm and October to May from 9am to 5pm; closed January 1, May 1, and December 25. Admission is 20F ($3.40) for adults and 10F ($1.70) for children under 16.

The **Musée Jean-Peské,** route de Port-Vendres (☎ **04-68-82-10-19**), has a collection of works by artists who migrated here to paint. It's open in July and August, daily from 10am to noon and 3 to 7pm; September to June, Wednesday to Monday from 10am to noon and 2 to 6pm. Admission is 12F ($2.05) for adults, 8F ($1.35) for children 12 to 16, and free for children 11 and under.

WHERE TO STAY

Casa Pairal. Impasse des Palmiers, 66190 Collioure. ☎ **04-68-82-05-81.** Fax 04-68-82-52-10. 28 units. MINIBAR TV TEL. 360F–760F ($61.20–$129.20) double; 810F–960F ($137.70–$163.20) junior suite. AE, MC, V. Parking 40F ($6.80). Closed Nov 2–Mar 27.

This is a small-scale, family-operated place, not too businesslike, but sort of charming. On sunny days the most alluring part of this 150-year-old house is an outdoor swimming pool in the shadow of century-old trees. The small to medium-sized bedrooms are comfortable and fitted with fine mattresses and filled with charming old antiques blended with more modern pieces. All the rooms come with a small bath, usually with a shower stall. The best doubles have a petit salon plus a small balcony. Only breakfast is served but there are many restaurants nearby. The hotel lies 150 meters from the port and the beach.

Hôtel Princes de Catalogne. Rue des Palmiers, 66190 Collioure. ☎ **04-68-98-30-00.** Fax 04-68-98-30-31. 29 units. A/C MINIBAR TV TEL. 340F–420F ($57.80–$71.40) double; 550F–650F ($93.50–$110.50) suite. AE, MC, V. Free parking.

This is a relatively modern hotel of little architectural interest, but its position is in the town center and it has a hardworking and cooperative staff. Bedrooms contain simple, angular furniture with touches of traditional Provençal upholsteries, a writing table, a hair dryer, a safe, and comfortable beds and mattresses; they are a bit more spacious than you might have expected. Bathrooms are tiled and small, with shower stalls only, but they are well cared for and have adequate shelf space. There's a cafe on the premises that specializes in tapas, but no bona fide restaurant.

✪ **Relais des Trois Mas et Restaurant La Balette.** Rte. de Port-Vendres, 66190 Collioure. ☎ **04-68-82-05-07.** Fax 04-68-82-38-08. 23 units. A/C MINIBAR TV TEL. 495F–1,295F ($84.15–$220.15) double; 1,235F–2,450F ($209.95–$416.50) suite. MC, V. Closed Nov 15–Dec 15. Parking 85F ($14.45).

Three antique houses were combined to create the town's premier hotel, which is also the restaurant of choice. The hotel's decoration of its beautiful rooms honors the famous artists who've lived at Collioure. Rooms have spacious baths with Jacuzzis, thick towels, and hair dryers. The large beds or twins have fine French mattresses and quality linens. The rooms open onto views of the water. Even if you aren't a guest, you may want to take a meal in the dining room, with its vistas of the harbor. Christian Peyre is unchallenged as the leading chef in town. His cooking is inventive—often simple, but always refined. There's an outdoor heated pool.

WHERE TO DINE

Note that the **Restaurant La Balette** (see above) is the best dining room in town.

L'Andalou. 10 rue de la République. ☎ **04-68-82-32-78.** Reservations recommended. Main courses 35F–125F ($5.95–$21.25). AE, MC, V. Thurs–Tues noon–2:30pm and 7pm–midnight. FRENCH/SPANISH.

Situated at the edge of Collioure's historic core, this cozy bistro and tavern is the creative statement of Manuel Fernandez, his wife Caroline, and extended members of their family. It's decorated with a hanging collection of flamenco dresses and depictions of the surrounding landscape. The menu offers succulent, well-prepared testimonials to the old-fashioned, savory seafood that fed many generations of Catalonians. Look for such Spanish-style dishes as a *parillade* of seafood, a spicy, garlic-laced *soupe de poissons,* or perhaps a portion of yellow Manchego cheese in a style you expect in Madrid. A particularly attractive bargain is the house *paella,* priced at 59F ($10.05) for one person, and at 175F ($29.75) for a full-blown celebration of the dish. Snails are usually drenched in butter and roasted garlic, while a *brochette Andaluz* brings grilled and herbed beef to succulent new heights. Also look for thin-sliced Serrano ham, the omelet-style cake made of eggs and peppers that locals refer to as *tortillas,* and several different preparations of mussels, including a grilled form *(à la plancha)* that's particularly delectable. A roster of French and Spanish wines (especially *riojas*) can accompany your meal.

Le Trémail. 16 bis rue Mailly. ☎ **04-68-82-16-10.** Reservations recommended. Main courses 84F–146F ($14.30–$24.80); set menu 120F ($20.40). DC, MC, V. Tues–Sun 12:15–2:15pm and 7:15–10:30pm. (Also open Mon for lunch and dinner between mid-June and mid-Sept.) CATALÁN/SEAFOOD.

Set on a narrow, cobble-covered alleyway in the oldest part of Collioure, this rustic and authentically Catalán restaurant functioned for many generations as the family home of the owner, Jean-Paul Fabre. Surrounded by stone walls, hand-painted Spanish tiles, and dangling fish nets, less than 60 feet from the edge of the sea, it specializes in grilled fish *(à la plancha),* invariably served with olive oil and herb-enriched vinaigrette. Examples include grilled anchovies with braised onions and peppers; a succulent version of whatever the day's catch from the local fishing fleet might be; and desserts like *crème Catalán* or a homemade pastry. A limited number of "noble fish"—sole and turbot—might be on hand as well as a limited roster of meat. Particularly succulent is *rondelles* of calamari with red wine.

9 Narbonne

525 miles (844.91km) SW of Paris, 38 miles (61.16km) E of Carcassonne, 58 miles (93.34km) S of Montpellier

Medieval Narbonne was a port to rival Marseille in Roman days, with its "galleys laden with riches." It was the first town outside Italy to be colonized by the Romans, but the Mediterranean, now 5 miles away, left it high and dry. It's an intriguing place, steeped in antiquity.

After Lyon, Narbonne was the largest town in Gaul. Even today you can see evidence of the town's former wealth. Too far from the sea to be a beach town, it attracts history buffs to its memories of a glorious past. Some 50,000 Narbonnais live in what is really a sleepy backwater. However, many locals are trying to make a go with their vineyards. Caves are open to visitors in the surrounding area (the tourist office will advise). If you want to go to the beach, you'll have to head to the nearby sands at the village of **Gruisson** and the beach (Gruisson-Plage) that adjoins it, or to the suburb of **St-Pierre la Mer** and its adjoining beach (Narbonne-Plage). Both lie 9 miles south of Narbonne. Buses from the town center are frequent, marked with their respective destinations.

Liberté, Egalité, Fraternité . . . Nudité

The municipality known as ✪ **Agde,** 25 miles northeast of Narbonne and 31 miles southwest of Montpellier, operates like every other *commune* in France, with one startling exception: its flourishing nudist colony. In the 1970s, the community's founder/matriarch, Mlle Geneviève Oltha, had the idea of promoting a simple pine grove beside the sea as a place for an escape from the stresses of urban life. Within less than 25 years, the site burgeoned into the largest nudist colony in Europe, with a roster of about 100 midwinter residents and a midsummer population usually approaching 50,000.

Don't expect everyone in Agde to be nude, since the town's four major subdivisions (Cité d'Agde, Cap d'Agde, Grau d'Agde, and La Tamarissière) offer options for the clothed as well. However, in the clearly signposted and, for the most part, fenced-in **Quartier Naturist Cap d'Agde,** nudity is required on the beaches and encouraged elsewhere. Stores, restaurants, shops (most selling everything except—you guessed it—clothing) are part of the setup. Those who arrive on foot at the compound's gate pay 15F ($3) for entrance; motorists with as many passengers as can be crammed into their cars pay 60F ($12). The **Agde Office de Tourisme,** Espace Molière, Centre Ville (☎ **04-67-94-29-68**), or its satellite branch, the **Office Municipal de Tourism,** Cap d'Agde, Les Plages (☎ **04-67-01-04-04**), long ago became accustomed to answering questions for the clothed, the unclothed, and the clothing indecisive.

Conveniently close to but not within the nudist zone are two museums. The **Musée Agathois,** rue de la Fraternité (☎ **04-67-94-82-51**), is noted for the homage it pays to (clothed) cultural models of the city's 19th-century fishing tradition and the region's handcrafts. The **Musée Ethèbe,** Mas de la Clape, Cap d'Agde (☎ **04-67-94-69-60**), showcases the artifacts dredged up by marine explorations of the nearby sea bottom. Its star exhibit and namesake is the nearly life-size **l'Ethèbe,** a graceful-looking Greek statue from the 6th century B.C. Admission to both museums costs 15F ($2.55).

ESSENTIALS

GETTING THERE   Narbonne has good rail connections, with 14 trains per day arriving from Perpignan (trip time: 50 mins.), 13 per day from Toulouse (trip time: 90 mins.), and 12 per day from Montpellier (trip time: 60 mins.). For **rail information** and schedules, call ☎ **08-36-35-35-35.** Buses arrive at a somewhat grubby-looking **Gare Routière** on the avenue Carnot (☎ **04-68-90-77-64**), and it is unlikely that there will be a staff member on the premises. If you're driving, Narbonne is located at the junction of A61 and A9, making it easily accessible from either Toulouse or the Riviera.

VISITOR INFORMATION   The **Office de Tourisme** is on place Roger-Salengro (☎ **04-68-65-15-60**).

EXPLORING THE TOWN

The town's sights are concentrated in the medieval Vielle Ville, a massive central labyrinth of religious and civic buildings.

THE CENTRAL COMPLEX

A *billet global,* good for 3 days, allows entrance into all the museums in the archbishop's palace plus the Musée Lapidaire. It costs 30F ($5.10) for adults, 10F ($1.70) for students and ages 12 to 18. The museums are free for children 11 and under.

The neo-Gothic **Hôtel de Ville** (town hall) in the complex was reconstructed by Viollet-le-Duc, the 19th-century architect who refurbished Notre-Dame de Paris between 1845 and 1850.

✪ **Cathédrale St-Just.** Place de l'Hôtel-de-Ville (enter on rue Gauthier). ☎ **04-68-32-09-52.** Admission free. Daily: Apr–Sept 9am–7pm; Oct–March 9am–noon and 2–6pm.

The cathedral's construction began in 1272 but it was never finished. Only the transept and a choir were completed. The choir is 130 feet high, built in the bold Gothic style of northern France. At each end of the transept are 194-foot towers from 1480. There's an impressive collection of Flemish tapestries. The cathedral is connected to the archbishop's palace by 14th- and 15th-century cloisters.

Donjon Gilles-Aycelin. Place de l'Hôtel-de-Ville. Admission 10F ($1.70) adults, 5F (85¢) students and ages 11–18. Apr–Sept, daily 11am–7pm. Oct–Mar, daily 10am–noon and 2–5pm.

If you happen to visit between mid-June and mid-September, you might want to participate in one of the occasional hikes up the steep steps of the watchtower. A watchtower and prison in the late 13th century, it has a lofty observation platform with a view of the cathedral, the surrounding plain, and the Pyrénées.

✪ **Palais des Archevêques (Archbishop's Palace, or Vieux-Palais).** Place de l'Hôtel-de-Ville. ☎ **04-68-90-30-30** or 04-68-90-30-54 for museum information. Admission: *billet global* or 10F ($1.70). Apr–Sept, daily 9:30am–12:15pm and 2–6pm; Oct–Mar, Tues–Sun 10am–noon and 2–5pm.

The palace was conceived as part fortress, part pleasure residence. It has three military-style towers from the 13th and 14th centuries. The Old Palace on the right dates from the 12th century, and the so-called "New Palace" on the left, from the 14th. It's said that the old, arthritic, and sometimes very overweight archbishops used to be hauled up the interior's monumental Louis XIII-style stairs on mules.

Today the once-private apartments of the former bishops contain three museums. The **Musée Archéologique** contains prehistoric artifacts, Bronze Age tools, 14th-century frescoes, and Greco-Roman amphorae. Several of the sarcophagi date from the 3rd century and some of the mosaics are of pagan origin. The **Musée d'Art et d'Histoire de Narbonne** is located three floors above street level in the archbishop's once-private apartments (the rooms where Louis XII resided during his siege of Perpignan). Their coffered ceilings are enhanced with panels depicting the nine Muses. A Roman mosaic floor and 17th-century portraits are on display. There's also a collection of antique porcelain, enamels, and a portrait bust of Louis XIV. In the **Horreum Romain,** you'll find a labyrinth of underground passageways, similar to catacombs but without burial functions, dug by the Gallo-Romans and their successors for storage of food and supplies during times of siege.

MORE SIGHTS

Basilique St-Paul-Serge. Rue de l'Hôtel-Dieu. ☎ **04-68-41-12-29.** Admission free. Apr–Sept, daily 9am–7pm; Oct–Mar, daily 9am–noon and 2–6pm.

This early Gothic church was built on the site of a 4th-century necropolis. It has an elegant choir with fine Renaissance wood carvings and some ancient Christian sarcophagi. The chancel, from 1229, is admirable. The north door leads to the Paleo-Christian Cemetery, part of an early Christian burial ground.

Musée Lapidaire. Place Lamourguier. ☎ **04-68-65-53-58.** Admission: *billet global* or 10F ($1.70). July–Aug, daily 9:30am–12:15pm and 2–6pm; rest of year by arrangement with tourist office.

Located in the 13th-century Notre-Dame de Lamourguier, this museum contains an important collection of Roman artifacts—broken sculptures and Latin inscriptions—

as well as relics of medieval buildings. You can also enter with your general admission ticket to the museums of the archbishop's palace.

WHERE TO STAY

Hôtel Languedoc. 22 bd. Gambetta, 11100 Narbonne. ☎ **04-68-65-14-74.** Fax 04-68-65-81-48. 40 units. TEL. 280F–425F ($47.60–$72.25) double; 525F ($89.25) suite. AE, DC, MC, V. Parking 30F ($5.10).

This oft-modernized turn-of-the-century hotel is near the canal de la Rhône. It offers well-equipped rooms with acceptably comfortable mattresses. As is typical of an old hotel of this era, rooms come in various shapes and sizes. About half the bathrooms have shower stalls; the others have tub-and-shower combinations, with hair dryers available from reception. The on-site restaurant specializes in regional dishes. The hotel's wine bar, Le Bacchus, is open daily noon to 2pm and 7 to 10pm. Specializing in the many esoteric vintages grown nearby, it sells wine by the glass and serves simple but flavorful dishes such as grilled salmon with anchovy butter, tender lamb cooked with beans, sautéed chicken chasseur, and fresh oysters. Set-price menus cost from 68F to 115F ($11.55 to $19.55).

La Résidence. 6 rue du 1er-Mai, 11100 Narbonne. ☎ **04-68-32-19-41.** Fax 04-68-65-51-82. 25 units. A/C MINIBAR TV TEL. 336F–457F ($57.10–$77.70) double. AE, MC, V. Parking 40F ($6.80).

Our favorite hotel in Narbonne is near the Cathédrale St-Just. The 19th-century La Résidence, converted from the premises of a once-stately villa, is decorated with antiques. Bedrooms range from small to spacious, each fitted with doubles or twins with quality French mattresses and fine linen. Bathrooms are small but well maintained with adequate shelf space. Most have a tub-and-shower combination; hair dryers are available on request. It doesn't have a restaurant but offers breakfast and a gracious welcome.

WHERE TO DINE

Aux Trois Caves. 4 rue Benjamin-Cremieux. ☎ **04-68-65-28-60.** Reservations recommended. Main courses 125F–200F ($21.25–$34); set-price menus 99F–230F ($16.85–$39.10). AE, DC, V. Daily noon–2pm and 7:30–10:30pm. FRENCH.

In a trio of interconnected medieval cellars, this is a well-managed restaurant with good food and a sense of history. One of the three Romanesque-style dining rooms has a single table suitable for two diners, and is an ideal spot for a romantic dinner. The menu focuses on the surrounding region—deliberately undercooked foie gras, served with a compôte of apples; a salad of local field greens with strips of magret of duckling and pine nuts; prawns in whisky sauce; and a mignon of veal strips with fresh morels. Especially succulent is the platter of grilled sardines, cooked in white wine; and the equally delectable grilled filets of turbot in a lemon-flavored butter sauce.

L'Alsace. 2 av. Pierre-Sémard. ☎ **04-68-65-10-24.** Reservations recommended. Main courses 90F–150F ($15.30–$25.50); fixed-price menus 98F–240F ($16.65–$40.80). AE, DC, MC, V. Mon noon–2:30pm, Wed–Sun noon–2:30pm and 7:30–10pm. FRENCH.

Across from the train station, this restaurant is Narbonne's most reliable restaurant. The comfortable dining room is done in English style, with wood paneling and a glass-enclosed patio. In spite of the restaurant's name, the cuisine isn't from Alsace-Lorraine, but is typical of southwestern France, with a focus on seafood. The Sinfreus, who own the place, offer a fry of red mullet, a savory kettle of bourride, and magret of duck with flap mushrooms. Especially delectable is this restaurant's specialty: sea wolf or other whole fish baked in a salt crust—a method that usually produces a delightfully pungent and flaky product.

✪ La Table St-Crescent. In the Palais des Vins, route de Perpignan. ☎ **04-68-65-10-24.** Reservations recommended. Main courses 50F–150F ($8.50–$25.50). Set menus 100F ($17; available only Mon–Fri); and 148F–248F ($25.15–$42.15). AE, MC, V. FRENCH/LANGUEDOCIENNE.

One of the most well-respected restaurants in this region of France is less than a mile east of the town center, beside the road leading to Perpignan. The restaurant is part of a complex of wine-tasting boutiques established by local wine growers, and tends to attract diners interested in wine. It's in a former small chapel, or oratory, whose foundations are said to date from the 8th century. It's outfitted in a nondescript way that's little more than a foil for the inspired cuisine of master chef Claude Giraud. His wife, Sabrine, is wine steward and social arbiter. The chef delivers a refined, brilliantly realized repertoire. Expect sublime sauces and sophisticated herbs and seasonings. Menu items change four times a year based on seasonality of ingredients and the inspiration of the owners. Examples include a *parmentier* of Norman potatoes with grated local truffles, bound together with a reduction of chicken stock; sea bass marinated with olives; and lasagne of grilled eggplant with a confit of tomatoes and oil of pistou. Especially succulent is roasted shoulder of lamb with crispy noodles and sweet garlic and sage sauce. If you want the staff to select which wines should accompany your set menus, they're available for a supplement of only 50F ($8.50) per person. Be assured that they'll be well chosen, usually local and sometimes rather obscure vintages.

NARBONNE AFTER DARK

The city has some routine dance clubs—nothing special. Check out the action, if any, at **Le Cassiopée,** chemin Rochegrise (☎ **04-68-41-75-61**), or at **Dancing GM Palace,** Centre Commercial Forum Sud, Route de Perpignan (☎ **04-68-41-59-71**).

10 Aigues-Mortes

466 miles (749.95km) SW of Paris, 39 miles (62.76km) NE of Sète, 25 miles (40.23km) E of Nîmes, 30 miles (48.28km) SW of Arles

South of Nîmes, you can explore much of the Camargue by car, mainly on the roads of the **Parc Regional de Camargue.** The most rewarding target is Aigues-Mortes, the city of the "dead waters." It is France's most perfectly preserved walled town. In the middle of dismal swamps and melancholy lagoons, Aigues-Mortes stands on four navigable canals. Although it is now 4 miles from the sea, it was once a thriving port, the first in France on the Mediterranean. Louis IX and his crusaders set forth from here on the Ninth Crusade.

ESSENTIALS

GETTING THERE   Five trains per day connect Aigues-Mortes and Nîmes (trip time: 1 hr.). For information and schedules, call ☎ **08-36-35-35-35.** Four buses a day arrive from Nîmes (trip time: 55 mins.), pulling into the **Gare Routière,** Route de Nîmes (☎ **04-66-53-74-74**), about a quarter-mile west of the town center. If you're driving, take D979 south from Gallargues, or A9 from Montpellier to Nîmes.

VISITOR INFORMATION   There's an **Office de Tourisme** at Porte de la Gardette (☎ **04-66-53-73-00**).

EXPLORING THE TOWN

The main allure in Aigues-Mortes is the city itself. A sense of medievalism still permeates virtually every building, every rampart, and every cobbled street, and the town is still enclosed by walls that were constructed between 1272 and 1300. The **Tour de Constance** (☎ **04-66-53-61-55**), which looks out on the marshes, is a model castle

Les Gardiens of the Camargue

Steamy, sweaty, and as flat as the plains of Nebraska, the marshy delta of the Rhône has been called a less fertile version of the Nile delta. The waterlogged flatlands encompassing the Grand and Petit Rhône were scorned by conventional farmers throughout the centuries because of their high salt content and root-rotting murk.

However, the area was considered a fit grazing ground for the local black-pelted longhorn cattle, so a breed of cowpokes and cowboys evolved on these surreal flatlands, whose traditions will make you think of Dodge City combined with primal hints of ancient Celtic lore. These French cowboys, caretakers of the cattle that survive amid the flamingos, ticks, hawks, snakes, and mosquitoes of the hot, salty wetlands, are known and loved by schoolchildren as *les gardiens*.

The monotonous terrain, whose highest point might be a mound of debris left from a medieval salt flat, however, does not evoke the romance associated with the wide open spaces of America's West. The tradition of *les gardiens* originated in the 1600s, when local monasteries began to disintegrate and large tracts of cheap land were bought by private owners. Wearing their traditional garb of leather pants and wide-rimmed black hats, the *gardiens* present a fascinating picture as they ride through the marshlands on their sturdy horses. They tend not to be overly communicative to outsiders; in speaking to one another, they use a clipped, telegraphic form of Provençal whose syntax would make Académie Française members shudder. Motor homes and caravans are beginning to appear in the area today, but once *les gardiens* lived in distinctive, single-story *cabanes* with thatched roofs and without windows. Bull's horns were positioned above each building's entrance as a means of driving away evil spirits. Many historians believe that the first real cowboys of North America were *gardiens,* imported from the Camargue to Louisiana to tend the flocks of the New World.

Their ally in the business of tending cattle is the strong, heavy-tailed Camargue horse, probably a descendant of Arabian stallions brought here by Moorish invaders after the collapse of the Roman Empire. Brown or black at birth, these horses develop a white coat, usually after their fourth year. Traditionally, they had no sheltered stables but were left to fend for themselves during the stifling summers and bone-chilling winters.

Today, in the world of modern tourism, the *gardiens* have become living symbols of an antique tradition that hasn't changed much—the cattle still run semi-wild, identified by the brand of their *manadier,* or owner.

Even bullfighting is alive and well in the Camargue. Bullfighters usually come in from Spain, but these high-energy odes to high jinx and high testosterone are

---

of the Middle Ages. At the top, which you can reach by elevator, a panoramic view unfolds. Admission is 32F ($5.45) for adults, 21F ($3.55) for youths ages 12 to 17, and free for children 11 and under. The monument is open every day: May to August 9:30am to 8pm; September 9:30am to 7pm; October to January 10am to 5pm; and February to April 10am to 6pm.

The city's religious centerpiece is the **Eglise Notre-Dame des Sablons,** rue Jean-Jaurès (☎ **04-66-53-86-73**). Originally constructed of wood in 1183, it was rebuilt in stone in 1246 in the ogival style. Its stained-glass windows are modern, having been installed in 1980 as replacements for the badly damaged and weather-beaten originals. The church is open daily from 8:30am to 6pm.

conducted in ways that aren't completely *espagnol.* Sometimes the bull is killed and sometimes it will mangle a local youth during a bullring celebration. Most *gardiens* are too shrewd to participate in a head-on confrontation with a bull, though there are likely to be at least one or two on horseback in or near the ring during the contest.

Today, expect to see fewer *gardiens* than in the past. They seem willing to participate in tourism only up to a point. Many reminders of their traditions remain in the form of felt-sided cowboy hats as well as commemorative saddles and boots whose style resembles that of cowherds on the faraway plains of Spain.

If observing unique wildlife or riding a horse through France's hottest and most legendary wetlands attracts you, you will enjoy a stay in France's cowboy country. Both hotels below will arrange a *ballade* on horseback for you, excursions that focus on the ecology and panorama of the marshlands. With equipment included, the cost ranges from 70F to 80F ($11.90 to $13.60) per hour. A full-day equestrian excursion that includes lunch is priced at 490F ($83.30).

At **L'Etrier Camarguais,** chemin bas des Launes, 13460 Les-Stes-Maries-de-la-Mer (☎ **04-90-97-81-14;** fax 04-90-97-88-11), about a mile north of Les-Stes-Maries-de-la-Mer, you'll find 28 rooms (with minibar, air-conditioning, TV, and phone) costing 840 to 980F ($142.80 to $166.60) for a double, half board included. In a compound surrounded by marshland, it resembles a combination log cabin/terra-cotta-and-stone farmhouse. The bar is decorated with saddles from around the world, the staff is accommodating, and the comfortably unpretentious rooms are outfitted in the Provençal style.

Offering a Camargue holiday on a somewhat grander scale is **Mas de la Fouque,** route d'Aigues-Mortes, 13460 Les-Stes-Maries-de-la-Mer (☎ **04-90-97-81-02;** fax 04-90-97-96-84). About 2 miles west of Les-Stes-Maries-de-la-Mer (about 3½ miles by car because of the meandering roads), its rooms face southern views over the marshy Etang des Launes. It's more appealing and has more amenities than its less expensive competitor. The 14 rooms (12 with air-conditioning, and all with TV, phone, and minibar) cost 2,160F ($367.20) for a double, half board included. The restaurant offers respite even for nonguests, with elegant fixed-price lunches and dinners for between 245F to 400F ($41.65 to $68). A tennis court and swimming pool are on the premises, and if you like to shoot, the hotels will help arrange the permits and guides for hunting small game during the autumn and winter.

WHERE TO STAY

Note that the **Restaurant Les Arcades** (see below) also rents rooms.

Hostellerie des Remparts. 6 place Anatole-France, 30220 Aigues-Mortes. ☎ **04-66-53-82-77.** Fax 04-66-53-73-77. 19 units. TEL. 300F–475F ($51–$80.75) double. AE, DC, V.

Established about 300 years ago, this weather-worn inn lies at the foot of the Tour de Constance, adjacent to the medieval fortifications. Popular and often fully booked (especially in summer), it evokes the Middle Ages with charm and a sense of nostalgia. The rooms with simple furniture are accessible via narrow stone staircases; 13 contain TVs. Each comes with a rather thin but reasonably comfortable mattress, plus a small bathroom with a shower stall. Breakfast is the only meal served.

Hôtel des Croisades. 2 rue du Port, 30220 Aigues-Mortes. ☎ **04-66-53-67-85.** 14 units. A/C TV TEL. 240F–320F ($40.80–$54.40) double. MC, V. Free parking.

Set within 250 yards of the medieval ramparts, adjacent to the canal ("le Chenal maritime") and the marina, this is a cozy, well-maintained hotel that's under the care of Mireille and Robert Thiers. It was originally built as a private home in the late 1800s, and was transformed in 1987 into the simple but decent and dignified hotel you'll see today. Bedrooms are well proportioned and clean, often with reproduction furniture that evokes old France, including oversize armoires and deep colors like bordeaux and terra-cotta. Each unit comes with a comfortable mattress and fine linen, plus a small bathroom with a shower stall and a combined tub and shower. Rooms 11, 12, 14, and 15 have the most panoramic views over the walled city and the marina. Breakfast is the only meal served.

✪ **Hôtel Les Templiers.** 23 rue de la République, 30220 Aigues-Mortes. ☎ **04-66-53-66-56.** Fax 04-66-53-69-61. 10 units. A/C TV TEL. 450F–800F ($76.50–$136) double. AE, DC, V. Closed Nov–Mar 22.

The town's leading inn is a gem of peace and tranquillity, along with luxurious comfort. Protected by the ramparts built by Saint Louis, king of France, this 17th-century residence has been tastefully converted to receive guests in all the comfort of a private home. The small to medium-size guest rooms are decorated in Provençal style with a homelike aura. Each comes with a firm mattress and fine linen on a comfortable French bed, plus a compact and efficiently organized private bathroom, most often with a shower stall, and all with good-sized towels. You can relax in the courtyard, where you can also enjoy breakfast. Arrangements can be made to take half board at the Le Maguelone restaurant across the street, costing 600F ($120) per person. The cookery is very regional, with fresh products from the surrounding area used effectively.

WHERE TO DINE

Restaurant les Arcades. 23 bd. Gambetta, 30220 Aigues-Mortes. ☎ **04-66-53-81-13.** Fax 04-66-53-75-46. Reservations recommended. Main courses 75F–165F ($12.75–$28.05); fixed-price menus 130F–220F ($22.10–$37.40). AE, DC, MC, V. Tues 7:30–9:30pm, Wed–Sun noon–2pm and 7:30–9:45pm (also open Mon night July–Aug). Closed 2 weeks in Feb and 2 weeks in Nov. FRENCH.

This restaurant has several formal sections with ancient beamed ceilings or intricately fitted stone vaults. Almost as old as the nearby fortifications, the place is especially charming on sultry days, when the thickness of the masonry keeps the interior cool. Good food is served at reasonable prices and is likely to include warm oysters, fish soup, pot-au-feu with three different meats, roasted monkfish in red-wine sauce, lobster fricassée, grilled filet of bull from the Camargue, and grilled duckling. Especially charming is a platter piled high with stuffed zucettini flowers served with pesto sauce.

The owner also rents 10 large, comfortable rooms upstairs, each with air-conditioning, TV, and phone. A double is 480F ($81.60), breakfast included.

11 Montpellier

471 miles (758km) SW of Paris, 100 miles (160.93km) NW of Marseille, 31 miles (49.89km) SW of Nîmes

The capital of Mediterranean (or Lower) Languedoc, this ancient university city is still renowned for its medical school, founded in the 13th century. Nostradamus qualified as a doctor here, and even Rabelais studied at the school. Petrarch came to Montpellier in 1317 and stayed for 7 years.

Today Montpellier is a bustling metropolis, one of southern France's fastest-growing cities thanks to an influx of new immigrants. Except for some dreary suburbs, the city has a handsomely laid out core, with tree-flanked promenades, broad avenues, and historic monuments. Students are about a quarter of the population, giving the city a lively, animated aura. In recent years many high-tech corporations, including IBM, have settled in Montpellier.

ESSENTIALS

GETTING THERE   Some 20 trains per day arrive from Avignon (trip time: 1 hr.), eight from Marseille (trip time: 1¾ hrs.), every 2 hours from Toulouse (trip time: 2 hrs.), and 10 per day from Perpignan (trip time: 1½ hrs.). From Paris there are eight trains per day (change in Lyon; trip time: 4½ hrs.). For **rail information** and schedules, call ☎ **08-36-35-35-35.** Two buses a day from Nîmes (trip time: 1¾ hrs.) pull into the **Gare Routière,** rue Jules-Ferry (☎ **04-67-92-01-43**), near the town center. For motorists, Montpellier lies off the A9 superhighway, heading west.

VISITOR INFORMATION   The **Office de Tourisme** is at 30 Allée Jean de Lattre de Tassigny (☎ **04-67-60-60-60**), adjacent to the most central plaza in town, place de la Comédie.

SPECIAL EVENTS   From the end of June to the beginning of July, the **Festival International Montpellier Danse** brings classical and modern dance performances to town. Tickets from 35F to 260F ($5.95 to $44.20) can be purchased through the Hôtel d'Assas, 6 rue de la Vieille Aiguillerie (☎ **04-67-60-83-60**). In late July, the **Festival de Radio France et de Montpellier** presents a variety of orchestral music, jazz, and opera, usually in the Corum Theater. Tickets range in price from 50F to 150F ($8.50 to $25.50), and can be purchased either by calling ☎ **04-67-02-02-01** or by contacting the Corum Theater at ☎ **04-67-61-67-61.**

EXPLORING THE TOWN

Called the Oxford of France because of its academic community, Montpellier is a city of young people, as you'll notice if you sit at one of the cafes on the heartbeat **place de la Comédie,** with its 18th-century Fountain of the Three Graces. It's the living room of Montpellier, the ideal place to chat, people-watch, or cruise.

Paul Valéry met André Gide in the **Jardin des Plantes,** 163 rue Auguste-Broussonnet (☎ **04-67-63-43-22**), and you might begin here, as it's the oldest such garden in France. It's reached from boulevard Henri-IV. This botanical garden, filled with exotic plants and a handful of greenhouses, was opened in 1593. Admission is free. It's open April to September, Tuesday to Sunday from 10am to 7pm; October to March, Monday to Friday from 10am to 5pm.

Nearby is the town's spiritual centerpiece, the **Cathédrale St-Pierre,** on place St-Pierre (☎ **04-67-66-04-12**), founded in 1364. Once associated with a Benedictine monastery, the cathedral suffered badly in the religious wars. (After 1795 the monastery was occupied by the medical school.) Today it has a somewhat-bleak western front with two towers and a canopied porch. In theory, the church can be visited daily from 9:30am to noon and 2:30 to 7pm, but know in advance that local authorities warn of fiscal cutbacks here, and these hours might be severely curtailed during the lifetime of this edition. If that is the case, call either the number listed above for information, or ☎ **04-67-91-11-00,** or, as a last resort, the tourist office.

Before leaving town, take a stroll along the 17th-century **promenade du Peyrou,** a terraced park with views of the Cévennes and the Mediterranean. This is a broad esplanade constructed at the loftiest point of Montpellier. Opposite the entrance is an Arc de Triomphe, erected in 1691 to celebrate the victories of Louis XIV. In the center of the promenade is an equestrian statue of Louis XIV, and at the end, the **Château d'Eau,** a pavilion with Corinthian columns that serves as a monument to 18th-century classicism. Water is brought here by a conduit, nearly 9 miles long, and an aqueduct.

✪ **Musée Fabre.** 39 bd. Bonne-Nouvelle. ☎ **04-67-14-83-00.** Admission 20F ($3.40) adults, 10F ($1.70) students and persons 20 and under. Tues–Fri 9am–5:30pm, Sat and Sun 9:30am–5pm.

One of France's great provincial art galleries, it occupies the former Hôtel de Massilian, where Molière once played for a season. The origins of the collection were an exhibition of the Royal Academy that was sent to Montpellier by Napoléon in 1803. The most important works of the collection, however, were given by François Fabre, a Montpellier painter, in 1825. After Fabre's death, many other paintings from his collection were donated to the gallery. Several of these he painted himself, but the more important works were ones he had acquired—including Poussin's *Venus and Adonis* and paintings from the Italian Renaissance. This generosity was followed by donations from others, notably Valedau, who in 1836 left the museum his collection of Rubens, Gérard Dou, and Téniers.

SHOPPING

Stroll down **place de la Comédie,** with its ultramodern Polygone shopping center, site of more than 120 independent boutiques, and **rue Jean-Moulin.** This town has a plethora of name-brand boutiques and department stores. For traditional regional delicacies, visit **Au Gourmets,** 2 rue Clos-René (☎ **04-67-58-57-04**); or visit **Pâtissier Schoeller,** 121 av. de l'Odàve (☎ **04-67-75-71-55**), for a plentiful supply of *grisettes de Montpellier* (licorice-and-honey candies) and *comédie de Montpellier* (melt-in-your-mouth almond paste candies).

WHERE TO STAY

Note that **Le Jardin des Sens** (see below) also rents rooms.

EXPENSIVE

Hôtel Metropole. 3 rue Clos-Rene, 34000 Montpellier. ☎ **04-67-58-11-22.** Fax 04-67-92-13-02. 84 units. A/C MINIBAR TV TEL. 680F ($115.60) double; 1,260F ($214.20) suite. AE, DC, MC, V. Parking 40F ($6.80).

In the heart of Montpellier, this 1898 monument adjacent to the town's railway station has an entrance with a soaring portal set into a dignified stone facade. In 1998 it underwent a radical renovation that retained the charming interior garden and the original detailing and added to the premises a small-scale fitness center. The well-furnished, contemporary-looking bedrooms range in size from medium to spacious, and are fitted with fine linens and quality mattresses. Each contains a roomy marble-sheathed private bath, often with a tub-and-shower combination. On the premises is a dignified-looking restaurant, La Closerie, open Monday to Friday for both lunch and dinner. Set menus cost 130F ($22.10) each.

MODERATE

✪ **Hôtel du Parc.** 8 rue Achille-Bège, 34000 Montpellier. ☎ **04-67-41-16-49.** Fax 04-67-54-10-05. 19 units. A/C TV TEL. 310F–425F ($52.70–$72.25) double. AE, V. Free parking.

One of the town's more charming moderately priced hostelries, this hotel lies in the heart of the city near the Palais des Congrès. It was a Languedocian residence in the 18th century but has been turned into a hotel with a lot of grace notes and French provincial charm. Rooms have been carefully decorated, including comfortable mattresses and streamlined baths with hair dryers and adequate numbers of good-size towels. A garden and flowering terrace offer you breakfast outside. Numerous restaurants surround the hotel.

La Maison Blanche. 1796 av. de la Pompignane, 34000 Montpellier. ☎ **04-99-58-20-70.** Fax 04-67-79-53-39. 38 units. A/C TV TEL. 490F ($83.30) double; 780F ($132.60) suite. AE, DC, MC, V. Free parking. A 5-min. drive southeast of Montpellier's center: Take bd. d'Antigone east until you reach the intersection with av. de la Pompignane; then head north until you come to the hotel, on your right.

This hotel seems to have worked hard to create a French Créole ambience—it's set in a modern clapboard motel whose balconies drip with ornate gingerbread and whose verdant gardens are bordered with lattices. The rooms are stylishly furnished in rattan and wicker, with comfortable beds and soft mattresses. Bathrooms are tiled and well maintained, with tub-and-shower combinations or shower stalls and good-sized towels. Parts of the interior, especially the dining room, might remind you more of the France of Louis XIII than Old Louisiana, but overall the place is charming and unusual. The in-house restaurant, open daily for lunch and Tuesday to Saturday for dinner, serves fixed-price menus at 110F to 160F ($18.70 to $27.20).

INEXPENSIVE

Hôtel du Palais. 3 rue du Palais, 34000 Montpellier. ☎ **04-67-60-47-38.** Fax 04-67-60-40-23. 26 units. A/C MINIBAR TV TEL. 330F–400F ($56.10–$68) double. Parking 60F ($10.20). AE, DC, MC, V.

One of the most historic hotels in town, the Palais is in the town center, amid a labyrinth of narrow streets. Built in the late 1700s, it has the kind of grandly symmetrical design associated with the *ancien régime.* Much of the decor dates from a restoration in 1983. Lots of fabrics, big curtains, and walls painted to resemble marble adorn the public rooms. Bedrooms are relatively large, cozy, and appealing; they feature antique reproductions. Maintenance is good, mattresses are comfortable, and each room comes with a compact bath equipped with a shower stall. Breakfast is the only meal served.

Les Arceaux. 33–35 bd. des Arceaux, 34000 Montpellier. ☎ **04-67-92-03-03.** Fax 04-67-92-05-09. 18 units. TV TEL. 300F–335F ($51–$56.95) double. AE, MC, V.

A hotel has stood at this prime location, right off the renowned promenade du Peyrou, since the turn of the century. The small to medium-sized rooms are pleasantly but simply furnished. A shaded terrace adjoins the hotel. Breakfast is the only meal served.

Ulysse. 338 av. de St-Maur, 34000 Montpellier. ☎ **04-67-02-02-30.** Fax 04-67-02-16-50. 27 units. MINIBAR TV TEL. 320F–350F ($54.40–$59.50) double. AE, DC, V. From bd. d'Antigone, head north along av. Jean-Mermoz to rue de la Pépinière; continue right for a short distance, then take a sharp left at the first intersection, which leads to av. de St-Maur.

One of the city's better bargains, Ulysse delivers a lot for the price. There's simplicity here, though the owners have worked hard—on a budget—to make the hotel as stylish as possible. Each room is individually decorated. The furnishings are functional but have a certain flair. Much in-room comfort is found here, including firm mattresses, fully equipped baths, and extra features like a minibar, unusual for a budget hotel. The housekeeping is first rate, even though the prices are not.

STAYING NEARBY

Demure des Brousses. Route de Vauguières, 34000 Montpellier. ☎ **04-67-65-77-66.** Fax 04-67-22-22-11. 17 units. TV TEL. 380F–580F ($64.60–$98.60) double. AE, DC, MC, V. Free parking. Take D-172E 2 miles east of the center.

This 18th-century country house stands in an impressive 5-acre park. The house was built by M. and Mme Brousse, who made their fortune as épiciers or spice merchants. A tranquil choice, it has been skillfully converted for guests. Rooms range from medium size to spacious, with each differently decorated in such 19th-century styles as French Empire. Well-fitted beds are equipped with quality mattresses and fine linens, and each room comes with a small tiled bathroom. Public rooms are decorated like those of a gracious French country house, making this an intimate retreat. It's about a 10-minute drive from the heart of Montpellier.

WHERE TO DINE

La Réserve Rimbaud. 820 av. de St-Maur. ☎ **04-67-72-52-53.** Reservations recommended. Main courses 90F–160F ($15.30–$27.20); fixed-price menus 160F–380F ($27.20–$64.60). AE, DC, MC, V. Tues–Sat noon–2pm and 8–10pm, Sun noon–2pm. Closed Jan–Mar 20. Take N113 (av. de Nîmes) northeast toward Nîmes and follow it to the intersection with av. St-Lazare, then turn left; the restaurant is on the right. FRENCH.

The most memorable restaurant in town is in a bulky, rectangular 19th-century manor house once owned by a prosperous local family, the Rimbauds. It offers about 30 seats in an early 1900s setting. Menu items—prepared and presented by English-speaking members of the Tarrit family—change with the season but are likely to include *gigot de mer* (a slab of monkfish with local herbs), curried crayfish, stuffed calamari, warm foie gras with apples, fricassée of sole with baby vegetables, and a thin-crusted *croustillant aux pommes* served with English cream.

Le Chandelier. Immeuble La Coupole Antigone, 267 rue Léon-Blum. ☎ **04-67-15-34-38.** Reservations recommended. Main courses 110F–210F ($18.70–$35.70); set-price menus 220F ($37.40; not available Sat night) and 290F–340F ($49.30–$57.80). AE, DC, MC, V. Mon–Sat noon–1:30pm and 7:30–10pm. FRENCH.

This is the most dramatic modern restaurant in Montpellier, on the 7th floor of a modern office building, with superb food as prepared by Gilbert Furland, superb service as choreographed by Jean-Marc Forest, and a sweeping view over an upscale residential neighborhood (l'Antigone). A large terrace becomes the main attraction during clement weather. The staff searches for "temptations of the palate," which means that you'll be presented with some unusual flavor combinations. Examples include a sophisticated version of calamari fried with fresh thyme; an escalope of foie gras in orange sauce; an award-winning ragout of lobster; and sautéed pigeon in a Provençal pistou. A particularly scrumptious dessert is a crispy *tarte* with caramelized mango.

✪ **Le Jardin des Sens.** 11 av. St-Lazare. ☎ **04-67-79-63-38.** Fax 04-67-72-13-05. E-mail: jardinsens@relaischateaux.fr. Reservations required. Main courses 160F–280F ($27.20–$47.60); fixed-price lunch (Mon–Fri) 230F ($39.10); fixed-price menu 380F–590F ($64.60–$100.30). AE, MC, V. Mon–Sat noon–2pm and 7:30–10pm. FRENCH.

If we could award more than one star, we'd grant two to this citadel of fine cuisine. The chefs—the biological twins Laurent and Jacques Pourcel—have taken Montpellier by storm. Michelin has awarded them three stars, thus bestowing its divine blessing. Post-nouvelle reigns here. The rich bounty of Languedoc is served in preparations designed to enhance its natural flavor. Meals often seem flawless. The cuisine could be almost anything, depending on where the chefs' imaginations roam. An appropriate starter might be ravioli stuffed with foie gras of duckling and flap mushrooms, floating in chicken bouillon fortified with truffles, broad beans, and crispy potatoes. A main course of note involves crisp-fried crayfish tails, served with a confit of pigeon and a fricassée of green peas with slices of Bayonne ham. A *tarte fine* with tomatoes, roasted monkfish, and essence of thyme is memorable, as is a filet of pigeon stuffed with pistachios. A dessert specialty is a gratin of limes with slices of pineapple *en confit*.

The Jardin des Sens also rents 12 deluxe guest rooms and two suites, designed in cutting-edge modernism by Bruno Borrione, a colleague of Philippe Starck. They cost 900F to 1,300F ($153 to $221) for a double and 1,600F to 2,500F ($272 to $425) for a suite.

✪ **L'Olivier.** 12 rue Aristide-Olivier. ☎ **04-67-92-86-28.** Reservations required. Main courses 80F–150F ($13.60–$25.50); fixed-price menus 170F–198F ($28.90–$33.65). AE, DC. Tues–Sat noon–1:30pm and 7:30–9:30pm. Closed Aug and holidays. FRENCH.

No restaurant, with the exception of Le Jardin des Sens, has improved more than this. Chef Michel Breton, assisted by his wife Yvette, is making his name known in restaurant guides to the south of France. Don't even dream of showing up here without a reservation: The establishment holds places for only 20 diners at a time. The subdued, rather bland-looking modern space is painted a clear yellow and accented with contemporary paintings. But you don't come here for background—you want to try Breton's "creative statements." Some dishes that might appear regularly are salmon with oysters, fricassée of lamb with thyme, warm monkfish terrine, frog's legs with wild mushrooms, haunch of rabbit stuffed with wild mushrooms, and salad of lamb sweetbreads with extract of truffles. The welcome is warm hearted and sincere.

MONTPELLIER AFTER DARK

After the sun sets, head for **place Jean-Jaurès, rue de Verdun,** and **rue des Ecoles Laïques;** or take a walk down **rue de la Loge** for its carnival atmosphere of talented jugglers, mimes, and musical artists.

Rockstore, 20 rue de Verdun (☎ 04-67-58-70-10), with its 1950s rock memorabilia and live concerts, draws lots of students. Upstairs, its disco pounds out techno and rock. The cover for the disco is 50F ($8.50).

An exotic cocktail bar is **Viva Brazil,** 7 rue de Verdun (☎ **04-67-58-63-33**), where you make your way through the lush rain-forest vegetation and friendly natives to reach the mirrored sanctuary of the dance floor. For the best jazz and blues in town, check out **JAM,** 100 rue Ferdinand-de-Lesseps (☎ **04-67-58-30-30**). In a noisy, smoky, and even gritty space, its regular concerts attract jazz enthusiasts from miles around. Concert tickets average 50F ($8.50).

A more recently inaugurated disco is **La Tipola,** Route de Palavas (☎ **04-67-65-62-95**), a modern, sparsely decorated bar and dance hall with enough bars to ensure that everyone can get a drink at any time, and a clientele that tends to be between 20 and 38 years old. Open every Wednesday to Sunday beginning around 10pm, it charges 50F ($8.50) entrance, a price that includes the first drink.

Gays and lesbians gather at the town's most animated gay bar and disco, **La Villa Rouge,** Route de Palavas, a short distance from La Tipola (see above), with which it shares the same phone. Both of them lie about 3 miles south of the town center.

The biggest and most up-to-date theater in town is **Le Corum,** in the Palais des Congrès, esplanade Charles-de-Gaulle (☎ **04-67-61-67-61**), in the heart of town. Plays, dance recitals, operas, and symphonic concerts are presented. For complete ticket information and schedules, contact either the Corum directly, or an organization its management, the **Opéra Comédie,** place de la Comédie (☎ **04-67-60-19-99**).

12 Nîmes

440 miles (708.11km) S of Paris, 27 miles (43.45km) W of Avignon

Nîmes, the ancient Nemausus, is a great place to view some of the world's finest Roman remains. The city grew to prominence during the reign of Caesar Augustus

(27 B.C to A.D. 14). Today it possesses one of the best-preserved Roman amphitheaters in the world and a near-perfect Roman temple. The city of 135,000 is more like Provence than Languedoc, and there's a touch of Pamplona (Spain) here in the festivals of the *corridas* (bullfights) at the arena. The Spanish image is even stronger at night, when the bodegas fill, usually with students, drinking sangría and listening to the sounds of flamenco.

By 1860 the togas of Nîmes's citizenry had given way to denim, the cloth de Nîmes. An Austrian immigrant, Leví-Strauss, started to export this heavy fabric to California for use as material for work pants for gold diggers in those boomtown years. The rest, as they say, is history.

ESSENTIALS

GETTING THERE   Nîmes is a major rail terminus for southern France. It lies on the main rail line between Marseille and Bordeaux. Six TGF trains a day arrive from Paris (trip time: 4½ hrs.); tickets are from 390F ($66.30) each way. For **rail information** and **schedules,** call ☎ **08-36-35-35-35.** The bus station, **Gare Routière,** is just behind the railway station, on the rue Ste-Félicité (☎ **04-66-29-52-00**). If you're driving, Nîmes can be reached from Lyon along A7 south to the town of Orange, connecting here to A9 into Nîmes.

VISITOR INFORMATION   The **Office de Tourisme** is at 6 rue Auguste (☎ **04-66-67-29-11**).

EXPLORING THE CITY

If you want to explore the city's monuments and museums, you can buy a *billet global,* sold at the ticket counter of any of the local museums and monuments. It provides access to all the cultural sites over a 3-day period, for an inclusive fee of 60F ($10.20) for adults and 30F ($5.10) for students and children 15 and under. Entrance is free for children under 10.

THE TOP SIGHTS

✪ **Amphithéâtre Romain.** Place des Arènes. ☎ **04-66-76-72-77.** Admission 28F ($4.75) adults, 20F ($3.40) students and children 15 and under. Daily 9am–noon and 2:30–6pm.

The elliptically shaped amphitheater is a better-preserved twin to the one at Arles, and is far more complete than the Colosseum of Rome. It's two stories high, each floor having 60 arches, and was built of huge stones painstakingly fitted together without mortar. One of the best preserved arenas from ancient times, it once held more than 20,000 spectators, who came to see gladiatorial combats and wolf or boar hunts. Today it's used for everything from ballet recitals to bullfights.

✪ **Maison Carrée.** Place de la Comédie. ☎ **04-66-36-29-76.** June–Sept, daily 9am–noon and 2:30–7pm; Oct–May, daily 9am–12:30pm and 2–6pm.

The pride of Nîmes, this is one of the most beautiful, and certainly one of the best-preserved, Roman temples of Europe. It was built during the reign of Caesar Augustus. Set on a raised platform with tall Corinthian columns, it inspired Thomas Jefferson as well as the builders of La Madeleine in Paris. A changing roster of cultural and art exhibits is presented, beneath an authentically preserved roof that the city of Nîmes repaired in 1996.

Carré d'Art/Musée d'Art Contemporain. Place de la Maison Carré. ☎ **04-66-76-35-35.** Admission 28F ($4.75) adults, 20F ($3.40) students and children 14 and under. Tues–Sun 11am–6pm.

Across the square stands the modern-day twin of the Maison Carrée, a sophisticated research center and exhibition space that contains a library, a newspaper kiosk, and an

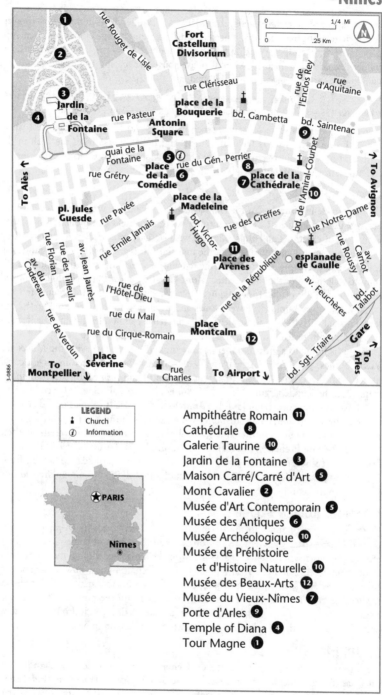

art museum. Its understated design from 1993 was inspired by (but doesn't overpower) the ancient monument nearby. The museum's permanent expositions are often supplemented with temporary exhibits of contemporary art. *Note:* The view from this modern building's terrace allows you to rise above the roaring traffic and presents a panorama of ancient monuments and medieval churches.

Musée des Beaux-Arts. Rue Cité-Foulc. ☎ **04-66-67-38-21.** Admission 28F ($4.75) adults, 20F ($3.40) students and children 14 and under. Tues–Sun 11am–6pm.

The city's largest museum contains French paintings and sculptures from the 17th to the 20th century as well as Flemish, Dutch, and Italian works from the 15th to the 18th century. Seek out in particular one of G. B. Moroni's masterpieces, *La Calomnie d'Apelle,* and a well-preserved Gallo-Roman mosaic.

MORE SIGHTS

The **Jardin de la Fontaine,** at the end of quai de la Fontaine, was laid out in the 18th century, using the ruins of a Roman shrine as an ornamental centerpiece. It was planted with rows of chestnuts and elms, adorned with statuary and urns, and intersected by grottos and canals—making it one of the most beautiful gardens in France. Adjoining it is the ruined **Temple of Diana** and the remains of some Roman baths. Within a 10-minute walk north of the town center, **Mont Cavalier,** a low but rocky hill, is topped by the sturdy bulk of the **Tour Magne,** the city's oldest Roman monument. You can climb it for a panoramic view over Nîmes and its environs. Admission is 15F ($2.55) for adults and 12F ($2.05) for students and children 14 and under. It's open daily: May to September from 9am to 7pm, and October to April from 9am to 5pm.

Nîmes is home to a great number of museums. If time allows, visit the **Musée du Vieux-Nîmes,** place de la Cathédrale (☎ 04-66-36-00-64), housed in an episcopal palace from the 1700s. It's rich in antiques. The museum is open Tuesday to Sunday from 11am to 6pm, charging 28F ($4.75) for adults and 20F ($3.40) for children.

A busy thoroughfare, boulevard de l'Amiral-Courbet, leads to the **Porte d'Arles**—the remains of a monumental gate built by the Romans during the reign of Augustus. Farther along, contained in the same stately building at 13 bis bd. l'Amiral-Courbet, are the **Musée de Préhistoire et d'Histoire Naturelle** (☎ 04-66-67-39-14), and the **Musée Archéologique** (☎ 04-66-67-25-57). Both are open Tuesday to Sunday from 11am to 6pm, and a fee of 28F ($4.75) for adults and 20F ($3.40) for children admits you to both museums.

A FAMOUS ROMAN BRIDGE

Outside the city, 14 miles to the northeast, the well-preserved, much-photographed **pont du Gard** spans the Gard River. Consisting of three tiers of arches arranged into gracefully symmetrical patterns, its huge stones are held together without mortar. It dates from about 19 B.C. and is a vivid reminder of the technical know-how of the ancient Romans. Frédéric Mistral, the national poet of Provence and Languedoc, recorded a medieval legend that the devil constructed the bridge with the proviso that he could claim the soul of the first person to go across it. Take Highway N86 from Nîmes to a point 2 miles from the village of Remoulins, where signs are prominently posted.

SHOPPING

Head to the center of town to the **rue du Général-Perrier, rue des Marchands, rue du Chapître,** and the pedestrian streets of **rue de l'Aspic** and **rue de la Madeleine.** A Sunday market is conducted from 8am to around 1pm in the parking lot of the **Stade des Castières,** adjacent to the boulevard Périphérique that encircles Nîmes, where the town's football (soccer) matches take place.

To appease your sweet tooth, go to just about any pastry shop in town and ask for the regional almond-based cookies called *croquants villaret* and *caladons*. They're great for a burst of energy. One of the best souvenirs you can buy in Nîmes (especially if you're not continuing east into Provence) is a *santon*—wood or clay figurines sculpted into characters from Provençal country life. You can collect a set that creates a uniquely country-French nativity scene. For a selection of santons in various sizes, visit the **Boutique Provençale,** 10 place de la Maison Carré (☎ **04-66-67-81-71**), or **Au Papillon Bleu,** 15 rue du Général-Perrier (☎ **04-66-67-48-58**).

WHERE TO STAY
MODERATE

Hôtel de Milan. 17 av. Feuchères, 30000 Nîmes. ☎ **04-66-29-29-90.** Fax 04-66-29-05-31. 33 units. TV TEL. 230F–280F ($39.10–$47.60) double. AE, DC, MC, V. Parking 10F ($1.70) per day in lot across street.

The three-story Hotel de Milan is just across the street from the railway station, and is especially convenient for Eurailpass holders on a tight budget. Rooms are basic—no frills, but clean and decent, with relatively banal furnishings in a bland, contemporary style. Rooms are small and mattresses a bit thin, but there is reasonable comfort here and good value for the price. The cramped bathrooms contain shower stalls and medium-sized towels. The only meal served on the premises is breakfast, but the staff will direct you to several restaurants within the neighborhood.

Hôtel l'Amphithéâtre. 4 rue des Arènes, 30000 Nîmes. ☎ **04-66-67-28-51.** Fax 04-66-67-07-79. 17 units. TV TEL. 230F–260F ($39.10–$44.20) double; 300F ($51) triple or quad. AE, MC, V. Closed Dec 20–Jan 25. Parking 50F ($8.50).

The core of this small-scale, old-fashioned hotel dates from the 18th century—it has functioned as a hotel for longer than anyone remembers. A stay here involves trekking to your room up steep flights of creaking stairs, and navigating your way through a labyrinth of upper corridors. Small bedrooms are outfitted in a deliberately old-fashioned way, usually with antiques or antique reproductions, wall-to-wall carpeting, and creaky but comfortable mattresses. Bathrooms are cramped but tidy affairs with shower stalls and rather thin towels. The hotel and staff are less than perfect, but at these prices, who's complaining?

Hôtel Vatel. 140 rue Vatel, B.P. 7128, 30913 Nîmes CEDEX. ☎ **04-66-62-57-57.** Fax 04-66-57-50. 46 units. A/C MINIBAR TV TEL. 600F ($102) double; 1,200F ($204) suite. AE, DC, MC, V. From the A4 autoroute, exit at "Nîmes Ouest."

This modern seven-story, four-star hotel, 2 miles north of the town center, is part of a group of buildings that include a technological university and a large hospital. Its student staff from the local hotel school work on site as part of their on-the-job training. Rooms are streamlined, tasteful, and modern, and include private terraces, safes, and marble-sheathed bathrooms with fluffy towels and hair dryers. Upholsteries are richly patterned, and comfortable beds have firm mattresses. In all, the modern format of this hotel provides levels of comfort that older hotels, in more historic settings, simply can't match. Les Palmiers is the more formal and expensive of the hotel's two restaurants. More casual is Le Restaurant Provençal, which occupies something akin to a greenhouse, and specializes in regional cuisine. Facilities include a swimming pool and health club, exercise room, solarium, sauna, tennis court, and conference and convention facilities.

Imperator Concorde. Quai de la Fontaine, 30900 Nîmes. ☎ **04-66-21-90-30.** Fax 04-66-67-70-25. www.occidental-hoteles.com. E-mail: madrid@occidental-hoteles.com. 63 units. A/C MINIBAR TV TEL. 550F–690F ($93.50–$117.30) double; 1,900F ($323) suite. AE, DC, MC, V. Parking 70F ($11.90).

This is the largest hotel in town, a member of the well-managed Concorde chain, and also a four-star property. Set behind the town's ancient Roman monuments, with a pale pink Italianate facade, it was much improved by renovations in the late 1990s. Bedrooms are artful and cozy, each outfitted in a monochromatic, jewel-toned color scheme of pink, ochre, or navy blue. Furniture is traditional French *ancien régime*, with fluted or cambriole details. Beds are comfortable, towels thick, and the up-to-date bathrooms have hair dryers. You can order a meal in the hotel's verdant rear gardens, or in a sun-flooded, high-ceilinged dining room, L'Enclos de la Fontaine. Set menus are priced from 145F to 380F ($24.65 to $64.60).

New Hôtel La Baume. 21 rue Nationale, 30000 Nîmes. ☎ **04-66-76-28-42.** Fax 04-66-76-28-45. 34 units. A/C MINIBAR TV TEL. 420F ($71.40) double. AE, DC, MC, V. Parking 40F ($6.80).

Our favorite nest in Nîmes is in a 17th-century mansion. The designers were careful to preserve the original architectural heritage during its conversion, and the result is a winning combination of modern and traditional. The 24 rooms are fitted out with exceptional charm in warm Provençal tones of ocher, burnt orange, and yellow, and, in almost every case, with king-size beds with firm mattresses. There are thoughtful extras like hair dryers and good-sized towels, and the plumbing is state-of-the art. The hotel restaurant is also worth a visit, turning out such dishes as fresh salmon flavored with anise, and chicken saltimbocca with ham. Set menus are reasonably priced at 80F ($13.60) each.

Novotel Atria Nimes Centre. 5 bd. de Prague, 3000 Nîmes. ☎ **04-66-76-56-56.** Fax 04-66-76-56-59. 119 units. A/C MINIBAR TV TEL. 540F ($91.80) double; 850F ($144.50) suite. AE, DC, MC, V. Parking 35F ($5.95).

Opened in mid-1995, this cost-conscious member of a nationwide chain occupies a desirable site in the heart of Nîmes, adjacent to the ancient arena. Its six floors wrap around a carefully landscaped inner courtyard. Each room contains a double bed, a single bed (which converts into a sofa), a well-equipped bath, and a wide writing desk. Half the rooms were renovated in the late 1990s; the remainder will be improved during the lifetime of this edition. Although in a rather sterile chain format, the medium-sized bedrooms come with a firm mattress and a small bathroom that is tiled and furnished with shower stall. The hotel offers a bar and an attractive restaurant, Les Sept Collines, which is open daily for lunch and dinner and charges 95F ($16.15) for a set-price meal.

WHERE TO DINE

The dining room at the **New Hôtel La Baume** (see above) is also a good choice.

✪ **Alexandre.** Rte. de l'Aéroport de Garons. ☎ **04-66-70-08-99.** Reservations required. Main courses 140F–190F ($23.80–$32.30). Set-price lunches 190F–450F ($32.30–$76.50); set-price dinners 285F–450F ($48.45–$76.50). AE, MC, V. July–Aug, Tues–Sat noon–1:45pm and 8–9:45pm. Sept–June, Tues–Sun noon–1:45pm and Tues and Thurs–Sat 8–9:45pm. Closed: Feb. From the town center, take rue de la République southwest to av. Jean-Jaurès, then head south and follow signs to the airport in the direction of Garons. FRENCH.

The most charming, amusing, and competent restaurant around is on the outskirts of Nîmes, 5½ miles south of the center. In its verdant setting, you'll discover the elegant but rustic domain of Michel Kayser, an exceptional chef who adheres to classic tradition, with subtle improvements. He's assisted in the dining room by his charming wife, Monique. Menu items are designed to amuse as well as delight the palate: Examples are *île flottante* with truffles and velouté of cèpe mushrooms, roasted pigeon stuffed with purée of vegetables and foie gras, and the region's most sophisticated version of an old country recipe, *pieds et paquets*. Especially appealing is the cheese trolley loaded with esoteric goat cheeses from the region and worthy cheeses from other parts of France. The dessert trolley is incredibly hard to resist.

Restaurant au Chapon Fin. 3 rue du Château-Fadaise. ☎ **04-66-67-34-73.** Reservations required. Main courses 82F–135F ($13.95–$22.95); fixed-price menus 75F ($12.75) at lunch, 120F ($20.40) at dinner. AE, MC, V. Mon–Fri noon–2pm and 7:30–10pm, Sat 7:30–10pm. Closed 2 weeks in Aug. FRENCH.

This tavern/restaurant, on a little square behind St-Paul's, is run by M. and Mme Grangier. It has beamed ceilings, small lamps, and a black-and-white stone floor. Madame Grangier is from Alsace, but don't scour the menu for Alsatian specialties— it is linked to the traditions of Languedoc. From the à la carte menu you can order foie gras with truffles, coq au vin, and entrecôte flambéed with morels. The proprietor makes his own *confit d'oie* (goose preserved in its own fat) from birds shipped in from Alsace.

San Francisco Steak House. 33 rue Roussy. ☎ **04-66-21-00-80.** Reservations required. Main courses 60F–150F ($10.20–$25.50). AE, DE, MC, V. Mon–Fri noon–1:30pm and Mon–Sat 8pm–midnight. Bus: 3 or 5. STEAK/FRENCH.

Near place de la Couronne, this popular theme restaurant is patterned on California. It serves the best steaks and seafood in Nîmes, always in generous portions with plenty of flavor, as well as succulent veal and lamb chops. Two trendy dishes are grilled ostrich steak and grilled bison steak. There is a full gamut of traditional beef dishes, including steak tartare. Begin your meal with a shrimp-stuffed avocado or a tender salad of grapefruit and crayfish segments.

Wine Bar Chez Michel. 11 place de la Couronne. ☎ **04-66-76-19-59.** Reservations not required. Main courses 55F–130F ($9.35–$22.10); fixed-price menus 77F ($13.10) at lunch, 80F–130F ($13.60–$22.10) at dinner. AE, DC, MC, V. Tues–Sat noon–2pm and Mon–Sat 7pm–midnight. FRENCH.

This place has mahogany panels and leather banquettes like those you might have found in a turn-of-the-century California saloon. An array of salads and platters is served, and at lunch you can order a "quick menu," including an appetizer, a garnished main course, and two glasses of wine. Typical dishes are magret of duckling and con-trefilet of steak with Roquefort sauce. You can now enjoy lunch on the terrace in the newly renovated courtyard. A restaurateur extraordinaire, Michel Hermet also makes his own wine; his vineyards that have been associated with his family for many generations. There are more than 300 other varieties of wine to choose from, by the glass or pitcher.

NIMES AFTER DARK

Once the warm weather hits, all sorts of activities take place at the arena, including concerts and theater under the stars. The Office de Tourisme (☎ 04-66-67-29-11) has a complete listing of events and schedules. Otherwise, for popular events that include football (soccer), bullfights, and rock concerts, you can contact the **Bureau de Location des Arènes,** 1 rue Alexandre-Ducros (☎ 04-66-67-28-02). Tickets for cultural events like symphonic or chamber-music concerts, theater, and opera performances are sold through **Hall du Théâtre,** 1 place de la Calade (☎ 04-66-36-02-04).

During the heat of midsummer, many of Nîmes's central squares burst out with recorded music, crowds of pedestrians and, on Thursday nights in July and August, markets with rich troves of used objects, paintings, crafts, and sculpture. Artists, musicians, and all kinds of locals gather in observance of the city's **Les Jeudis de Nîmes.** Of special interest are the place de l'Horloge, the place du Marché, and the place aux Herbes.

Other streets to explore for a healthy dose of nocturnal good times on any night of the week include **impasse Porte-de-France** and **boulevard Victor-Hugo.**

If you like hanging out with a mixture of French students and French soldiers, check out a local spot where they seem to congregate together, **Café Le Napoléon,** 46 bd. Victor-Hugo (☎ **04-66-67-20-23**). Popular with the intelligentsia is the **Haddock Café,** 13 rue de l'Agau (☎ **04-66-67-86-57**), with its weekly live rock concerts. But if you simply want to tank down some brew and have a rip-roaring good time, go to the **Queen's Beer,** 1 bis rue Jean-Reboul (☎ **04-66-67-81-10**).

Local jazz aficionados know that **Le Diagonal,** 41 bis rue Emile-Jamais (☎ **04-66-21-70-01**), hosts the area's best jazz and blues concerts. The flashy, sexy, and hip **La Comédie,** 28 rue Jean-Reboul (☎ **04-66-73-13-66**), is the hands-down best for dancing and attracts a pretty crowd of youthful danceaholics. A little less flashy, but a lot more fun, **Lulu Club,** 10 impasse de la Curaterie (☎ **04-66-36-28-20**), is the gay and lesbian stronghold in Nîmes.

A newer nightlife contender attracting the city's young and restless is **Le C.K.F.,** 20 rue de l'Etoile (☎ **04-66-21-59-22**). Open every Wednesday to Saturday, beginning after 11pm, it rocks and rolls to music from Los Angeles and London, as clients dance, dance, dance. Clubs with dancing and/or entertainment generally impose a cover of 50F to 70F ($8.50 to $11.90), depending on the night.

Provence 4

Provence has been called a bridge between the past and the present, where yesterday blends with today in a quiet, often melancholy way. Peter Mayle's best-selling *A Year in Provence, Toujours Provence* and *Encore Provence* have played no small part in the burgeoning popularity this sunny corner of southern France has enjoyed during recent years.

The Greeks and Romans filled the landscape with cities boasting Hellenic theaters, Roman baths, amphitheaters, and triumphal arches. These were followed in medieval times by Romanesque fortresses and Gothic cathedrals. In the 19th century Provence's light and landscapes attracted illustrious painters like Cézanne and van Gogh. Despite the changes over the years, the howling mistral will forever be heard through the broad-leaved plane trees.

Provence has its own language and its own customs. The region is bounded on the north by the Dauphine, on the west by the Rhône, on the east by the Alps, and on the south by the Mediterranean. We'll focus in the next chapters on the part of Provence known as the glittering French Riviera or Côte d'Azur.

EXPLORING THE REGION BY CAR

Here's how to link together the best of the region if you rent a car.

Day 1   Beginning in **Orange,** tour the Roman ruins and the Musée Municipal, then drive south for 8 miles along A9 to **Châteauneuf-du-Pape** for a visit to the village's famous wineries and the Musée des Vieux Outils de Vignerons. Continue south for 8 miles along any of three highways marked AVIGNON. Spend the night in Avignon.

Day 2   This day is devoted to **Avignon,** where you can tour the Palais des Papes and walk among the sights of place du Palais, the Quartier de la Balance, and Old Avignon. Spend another night here.

Day 3   Head west, following A100 for 20 miles, past Remoulins to the pont du Gard; get on Rte. 981 going northwest for 12 miles to **Uzès,** the beautiful medieval town where you'll spend the day and night. Start your tour at Le Duché, then visit the town's 4th-century crypt and Cathédrale St-Théodorit, and end with a stroll through the asymmetrical place aux Herbes.

Day 4   In the morning, drive southwest for 12 miles along Rte. 981 to the pont du Gard, then take Rte. 986 10 miles south to Beaucaire and 1 mile east on Rte. 999 to **Tarascon.** Spend the morning touring the Château du Roi René and admiring the art in the Eglise

Ste-Marthe, then take Rte. 970 south for 2 miles, continuing south on A570 for 7½ miles to **Arles.** Spend the afternoon touring the Roman ruins, the museums, and the necropolis, then stay here overnight.

Day 5 Leave Arles along D17, driving north for 6½ miles to **Fontvieille.** The morning is a tribute to the author Alphonse Daudet. Begin by touring the Château de Montauban, a museum in his honor, and the Moulin de Daudet, the windmill that inspired his *Lettres de Mon Moulin.* Also view the Roman aqueducts. Then head 5 miles west on Rte. 17 to **Les Baux,** where you can contrast the buildings of the living village with the ruins of the ghost village. Drive on to **St-Rémy-de-Provence,** 6 miles north along the road marked ST-RÉMY, to spend the night.

Day 6 In the morning, tour St-Rémy's Roman monuments and Musée Archéologique, then stroll the streets, admiring its historic buildings. A 10-mile drive east along Rte. 99 brings you to **Cavaillon,** where you'll spend the afternoon and night. A tour of the town can include the vegetable markets, the reconstructed 1st-century A.D. Roman arch, the medieval Chapelle St-Jacques, the Musée Archéologique, and the 18th-century synagogue housing a small Jewish museum.

Day 7 Drive to **Gordes,** taking D2 north for 10 miles. Visit the 12th-century Château de Gordes, home to the Musée Didactique Vasarély; Frédérique Duran's Moulin des Bouillons, with its Museum of Stained Glass; and the mysterious Village des Bories or the isolated Cistercian Abbaye de Sénanque. Then take the route de Roussillon 10 miles east to **Roussillon,** where you can admire the scenic village and the Giants' Causeway, before continuing along the route de Bonnieux for 7 miles south to **Bonnieux.** Follow Rte. 36 for 7½ miles to the intersection with Rte. 943 and continue on that road 6 miles south, past the grave of Albert Camus, to Cadenet. Here transfer to Rte. 543 south and drive 10 miles to Lignane, where a 4-mile drive southeast on Rte. 7 will lead into **Aix-en-Provence,** your destination for the night.

Day 8 Explore Aix, admiring the countryside that inspired Cézanne and Old Aix, as well as tour the Musée Granet. Spend a second night.

Day 9 Take A8 south for 17 miles to **Marseille,** where you can spend the day exploring the many sights, including its churches and museums. Stay here for the night.

Day 10 Drive to **Toulon,** taking A50 east for 42 miles. You can spend the night here after a day of seeing the Musée de l'Histoire Naturelle and the Musée de Toulon. Or you can boat to the **Iles d'Hyères** for an overnight stop.

Day 11 You'll need a full day if you want to explore the **Grand Canyon du Verdon.** The Verdon River, a tributary of the Durance, has cut Europe's biggest canyon into a limestone plateau. The canyon covers a distance of 13 miles east to west and is one of the most spectacular natural sights in France. Once you get there, for safety reasons it's best to go on guided hikes.

1 Orange

409 miles (658.22km) S of Paris, 34 (54.72km) miles NE of Nîmes, 16 miles (25.75km) S of Avignon

Orange gets its name from the days when it was a dependency of the Dutch House of Orange-Nassau, not because it's set in a citrus belt. Actually, the last orange grove departed 2,000 years ago. The juice that flows in Orange today comes from its fabled vineyards, which turn out a Côtes du Rhône vintage, and many *caves* are spread throughout the district, some of which offer *dégustations* to paying customers. The tourist office (see "Essentials," below) will provide you with a list.

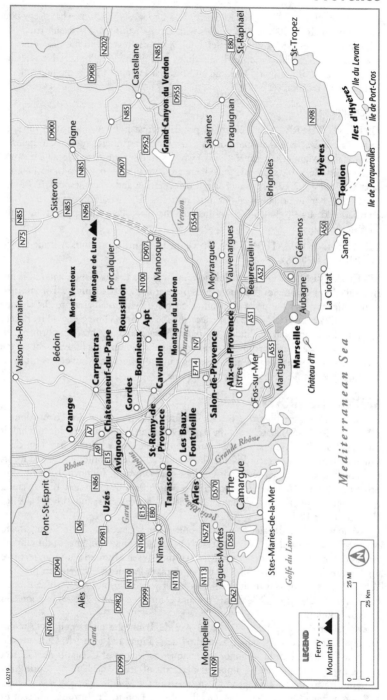

Mediterranean Sea

Golfe du Lion

LEGEND
Ferry
Mountain

113

E-0219

Overlooking the Valley of the Rhône, today's Orange, with a somewhat sleepy population of about 30,000, tempts visitors with Europe's third-largest extant triumphal arch and best-preserved Roman theater. Louis XIV, who toyed with the idea of moving the theater to Versailles, said, "It is the finest wall in my kingdom." UNESCO has placed the arch on its World Cultural and Natural Heritage List in the hopes that it can be preserved "forever."

ESSENTIALS

GETTING THERE Some 20 trains per day arrive from Avignon (trip time: 17 mins.); a one-way fare is around 36F ($6.10). From Paris there are 14 TGV trains to Valence and Avignon (trip time: 4½ hrs.) where you can transfer to a local; a one-way fare is 410F ($69.70). From Marseille there are 14 trains per day (trip time: 1½ hrs.); fares are 130F ($22.10) one-way. For **rail information** and schedules, call ☎ 08-36-35-35-35. For information about bus routes and schedules, contact the **Gare Routière** (☎ 04-90-34-15-59), located on the place Pourtoules, just behind the Théâtre Antique.

VISITOR INFORMATION The **Office de Tourisme** is on cours Aristide-Briand (☎ 04-90-34-70-88).

SPECIAL EVENTS From mid-July to mid-August, a drama, dance, and music festival called **Les Chorégies d'Orange** takes place at the Théâtre Antique. For information or tickets, visit the permanent office on place Sylvain, adjacent to the antique theater; call ☎ 04-90-34-24-24; or check the Net at **www.choregies.asso.fr**. Recent opera performances have included *Turandot, Norma,* and a concert performance of *Tristan und Isolde* (there are only six operas during the month-long festival). Part of the excitement of this particular festival is seeing musical events staged in one of the most historically evocative ancient theaters in Europe.

SEEING THE SIGHTS

In the southern part of town, the ✪ **Théâtre Antique,** place des Frères-Mounet (☎ 04-90-51-17-60), dates from the days of Augustus. Built into the side of a hill, it once held 8,000 spectators in tiered seats divided into three sections based on class. Carefully restored, the nearly 350-foot-long and 125-foot-high theater is noted for its fine acoustics and is used today for outdoor entertainment. It's open daily: April to September 9am to 6:30pm and October to March 9am to noon and 1:30 to 5pm. Admission is 30F ($5.10) for adults, 25F ($4.25) for students, and 10F ($1.70) for children under 18.

To the west of the theater once stood one of the biggest temples in Gaul, which, with a gymnasium and the theater, formed one of the greatest buildings in the empire. Across the street on place des Frères-Mounet, the **Musée Municipal d'Orange,** place du Théâtre-Antique (☎ 04-90-51-18-24), displays fragments excavated in the area. Your ticket to the ancient theater will also admit you to this museum, which is open daily: April to September 9:30am to 7pm and October to March 9:30am to noon and 1:30 to 5:30pm.

Even older than the theater is the ✪ **Arc de Triomphe** on avenue de l'Arc-de-Triomphe. It has decayed, but its sculptural decorations and other elements are still fairly well preserved. Built to honor the conquering legions of Caesar, it rises 72 feet and is nearly 70 feet wide. Composed of a trio of arches held up by Corinthian columns, it was used as a dungeon for prisoners in the Middle Ages.

Before leaving Orange, head for the hilltop park, **Colline St-Eutrope,** adjacent to the théâtre antique for a view of the surrounding valley with its mulberry plantations.

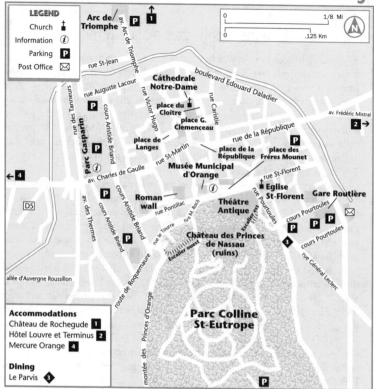

Orange

LEGEND
- ✝ Church
- ⓘ Information
- 🅿 Parking
- ✉ Post Office

WHERE TO STAY

Hôtel Louvre et Terminus. 89 av. Frédéric-Mistral, 84100 Orange. ☎ **04-90-34-10-08.** Fax 04-90-34-68-71. 32 units. A/C MINIBAR TV TEL. 280F–420F ($47.60–$71.40) double; 450F ($76.50) suite. AE, DC, MC, V. Parking 30F ($5.10) in garage.

Surrounded by a garden terrace, this conservatively decorated Logis de France offers good value in a much-renovated building begun around 1900. Don't expect grandeur: everything is simple, efficient, and rather brusque. The hotel also has a modest but worthy restaurant, serving meals daily at both lunch and dinner. Set-price menus cost from 88F to 135F ($14.95 to $22.95). Bedrooms, ranging from small to medium in size, have all the basic necessities, plus fine mattresses on the beds, most often doubles or twins. Each unit comes with a small private bathroom in tile, each containing a shower stall and hair dryer.

Mercure Orange. 80 Rte. de Caderousse, 84100 Orange. ☎ **04-90-34-24-10.** Fax 04-90-34-85-48. 99 units. MINIBAR TV TEL. 480F–620F ($81.60–$105.40) double. AE, DC, MC, V. Drive half a mile west of Orange's center, following the directions to Caderousse. Free parking.

This comfortable modern hotel lies about a mile west of the edge of the city, in a 20-year-old building whose wings curve around a landscaped courtyard. Its well-furnished rooms are arranged around a series of gardens, the largest of which contains a pool. Fixed-price menus are served in the poolside restaurant. This is your best bet for general overnight comfort far from the madding crowd. It was completely renovated in 1999, with an upgrade of many of the bedrooms and mattresses. Bathrooms are small but efficiently organized with shower/tub combinations.

Driving Les Routes de la Lavande

As characteristic of Provence as heather is of the Yorkshire moors, lavender has played a major role here for hundreds of years. When it was part of the Roman Empire, Provence produced the flowers to scent the public baths. In the Middle Ages, villages burnt piles of the plant in the streets, the prevalent medical theory being that disease was spread by vapors in the air. But it was during the Renaissance that the current industry took root, linked to the Médicis, who padded their wealth with a brisk trade in the distillation of the flower's essential oils. Today lavender production and distillation are more than just trades—they're a way of life for many families.

The heart of lavender production lies in Provençal fields stretching from the foothills of the Vercors mountains to the Verdon canyons and from Buech to the Luberon range. Plants grown and distilled in this area are sold under the Haute-Provence label, renowned for its quality. A drive through the region is most scenic just before the midsummer harvest, when the countryside is a purplish hue from the blossoms of the lavender plants, spread out in seemingly endless rows to the horizon. You can not only take in the sight and scent of the flowers but also tour the distilleries and farms. Some of these facilities are open only during summer, when the year's harvest is undergoing distillation. Those that are open all year offer tours. They also sell the plants themselves as well as the essential oils and dried flowers of the plant (used in Provençal cooking), perfumes, honey, and herbal teas.

One of the best places to visit lavender farms and distilleries is **Nyons,** 26 miles northeast of Orange. From Orange, take A7 northwest for 1¾ miles to Rte. 976 and drive northeast for 8 miles to St-Cécile-les-Vignes, where the road becomes Rte. 576. Continue northeast for 3¾ miles to Tulette, turn right onto Rte. 94, and go 13½ miles northeast to Nyons. Stop at the **Office de Tourisme,** place Libération (☎ **04-75-26-10-35**), to pick up the brochure *Les Routes de la Lavande,* offering a brief explanation and history of lavender production and a map of the region and its production facilities, with addresses, phone numbers, and hours.

On the outskirts of Nyons, start out at the **Jardin des Arômes (Garden of Scents),** promenade de la Digue (☎ **04-75-26-04-30**), with its collection of

WHERE TO DINE

Le Parvis. 3 cours Pourtoules. ☎ **04-90-34-82-00.** Reservations required. Main courses 65F–110F ($11.05–$18.70); fixed-price menus 105F–256F ($17.85–$43.50). AE, DC, MC, V. Tues–Sun noon–2:30pm and Tues–Sat 7–9:30pm, Sun noon–2:30pm. Closed Nov 1–15. FRENCH.

Jean-Michel Berengier sets the best table in Orange, though the dining room is rather austere. He bases his cuisine not only on well-selected vegetables but also on the best ingredients from "mountain or sea." Try his escalope of braised sea bass with fennel or feuilleté of asparagus, or his roasted sea bass with bacon and celeriac. A year-round can't-miss dish is the foie gras of the chef, which could be flavorfully followed by lamb whose preparation varies according to the season. (The staff prides itself on dozens of preparations.) The service is efficient and polite. A special children's menu is offered for 60F ($10.20).

WHERE TO STAY & DINE NEARBY

✪ **Château de Rochegude.** 26790 Rochegude. ☎ **04-75-97-21-10.** Fax 04-75-04-89-87. www.relaischateaux.fr/rochegude. 29 units. A/C MINIBAR TV TEL. 700F–1,850F ($119–$314.50) double; 2,050F–2,550F ($348.50–$433.50) suite. AE, DC, MC, V. Closed

aromatic plants and lavenders; it's open around the clock throughout the year and charges no admission. To reach it from Nyons, follow the road signs pointing to Gap. After viewing and enjoying the scent of the living plants in close proximity, go to **Bleu Provence,** 58 promenade de la Digue (☎ **04-75-26-10-42**), a family-owned distillery founded in 1926, for thyme, rosemary, lavender, and "every other spice that's Provençal." There's a shop on the premises where you can buy the essential oils, soaps, and unguents as well as staff that will take you on a guided English or French-language tour. If you walk around the premises on your own, the visit is free; to participate in the guided tours (duration is 45 minutes), the cost is 15F ($2.55) per person. It's open daily except Monday morning, from 9:30am to 12:15pm and 2:30 to 6:30pm (till 7pm between June and September).

In St-Nazaire-le-Desert, northeast of Nyons, you can visit **Gérard Blache,** in the village center next to the Auberge du Desert (☎ **04-75-27-51-08**), place de la Fontaine, a shop that sells all things lavender in July and August, daily from 10am to 7:30pm. From here, head southeast to Rosans, where the distillery of the **Cooperative des Producteurs de Lavande des Alpes (Lavender Cooperative of the Alps),** on D94 west of Rosans (☎ **04-92-66-60-30**), offers short guided tours and sales of essential oils from mid-June to August, daily from 10am to noon and 2 to 6pm. Southwest of here is Buis-les-Baronnies, where the **Shop Bernard Laget,** in the village center on place aux Herbes (☎ **04-75-28-12-01**), includes lavender products among its medicinal and aromatic plants; it's open Tuesday to Sunday from 9:30am to noon and 3:30 to 7pm. Finally, head southeast of Buis to Savoillan, where the **Ferme St-Agricole (St. Agricol Farm)** (☎ **04-75-28-86-57**) boasts botanical paths leading through an experimental garden, a species preservation garden, and a greenhouse. Its shop sells lavender products. The farm is open daily: June 15 to September 15 from 10:30am to 1pm, and September 16 to June 14 from 10:30am to 1pm and 2 to 6pm. Admission is 20F ($3.40).

Jan–Feb. It lies 8 miles north of Orange; take D976, following the signs toward Gap and Rochegude. Free parking.

This Relais & Châteaux stands on 25 acres of parkland. The stone castle is at the edge of a hill, surrounded by Rhône vineyards. Throughout its history this 12th-century turreted residence has been renovated by a series of distinguished owners, ranging from the pope to the dauphin. The current owners have made many 20th-century additions, but ancient touches still survive. Each room is done in a traditional Provençal style, with fabrics and furniture influenced by that region's 18th- and 19th-century traditions. As befits a château, bedrooms come in many shapes and sizes, some quite spacious. Each has a sumptuous bed with quality mattresses, fine linen, and elegant fabrics. Bathrooms are tiled or clad in marble, each with thick towels and a shower/tub combination. The food and service are exceptional. You can enjoy meals surrounded by flowering plants in the stately dining room. There are also a barbecue by the pool and sunny terraces where refreshments are served. In the restaurant, fixed-price menus range from 200F to 600F ($34 to $102). This latter is for a dining experience richly accessorized with truffles.

Hostellerie Le Beffroi. Rue de l'Evèché, 84110 Vaison-la-Romaine. ☎ **04-90-36-04-71.**
Fax 04-90-36-24-78. 22 units. MINIBAR TV TEL. 410F–655F ($69.70–$111.35) double. AE,
DC, MC, V. Closed Feb 15–Mar 20 and Nov 10–Dec 21. Parking 40F ($6.80). From Orange,
drive 21 miles northeast, following the signs to Vaison-la-Romaine. The hotel is in Vaison's
medieval core (Cité Médiévale).

This charming 16th- and 17th-century hotel boasts ocher walls and original detailing
on the exterior, and flowered wallpaper, heavy ceiling beams, plaster detailing, and
fireplaces in the rustic interior. The elegantly furnished rooms display 19th-century
antiques. Bedrooms come in a variety of shapes and sizes, but each is fitted with a
quality mattress and fine linen on a comfortable French bed, most often doubles or
twins. Bathrooms are small but efficiently organized with adequate shelf space. There's
a garden with a view of the town where you can order meals under a giant fig tree;
fixed-price menus are 98F to 195F ($16.65 to $33.15). For your convenience, the
hotel, across from the chiseled fountain in the Haute-Ville sector, maintains a limited
number of parking spaces.

The town itself is worth exploring, for it contains some fascinating reminders of its
former Roman occupation, including Les Ruines Romaines, two areas that've been
excavated—the Quartier Puymin and Quartier Villasse.

2 Châteauneuf-du-Pape

417 miles (671.1km) S of Paris, 12 miles (19.31km) N of Avignon, 8 miles (12.87km) S of
Orange

Near Provence's north border, the **Château du Pape** was built as the Castelgandolfo,
the country seat of the French popes of Avignon, during the 14th-century reign of
Pope John XXII. Now in ruins, it overlooks the vast acres of vineyards that the popes
planted, the start of a regional industry that today produces some of the world's best
reds as well as an excellent white.

ESSENTIALS

GETTING THERE There's no rail station in Châteauneuf, so train passengers must
get off at Sorgues (4½ miles south) or Orange (8 miles north). For **rail information,**
call ☎ **08-36-35-35-35.** About three buses a day arrive from both towns. Buses from
Avignon are also a possibility. Bus passengers are deposited and retrieved in place de la
Bascule, behind Châteauneuf's post office. The tourist office (below) is the best source
for schedules and information about bus access.

VISITOR INFORMATION The **Office de Tourisme** is at place du Portail (☎ **04-
90-83-71-08**).

A SPECIAL EVENT Since the Middle Ages the annual **Fête de la Véraison** has
been held in early August. See below for details.

WINE LURE & LORE

What makes the local wines distinctive is the blending of 13 varieties of grapes, grown
on vines surrounded by stones that reflect heat onto them during the day and keep
them warm in the cool night. As a result, the wines produced in the district's vineyards
are among the most potent in France, with an alcohol content of at least 12.5% and,
in many instances, as high as 15%. The region played a central role in the initiation
of the Appellation d'Origine Contrôlée, France's strict quality-control system. This
was formed when the late Baron Le Roy de Boiseaumarie, the most distinguished of
the local vintners, initiated geographical boundaries and minimum standards for the
production of wines given the Châteauneuf-du-Pape label. In 1923, local producers

won exclusive rights to market their Côtes du Rhônes under that label, and thus paved the way for other regions to identify and protect their distinctive wines. You'll see a plaque devoted to his memory in the town's **place de la Renaissance.**

To learn about the town's wine-related lore, there are two major *associations de vignerons,* each representing a consortium of individually owned vineyards whose owners pool their marketing, advertising, and bottling programs. Open Monday to Friday from 8am to noon and 2 to 6pm, **Syndicat Reflets,** 2 chemin du Bois de la Ville (☎ **04-90-83-71-07**), represents six vintners, and **Prestige et Tradition,** 3 rue de la République (☎ **04-90-83-72-29**), represents 10. They offer *dégustations* and sales.

Another useful source is **La Vinothèque,** 9 rue de la République (☎ **04-90-83-74-01**). A sales and marketing outlet for Mme Carre, matriarch of the Comtes d'Argelas vineyards, it's open for wine tasting and sales daily from 9am to 7pm. On the premises is **La Boutique de la Vinothèque,** where wine accessories (corkscrews, racks, decanters) are sold.

TOURING & TASTING THE WINES

A map posted in the village square, **place du Portail** (but called **place de la Fontaine** by just about everyone), pinpoints 14 wineries open for touring and tasting. The best known is **Domaine de Mont-Redon,** on D68 about 3 miles north of the town center (☎ **04-90-83-72-75**). It offers samplings of recent vintages of red and white wines and sales of *eau-de-vie,* a clear grape liqueur produced in a limited batch of 2,000 bottles annually. A noteworthy competitor is **Clos des Papes,** avenue Le Bienheureux Pierre de Luxembourg, in the town center (☎ **04-90-83-70-13**), where humidified cellars produce what many connoisseurs consider the region's best wine. Both establishments prefer advance notice before your arrival.

The town's only museum devotes all its exhibition space to wine making. The **Musée des Vieux Outils de Vignerons** of the **Caves du Père-Anselme,** avenue Le Bienheureux Pierre de Luxembourg (☎ **04-90-83-70-07**), contains the history and artifacts of local wine production, including a 16th-century winepress, wine makers' tools, barrel-making equipment, and a tasting cellar. It's open daily: mid-June to mid-September from 9am to 7pm and the rest of the year from 9am to noon and 2 to 6pm. Admission and tastings are free.

A WINE FESTIVAL   During 3 days in early August the village hosts the annual **Fête de la Véraison,** a medieval fair. It includes tasting stalls set up by local wine makers, actors impersonating Provençaux troubadours, bear-baiters (who are much kinder to their animals than their medieval counterparts), falconers with their birds, lots of merchants selling locally made handcrafts, battered flea market kiosks, and food. Don't expect dancing—what you'll get is a festival where the antique fountain on place du Portail spurts out wine, and vast amounts of that beverage are consumed. If you attend, you can drink all the wine you want for the price of a *verre de la Véraison.* This souvenir glass, filled on demand at any vintner who participates, costs 16F ($2.70) and is sold at strategically positioned kiosks around town.

WINE FOR CHOCOLATES

One of the newest industries in Châteauneuf is the **Chocolaterie Castelain,** whose factories and showrooms lie on the Route d'Avignon (☎ **04-90-83-54-71**), about 2 miles south of town. They've become known for a popular type of black chocolate (*la ganache*) flavored with a distilled version (*vieu marc de Châteauneuf*) of the red wine produced in local vineyards. The brand name of their chocolates is **Palet des Pâpes.** The chocolates taste extremely good when consumed with any of the local vintages.

WHERE TO STAY

✪ **Hostellerie du Château des Fines-Roches.** Rte. d'Avignon, 84230 Châteauneuf-du-Pape. ☎ **04-90-83-70-23.** Fax 04-90-83-78-42. 6 units. A/C MINIBAR TV TEL. 750F–950F ($127.50–$161.50) double. AE, MC, V. From the center of town, drive 2 miles south, following the signs to Avignon.

This medieval-inspired manor house was built late in the 19th century by local landowners. Named for the smooth rocks *(fines roches)* found in the soil of the nearby vineyards, the château devotes its huge cellars to the storage of thousands of bottles of local wines. The guest rooms on the upper floors of this charming hotel were renovated in 1997 and include Provençal styling with a scattering of antiques. Each bedroom comes with a quality mattress and fine linen plus a small but well-organized bathroom with shower/tub combination.

A meal in the restaurant is highly recommended. Menu items, carefully crafted and flavorful, include filets of red mullet prepared with aromatic herbs and garnished with its own liver marinated in vinaigrette, barigoule of crayfish tails with artichokes, filet of bull from the Camargue marinated in a particular vintage *(syrah)* of strong red wine, and roast rack of local lamb with a gratin of eggplant and sheep's cheese. Fixed-price menus are 210F to 340F ($35.70 to $57.80) and main courses are 95F to 160F ($16.15 to $27.20). The wine list focuses on local vintages, particularly those from the village. Between mid-June and September it's closed Monday at lunch; the rest of the year it's closed Sunday night and all day Monday.

WHERE TO DINE

La Mère Germaine. Place de la Fontaine, 84230 Châteauneuf-du-Pape. ☎ **04-90-83-54-37.** Fax 04-90-83-50-27. Reservations recommended. In the bistro, platters 69F–125F ($11.75–$21.25); in the restaurant, set-price menus 155F–380F ($26.35–$64.60). AE, DC, MC, V. Thurs–Tues noon–2:30pm and 7–9:30pm. PROVENÇALE.

Named after the matriarch who established this place several generations ago, this restaurant contains both a restaurant gastronomique and a simple bistro. Both enjoy sweeping panoramas from terraces where tables are set out in the summer months. Cuisine in both establishments is based on the traditions of Provence. In the bistro, you're likely to find simple platters of grilled fish, stews, casseroles, and grilled meats, but in the restaurant, cuisine is more elaborate, intricate, and tuned to the seasons. Dishes in the restaurant include zucchini flowers stuffed with mushrooms and drizzled with ratatouille juice, roasted rabbit stuffed with black-olive tapenade and fresh tomatoes, filet of turbot with *barigoule* (Provençal vinaigrette), and crispy rack of lamb scented with herbs from the surrounding *garrigue* (scrubland). Of special interest is the 380F ($64.60) *menu dégustation,* with each course accompanied by an appropriate wine or liqueur from Châteauneuf.

Eight simple, well-scrubbed bedrooms on the premises rent for 290F to 320F ($49.30 to $54.40) each. None has a TV, phone, or elaborate amenities, but for a comfortable sojourn after a meal in the restaurant, they offer good value and a sense of comfort and efficiency.

3 Avignon

425 miles (683.97km) S of Paris, 50 miles (80.47km) NW of Aix-en-Provence, 66 miles (106.22km) NW of Marseille

In the 14th century Avignon was the capital of Christendom—the popes lived here instead of in Rome. The legacy left by their "court of splendor and magnificence" makes Avignon one of the most interesting and beautiful of Europe's medieval cities.

In case you want to see the world.

At American Express, we're here to make your journey a smooth one. So we have over 1,700 travel service locations in over 130 countries ready to help. What else would you expect from the world's largest travel agency?

do more

Travel

Call 1 800 AXP-3429 or visit
www.americanexpress.com/travel

In case you want to be welcomed there.

We're here to see that you're always welcomed at establishments everywhere. That's why millions of people carry the American Express® Card – for peace of mind, confidence, and security, around the world or just around the corner.

do more

Cards

In case you're running low.

We're here to help with more than 190,000 Express Cash locations around the world. In order to enroll, just call American Express at 1 800 CASH-NOW before you start your vacation.

do more

Express Cash

And in case you'd rather be safe than sorry.

We're here with American Express® Travelers Cheques. They're the safe way to carry money on your vacation, because if they're ever lost or stolen you can get a refund, practically anywhere or anytime. To find the nearest place to buy Travelers Cheques, call 1 800 495-1153. Another way we help you do more.

do more

Travelers Cheques

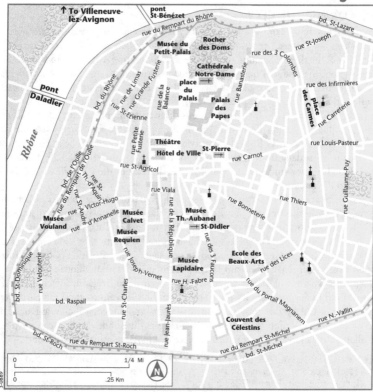

The popes are long gone, but life goes on exceedingly well. Today this walled city of some 100,000 residents reaches its peak celebration time during the famous **Festival d'Avignon,** a 3-week stint of music, art, and theater when bacchanalia reigns in the streets (see "Special Events" below). Avignon at any time of the year is a major stopover on the route from Paris to the Mediterranean. Lately, it has become well known as a cultural center. Artists and painters in increasing numbers have been moving here. Experimental theaters, painting galleries, and art cinemas have brought diversity to the inner city, especially rue des Teinturiers.

ESSENTIALS

GETTING THERE   Avignon is a junction for bus routes throughout the region, and train service from other towns is frequent. The TGV trains from Paris arrive at the Gare SNCF, on the Bd. Saint-Roche, 21 times per day (trip time: 3½ hrs.), and 12 trains per day arrive from Marseille (trip time: 1½ hrs.). For **rail information** and schedules, call ☎ **08-36-35-35-35.** For information about bus arrivals in Avignon, contact the **Gare Routière,** bd. St-Michel (☎ 04-90-82-07-35).

VISITOR INFORMATION   The **Office de Tourisme** is at 41 cours Jean-Jaurès (☎ **04-90-82-65-11**).

SPECIAL EVENTS   The 3-week **Festival d'Avignon** takes place in July. For information about dates, tickets, and special events for the year 2000, contact the **Bureaux du Festival,** 8 bis rue de Mons, 84000 Avignon (☎ **04-90-27-66-50**).

EXPLORING THE CITY

Even more famous than the papal residency is the French nursery ditty *"Sur le pont d'Avignon, l'on y danse, l'on y danse."* Ironically, pont St-Bénézet was far too narrow for the *danse* of the rhyme. Spanning the Rhône and connecting Avignon with Villeneuve-lèz-Avignon, the bridge is now only a fragmented ruin, with only four of its original 22 arches still extant. According to legend, the vision of a shepherd named Bénézet, while tending his flock, inspired its construction. Actually, the bridge was built between 1117 and 1185. It suffered various disasters from then on. In 1669, half the bridge toppled into the river. On one of the piers is the two-story **Chapelle St-Nicolas**—one story is in Romanesque style, the other in Gothic. The remains of the bridge are open daily from 9am to 6:30pm. Admission costs 18F ($3.05) for adults and 9F ($1.55) for students and children. The interior of the Chapelle-St-Nicolas is closed to the public.

It's worth at least an hour to walk through the **Quartier de La Balance,** where the Gypsies lived in the 1800s. Over the years La Balance had grown seedy, but since the 1970s major renovations have taken place. Start at place du Palais, going along rue de La Balance, detouring, if possible, into the historically evocative rue de la Grande Fusterie and the rue des Grottes. The main interest here is the restoration of the old town houses with their renewed elegant facades, many graced with mullioned windows. In the district are some of the ramparts that used to surround Avignon, stretching for 2¾ miles. Built in the 14th century by the popes, in the 19th century these ramparts were partially restored by that busy restorer of medieval monuments, Viollet-le-Duc. The most intriguing section is along rue du Rempart-du-Rhône, leading east to place Crillon. After a look, you can return to place de l'Horloge via rue St-Etienne.

✪ **Palais des Papes.** Place du Palais. ☎ **04-90-27-50-74.** Admission 45F ($7.65) adults; 36F ($6.10) students, children, and seniors. A 10F ($1.70) supplement is charged when there is a special exhibition. Tours: 45F ($7.65) adults, 36F ($6.10) children and students. Apr–Oct, daily 9am–7pm; Nov to mid-March, daily 9:30am–5:45pm. Last 2 weeks of March, daily 9:30am–6:30pm.

Dominating Avignon from a hill is one of the most famous (and/or notorious, depending on your point of view) palaces in the Christian world. Headquarters of a schismatic group of cardinals who came close to toppling the authority of the popes in Rome, it is part fortress, part showplace. It all began in 1309, when Pope Clement V fled to Avignon to escape political infighting in Rome. His successor, John XXII chose to stay in Avignon. The third Avignon pope, Benedict XII, was the one responsible for the construction of this magnificent palace. Avignon became, for a time, the Vatican of the north. During the period, dubbed "the Babylonian Captivity" by Rome, the popes held extravagant court in the palace; art and culture flourished—and so did prostitution and vice. When Gregory XI was persuaded to return to Rome in 1376, Avignon proceeded to elect its own rival pope, and the Great Schism split the Christian world. The real struggle, of course was about the wealth and power of the papacy. The reign of popes in Rome and antipopes in Avignon finally ended in 1417 with the election of Martin V, and the papal court here was disbanded.

The **Chapelle St-Jean** is known for its beautiful frescoes, attributed to the school of Matteo Giovanetti, and painted between 1345 and 1348. The frescoes present scenes from the life of John the Baptist and John the Evangelist. More Giovanetti frescoes can be seen above the Chapelle St-Jean in the **Chapelle St-Martial.** The frescoes here depict the miracles of St. Martial, patron saint of Limousin.

The **Grand Tinel (Banquet Hall)** is about 135 feet long and 30 feet wide, and the pope's table stood on the southern side. The pope's bedroom is on the first floor of the Tour des Anges. Its walls are entirely decorated in tempera with foliage on which birds

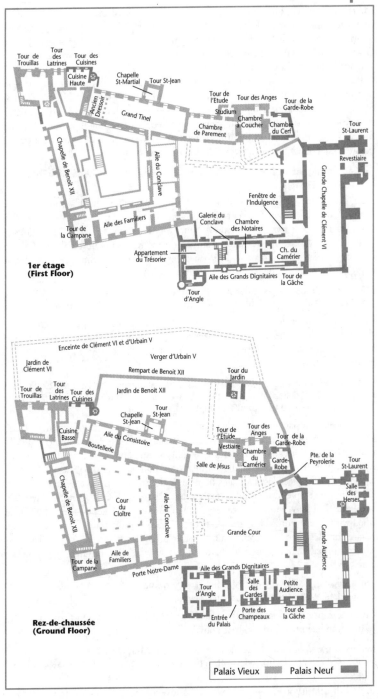

1er étage (First Floor)

Tour de Trouillas
Tour des Latrines
Tour des Cuisines
Cuisine Haute
Chapelle St-Martial
Tour St-Jean
Ancien Dressoir
Grand Tinel
Tour de l'Étude
Tour des Anges
Tour de la Garde-Robe
Studium
Chambre à Coucher
Chambre du Cerf
Tour St-Laurent
Chambre de Parement
Revestiaire
Chapelle de Benoît XII
Aile du Conclave
Grande Chapelle de Clément VI
Fenêtre de l'Indulgence
Galerie du Conclave
Chambre des Notaires
Tour de la Campane
Aile des Familiers
Appartement du Trésorier
Ch. du Camérier
Aile des Grands Dignitaires
Tour de la Gâche
Tour d'Angle

Rez-de-chaussée (Ground Floor)

Enceinte de Clément VI et d'Urbain V
Verger d'Urbain V
Jardin de Clément VI
Rempart de Benoît XII
Tour du Jardin
Tour de Trouillas
Tour des Latrines
Tour des Cuisines
Jardin de Benoît XII
Chapelle St-Jean
Tour St-Jean
Cuisine Basse
Aile du Consistoire
Boutellerie
Tour de l'Étude
Tour des Anges
Tour de la Garde-Robe
Vestiaire
Chambre du Camérier
Salle de Jésus
Garde-Robe
Pte. de la Peyrolerie
Tour St-Laurent
Chapelle de Benoît XII
Cour du Cloître
Aile du Conclave
Salle des Herses
Grande Cour
Grande Audience
Tour de la Campane
Aile de Familiers
Porte Notre-Dame
Aile des Grands Dignitaires
Tour d'Angle
Salle des Gardes
Petite Audience
Entrée du Palais
Porte des Champeaux
Tour de la Gâche

Palais Vieux   Palais Neuf

and squirrels perch; birdcages are painted in the recesses of the windows. In a secular vein, the **Studium (Stag Room)**—study of Clement VI—was frescoed in 1343 with hunting scenes. Added under the same Clement, who had a taste for grandeur, the **Grande Audience (Great Audience Hall)** contains frescoes of the prophets; these are also attributed to Giovanetti, and were painted in 1352.

Between two and four French-language guided tours are offered every day at schedules that vary widely according to the season and day of the week. Tours usually last 50 minutes, and aside from the exceptions mentioned above, they are somewhat monotonous, since most of the rooms have been stripped of their once-legendary finery. Self-guided tours in English, using a pre-recorded tape cassette and a portable tape recorder, are available anytime during opening hours.

✪ **Cathédrale Notre-Dame des Doms.** Place du Palais. ☎ **04-90-86-81-01.** Admission free. Daily 11am–6pm.

Near the palace is the 12th-century cathedral, containing the Flamboyant Gothic tomb of some of the apostate popes. Crowning the top is a gilded statue of the Virgin from the 19th century. The cathedral's hours vary according to whatever religious ceremony is scheduled, but generally it's open during the hours noted above. From the cathedral, enter the promenade du Rocher-des-Doms to stroll through its garden and enjoy the view across the Rhône to Villeneuve-lèz-Avignon.

Musée Calvet. 65 rue Joseph-Vernet. ☎ **04-90-86-33-84.** Admission 30F ($5.10) adults, 15F ($2.55) children. June–Sept, Wed–Mon 10am–7pm; Oct–May 10am–1pm and 2–6pm.

An extensive collection of ancient silver is housed in this lovely 18th-century neo-classical mansion. The museum displays works of Vernet, David, Corot, Manet, and Soutine. Our favorite oil is by Brueghel the Younger, *Le Cortège nuptial (The Bridal Procession).*

✪ **La Foundation Angladon-Dubrujeaud.** 5 rue Laboureur. ☎ **04-90-82-29-03.** Admission 30F ($5.10) adults, 15F ($2.55) students and persons 12 to 18, free for children under 12. May–Sept, Wed–Sun 1–7pm; Oct–Apr, Wed–Sun 1–6pm.

This museum, opened in 1995, contains the magnificent art collection of Jacques Doucet, renowned Parisian haute couture designer and belle époque dandy and dilettante. Doucet cultivated a number of young artists, among them Picasso, Braque, Max Jacob, Marcel Duchamp, and Guillaume Apollinaire, and began to collect their early works. For decades, Doucet's heirs kept the treasure trove a relative secret and lived in quiet splendor amid canvases by Cézanne, Sisley, Derain, Degas, and Modigliani. Today you can wander through Doucet's former abode, which is also filled with rare antiques and art objects that include 16th-century Buddhas and Louis XVI chairs designed by Jacob. Doucet died in 1929 at the age of 76, his own fortune so diminished that his nephew paid for his funeral. But his rich legacy lives on here.

Musée Lapidaire. 18 rue de la République. ☎ **04-90-85-75-38.** Admission 10F ($1.70), children free. Wed–Mon 10am–1pm and 2–6pm.

An important collection of Gallo-Roman sculptures is displayed in this 17th-century Jesuit church. Enter at the address above.

Musée Louis-Vouland. 17 rue Victor-Hugo. ☎ **04-90-86-03-79.** Admission 20F ($3.40) adults, 10F ($1.70) students. June–Sept, Tues–Sat 10am–noon and 2–6pm; Oct–May, Tues–Sat 2–6pm.

In a 19th-century mansion opening onto a lovely garden, Avignon's treasure trove of lavish 17th- and 18th-century antiques and objets d'art is displayed. The collection includes Sèvres porcelain, the comtesse du Barry's tea set, great tapestries from

Aubusson and Gobelins, glittering chandeliers, and commodes to equal those at Versailles. Our favorites are the Louis XV inkpots with silver rats holding the lids.

Musée du Petit-Palais. Place du Palais. ☎ **04-90-86-44-58.** Admission 30F ($5.10) adults, 15F ($2.55) students and youths 12 to 18, free for children 11 and under. Daily 9:30am–noon and 2–6pm.

This was the bishop's palace where the first two Avignon popes lived until Benedict XII constructed Palais des Papes. It holds an important collection of paintings from the Italian schools of the 13th to the 16th centuries, including works from Florence, Venice, Siena, and Lombardy. In addition, salons display 15th-century paintings done in Avignon, and several galleries are devoted to Roman and Gothic sculptures.

Musée Requien. 61 rue Joseph-Vernet. ☎ **04-90-82-43-51.** Admission free. Tues–Sat 9am–noon and 2–6pm.

This tiny natural history museum holds the very personal displays (on local geology, botany, natural history, and zoology) of Avignon-born naturalist Esprit Requien.

SEEING VILLENEUVE-LÉZ-AVIGNON

The modern world is impinging on Avignon, but across the Rhône at Villeneuve-lèz-Avignon the Middle Ages slumber on. When the popes lived in exile at Avignon, wealthy cardinals built palaces (*livrées*) across the river. Crowning the town is the **Fort St-André,** Mont Andaon (☎ **04-90-25-45-35**), founded in 1360 by Jean-le-Bon to serve as a symbol of might to the pontifical powers across the river. The Abbaye St-André, now privately owned, was installed in the 18th century. You can visit the tranquil formal garden encircling the mansion, with its rose-trellis colonnade, fountains, and flowers. It's open daily: April to September, 10am to 12:30pm and 2 to 6pm; from October to March, it closes at 5pm. Entrance costs 25F ($4.25) for adults, 15F ($2.55) for ages 12 to 25; free for children under 12.

Many visitors prefer to stay or dine here rather than in Avignon (see our recommendations below). For additional information, contact the **Office de Tourisme,** place Charles-David (☎ **04-90-25-61-33**).

Chartreuse du Val-de-Bénédiction. 60 rue de la République. ☎ **04-90-15-24-24.** Admission 32F ($5.45) adults, 21F ($3.55) children 12–17, and free for children 11 and under. Daily 9am–6:30pm.

France's largest Carthusian monastery (or charterhouse), and once the country's most powerful, was built in 1352. The complex contains a church, three cloisters, and rows of cells that housed the medieval monks. The Centre National d'Ecritures et du Spectacle that now occupies the premises offers artists and writers the opportunity to live and work rent-free in the monastic cells for up to a year. Exhibitions of photography and painting are presented throughout the year.

Pope Innocent VI, whose tomb is here, founded this charterhouse. Don't miss the chapel that contains a remarkable *Coronation of the Virgin* by Enguerrand Charonton—the section of the 1453 masterpiece that depicts the denizens of hell is Bosch-like in its horror. The 12th-century graveyard cloister is lined with cells where the former fathers prayed and meditated.

Tour Philippe le Bel. Rue Montée-de-la-Tour (at av. Gabriel-Péri). ☎ **04-90-27-49-68.** Admission 10F ($1.70) adults, 6F ($1) students and ages 12 to 17, free for children under 12. Mid-June to mid-Sept, daily 10am–12:30pm and 3–7pm; Apr–May and mid-Sept to Oct 1, same hours but closed Mon. Oct–Jan and Mar, Tues–Sun 10am–noon and 2–5:30pm. Closed February.

Constructed by Philippe the Fair in the 13th century, when Villeneuve became a French possession, the tower served as a gateway to the kingdom. If you have the stamina, you can climb to the top for a panoramic view of Avignon and the Rhône Valley.

Eglise Notre-Dame. Place Meissonier. Admission to church free; to cloisters, 7F ($1.20) adults, 5F (85¢) students and ages 12 to 17. Same hours as the tower; see above.

One of the great French treasures is in this church, a 14th-century ivory Virgin. The church was founded in 1333 by Cardinal Arnaud de Via.

SHOPPING

Since the 1960s, **Antiquités Bourret,** 5 rue Linas (☎ 04-90-86-65-02), has earned a reputation as a repository for 18th- and 19th-century Provençal antiques. ✪ **Véronique Pichon,** place Crillon (☎ 04-90-85-89-00), is the newest branch of a porcelain manufacturer whose colorful products have been a regional fixture since the 1700s. Manufactured in the nearby town of Uzès, the tableware, decorative urns, statues, and lamps are priced well enough to be shipped virtually anywhere.

The Avignon branch of **Les Olivades,** 28 rue des Marchands (☎ 04-90-86-13-42), is part of the Pierre Deux chain. Look for fabrics by the yard, bedcovers, slip-covers, draperies, and tablecloths. The fabrics, printed in a factory only 6 miles from Avignon, tend to feature intricate designs in colors inspired by 19th-century models or Créole designs with butterflies, pineapples, bananas, and flowers.

The idea that launched ✪ **Les Indiens de Nîmes,** 4 rue du College-de-Roure (☎ 04-90-86-32-05), was the duplication of 18th- and 19th-century Provençal fabric patterns. Fabrics are sold by the meter as well as made into clothing. Available as well are kitchenware and a selection of furniture inspired by Provence. **Souleiado,** 5 rue Joseph-Vernet (☎ 04-90-86-47-67), also has Provençal-inspired clothing, mostly for women. The shop's name ("first ray of sunshine after a storm") evokes its spirit. Fabrics are also sold by the meter.

Hervé Baume, 19 rue Petite Fusterie (☎ 04-90-86-37-66), is for those who'd like to set a Provençal table. It's stocked with merchandise that ranges from Directoire dinner services to French folk art, including modern classics like handblown crystal hurricane lamps. If you're desperate for a potbellied tureen for your *aïgo boulido,* that regional garlic soup, head for **Terre è Provence,** 26 rue République (☎ 04-90-86-31-59). You can also pick up wonderful kitsch here—perhaps terra-cotta plates decorated with three-dimensional cicadas.

Jaffier-Parsi, 42 rue des Fourbisseurs (☎ 04-90-86-08-85), is known for its copper saucepans, shipped from the Norman town of Villedieu-les-Poèles, where they have been made since the Middle Ages.

WHERE TO STAY
VERY EXPENSIVE

✪ **La Mirande.** 4 place Amirande, 84000 Avignon. ☎ 04-90-85-93-93. Fax 04-90-86-26-85. www.la-mirande.fr. 20 units. A/C MINIBAR TV TEL. 1,700–2,400F ($289–$408) double; 3,200F ($544) suite. AE, DC, V.

In the heart of Avignon, behind the Palais des Papes, this restored 700-year-old town house is one of France's grand little luxuries, the best thing in town. The hotel treats you to two centuries of decorative art—from the 1700s Salon Chinois to the Salon Rouge, its striped walls in Rothschild red. In 1987, Achim and Hannelore Stein transformed the house into this citadel of opulence. The most sought-out room is no. 20, whose lavish decor opens directly onto the garden. But all the rooms are stunning— the exquisite taste of the decorators is reflected in every individually designed bedroom. Most are quite spacious. Rooms have bedside controls, hand-printed fabrics on the walls, antiques, and art, along with deluxe mattresses. Baths are sumptuous, with huge bathtubs, hair dryers, make-up mirrors, thick towels, and luxurious toiletries. The restaurant earns its one Michelin star—Chef Daniel Hébet has a light, sophisticated touch. Fixed-price menus are 210F to 480F ($35.70 to $81.60). The restaurant is open daily, June to September for both lunch and dinner. From October to May, it's closed Tuesday and Wednesday for lunch.

EXPENSIVE

✪ **Hôtel d'Europe.** 12 place Grillon, 84000 Avignon. ☎ **04-90-14-76-76.** Fax 04-90-85-43-66. www.hotel-d-europe.fr. E-mail: reservations@hotel-d-europe.fr. 47 units. A/C TV TEL. 660F–1,980F ($112.20–$336.60) double; 2,700F–3,000F ($459–$510) suite. AE, DC, MC, V. Parking 55F ($9.35).

The vine-covered Hôtel d'Europe has been in operation since 1799. You enter through a courtyard, where tables are set in the warmer months. The grand hall and salons boast tastefully arranged antiques. The good-size guest rooms have handsome decorations, period furnishings, and tile or marble bathrooms, shower/tub combinations, deluxe toiletries, thick towels, and hair dryers. Three suites perched on the roof have views of the Palais des Papes. In some twin-bedded rooms the beds are a bit narrow, but comfortable overall. The restaurant, La Vieille Fontaine, is one of the most distinguished in Avignon. Meals are served in elegant dining rooms or a charming inner courtyard. Set menus cost 230F to 400F ($39.10 to $68). The wine list is impressive but celestial in price.

MODERATE

Hôtel Bristol. 44 cours Jean-Jaurès, 84009 Avignon. ☎ **04-90-82-21-21.** Fax 04-90-86-22-72. 66 units. TV TEL. 550F–930F ($93.50–$158.10) double. Rates include breakfast. AE, DC, MC, V. Closed Feb 13–Mar 7. Parking 50F ($8.50).

In the center of Avignon, on one of the principal streets leading to the landmark place de l'Horloge and the Palais des Papes, the Bristol is one of the town's better bets. A traditional hotel, it offers comfortably furnished well-maintained rooms, most recently renovated in the early 1990s. Bedrooms are moderate in size, usually with twin beds fitted with quality mattresses. Three units are suitable for persons with disabilities. Bathrooms are compact and tiled, each with a hair dryer and a shower-and-tub combination. Breakfast is the only meal served. Though it's not the most atmospheric place in Avignon, it offers good, solid value in an expensive city.

Hôtel Cité-des-Papes. 1 rue Jean-Vilar, 84000 Avignon. ☎ **04-90-86-22-45.** Fax 04-90-27-39-21. 75 units. A/C MINIBAR TV TEL. 550F–595F ($93.50–$101.15) double. 3rd and 4th occupants 85F ($14.45) each. AE, DC, MC, V. Parking 47F ($8).

Nearly adjacent to the Palais des Papes, this five-story modern building offers bedrooms that offer solid comfort, though they are not particularly stylish. Views from many of its windows extend over the place de l'Horloge. Rooms were renovated in 1998. In 1999, its management added another dozen on the upper floors by taking over the premises of a next-door restaurant. Rooms have beds with good mattresses, plus tiled bathrooms with shower/tub combinations. The restaurant, La Table de Provence, is open daily for lunch and dinner.

Quality Hotel Cloître Saint-Louis. 20 rue Portail Boquier, 84000 Avignon. ☎ **04-90-27-55-55.** Fax 04-90-82-24-01. 80 units. TV TEL. 450F–860F ($76.50–$146.20) double; 820F–1,145F ($139.40–$194.65) suite. AE, MC, V.

This unusual hotel is in a former Jesuit school, built in the late 1580s. It's not far from the railroad station, and the venerable building has a grandly baroque facade, wraparound arcades, and soaring ceiling vaults. While public areas retain many original features, bedrooms are more functional. Their decor is rather dull and severe;

some have sliding glass doors overlooking the patio. A new wing has been added, designed by world-class architect Jean Nouvel, who is responsible for the new wing of the Institut du Monde Arabe in Paris. Rooms range from medium sized to spacious, with sleek modern lines and twin or double beds. Extras include automatic alarm clocks and private safes; bathrooms have shower/tub combinations or shower stalls. The staff is hardworking, and maintenance is tidy.

INEXPENSIVE

Hôtel d'Angleterre. 29 bd. Raspail, 84000 Avignon. ☎ **04-90-86-34-31.** Fax 04-90-86-86-74. 40 units, 35 with bath. TV TEL. 210F ($35.70) double without bath, 280F–330F ($47.60–$56.10) double with bath. DC, MC, V. Closed Dec 28–Jan 28. Free parking.

In the heart of Avignon, this art deco, circa 1929 structure is the city's best budget hotel. The rooms are comfortably but basically furnished with adequate mattresses and good-quality towels. Breakfast is the only meal served.

✪ **Hôtel Danieli.** 17 rue de la République, 84000 Avignon. ☎ **04-90-86-46-82.** Fax 04-90-27-09-24. www.avignonetprovence.com/fr/danieli. 29 units. TV TEL. 405F–455F ($68.85–$77.35) double. AE, DC, MC, V. Parking 45F ($7.65).

This hotel's Italian influence is clear in its arches, chiseled stone, tile floors, and baronial stone staircase. Built during the reign of Napoléon I, it's classified as a historic monument in its own right. Its small, informal public rooms are outfitted mostly in antiques acquired by the history-conscious owner. The guest rooms, however, have painted bamboo furnishings and acceptably comfortable mattresses. Tiled bathrooms are compact and efficiently organized, with shower stalls or shower/tub combinations. Hair dryers are available from the reception. Unless special arrangements are made for a group (and this hotel accepts many), breakfast is the only meal served.

Hôtel le Médiéval. 15 rue Petite Saunerie, 84000 Avignon. ☎ **04-90-86-11-06.** Fax 04-90-82-08-64. 35 units. TV TEL. 240F–350F ($40.80–$59.50) double. Extra bed 50F ($8.50). V.

About 3 blocks south of the Palais des Papes, this hotel is in a three-story town house from the late 1600s. It is clean, simple, and uncomplicated. Under beamed ceilings, most rooms are medium to spacious in size, each offering good comfort and generally large beds, each fitted with quality mattresses. The rooms that are the most quiet and peaceful overlook the small inner courtyard, with its pots of flowers and flowering shrubs. Others that overlook a congested medieval street corner might be a bit noisier, but are not without a rough-and-ready charm of their own. Bathrooms are tiled and a bit small but still have adequate shelf space, most with a shower/tub arrangement. Don't look for either a bar or a restaurant on the premises. There is no breakfast room; breakfast is served in the bedrooms.

WHERE TO DINE

✪ **Brunel.** 46 rue de La Balance. ☎ **04-90-85-24-83.** Reservations required. Main courses 140F–182F ($23.80–$30.95); fixed-price menus 170F–330F ($28.90–$56.10). MC, V. Tues–Sat noon–1:30pm and 7:30–9:30pm. PROVENÇAL.

In the historic heart of Avignon, this elegant, flower-filled, air-conditioned restaurant is managed by the Brunel family. It offers such specialties as warm pâté of duckling and breast of duckling with apples. The chef prepares a superb plate of ravioli stuffed with wild mushrooms served with roasted foie gras. Grilled John Dory is accompanied by artichoke hearts, and even the lowly pig's feet emerge with a sublime taste. Desserts are excellent and prepared fresh daily. House wines can be ordered by the carafe.

✪ **Christian Etienne.** 10 rue Mons. ☎ **04-90-86-16-50.** Reservations recommended. Main courses 140F–250F ($23.80–$42.50); fixed-price menus 170F–500F ($28.90–$85). AE,

DC, MC, V. July, daily noon–2:30pm and 8–10:30pm; the rest of the year, Tues–Sat noon–1:30pm and 7:30–9:30pm, Sat 8–10:30pm. PROVENÇALE.

The stone house containing this restaurant was built in 1180, around the same time as the Palais des Papes. The dining room contains early 15th-century frescoes honoring the marriage of Anne de Bretagne to the French king in 1491. Owner Christian Etienne is the star chef of Avignon; he continues to explore the depths of his culinary repertoire. Several of the fixed-price menus have specific themes: The two 300F ($51) menus feature tomatoes or vegetables; the 430F ($73.10) menu offers preparations of lobster; and the 500F ($85) menu relies on the chef's discretion *(menu confiance)* to come up with unusual combinations. Note for strict vegetarians: The vegetable menus are among the most creative of their kind but are flavored with small amounts of meat or fish or, sometimes, meat drippings. In summer, look for a vegetable menu where every course is based on ripe tomatoes—the main course is a mousse of lamb, eggplant, tomatoes, and herbs. À la carte specialties include filet of red snapper with a black-olive coulis, rack of lamb with fresh thyme and garlic essence, and a dessert specialty of fennel sorbet with saffron-flavored English cream sauce.

✪ **Hiély-Lucullus.** 5 rue de la République. ☎ **04-90-86-17-07.** Reservations required. Fixed-price menus 160F–220F ($27.20–$37.40). MC, V. Wed–Sun noon–1:30pm and Tues–Sun 7:30–9:30pm. Closed 2 weeks in July and 2 weeks in Jan. FRENCH.

This Relais Gourmand used to reign supreme in Avignon before the arrival of Christian Etienne. It's still going strong and richly deserves its star, even if it's no longer as trendy as it was. The town's fabled chef, Pierre Hiély, has retired, though he drops in occasionally to check on how his former sous chef, André Chaussy, is doing—he's doing just fine. Reasonably priced fixed-price menus are offered—no à la carte. The cuisine hasn't changed, but occasional creative touches are added. Try one of his special appetizers, like petite marmite du pêcheur, a savory fish soup ringed with black mussels. Main-dish specialties are *pintadeau* (young guinea hen) with peaches, and roasted salted cod fish with olive oil and juniper berries. The *pièce de résistance* is *agneau des Alpilles grillé* (grilled alpine lamb). Carafe wines include Tavel Rosé and Châteauneuf-du-Pape.

La Fourchette. 7 rue Racine. ☎ **04-90-85-20-93.** Fixed-price menus 110F–158F ($18.70–$26.85) at lunch, 158F ($26.85) at dinner. MC, V. Mon–Fri noon–2pm and 7:30–9:30pm. Closed Aug 5–29. FRENCH.

Creative cooking at a moderate price is offered here in two dining rooms, one like a summer house with walls of glass, the other a tavern with oak beams. You might begin with fresh sardines flavored with citrus, or a parfait of chicken livers with a spinach flan and a confiture of onions. For a main course we'd recommend the blanquette of monkfish with endives or daube of beef prepared in the local style with a gratin of macaroni.

Piedoie. 26 rue des Trois-Faucons. ☎ **04-90-86-51-53.** Reservations recommended. Main courses 80F–100F ($13.60–$17); set-price lunches 90F–180F ($15.30–$30.60); set-price dinners 120F–180F ($20.40–$30.60). MC, V. Thurs–Tues noon–2pm and 7–9:30pm. Closed 2 weeks in Feb and 2 weeks in Nov. FRENCH.

In an intimate, yellow-and-ochre-colored dining room behind the city ramparts, this place is the creative statement of its namesake, Thierry Piedoie, a chef who takes his food seriously. Menu items change with the seasons and availability of ingredients, but are likely to include a warm tartlet of asparagus tips and Serrano ham; a platter with smoked Scottish salmon, black Provençal olives, and herb salad; sweetbreads with glazed ginger and a confit of lemons; and filet of sole served with sesame seeds and grapefruit segments.

STAYING & DINING IN VILLENEUVE-LEZ-AVIGNON

Best Western La Magnaneraie. 37 rue Camp-Bataille, 30400 Villeneuve-lèz-Avignon. ☎ **04-90-25-11-11.** Fax 04-90-25-46-37. www.avignon-et-provence.com/la-magnaneraiebestwestern.fr. E-mail: magnaneraie@gulliver.fr. 28 units. A/C MINIBAR TV TEL. 500F–1,200F ($85–$204) double; 600F–1,800F ($102–$306) suite. AE, DC, MC, V.

One of the most charming accommodations in the region is this place on 2 acres of gardens, under the direction of Gérard and Eliane Prayal. Tastefully renovated and enlarged with a new wing in the 1980s, the place is furnished with antiques and good reproductions. The bedrooms, mostly medium size, have fine linens and quality mattresses. Baths are neatly arranged; most have a shower/tub combination and all have hair dryers. Many guests who arrive for only a night remain for many days to enjoy the good food and atmosphere, garden, tennis court, and landscaped pool. In 1993 the government rating of this inn was increased to four stars, based mostly on M. Prayal's excellent cuisine. His fixed-price menus range from 170F ($28.90) for a celebration of traditional Provençal recipes to 450F ($76.50) for a *menu dégustation.* Menu items may include zucchini flowers stuffed with mushroom-and-cream purée, feuilleté of foie gras and truffles, croustillant of red snapper with basil and olive oil, and rack of lamb with thyme. Dessert might be gratin of seasonal fruits with sabayon of lavender-flavored honey.

Hôtel de l'Atelier. 5 rue de la Foire, 30400 Villeneuve-lèz-Avignon. ☎ **04-90-25-01-84.** Fax 04-90-25-80-06. 19 units. TV TEL. 250F–460F ($42.50–$78.20) double. AE, DC, MC, V. Parking 25F ($4.25) in nearby garage, free on street.

Villeneuve's budget offering is this 16th-century village house that has preserved much of its original style. Inside is a tiny duplex lounge with a large stone fireplace. Outside, a sun-filled rear garden, with potted orange and fig trees, provides fruit for breakfast. The immaculate accommodations are comfortable and informal, but a bit dowdy. All are fitted with a comfortable French mattress. Bathrooms are small but nicely arranged, most with a shower/tub combination, and all equipped with hair dryers. In the old bourgeois dining room, a continental breakfast is the only meal served.

○ **Le Prieuré.** Place du Chapitre, 30400 Villeneuve-lèz-Avignon. ☎ **04-90-15-90-15.** Fax 04-90-25-45-39. www.relaischateaux.fr/leprieure. 36 units. A/C MINIBAR TV TEL. 570F–1,300F ($96.90–$221) double; 1,500F–1,800F ($255–$306) suite. AE, DC, MC, V. Free parking. Closed Nov–Mar.

This small, charming, well-managed property was built in 1322 as a cardinal's residence. Roger Mille purchased it in 1943 and three generations of his family have been running it. Adjacent to the village church, it has an ivy-covered stone exterior, green shutters, a tiled roof, and a series of rustic but plush public rooms. Bedrooms were renovated in mid-1990 in a cozy, well-upholstered, well-padded style. Rooms have comfortable mattresses, well-designed bathrooms, and plenty of thick towels.

   Dining/Diversions: The in-house restaurant is sought after for the excellence of its cuisine and its charm. Set menus cost from 200F to 480F ($34 to $81.60) each, and are served daily at both lunch and dinner. Advance reservations for non-residents are recommended. Between June and September, lunches, including an array of cold salads, are served on the terrace adjacent to the swimming pool at around 100F ($17) per main course.

STAYING & DINING NEARBY

○ **Auberge de Cassagne.** 450 allée de Cassagne, Rte. de Vèdene (D62), Le Pontet, 84130 Avignon. ☎ **04-90-31-04-18.** Fax 04-90-32-25-09. www.valruges-cassagne.com. E-mail: cassagne@wanadoo.fr. 35 units. A/C MINIBAR TV TEL. 590F–1,340F ($100.30–$227.80) double; from 1,180F ($200.60) suite. AE, DC, MC, V. Parking 20F ($3.40). Take N7 and D62 for 4 miles northeast.

This could be your best bet for food and lodging in the Avignon area. The hotel, set in a park, is an enchanting little Provençal inn with country-style rooms. Rooms have been recently renovated, with comfortable beds and roomy bathrooms that are handsomely maintained, each with a shower/tub combination, generous shelf space, deluxe toiletries, thick towels, and a hair dryer. The cuisine is exceptionally good, much of it in the style of Paul Bocuse. You can enjoy your meals in an elegantly rustic dining room or at a table in the garden. The kitchens feature dishes like a duo of turbot and salmon served with a ragout of mushrooms, foie gras braised in port wine, and tagliatelle with a confit of tomatoes and olive oil. The fixed-price meals, 195F to 480F ($33.15 to $81.60), are available to nonguests, and reservations are required. There's a swimming pool within the garden, plus a tennis court and a Jacuzzi.

✪ **Auberge de Noves.** 13550 Noves. ☎ **04-90-24-28-28.** Fax 04-90-90-16-92. www. aubergedenoves.com. E-mail: noves@relaischateaux.fr. 23 units. A/C MINIBAR TV TEL. 950F–1,650F ($161.50–$280.50) double; 1,700F–1,950F ($289–$331.50) suite. AE, DC, MC, V. Follow Rte. 571 for 10 miles southeast. Free parking.

This is an attractive and peaceful Relais & Châteaux that looks like a cross between a neoclassical villa on the Riviera and a vintage Beverly Hills mansion from the 1920s. After millions of francs of investment by the Lalleman family, it's one of the finest luxury country estates in Provence. Bedrooms are attractive and sunny, with antiques or good reproductions, comfortable mattresses, and plush bathroom amenities, including lots of thick towels. Some rooms have terraces, and most have exceptional views. On-site, within a pine-studded garden, there's a tennis court and a swimming pool.

The food is among the area's best, including herb-flavored *filet d'agneau* (lamb), chicken-liver mousse, superb sole, veal kidneys Printaneir, and rabbit in mustard sauce. From the first-class wine cellar come selections like Châteauneuf-du-Pape and Lirac. The restaurant doesn't serve lunch on Wednesday, and reservations are required. Fixed-price meals are 275F to 535F ($46.75 to $90.95).

Les Agassins. 52 av. Charles-de-Gaulle, Le Pigeonner, route d'Avignon, 84130 le Pontet. ☎ **04-90-32-42-91.** Fax 04-90-32-08-29. www.agassins.com. 26 units. A/C MINIBAR TV TEL. 890F–1,200F ($151.30–$204) double; 1,900F ($323) suite. AE, DC, MC, V. Free parking. Closed Jan to mid-Feb. Take the N7 for 3 miles NE of Avignon.

Part of the appeal of a stay here are the parks and breathtaking gardens of this Provençal manor house. It takes its name from the *agassins* (magpies) that used to be raised as a food source on the property during the Middle Ages. Although it has been much altered over the years, the original manor was built for Guillaume de Fargis, nephew of Pope Clement V. The hotel as you'll see it today dates from the early 1970s. Public areas are lavishly outfitted with antiques, balconies are usually ringed with flowers, floors are layered with gracefully worn terra-cotta tiles, and a collection of interesting paintings lines the walls. Bedrooms are beautifully decorated, with comfortable beds and mattresses; stone or tile-sheathed bathrooms have lots of thick towels. Most have a private balcony or terrace.

Dining/Diversions: The in-house restaurant, La Table des Agassins, is open daily for lunch and dinner between May and September. The rest of the year, it's closed only during Saturday lunch and all day Sunday. A set menu costs 220F ($37.40).

AVIGNON AFTER DARK

Near the Palais des Papes is **Le Grand Café,** La Manutention (☎ **04-90-86-86-77**), a restaurant/bar/cafe that might quickly become your favorite watering hole. For dancing, **Les Ambassadeurs,** 27 rue Bancasse (☎ **04-90-86-31-55**), is more animated than its more subdued competitor, **Piano Bar Le Blues,** 25 rue Carnot

(☎ **04-90-85-79-71**); the cover at both is 10F ($2). Near Le Blues is a restaurant, **Red Zone,** 27 rue Carnot (☎ **04-90-27-02-44**), whose bar area is the site of live performances from whatever techno-punk band happens to be in town.

Winning the award for having the most unpronounceable name is **Le Woolloomoolloo** (it means "Black Kangaroo" in an Aboriginal dialect of Australia), 16 bis rue des Teinturiers (☎ **04-90-85-28-44**). Here a bar and cafe complement a restaurant that serves both French cuisine and a changing roster of cuisines from Asia, Africa, and South America. Another option for late-night dancing and drinking is **Le Kiproko,** 22 bd. Lambert (☎ **04-90-82-68-69**), open Wednesday to Saturday after around 10:30pm. An alternative choice is **Bokao's Café,** 9 quai St-Lazare (☎ **04-90-82-47-95**), which offers both a restaurant and a disco as diversions during long sultry nights in Avignon.

For lesbians and gays, **L'Esclav,** 12 rue de Limas (☎ **04-90-85-14-91**), is a bar and disco that's the focal point of the city's gay community.

4 Uzès

424 miles (682.36km) S of Paris, 24 miles (38.62km) W of Avignon, 31½ miles (50.69km) NW of Arles

This scenically beautiful village is set on a limestone plateau that straddles the line between Provence and the Garrigues region. It is famous for the long-standing House of Uzès, home of France's highest-ranking ducal family, who still live in the ducal palace of Le Duché that dominates the town.

Jean Racine lived here in 1661, sent by his family to stay with an uncle, the vicar general of Uzès, in hopes that his dramatic ambitions might be dispelled. They weren't, and he went on to claim his place as one of France's great dramatists/poets. More recently, Uzès was the setting of Jean-Paul Rappeneau's version of *Cyrano de Bergerac,* in which Gérard Depardieu played the part of the soldier-poet.

In 1962, the village was named one of France's 500 *villes d'art* and has since taken good advantage of preservation funds set aside for restoration of its historic district. However, the designation has been viewed as a mixed blessing since many visitors, notably Parisians taking a break from city life, have discovered the charms of the village.

ESSENTIALS

GETTING THERE   There's no rail station in Uzès. Train passengers must get off at Avignon (a 45-min. bus ride) or Nîmes (a 35-min. bus ride). For **rail information** and schedules, call ☎ **08-36-35-35-35.** There are about eight buses a day from both places. For information, contact the **Gare Routière d'Uzès,** avenue de la Libération (☎ **04-66-22-00-58**).

VISITOR INFORMATION   The **Office de Tourisme** is on place Albert-1er (☎ **04-66-22-68-88**).

SEEING THE SIGHTS

In the old part of town, every building is worth a moment or two of consideration. A pleasant square for a stroll, the asymmetrical **place aux Herbes** is defined by the medieval homes and sheltered walkways along its edges. The **Cathédrale St-Théodorit,** place de l'Evêché (☎ **04-66-22-13-26**), still utilizes its original 17th-century organ, a remarkable instrument composed of 2,772 pipes. The cathedral is open daily from 9am to 6:30pm. If you're lucky enough to be here during the last 2 weeks of July, you can attend one of the organ concerts that highlight the **Nuits Musicales d'Uzès** festival.

Adjacent is the circular six-story **Tour Fenestrelle,** all that remains of the original 12th-century cathedral that was burnt by the Huguenots. It's closed to the public.

Le Duché. Place du Duché. ☎ **04-66-22-18-96.** Admission 50F ($8.50) adults, 35F ($5.95) students and teens 12 to 16, 20F ($3.40) children 7 to 11, free for children 10 and under. The complex is open daily: June–Sept, daily 10am–6:30pm; Oct–May, daily 10am–noon and 2–6pm.

The palace is in a massive conglomeration of styles, the result of nearly continuous expansion of the residence in direct correlation to the rising wealth and power of the duke and duchess. The Renaissance facade blends Doric, Ionic, and Corinthian elements. Easily seen from below is the **Tour de la Vicomté,** a 14th-century watchtower recognizable by its octagonal turret.

Large segments of the compound, most notably its sprawling annex, are occupied by the comte and comtesse de Crussol d'Uzès and cannot be visited. You can climb the winding staircase in the square 11th-century **Tour Bermonde** for a sweeping view over the countryside from its elevated terrace. The **11th-century cellar,** noted for its huge dimensions and vaulted ceilings, contains casks of wine from the surrounding vineyards. Tours of the site end with a *dégustation* of the reds and rosés of the Cuvée Ducale. The building's showcase apartments include a dining room with Louis XIII and Renaissance furnishings, a great hall (Le Grand Hall) done in the style of Louis XV, a large library that includes family memoirs, and the 15th-century **Chapelle Gothique.** Visits are usually part of an obligatory French-language tour, but you can follow the commentary in an English-language pamphlet.

4th-century crypt. Place du Duché. Admission 25F ($4.25) adults, 15F ($2.55) students and children 15 and under. June 15–Sept 15, Mon and Fri 10am, Wed 4pm. Other times of year, prearranged group tours available.

Adjacent to the palace, but completely independent of its jurisdiction, stands one of Provence's oldest early Christian monuments. The claustrophobic meeting place has walls with niches to hold the semipagan cult objects the new religion had not yet abandoned. The crypt is under the auspices of the tourist office, and schedules change frequently, so call ☎ **04-66-22-68-88** for information and to confirm the hours.

WHERE TO STAY

Hôtel d'Entraigues. 8 rue de la Calade, 30700 Uzès. ☎ **04-66-22-32-68.** Fax 04-66-22-57-01. www.lcm.fr/savry. 35 units. MINIBAR TV TEL. 290F–525F ($49.30–$89.25) double. AE, DC, MC, V. Parking 50F ($8.50).

The core of this hotel is a 15th-century manor house, expanded into two separate buildings, and much of it looks as it did 300 years ago. It's nestled in a Mediterranean garden adjacent to the cathedral. Room furnishings vary from comfortably old-fashioned to modern contemporary. Bathrooms were redone in ceramic tiles in 1998. Mattresses are standard and firm; towels are of medium quality. The hotel's restaurant, Les Jardins de Castile, features open-air dining and fixed-price menus that cost from 80F to 175F ($13.60 to $29.75) at lunch, and from 125F to 175F ($21.25 to $29.75) for dinner.

Hôtel Marie d'Agoult (Château d'Arpaillargues). Arpaillargues, 30700 Uzès. ☎ **04-66-22-14-48.** Fax 04-66-22-56-10. 29 units. A/C TV TEL. 500F–850F ($85–$144.50) double; 900F–1,000F ($153–$170) suite. AE, MC, V. Closed Nov–Mar. Drive 2½ miles west of Uzès, following the signs to Andouze-Arpaillargues.

The foundations of this place are believed to date from a 3rd-century fortress, making it as old as the Gallo-Roman occupation of Provence. The combination of rough and chiseled stone construction you see today is from the late 1600s and early 1700s, and was a site where silkworms were raised when this area was a silk-making center. The hotel is named for a former occupant, Marie d'Agoult, mistress of Franz Liszt and mother of Richard Wagner's wife, Cosima. All rooms except five have air-conditioning. The five, on the ground floor, have vaulted ceilings with exposed brick. The place offers a sleepy and rather passive insight into a way of life of long ago. Beds are soft and comfortable, and bathrooms are small but tidily cared for with shower/tub combinations.

WHERE TO DINE

If you'd like to dine in town, consider the Jardins de Castille, the restaurant of the **Hôtel d'Entraigues** (see above). However, the area's best place to dine is in the hamlet of St-Maximin, 3½ miles southeast of Uzès. To reach it from Uzès, follow the signs to St-Maximin.

Les Fontaines. 6 rue Entre les Tours. ☎ **04-66-22-41-20.** Reservations recommended. Main courses 65F–85F ($11.05–$14.45); set menus 95F–120F ($16.15–$20.40). MC, V. Fri–Tues noon–2:30pm and 7–10pm. Open daily for lunch and dinner July–Aug. Closed Feb. MEDITERRANEAN.

In a 12th-century building in the heart of Uzès, you can enjoy thoughtful service and a well-seasoned roster of mostly Mediterranean dishes. Examples include chicken with garlic and goat cheese; a Moroccan *tagine* of lamb garnished with dried fruits; eggplant caviar; and a huge array of fresh-caught grilled fish, including a succulent version of monkfish with a pistous served over the top. The courtyard contains a scattering of summertime tables and a pair of verdant fig trees.

5 Tarascon

10 miles (16.09km) W of St-Rémy, 11 miles (17.70km) N of Arles, 15 miles (24.14km) E of Nîmes

On the banks of the Rhône, this former port is rich in lore if not much else. Legend has it that the earliest inhabitants in pagan times were terrorized by a blood-thirsty dragon called "the Tarasque," which devoured children and cattle. The town was saved by St. Martha, who landed in Provence with the St. Marys shortly after Jesus's resur-rection. She called out to the Tarasque, made the sign of the cross, sprinkled it with holy water, and led it into town. The citizens of Tarascon promptly fell upon the Tarasque with all manner of weapons and killed it with a savage vengeance. St. Martha, seeing that her work was cut out for her, settled in the town and converted the pagans to Christianity.

Since the 1400s the **Fête de la Tarasque** has taken place on the final Sunday in June to commemorate this victory over the dragon. Young men parade down the streets operating a huge 18-foot Tarasque puppet. Fringe elements of the festival go on for several days, and include arts events, bullfights, and dancing.

Another legend of sorts was invented by Alphonse Daudet in the 19th century: Taratin de Tarasque, a harmless and comical character along the lines of Don Quixote. Today Taratin is a cartoon that holds a special place in the hearts of all French children.

ESSENTIALS

GETTING THERE   Tarascon is easily accessible by train, bus, and car. Seven daily trains come from Arles (trip time: 10 mins.), averaging 17F ($2.90) one-way, and 13 daily trains from Avignon (trip time: 10 mins.), costing 22F ($3.75) one-way. Two buses per day depart Arles for the half-hour trip, costing 17F ($2.90) one-way, and three buses make the half-hour trip from Avignon, costing 22F ($3.75) one-way. For **rail information** and schedules, call ☎ **08-36-35-35-35;** for bus schedules, ☎ **04-66-29-27-29.**

VISITOR INFORMATION   The **Office de Tourism** is at 59 rue des Halles (☎ **04-90-91-03-52**).

SEEING THE SIGHTS

Château de Tarascon. Boulevard du Roi-René. ☎ **04-90-91-01-93.** Admission 32F ($5.45) adults, 21F ($3.55) ages 12–25, free for children 11 and under. Apr–Sept, daily 9am–7pm; Oct–Mar, daily 9am–noon and 2–7pm.

Standing as a lone sentinel on the Rhône, with imposing stone walls and classic fairy-tale towers, this 15th-century castle was built by Provence's good King René and his father, Louis II of Anjou. It served as a border defense between France and the proudly independent Provence. After Louis's death, the castle was turned into a pleasure palace by René, who was addicted to festivities on the grand scale. He played host to artists, musicians, and dancers, and gave all sorts of lavish parties. Alas, shortly after his death France annexed Provence and the castle was turned into a dreary prison. It remained a prison until 1926 and you can still see graffiti and messages carved into the walls by the desperate prisoners. Today, while you can see the royal apartments, courtyard, garden, and old apothecary, you won't be treated to any of the fine trappings from René's day.

Collégiale Ste-Marthe. Boulevard du Roi-René. ☎ **04-90-91-09-50.** Admission free. Daily 8am–noon and 2–6pm, except during masses.

Since St. Martha has played such a pivotal role in legend and history, try to see this church across from the castle. It dates from the late 1100s and has been badly damaged by centuries of war and revolution. However, it still houses in the crypt a tomb that's said to be that of the famous saint.

Maison de Tartarin. 55 bis bd. Itam. ☎ **04-90-91-05-08.** Admission 10F ($1.70) adults, 5F (85¢) children 7–16, free for children 6 and under. Mid-Apr to Sept, Mon–Sat 10am–noon and 2–7pm; mid-Mar to mid-Apr and Oct to mid-Dec, Mon–Sat 10am–noon and 1:30–5pm.

For a whimsical break, visit this museum and shrine of sorts to the life of Tartarin de Tarascon, the satirical character created in the 19th century by Alphonse Daudet in his *New Don Quixote*. In the beginning, residents felt that Daudet's Tartarin was an insulting slap in the face to the town and its citizens; however, when they saw this fictional hero become popular, they had a change of opinion. The museum houses displays, models, and memorabilia tracing Tartarin's history to the present.

Musée Souleiado. 39 rue Proudhon. ☎ **04-90-91-08-80.** Admission 30F ($5.10) adults and 15F ($2.55) children 15 and under. Mon–Fri 8:30am–noon and 1:30–6pm. By private tour only; arrange 1 week in advance.

For a glimpse into the history behind the popular hand-decorated fabrics known as *souleiado*, take a tour of this museum. *Souleiado* is a Provençal word that means "sunbeam" and is used to describe these brightly colored calico fabrics. The designs that decorate the fabric are carved on blocks of pear wood. The museum contains a display of more than 40,000 of these pear blocks, some more than 200 years old.

WHERE TO STAY & DINE

Hôtel des Echevins. 26 bd. Itam, 13150 Tarascon. ☎ **04-90-91-01-70.** Fax 04-90-43-50-44. 39 units. TV TEL. 290F–315F ($49.30–$53.55) double. AE, MC, V. Closed late Nov to mid-Mar. Parking 30F ($5.10).

The subtle pink exterior of this private residence from the 17th century gives way to a refreshingly cool lobby with a mix of dark-wood period reproductions and antiques. A standout is the central stone staircase with its ornate black-and-gold wrought-iron banister. The rooms are average in both size and furnishings but provide a comfortable beds and views onto the surrounding houses. Bathrooms are small but tidy, with shower stalls. Some even offer glimpses of the château in the distance. The hotel also contains the town's best dining choice, Le Mistral. Cookery here is solid and reliable, with an emphasis on fresh ingredients and regional produce. Set-price menus cost 87F to 120F ($14.80 to $20.40). Reservations are recommended.

Hôtel Les Mazets des Roches. Rte. de Fontvieille, 13150 Tarascon. ☎ **04-90-91-34-89.** Fax 04-90-43-53-29. 39 units. AC TV TEL. 350F–750F ($59.50–$127.50) double, 690F–900F ($117.30–$153) double with half board; from 900F ($153) suite, 1,140F ($193.80) suite with half board. AE, DC, MC, V. Closed Nov–Mar. Take D33 for 4 miles south of town, following the signs to Fontvieille.

This oasis of modern luxury, set on 30 acres of countryside, originated about a century ago. Guest rooms are brought to life in a palette of earth tones and coordinating fabrics, light rattan furnishings, and a bounty of natural light streaming in through the windows. They are small to medium in size, each with a good mattress and a well-maintained private bathroom with a shower stall—sometimes with a shower/tub combination. The public areas include a fully stocked bar, lots of flowers, and an inviting sitting room. The impressive grounds include two tennis courts and an immense pool. If an athletic routine is not your style, simply sun yourself on the terrace or relax with a drink or light meal in the shade of the garden. The hotel boasts a restaurant of merit (open for lunch and dinner) offering a complete menu of Provençale specialties. Set menus cost 95F to 175F ($16.15 to $29.75).

6 Arles

450 miles (724.20km) S of Paris, 22 miles (35.41km) SW of Avignon, 55 (88.51km) miles NW of Marseille

Arles has been called "the soul of Provence," and art lovers, archaeologists, and historians are all attracted to this town on the Rhône. Many of the scenes painted so luminously by van Gogh remain to delight. The great Dutch painter left Paris for Arles in 1888. He was to paint some of his most celebrated works in this Provençal town.

The Greeks are said to have founded Arles in the 6th century B.C. Julius Caesar established a Roman colony here in 46 B.C. Under Roman rule Arles prospered. Constantine the Great named it the second capital in his empire in A.D. 306, when it was known as "the little Rome of the Gauls." It wasn't until 1481 that Arles was incorporated into France.

Though Arles isn't quite as lovely as it was when van Gogh came here, it has enough antique charm to keep the appeal alive. Its first-rate museums, excellent restaurants, and summer festivals (such as the early June international photography festival) make a visit rewarding.

ESSENTIALS

GETTING THERE   Arles lies on the Paris-Marseille and the Bordeaux–St-Raphaël rail lines, so it has frequent connections from most cities of France. Ten trains arrive daily from Avignon (trip time: 20 mins.) and 10 per day from Marseille (trip time: 1 hr.). From Aix-en-Provence, there are at least 10 trains, routed through Marseille (trip time: 1¾ hrs.). For **rail information** and schedules, call ☎ **08-36-35-35-35.**

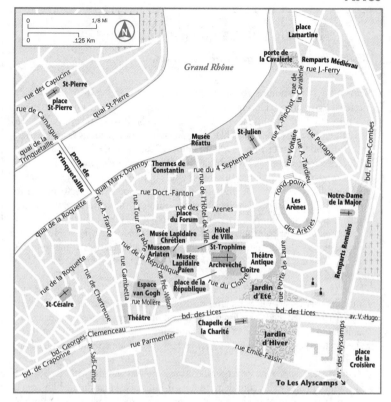

There are about five buses per day from Aix-en-Provence (trip time: 1¾ hrs.). For **bus information** and schedules, contact the Gare Routière, avenue Paulin-Talabot (☎ 04-90-49-38-01), opposite the railway station.

VISITOR INFORMATION   The **Office de Tourisme,** where you can buy a *billet global* (see below), is on the esplanade des Lices (☎ 04-90-18-41-20).

EXPLORING THE TOWN

Go to the tourist office, where you can purchase a *billet global,* the all-inclusive pass that admits you to the town's museums, Roman monuments, and all the major attractions, at a cost of 60F ($10.20) for adults and 40F ($6.80) for children.

The town is full of monuments from Roman times. The general vicinity of the old Roman forum is occupied by **place du Forum,** shaded by plane trees. Once the Café de Nuit, immortalized by van Gogh, stood on this square. You can see two columns in the Corinthian style and pediment fragments from a temple at the corner of the Hôtel Nord-Pinus. South of here is **place de la République,** the principal plaza, dominated by a 50-foot-tall blue porphyry obelisk. On the north is the impressive **Hôtel de Ville** (town hall) from 1673, built to Mansart's plans and surmounted by a Renaissance belfry.

Eglise St-Trophime. Place de la République. ☎ 04-90-96-07-38. Admission 15F ($2.55) adults, 9F ($1.55) students and children under 12. Church: Daily 9am–7pm. Cloister: mid-June to mid-Sept, daily 9am–7pm; rest of year daily 9am–12:30pm and 2–7pm.

In Search of van Gogh's "Different Light"

What strikes me here is the transparency of the air.

—Vincent van Gogh

Before the impressionists found refuge in Provence, the district had already attracted many artists. During the pope's residency at Avignon, a flood of Italian artists frescoed the papal palace in a style worthy of St. Peter's, and even after their departure, Provençal monarchs like King René imported painters from Flanders and Burgundy to adorn his public buildings. This continued to the 18th and 19th centuries, as painters drew inspiration from the dazzling light of Provence.

But it wasn't until 19th century that the role of Provence as an artistic catalyst became fully recognized. Dutch-born Vincent van Gogh (1853–90) moved to Arles in 1888 and spent 2 years migrating through the historic towns of Les Baux, St-Rémy, and Stes-Maries, recording through the filter of his incipient psychosis the dozens of paintings now prized by museums everywhere. His search, he said, was for "a different light," which led to the generation of masterpieces like *Starry Night, Cypresses, The Night Café, The Bridge at Arles,* and *Boats Along the Beach.*

Van Gogh wasn't alone in his pursuit of Provençal light: Gauguin joined him 8 months after his arrival. Soon afterwards, however, the two artists had a violent quarrel, which reduced the Dutchman to a morbid depression. Eventually van Gogh had to be hospitalized in a local sanitarium. He continued to paint there, but within 2 years van Gogh returned to Paris, where he committed suicide in July 1890.

Things went somewhat better for Cézanne, who was familiar with the beauties of Provence thanks to his childhood in Aix-en-Provence. He infuriated his father, a prominent Provençal banker, by abandoning his studies to pursue painting. Later, his theories about line and color were publicized around the world. Although he spent time in Paris, he rarely set foot outside Provence from 1890 until his death in 1904. Some critics have asserted that Cézanne's later years were devoted to one obsession: recording the line, color, and texture of Montagne-St-Victoire, a rocky knoll a few hours' horse ride east of Aix. He painted it more than 60 times without ever grasping its essence the way he'd hoped. The bulk of the Provençal mountain, however, as well as the way shadows moved across its rocky planes, were decisive in affecting the cubists, whose work Cézanne directly influenced.

On the east side of the square, this church's 12th-century portal is one of the finest achievements of the southern Romanesque style. In the pediment, Christ is surrounded by the symbols of the Evangelists. Frederick Barbarossa was crowned king of Arles on this site in 1178. The cloister, in both the Gothic and Romanesque styles, is noted for its medieval carvings. Be warned that the hours listed above are sometimes unpredictable; hours sometimes change at the whim of the custodial staff.

✪ **Les Alyscamps.** Rue Pierre-Renaudel. ☎ **04-90-49-36-87.** Admission 15F ($2.55) adults, 9F ($1.55) children. Daily 9am–7pm.

This is one of the most famous necropolises of the western world. Its fame began when Genesius, a Roman civil servant, refused to write down an edict calling for persecution of Christians. For this, he was beheaded in 250; later he was made a saint when it was said that miracles began to happen on this site. In time the fame of Les Alyscamps spread throughout the Christian world; more and more of the faithful wanted to be buried here, and coffins were shipped down the Rhône for burial. By the 10th century the legend spread that the heroes of Roncevaux—Roland and Olivier—were also entombed here, which brought the place even more fame. Dante even mentioned it in his *Inferno*. In the Middle Ages there were 19 churches and chapels on the site. After the Renaissance, the graveyard was desecrated: tombs were removed and stones taken to construct other buildings. For an evocative experience, walk down L'Allée des Sarcophages, where 80 generations have been buried over 2,000 years. The lane is lined with sarcophagi under tall poplar trees.

Musée de l'Arles Antique. Presqu'île du Cirque Romain (½ mile south of the center). ☎ **04-90-18-88-88.** Admission 35F ($5.95) adults, 25F ($4.25) students and ages 12–18. Free for children under 12. Apr to mid-Sept, daily 9am–7pm; mid-Sept to Mar, daily 9:30am–noon and 1:30–6pm.

Opened in 1995, the museum holds one of the world's most famous collections of Roman Christian sarcophagi as well as a rich ensemble of sculptures, mosaics, and inscriptions from the Augustinian period to the 6th century A.D. Eleven detailed models show ancient monuments of the region as they existed in the past.

Museon Arlaten. Enter at 29 rue de la République. ☎ **04-90-96-08-23.** Admission 20F ($3.40) adults, 15F ($2.55) children 12–18, free for children under 12. Apr–Oct, daily 9am–noon and 2–6:30pm; Nov–Mar, Tues–Sun 9am–noon and 2–5pm.

The museum was founded by Frédéric Mistral, the Provençal poet who led a movement to establish modern Provençal as a literary language, using the money from his Nobel Prize for Literature in 1904. This is really a folklore museum, with regional costumes, portraits, furniture, dolls, a music salon, and a room devoted to mementos of Mistral. Among its curiosities is a letter (in French) from President Theodore Roosevelt to Mistral, bearing the letterhead of the Maison Blanche in Washington, D.C.

Théâtre Antique. Rue du Cloître. ☎ **04-90-96-93-30.**
Amphitheater (Les Arènes). Rond-pont des Arènes. ☎ **04-90-49-36-86.** Admission to each site: 15F ($2.55) adults, 9F ($1.55) children. Daily 9am–7pm (hours can be unpredictable).

These are the city's two great classical monuments. The Roman theater, begun by Augustus in the 1st century, was mostly destroyed and only two Corinthian columns remain. Here the famous *Venus of Arles* was discovered in 1651. A copy of a masterpiece of Hellenistic statuary, it was broken into three pieces and armless when discovered. Arles offered it to Louis XIV, who had it restored, and today it is in the Louvre. To reach the theater, take rue de la Calade from the city hall.

Nearby, also built in the 1st century, the Amphitheater seats almost 25,000 and still hosts bullfights in summer. The government warns you to visit the old monument at your own risk, since the stone steps are uneven and much of the masonry is worn down to the point where it might be a problem for older travelers or for those with disabilities. For a good view, you can climb the three towers that remain from medieval times when the amphitheater was turned into a fortress. Note that the theater and Les Arènes maintain the same hours and the same fluid scheduling as Eglise St-Trophime.

Thermes de Constantín. Rue Dominique-Maisto. ☎ **04-90-49-35-40.** Admission 15F ($2.55) adults, 9F ($1.55) children.

Today, near the banks of the Rhône, only the baths *(thermae)* remain of a once-grand imperial palace. Visiting hours are the same as at Les Alyscamps.

Musée Réattu. 10 rue du Grand-Prieuré. ☎ **04-90-49-37-58.** Admission 15F ($2.55) adults, 9F ($1.55) students and ages 12–18, free for children under 12. Apr–Sept, daily 9am–12:30pm and 2–7pm; Mar and Oct, daily 10am–12:30pm and 2–6:30pm; Nov–Feb, daily 10am–12:30pm and 2–5:30pm.

The town's museum is named for the rather mediocre local painter Jacques Réattu, but it contains more important works—etchings and drawings by Picasso, and paintings by Alechinsky, Dufy, Léger, Henri Rousseau, and Zadkine. Note the Arras tapestries from the 16th century.

SHOPPING

In a somewhat isolated position 7½ miles north of Arles, ✪ **Les Olivades Factory Store,** chemin des Indienneurs, St-Etienne-du-Grès (☎ **04-90-49-19-19**), stands beside the road that's signposted to Tarascon and Avignon. Because of the wide array of art objects and fabrics inspired by the traditions of Provence, it's worth your while to make a trek out here. Fabrics, dresses, shirts for men and women, table linens, and fabric by the yard are all available at retail outlets of the Olivades chain throughout Provence, but here the selection is a bit cheaper and more diverse.

WHERE TO STAY
EXPENSIVE

✪ **Hôtel Jules César et Restaurant Lou Marquês.** 9 bd. des Lices, 13631 Arles CEDEX. ☎ **04-90-93-43-20.** Fax 04-90-93-33-47. 58 units. MINIBAR TV TEL. 700F–1,250F ($119–$212.50) double; from 1,600F ($272) suite. AE, DC, MC, V. Closed Nov 12–Dec 23. Parking 60F ($10.20).

In the center of Arles, this 17th-century former Carmelite convent has been skillfully transformed into a stately country hotel, with the best restaurant in Arles. Though this is a noisy neighborhood, most rooms face the quiet, unspoiled cloister. The antique Provençal furnishings are luxurious, and you wake to the scent of roses and the sound of birds singing.

Throughout, you'll find a blend of antique neoclassic architecture and postmodern amenities. Rooms have recently been renewed with fresh carpeting and curtains. The interior rooms are the most tranquil but also the darkest. Bright fabrics enliven them. Most downstairs rooms are spacious, but those upstairs are small, though with an old world charm. Rooms in the modern extensions are spacious and comfortable, but lack much character. Tiled bathrooms are well maintained and supplied with deluxe toiletries, thick towels, and hair dryers. All but 18 have a shower/tub combination.

The restaurant, Lou Marquês, has tables outside on the front terrace. The food is extremely fresh. From the à la carte menu, we recommend *bourride à la Provençale* or Arles lamb. Fixed-price menus are 210F to 320F ($35.70–$54.40), with à la carte dinners averaging 300F ($60).

MODERATE

✪ **Grand Hotel Nord Pinus.** Place du Forum, 13200 Arles. ☎ **04-90-93-44-44.** Fax 04-90-93-34-00. www.nord-pinus.com. E-mail: info@nordpinus.com. 23 units. MINIBAR TV TEL. 840F–990F ($142.80–$168.30) double; 1,700F ($289) suite. Parking 50F ($8.50) per night. AE, MC, V.

Few hotels in Arles manage to evoke Provence's 19th-century charm as effectively as this one. Occupying an antique townhouse on a tree-lined square in the heart of town, it has public rooms filled with antiques and an ornate staircase lined with graceful wrought-iron balustrades. In a range of shapes and sizes, bedrooms are glamorous, even theatrical, filled with rich upholsteries, with thick curtains artfully arranged around the oversized French doors. Each comes with a fine mattress and quality linen, usually on twin or double beds. All have tidily maintained tiled baths with adequate shelf space and a shower/tub combination. Many bullfighters and artists have stayed here—you'll see their photographs and framed artworks in many of the public areas. There's an on-site bar and restaurant, open daily for lunch and dinner.

INEXPENSIVE

✪ **Hôtel Calendal.** 22 place du Docteur-Pomme, 13200 Arles. ☎ **04-90-96-11-89.** Fax 04-90-96-05-84. 27 units. TEL. 265F–450F ($45.05–$76.50) double. AE, DC, MC, V. Bus: 4.

On a quiet square not far from the arena, the Calendal offers spacious to medium-sized rooms. Recently redecorated with sunny colors, they have high ceilings, comfortable beds, and well-maintained bathrooms. Most have views over one of the hotel's best feature, a shaded garden filled with palms and palmettos. Because of its reasonable rates, the Calendal has long been a bargain hunter's favorite. On the premises is a restaurant with a limited menu featuring omelets, soups, and platters inspired by the cuisine of France and Provence.

Hôtel d'Arlatan. 26 rue du Sauvage, 13631 Arles. ☎ **04-90-93-56-66.** Fax 04-90-49-68-45. www.hotelarlatan.fr. E-mail: hotel-arlatan@provnet.fr. 40 units. A/C MINIBAR TV TEL. 498F–698F ($84.65–$118.65) double; 798F–1,450F ($135.65–$246.50) suite. AE, DC, MC, V. Parking 70F ($11.90).

In the former residence of the comtes d'Arlatan de Beaumont, near place du Forum, this hotel has been managed by the same family since 1920. It was built in the 15th century on the ruins of an old palace begun by Constantine—in fact, there's still a wall from the 4th century. Rooms are furnished with Provençal antiques and reproductions, the walls covered in patterned wallpaper and in some rare instances, tapestries in the style of Louis XV and Louis XVI. The most appealing rooms overlook the garden. As this was a former private residence, accommodations range from small (on the upper floors) to more spacious on the ground floor. The bathrooms are efficiently organized with adequate shelf space, hair dryers, tiled walls, and often a shower/tub combination.

Hôtel de la Muette. 15 rue des Suisses, 13200 Arles. ☎ **04-90-96-15-39.** Fax 04-90-49-73-16. E-mail: hotel.muette@wanadoo.fr. 18 units. TV TEL. 220F–300F ($37.40–$51) double. AE, MC, V. Parking 35F ($5.95).

A short walk from the city's ancient Roman arena, this hotel occupies an old building that has been an inn since the 1100s. Extensively renovated and restored, it presents a severe-looking stone facade to the outside world, and an interior that retains the ancient ceiling beams and rough-textured masonry walls. Cheerfulness is added in the form of many coats of white paint and traditional Provençal fabrics in sunny colors of maize, red, and blue. Overall, the place is comfortable, if a bit cramped, representing good value for the money. Mattresses are soft and cushiony, and bathrooms are small with shower stalls and barely adequate shelf space.

Hôtel Le Cloître. 16 rue du Cloître, 13200 Arles. ☎ **04-90-96-29-50.** Fax 04-90-96-02-88. www.home.sprintmail.com/njanvier/lecloitre. 30 units. TEL. 260F–305F ($44.20–$51.85) double; 375F–405F ($63.75–$68.85) triple. AE, MC, V. Closed Nov–Feb. Parking 30F ($5.10). Bus: 4.

Set between the ancient theater and the cloister, this hotel is a great value. Originally part of a 12th-century cloister, it still has its original Romanesque vaultings. The atmosphere is Provençal—pleasant rooms with high ceilings, comfortable mattresses, reasonably plush towels, and lots of charm. Some, but not all, have their own TVs, and there's a TV lounge for everyone else.

Hôtel Mirador. 3 rue Voltaire, 13200 Arles. ☎ **04-90-96-28-05.** Fax 04-90-96-59-89. E-mail: hotelmirador@europost.org. 15 units. TV TEL. 190F–260F ($32.30–$44.20) double. AE, MC, V. Free parking.

Just a minute's walk north of Arles' Roman arena, this is a pleasant, family-run two-star hotel in a central location. Bedrooms are slightly cramped but well maintained and cozy, with good mattresses plus adequate bathrooms with shower stalls. Public areas are outfitted in a *faux-antique* decor of exposed wood and flower-patterned fabrics. You'll be happiest here if you don't expect grandeur, but accept small inconveniences with a sense of humor.

WHERE TO DINE

For a truly elegant meal, consider dining at the **Restaurant Lou Marquês** at the Hôtel Jules César (see above).

La Côte d'Adam (Adam's Rib). 12 rue de la Liberté. ☎ **04-90-49-62-29.** Reservations required in summer. Main courses 75F–90F ($12.75–$15.30); fixed-price menus 85F–125F ($14.45–$21.25). AE, MC, V. Mon 7:15–9:30pm, Tues–Sun noon–2pm and 7:15–9:30pm. Closed Nov 15–30. PROVENÇAL.

In the historic center of town, this completely unpretentious restaurant has a rustic interior, a beamed ceiling, and a high carved-stone fireplace. It holds 40 and serves such dishes as aiguillettes of duck and John Dory with a confit of pear. Many dishes are imbued with fragrant olive oil. Between May and September the place is likely to be open daily.

Le Vaccarès. Place du Forum, 9 rue Favorin. ☎ **04-90-96-06-17.** Reservations required. Main courses 95F–140F ($16.15–$23.80); fixed-price menus 150F–320F ($25.50–$54.40). AE, MC, V. Tues–Sat noon–2pm and 7:30–9:30pm, Sun noon–2pm. Closed Jan 15–Feb 15 and all day Sun July–Aug. PROVENÇAL.

Le Vaccarès offers southern French elegance and the finest food in town, in a setting whose outdoor terrace (used during clement weather) opens onto the market of Arles. Its staff and two generations of the Dumas family use unusual ingredients to create innovative Provençal dishes. Specialties are sauté of lamb with basil, poached sea wolf with confit of lemon and orange, mussels with fresh herbs, croquette of squid, seadevil soup, elegantly simple steamed sea bass garnished only with olive oil, and émincé of beef with Châteauneuf. Its selection of wines is impressive (especially the Rhône Valley and Var).

ARLES AFTER DARK

Because of its relatively small population of around 50,000, Arles doesn't offer as many nightlife options as Aix-en-Provence, Avignon, Nice, or Marseille. The town's most appealing choice is the bar/cafe/music hall **Cargo de Nuit,** 7 av. Sadi-Carnot, route pour Barriol (☎ **04-90-49-55-99**). The cover charge is between 35F ($5.95) and 45F ($7.65); the place provides a rich diet of recorded blues, salsa, reggae, and Cubano music and access to a sprawling bar and a restaurant.

A good option farther from the city center, particularly for those in their 40s and 50s, is the very large **Le Krystal,** route de Pont-de-Crau (☎ **04-90-98-32-40**), about 6 miles south of Arles. The town's most animated cafe, and the one where most of the available single people go, is **Le Café van Gogh,** 11 place du Forum (☎ **04-90-96-44-56**). Overlooking the most attractive plaza in Arles, it features live music and an ambience that the almost-young and restless refer to as *super-chouette* or "super cool."

7 Fontvieille

449 miles (722.60km) S of Paris, 6½ miles (10.46km) N of Arles, 18½ miles (29.77km) S of Avignon

This sleepy village is best known for the Moulin de Daudet, the windmill that inspired Alphonse Daudet to write his *Lettres de Mon Moulin,* a philosophical and anecdotal

Impressions

All this beautiful Provençal landscape lives on light alone.

—Alphonse Daudet

tract still popular in France (and often required reading for foreign students of the French language). The book took as its theme the death of rural life in Provence, and today the windmill, spared because of its association with the author, illustrates his point—it's the only one surviving for miles around.

ESSENTIALS

GETTING THERE   As there's no train station in Fontvieille, rail passengers arrive at Avignon, 13½ miles away, where you can rent a car. You can also take a train to Arles, 6½ miles away, where taxis line up at the train station; one-way fare to Fontvieille is around 150F ($25.50). For **rail information** and schedules, call ☎ 08-36-35-35-35.

Note that there are infrequent and difficult-to-decipher bus schedules from both Arles and Avignon, between two and six per day, depending on the day of the week and the season. At press time, there were plans to re-establish the railway spur between Arles and Fontvieille. For bus and railway information and scheduling, call ☎ 08-36-35-35-35.

VISITOR INFORMATION   The **Office de Tourisme** is on place Honorat (☎ 04-90-54-67-49).

SEEING THE SIGHTS
PAYING HOMAGE TO DAUDET

Moulin de Daudet. On D33 (about ½ mile south of the village center). ☎ **04-90-54-60-78.** Admission 10F ($1.70), includes exhibit on Daudet's life in the Château de Montauban (see below). June–Sept, daily 9am–7pm; Oct–Dec and Feb–May, daily 10am–noon and 2–5pm. Closed Jan.

The mill is clearly signposted from the village center and makes a perfect destination for a pleasant stroll. Upstairs the workings of the milling system are illustrated, and the basement holds a museum dedicated to Daudet that includes photographs, letters, and documents. A patron of the young Proust, he died in 1897 at age 57, a victim of the venereal disease he contracted during his promiscuous life.

Château de Montauban. Rue de Montauban. ☎ **04-90-54-75-12.** Admission 10F ($1.70), includes Moulin de Daudet. Apr–Sept, daily 9am–7pm. Closed Oct–Mar.

Less evocative than the mill is the château where Daudet often stayed. In the town center, it was built around 1812 and most of its interior is used by the public-service organizations for the region. However, you can visit a room containing 46 illustrations on the life of Daudet, along with some of his memorabilia.

MORE SIGHTS

Standing in contrast to the Moulin de Daudet (just over a mile south of it on D33) are two **Roman aqueducts** whose waters long ago turned the wheels of 16 water mills. They stretch in a ruined, barely recognizable row that's signposted from the roadside—testimonials to the prosperity of Provence during the Roman occupation.

Also of historic significance are the quartet of **prayer stations (oratories)** that mark the northern, southern, eastern, and western entrances to the town. Built of stone and terra-cotta roof tiles in 1721, but with origins much older than that, their function was to invoke the help of various saints as a means of warding off pestilence, leprosy, famine, and various forms of malfeasance.

WHERE TO STAY

Hostellerie St-Victor. Chemin des Fourques, 13990 Fontvieille. ☎ **04-90-54-66-00.** Fax 04-90-54-67-88. 14 units. A/C MINIBAR TV TEL. 395F–595F ($67.15–$101.15) double; 995F ($169.15) suite. AE, DC, MC, V. From town, drive ¹/₃ mile west, following the signs to Arles. Free parking.

This stone farmhouse, a 1980s reproduction of a Provençal *mas*, makes a romantic inn. Its lounge boasts a large fireplace, a beamed ceiling with hand-hewn beams, and padded leather furniture. There's also a colonnaded terrace and a breakfast room over-looking landscaped shrubbery and flowers to the countryside beyond. A staircase with ornate posts leads to the rooms on the second floor. The earth tones that prevail are offset by pots of bright flowers. The graciously large rooms are furnished with a mix of antiques, comfortable mattresses, and efficient but not overly large bathrooms. The hotel also features a bar and a pool with a flagstone terrace and several acres of orchards devoted to cherries and apricots.

✪ **Hôtel La Rédgalido.** Rue Frédéric-Mistral, 13990 Fontvieille. ☎ **04-90-54-60-22.** Fax 04-90-54-64-29. www.relaischateaux.fr/regalido. 15 units. A/C TV TEL. 490F–1,230F ($83.30–$209.10) double; 1,640F ($278.80) suite. AE, MC, V. Closed Jan. Free parking.

This stylish Relais & Châteaux occupies a converted 19th-century olive mill, sur-rounded by an abundance of fig and palm trees, magnolias, lavender, and roses. All these, combined with ivy climbing the exterior, seemingly swallow the inn in an impressive garden. Its plushly comfortable rooms are inspired by old Provence. Each is well maintained, with plush mattresses and thick towels. Some of the best cuisine in the region is served in the vaulted formal dining room (see below).

WHERE TO DINE

✪ **Auberge de la Régalido.** Rue Frédéric-Mistral. ☎ **04-90-54-60-22.** Reservations rec-ommended. Fixed-price meals 165F–410F ($28.05–$69.70) at lunch, 270F–410F ($45.90–$69.70) at dinner. AE, MC, V. July–Sept, Wed–Sun noon–1:30pm; Oct–June, Wed–Sun noon–1:30pm and Tues–Sun 7:30–9pm. FRENCH/PROVENÇAL.

A stroll through the garden, praised for its junglelike verdancy, is a wonderful preface to a meal at this Relais & Châteaux. Its vaulted dining room has space for only 45 diners, who can move onto a small veranda on sultry days or nights. Menu items are carefully conceived, and include gratin of mussels with spinach, *papeton* (flan) of egg-plant with herbs, sliced roast lamb in a casserole with bracing quantities of garlic, and sea-wolf stew infused with olive oil. Dessert might be a moist chocolate cake.

8 Les Baux

444 miles (714.55km) S of Paris, 12 miles (19.31km) NE of Arles, 50 miles (80.47) N of Mar-seille and the Mediterranean

Cardinal Richelieu called Les Baux a "nesting place for eagles." In its lonely position high on a windswept plateau overlooking the southern Alpilles, Les Baux seems to be part of the mysterious, shadowy rock formations. Once it was the citadel of the pow-erful seigneurs of Les Baux, who ruled with an iron fist and sent their conquering armies as far as Albania. In medieval times, the flourishing culture of Les Baux attracted troubadours from all over Europe to the "court of love." Later on, Les Baux was ruled by the notorious "Scourge of Provence," Raymond de Turenne, who sent his men throughout the land to kidnap people. If a victim's friends and family could not pay ransom, the poor wretch was forced to walk a gangplank over the cliff's edge.

When Les Baux became a Protestant stronghold in the 17th century, Richelieu, fed up with its constant rebellion against Louis XIII, commanded his armies in 1632 to destroy the "eagle's nest." Today the castle and ramparts are a mere shell, though you can see remains of great Renaissance mansions.

With its dramatic situation, Les Baux is one of the most visited sites in southern France. More than a million visitors come here every year.

ESSENTIALS

GETTING THERE   From Arles there are six buses daily from March to September, but only one bus per day from October to February (trip time: 30 mins.). The fare is 32F ($5.45) one-way. For **bus information** and schedules, phone ☎ **04-90-49-38-01** in Arles.

VISITOR INFORMATION   The **Office de Tourisme** is on Rue Frédéric-Mistral (☎ **04-90-54-34-39**).

EXPLORING THE AREA

Les Baux has two aspects: the inhabited and carefully preserved medieval village and the evocative ruins of its fortress, the "dead" village. Visitors enter the city through the 19th-century Port Mage, but in medieval times, the monumental **Porte Eyguières** was the only entrance to the fortified city.

From **place St-Vincent** are sweeping views over the Vallon de la Fontaine. This is the site of the 12th-century **Eglise St-Vincent** (no phone), with its beautiful campanile, called La Lanterne des Morts ("Lantern of the Dead"). The stained-glass windows were a gift from Rainier of Monaco, in his capacity as the marquis des Baux. They are modern, based on designs of French artist Max Ingrand. The church is open April to October daily 9am to 6:30pm, and November to March 10am to 5:30pm.

The **Yves Brayer Museum,** at the intersection of rue de la Calade and rue de l'Eglise (☎ **04-90-54-36-99**), holds a retrospective collection of the works of Yves Brayer (1907–1990), a figurative painter and Les Baux's most famous native son (he's buried in the village cemetery). He painted scenes of Italy, of Morocco and, in Spain, of many bullfights, working mainly in shades of red, ocher, and black. Brayer also decorated the restored 17th-century **La Chapelle des Pénitents Blancs,** which stands close to the Church of St. Vincent, with frescoes of the Annunciation, the Nativity, and Christ in Majesty. The museum is open daily: April to October 10am to 6:30pm; the rest of the year 10am to noon and 2 to 5:30pm. Admission is 20F ($3.40) for adults, 10F ($1.70) for students and children.

The Renaissance-era **Hôtel de Manville,** rue Frédéric-Mistral, functions today as the **Mairie (Town Hall).** Only its courtyard can be visited. The town's ancient town hall on place Louis Jou now contains the **Musée des Santons** (no phone), a collection of antique creche figures. It's open April to October daily from 9am to 6:30pm, and November to March from 10am to 5:30pm.

In the Renaissance-era **Hôtel Jean-de-Brion,** rue Frédéric-Mistral (☎ **04-90-69-88-03** or 04-90-54-34-17) is the **Fondation Louis Jou,** which can only be visited by special arrangement. It has engravings and serigraphs by the artist. The 1569 **Hôtel des Porcelles** contains a collection of contemporary artists who have worked in Les Baux and in Provence.

Château des Baux. ☎ **04-90-54-55-56.** Admission 36F ($6.10) adults, 23F ($3.90) students and ages 15 and under. July–Aug, daily 9am–8:30pm; Mar and Sept–Oct, daily 10am–7pm; other months, daily 10am–5:30pm.

This complex of evocative, mostly ruined buildings was carved out of the rocky mountain peak. *La ville morte* (the "ghost village") is at the upper (northern) end of town. It's accessible via the rue du Château, at the **Hôtel de la Tour du Brau,** which contains a small archaeological and lapidary museum. Inside the compound is the ruined château des Baux with its tower-shaped *donjon* and surrounding ramparts, and the two towers, Tour Paravel and Tour Sarascenes. The collection of replicated medieval siege engines were built from the original plans. The ruined chapel of St-Blaise houses a little museum devoted to the olive. The site of the former castle covers an area at least five times that of the present village of Les Baux. As you stand here you can look out over the "Valley of Hell" and even glimpse the Mediterranean in the distance.

A DRIVE THROUGH HELL

Below Les Baux is a jagged and irregular gorge, **Val d'Enfer** (Valley of Hell). You can access the valley by D27 and D78G and drive through this bleak and rugged scenery. Centuries ago, caves in the gorge were inhabited by humans. The gorge is the source of many Provençal legends—witches, sprites, and fairies are said to live in the caves.

On your way to the valley, you can stop at the **Cathédrale d'Images** (☎ 04-90-54-38-65), off Route duVal d'Enfer (D27), a half mile north of the village, in a former quarry. In the interior is a rather bizarre audio-visual show—the limestone surfaces of the large rooms become three-dimensional screens for projectors that splash images from all directions. The site was created by photographer Albert Plecy. In various offshoot caves are changing exhibitions of modern art. The site is open daily in summer from 10am to 7pm; closed mid-January to mid-March. Admission is 43F ($7.30) for adults, 35F ($5.95) for students, and 25F ($4.25) for children under 12.

WHERE TO STAY

Note that **La Riboto de Taven** (see below) has two rooms for rent.

VERY EXPENSIVE

✪ **L'Oustau de Beaumanière.** Les Baux, 13520 Maussane-les-Alpilles. ☎ **04-90-54-33-07.** Fax 04-90-54-40-46. www.oustaudebeaumaniere.com. E-mail: oustau@relais-chateaux.fr. 22 units. A/C MINIBAR TV TEL. 1,385F–1,485F ($235.45–$252.45) double; 2,080F–2,180F ($353.60–$370.60) suite. AE, DC, MC, V. Closed Jan 3–Mar 10; Nov–Apr 1, hotel and restaurant closed Wed and Thurs to 4pm.

This Relais & Châteaux is one of southern France's most legendary hotels. On the premises of a Provençal *mas* (farmhouse) bought in 1945 by the late Raymond Thuilier, it became a rendezvous for the glitterati in the 1950s and 1960s and continues today, in a less spectacular kind of glamour, under the founder's grandson, Jean-André Charial. The hotel consists of three stone houses draped in flowering vines at the base of the rocky hill on which the fortified town rises. The plush guest rooms evoke the 16th and 17th centuries. All contain large sitting areas, and no two are alike. Most beds are twins or queen size, with new, very comfortable mattresses. The hotel has three annexes with comparable comfort, but less style—Le Manor is the most appealing. The sumptuous marble baths come with shower-and-tub combinations, hair dryers, robes, and thick towels. In the stone-vaulted dining room, the chef serves specialties like ravioli of truffles with leeks, and *rossini* (stuffed with foie gras) of veal with fresh truffles. The award-winning *gigot d'agneau* (lamb) *en croûte* has become this place's trademark and is particularly succulent. For dessert, consider a soufflé of red fruits. Service is daily from noon to 3pm and 7:30pm to midnight when the hotel is open (see above). Reservations are essential. Set menus cost from 490F to 750F ($83.30 to $127.50).

EXPENSIVE

La Cabro d'Or. 13520 Les Baux de Provence. ☎ **04-90-54-33-21.** Fax 04-90-54-45-98. 31 units. A/C MINIBAR TV TEL. 1,450F–1,950F ($246.50–$331.50) double; 2,140F–2,550F ($363.80–$433.50) suite. Rates include half board. AE, MC, V.

This is the less celebrated sibling of the Oustau de Beaumanière, located about a half mile away. It was built in the 1700s as a farmhouse and consists of about five low-slung, stone structures. The decor in these very comfortable accommodations evokes old-timey Provence. Some have sweeping views over the surrounding countryside, and all have unusual art, deluxe mattresses, and in most cases, recently upgraded bathrooms. Bathrooms are equipped with tub and shower, deluxe toiletries, hair dryers, and fluffy towels. The in-house restaurant is in a barn from the 1800s that has massive ceiling beams that are works of art in their own right. It's flanked with a vine-covered terrace that overlooks an ornamental pond and garden, with a farther view of a rocky, barren landscape that has been compared to the surface of the moon, it. On the premises are a swimming pool and two tennis courts.

MODERATE

Auberge de la Benvengudo. Vallon de l'Arcoule, Rte. d'Arles, 13520 Les Baux. ☎ **04-90-54-32-54.** Fax 04-90-54-42-58. 20 units. A/C TV TEL. 630F–750F ($107.10–$127.50) double; 950F ($161.50) suite. AE, MC, V. Closed Nov–Jan. Take RD78 for a mile southwest of Les Baux, following the signs to Arles.

This auberge is a tastefully converted 19th-century farmhouse surrounded by sculptured shrubbery, towering trees, and parasol pines. Rooms are about equally divided between the original building above the restaurant, and an attractive stone-sided annex. Bedrooms are sunny, well maintained, clean, and recently renovated. Each has a private terrace or balcony, and in some cases, an antique four-poster bed. The inn serves a delectable cuisine, with menu items that include a fillet of hogfish with saffron, fillet of red mullet with a concasse of tomatoes; grilled lamb chops with ratatouille, Mediterranean sole filet fried with rosemary, and osso buco Provençal. The 260F ($44.20) fixed-price menu changes daily except Sunday and is now joined by an à la carte menu. Lunch is served in summer. Extras include a pool, a tennis court, and an expansive terrace redolent of lavender and thyme.

Mas de L'Oulivié. 13520 Les Baux de Provence. ☎ **04-90-54-35-78.** Fax 04-90-54-44-31. E-mail: masdeloulivie@gulliver.fr. 20 units. A/C MINIBAR TV TEL. 620F–1,400F ($105.40–$238) double; 2,300F ($391) suite. AE, MC, V. Closed Nov–Mar.

This picturesque salmon-colored complex of traditional Provençal buildings, capped with terra-cotta roofs, is about a mile from town. Lounges have beamed ceilings, terra-cotta floor tiles, and comfortable provincial furnishings. The high-ceilinged bedrooms are decorated in traditional motifs in tones of peach, champagne, and beige, with casement doors that open onto the garden. They vary in size and shape—some are quite spacious—with a corresponding wide difference in price. You can live here expensively or moderately. Each unit is fitted with quality mattresses and fine linen, and has a bathroom that is tiled and roomy, most often with a shower/tub combination. Breakfast and lunch are the only meals served. There is a gracefully paneled bar, and lunch is served around the free-form swimming pool.

INEXPENSIVE

Hostellerie de la Reine-Jeanne. Grand-Rue, 13520 Les Baux. ☎ **04-90-54-32-06.** Fax 04-90-54-32-33. 10 units. TEL. 270F–360F ($45.90–$61.20) double. MC, V. Closed Nov 15–Feb 15 (open during Christmas holidays). Free parking.

This warm, well-scrubbed inn is the best bargain in Les Baux. You enter through a typical provincial French bistro. All the rooms are Spartan but comfortable, and three have their own terraces. Bathrooms are cramped, with only a shower stall and rather thin towels. Fixed-price menus are sumptuously prepared by the chef.

Hôtel Bautezar. Rue Frédéric-Mistral, 13520 Les Baux. ☎ **04-90-54-32-09.** Fax 04-90-54-51-49. 11 units. TEL. 350F–500F ($59.50–$85) double. MC, V. Closed Jan to Mar 15.

The entrance of this inn takes you down a few steps into the large medieval vaulted dining room, where you'll find Provençal furnishings and cloth tapestries hanging from the white stone walls, and a terrace with a view of the Val d'Enfer. The well-maintained guest rooms are decorated in Louis XVI style and come with comfortable mattresses. Bathrooms are small but well maintained with shower/tub combinations. The food is good—fixed-price menus begin at 165F ($28.05) and represent good value.

WHERE TO DINE

Two cafes near place St-Vincent offer refreshments and panoramic views: the **Hostellerie de la Reine Jeanne,** rue Frédéric-Mistral (☎ **04-90-54-32-06**), and the **Café/Restaurant Bautezar,** rue Frédéric-Mistral (☎ **04-90-54-32-09**). Note also that **L'Oustau de Beaumanière** (see above) boasts an excellent dining room.

✪ **La Riboto de Taven.** Le Val d'Enfer, 13520 Les Baux. ☎ **04-90-54-34-23.** Fax 04-90-54-38-88. Reservations required. Main courses 140F–170F ($23.80–$28.90); fixed-price menus 220F–300F ($37.40–$51) at lunch, 300F ($51) at dinner. AE, DC, MC, V. Tues noon–2pm, Thurs–Mon noon–2pm and 7:30–10pm. Closed Jan 3–Mar 15. FRENCH.

This 1835 farmhouse outside the medieval section of town has been owned by two generations of the Novi family—Christine and Philippe Theme are the English-speaking daughter and son-in-law. In summer you can sit outdoors at the beautifully laid tables; one is an old millstone. Menu items may include sea bass in olive oil, fricassée of mussels flavored with basil, and lamb en croûte with olives—plus homemade desserts. The cuisine is a personal statement of Jean-Pierre Novi, whose cookery is filled with brawny flavors and the heady perfumes of Provençal herbs.

It's also possible to rent two rooms so large they're like suites, for 1,100F ($187), breakfast included. Both have very comfortable beds, a cozy decor, and enough fluffy towels to make bathtime happy.

✳ 9 St-Rémy-de-Provence

438 miles (704.89km) S of Paris, 16 miles (25.75km) NE of Arles, 12 miles (19.31km) S of Avignon, 8 miles (12.87km) N of Les Baux

Nostradamus, the famous French physician/astrologer, was born here in 1503. Though he has many fans today, he also has detractors of his more than 600 obscure verses. In 1922 Gertrude Stein and Alice B. Toklas found St-Rémy after "wandering around everywhere a bit," as Ms. Stein wrote to Cocteau. But mainly St-Rémy is associated with Vincent van Gogh. He committed himself to an asylum here in 1889 after cutting off his left ear. Between moods of despair, he painted such works as *Olive Trees* and *Cypresses.*

Come to sleepy St-Rémy today not only for its memories and sights but for an experience of Provençal small-town living that you won't find in Aix or Avignon. It's a market town of considerable charm, and attracts the occasional celebrity who "hides out" here away from the hordes.

LES JARDINS

D5

MONTPLAISIR

chemin de Montplaisir

av. Albert Schweitzer

av. Plaisance du Touch

Ariaude

av. du Général Koening

place du
Général
de Gaulle

av. du Maréchal Juin

av. du Dix-Neuf Mars 1962

chemin de St-Bernard

LES MAGNANARELLES

av. Maréchal de Lattre

L'AUTIN

chemin de Ranjarde

av. Félix Gras

av. Louis Mistral

av. Gabriel St-René
Taillandier

av. Charles Mauron

rue Bertrand Dauvin

chemin des Figuières Folles

Arène
Barnier

Stade du
Sans Souci

chemin de Barrielle

av. Albert Gleizes

Musée
Archéologique

blvd. Gambetta

rue du Parage

Musée des
Aromes

SANS SOUCI

blvd. Marceau

rue Carnot

blvd. Mirabeau

Fontaine
Nostradamus

LE ROUGADOU

Musée
des
Alpilles

av. Fauconnet

Eglise
St-Martin

rue Lafayette

av. de la Liberation

chemin de St-Joseph

chemin de la Combette

blvd. Victor Hugo

rue Etienne Astier

Office
de
Tourisme

ST-JOSEPH

av. Jean de Servières

chemin de la L'Oratoire

chemin du Souvenir Francais

av. Durand Maillane

av. Pasteur

chemin de la Combette

chemin de la Croix d'Arles

Cimetière

Canal

des

Alpilles

av. Pierre Barbier

QUATRE
CANTONS

chemin Gaulois

av. Joseph d'Arbaud

av. Folco de Baroncelli

av. J. Baltus

chemin du Tor Blanc

D5

chemin Romain

av. Antoine de Salle

av. Vincent van Gogh

av. Edgar-le-Roy

av. Marius Girard

av. Marius Gasquet

Gaudre du Barrage

Monastère
de St-Paul-
de-Mausolée

des

Carrieres

chemin

LEGEND
Church †
Information ⓘ
Parking 🅿

To Ruins de Glanum ↓

ESSENTIALS

GETTING THERE Local **buses** from Avignon (a 45-min. ride) pull into the place de la République, in the town center. The fare is 36F ($6.10) one-way. For bus information and schedules, call ☎ 04-90-14-59-00.

VISITOR INFORMATION The **Office de Tourisme** is on place Jean-Jaurès (☎ 04-90-92-05-22).

SEEING THE SIGHTS

The cloisters of the asylum at the 12th-century **Monastère de St-Paul-de-Mausolée,** avenue Edgar-le-Roy (☎ 04-90-92-77-00), were made famous by van Gogh's paintings. Now a psychiatric hospital, the former monastery is east of D5, a short drive north of Glanum (see below). You can't visit the cell where this genius was confined from 1889 to 1890, but it's still worth coming here to see the Romanesque chapel and the cloisters with their circular arches and columns and beautifully carved capitals. The cloisters are open every Tuesday to Saturday from 9am to 7pm, except in February. Admission is 15F ($2.55) for adults, and 10F ($1.70) for students and persons ages 12 to 16. It's free for kids under 12. Adjacent to the church, you'll see a commemorative bust of van Gogh.

In the center of St-Rémy, the **Musée Archéologique,** in the Hôtel de Sade, rue du Parage (☎ 04-90-92-64-04), displays sculptures and bronzes from the ancient Roman excavations at nearby Glanum. April to September, it's open daily from 10am to noon and 2 to 6pm; February to March and October to December, from 10am to noon and 2 to 5pm. During January, it's open only by appointment; call directly or contact the local tourist office. Entrance costs 20F ($3.40) for adults, 15F ($2.55) for students and ages 12 to 17, free for children 11 and under.

Site Archéologique de Glanums (Ruins de Glanum). Av. Vincent-van-Gogh. ☎ 04-90-92-23-79. Admission 32F ($5.45) adults, 21F ($3.55) students and ages 17 to 25, free for ages 16 and under. Apr–Sept, daily 9am–7pm; Oct–Mar, daily 9am–noon and 2–5pm.

A Gallo-Roman settlement thrived here during the final days of the Roman Empire. Its historic monuments include an Arc Municipal, a triumphal arch dating from the time of Julius Caesar, and a cenotaph called the Mausolée des Jules. Garlanded with sculptured fruits and flowers, the arch dates from 20 B.C. and is the oldest in Provence. The mausoleum was raised to honor the grandsons of Augustus and is the only extant monument of its type. Entire streets and foundations of private residences from the 1st-century town can be seen. Some of the remains are from a Gallo-Greek town from the 2nd century B.C. To get there from the town center, follow the signs to LES ANTIQUES/LES BAUX—it's a half-mile south of St-Rémy on D5.

WHERE TO STAY

Note that the **Bar/Hôtel/Restaurant des Arts** (see below) also rents rooms.

✪ **Château de Roussan.** Rte. de Tarascon, 13210 St-Rémy-de-Provence. ☎ 04-90-92-11-63. Fax 04-90-92-50-59. 21 units. TEL. 440F–750F ($74.80–$127.50) double. AE, MC, V.

Although there are more lavish château hotels in the district, this one is more evocative of another time and place. This château's most famous resident, the Renaissance seer Nostradamus, lived in a rustic outbuilding a few steps from the front door. An archway of 300-year-old trees leads to the 1701 neoclassical facade of softly colored local stone. Most bedrooms are spacious, with mattresses that are well worn but still comfortable enough. Bathrooms have old-timey plumbing that still works. As you wander around the grounds you'll be back in history, especially when you come on the baroque sculptures lining the basin, fed by a stream. The restaurant, open daily for

A Countryside Drive

This 40-mile drive northeast of Arles passes through contorted limestone hills, the **Chaîne des Alpilles,** which is surrounded by olive and fruit orchards. Head south out of St-Rémy on D5, past the Monastère St-Paul-de-Mausolée on the left and Les Antiques, two Roman monuments, on the right, before climbing into the hills. Take a left turn at **La Plateau de La Caume,** the highest (422 feet) of the many rock-faced hills in the region. From here you can see the distant Parc Naturel Régional de Camargue and Mont Ventoux. After descending the far side of the slope, take a right on D27A to Les Baux, driving past the town to view the bleak **Val d'Enfer** (Valley of Hell). Then backtrack and continue south on D27/D78F until it dead-ends at D17.

A right turn takes you to **Fontvieille,** where you can pay tribute to the author Alphonse Daudet, whose *Lettres de Mon Moulin* were inspired by the Moulin de Daudet (windmill) here. To reach the windmill, take D33 (avenue des Moulins). Stop at the nearby Château de Montauban, which is now a museum in his honor. Continue south on D33 to D82 and turn left, stopping to walk along the road and view the ruins of the **Aqueducs de Barbegal** that supplied water between Arles and Eygalières when the area was part of the Roman Empire.

Backtrack to the main road and veer left on D78E to Paradou, where the road changes to D17. Keep driving straight, stopping if you wish in the village of **Maussane-les-Alpilles.** East of town, stay on the main road, which now becomes D78. At Le Destet, make a left turn to head northeast on D24. A change of perspective now allows you to view La Caume, on the left, from a distance. Keep driving past the D25 intersection and turn right on D24B to reach the ancient village of **Eygalières,** with its medieval castle and church. Just beyond it, at the junction of D24B and D74A, there is a sweeping view from the Romanesque **Chapelle St-Sixte.** A left on D74A takes you north to D99, where another left provides you with a pleasant country drive back to St-Rémy.

---

lunch and dinner, serves fixed-price menus at 165F ($28.05). Be warned that the staff here can be off-putting, but the sense of mysticism and the historical importance of the place usually compensates for Gallic crabbiness.

✪ **Hôtel Château des Alpilles.** Ancienne Rte. du Grès, 13210 St-Rémy-de-Provence. ☎ **04-90-92-03-33.** Fax 04-90-92-45-17. E-mail: chateau.alpilles@wanadoo.fr. 21 units. MINIBAR TV TEL. 900F–1,080F ($153–$183.60) double; from 1,400F ($238) suite. AE, DC, MC, V. Closed Jan 5–Feb 17 and Nov 20–Dec 18.

When she converted this mansion in 1980, Françoise Bon wanted to create a "house for paying friends." When it was built in 1827 by the Pichot family, it housed Chateaubriand and a host of other luminaries. To reach it, you pass beneath the 300-year-old trees that surround the neoclassic exterior. The spacious rooms have combined the best of an antique framework with plush upholstery, rich carpeting, and vibrant colors. Each boasts whimsical accessories, like the pair of porcelain panthers flanking one of the carved mantels. Travertine-trimmed baths with large windows have hair dryers, and lots of soft towels. Some are in a gracefully renovated 19th-century annex. Mme Bon has installed an elevator, but you may prefer to descend the massive stone staircase. In the garden are an outdoor pool, two tennis courts, a sauna, and a grill where you can order lunch in summer. In the evening, set menus cost 197F ($33.50) each.

Hôtel van Gogh. 1 ave. Jean Moulin, 13210 St-Rémy de Provence. ☎ **04-90-92-14-02.** Fax 04-90-92-09-05. 21 units. TEL. 320F–380F ($54.40–$64.60) double. Free parking. AE, MC, V.

Set 200 yards east of the town's historic center, beside the highway leading to Cavaillon, this is a low-slung and pleasant hotel covered with ivy. Built in 1974, and renovated several times since then, it offers reception areas with a fireplace, parquet floors, and traditional furniture, and clean, well-maintained bedrooms with a minimum of furniture but with patterned curtains and comfortable mattresses. Bathrooms are small. Breakfast, which takes place on a backyard veranda with a striped canopy, is the only meal served. There is a rectangular swimming pool in an enclosed courtyard.

Les Antiques. 15 av. Pasteur, 13210 St-Rémy-de-Provence. ☎ **04-90-92-03-02.** Fax 04-90-92-50-40. 27 units. MINIBAR TEL. 370F–750F ($62.90–$127.50) double. AE, DC, MC, V. Closed mid-Oct to mid-Apr.

This moderately priced, stylish, 19th-century villa is in a 7-acre park with a pool. It contains an elegant reception lounge, which opens onto several salons, all furnished in Napoléon III. Some accommodations are in a private modern pavilion, with direct access to the garden. The rooms are handsomely furnished, usually in pastels with flowered wallpapers. In the main building, they come in a variety of styles and shapes. Those in the modern pavilion are more comfortable and larger, but have less character. In all, you get first-rate mattresses and fine linen on comfortable French beds. Bathrooms are small but efficiently organized and well maintained, with adequate shelf space, luxury toiletries, and a set of fluffy towels. In summer you're served breakfast (the only meal) in what used to be the Orangerie.

✪ **Vallon de Valrugues.** Chemin Canto-Cigalo, 13210 St-Rémy-de-Provence. ☎ **04-90-92-04-40.** Fax 04-90-92-44-01. 53 units. MINIBAR TV TEL. 740F–1,580F ($125.80–$268.60) double; 1,980F–4,900F ($336.60–$833) suite. AE, DC, MC, V. Free parking.

Surrounded by a park, this Mediterranean hotel has not only the best accommodations but the best restaurant in town. The owners, Françoise and Jean-Michel Gallon, offer beautifully furnished rooms and suites, all with built-in safes. Rooms have recently been enlarged and renovated, with marble baths added and comfortable mattresses. The dining terrace is so pleasant it almost competes with the cuisine, which is winning praise for innovative light dishes such as John Dory with truffles and frozen nougat with a confit of fruits. Facilities include a pool, tennis courts, a sauna and gym, and a horseback-riding ring with instructors (for which you pay extra).

WHERE TO DINE

A great dining choice is the restaurant at **Vallon de Valrugues** (see above).

Bar/Hôtel/Restaurant des Arts. 32 bd. Victor-Hugo, 13210 St-Rémy-de-Provence. ☎ **04-90-92-08-50.** Reservations recommended. Main courses 75F–135F ($12.75–$22.95); fixed-price menus 120F–145F ($20.40–$24.65). AE, DC, MC, V. Wed–Mon noon–2pm and 7:30–9:30pm. Closed Feb and Nov 1–12. FRENCH.

This old-style cafe/restaurant evokes the earthy pleasures of *gitanes* and *pastis,* and in many ways it hasn't changed a lot since the days of Albert Camus. The wait for dinner can be as long as 45 minutes, so you may want to spend some time in the bar, with its wooden tables, pine paneling, copper pots, and slightly faded decor. Don't expect cutting-edge cuisine or a modern point of view, as everything about this place (including the speech of the all-Provençal staff), is immersed in the Midi of long ago. The menu lists specialties like rabbit terrine, pepper steak with champagne, tournedos with madeira and mushrooms, duckling in orange sauce, and three preparations of trout.

Warning: Always call before heading here and don't take the opening hours above too literally. The aging owner recently told us she reserves the right to close whenever she is tired.

La Maison Jaune. 15 rue Carnot. ☎ **04-90-92-56-14.** Reservations recommended. Set-price lunches 120F–285F ($20.40–$48.45); set-price dinners 175F–285F ($29.75–$48.45). MC, V. June–Sept, Wed–Sun noon–2pm and Tues–Sun 7:30–9:30pm. Oct–May, Tues–Sat noon–2pm and Mon–Sat 7:30–9:30pm. FRENCH/PROVENÇAL

The pair of dining rooms in this 18th-century mansion are among the most popular in town. The cuisine is prepared and served with flair by François and Catherine Perraud. In good weather, you can dine on an outdoor terrace overlooking the Hôtel de Sade. Menu items include pigeon roasted in wine from Les Baux; grilled sardines served with candied lemon and raw fennel; artichoke hearts marinated in white wine and offered with tomatoes; and a succulent version of roasted rack of lamb served with a tapenade of black olives and pulverized anchovies.

Le Jardin de Frédéric. 8 bd. Gambetta. ☎ **04-90-92-27-76.** Reservations required. Main courses 90F–110F ($15.30–$18.70); fixed-price menus 135F–175F ($22.95–$29.75). MC, V. Thurs–Tues noon–2pm and 7:30–9:30pm. Closed Feb. FRENCH.

Charming, with a good-humored atmosphere, this restaurant occupies a green-painted villa that was built on the site of a garden where Frédéric Mistral, "national poet" of Provence, wrote part of his opus. Menu items are innovative and reflect culinary techniques both from local sources and the grand restaurants of faraway Paris. Savor the seductive, succulent soufflé of codfish, served with saffron and garlic sauce; or carpaccio of duckling with foie gras. Try the tender rack of Sisteron lamb with a creamy garlic sauce; or filet of sea bass with basil sauce. Dessert might be a chocolate mousse with vanilla sauce. In summer, the dining room expands, perhaps in a style that would have been appreciated by Mistral himself, outside into the open air.

10 Cavaillon

436 miles (701.67km) SE of Paris, 17 miles (27.36km) SE of Avignon, 26 miles (41.84km) NE of Arles, 36½ miles (58.74km) NW of Aix-en-Provence

In the fertile Durance Valley, Cavaillon is the site of France's largest vegetable market, the **Marché d'Intért National,** a clearing house for the more than 880,000 tons of fruits and vegetables produced annually in the fields and gardens surrounding the town. Only wholesale buyers and sellers can actually trade in the drab, industrial-looking sprawl that begins about a mile south of the town center. If you want an idea of the marketplace's scope and scale, follow the signs from the town center pointing to MIN. Morning is the busiest time, between 9am and noon, Monday to Friday. The most famous local agrarian product is the *charentais,* better known as the melon de Cavaillon, a yellowish-green ribbed melon with sweet, bright-orange flesh. The French passion for the melon is illustrated by an agreement between the author Alexandre Dumas père and the Cavaillon library: On November 15, 1864, Dumas agreed to donate the 194 volumes of writings to the local library in return for a lifetime yearly annuity of a dozen melons.

The area's thriving agriculture can be traced back to François I, who authorized the use of the Durance River for irrigation in 1537. This action facilitated a change—the region's dry grain fields gave way to the cornucopia of vegetables that is produced today.

ESSENTIALS

GETTING THERE   Cavaillon is connected to the rail lines of the SNCF via a spur line from Avignon that operates only once or twice a day in either direction. A taxi from the Avignon rail station costs around 150F ($25.50). About 10 buses a day leave the Avignon train station, arriving in Cavaillon at a parking lot on the avenue Pierre Sémard. Fares are 25F ($4.25) per person each way. For bus schedules and information, contact the tourist office.

VISITOR INFORMATION   The **Office de Tourisme** is on place François-Tourel (☎ 04-90-71-32-01).

SEEING THE SIGHTS

In its early days, Cavaillon was a Roman trading center, and a reconstructed 1st-century A.D. **Roman arch** on place du Clos pays tribute to that epoch. A steep path behind the arch leads up the Colline St-Jacques to the medieval **Chapelle St-Jacques,** which offers a superb view of the farm valley, river, and distant mountains. Although the 12th-century chapel is permanently closed, the verdant gardens that surround it give perspective to its squat and rather bulky dimensions.

The **Musée de l'Hôtel Dieu** (also known as the **Musée Archéologique**) is in the chapel of the Ancien Hôtel-Dieu, porte d'Avignon (☎ 04-90-76-00-34). It displays artifacts of previous settlements, including Neolithic and Roman objects, and screens films documenting the town's history. It's open Monday, Wednesday, and Sunday from 10am to noon and 2 to 5pm, with an admission charge of 20F ($3.40).

The **Cathédrale Notre-Dame et St-Véran** (☎ 04-90-76-00-34), dates to the 12th century, with 17th-century updates to the interior. It's presently in a state of disrepair, and might even be closed during the lifetime of this edition, but until further notice, it's open Wednesday to Monday 9am to 12:30pm and 2:30 to 6:30pm. Inside, you'll find minor paintings by Mignard and Parrocel.

The 18th-century **synagogue,** rue Hébraïque, houses the **Musée Juif Comtadin** (☎ 04-90-76-00-34), a small museum of ritualistic objects. However, the museum does not document the papal persecution of the once-sizable Jewish community, which was confined to a small ghetto surrounding the synagogue. Although small scale, the synagogue's interior is quite beautiful—here a colony of Jews that never exceeded 200 attended services against a backdrop of Louis XV–style paneling and wrought-iron balustrades. In recent years restorers have exposed the synagogue's original colors: blue and yellow designs on a gray background. From October to March, the museum is open Wednesday to Monday 10am to noon and 2 to 4:30pm. April to September, it's open Wednesday to Monday 9:30am to 12:30pm and 2:30 to 6:30pm. The price of admission is included in the cost of the ticket to the Musée de l'Hôtel Dieu (see above).

WHERE TO STAY

Hôtel du Parc. 183 place François-Tourel, 84300 Cavaillon. ☎ **04-90-71-57-78.** Fax 04-90-76-10-35. 40 units. A/C TV TEL. 250F–275F ($42.50–$46.75) double. MC, V. Parking 26F ($4.40).

The town's most appealing hotel occupies a pair of buildings: one a private house built in the 18th century, the other a modern structure. Both face a landscaped courtyard with a fountain. All rooms here are comfortable, done in a country-rustic theme. Each was repainted and upgraded in 1998 and 1999. Bathrooms are tiled in pale brown or pale blue tiles, with adequate numbers of good-sized towels, and mattresses are firm and comfortable. Breakfast is the only meal served (in summer in the courtyard), but the cheerful owners will direct you to a restaurant choice nearby. The Fin de Siècle (see below) is very close to the hotel.

WHERE TO DINE

✪ **Alain Nicolet.** Route de Pertuis, Cheval Blanc. ☎ **04-90-78-01-56.** Reservations recommended. Main courses 145F–170F ($24.65–$28.90); fixed-price menus 150F–360F

($25.50–$61.20). AE, DC, MC, V. Tues–Sat noon–2pm and 7:30–9:30pm, Sun noon–2pm; also Sun–Mon 7:30–9:30pm July–Aug. Closed 1 week in Oct. From town, drive 2½ miles south, following the signs to Cheval Blanc. PROVENÇAL.

In an authentic replica of a stone-sided Provençal *mas*, this gourmet restaurant serves picture-perfect dishes made with the freshest seasonal ingredients. In summer, an olive-shaded terrace offers vistas over olive groves, the surrounding countryside, and the Alpilles. There's a trio of dining rooms, each containing only four tables, discreetly supervised by Mireille, the wife of owner/chef Alain Nicolet. Menu items include cray-fish with spices and onion-and-tomato marmalade, lobster ravioli with spinach, stuffed rabbit with Provençal herbs, and roast leg of lamb with its own juice and rata-touille. Dessert might be palette à la Nicolet, which is likely to include nougat glacé, a fondant of chocolate, a tulipe of strawberries, and a lemon or a chocolate tart. The cellars contain more than 300 vintages, mostly from Provence; at least 30% sell for under 150F ($25.50).

✪ **Prévot.** 353 av. de Verdun. ☎ **04-90-71-32-43.** Reservations recommended. Main courses 70F–200F ($11.90–$34); fixed-price menus 160F–350F ($27.20–$59.50) at lunch, 230F–360F ($39.10–$61.20) at dinner. AE, MC, DC, V. Tues–Sat noon–2pm and 7:15–9:30pm, Sun 12:30–3pm. PROVENÇAL.

This is Cavaillon's most sophisticated and endearing restaurant and has flourished since 1981 under the administration of Jean-Jacques Prévot and a well-trained staff. You'll dine in a 200-year-old building whose rooms contain so many references to melons and their cultivation that the municipal government often cites the decor as the town's unofficial "Museum of the Melon."

Menu items change with the season but usually include cured ham of wild boar, thinly sliced and served with slices of melon arranged into a daisy; a platter with two preparations of foie gras (one with fennel, the other with apples, cinnamon, and a confit of onions); soufflé of artichokes prepared with foie gras and barigoule sauce; a succulent tart layered with anchovies, tomato confit, and parmesan cheese; and a "trilogy" of scallops. Most controversial of all is a recipe that elevates the region's obses-sion with melons to heights that lesser chefs would never attempt: filet of red mullet baked with melon. According to the chef, the success of the dish depends entirely on knowing how to select a melon just firm enough and ripe enough to make the dish a success. Selections from the cellar are usually excellent.

Restaurant Fin de Siècle. 46 place du Clos (upstairs). ☎ **04-90-71-12-27.** Reservations recommended. Fixed-price menus 90F–210F ($15.30–$35.70). AE, DC, MC, V. Tues noon–2pm, Thurs–Mon noon–2pm and 7–9:30pm. Closed Aug. FRENCH.

This restaurant is one floor above street level in a turn-of-the-century building near the heart of town. On its ground floor is another place with virtually the same name (see below), so you're likely to hear a lot about its role as a *restaurant gastronomique,* a name it deserves for its cultivated finesse. You can order such Toulouse-derived dishes as cassoulet, confit of duckling, and magret of duckling with fruits; and upscale Provençal plates like red mullet in puff pastry, goat-cheese mousse with thyme-flavored cream sauce, and gâteau of eggplant with sweet-pepper/cream sauce. The dozen or so desserts include a succulent chocolate suprème served with a confit of oranges.

Bar/Brasserie Fin de Siècle. 46 place du Clos (ground floor). ☎ **04-90-71-28-85.** Lunch only: 48F–60F ($8.15 to $10.20), fixed-price menu 70F ($11.90). Mon–Sat noon–2pm; coffee and drinks: daily 7am–1am.

On the ground floor of the same building (see above) is our favorite cafe in Cavaillon. It's run by the Tallard family and has a striking sculpted and frescoed Napoléon III ceiling. If you phone in advance and the staff isn't too busy, you can dine here as well. Menu items include two-fisted versions of spaghetti carbonara, roast guinea fowl with vegetables and French fries, brochettes of blood sausage, and sliced roast lamb. You might order one of those anise-flavored drinks, such as Ricard, elbow to elbow with some of the town's lorry drivers and greengrocers.

11 Gordes

443 miles (712.94km) SE of Paris, 22 miles (35.41km) E of Avignon, 10 miles (16.09km) NE of Cavaillon, 40 miles (64.37km) N of the Marseille airport

Gordes is a colorful village, whose twisted narrow cobblestone streets circle a rocky bluff above the Imergue Valley. By the turn of the century, as its residents migrated toward cities and factory jobs, it suffered from the kind of attrition that was affecting agrarian communities all over Europe.

The 12th-century village was saved by modern art. Cubist painter André Lhote discovered the hamlet in 1938, and renowned artists like Marc Chagall began visiting and summering here. The late Victor Vasarély, one of the founders of op art, became its most famous full-time resident.

ESSENTIALS

GETTING THERE   There's no rail station in Gordes. Trains arrive at nearby Cavaillon, where taxis wait at the railway station; the trip into Gordes costs around 150F ($25.50). For **rail information** and schedules in Cavaillon, call ☎ **08-36-35-35-35.** There are no local buses. The village itself is closed to cars, but large parking lots are along its edge.

VISITOR INFORMATION   The **Office de Tourisme** is in the Salle des Gardes du Château, place du Château (☎ **04-90-72-02-75**).

SEEING THE SIGHTS

Dominating the skyline, the **Château de Gordes** is a fortified 12th-century structure whose dramatic silhouette contributed to the town's nickname as "the Acropolis of Provence." The château was really a fortress with crenellated bastions and round towers in each of its four corners. This is home to a museum, **Musée du Château de Gordes** (☎ **04-90-72-02-89**), site of a collection of works by Flemish-born painter Pol Mora (d. 1998). Be warned that this collection may or may not be replaced with the *oeuvres* of other painters during the lifetime of this edition, including some by surrealist and geometric master Vasarély. It's open Wednesday to Monday 10am to noon and 2 to 6pm. Adults pay 25F ($4.25) admission; students and persons ages 11 to 18 pay 20F ($3.40). Entrance is free for children under 10.

Some 2½ miles south of the village, surrounded by a rocky, arid landscape that supports only stunted olive trees and gnarled oaks (the Provençaux refer to this type of terrain as *la garrigue),* stands the **Moulin des Bouillons,** route de St-Pantaléon (☎ **04-90-72-22-11**), an olive-oil mill so ancient it was mentioned in the 1st-century writings of Pliny the Elder. It's now owned by the stained-glass artist Frédérique Duran, and its interior boasts the original Roman floors and the base of the olive press. In the garden is the **Musée du Vitrail** (Museum of Stained Glass), tracing the history of its manufacture. There's also an art gallery showing pieces by Duran and other artists. Year-round, except between November and March, when it's closed, the complex is open Wednesday to Monday 10am to noon and 2 to 6pm. A ticket granting admission to both the mill and the museum costs 30F ($5.10).

Cousin to the *trullis* of Italy are the reconstructed bories in the **Village des Bories,** Les Savournines (☎ **04-90-72-03-48**), 2 miles southwest of town. These mysterious stone beehive structures are composed of thin layers of stone that spiral upward into a dome. The substantial buildings were constructed without mortar, and are surrounded by stone boundary walls of similar construction. Their origin and use is a mystery— some sources claim they're Neolithic. What is known is that they were inhabited until the early 1800s. Their form suggests they were developed by shepherds and goat herders as shelter for themselves and their flocks. To get here, take D15, veering right beyond a fork at D2. A sign marks another right turn toward the village, where you must park and walk for about 45 minutes to visit the site. The village is open February to mid-November, daily from 9am to dusk; mid-November to January, Saturday and Sunday from 10am to dusk. Admission is 30F ($5.10) for adults and 20F ($3.40) for children.

Founded in 1148, the **Abbaye de Sénanque,** a Cistercian monastery 2½ miles north of Gordes on D15/D177 (☎ **04-90-72-05-72**), sits in isolation surrounded by lavender fields. It was abandoned during the Revolution, reopened in the 19th century, closed again in 1969, and reopened yet again (by the Cistercians) in 1988. The influential 20th-century writer and Catholic theologian Thomas Merton can be counted among those who found peace here. One of Provence's most beautiful medieval monuments, it's open Monday to Saturday from 10am to noon and 2 to 6pm and Sunday from 2 to 6pm. Admission costs 25F ($4.25) for adults, 20F ($3.40) for students, and 10F ($1.70) for persons ages 12 to 18. It's free for persons under 12. Be aware that this is a working monastery, not merely a tourist site. You can attend any of five masses per day, buy religious souvenirs and texts in the gift shop, and generally marvel at a medieval setting brought back to life.

WHERE TO STAY

Hôtel la Gacholle. Route de Murs, 84220 Gordes. ☎ **04-90-72-01-36.** Fax 04-90-72-01-81. E-mail: la.gacholle.gordes@wanadoo.fr. 12 units. MINIBAR TV TEL. 450F–750F ($76.50–$127.50) double. AE, MC, V. Closed Jan 15–Mar 15. From town, drive ³/₄ mile northeast, following the only road with signs for Murs.

Built in the 1960s in the form of an earth-toned Provençal *mas* (farmhouse), this inn combines stone walls, wooden beams, a tiled roof, brick floors, and flagstone terraces into an intimate setting. It stands in a grove of holm oak, offering a great view over the Luberon valley from its pool and dining terrace. The guest rooms are cozy, comfortable, and designed for a maximum of peace and quiet.

In 1998, the entire place was renovated, repainted, and redecorated by hardworking new owners. A heating mechanism was added to the existing swimming pool, the tennis court was upgraded, and improvements made to the quality of both the bedroom mattresses and the towels. In addition, the restaurant hours were extended. Here, within a room with a blazing fireplace, flanked with rough-hewn stone and accented with elegant linen, crystal, and china, you'll enjoy dishes that include panfried foie gras with figs and honey; crisp-fried local fish served with a "caviar" of eggplant and fresh Provençal herbs; and a ragout of Provençal lamb. In season, the fresh asparagus, prepared either hot or cold in a variety of ways, is heavenly. Set-price menus cost 85F ($14.45) at lunch and 195F ($33.15) at dinner.

✪ **Hôtel La Bastide de Gordes.** Le Village, 84220 Gordes. ☎ **04-90-72-12-12.** Fax 04-90-72-05-20. www.provenceguide.com. E-mail: bastide-gordes@avignon.pacwan.net. 31 units. A/C MINIBAR TV TEL. 700F–1,500F ($119–$255) double; 1,450F–1,850F ($246.50–$314.50) suite. AE, MC, V. Closed Nov 4–Mar 14. Free parking.

This hotel occupies what was a 17th-century manor house that was enlarged after World War II to become the headquarters for the town's gendarmerie. In 1988 it was transformed into a tasteful four-star hotel in a building staggered uphill near the town's summit. Some rooms have views over the valley of the Luberon. Bedrooms are luxurious and tasteful, with contemporary, antique, and reproduction furnishings and soft colors. Mattresses are firm and up to date. In 1999, management added a well-managed restaurant ("Les Terrasses") to the premises to supplement the already-existing swimming pool, sauna, and exercise facilities. Set-price lunches cost from 195F to 295F ($33.15 to $50.15); set-price dinners 245F to 295F ($41.65 to $50.15). The restaurant is open for lunch and dinner daily except Tuesday and Wednesday. During July and August, it's open daily.

✪ **Hôtel Les Bories.** Route de l'Abbaye de Sénanque, 84220 Gordes. ☎ **04-90-72-00-51.** Fax 04-90-72-01-22. www.euhotels.com/les bories. E-mail: lesbories@aol.com. 18 units. A/C MINIBAR TV TEL. 780F–2,100F ($132.60–$357) double; 1,700F–2,100F ($289–$357) suite. AE, DC, MC, V. Closed mid-Nov to mid-Feb. From town, drive 1½ miles north, following the signs to Abbaye de Sénanque or Venasque.

This is Gordes's best accommodation, a modern hotel clad in rough stone and built around the core of an old Provençal *mas*. It takes advantage of its hillside setting, offering vistas from the dining terrace, outdoor pool and terrace, glass-fronted lobby, and indoor pool. The garden ties into the valley with olive, holm oak, and lavender. The decor was inspired by high-tech Milanese design, with streamlined furniture, tile floors, and Oriental rugs in both public spaces and the spacious guest rooms. Rooms come equipped with fine linen and firm mattresses, plus bathrooms with adequate shelf space and shower/tub combinations. The cozy dining room is in a nook rising into a craggy stone vault, and the matching fireplace is topped by a mantle of massive rugged beams. The sophisticated in-house restaurant is open daily for dinner and Wednesday to Sunday for lunch: Fixed-price lunches are 195F to 390F ($33.15 to $66.30) and fixed-price dinners are 240F to 390F ($40.80 to $66.30).

WHERE TO DINE

The area's best cuisine is served at the **Hôtel Les Bories.** Also excellent is the restaurant at the **Hôtel de la Gacholle** (see above).

✪ **Comptoir de Victuailler.** Place du Château. ☎ **04-90-72-01-31.** Reservations required. Main courses 120F–220F ($20.40–$37.40); fixed-price lunch 175F–200F ($29.75–$34). DC, MC, V. Thurs–Tues 12:30–2:30 and Thurs–Mon 8–9:30pm. During July and August, daily 12:30–2:30 and Wed–Mon 8–9:30pm. Closed Nov–Easter. PROVENÇAL.

Our favorite restaurant in Gordes occupies a 200-year-old once-private home near the town's summit. It was opened in 1985 by its present owner, Jean-Michel Schmitt. The restaurant has only eight tables and—amazingly—only one chef, the good-natured Joelle Chaudat, who has single-handedly prepared all the meals from a cramped kitchen in back since the restaurant opened.

You'll dine in a setting like that of a generously stocked Provençal épicerie. Look for jars of olive oil and especially Côtes du Rhône wine, of which the owner is especially enamored. He knows most of the region's growers as well as their individual virtues. Menu items are classic and savory, like a rouelle of lamb that, according to the owners, must be made with new garlic; a best-selling codfish with sweet peppers; and a sophisticated recipe for roast guinea fowl with raspberries. Desserts may be a traditional recipe for chocolate cake or a more labor-intensive St-Honoré aux Trois Crèmes (puff pastry stuffed, frosted, and slathered with three cream-based sauces). The result is never "vulgar and heavy," in the words of the owner, but instead elicits rave reviews.

Le Mas Tourteron. Chemin de St-Blaise, Les Imberts. ☎ **04-90-72-00-16.** Fixed-price lunch 160F ($27.20) Wed–Fri; otherwise, set menus 200F–290F ($34–$49.30). AE, MC, V. Wed–Sun noon–2pm; Tues–Sat 7:30–9:30pm. Closed mid-Nov to mid-Feb. Take D2 for 4 miles southwest of Gordes. PROVENÇAL.

On the outskirts of the village of Les Imberts, this restaurant occupies an 18th-century Provençal *mas* whose cherry trees and vines still produce good fruit. There's just one dining room, a sun-flooded space, with additional seating that spills over into the verdant garden. Menu items are based on fresh ingredients and include cassolette of asparagus and herbs with a medley of other (strictly seasonal) ingredients, charlotte of lamb with Provençal herbs, and a *tarte à l'envers* (upside-down tart) of roast rabbit with black-olive tapenade. Things here are small-scale and just a wee bit fussy, but overall, the food is very good and the staff is well-meaning.

12 Carpentras

422 miles (679.14km) S of Paris, 32 miles (51.50km) N of Salon-de-Provence, 16 miles (25.75km) NE of Avignon, 16 miles (25.75km) SE of Orange

The bustling medieval market town of Carpentras is at the heart of a fruitful area of Provence known for its truffles and *berlingots* (sweets). Today it has a population of 30,000 and the city is ringed with boulevards on the site of its former medieval ramparts.

ESSENTIALS

GETTING THERE   There is no passenger train service. However, there are bus links if you're in Marseille. Bus links are provided by **Cars Arnaud Buses** (☎ **04-90-63-01-82**). Four or five of this line's buses head north per day.

If you're driving, take D942 northeast of Avignon.

VISITOR INFORMATION   The **Office de Tourisme** is at 170 av. Jean-Jaurès (☎ **04-90-63-00-78**).

EXPLORING THE TOWN

Porte d'Orange, from the 14th century, is a massive fortified gateway at the north side of the old town—all that's left of Pope Innocent VI's medieval defense wall that once had 32 towers and 4 gates. Across the street from the gateway is an ancient fountain on boulevard du Nord.

The **Palais de Justice** from 1640 is a former archbishop's palace modeled after the Farnese Palace in Rome, with some interesting frescoes from the 17th and 18th centuries. The concierge will usually let you look inside. Behind it is a Roman **Arc de Triomphe,** the only vestige remaining from the Roman era. It was built in the first century of Augustus Caesar's reign to commemorate the victory of Rome over the barbarians. Some very beautiful sculptures still decorate its east and west sides.

Cathédrale St-Siffrein. Place St-Siffrein. ☎ **04-90-63-08-33.** Free admission. Mon–Sat 8am–6pm and Sun 8am–1pm.

The cathedral was built on 1405 on the site of three previous churches. It has a 12th-century dome, and other Romanesque features. Construction was carried on for more than a century, which explains its different styles. It was finished in 1519. The west door is Renaissance but the south door is in a flamboyant Gothic style. You'll notice the decorated pediments, the capitals representing local vegetation, and a medieval fable of Goupil the fox. The cathedral is also rich in stained glass. To the left of the altar is a triptych of St. Siffrein, the town's patron, from the 15th century.

La Synagogue. Place Maurice Charretier. ☎ **04-90-63-39-97.** Free admission (donations appreciated). Mon–Thurs 10am–noon and 3–5pm, Fri 10am–noon and 3–4pm.

One of oldest synagogues in France, it dates from 1367, when the Jews were financiers to the Avignon popes, who consequently gave refuge to Jews expelled from other parts of France and Provence. The synagogue was rebuilt in the 18th century and is still in use even though few Jews remain in town. It has a rich rococo interior. You can see the ritual bath *(cabussadou)* in the basement, and an oven for baking unleavened bread. In 1990 the Jewish cemetery here suffered an attack by right-wing vandals.

SHOPPING

The most amazing candy creations, based on the abundance of nearby fields and gardens, is for sale at **Confiserie Clavel,** rue Porte d'Orange (☎ **04-90-63-07-59**). The specialty here—fashioned from figs, melons, and clementines—is berlingot, a hard caramel candy. The display window is filled with the latest creations to devour. The shop owner holds the world's Guinness record for the largest berlingot creation, weighing 56 kg. You'll fall in love with this shop and want to take it home after sampling truffles au Grand Marnier or truffles au calva (Calvados).

WHERE TO STAY

Hostellerie Blason de Provence. 515 Route de Provence, 84170 Monteux. ☎ **04-90-66-31-34.** Fax 04-90-66-83-05. 19 units. A/C TV TEL. 325F–440F ($55.25–$74.80) double. AE, MC, V. Take D942 2½ miles north of Carpentras. Closed Jan–Mar.

Set in the hamlet of Monteux, 2½ miles south of Carpentras, this large, rambling, generously proportioned country house preserves much of its original grace and style and architectural interest. On the grounds grounds is a flowering terrace with a striped canopy where tea is served throughout the afternoon. Bedrooms are simple but comfortable, in pale colors, with big windows overlooking the grounds. Bedrooms are medium size and have a real French provincial feeling. Beds are equipped with firm mattresses and fine linen. Bathrooms are small but have shower/tub combinations. On the premises are a restaurant, a tennis court, and a kidney-shaped swimming pool ringed with chaise longues and potted flowers.

Hôtel du Fiacre. 153 rue Vigne, 84200 Carpentras. ☎ **04-90-63-03-15.** Fax 04-90-60-49-73. 20 units. TV TEL. 290F–480F ($49.30–$81.60) double. MC, V.

The hotel is named after the carriages *(fiacres)* that used to unload 18th-century travelers here. The neoclassical front of the place is still elegant and formal, reminding you of that era, but our preferred spot is within the garden in back, where blankets of ivy sheath the rear of the house. Rooms are medium size and high-ceilinged, and often contain at least one old piece of furniture. They have exceedingly comfortable quality mattresses and fine linen; bathrooms are small but well kept, with adequate shelf space and good-sized towels. Public rooms are airy and relatively formal, and include a breakfast area with hanging tapestries, antique armoires, and a welcome kind of humor on the part of the Roll family, the owners/managers.

WHERE TO DINE

Rives d'Auzon. 47 bd. Du Nord. ☎ **04-90-60-62-62.** Reservations recommended. Main courses 70F–90F ($11.90–$15.30). Set menus 130F–190F ($22.10–$32.30). MC, V. Tues–Thurs noon–1:30pm and 7:30–9:30pm.

Just outside the Port d'Orange in a turn-of-the-century ocher-colored stucco house, you can enjoy some of the dishes that are known throughout Provence in a Provençale setting of oversize bay windows and a decor of lavender, gold, and cream. The menu varies widely according to the season. You might begin with freshly made soup laden with fresh Provençal vegetables or savory *petits farcis* (stuffed and deep-fried vegetables). For a main course selection, consider roast pigeon with sweet garlic; noisettes of lamb with risotto; a savory version of roast codfish with fresh vegetables and garlic-flavored mayonnaise; or fresh grilled fish.

13 Roussillon & Bonnieux

These villages lie so close to each other that you can visit both in a long morning or afternoon.

ROUSSILLON

28 miles (45.06km) E of Avignon, 6 miles (9.66km) E of Gordes

Color—17 shades of ocher, to be more precise—has proven to be this village's lifeblood. From as far back as Roman times, the area's rich deposits of ocher have been valued. Beginning in the late 1700s Roussillon's ocher powders were shipped around the world from nearby Marseille. Though the mining industry has dried up, hordes of artists and visitors still flock here to marvel and be inspired by the gorgeous ranges of the vibrant warm tones. Roussillon also served as a giant laboratory of sorts for the famous American sociologist William Wylie, who packed up his family and moved here for a year to study the village's complex life of work and fun, love and family feuds, and simple day-to-day existence. Later he published his study as *A Village in the Vaucluse.*

ESSENTIALS

GETTING THERE   From Avignon, drive east on N7 to D973, then to D22. Finally, turn north on D149 and follow the signs to Roussillon. The trip takes about 45 minutes. There's no train or bus service.

VISITOR INFORMATION   The **Office de Tourisme** is on place de la Poste (☎ **04-90-05-60-25**).

SEEING THE SIGHTS

Take time to explore the narrow, steep streets, soaking in the rusts, reds, and ochers of the stone used in the construction of the houses. From the **Castrum,** at the high point along rue de l'Eglise, you'll see a magnificent vista. Face north and gaze across the Vaucluse plateau and to Mont Ventoux. Turn south to see the Coulon valley and the Grand Luberon.

   You can reach the old ocher quarries with their sunburned exposed rocks by taking a 40-minute scenic walk east of the village. Paths to the quarries start at the tourist office (see "Essentials," above). Another panorama is the huge red cliffs of **Chaussée des Géants.** To view them, take the path southeast of the tourist office. The walk is about 45 minutes and includes a great look back at Roussillon.

   About 3 miles south of town on D149 is the **pont Julien.** Built more than 2,000 years ago, this three-arched Roman engineering feat of precisely hewn stone spans the Calavon River without the use of any mortar. It's thought to have been named in honor of the nearby Roman town of Apta Julia, known today as Apt.

WHERE TO STAY

Le Mas de Garrigon. Route de St-Saturnin d'Apt, 84220 Roussillon. ☎ **04-90-05-63-22.** Fax 04-90-05-70-01. www.masdegarrigon@wanadoo.fr. E-mail: garrigon@aol.com. 9 units. MINIBAR TV TEL. 650F–800F ($110.50–$136) double; 920F–970F ($156.40–$164.90) suite. AE, DC, MC, V.

This sprawling country estate house has been transformed into an inviting inn with an authentic Provençal feel. The well-scrubbed rooms are spacious, with dark exposed beams, warm-colored walls, and beautiful, contrasting fabrics. All have private south-facing terraces that look out onto the Luberon. There's a well-stocked library with comfortable armchairs, a sitting room with a large terra-cotta mantel and fireplace, and an intimate dining room with rustic antique furniture, where excellent meals are served. The grounds consist of an outdoor pool and patio surrounded by the shimmering greens and silvers of pine, aspen, almond, and olive trees. Staff here is not particularly well informed, but well-meaning nonetheless.

Le Mas de la Tour. 84400 Gargas. ☎ **04-90-74-12-10.** Fax 04-90-04-83-67. 33 units. TV TEL. 225F–500F ($38.25–$85) double. MC, V. Closed Oct–Mar. From Gargas, drive 2 miles south, following the signs to Apt.

The history of this *mas* on the outskirts of town dates back some 800 years. In 1985 it was completely renovated with all modern amenities added, including a large enticing pool. The rooms run the gamut from matchbox-sized to palatial. The smaller ones have exterior entrances and are somewhat reminiscent of those found in simple motels; the larger ones have bathtubs and terraces. Each has firm, comfortable mattresses and good-sized towels. The common areas, with heavy exposed beams and stone walls, include a billiards room, a library, an English bar, and a restaurant where you can enjoy a well-prepared dinner for 125F to 180F ($21.25 to $30.60).

WHERE TO DINE

David. Place de la Poste. ☎ **04-90-05-60-13.** Reservations recommended. Main courses 80F–130F ($13.60–$22.10); fixed-price menus 135F–270F ($22.95–$45.90). MC, V. Tues–Sun noon–2pm and 7:30–9pm. Closed from the end of Nov to mid-Mar. PROVENÇAL.

The town's most popular restaurant, it creates a pleasurable experience with its airy dining area and panoramic views of the red cliffs and hills of the Vaucluse. In the warmer months, dining is *en plein air* on the flowered terrace. The talented chef/owner Jean David is a traditional restaurateur who takes pride in his art, which he's been practicing since the 1950s. He works alongside his wife, son, and daughter in this family-run place. Menu items include a rice casserole of scallops and spinach, grilled country lamb flank rubbed with rosemary and served with an assortment of seasonal vegetables, and a tender beef filet with dark morel sauce. The light homemade fruit sorbets are a perfect end to a satisfying meal.

Le Bistro de Roussillon. Place de la Mairie. ☎ **04-90-05-74-45.** Reservations recommended. Main courses 90F–130F ($15.30–$22.10); fixed-price menu 105F ($17.85). MC, V. Daily noon–2:30pm and 7–9pm. Closed Jan and mid-Nov to mid-Dec. PROVENÇAL.

Here's a place where the vibrancy of a fast-paced Paris bistro collides with relaxed Provençal *savoir-vivre*. The result is a superlative ambience of hearty meals, intriguing chatter, and festive, friendly service. The bistro has one intimate dining room and two terraces—one with a vista of valley and hills and the other facing the square. Menu items vary from light salads to regional fare like *daube* (a traditional beef-and-vegetable stew often served over pasta), roast rack of pork with honey and spices, and grilled filet of hogfish.

BONNIEUX

7 miles (11.27km) S of Roussillon, 28 miles (45.06km) N of Aix-en-Provence

This romantic hill town, nestled in the heart of the Petit Luberon, commands views of nearby Roussillon, the whole Coulon Valley, and the infamous **Château de Lacoste,** whose ruins bear testament to the life of its disturbed owner, Donatien

Alphonse François, comte de Sade (also known as the marquis de Sade), who lived there in the 1770s. The celebrated marquis, who gave us the term "sadism," died in a lunatic asylum. Because of the danger of falling stones, the ruins of the château cannot be visited—even by the most devoted aficionados of de Sade—but merely admired from afar.

Strategically located between Spain and Italy, Bonnieux has had a bloody history of raids and battles since its beginnings in Roman times, when it stood closer to the valley floor. To better defend itself, the town was moved farther up the hill during the 1200s, when it also received sturdy ramparts and sentry towers. In the 16th century, Bonnieux grew into a Catholic stronghold and often found itself surrounded by Protestants who were suspicious and jealous of its thriving economy. Since its streets were lined with mansion after mansion belonging to prominent bishops, allegations swirled around that the town received particular "favors" to bolster its standing. Envy and zeal got the best of the Protestants and they eventually laid siege to the town, killing approximately 3,000 of the 4,000 inhabitants. Even though Bonnieux is the largest hill town in the area, its population never truly recovered and continues to hover around 1,500.

ESSENTIALS

GETTING THERE From Roussillon, drive south along D149 directly to Bonnieux. The trip takes about 15 minutes. There's no train or bus service.

VISITOR INFORMATION The **Office de Tourisme** is at 7 place Carnot (☎ **04-90-75-91-90**).

SEEING THE SIGHTS

You'll most likely want to work with gravity and not against it when exploring this steep village. Start at the summit with the **Vieille Eglise (Old Church)** and its cemetery. The grounds of stately cedars surrounding this Romanesque church, which dates from the 1100s, provide the best vantage point from which you can view the valley's hill towns. Hours of this church are erratic, corresponding to the whims of the priest who performs mass here at irregular intervals. Farther down the incline is the **Musée de la Boulangerie,** 12 rue de la République (☎ **04-90-75-88-34**), dedicated to the authentic portrayal of the art of French breadmaking. Exhibits show all stages of the process, from planting and harvesting the grain to the final mixers and ovens that turn the flour, water, salt, and yeast mixture into warm, crusty loaves. The museum is open April to September, Wednesday to Monday from 10am to noon and 3 to 6:30pm; in October, Saturday and Sunday from 10am to noon and 3 to 6:30pm. It's closed throughout the rest of the year. Admission is 12F ($2.05) for adults and 6F ($1) for children 12 and under.

At the lower extreme of town, clearly signposted from the center, is the **Eglise Neuve (New Church),** from the late 1800s. Many people find the architecture of this church to be less than inspiring. You visit it, however, to admire the four beautiful panels from the Old Church. They date from the 1500s and are painted in the brightly colored German style to show the intensity of the Passion of Christ. It's open daily from 9am to 6pm.

WHERE TO STAY

Auberge de l'Aiguebrun. Off D943, 84480 Bonnieux. ☎ **04-90-04-47-00.** Fax 04-90-04-47-01. TV TEL. 650F–680F ($110.50–$115.60) double, 880F–1,020F ($149.60–$173.40) suite. MC, V. Closed Jan–Feb. From town, drive 4 miles southeast, following the signs to Lourmarin. Free parking.

To relax in one of the most tranquil settings in Provence and soak up that special, surreal sunlight, come here. Artists and lovers seek out this remarkable 19th-century manor house enclosed by the Luberon hills and a mountain river. The intimate guest

The Libertine Trail of the Marquis de Sade

Denounced by some and a cult figure to others even today, Donatien Alphonse François, comte de Sade (1740–1814), is, of course, better known as the "marquis de Sade." The term *sadism* was coined from his name, and this "freest spirit who ever was" led a life devoted to an unleashed libido. By 1764, a police alert advised brothel madames to "refrain from providing the marquis with girls to go to any private chambers with him." Because of his prolonged sexual orgies that combined various kinds of torture (willing or unwilling), and especially because he recorded his controversial ideas for public consumption, he was often in and out of prison.

The marquis and his wife, the very plain but very wealthy Renée-Pélagie de Montreuil, hated Paris and court life and sought a secluded place in the country for their family of three. His wife, who was at first totally devoted to him, apparently overlooked his "deviant behavior" and so he was supposedly a "happily married man."

The marquis grew up in the area around Lacoste. Banished from home because of his violent rages, he spent 6 years of his childhood with his uncle, the noted cleric/scholar Abbé de Sade (who also happened to be a libertine) at the Abbé's castle at Saumane-de-Vaucluse, halfway between Lacoste and Mazan.

This crenellated fortress was a gift from the popes at Avignon, and it still stands in the hilltop village of Saumane-de-Vaucluse, to the west of Lacoste. The castle has been restored and you can visit it. It is believed that the fictional Château de Silling, depicted in *The 120 Days of Sodom,* was based on this castle, where "all that the cruelest art and most refined barbarity could invent in the way of atrocity" was concealed for orgies and torture.

When the marquis returned to Paris, he attended the prestigious Lycée Louis Le Grand, where flagellation was the school's accepted form of punishment. He related to this on an erotic level, and the experience was the catalyst for his lifelong obsession with the exploration of the pain of pleasure and the pleasure of pain.

De Sade country really begins some 25 miles east of Avignon and not far from Ménerbes. The little village of Lacoste, surmounted by the marquis's ancestral castle, exists in a kind of time pocket, with a population that is about the same as it was back in the days of history's most articulate libertine. The château itself (not open to the public) isn't in good shape—just a moat, a few walls, some ramparts, and a scattering of rooms. More interesting is the panoramic view—on a clear day, you can even see Bonnieux. As you stand here, it's easy to imagine the marquis's world of tortured damsels and debauched noblemen coming alive again in such a remote spot in a foreboding landscape.

rooms look out over the river or the hills. They are individually decorated in the Provençal style with tawny colors, and have comfortable mattresses and bathrooms with up-to-date accessories and good-sized towels. In the public rooms, attention is lovingly paid to every detail, from the crackling fire on cooler evenings to the soft and classical music wafting from room to room. Au Relais de la Rivière also has a superb restaurant with its own garden; it's open Wednesday to Monday (closed Wednesday at lunchtime), with set-price menus costing around 200F ($34) each. Regrettably, a well-meaning new management imbues this place with a bit more pretentiousness than it deserves.

Though he spent 1771 worrying about "garden, farmyard, cheeses, and fire-wood," in 1772 the marquis found himself deep in trouble. His manservant, Latour, had arranged for four girls to meet with the marquis. De Sade had prepared some sweets whose sugar had been soaked in extract of Spanish fly (an actual aphrodisiac); later on, some of the girls complained to the police that they'd been poisoned, and accused Latour and de Sade of homosexual sodomy. The marquis fled but in *absentia* was found guilty of poisoning and sodomy. The punishment under law was decapitation—de Sade and Latour were later executed in effigy at Aix-en-Provence.

In 1778, de Sade's days of indulgence came to an end. His mother-in-law, outraged at his behavior, had him legally imprisoned for life. He wrote his novels, including *Justine* and the *120 Days of Sodom,* in prison. Freed in 1790 following the onset of the Revolution, he found that his wife had finally abandoned him forever. Napoléon ordered that the marquis be placed in a mental institution, where he died in 1814 at age 74, leaving scores of unpublished manuscripts that were not to see print for more than a century.

In time, this "abominable assemblage of all crimes and obscenities" won an adoring public. Sadists looked to him as the father of their cult. Foreigners attracted to the marquis's reputation have turned Lacoste into a lively place. An American art school was founded here in the 1970s, and—surprise, surprise—many locals are proud of their hometown boy. A small theater has been built in a stone quarry just below the château, and so the marquis's long-cherished wish to make Lacoste into a mecca for thespians has come true. **Théâtre de Lacoste** now draws some 1,600 patrons at a time, equaled in size in the region only by Avignon's outdoor theater. Believe it or not, one recent production dramatized a fictional love affair between the marquis and St. Theresa of Avila. Don't expect comfort or even high-tech acoustics when you come to a production at this theater: Seats are lined up on stone ledges, and the audience is subject to the vagaries of wind and weather. For information about tickets and performances, contact the Mairie (Town Hall) of Lacoste at ☎ **04-90-75-82-04.**

In Lacoste, you can stay at the **Relais du Procurer,** rue Basse (☎ **04-90-75-82-28**), where a double rents for 600F ($102). The most popular bar/restaurant is the **Café de Sade,** rue Basse in the center of town (☎ **04-90-75-82-29**); dinner costs from 85F ($14.45), and you can accompany your meal with a local vintage, Cuvée du Divin Marquis.

In the 1990s, de Sade entered the modern age: His admirers now maintain a host of Web sites on the Internet.

Hostellerie du Prieuré. Rue J.-B.-Aurard, 84480 Bonnieux. ☎ **04-90-75-80-78.** Fax 04-90-75-96-00. 10 units. TEL. 540F–670F ($91.80–$113.90) double. MC, V. Closed Nov–Feb. On-street parking free, in garage 10F ($1.70).

Protected in the shadows of Bonnieux's medieval ramparts, this is an 18th-century abbey turned hotel. The medium-to-large rooms are individually furnished in a simple manner befitting the style of the building and overlook the hotel garden or the ramparts. Despite their simplicity, they have a severe kind of dignity, and contain firm mattresses. Depending on the weather and the season, breakfast is served either inside, next to the blazing fireplace, or in the verdant, lushly landscaped garden. The in-house restaurant serves set-price menus ranging in cost from 98F to 200F ($16.65 to $34) each, featuring such dishes as a chartreuse of lamb with a confit of eggplant, red snapper filets with pistou, and a dessert *fondant* of bitter chocolate. The restaurant is closed Wednesday all day, and Thursday at lunchtime.

Warning: Despite this inn's provincial French charm and grace, you might not like its policy of locking up at night until 8am the next morning. You're given a key if you plan to arrive late, but then you can't go out again. Some readers find this measure "draconian," others like the feeling of safety.

WHERE TO DINE

You can also consider dining at the two inns listed above.

Le Fournil. 5 place Carnot. ☎ **04-90-75-83-62.** Reservations recommended. Main courses 75F–90F ($12.75–$15.30); fixed-price menus 125F–180F ($21.25–$30.60). MC, V. Sept–June, Tues 7:30–9:30pm, Wed–Sun 12:15–2pm and 7:30–9:30pm; July–Aug, Tues–Sun 12:30–1:45pm and 7:30–9:30pm, Sat 7:30–9:30pm. Closed Jan to mid-Feb and mid-Nov to mid-Dec. PROVENÇAL.

Charming and completely without pretension, this restaurant occupies the premises of a clean, dry, well-swept cave opening on a small-scale square graced with a 12th-century fountain. The inventive chefs, Guy Malbec and Jean-Christophe Lèche, have taken recipes of long standing and given them a new and livelier taste. The menu varies with the season and the inspiration of the chefs, but might include crispy-skinned supreme of stuffed guinea fowl with baby vegetables, a confit of fruit, and parsley sauce; a platter of roasted and grilled baby goat, featuring two cooking techniques on one platter, with a confit of lemon; and filet of monkfish with sweet garlic and served with a purée of potatoes and olive oil. The wine list contains 35 to 40 selections, mainly regional choices like Côtes du Rhône and Côte de Luberon.

14 Apt

32 miles (51.50km) W of Avignon, 32 miles (51.50km) N of Aix-en-Provence, and 451 miles (725.81km) S of Paris

Known as *Colonia Apta Julia,* this was an important Gallo-Roman city and today is a large, bustling market town. Ignore the modern industrial area and head for the Vieille Ville to capture the beauty of Apt. Here you can walk long narrow streets that wind between old houses where every nook and cranny offers something waiting to be discovered.

Apt is known for its wines—it's a region of the Rhône Valley where the grapes that go into Côte de Luberon and Côtes de Ventoux are grown. It is also known for its basket and wicker work and has been a producer of hats since the 17th century, and it is the capital of crystallized fruit or *fruit-confits,* so beloved in Provence.

The old Roman city faded into history and was eventually deserted and covered by silt from the river and the hillsides. Roman remains are still buried around 16 to 33 feet below the current town.

ESSENTIALS

GETTING THERE   Apt has no railway station. From Avignon five buses per day make the 75-minute trek to Apt; a one-way ticket is around 41F ($6.95). Bus passengers are deposited in a parking lot beside the Route de Digne (☎ **04-90-74-20-21**), at the eastern periphery of town. The best way to reach Apt is by driving; follow the N100 east from Avignon.

VISITOR INFORMATION   The **Office de Tourism** is at 20 av. Philippe-de-Girard (☎ **04-90-74-03-18**).

EXPLORING THE AREA

Apt, capital of Le Luberon, proclaims itself "the world capital of crystallized fruits." The town is filled with Les Confiseurs selling this treat (see "Shopping," below). The best time to visit Apt is for its **Saturday morning market** centered around place de la Bouquerie, voted one of the 100 most appealing village markets in France. The streets are literally packed with market stalls and lined with temporary shops. Lavender growers, purveyors of goat cheese, potters, local beekeepers, and craftspeople who look like leftovers from the '60s invade the town to peddle their wares. The **Tour de l'Horloge,** dating from the 1500s and straddling the rue des Marchands, is a particularly active area for the Saturday market. On market days, the town fills with jazz musicians, barrel organ players, stand-up comics, and what one local merchant calls "assorted freaks."

Cathédrale Ste-Anne. Vieille Ville. No phone. Free admission. Mon–Sat 10am–noon and 4–6pm, Sun 10am–noon. Ask the caretaker for entrance to the Sacristy.

This major monument is known for its ancient two-level crypt. According to legend, the bones of the legendary Ste-Anne, mother of the Virgin Mary, were miraculously discovered in this crypt in the 8th century, occasioning the building of the cathedral. Her life is depicted in a beautiful set of 14th-century stained-glass windows at the end of the apse. Her shroud is also displayed among the reliquaries of the treasury. Scholars speculate that Anne was not the biblical figure, but a dim memory of the primeval pan-European mother goddess sometimes known as Ana or Anna Perenna to the Romans.

In the 13th century the present church was enlarged, and in the 18th century the floor was raised and the broken barrel vault turned into a higher ogee vault. The oldest part of the cathedral is the tower crypt, which still has a funerary monument honoring a priest in the time of Apia Julia and Carolingian flagstones. The church and its treasury are filled with rare ecclesiastical artifacts. In the chapel of St. John the Baptist you can see an early Christian marble sarcophagus from the Pyrenees. Among the treasures in the sacristy are 11th- and 12th-century manuscripts, elaborate vestments, and an 11th-century Arab standard brought back from the First Crusade. The nave is adorned with scenes from the life of Christ, painted by Pierre and Christophe Delpech in the 18th century.

To see the **Sacristy,** you must ask Mlle Claude Pion, the church caretaker. She is constantly on-site during opening hours (see above), and will open it according to the schedule of daily masses or the priorities of the priests. If she does, a donation to the maintenance of the church is appreciated.

Musée Archéologique. Place Carnot. ☎ **04-90-74-00-43.** Admission 9.60F ($1.65). July–Aug, Wed–Mon 10am–noon and 2:30–5:30pm; Sept–June, Wed–Mon 10am–noon and 2:30–4:30pm.

The town's major museum contains Roman objects found in local excavations, including pieces of mosaics, sarcophagi, coins, and even oil lamps from the 2nd century B.C. It also displays sacred and decorative art by faience makers from the 17th and the 19th centuries.

Hôtel Colin d'Albertas. Rue de la République. ☎ **04-90-74-02-40.** Tours: 25F ($4.25). June–Sept, daily 3pm and 5pm.

The antique lavish 17th-century baroque interior of this building was opened for hour-long daily guided tours in 1999. It contains some of the most spectacular plaster and stucco work in the region, and is a museum in its own right.

OUTDOORS IN LUBERON NATIONAL PARK

The information office for the Luberon National Park is in an 18th-century house, **La Maison du Parc,** 1 place Jean-Jaurès (☎ **04-90-04-42-00**). The office provides maps, details of hiking trails in the park, and other outdoor activities in the area. Much of the land in the Luberon area is privately owned, but trails in the park are open to the public. In summer there are tastings of the regional produce here. On site is a small Museum of Paleontology, of only specialist interest. Admission is 8F ($1.35), and it's open May to October, Monday to Saturday from 8:30am to noon, and the rest of the year Monday to Friday from 1:30 to 6pm.

SHOPPING

The large town is filled with confiseurs selling candied fruits. The best are **Confiserie Marcel Richaud,** 48 quai de la Liberté (☎ **04-90-74-13-56**), and **Confiseur Le Coulon/Jean Ceccon,** 24 quai de la Liberté (☎ **04-90-74-21-90**).

WHERE TO STAY & DINE

Auberge du Luberon. 8 place Faubourge du Ballet, 84400 Apt. ☎ **04-90-74-12-50.** Reservations recommended. Main courses 90F–230F ($15.30–$39.10), set-price menus 155F–450F ($26.35–$76.50). AE, MC, V. Oct–June, Tues–Sun noon–1:45pm and Tues–Sat 7:30–9:30pm. July–Sept, Tues–Sun noon–1:45pm and daily 7:30–9:30pm. AE, MC, V. FRENCH.

Though mainly a restaurant, this place is also a hotel. It's in the heart of the city's historic center, in a century-old building. The menu reflects old-fashioned culinary virtues and style. Specialties include foie gras with a confit of fruits, in the style that Apt is famous for; a charlotte of lamb with eggplant; John Dory with artichoke hearts *barigoules;* and a trolley laden daily with 13 different desserts.

There are 11 bedrooms, about half in a nearby annex. All have TVs and telephones, and some have air-conditioning. Doubles without air conditioning cost 295F ($50.15); doubles with air conditioning 340F–450F ($57.80–$76.50).

Relais de Roquefure. Along N000, 84400 Apt. ☎ **4-90-04-88-88.** Fax 04-90-74-14-86. 15 units. TEL. 230F–500F ($39.10–$85) double. Half board 410F–640F ($69.70–$108.80) double. V.

Lying 3½ miles north of the center, this Logis de France country hotel in the Luberon Nature Reserve is the finest place to stay in the area. It offers good food and a good night's sleep, all at a fair price. Georges and Jeannine Rousset, the owners, are hospitable hosts. Rooms are small but comfortable, with fine, soft beds. Bathrooms are small but equipped with plenty of good-sized towels. In summer, guests can sit under the shade trees or jump into the swimming pool. The food is some of the best in the area, emphasizing regional produce. Horses and bikes can be rented.

15 Salon de Provence

29 miles (46.67km) SE of Avignon, 23 miles (37.01km) NW of Aix-en-Provence, 33 miles (53.11km) NW of Marseille

The hometown of Nostradamus is centered between Aix-en-Provence and Avignon, and makes an excellent stopover between these towns. Today a busy modern town, it grew up as a fortified hilltop fortress centering around **Château de l'Empéri.** With a population of some 35,000, it has been a center of the olive oil industry since the 15th century, although it owes much of its prosperity to the French Air Force's officer training school centered here.

Salon-de-Provence was the birthplace of Adam de Craponne (1527–76), creator of the famous canal, bearing his name today, that irrigates the region of Crau.

ESSENTIALS

GETTING THERE   Train connections, about seven a day from Avignon, are the best and most direct (40 mins. each way). For information and schedules, contact the local tourist office. From Aix-en-Provence, there are about 7 daily buses (trip time between 30 and 45 mins.) to downtown Salon de Provence's place Morgan. For information on bus travel into and around Salon de Provence, contact the Gare Routière in Aix-en-Provence (☎ **04-42-27-17-91**). Train connections from Aix are less convenient, and require a transfer in Marseille.

If you're driving, Salon de Provence is strategically located at the junction of highways connecting Avignon with Aix-en-Provence (N7), Marseille with Arles and Nîmes (N113), and the A7 and A54 autoroutes.

VISITOR INFORMATION   The **Office de Tourisme** is at 56 cours Gimon (☎ **04-90-56-27-60**).

EXPLORING THE TOWN

A major attraction in the town is the **Fontaine Moussue** on the place Croussilat just outside the Porte de l'Horloge. Covered by a thick mound of moss, this much-photographed fountain dates from the 18th century. It is surrounded by plane trees planted to commemorate events over the centuries. One was planted in 1799 to mark the end of the Revolution, another in 1919 to mark the end of World War I.

Château de l'Empéri. Montée du Puech. ☎ **04-90-56-22-36.** Admission 25F ($4.25) adults, 15F ($2.55) ages 7 to 18, free for ages 6 and under. Wed–Mon 10am–noon and 2:30–6:30pm.

This chateau is surrounded by ancient circular walls. You can enter through the 17th-century Porte de l'Horloge or the Porte Bourg Neuf. The chateau dates from the 10th century and is one of the most beautiful in Provence, with its courtyards, towers, and walls. Once this was the residence of the archbishops of Arles, lords of Salon. Both François I, in 1516, and Marie de Médici, in 1600, visited and stayed here. From 1831 it was used as a barracks and severely damaged in an earthquake in 1909. Over the years it has been gradually and attractively restored.

The château houses the **Musée de Art et d'Histoire Militaire,** with a collection of more than 10,000 artifacts, including military uniforms, weapons, waxwork figures, and military flags. The museum covers the era from Louis XIV, the Sun King, up to France's entry into World War II.

Musée Nostradamus. 11 rue Nostradamus. ☎ **04-90-56-64-31.** Admission 25F ($4.25). Mid-June to mid-Sept, daily 10am–noon and 3–8pm. Rest of year, daily 10am–noon and 2–6pm.

Nostradamus (1503–66), who was born at St-Rémy-de-Provence, spent the last 19 years of his life at this little house close to the chateau. It's now a museum devoted to him and his famous enigmatic predictions of the future. A series of fairly unconvincing tableaux depict scenes from his life, with a rambling commentary on portable CD players.

Nostradamus was born into a family of converted Jews and trained as a doctor in Montpellier. He treated plague victims n Lyon and Aix. He married a woman from Salon in 1547 and settled here, where he studied astrology, publishing almanacs and inventing new recipes for cosmetics. Written in the future tense, his *Centuries* in rhyming quatrains was published in 1555, bringing him instant celebrity. Nostradamus is buried in the interesting 14th-century **Eglise St-Laurent,** which lies just to the north of the town center.

Musée Grevin de la Provence. Place du Puits de Jacob. ☎ **04-90-56-36-30.** Admission 25F ($4.25). Mid-June to mid-Sept, daily 10am–noon and 3–8pm. Rest of year, daily 10am–noon and 2–6pm.

In this wax museum, lifelike tableaux capture the region's many historical figures.

WHERE TO STAY

Abbaye de Sainte-Croix. Val de Cuech, 13300 Salon de Provence. ☎ **04-90-56-24-55.** Fax 04-90-56-31-12. E-mail: saintecroix@relaischateaux.fr. 24 units. A/C MINIBAR TV TEL. 800F–1,080F ($136–$183.60) double; 1,265F–2,400F ($215.05–$408) suite. AE, MC, V. Closed Nov to mid-Mar.

Few hotels in the region can boast origins as authentic and charming as this ancient one-time monastery from the 1100s, 2½ miles north of the city center. A Relais & Châteaux hotel, it boasts thick stone walls, most of its original arches and vaults, and a severely dignified, sometimes forbidding kind of grandeur evocative of the Middle Ages. Bedrooms come in a variety of sizes and shapes, although they are usually spacious. They feature a simple elegance: lovely old furniture, terra-cotta floors, and sometimes spectacular views over fields of lavender and rugged, much-eroded hills. Each has a safe, hair dryer, quality mattress, and fine linen, along with a compact tiled bathroom with adequate shelf space and shower/tub combination. On the site is a swimming pool. The place is more famous as a restaurant than as a hotel—see "Where to Dine," below.

Hôtel d'Angleterre. 98 Cours Carnot, 13300 Salon de Provence. ☎ **04-90-56-01-10.** Fax 04-90-56-71-75. 26 units. TV TEL. 255F–305F ($43.35–$51.85) double. MC, V.

Set on the northwestern fringe of the peripheral boulevard (Cours Carnot) that flanks the edge of town (a 10-min. walk from the center), this is a conservative, not particularly exciting three-story hotel with roots in memories of British tourism during the early 1900s. Everything has been radically modernized from its original turn-of-the-century charm, with touches of kitsch and an overwhelming sense of bourgeois, and somewhat tense propriety. One of the few appealing touches is the circular skylight in the breakfast room. Come here for the relatively low rates, as bedrooms are Spartan and not particularly cozy. They range from small to medium, and are reasonably comfortable. Bathrooms are a bit cramped but have shower stalls and good-sized towels.

WHERE TO DINE

Abbaye de Sainte-Croix. Val de Cuech, 13300 Salon-de-Provence. ☎ **04-90-56-24-55.** Reservations recommended. Main courses 150F–210F ($25.50–$35.70). Set-price menus at lunch 330F–560F ($56.10–$95.20); set-price menus at dinner 410F–560F ($69.70–$95.20). AE, MC, V. FRENCH. Closed Nov to mid-Mar.

In the hotel recommended above, this restaurant serves the best-recommended food in the region. Part of its appeal comes from its architecture of medieval soaring vaults and high perpendicular lines. From its terrace is a view over the low hills of the Alpilles. Menu items change with the season and the inspiration of the chef, and include such delectable items as lobster salad with a walnut oil vinaigrette; sliced sea wolf with a fondant of green and red peppers, basil, and locally produced olives and olive oil; thin-sliced roasted lamb with truffles from the Luberon in clarified butter; turbot with morels; and aiguillette of duck with a tapenade of olives.

Mas du Soleil (Restaurant Francis Robin). 38 chemin St-Côme, Salon-de-Provence. ☎ **04-90-56-06-53.** Reservations recommended. Main courses 85F–220F ($14.45–$37.40). Set-price menus 180F–650F ($30.60–$110.50). AE, MC, V. Tues–Sun noon–2pm, Tues–Sat 7:30–9pm. FRENCH.

In an 1850s stone-sided farmhouse, the ocher-colored facade of this inn is a 5-minute walk from the center of town. The critically acclaimed cuisine of Francis Robin changes according to the season and the availability of the ingredients. Menu items include such treats as a rosemary-infused rack of lamb for two, filet of beef layered with escalope of foie gras, warm salad of filet of red snapper, and a medley of grilled Mediterranean fish. One particularly tempting main course that the chef is particularly proud of is a *civet* (stew) of lobster. Dining room windows overlook a swimming pool in the garden.

An upper floor contains 10 well-maintained bedrooms outfitted with flowered wallpaper, traditional furniture, air-conditioning, TVs, and telephones. Each has a bay window overlooking the garden and terrace or a private patio. Depending on the season and the room, doubles range in price from 530F–1,350F ($90.10 to $229.50).

16 Aix-en-Provence

469 miles (754.78km) S of Paris, 50 miles (80.47km) SE of Avignon, 20 miles (32.19km) N of Marseille, 109 miles (175.42km) W of Nice

The most charming center in all Provence, this faded university town was once a seat of aristocracy, its streets walked by counts and kings. Founded in 122 B.C. by a Roman general, Caius Sextius Calvinus, who named it *Aquae Sextiae* after himself, Aix (pronounced "ex") has been in turn a Roman military outpost, a civilian colony, the administrative capital of a province of the later Roman Empire, the seat of an archbishop, and the official residence of the medieval comtes de Provence. After the union of Provence with France, Aix remained until the Revolution a judicial and administrative headquarters.

The celebrated son of this old capital city of Provence, Paul Cézanne, immortalized the countryside nearby. Just as he painted it, Montagne Ste-Victoire looms over the town today, though a string of high-rises has now cropped up on the landscape.

The Université d'Aix has been attracting international students since 1413. Today absinthe has given way to pastis in the many cafes scattered throughout the town.

This city of some 150,000 is reasonably quiet in winter, but active and bustling when the summer hordes pour in. Summer brings frequent cultural events, ranging from opera to jazz, from June to August. Increasingly, Aix is becoming a "bedroom community" for urbanites fleeing Marseille after 5pm.

ESSENTIALS
GETTING THERE   Aix is a rail and highway junction. Trains arrive hourly from Marseille (a 40-min. trip). For **rail information** and schedules, call ☎ **08-36-35-35-35.** Several independent bus companies service the routes into Aix-en-Provence; for information about routes and companies, call the **Gare Routière,** Rue Lapierre (☎ **04-42-27-17-91**). SATAP (☎ **04-42-26-23-78**) operates up to four buses a day between Aix and Avignon. Aix lies off the main route (E80) between Nîmes and Cannes.

VISITOR INFORMATION   The **Office de Tourisme** is at 2 place du Général-de-Gaulle (☎ **04-42-16-11-61**).

SPECIAL EVENTS   Aix has the liveliest music scene in the south of France. Four midsummer festivals showcase concerts, opera, and dance. They include the **Saison d'Aix** (June to August) that focuses on symphonic and chamber music. A well-attended open-air **Jazz Festival** (late June to mid-July) brings in important musicians from virtually everywhere. For information, call the **Office des Fêtes et de la Culture,** Espace Forbin, Cours Gambetta (☎ **04-42-63-06-75**).

The **Festival International de Danse** is a 6-week festival that features classical and modern dance troupes from throughout Europe and the world. For information, call ☎ **04-42-96-05-01.** The **Festival d'Art Lyrique** features opera performances during 3 weeks in July, usually around the 6th to the 30th. Its administrative headquarters is at place de l'Archêveché, 13100 Aix-en-Provence (☎ **04-42-17-34-34**).

EXPLORING THE CITY

A particularly stately looking thoroughfare that's sometimes compared to La Canébière in Marseilles, or even the Champs-Elysées in Paris, is ✪ **cours Mirabeau,** named for the revolutionary and statesman. The street begins at the 1860 landmark fountain on place de la Libération. The branches of the plane trees make an arch overhead, shading the street from the hot Provençal sun and filtering the light so that shadows play upon the rococo fountains below. On one side are shops and sidewalk cafes, on the other richly embellished sandstone *hôtels particuliers* (mansions) from the 17th and 18th centuries.

Atelier de Cézanne. 9 av. Paul-Cézanne. ☎ **04-42-21-06-53.** Admission 25F ($4.25) adults, 10F ($1.70) children. Daily 10am–noon and 2:30–6pm (closes 5pm Oct–Mar).

Outside town is the studio of the painter who was the major forerunner of cubism, surrounded by a wall. The house was restored by American admirers. It remains much as Cézanne left it in 1906: "his coat hanging on the wall, his easel with an unfinished picture waiting for a touch of the master's brush," as Thomas R. Parker wrote.

Cathédrale St-Sauveur. Place des Martyrs de la Résistance. ☎ **04-42-23-45-65.** Daily 8:30am–noon and 2–6pm. Masses Sun at 9am, 10:30am, and 7pm.

The architecture of the cathedral covers many eras: Notable is the **baptistery,** which dates from the 4th or 5th century; Romanesque and Gothic stand side-by-side in a double nave. Its greatest treasure is the brilliant 15th-century triptych by Nicolas Froment, *The Burning Bush.* It shows Good King René and his second wife, Jeanne de Laval, kneeling before the Virgin, who is poised above the burning bush. The delicate oil and tempera painting is usually closed to the public—for a tip the custodian may open it for you.

Chapelle Penitents-gris (Chapelle des Bourras). 15 rue Lieutaud. ☎ **04-42-26-26-72.** Admission free (voluntary donation). July–Aug, Sat 4:30–6pm; Sept–June, Sat 2:30–4:30pm.

This 16th-century chapel honoring St. Joseph was built on the ancient Roman Aurelian road linking Rome and Spain. The chapel was restored by Herbert Maza, founder and former president of the Institute for American Universities. Visits can be pre-arranged with Mr. Borricand, rector of a group of local ecclesiastics.

Musée des Tapisseries. 28 place des Martyrs de la Résistance. ☎ **04-42-23-09-91.** Admission 12F ($2.05). Fri–Wed 10am–noon and 2–6pm.

This museum is in a former archbishop's palace. Lining its gilded walls are three series of tapestries from the 17th and 18th century, collected by the archbishops to decorate the palace: *The History of Don Quixote* by Natoire, *The Russian Games* by Leprince, and *The Grotesques* by Monnoyer. In addition, the museum exhibits rare furnishings from the 17th and 18th centuries.

Musée Granet (Musée des Beaux-Arts). Place St-Jean-de-Malte. ☎ **04-42-38-14-70.** Admission 10F ($1.70). Wed–Mon 10am–noon and 2:30–6pm.

A former director once claimed that the walls of this museum "would never be sullied by a Cézanne." Fortunately that's not true—the museum owns eight paintings by Cézanne, none of them major. The great painter had a famously antagonistic rela-

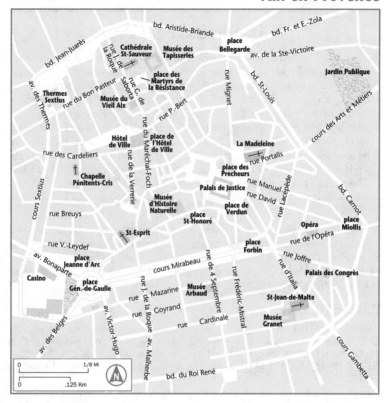

tionship with the people of Aix. The museum is housed in the former center of the Knights of Malta, and contains works by van Dyck, van Loo, and Rigaud; portraits by Pierre and François Puget; and an interesting *Jupiter and Thetis* by Ingres. Ingres also did an 1807 portrait of the museum's namesake, François Marius Granet. Granet's own works abound.

SHOPPING

For a good selection of art objects and fabrics inspired by the traditions of Provence, head for **Les Olivades,** 15 rue Marius-Reinaud (☎ **04-42-38-33-66**). It sells tasteful fabrics, shirts for both women and men, fashionable dresses, and table linens.

Opened a century ago, **Bechard,** 12 cours Mirabeau (☎ **04-42-26-06-78**), is the town's most famous bakery. On the ground floor of a building on the main street, it takes its work so seriously that it refers to its underground kitchens as a *laboratoire* (laboratory). The pastries are truly delectable; in most cases they are made fresh every day.

La Boutique du Pays d'Aix, in the Office de Tourisme, 2 place du Général-de-Gaulle (☎ **04-42-16-11-61**), carries a large selection of silk scarves in Provençal motifs, commemorative T-shirts, souvenir magnets for decorating the front of your refrigerator, and small-scale replicas of Provençal cottages. There's also a tempting array of *calissons,* sugared confections made with almonds and a confit of melon.

Founded in 1934 on a busy boulevard about half a mile from the center of Aix, the showroom and factory of ✪ **Santons Fouque,** 65 cours Gambetta, route de Nice, RN7 (☎ **04-42-26-33-38**), stocks the largest assortment of *santons* (creche figures) in Aix. More than 1,800 figurines are cast in terra-cotta, finished by hand, then

Walking the Route de Cézanne

If you want to experience the Aix area Cézanne did, walk the length of the carefully signposted route de Cézanne (D17), which winds through the Provençal
countryside toward Ste-Victoire. From the east end of cours Mirabeau, take rue
du Maréchal-Joffre across boulevard Carnot to boulevard des Poilus, which
becomes avenue des écoles-Militaires and finally D17. The stretch between Aix
and the hamlet of Le Tholonet is full of twists and turns where Cézanne often set
up his easel. It's a hike of 3½ miles, but you can do it in a relatively relaxed way
by starting early in the morning. In Le Tholonet you can refresh yourself at a cafe
while waiting for one of the frequent buses back to Aix. The best cafe is **Chez
Thomé,** La Plantation, Tholonet (☎ **04-42-66-90-43**).

decorated with oil-based paint according to 18th-century models. All the trades once
practiced in medieval Provence are represented—there are grizzled but awestruck shoe-
makers, barrel makers, coppersmiths and ironsmiths, and rope makers, each poised to
welcome the newborn Jesus. Depending on size and complexity, figurines range from
50F to 6,000F ($8.50 to $1,020).

WHERE TO STAY
VERY EXPENSIVE

✪ **Villa Gallici.** Av. de la Violette (impasse des Grands Pins), 13100 Aix-en-Provence. ☎ **04-
42-23-29-23.** Fax 04-42-96-30-45. E-mail: villagallici@wanadoo.fr. 23 units. A/C MINIBAR TV
TEL. 1,000F–2,550F ($170–$433.50) double; 2,050F–2,950F ($348.50–$501.50) suite. AE,
DC, MC, V.

This elegant, relentlessly chic inn has been stylishly decorated by its creators (architects and interior designers Messrs. Dez, Montemarco, and Jouve). It was originally
hailed as "divinely over the top." Each room has an individualized decor of subtlety
and charm; some boast a private terrace or garden. Beds are hung with "waterfalls" of
sprigged and striped cotton, mattresses are decadently comfortable, towels pre-
dictably plush, and each room has a safe. The villa sits in a large enclosed garden in
the heart of town, close to one of the best restaurants, Le Clos de la Violette (see
below), and a 5-minute walk from the town center. Despite its grand reputation as a
place that requires ironbound advance reservations, and where famous people bask in
sybaritic anonymity, some of the staff are not as well trained or as well informed as
they might be. But that is only a minor distraction in an otherwise well-orchestrated
symphony.

   Dining: On the premises is an airy in-house restaurant, open daily for lunch and
dinner.

   Amenities: A limited array of spa facilities, plus a swimming pool.

EXPENSIVE

Hôtel des Augustins. 3 rue de la Masse, 13100 Aix-en-Provence. ☎ **04-42-27-28-59.** Fax
04-42-26-74-87. 29 units. A/C MINIBAR TV TEL. 600F–1,500F ($102–$255) double. AE, DC,
V. Parking 50F ($8.50).

Converted from the 12th-century Grands Augustins Convent, this hotel has been
beautifully restored, with ribbed-vault ceilings, stained-glass windows, stone walls,
terra-cotta floors, and Louis XIII furnishings. The reception desk is in a chapel, and
oil paintings and watercolors decorate the public rooms. Before its transformation into
a hotel in 1892, this site won a place in history by sheltering an excommunicated

Martin Luther on his return from Rome. The spacious soundproof guest rooms—two with terraces—all have automatic alarm-call facilities. They are outfitted in a severe kind of monastic dignity, with dark-grained wooden furniture and high ceilings. Touches of luxury, however, appear with the firm, very comfortable mattresses (a lot cozier than what was used by the monks of long ago), and big bathrooms with thick towels. There's no full-fledged restaurant on the premises; consequently, breakfast is the only meal served. The hotel has a private garage on the other side of place de la Rotonde, where you can rent a space for your car.

Hôtel Pigonnet. 5 av. du Pigonnet, 13090 Aix-en-Provence. ☎ **04-52-59-02-20.** Fax 04-42-59-47-77. www.hotelpigonnet.com. E-mail: reservation@hotelpigonnet.com. 52 units. A/C MINIBAR TV TEL. 800F–1,550F ($136–$263.50) double; 1,800F–2,000F ($306–$340) suite. AE, DC, MC, V. Free parking.

This pink-sided Provençal mansion on the edge of town is surrounded by gardens, a swimming pool, and memories of Paul Cézanne, who used to visit there. Many renovations were completed here during 1998. The high-ceilinged bedrooms contain antique and reproduction French provincial furnishings, elaborate curtains, comfortable mattresses, plenty of thick towels, and a pervasive sense of country elegance. Breakfast is served on a colonnaded veranda overlooking a reflecting pool in the courtyard. In summer, the in-house restaurant expands outward into the garden, featuring such dishes as a terrine of house-made foie gras; roasted Provençal lamb in a honey-flavored rosemary sauce; and a roulade of chicken with crayfish in shellfish sauce. Set-price menus range from 220F to 330F ($37.40 to $56.10) each.

Mercure Paul-Cézanne. 40 av. Victor-Hugo, 13100 Aix-en-Provence. ☎ **04-42-26-34-73.** Fax 04-42-27-20-95. 55 units. A/C MINIBAR TV TEL. 530F–580F ($90.10–$98.60) double; 620F–900F ($105.40–$153) suite. AE, DC, MC, V. Parking 50F ($8.50).

The refined interior of this place is more tasteful than you'd expect in a member of a nationwide chain. Since being sold by its former owner, however, it has lost its top position to the much more stylish and tranquil Gallici, and there have been increasing complaints about a less-than-cooperative staff. The lounge seems more like a private sitting room than a hotel lobby. Many of the rooms have mahogany Victorian furniture, Louis XVI chairs, marble-top chests, gilt mirrors, and oil paintings. All baths have hand-painted tiles. And mattresses that, while not exactly plush, are at least comfortable. Breakfast is served in a small room opening onto a rear courtyard.

MODERATE

Grand Hôtel Nègre Coste. 33 cours Mirabeau, 13100 Aix-en-Provence. ☎ **04-42-27-74-22.** Fax 04-42-26-80-93. 37 units. A/C TV TEL. 400F–650F ($68–$110.50) double. AE, DC, V.

This hotel, a former 18th-century town house, is so popular with the dozens of musicians who flock to Aix for the summer festivals that it's usually difficult to get a room at any price. Such popularity is understandable. Outside, flowers cascade from jardinières, and windows are surrounded with 18th-century carvings. Inside, there's a wide staircase, marble portrait busts, and a Provençal armoire. The medium-sized and soundproof rooms contain interesting antiques, firm mattresses, and recently renovated bathrooms with good-sized towels. The higher floors overlook cours Mirabeau or the old city.

Résidence Rotonde. 15 av. des Belges, 13100 Aix-en-Provence. ☎ **04-42-26-29-88.** Fax 04-42-38-66-98. 42 units. MINIBAR TV TEL. 360F–480F ($61.20–$81.60) double. AE, DC, MC, V. Closed Dec. Free parking.

A contemporary hotel in the town center, the Rotonde provides cheerful, streamlined accommodations. Occupying part of a residential building, it has an open spiral can-tilevered staircase and molded-plastic and chrome furniture. The rooms have ornate wallpaper, Nordic-style beds, and adequately comfortable mattresses. Bathrooms are a bit small but adequate for the job, with suitable shelf space and mostly shower/tub combinations. There's no restaurant, but breakfast is served.

INEXPENSIVE

Hôtel des Quatre Dauphins. 54 rue Roux Alphéran, 13100 Aix-en-Provence. ☎ **04-42-38-16-39.** Fax 04-42-38-60-19. 13 units. A/C TV TEL. 335F–420F ($56.95–$71.40) double. Nearby parking 55F ($9.35). AE, DC, MC, V.

This hotel is in an 18th-century five-story former town house, a short walk from the place des Quatre Dauphins and the Cours Mirabeau. Despite frequent modernization, some of the original motifs remain. The medium-sized bedrooms were recently refur-bished in a simplified Provençal style. Some have painted ceiling beams and casement windows that overlook the street outside. Space is not overly abundant, but mattresses are comfortable, and many clients find the blue-and-white color schemes soothing. Bathrooms are just adequate for the job, with shower stalls and tidy maintenance. Breakfast is served in your bedroom or within a small breakfast salon.

Hôtel La Caravelle. 29 bd. du Roi-René (at cours Mirabeau), 13100 Aix-en-Provence. ☎ **04-42-21-53-05.** Fax 04-42-96-55-46. 32 units. A/C TV TEL. 275F–450F ($46.75–$76.50) double. AE, DC, MC, V.

A 3-minute walk from the center is this conservatively furnished three-star hotel with a bas-relief of a three-masted caravelle on the stucco facade. The hotel is run by M. and Mme Henri Denis in a continuing tradition of warm hospitality. The majority of the rooms were restored between 1995 and 1998; they have double-glazed windows to help muffle the noise. Mattresses are relatively comfortable, and most bathrooms have shower only, although eight come with a shower/tub combination; all contain a hair dryer. Breakfast is served in the stone-floored lobby.

STAYING & DINING NEARBY
IN VAUVENARGUES

This town is the burial place of **Pablo Picasso.** It was here that the artist, who died at 91, painted his *Luncheon on the Grass* and did a red-and-black portrait of his wife, Jacqueline, who's also interred here. The town is named for the aristocratic Vauvenar-gues family, in whose turreted **château** Picasso lived from 1959 to 1961. The château has 14th-century ocher stone walls, with 16th- and 17th-century additions. The coat-of-arms of the Vauvenargues can be seen above the Louis XIII porch. They owned the château from 1790 to 1947; it was later purchased by antiques dealers who sold all the furnishings. Picasso acquired it in 1958. You aren't allowed inside but can see some of the artist's sculptures in the castle park.

Au Moulin de Provence. Rue des Maquisards, 13126 Vauvenargues. ☎ **04-42-66-02-22.** Fax 04-42-66-01-21. www.multimedia.net/gastronomic/moulin-provence.htm. E-mail: moulin.provence@wanadoo.fr. 12 units. TEL. 250F–280F ($42.50–$47.60) double. MC, V. Closed Jan–Feb. Take D110 10 miles east of Aix.

Cozy and homelike, in the best tradition of a Provençal inn, this is Vauvenargues's only major hotel. The English-speaking host, Magdeleine Yemenidjian, welcomes her guests, most of whom were attracted here by the Picasso legacy. The good-sized rooms have balconies with views of Mont Ste-Victoire, the mountain range that inspired many artists, including Cézanne. Beds are comfortable and firm; bathrooms are adequate. The inn serves a good meal for 100F ($17) and up.

IN MEYRARGUES

○ **Château de Meyrargues.** 13650 Meyrargues. ☎ **04-42-63-49-90.** Fax 04-42-63-49-92. 11 units. TV TEL. 700F–1,300F ($119–$221) double; 2,000F ($340) suite. AE, MC, V. From Aix, take A51 for 10½ miles northeast, following the signs for Sisteron and Pertuis; get off at exit 14, then follow the signs to the château.

This 12th-century château is one of France's oldest fortified sites, having been a Celtic outpost in 600 B.C. Once the lords of Les Baux lived here, but now it's an award-winning holiday retreat. The entrance is imposing, with a reflecting pool and twin stone towers flanking a sweeping set of balustraded steps. From its terraces and rooms you can enjoy a panoramic view of the valley of the Durance. The spacious accommodations feature canopied beds with firm and comfortable mattress, fabrics inspired by Provençal designs and colors, worthy antiques, and tiled bathrooms with floods of hot water and lots of thick towels. The hotel was completely renovated and upgraded between 1994 and 1995.

Meals are served in a baronial-looking dining room with a large fireplace, near a bar with a private terrace. Set-price menus, which tend to emphasize grilled fish and roasted versions of Provençal lamb, begin at 250F ($42.50) each. The restaurant is open daily, year-round, for lunch and dinner. There are 12 acres of private terrain around the château, wherein patches of verdant gardens are interspersed with a swimming pool and lots of rocky outcroppings.

IN BEAURECUEIL

Mas de la Bertrande. 13100 Beaurecueil. ☎ **04-42-66-75-75.** Fax 04-42-66-82-01. 10 units. MINIBAR TV TEL. 380F–550F ($64.60–$93.50) double. AE, DC, V. Closed Feb 15–Mar 15. From Aix, drive 6 miles southeast, following the signs to Trets.

This charming three-star hotel has a setting that looks like a Cézanne canvas, at the foot of Montaigne Ste-Victoire. The former stable has ceiling beams, a country fireplace, and plush furniture. The hotel's staff is very attentive, and rooms are cozily outfitted with Provençal furniture and comfortable mattresses. Bathrooms are well equipped and tidily maintained; all have hair dryers.

The cuisine is one of the primary reasons for a stop here. The chef's innovative specialties are served on the terrace or in the dining room, both ringed with flowers. Specialties are herb-flavored lamb, stuffed sole, bisque of mussels, truffled chicken, rockfish soup, foie gras of the region, and an excellent tarte Tatin. The cheese board has selections from all over France. Fixed-price menus cost 150F ($25.50). The restaurant is closed Sunday night and Monday.

WHERE TO DINE
EXPENSIVE

Le Clos de la Violette. In the Villa Gallici, 10 av. de la Violette. ☎ **04-42-23-30-71.** Reservations required. Main courses 185F–200F ($31.45–$34); fixed-price menus 270F–550F ($45.90–$93.50) at lunch, 370F–550F ($62.90–$93.50) at dinner. AE, V. Mon 7:30–9:30pm, Tues–Sat noon–1:30pm and 7:30–9:30pm. FRENCH.

The restaurant is in an elegant residential neighborhood that is best reached by taxi. Le Clos de la Violette is a creative and innovative restaurant whose cuisine is usually a bit better than the attention span of its sometimes inexperienced staff. The imposing Provençal villa has an octagonal reception area and several modern dining rooms. Menu items are stylish and seasonal, richly tuned to the flavors of Provence. Examples include local goat's cheese in puff pastry with a confit of fresh celery; braised sea wolf with beignets of fennel; warm onion brioche with a fig-flavored vinaigrette and balsamic vinegar; and roasted Provençal lamb in puff pastry. An absolutely superb dessert might be a "celebration" of Provençal figs—an artfully arranged platter containing a galette of figs, a tart of figs, a parfait of figs, and a sorbet of figs.

MODERATE

Chez Maxime. 12 place Ramus. ☎ **04-42-26-28-51.** Reservations recommended. Main courses 85F–160F ($14.45–$27.20); fixed-price lunches 95F–270F ($16.15–$45.90); fixed-price dinners 130F–270F ($22.10–$45.90). MC, V. Mon 8–11pm, Tues–Sat noon–2pm and 8–11pm. Closed Jan 15–31. GRILLS/PROVENÇAL.

This likeable restaurant reflects the skills and personality of its owner/namesake, Felix Maxime. It's in the pedestrian zone with a terrace on the sidewalk. The most important element here is the cuisine. Redolent with the flavors of Provence, a *tian*—layers of eggplant, peppers, and Mediterranean herbs in a terra-cotta pot, infused with garlic, aromates, and olive oil, and baked until bubbly—is a superb beginning. Another fine appetizer is *rillettes* (like a roughly textured pâté) of sea wolf with a garlicky rouille mayonnaise. Specialties include as many as 19 kinds of grilled meat or fish cooked over an oak-burning fire, and several preparations of lamb. A staff member will dress your cut of meat next to your table. The wine list features more than 500 vintages, including many esoteric bottles from the region.

Trattoria Chez Antoine Côte Cour. 19 rue Mirabeau. ☎ **04-42-93-12-51.** Reservations recommended. Main courses 65F–140F ($11.05–$23.80). DC, MC, V. Tues–Sat noon–2:30pm and Mon–Sat 7:30pm–midnight. PROVENÇAL/ITALIAN.

In 1997 this popular trattoria moved into new quarters—an 18th-century town house a few steps from place Rotonde—and managed to lure most of its regulars along. These include Emanuel Ungaro as well as many other film and fashion types, who mingle smoothly with old-time "Aixers." Despite the grandeur of the setting, the ambiance is unpretentious, even jovial. Crusty bread and small pots of aromatic purées (anchovy and basil) are placed at your table before your order is taken. A simple wine, such as Côtes du Rhône, will go nicely with the kind of hearty Mediterranean food that's de rigueur. Examples are a memorable version of *pastis* (pasta Romano flavored with calf's liver, flap mushrooms, and tomato sauce), *osso buco* (veal shank layered with salty ham), a selection of *légumes farcies* (such as eggplant and zucchini stuffed with minced meat and herbs), and at least half a dozen kinds of fresh fish.

INEXPENSIVE

Brasserie Royale. 17 cours Mirabeau. ☎ **04-42-26-01-63.** Reservations not needed. Main courses 55F–105F ($9.35–$17.85); fixed-price menus 69F–100F ($11.75–$17). MC, V. Daily noon–2pm and 7pm–1am. FRENCH.

Located on a tree-lined boulevard, the informal Brasserie Royale offers excellent, unpretentious regional cooking at reasonable prices. It's a modernized, animated, and invariably crowded place with an interior dining room and a popular glass-enclosed, canopied section on the sidewalk. You're served such hearty fare as tripe Provençal, daube Provençal (a favorite dish here), and bourride Provençale. The daube consists of succulent chunks of beef braised in a rich red wine stock, enriched with various fresh vegetables, and well-seasoned with herbs. The bourride is a savory fish stew richly spiced with garlic and a bouquet garni and served in a tureen on slices of fresh bread with the fish on the side. Gigot of tender alpine lamb is another specialty; the meat is perfumed with the fresh herbs of Provence. The chef is known for his *plats du jour,* which on our last visit included *lapin* (rabbit) chasseur, paella, osso buco, and couscous. If you're dining light, you might enjoy one of the omelets. Wines of Provence come by the half or full bottle. The brasserie is also a *glacier* during the afternoon, serving several different ice-cream specialties, milk shakes, and Irish coffee.

Le Bistro Latin. 18 rue de la Couronne. ☎ **04-42-38-22-88.** Reservations recommended. Fixed-price menus 89F ($15.15) Tues–Fri, 119F–179F ($20.25–$30.45) at dinner. MC, V. Mon 7–10:30pm, Tues–Sat noon–2pm and Mon–Sat 7–10:30pm. PROVENÇAL.

The best little bistro in Aix-en-Provence (for the price) is run by Bruno Ungaro and his partner, Gilles Holtz, who pride themselves on their fixed-price menus. They offer two intimate dining rooms, a street-level room, and another in the cellar decorated in Greco-Latin style. The staff is young and enthusiastic, and Provençal music plays in the background. Try the chartreuse of mussels, one of the meat dishes with spinach-and-saffron/cream sauce, or crêpe of hare with basil sauce. We've enjoyed the classic cuisine on all our visits, particularly the scampi risotto.

AIX AFTER DARK

Aix's role as a university town, and its status as one of Provence's largest towns (after Marseille and Nice), almost guarantees an animated roster of nightlife options.

Rockers head for **Le Mistral,** 3 rue Frédéric-Mistral (☎ 04-42-38-16-49), where techno and house music blare long and loud. Its slightly more subdued competitor, **Le Richelme,** 24 rue de la Verrerie (☎ 04-42-23-49-29), plays the same music but sometimes dips into 1970s and 1980s disco. Nearby, a woodsy-looking English pub that plays rock videos, **Bugsy,** 25 rue de la Verrerie (☎ 04-42-38-25-22), is where the good times are punctuated with bouts at billiard tables.

Less competitive and favored by those over 30 is the **Scat Club,** 11 rue de la Verrerie (☎ 04-42-23-00-23), where a pianist and a jazz trio provide music live (jazz, soul, blues, and rock and roll) to drink to. (Where did this relatively wholesome club gets its controversial name? From the popular French dance, of course.) Its rival is **Hot Brass,** chemin de la Pleine des Vergueiers (☎ 04-42-21-05-57), attracting lots of off-duty photographers, artists, actors, and literary types who appreciate the drinks and live music. Both these places boast two floors, each with its own bar, and live acts that include healthy doses of rhythm and blues.

If you're a university student or want to act like one, head for the **Jungle Café,** 4 bd. Carnot (☎ 04-42-21-47-44), where live music enhances an everyday preoccupation with dating and mating. The town's most animated gay disco is **M.P.** (an abbreviation for "Mary Poppins"), in the rue des Bernardins (no phone).

17 Marseille

479 miles (770.88km) S of Paris, 116 miles (186.68km) SW of Nice, 19 miles (30.58km) S of Aix-en-Provence

Bustling Marseille, with more than a million inhabitants, is the second-largest city in France (its population surpassed that of Lyon in the early 1990s) and France's premier port. It's been called France's New Orleans. A crossroads of world traffic—Dumas called it "the meeting place of the entire world"—the city is ancient, founded by Greeks from the city of Phocaea, near present-day Izmir, Turkey, in the 6th century B.C. Marseille is a place of unique sounds, smells, and sights. It has seen wars and much destruction, but trade has always been its raison d'être.

Perhaps its most common association is with the national anthem of France, "La Marseillaise." During the Revolution, 500 volunteers marched to Paris, singing this rousing song along the way. The rest is history.

Although in many respects Marseille is big and sprawling, dirty and slumlike in many places, there's much elegance and charm here as well. The Vieux Port, the old harbor, is especially colorful, compensating to an extent for the dreary industrial dockland nearby. Marseille has always symbolized danger and intrigue, and that reputation

It's been called seedy, low-rent . . . not comme il faut (remember The French Connection?). But drugs are no longer king in Marseille, and this multi-ethnic city by the sea is fast becoming France's new repository of cool. Hip fusion music is recorded here, fashion is booming, tourism is rising, and the seafood restaurants just can't be beat.
—Amy Wilentz, 1999

is somewhat justified. It's also the goal of literally thousands of North and sub-Saharan Africans, creating a lively medley of races and creeds. One-quarter of the population of Marseille is of North African descent.

Marseille today actually occupies twice the amount of land space as Paris, and its age-old problems remain, including a declining drug industry, smuggling, corruption (often at the highest levels), the Mafia, and racial tension. Unemployment, as always, is on the rise. But in spite of all these difficulties, it's a bustling, always-fascinating city unlike any other in France. A city official proclaimed recently that "Marseille is the unbeloved child of France. It's attached to France, but has the collective consciousness of an Italian city-state, like Genoa or Venice."

ESSENTIALS

GETTING THERE   The Marseille **airport** (☎ 04-42-14-14-14), 18 miles north of the center in Marignane, receives international flights from all over Europe. From the airport, blue-and-white minivans *(navettes)* make the trip from a point in front of the arrivals hall to Marseille's St-Charles rail station near the Vieux Port for a one-way fee of 45F ($7.65) per person. The minivans run daily at 20-minute intervals, 6:20am to 10:50pm.

The city is the terminus for the TGV bullet train, which departs daily from Paris's Gare de Lyon (trip time: 4¾ hrs.). Local trains from Paris arrive almost every hour. Marseille has especially good train connections to and from Italy. For **rail information** and schedules call ☎ 08-36-35-35-35. Buses pull into the **Gare Routière,** on the place Victor Hugo (☎ 04-91-08-16-40), adjacent to the St. Charles railway station. Take the A7 autoroute into Marseille.

VISITOR INFORMATION   The **Office de Tourisme** is at 4 La Canebière (☎ 04-91-13-89-00).

EXPLORING THE CITY

Many visitors never bother to visit the museums, preferring to absorb the unique spirit of the city as reflected by its busy streets and at its sidewalk cafes, particularly those along the main street, **La Canebière.** Known as "can of beer" to World War II GIs, it's the spine and soul of Marseille, but the seediest main street in France. Lined with hotels, shops, and restaurants, the street is filled with sailors of every nation and a wide range of foreigners, especially Algerians, some of whom live in souklike conditions. La Canebière winds down to the **Vieux Port,** dominated by the massive neoclassical forts of St-Jean and St-Nicholas. The port is filled with fishing craft and yachts and ringed with seafood restaurants.

Motorists can continue along to the corniche **Président-J.-F.-Kennedy,** a promenade running for about 3 miles along the sea. You pass villas and gardens along the way and have a good view of the Mediterranean. To the north, the **Port Moderne** (also known simply as "La Joliette," or "the gateway to the East") is a man-made labyrinth of nautical engineering. Its construction began in 1844, and a century later, the Germans destroyed it. Today, it's one of the busiest ports in the Mediterranean.

Marseille

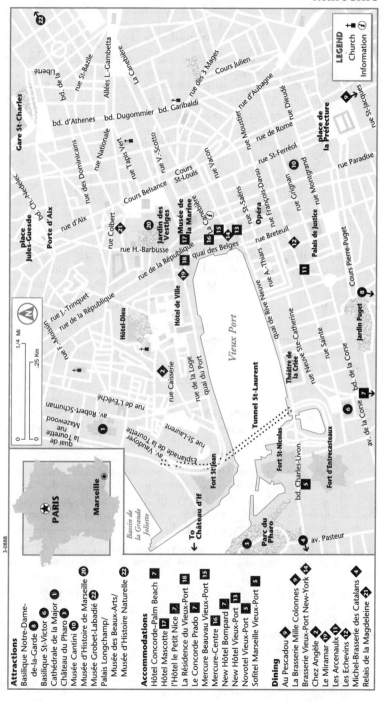

Attractions
Basilique Notre-Dame-de-la-Garde ❽
Basilique St-Victor ❻
Cathédrale de la Major ❶
Château du Pharo ❸
Musée Cantini ❿
Musée d'Histoire de Marseille ❷⓿
Musée Grobet-Labadié ❷❷
Palais Longchamp/
Musée des Beaux-Arts/
Musée d'Histoire Naturelle ❷❷

Accommodations
Hôtel Concorde-Palm Beach ❼
Hôtel Mascotte ⓱
l'Hôtel le Petit Nice ❼
La Résidence du Vieux-Port ⓲
Le Concorde Prado ❼
Mercure Beauvau Vieux-Port ⓯
Mercure-Centre ⓰
New Hôtel Bompard ❼
New Hôtel Vieux-Port ⓭
Novotel Vieux-Port ❺
Sofitel Marseille Vieux-Port ❺

Dining
Au Pescadou ◆❾
La Brasserie Mille Colonnes ◆❾
Brasserie Vieux-Port New-York ◆⓮
Chez Angèle ◆❷
Le Miramar ◆⓳
Les Arcenaulx ◆⓱
Les Echevins ◆⓲
Michel-Brasserie des Catalans ◆
Relais de la Magdeleine ◆❷

181

Exploring the Massif des Calanques

You can visit the Massif des Calanques, a wild and rugged terrain, from either Marseille or Cassis. This craggy coastline lies between the two ports, directly south of Marseille and to the west of Cassis. With its highest peak at 1,850 feet, the Calanques stretch for some 12½ miles of dazzling limestone whiteness. This is one of France's great natural beauty areas.

Exactly what is a *calanque?* The word comes from the Provençal *cala,* meaning steep slopes. Nature has cut steep coastal valleys into solid rock, creating rivers. Most of these gorges extend less than a mile inland from the Mediterranean. They're similar to fjords, created by glaciers, but these gorges have been created by the raging sea. The needlelike rocks and cliff faces overhanging the sea attract rock climbers and deep-sea divers.

In July and August the **Société des Excursionnistes Marseillais,** 16 rue de la Rotonde (☎ **04-91-84-75-52**), conducts free walking tours of the Calanques twice a week. Call for information, since the days of these walking tours can vary depending on weather. This outfit also conducts boat trips daily in summer, leaving from quai des Belges in Marseille and costing 100F ($17). Trips are conducted in a combination of French and English, and last for about 2½ hours.

The highlight of the Calanques is **Sormiou,** with its beach, seafood eateries, and small harbor. Sormiou is separated from another small but enchanting settlement at **Morgiou** by **Cap Morgiou,** which offers a panoramic belvedere with splendid views of both the Calanques and the eastern side of the massif. At Morgiou there are tiny creeks for swimming.

SEEING THE TOP ATTRACTIONS

Basilique Notre-Dame-de-la-Garde. Rue Fort-du-Sanctuaire. ☎ **04-91-13-40-80.** Free admission. Mid-June to mid-Sept daily 7am–8pm; late Sept to early June daily 7am–7pm. Métro: Vieux-Port. Bus: 60.

This landmark church crowns a limestone rock overlooking the southern side of the Vieux-Port. It was built in the Romanesque-Byzantine style popular in the 19th century and topped by a 30-foot gilded statue of the Virgin. Visitors come here not so much for the church as for the view—best seen at sunset—from its terrace. Spread out before you are the city, the islands, and the sea.

Basilique St-Victor. Place St-Victor. ☎ **04-96-11-22-60.** Admission to crypt 10F ($1.70). Crypt daily 8am–7pm. Head west along quai de Rive-Neuve (near the Gare du Vieux-Port). Métro: Vieux-Port.

For a city as ancient as Marseilles, antique monuments are few, thanks to the waves of building that have always reflected this city's role as a major commercial center. This semifortified basilica is one of the most noteworthy. It was built above a crypt from the 5th century foundation of the church and abbey founded by St. Cassianus. You can visit the crypt, which also reflects work done in the 10th and 11th centuries.

Cathédrale de la Major. Place de la Major. ☎ **04-91-90-53-57.** Free admission. Tues–Thurs 9am–noon and 2–5:30pm, Fri 9am–noon and 2–6:30pm, Sat–Sun 9am–noon and 2:30–6pm. Closed Mon. Métro: Joliette.

This was one of the largest cathedrals (some 450 feet long) built in Europe in the 19th century. Its interior is adorned with mosaic floors and red-and-white marble banners, and the exterior is in a bastardized Romanesque-Byzantine style. The domes and cupolas may remind you of Istanbul. This vast pile has almost swallowed its 12th-century Romanesque predecessor (originally a baptistery) built on the ruins of a Temple of Diana.

Musée des Beaux-Arts. In the Palais Longchamp, place Bernex. ☎ **04-91-14-59-30.** Admission 12F ($2.05) adults, 6F ($1) students and ages 12–18. Free for children under 12. June 15–Sept 15, Tues–Sun 11am–7pm; Sept 16–June 14, Tues–Sun 10am–5pm. Metro: Cinq av. Longchamp or Réfomés.

One of the most scenic sights is **Palais Longchamp,** with its spectacular fountain and colonnade, built during the Second Empire. This museum, housed in a northern wing of the palace, displays a vast array of paintings from the 16th to the 19th centuries. They include works by Corot, Millet, Ingres, David, and Rubens. Some 80 sculptures and objets d'art were bequeathed to the museum as well; particularly interesting is a gallery of Pierre Puget sculpture. One salon is devoted to Honoré Daumier, born in Marseille in 1808.

Musée Cantini. 19 rue Grignan. ☎ **04-91-54-77-75.** Admission 18F ($3.05) adults, 10F ($1.70) students, free for seniors and children 10 and under. June–Sept Tues–Sun 11am–6pm; Oct–May Tues–Sun 10am–5pm. Métro: Estrangin Préfecture.

The temporary exhibitions of contemporary art staged here are often as good as the permanent collection. This museum is devoted to modern art, with masterpieces by Derain, Marquet, Ernst, Masson, Balthus, and others. It also owns a selection of works by important young international artists.

Musée Grobet-Labadié. 140 bd. Longchamp. ☎ **04-91-62-21-82.** Admission 12F ($2.05) adults, 6F ($1) students and ages 11–18. Free for children under 11., June–Sept, Tues–Sun 11am–6pm; Oct–May, Tues–Sun 10am–5pm. Métro: Réfomés.

This private collection, bequeathed to the city in 1919, includes exquisite Louis XV and Louis XVI furniture, as well as an outstanding collection of medieval Burgundian and Provençal sculpture. Other exhibits are 17th-century Gobelin tapestries; 15th- to 19th-century German, Italian, French, and Flemish paintings; and 16th- and 17th-century Italian and French faïence.

Musée de la Faïence. In the Château Pastré, 157 av. de Montredon. ☎ **04-91-72-43-47.** Admission 12F ($2.05) adults, 6F ($1) students and ages 11–18, free for children under 11. June–Sept, Tues–Sun 11am–6pm; Oct–May, Tues–Sun 10am–5pm.

This museum contains one of the largest collections of porcelain in France. Its collections date from Neolithic times to the present. Especially numerous are the delicate and richly ornate ceramics that graced the tables of local landowners during the 18th and 19th centuries. The museum is about 3 miles south of the center of Marseille, in a stately manor house (Château Pastré) that was built by a local ship owner in 1864.

Musée d'Histoire de Marseille. Centre Bourse, square Belsunce. ☎ **04-91-90-42-22.** Admission 12F ($2.05) adults, 6F ($1) students and ages 11–18. Free for children under 11. Mon–Sat noon–7pm. Métro: Vieux-Port.

You're allowed to wander through an archaeological garden where excavations are still going on, as scholars attempt to learn more about the ancient town of Massalia, founded by Greek sailors. Of course, many of the exhibits, such as old coins and fragments of pottery, only suggest their former glory. To help you more fully realize the era, you're aided by audiovisual exhibits and a free exhibition room. A medieval quarter of potters has been discovered, and the Louis XIV town is open to the public. You can also see what's left of a Roman wreck that was excavated from the site.

Musée d'Histoire Naturelle. In the Palais Longchamp, place Bernex. ☎ **04-91-14-59-50.** Admission 12F ($2.05) adults, 6F ($1) students and ages 12–18, free for children under 12. Mid-June to Sept, Tues–Sun 10am–5pm; Oct to mid-June, Tues–Sun 11am–6pm.

The same building as the Musée des Beaux-Arts, the natural history museum contains exhibits on geology, mineralogy, botany, and zoology, particularly as they affect the Mediterranean coastline around Marseille.

PANORAMIC VIEWS

Basilique Notre-Dame-de-la-Garde, rue Fort-du-Sanctuaire (☎ 04-91-13-40-80), crowns a limestone bluff overlooking the southern flank of the Vieux Port. Built in 1864 in the Romanesque-Byzantine style, and capped with a 30-foot gilded statue of the Virgin, it sits atop the foundations of a fortress that was commissioned during the Renaissance by French monarch François 1er. Although the architecture shows France's gilded age at its most evocative, visitors come here not so much for the church as for the view—best seen at sunset—from its terrace. Spread out before you are the city, the islands, and the sea. The church is open daily: mid-June to mid-September from 7am to 8pm and the rest of the year from 7am to 7pm.

Another vantage point for a panoramic view is the **Parc du Pharo,** a promontory facing the entrance to the Vieux Port. Most people visit this park to escape the urban congestion of Marseille, but if you're in the mood for some history, check out the gray-stone facade of the **Château du Pharon** (☎ 04-91-14-64-95). Built in the 1860s by Napoléon III for his empress, Eugénie (who is reputed not to have liked it and seldom visited), it's owned and maintained by the city of Marseille as a convention center and—less frequently—as a concert hall. The building has no regular hours, but if nothing is going on, you can enter the lobby and ask for a quick glance at the **Salon des Génies.**

BOATING TO CHÂTEAU D'IF

From quai des Belges at the Vieux Port you can take a ride to the infamous Château d'If. Boats leave the quai about every 60 to 90 minutes, depending on the season, for the 20-minute ride (cost is 50F/$8.50). Contact the **Groupement des Armateurs Côtiers;** its office on quai des Belges (☎ 04-91-55-50-09) is open daily from 7am to 7pm.

On the sparsely vegetated island of **Château d'If** (☎ 04-91-59-02-30), François I built a fortress to defend Marseille and its port. The site later housed a state prison; carvings by Huguenot prisoners can still be seen inside some of the cells. Alexandre Dumas used the château as a setting for his novel, *The Count of Monte Cristo.* The château is open Tuesday to Sunday: April to September from 9am to 7pm and October to March from 9am to 5:30pm. Admittance to the island costs 25F ($4.25) for adults, and 15F ($2.55) for students and children 12 to 18. It's free for children under 12.

SHOPPING

Only Paris and Lyon can rival Marseille in breadth and diversity of merchandise. Your best bet is a trip to the **Vieux Port** and the streets surrounding it for a view of the folkloric objects that literally pop out of the boutiques.

ART & ANTIQUES   The sunlight of Provence has always been cited by artists for its luminosity, and so Marseille has a handful of well-respected art galleries. The most internationally minded of the lot is **Galerie Cargo,** 55 rue Grignan (☎ 04-91-54-84-84), where paintings from medium- to top-echelon international artists are exhibited and sold. Its most powerful competitor is **Galerie Roger-Pailhas,** 61 cours Julien

(☎ 04-91-42-18-01). Antiques from around Provence are sold at **Galerie Wulfram-Puget,** 39 rue de Lodi (☎ **04-91-92-06-00**), and **Antiquités François-Décamp,** 302 rue Paradis (☎ **04-91-81-18-00**).

FASHION   You don't normally think of Marseille as a place to go to shop for fashion, but the local fashion industry is booming. The fashion center is found along **Cours Julien,** where you'll find dozens of boutiques and ateliers. Much of the clothing reflects North African influences, although there is a vast array of French styles as well. The basic style of much of this clothing at the millennium is rich, brocaded, ethnic, and cut close to the body.

For hats, at **Felio,** 4 place Gabriel-Péri (☎ **04-91-90-32-67**), you'll find large-brimmed numbers that would've thrilled ladies of the belle époque or guests at a stylish wedding inspired in the 1920s by Lanvin. There's a selection of *casquettes Marseillaises* (developed for men as protection from the *soleil du Midi*) and berets that begin at 150F ($25.50).

FOLKLORE & SOUVENIRS   Especially popular are the *santons* (carved wooden crèche figurines). The best place for acquiring these artifacts is just above the Vieux Port, behind the Théâtre National de la Criée. At **Ateliers Marcel Carbonel,** 47 rue Neuve-Ste-Catherine (☎ **04-91-54-26-58**), more than 600 figures, available in half a dozen sizes, sell at prices beginning at 60F ($10.20).

All the souvenir shops along the pedestrian **rue St-Féréol,** running perpendicular to La Canebière, sell folkloric replicas of handcrafts from Old Provence, including the cream-colored or pale-green bars of the city's local soap, savon de Marseille. Infused with a healthy dollop of olive oil, it's known for its kindness to skin dried out by the sun and mistral. A large selection is available at **La Savonnerie du Sérail,** 50 bd. Anatole de la Forge (☎ **04-91-98-28-25**).

FOOD & CHOCOLATE   At **Amandine,** 69 bd. Eugène-Pierre (☎ **04-91-47-00-83**), a photograph or a work of graphic art can be reproduced in various shades of chocolate on top of a delicious layer cake in any flavor you specify in advance. If you don't happen to have your scrapbook with you, you can buy a cake emblazoned with scenes of the Vieux Port or whatever. More traditional pastries and chocolates are found at **Puyricard,** 25 rue Francis-Davso (☎ **04-91-54-26-25**), with another location at 155 rue Jean-Mermoz (☎ **04-91-77-94-11**). The treats available here include chocolates stuffed with almond paste *(pâté d'amande)* or *confits de fruits,* along with a type of biscuit called *une Marseillotte.*

Since medieval times, Marseille has thrived on the legend of Les Trois Maries—three saints named Mary who, assisted by awakened-from-the-dead St. Lazarus, reportedly came ashore at a point near Marseille to Christianize ancient Provence. In commemoration of their voyage, small boat-shaped cookies *(les navettes)* are flavored with secret ingredients (that include orange zest, orange-flower water, and sugar); they are forever associated with Marseille. They're sold throughout the city, notably at **Le Four des Navettes,** 136 rue Sainte (☎ **04-91-33-32-12**). It opened in 1791 and is dedicated to perpetuating the city's most cherished medieval myth and ferociously guarding the secret of how the pastries are made. The boat-shaped cookies are sold for 45F ($7.65) per dozen

Two of the city's most sophisticated emporiums for takeout food include **Fromagerie Blanc,** 19 av. du prado (☎ **04-91-79-21-00**), where you can acquire ingredients for a picnic: pâtés, cheeses, breads, pastries, and a succulent array of pre-cooked platters. A competitor with an even greater selection of cheeses (whose variety confused even the ultimate francophile, Charles de Gaulle) is **La Fromagerie Marou,** 2 bd. Baille (☎ **04-91-78-17-68**).

A MARSEILLE MALL Looking for something that approximates, with a Provençal accent, a sun-flooded mall in California? Head for the most talked-about real-estate development in the city's recent history, **L'Escale Borély,** avenue Mendès-France. Within a 25-minute transit (take the Métro to rond-point du Prado, then transfer to bus no. 19) south of Marseille, it incorporates shops, cafes, bars, and restaurants. Note the newest fad from your seat on a terrace as you sip pastis—in-line skating. For more on L'Escale Borély, see "Marseille After Dark," below.

A DAY AT THE BEACH

Bus 83 leaves form the Vieux-Port heading for the public beaches outside Marseille. This bus will take you to both plage du Prado and plage de la Corniche, the best bets for swimming and sunning. The sands are a bit gray and sometimes rocky, but the beaches are wide and the water is generally clear. These beaches are set against a scenic backdrop of the cliffs of Marseille.

WHERE TO STAY
VERY EXPENSIVE

✪ **Hôtel Le Petit Nice.** Corniche Président-J.-F.-Kennedy/Anse-de-Maldormé, 13007 Marseille. ☎ **04-91-59-25-92.** Fax 04-91-59-28-08. www.relaischateaux.fr. 15 units. A/C MINIBAR TV TEL. 1,200–2,600F ($204–$442) double; 4,300F–5,500F ($731–$935) suite. AE, DC, MC, V. Parking 100F ($17) in garage. Free in a supervised outdoor parking lot. Métro: Vieux-Port.

This is the best in Marseille, with the finest restaurant. The Résidence opened in 1917 when the Passédat family joined two villas. The narrow approach takes you past what looks like a row of private villas, in a secluded area below the street paralleling the beach. Rooms are decorated with tasteful fabrics and quality carpeting, plus such extras as private safes, and all come equipped with luxury mattresses on fine beds. Units in the main house are modern and even avant-garde—four units were inspired by the Cubism and have geometric appointments and bright colors. The spacious Marina Wing across from the main building offers individually decorated rooms in the antique style, opening onto sea views. Marble baths are quite sumptuous and come with deluxe toiletries and fluffy towels.

The beautiful restaurant has a view of the shore and the rocky islands off the coast. In summer, dinner is served in the garden facing the sea. It's run by Jean-Paul Passédat and his son Gerald, whose imaginative culinary successes include sliced sea wolf in the style of the Passédat family matriarch, Lucy; vinaigrette of *rascasse* (hogfish); and sea devil with saffron and garlic. It's open daily from April 18 to October; off-season it's closed all day Sunday and Monday. Set menus cost 350F to 620F ($59.50 to $105.40) at lunch and 620F ($105.40) at dinner. There's also a seawater pool and a solarium.

EXPENSIVE

Sofitel Marseille Vieux-Port. 36 bd. Charles-Livon, 13007 Marseille. ☎ **04-91-15-59-00.** Fax 04-91-15-59-50. www.sofitel.com. E-mail: Ho542@accor-hotels.com. 130 units. A/C MINIBAR TV TEL. 990F–1,400F ($168.30–$238) double; 2,500–3,800F ($425–$646) suite. AE, DC, MC, V. Parking 65F ($11.05). Métro: Vieux-Port.

This seven-story Sofitel looms above the massive embankments of the old port. Though lacking the charm, grace, and atmosphere of Le Petit Nice, it's still the choice address among the city's chain hotels, where you get good value. Rooms may look out on the boulevard traffic or on one of the best panoramic views of the port of Old Marseille. They're fairly generous in size, up-to-date, and recently furnished in Provence style. Bright and modern and inviting, they have fashionable fabrics, thick carpets, small closets, and well-fitted beds—most often doubles or twins—with quality mattresses and fine linens. Bathrooms come with hair dryers and most often shower/tub combinations, with thick towels. Some of the superior rooms also have robes. There are a pool, an elegant bar, and Les Trois Forts, a restaurant with views of the harbor and its defenses. Meals are served daily from noon to 2pm and 7 to 10:30pm. In the same building is the three-star Novotel (see below).

MODERATE

Hôtel Concorde–Palm Beach. 2 promenade de la Plage, 13008 Marseille. ☎ **04-91-16-19-00.** Fax 04-91-16-19-39. www.palmbeach-hotel.com. E-mail: reservation@palmbeach-hotel.com. 145 units. A/C MINIBAR TV TEL. 590F–730F ($100.30–$124.10) double, 1,680F ($285.60) suite. AE, DC, MC, V. Parking 45F ($7.65). From the town center, take corniche J.-F.-Kennedy for 1½ miles east, following the signs DIRECTION PLAGES.

Popular with commercial travelers, this modern hotel complex and seaside resort was radically renovated in 1999. The interior is a tasteful blend of big windows, expansive terraces, and soothing colors. Rooms are airy, relatively spacious, and summery, each with a private terrace, a recently replaced mattresses, and bathrooms with adequate numbers of good-sized towels, plus a hair dryer. Meals in Les Voilliers, a grill room specializing in buffets, begin at around 100F ($17); more elegant meals in the seafood restaurant, La Réserve, cost from 180F to 210F ($30.60 to $35.70) for a set-price menu. On the premises are an outdoor pool and a solarium.

Mercure Beauvau Vieux-Port. 4 rue Beauvau, 13001 Marseille. ☎ **800/223-6800** in the U.S., or 04-91-54-91-00. Fax 04-91-54-15-76. 71 units. A/C MINIBAR TV TEL. 650F–780F ($110.50–$132.60) double. AE, DC, MC, V. Parking 30F ($5.10) extra.

Located at the edge of the Vieux-Port, this six-story member of the nationwide chain was renovated in 1996, and today offers comfortable and well-positioned rooms in the heart of the touristic zone. The lobby has a Provençal decor, and rooms are outfitted in modernized versions of either Louis-Philippe or Provençal with touches of Napoléon III. They are medium size and well maintained, with double or twin beds with firm mattresses. The tiled bathrooms have adequate shelf space, most often a shower/tub combination, and a rack of good-sized towels. Breakfast is the only meal served.

Mercure-Centre. Rue Neuve-St-Martin, 13001 Marseille. ☎ **04-91-39-20-00.** Fax 04-91-56-24-57. 199 units. A/C MINIBAR TV TEL. 490F–590F ($83.30–$100.30) double, 980F ($166.60) suite. AE, DC, MC, V. Parking 65F ($11.05). Métro: Colbert.

One of the most modern hotels in town, this bronze building looks out over the Greco-Roman ruins of the Jardin des Vestiges, a 2-minute walk from the Old Port, and near a collection of boutiques, the Centre Bourse. The well-kept rooms are medium in size and furnished in a functional chain-style format, with twin or double beds and good mattresses. Tiled bathrooms are compact but have adequate shelf space and shower/tub combinations. There are both a formal and an informal restaurant and a bar where many of Marseille's shoppers go. The more upscale choice is the **Oursinade,** open daily for lunch and dinner; the less formal, less expensive bistro, **l'Oliveraie,** is open daily from noon to midnight. Many staff members speak English.

Novotel Vieux-Port. 36 bd. Charles-Livon, 13007 Marseille. ☎ **04-91-59-22-22.** Fax 04-91-31-15-48. E-mail: H0911@accor-hotels.com. 90 units. A/C MINIBAR TV TEL. 560F–660F ($95.20–$112.20) double. AE, DC, MC, V. Parking 45F ($7.65). Métro: Vieux-Port.

In the same building as the more upscale Sofitel (see above), this Novotel was created in 1987. Bedrooms are outfitted in a chain-hotel format—services are less extensive, amenities less plush, and spaces a bit more cramped than those at the Sofitel, but this is one of the most reasonably priced, good-value hotels in town. Each room contains both a double and a single bed (which also serves as a couch) and a desk, and has an efficiently designed bathroom. The rooms overlooking the old port tend to fill up first.

The lattice-decorated restaurant (Côte Jardin) serves solid and basic meals, daily from 6am to midnight.

INEXPENSIVE

Hôtel Mascotte. 5 la Canebière, 13001 Marseille. ☎ **04-91-90-61-61.** Fax 04-91-90-95-61. 45 units. A/C TV TEL. 435F–525F ($73.95–$89.25) double. AE, MC, V. Parking in a nearby public lot, 110F ($18.70) a day.

Everything about this hotel evokes the tenuous grandeur of 19th-century port life in Marseille. It's less than 2 blocks from the inner sanctums of the Vieux-Port, behind a battered Beaux-arts facade whose ornate corbels and cornices have seen the sun and mistrals of many, many seasons. Inside, a series of renovations have stripped the bedrooms of some of their old-fashioned charm but have left behind clean, efficient, soundproofed spaces that are sometimes larger than you might expect. Each accommodation is well maintained and equipped, with firm mattresses on the twin or double beds. Bathrooms are small but tidily kept, each with a shower/tub combination or a shower stall. Breakfast is the only meal served, but considering the many dining options in the surrounding neighborhood, no one seems to care.

La Résidence du Vieux-Port. 18 quai du Port, 13001 Marseille. ☎ **04-91-91-91-22.** Fax 04-91-56-60-88. 41 units. A/C MINIBAR TV TEL. 560F–660F ($95.20–$112.20) double; 765F ($130.05) suite. AE, DC, MC, V. Parking 30F ($5.10). Métro: Vieux-Port.

Old-fashioned, with a touch of raffish charm and an unbeatable location directly beside the harbor, this eight-story hotel's guest rooms have loggia-style terraces opening onto the port. They are simple but serviceable, with comfortable mattresses and sufficient towels. A restoration was completed in 1997. The conscientious staff tend to guests appropriately. The hotel has a cafe and a breakfast room on the second floor, and a bar behind the lobby.

Le Concorde Prado. 11 av. de Mazargues, 13008 Marseille. ☎ **04-91-76-51-11,** or 212/752-3900 for reservations in the U.S. Fax 04-91-77-95-10. 47 units. A/C MINIBAR TV TEL. 595F ($101.15) double. Free parking. Métro: Rond-Point du Prado. Bus: 83.

Set near Marseille's congress and convention center (from which it gets a lot of business), a 10-minute subway ride east of the center, this small-scale hotel was built in the 1970s in a dramatic contemporary design. It has bronze-faced elevators, and its yellow and blue guest rooms are outfitted in a modern interpretation of traditional Provençal styling. Each has large reading lamps and comfortably oversized armchairs that add a sense of coziness to the otherwise contemporary format. You'll have a choice of rooms overlooking either the busy avenue or the garden with its reflection pools. Mattresses are firm, tiled bathrooms are moderate in size and have shower/tub combinations along with a rack of good-sized towels. Newer units have makeup mirrors and hair dryers.

New Hôtel Bompard. 2 rue des Flots-Bleus, 13007 Marseille. ☎ **04-91-52-10-93.** 46 units. A/C MINIBAR TV TEL. 445F–460F ($75.65–$78.20) double. Free parking. Bus: 61 or 83.

This tranquil retreat is set atop a cliff along the corniche, about 1½ miles east of Vieux Port. Partly because of its elegant garden, it might remind you of a well-appointed private home. Bedrooms have conservatively traditional furniture, tasteful and subdued color schemes, and balconies or terraces overlooking the grounds. Most of the accommodations are medium size, and they are well maintained, with comfortable beds fitted with firm mattresses and quality linen. The small bathrooms have just adequate shelf space and are most often equipped with a shower/tub combination. There's a bistro on the premises, Le Lautrec, which serves lunch and dinner daily, with main courses priced at 55F to 95F ($9.35 to $16.15) each.

New Hôtel Vieux-Port. 3 bis rue Reine-Elisabeth, 13001 Marseille. ☎ **04-91-00-51-42.** Fax 04-91-90-76-24. E-mail: marseillevieux-port@new-hotel.com. 47 units. TV TEL.

Mon–Thurs 440F ($74.80) double; Fri–Sun 350F ($59.50) double. Bus 50F ($8.50). Parking 30F ($5.10). Bus: 83.

Located close to the port, in a six-story turn-of-the-century building that was completely renovated between 1994 and 1997, this hotel offers clean and comfortable rooms and a hardworking, English-speaking staff. Rooms that overlook the port are outfitted in a traditional way; the more contemporary-looking accommodations look out over the commercial neighborhood nearby. This hotel offers exceptional value for Marseille, although most of the accommodations are small. Each comes with a firm mattress on twin or double beds; bathrooms are compact but well cared for, some with a shower/tub, some with just a shower, and all with good-sized towels.

WHERE TO DINE
EXPENSIVE

Au Pescadou. 19 place Castellane. ☎ **04-91-78-36-01.** Reservations recommended. Main courses 90F–120F ($15.30–$20.40); bouillabaisse 230F ($39.10) per person; fixed-price menus 158F–198F ($26.85–$33.65). AE, DC, MC, V. Mon–Sat noon–2pm and 7–11pm, Sun noon–2pm. Closed July–Aug. Métro: Castellane. SEAFOOD.

This is one of Marseille's finest seafood restaurants. It's now run by the three multilingual sons of the original owner, Barthélémy Mennella. The venue is rough-edged but civil. Beside a busy traffic circle downtown, it overlooks a fountain and a sidewalk display of fresh oysters. For an appetizer, try almond-stuffed mussels or "hors d'oeuvres of the fisherman." Main-dish specialties are bouillabaisse, *gigot de lotte* (monkfish stewed in cream sauce with fresh vegetables), and scallops cooked with morels.

Adjacent to the main restaurant, and under the same management, is an informal newcomer, **La Brasserie Mille Colonnes,** 21 place Castellane (☎ **04-91-78-18-10**). Bustling and gregarious, it serves platters of grilled fish as well as blanquettes of veal, steak *(a bac),* and pastas. Full meals, without wine, rarely exceed 140F ($23.80); and *plats du jour* cost from 45F to 65F ($7.65 to $11.05).

✪ **Le Miramar.** 12 Quai du Port. ☎ **04-91-91-10-40.** Reservations recommended. Main courses 170F–255F ($28.90–$43.35); bouillabaisse 250F ($42.50) per person (minimum of 2 diners). AE, DC, MC, V. Mon–Sat 12:15–2pm and 7:15–10pm. Closed 2 weeks in Jan and 3 weeks in Aug. Métro: Vieux-Port/Hôtel-de-Ville. SEAFOOD.

Since the mid-1960s, aficionados of bouillabaisse have been flocking here for a taste of the famous savory fish soup. When you try it here, you may exclaim, "Ah, bouillabaisse!" Savoring the delights of this fine restaurant will be one of the culinary highlights of your trip. It's hard to imagine that bouillabaisse was once a rough-and-tumble recipe favored by local fisherfolk. It was actually devised as a way of using the least desirable portion of their catch. Actually it's two dishes—beginning with a saffron-tinted soup followed by the various fish poached in the soup. It's consumed with a large dollop of *rouille,* a sauce of red chilies, garlic, olive oil, egg yolk, and cayenne. For the version served here, the chef considers rascasse or hogfish essential, but views lobster as a "silly frill that adds nothing to the soup but plenty to the bill." The setting is a large, big-windowed room with frescoes of underwater life, linked to an outdoor terrace that overlooks Marseilles' most famous church, Notre-Dame-de-la-Garde.

Michel-Brasserie des Catalans. 6 rue des Catalans. ☎ **04-91-52-30-63.** Reservations recommended. Main courses 180F–200F ($30.60–$34). AE, DC, MC, V. Daily noon–2pm and 7:30–10pm. Bus: 81 or 83. SEAFOOD.

Although it's decorated with shellacked lobsters and starfish, this restaurant serves a fine bouillabaisse. Just beyond the Parc du Pharo, next to the Old Port, it's one of the best old-time restaurants in town. The cooking emphasizes the taste of the seafood rather than fancy sauces. In addition to the bouillabaisse, it offers a good *bourride* (fish stew with aïoli sauce). The waiter brings you an array of fresh fish from which you make your selection. There's a kind of raffish insouciance here that you might find very appealing.

MODERATE

Brasserie Vieux-Port New-York. 33 quai des Belges. ☎ **04-91-33-91-79.** Reservations recommended at lunch. Main courses 60F–160F ($10.20–$27.20); fixed-price menu 145F ($24.65); bouillabaisse 250F ($42.50). DC, MC, V. Brasserie, daily noon–2:30pm and 7:30–11:30pm; bar and cafe, daily 6:30am–3:30am. Métro: Vieux-Port. FRENCH/PROVENÇAL.

This time-honored brasserie sits on one of the quays overlooking the city's ancient harbor. Many locals consider it their favorite cafe, taking advantage of its dawn-to-dusk hours for a glass of midmorning wine, afternoon coffee, or pastis in its congenially battered art deco interior. You can enjoy a *farci du jour* (stuffed vegetable of the day, tomatoes, peppers, or onions, usually served as part of a main course); grilled fish (monkfish with artichokes is especially flavorful); côte de boeuf with marrow sauce; or a succulent version of bouillabaisse. Also available are pizzas, salads, and grilled meats. Service is more perfunctory on the terrace than at tables inside. Wines focus on Provence. Friday and Saturday nights, from 9pm till closing, waiters are encouraged to sing as they serve.

✪ **Les Arcenaulx.** 25 cours d'Estienne d'orves. ☎ **04-91-59-80-30.** Reservations recommended. Main courses 68F–110F ($11.55–$18.70); fixed-price menus 135F–285F ($22.95–$48.45). AE, DC, MC, V. Mon–Sat noon–2:30pm and 8–11:30pm. Métro: Vieux-Port. PROVENÇAL.

These bulky stone premises were built by the navies of Louis XIV. Close to the water near the Vieux Port, they contain this restaurant and two bookstores (one for French classics, one for modern titles), all directed by the hardworking and charming sisters, Simone and Jeanne Laffitte. Look for authentic and hearty Provençal cuisine with a Marseillais accent. Dishes include a *baudroie à la Raimu*—a kettle of seasonal fish, named for a popular 20th-century actor (similar to bouillabaisse). Equally tempting are artichokes *barigoule* (loaded with aromatic spices and olive oil), a charlotte of crabs, and a worthy assortment of *petites légumes farcies* (Provençal vegetables stuffed with chopped meat and herbs).

Les Echevins. 44 rue Sainte. ☎ **04-91-33-08-08.** Reservations recommended. Main courses 85F–185F ($14.45–$31.45); fixed-price menus 120F–300F ($20.40–$51). AE, DC, MC, V. Mon–Fri noon–2:30pm and 7:30–11:30pm, Sat 7:30–11:30pm. Métro: Vieux-Port. PROVENÇAL/SOUTHWESTERN FRENCH.

On the opposite side of the same building that contains Les Arcenaulx, this restaurant occupies premises that were once a dorm for the prisoners who were forced to row the ornamental barges of Louis XIV during his rare inspections of Marseille's harbor facilities. Today the setting is one of crystal chandeliers, plush carpets, enviable antiques, and massive beams. You'll get a lot for your money—prices are relatively reasonable, and the owners use fresh ingredients prepared at the last possible minute. Inspiration for menu items (cassoulet, magret of duckling, and foie gras) comes from the southwest of France or Provence, specifically Marseille. Provençal dishes include a succulent version of baked sea wolf prepared as simply as possible—just with herbs and olive oil. There's also roast codfish with aïoli and a succulent version of *baudroie* (a simpler version of bouillabaisse).

INEXPENSIVE

Chez Angèle. 50 rue Caisserie. ☎ **04-91-90-63-35.** Reservations recommended. Pizzas, pastas, and salads 50F–95F ($8.50–$16.15); fixed-price menu 110F ($18.70). MC, V. Mon–Fri noon–2:30pm and daily 7–11pm. Closed July 20–Aug 20. Métro: Vieux-Port. PROVENÇAL/PIZZA.

A local friend guided us here, and though most of Marseille's cheap eating places aren't recommendable, this one is worthwhile if you're watching your francs. Small and unpretentious, with a raffish kind of amiability on the part of the owner, it's a pizzeria-restaurant, with a more-than-average comprehensive menu. Pizza (the best are pistou, fresh seafood, or cèpe mushrooms), well-prepared ravioli, tagliatelle, osso buco, and grilled shrimp, squid, and daurade Provençal style are available. For something really ethnic, ask for Francis's version of *pieds et paquets,* a country recipe savored by locals—equal portions of grilled sheep's foot and sheep's intestines stuffed with garlic-flavored bread crumbs, herbs, and chopped vegetables. Note that this place lies on the route between Marseille and Aix.

STAYING & DINING NEARBY

Relais de la Magdeleine. Route d'Aix, 13420 Gemenos. ☎ **04-42-32-20-16.** Fax 04-42-32-02-26. 24 units. TV TEL. 595F–890F ($101.15–$151.30) double; 1,200F ($204) suite. MC, V. Closed Dec–Mar 15. Free parking. Head east of Marseille for 15 miles along A50.

In a stone-sided, early-18th-century country mansion at the foot of the Ste-Baume mountain range, this hotel is surrounded by large homes, open fields, and woodlands. It's near the venerated spot where, according to medieval legend, Mary Magdalene is believed to have died. The inn has striking architectural details; note a carving of St. Roch, with his dog above the entrance. The decor is upscale, with antiques and worthy reproductions. Guest rooms are individually furnished, in Directoire, Provençal, and Louis styles. Mattresses are firm and comfortable, towels adequate and plentiful. The relais also serves savory and well-prepared meals daily at lunch and dinner. Fixed-price menus cost 250F ($42.50); at lunch Monday to Friday there's also a menu for 160F ($27.20). Specialties include lamb cooked with Provençal honey and thyme, and filet of sole Beau with red wine butter and a fondue of leeks. A good-sized pool is on the premises, and tennis courts, a golf course, and the beach are nearby.

MARSEILLE AFTER DARK

You can get an amusing (and relatively harmless) exposure to the town's saltiness by walking around the **Vieux Port,** with its cafes and restaurants. Select one that strikes your fancy (or just park yourself by the waterfront for a view of the passing parade). But for a sure bet, head for the bar area of the previously recommended **Brasserie Vieux-Port New-York,** 33 quai des Belges (☎ **04-91-33-91-79**). Joining you are likely to be members of Marseille's arts community who gather here to chat with friends.

A modern-day equivalent of the Vieux Port is a 20-minute Métro ride away: **Escale Borély,** avenue Mendès-France, a waterfront development south of the town center. You'll find about a dozen cafes as well as restaurants of every possible ilk, in-line skaters on the promenade in front, and the potential for dialogues with friendly strangers. An especially good place is **L'Assiette Marine** (☎ **04-91-71-04-04**), a seafood restaurant with a separate bar area where fresh oysters, clams, and chilled lobster accompany your drink.

Unless the air-conditioning is very powerful, Marseille's dance clubs produce a lot of sweat. The best of them is the **Café de la Plage,** in the Escale Borély (☎ **04-91-71-21-76**), where a 35-and-under crowd dance in an environment that's safer and healthier than at many of its competitors. Closer to the Vieux Port, you can dance and drink at the **Metal Café,** 20 rue Fortia (☎ **04-91-54-03-03**), where 20- to 50-year-olds listen to recent releases from London and Los Angeles. The nearby **Trolley Bus,** 24 quai de Rive-Neuve (☎ **04-91-54-30-45**), is best known for its techno, house, punk rock, and retro music, but the arts community especially appreciates the dramatic readings and philosophical debates held the first Tuesday of every month. (Call ahead for the highly flexible and changing schedules.) Also appealing, if only because people here seem to have more fun than at the usual run-of-the-mill pastis dive, is **Pêle-Mêle,** 8 place aux Huiles (☎ **04-91-54-85-26**), a many-faceted bar/disco/cafe and host of occasional live music.

If you miss free-form modern jazz and don't mind taking your chances in the less-than-savory neighborhood adjacent to the city's rail station (La Gare St-Charles—a taxi here and back is recommended), consider dropping into **La Cave à Jazz,** rue Bernard-du-Bois (☎ **04-91-39-28-28**). If you're a single male looking for opposite-sex strangers who are no strangers to the art of entertaining foreign men, consider a brief encounter at **The Bunny Club,** 2 rue Corneille (☎ **04-91-54-09-20**), but be alert that this is a very, very adult venue that may not be altogether savory. Equivalent in texture and tone is the **Bar Eden,** 7 rue Curiol (☎ **04-91-47-30-06**). From year to year, it swings between encouraging cross-dressing men or sex-industry women. At press time it had reverted to its old-fashioned heterosexual format—you can be sure that no straight male venturing inside will lack for immediate feminine companion-ship.

A cabaret that presents sexy performers, broad humor, and occasional political satire is **Le Chocolat Théâtre,** 59 cours Julien (☎ **04-91-42-19-29**). The venue and hours change week by week, so phone in advance for what's scheduled. There's also a restaurant here.

Gay and hopeful? The gay scene here isn't as interesting as it is in Nice, in spite of the number of gay bars and saunas. Nonetheless, **MP Bar,** 10 rue Beauveau (☎ **04-91-33-64-79**), *is* le gay bar in Marseille. It is open nightly from 6pm to sunrise. **L'Enigme (Le Kempson),** 22 rue Beauvau (☎ **04-91-33-79-20**), is the kind of bar where over-40 gay males might appreciate the jokes and randiness of more than 20-somethings. It has the ambiance of a French-speaking British pub where 98% of the crowd happens to be gay, male, and into denim or leather. The youth-conscious **New Can Can,** 3–5 rue Sénac (☎ **04-91-48-59-76**), is an enormous venue that's every-body's favorite dance emporium every Thursday to Sunday, from around 11pm till dawn. An alternative gay bar and disco, conveniently located in the sultry central neighborhood near the Vieux Port, was **Le Crazy,** rue du Chantier (no phone), where lots of the regulars seem to have known one another since forever, and where a sailor or student from abroad will probably not buy his own drinks for very long. Its bar area and dance floor are especially busy every night from around 9pm till 2am.

18 Toulon

519 miles (835.25km) S of Paris, 79 miles (127.14km) SW of Cannes, 42 miles (67.59km) E of Marseille

This fortress and modern town is the principal naval base of France: the headquarters of the Mediterranean fleet, with hundreds of sailors wandering the streets. With its beautiful harbor, it's surrounded by hills and crowned by forts. A large breakwater pro-tects it on the east, and the great peninsula of Cap Sicié is on the west. Separated by the breakwater, the outer roads are known as the **Grande Rade** and the inner roads the **Petite Rade.** On the outskirts is a winter resort colony. Although not as dangerous or as intriguing as Marseille, Toulon also has a large Arab population from North Africa. Note that there's racial tension here, worsened by the closing of the shipbuilding yards.

Park your vehicle underground at place de la Liberté, then go along boulevard des Strasbourg, turning right onto rue Berthelot. This will take you into the **pedestrian zone** in the core of the old city centered around the rue d'Alger. This area is filled with shops, hotels, restaurants, and cobblestone streets but can be dangerous at night. The best beach, **Plage du Mourillon,** is 1¼ miles east of the heart of town.

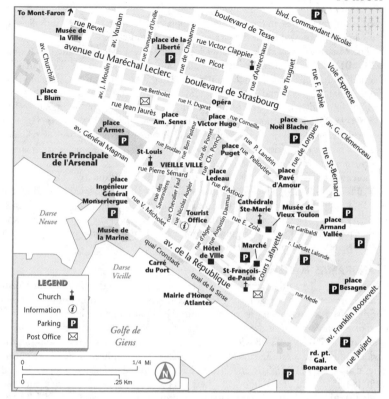

ESSENTIALS

GETTING THERE   Trains arrive from Marseille about every 30 minutes (trip time: 1 hr.). If you're on the Riviera, frequent trains arrive from Nice (trip time: 2 hrs.) and from Cannes (trip time: 80 mins.). For **rail information** and schedules, call ☎ 08-36-35-35-35. Three buses per day arrive from Aix-en-Provence (trip time: 75 mins.). For **bus information** and **schedules,** call either of the two bus companies that service the routes into Toulon. They are **Cie Sodetrav** (☎ 04-94-12-55-12) and **Littoral Cars** (☎ 04-94-74-01-35).

VISITOR INFORMATION   The **Office de Tourisme** is on place Raimu (☎ 04-94-18-53-00).

EXPLORING THE TOWN

In **Vieux Toulon,** between the harbor and boulevard des Strasbourg (the main axis of town), are many remains of the port's former days. The site where the city's raffish and gutsy style might best be appreciated is the open-air fruit and vegetable market, **Le Marché,** which spills over onto the narrow, plantain-lined streets around cours Lafayette every morning from 7:30am till around 2:30pm. Also in Old Toulon is the **Cathédrale Ste-Marie-Majeure (St. Mary Major),** rue Emile Zola (☎ 04-92-92-28-91), which was built in the Romanesque style in the 11th and 12th centuries, then much expanded in the 17th century. Its badly lit nave is Gothic, and the belfry and facade are from the 18th century. It's open daily from 8am to 6pm.

In contrast to the cathedral, tall modern buildings line quai Stalingrad, opening onto **Vieille d'Arse.** On place Puget, look for the **atlantes** (caryatids), figures of men used as columns. These interesting figures support a balcony at the Hôtel de Ville (city hall) and are also included in the facade of the naval museum.

The **Musée de la Marine,** place du Ingénieur-Général-Monsenergue (☎ **04-94-02-02-01**), contains many figureheads and ship models. It's open Wednesday to Monday: July and August from 9:30am to noon and 3 to 7pm, and September to June from 9:30am to noon and 2 to 6pm. Admission is 29F ($4.95) for adults and 19F ($3.25) for students. The **Musée de Toulon,** 113 bd. du Général-Maréchal-Leclerc (☎ **04-94-93-15-54**), shows works from the 16th century to the present. There's a particularly good collection of Provençal and Italian paintings, as well as religious works. The latest acquisitions include New Realism pieces and minimalist art. It's open daily from 1 to 6pm; admission is free.

Somewhat less interesting is the **Musée du Vieux Toulon,** 69 cours Lafayette (☎ **04-94-92-29-23**), which is not to be confused with the above-mentioned Musée de Toulon. Its exhibits pertain to the role of commerce, shipbuilding, and the French military during the development of Toulon, with tableaux of the historic figures who either protected or fostered its growth from medieval times to the present. It's open Monday to Saturday from 2 to 6pm. Entrance is free.

PANORAMAS & VIEWS

We suggest taking a drive, an hour or two before sunset, along the **corniche du Mont-Faron.** It's a scenic boulevard along the lower slopes of Mont Faron, providing views of the busy port, the town, the cliffs, and, in the distance, the Mediterranean.

For a panoramic view over the dry, sun-flooded landscapes, consider boarding a **funicular** (☎ **04-94-92-68-25** for information) which departs from a point on the bd. l'Amiral Vence near the Hotel La Tour Blanche. The **télépherique** (cable car) operates daily from 9 to 11:45am and 2:15 to 6:30pm, costing 40F ($6.80) for adults and 25F ($4.25) for children round-trip. Once you get to the top, enjoy the view and then visit the **Memorial du Débarquement en Provence,** Mont Faron (☎ **04-94-88-08-09**), which, among other exhibits, documents the Allied landings in Provence in 1944. It's open in summer, daily from 9:30 to 11:45am and 2:30 to 5:45pm; in winter, Tuesday to Sunday from 9:30 to 11:30am and 2 to 4:30pm. Admission is 25F ($4.25) for adults, 10F ($1.70) for children 5 to 12, and free for children 4 and under.

WHERE TO STAY

Hôtel La Corniche. 1 littoral Frédéric-Mistral (at Le Mourillon), 83000 Toulon. ☎ **800/528-1234** in the U.S., or 04-94-41-35-12. Fax 04-94-41-24-58. 23 units. A/C MINIBAR TV TEL. 400F–550F ($68–$93.50) double; 450F–820F ($76.50–$139.40) suite. AE, DC, MC, V. Parking 40F ($6.80). Bus: 3, 13, or 23.

An attractive hotel near the town's beaches, with an interior garden, La Corniche offers a pleasant staff, two restaurants, and comfortable accommodations. Those at the front have sea views and loggias and are more expensive. Room decoration is in Provençal style, and bathrooms have hair dryers and good-sized towels. The more formal of the two restaurants is the Bistro; it features a trio of pine trees growing upward through the roof and a large bay window overlooking the port. The simpler restaurant is the cramped but cozy Rôtisserie, which is under a different management. Both emphasize fish among their offerings. A fairly good but limited wine list complements the food, which is perfectly adequate and much-improved in recent years. You'll find this place in the neighborhood known as Le Mourillon, a 15-minute walk from the congested commercial center of Toulon.

Hôtel Maritima. 9 rue Gimelli, 83000 Toulon. ☎ **04-94-92-39-33.** 40 units, 21 with bath or shower. TEL. 140F ($23.80) double without bath, 240F ($40.80) double with bath. MC, V. Free parking. Bus: 3.

The most decent bargain hotel in Toulon stands near the railway station and Jardin Alexandre-1er. Built in the late 1800s, it has been frequently renovated and altered over the years. Furnishings are blandly traditional but serviceable; it's modest but well maintained. Mattresses have slept many guests, but are still reasonably comfortable. Only 11 rooms have TVs. Bathrooms are small and short on shelf space and have rather thin towels but are tidily maintained. There's no restaurant, although several lie right outside the door. Only breakfast is served on site.

New Hôtel Tour Blanche. bd. de l'Amiral-Vence, 83200 Toulon. ☎ **04-94-24-41-57.** Fax 04-94-22-42-25. www.new-hotel.com. E-mail: toulontourblanche@new-hotel.com. 91 units. A/C MINIBAR TV TEL. 390F–440F ($66.30–$74.80) double. AE, DC, MC, V. Free parking. Bus: 40. From the town center, follow the signs to the Mont Faron *téléphérique* and you'll pass the hotel en route.

With excellent modernized accommodations, attractive gardens with terraces, and a pool, this seven-story hotel is the best in Toulon. In the rocky hills about a half-mile mile north of the town center, it has sweeping views from even the lower floors out over the town to the port and the sea. Many rooms, especially those overlooking the bay, have balconies, and each is simply outfitted in an international modern style, with comfortable mattresses. Bathrooms are tiled and compact, with shower/tub combinations or shower stalls. The restaurant, Les Terrasses, offers a panoramic view, set-menus priced at 100F to 180F ($17 to $30.60) each, and food and wine whose selection is inspired by the culinary traditions of Provence and the Midi.

WHERE TO DINE

✪ **La Chamade.** 25 rue Denfert-Rochereau. ☎ **04-94-92-28-58.** Reservations recommended. Fixed-price menu 185F ($31.45). AE, MC, V. Mon–Fri noon–2:30pm and 7–9:30pm, Sat 7–9:30pm. Closed Aug 1–25. Bus: 1 or 21. FRENCH.

In the town center, in a relatively nondescript building whose thick walls hint at its age, this restaurant simplified its culinary offerings in 1996 by having a single option—a 175F ($35) fixed-price menu that includes a choice of three appetizers, three main courses, and three desserts. You'll be seated in a labyrinth of several small, appealing modern dining rooms to enjoy the carefully cultivated cuisine of Francis Bonneau, former disciple of some of the grand restaurants of Paris and Brittany. Menu items change with the season and the availability of ingredients but might include stuffed and deep-fried zucchini blossoms, filet of sea bass with basil-flavored butter sauce, and roast whitefish garnished with ham and risotto with local herbs. Desserts often include a craqueline of dates served with gentian, a herb that flourishes on Provence's arid hillsides; or frozen custard garnished with local strawberries marinated in red wine.

TOULON AFTER DARK

A town that's the temporary home of thousands of French and foreign sailors is bound to have an earthy and rather raunchy nightlife scene. An appealing but rough-and-ready bar that sports stiff drinks, live music, and a complete lack of pretension is **Le Bar 113,** 113 avenue de Infanterie de la Marine (☎ **04-94-03-42-41**). Adjacent to the port is the **Bar La Lampa,** Port de Toulon (☎ **04-94-03-06-09**), where a choice of *tapas* and bouts of live music accompany copious amounts of beer. An even less formal hangout is **Bar à Thym,** 32 bd. Cuneo (☎ **04-94-41-90-10**), where everybody seems to drink beer, gossip, and listen to live music.

Toulon is also home to one of the Azure Coast's best-known gay discos, **Boy's Paradise,** 1 bd. Pierre-Toesca (☎ **04-94-09-35-90**), near the city's railway station, where groups of gay men include a scattering of off-duty French sailors and, to a lesser degree, gay women.

But if you feel claustrophobic in a town noted for its heavy industry and want a resortlike place, you might be happy at Hyère, about 16 miles east of Toulon, where there's an upscale disco, **Le Fou du Roy,** in the Casino des Palmiers (☎ **04-94-12-80-80**). It attracts a relatively lively crowd that likes to dance, dance, dance. About 9 miles west of Toulon, in the small port town of Sanary, is a disco attracting dancers under age 30: **Mai-Tai,** route de Bandol (☎ **04-94-74-23-92**).

19 Hyères

529 miles (852km) S of Paris; 62 miles (100km) SE of Aix-en-Provence, 76 miles (122km) SW of Cannes, 11 miles (17.70km) E of Toulon

The broad avenues of Hyères, shaded by date palms, still evoke the lazy belle époque. The full name of the town is Hyères-les-Palmier, as it is known for its production of palm trees. Believe it or not, many of these trees are exported to the Middle East.

Hyères is the oldest resort along the Côte d'Azur, having once been frequented by the likes of Queen Victoria, Napoléon, Leo Tolstoy, and Robert Louis Stevenson. It was particularly popular with the British before 1939. It has changed so little from its heyday that many French film directors have used it as locations for period pieces; for example, Jean-Luc Godard *(Pierrot le fou)* and François Truffaut, who shot his last film here (*Vivement dimanche,* released as *Confidentially Yours* in the U.S.). Today it lives off its past glory and its memories.

As a visitor, you'll find the most interesting section of Hyères to be the Vieille Ville, which lies 3 miles inland from the sea on a hill. Try to arrive early to attend a bustling morning market around place Massillon. The more modern town and the nucleus of the 19th-century resort stretch toward the sea.

ESSENTIALS

GETTING THERE   The Toulon-Hyères airport lies between the town center and the beach. Rail connections are fairly easy, as Hyères lies on the main Nice-Lyon-Paris line. Local trains connect Hyères with Toulon. There are two buses per day from Toulon, Cannes, and Nice. For information about schedules, call **Phoceens Car,** 2 place Massena in Nice at ☎ **04-93-85-66-61.**

If you're driving, A5 goes through Toulon to Marseille and points north and west, and A57 goes northeast to join A8, the autoroute between Nice and Aix-en-Provence.

VISITOR INFORMATION   The **Office de Tourisme,** at Rotonde Jean-Salusse and avenue de Belgique (☎ **04-94-65-18-55**), dispenses information about the town and the area.

EXPLORING THE AREA

The land lying between the city and the sea is unattractive, and the beaches are a bit polluted, but there are some swimming possibilities here, notably at **Hyères-Plage.** There is also a yacht marina at Port d'Hyères. We find the parks and old town of Hyères more interesting than its beachfront.

Heading into town from the beach, go along the wide avenue Gambetta shaded by double rows of palms. At the end of Gambetta, continue along rue Rabaton to **place Massillon,** the beginning of the old town and the site of many good terrace cafe-restaurants. The daily market also takes place here. The 12th-century **Tour St-Blaise** which stands on the square was once a command post of the Knights Templar.

Above place Massillon is a warren of intriguing old streets climbing the hillside. Many are cobblestoned and bordered by stone walls, with an abundance of flowers in summer. Look for the medieval arched *portes.* Most of the Vieille Ville houses have

Edith Wharton's Unknown Masterpiece

Though the world is familiar with Edith Wharton's masterful novel *The Age of Innocence,* as well as her other major works *(The House of Mirth, Ethan Frome),* many of her fans are unaware that she created another masterpiece in the Riviera resort of Hyères. Here the wealthy American novelist rented a villa, **Castel-Ste-Claire,** sometimes called "La Solitude," rue Victor-Basch, in the Parc de Castel Ste-Claire. Another famous novelist, Robert Louis Stevenson, once rented this house, and wrote *A Children's Garden of Verse* here. Ms. Wharton purchased the villa in 1927, and on the 28 terraced acres, created spectacular gardens that were a botanical fantasy. She imported workers for the task, and even had plants shipped from all over the world.

The gardens are supposedly not so impressive as they were in Wharton's day. Today they are called **Parc Ste-Claire,** and are located along the appropriately named avenue Edith Wharton. The Wharton villa is the headquarters of the **Parc National de Porquerolles** (☎ **04-94-12-92-30**), and is open daily from 9am to 5:30pm.

The villa was originally built in 1849 by one of the most famous marine archeologists of his day, Olivier Voutier, who was instrumental in the excavation of the famous statue in the Louvre, *Venus de Milo.* As you explore the garden terraces, you'll also be following in the footsteps of the avant-garde of yesterday: "those Surrealist scandals," Buñuel and Dalí, even Man Ray and André Gide. Giacometti and Jean Cocteau also showed up in time.

been restored, often painted in lovely Mediterranean pastels with contrasting shutters and doors.

Part of the ramparts have survived although most of them have been torn down; they date from the 12th century. All that remains of the south "curtain wall" are Porte-St-Paul, next to the Collegiate Church, and Porte Baruc. A trio of lovely old towers have survived from the north curtain wall.

Steep narrow streets lead up behind Tour St-Blaise to the 18th-century **Le Collegiale St-Paul,** place St-Paul (☎ **04-94-65-83-30**). In the Romanesque narthex are 400 fragments from the Church of Notre-Dame-de-Consolation, destroyed in bombing raids in 1944. The Gothic nave dates from the 15th and 16th centuries. The church is flanked by an elegant turreted Renaissance house constructed above one of the medieval city gates. The church is open Wednesday to Saturday from April to October 10:30am to noon and 3:30 to 6pm. From November to March, it is open Wednesday to Saturday 3 to 5pm.

Artifacts left behind by the Greeks and Romans can be examined at the **Musée Municipal,** place Lefebvre (☎ **04-94-35-90-42**). The museum is often the venue for special exhibitions. Entrance is free, and it is open Monday, Wednesday, Thursday, and Friday from 10am to noon and 3 to 6pm. If there's a special exhibition, it is also open Saturday and Sunday from 3 to 6pm.

The main attraction of the town is **Parc St-Bernard,** 12½ miles east of Toulon by N98, on the hill above Hyères. It is open all year daily from 8am to 6pm. To reach the park, go up rue Saint Esprit to where it becomes rue Barbacane. Charles and Marie-Laure de Noailles, great patrons of the arts, commissioned a modern Cubist-style villa here in 1924 and brought in garden designer Gabriel Guevrekian, who created an extensive garden in the shape of an isosceles triangle, pointing away from the end of the villa. The Noailles played a role in nurturing the avant-garde artists of the Jazz Age, including F. Scott Fitzgerald. Edith Wharton was a devoted friend of the family. The villa is currently being restored, but you can visit the terraced gardens where olives and pines provide shade and there are benches for sitting. Also in the park are the ruins of Château d'Hyères, above the medieval old town. Signposts and arrows lead visitors on a self-guided walk through the ruins, which have unrestricted access.

WHERE TO STAY

Hôtel du Soleil. Rue du Rempart (place Clemenceau), 83400 Hyères. ☎ **04-94-65-16-26.** Fax 04-94-35-46-00. www.citotel.com/hotels/soleil.html. E-mail: hotel.du.soleil@infonie.fr. 20 units. TEL. 220F–340F ($37.40–$57.80) double. AE, DC, MC, V.

The foundations of this hotel date from the 11th century, when they were lodgings for the guards who defended the once-formidable fortress of Hyères. What you'll see, however, dates from around 1900—a boxy-looking *bastide* (masonry building) atop the old foundations. Over the years, a sheathing of ivy has softened the angles a bit, and the interior has been kept up to date with frequent modernizations. Bedrooms are cozy, if somewhat small, with Provençal furniture and casement windows; from the back are views of the sea, and in front, views of upscale villas on a nearby hill. Rooms have comfortable French beds (often doubles), plus well-maintained tiled bathrooms with shower/tub combinations. Other than breakfast, no meals are served, although there are several places to eat (including the Bistro Marius, below) within a 3-minute walk.

Hôtel les Pin d'Argent. Bd. de la Marine, 83400 Hyères. ☎ **04-94-57-63-60.** Fax 04-94-38-33-65. E-mail: pins.dargent@wanadoo.fr. 20 units. MINIBAR TV TEL. 330F–530F ($56.10–$90.10) double; 420F–620F ($71.40–$105.40) suite. AE, MC, V. Closed Nov–Mar.

This place is desirably located between the coastal road and the port, near the town center, in a pine and palm-studded garden. The building is in an 1850s Italianate style, and the landscaped grounds are enhanced with a stone-ringed swimming pool and an outdoor terrace. Bedrooms have high ceilings, soaring casement windows, and hints of the building's aristocratic origins. Most of the units are rather spacious and all are tidily maintained, equipped with simple but comfortable beds and mattresses, and bathrooms that are a bit cramped but have adequate shelf space and shower/tub combinations. A modern extension near the pool contains a big-windowed restaurant, open only from April to September.

Ibis Hyères-Plage. Allée de la Mer, La Capte, 83400 Hyères-Plage. 96 units. A/C TV TEL. 460F–610F ($78.20–$103.70) double. AE, DC, MC, V.

This hotel is located between the coastal road and the beach, on the eastern edge of the land bridge that stretches between the French mainland and the Gien peninsula. It places emphasis on resort life. The rectangular swimming pool is filled with heated Mediterranean saltwater, and there is a spa (thalassotherapy) facility. The hotel is designed in a horseshoe shape, with the open end of the U facing the beach. Bedrooms are larger than in the Novotel and Mercure chains, and decorated in a standardized format that includes one double bed and one single bed, both with good mattresses, a writing table, and a soothing color scheme of blue-gray. Bathrooms are motel standard, with shower/tub combinations and tidy maintenance. There's a bar, and also a restaurant serving lunch and dinner daily (closed for 3 weeks in January). The spa facility offers a roster of algae rubs, mud packs, massage, and steam or hydrotherapy treatments. Don't come expecting a half-hour quickie fix—the team insists on a minimum of a full day, and preferably a full week. Daily treatments begin at 515F ($87.55). There is also a downtown Ibis hotel.

WHERE TO DINE

Bistrot de Marius. 1 place Massillon. ☎ **04-94-35-88-38.** Reservations recommended. Main courses 95F–195F ($16.15–$33.15); set-price menus 92F–190F ($15.65–$32.30). AE, DC, MC, V. Sept–June, Wed–Mon noon–3pm and 7–11pm. July–Aug, daily noon–3pm and 7–11pm. PROVENÇAL/SEAFOOD.

Set almost adjacent to the Tour des Templiers, this restaurant was established in 1910 in a building whose foundations date from the 13th century. Its trio of dining rooms (one is upstairs) have exposed stone and paneling and a sense of historic charm. Fish, especially grilled sea bass, monkfish, dorado, and tuna, are specialties here, along with mussels and oysters. Sauce choices include a red wine–based sauce, *marchand de vin*, and lemon-butter and basil-flavored vinaigrette. A succulent version of *bouillabaisse*, priced at 195F ($33.15), is a meal in itself, and there is a limited selection of chicken, veal, and beef.

Crèche Provençale. 15 route de Toulon. ☎ **04-94-65-30-28.** Reservations required. Main courses 85F–145F ($14.45–$24.65); set-price lunches 130F–260F ($22.10–$44.20); set-price dinners 160F–260F ($27.20–$44.20). MC, V. Tues–Fri and Sun noon–2:30pm, and Tues–Sun 7–9:30pm. PROVENÇAL.

In a century-old inn with exposed structural beams and stone, you can order time-tested Provençal dishes. Tables are elaborately laid with rich naperies, porcelain, and crystal. Dishes include a terrine of leeks with a confit of tomatoes; roasted red snapper with thyme-flavored cream sauce, a tapenade of black olives, and paper-thin slices of cured ham; and deboned pigeon with braised cabbage and balsamic vinegar.

20 Iles d'Hyères

24 miles (38.62km) SE of Toulon, 74 miles (119.09km) SW of Cannes

Off the Riviera in the Mediterranean is a little group of islands enclosing the southern boundary of the Hyères anchorage. During the Renaissance they were called the Iles d'Or, from a golden glow sometimes given off by the rocks in the sunlight. Nothing in the islands today will remind you of the turbulent time when it was attacked by pirates and Turkish galleys, or even of the Allied landings here in World War II.

Mass tourism has arrived on these sun-baked islands, with some of the tackiness that goes with it. Cars are forbidden on all three major islands, and they cannot be transported on any of the ferryboats. Expect a summer holiday spirit not unlike a Gallic version of Nantucket, with thousands of midsummer day-trippers arriving, often with children, for a day of sun, sand, and people-watching.

Which island is the most appealing? Ile des Porquerolles is the most beautiful. Thinking of heading to Le Levant? You may want to steer clear—only 25% of the island is accessible to visitors—three-quarters belongs to the French army, and it is used frequently for testing missiles.

ESSENTIALS

GETTING THERE   Ile de Porquerolles   Ferryboats leave from at least three points along the Côte d'Azur. The most frequent, convenient, and shortest trip sails from the harbor of La Tour Fondue on the peninsula of Gien, a 20-mile drive east of Toulon. Depending on the season, there are 4 to 20 departures a day for a 15-minute crossing. Round-trip fares are 80F ($13.60). For information, call the **Transports Maritimes et Terrestres du Littoral Varois,** La Tour Fondue, 83400 Giens (☎ **04-94-58-21-81**). The next-best option is the ferryboat from Toulon. There are infrequent boats (usually only twice a day, April to September) from the ports of Le

Lavandou and Cavalaire. For information on rides from these ports and from Toulon, call **Trans-Med 2000,** quai Stalingrad, 83000 Toulon (☎ 04-94-92-96-82).

Ile de Port-Cros   The most popular route is the 35-minute crossing from Le Lavandou, departing 3 to 10 times daily, depending on the season. (Between November and March, there are only three per week.) For information, call the **Compagnie Maritime des Vedettes "Iles d'Or,"** 15 quai Gabriele-Peri, 83980 Le Lavandou (☎ 04-94-71-01-02). Round-trip fares are 122F ($20.75) for adults and 80F ($13.60) for children 4 to 11. The same company also offers less convenient and longer crossings from Cavalaire, but only from April to September. For no additional fee, you can be dropped off at the military installations at Le Levant.

VISITOR INFORMATION   Other than temporary, summer-only kiosks without phones that distribute brochures and advice near the ferry docks of Porquerolles and Port-Cros, there are no tourist bureaus on the islands. Consequently, the mainland tourist offices in Toulon and Hyères try to fill in the gaps. Contact the **Office de Tourisme,** Rotonde J.-Salusse, avenue de Belgique, Hyères (☎ 04-94-65-18-55), or the **Office de Tourisme,** place Raimu, Toulon (☎ 04-94-18-53-00).

ILE DE PORQUEROLLES

This is the largest and westernmost of the Iles d'Hyères. It has a rugged south coast, but the north strand, facing the mainland, is made up of **sandy beaches** bordered by heather, scented myrtles, and pine trees. The island is about 5 miles long and 1¼ miles wide and is 3 miles from the mainland.

The population is only 400. The island is said to receive 275 days of sunshine annually. It's a land of rocky capes, pine forests twisted by the mistral, sun-drenched vineyards, and pale ocher houses. The "hot spots," if there are any, are the cafes around **place d'Armes** where everybody gathers.

The island has had a violent history of raids, attacks, and occupation by everybody from the Dutch, English, and Turks to the Spaniards. Ten forts, some in ruins, testify to a violent past. The most ancient is **Fort Ste-Agathe,** built in 1531 by François I. In time it was a penal colony and a retirement center for soldiers of the colonial wars.

The French government in 1971 purchased the largest hunk of the island and turned it into a national park and botanical garden.

WHERE TO STAY & DINE

Le Relais de la Poste. Place d'Armes, 83540 Porquerolles. ☎ **04-94-58-30-26.** Fax 04-94-58-33-57. 30 units. TEL. 456F–676F ($77.50–$114.90) double. No credit cards. Closed late Sept to Mar.

On a small square in the heart of the island's main settlement, this pleasant and unpretentious hotel is the oldest on the island—it opened "sometime in the 19th century" and is today managed by the good-natured sixth generation of its founding family. It offers Provençal-style rooms with loggias. Most rooms are small to medium in size, but each comes with a comfortable mattress and fine linen on a twin or double bed. Bathrooms are compact and well organized with shower stalls. The hotel has a billiard table and a crêperie that sells only sugared snack-style dessert crêpes and fresh fruit juices. It maintains a kiosk that rents bicycles for 50F ($8.50) per day.

✪ **Mas du Langoustier.** 83400 Porquerolles. ☎ **04-94-58-30-09.** Fax 04-94-58-36-02. www.langoustier.com. E-mail: langoustier@compuserve.com. 50 units. TV TEL. 1,499F–1,589F ($254.85–$270.15) double. Rates include half board. AE, DC, MC, V. Closed mid-Oct to Apr 25.

In a large park on the island's western tip, this tranquil resort hotel is actually an old Provençal *mas* (farmhouse) with a view of a lovely pine-ringed bay. Employees greet guests in a covered wagon by the jetty. In an antique Provençal style, bedrooms are the most elegantly decorated on the island, furnished with quality mattresses and fine linen on the comfortable beds. Bathrooms are roomy, most often with a shower/tub combination, plus a hair dryer and an assortment of thick towels. Should you visit only for a meal, prices begin at 350F ($59.50). The menu is the finest in the islands, mainly seafood in a light nouvelle style. Try the *loup* (sea bass) with Noilly Prat in puff pastry or tender kid with dried tomatoes roasted in casserole. The house wine is an agreeable rosé. You can drink and dine on the terraces. The hotel also has tennis courts.

ILE DE PORT-CROS

Lush subtropical vegetation reminiscent of a Caribbean island makes this a green paradise, 3 miles long and 1¼ miles wide. The most mountainous of the archipelago, Port-Cros has been a French national park since 1963. Although a fire in 1892 devastated the island, it has bounced back with pine forests and ilexes. Bird-watchers flock here to observe nearly 100 different species. There are many marked trails, mainly for day-trippers. The most popular and scenic is *sentier botanique;* the more adventurous and athletic take the 6-mile *circuit historique* (you'll need a packed lunch for this one). Divers follow a 300-yard trail from Plage de la Palud to the islet of Rascas, where a plastic guide sheet identifies the underwater flora. Thousands of pleasure craft call here annually, which does little to help the island's fragile environment.

WHERE TO STAY & DINE

✪ **Le Manoir.** 83400 Ile de Port-Cros. ☎ **04-94-05-90-52.** Fax 04-94-05-90-89. 23 units. TEL. 1,500F–1,800F ($255–$306) double; 1,800F–2,060F ($306–$350.20) duplex apartment for 2. Rates include half board. MC, V. Closed Oct–May.

This is the only bona-fide hotel on the island, but despite lack of competition, its owners work hard to make their guests as comfortable as possible. It consists of an 18th-century manor house, plus an annex that holds most of the guest rooms. Accommodations are simple and clean, with acceptable mattresses and adequate numbers of good-sized towels. The terrace and its swimming pool, shaded by bamboo, eucalyptus, and oleander, overlook the bay of Port-Cros. Chef Sylvain Chaduteau serves lobster-and-fish terrine, several seasoned meats, and fresh local fish with baby vegetables, as well as regional goat cheese and velvety mousses. The dining room is open daily, from May to October, for both lunch and dinner, with set dinners for nonresidents priced at 260F ($44.20) each.

21 Grand Canyon du Verdon

Trigance: 45 miles (72.42km) S of Digne-les-Baines; 12½ miles (20.12km) W of Castellane; 27 miles (43.45km) NW of Draguignan; 53 miles (85.30km) E of Manosque. La-Palud-sur-Verdon: 40 miles (64.37km) S of Digne-les-Baines; 15½ miles (24.94km) W of Castellane; 37 miles (59.55km) NW of Draguignan; 41 miles (65.98km) E of Manosque

Over the centuries the Verdon River, a tributary of the Durance, has cut Europe's biggest canyon into the surrounding limestone plateau. The canyon runs from pont de Soleils to Lac Ste-Croix, a distance of 13 miles east to west. The upper section of the gorge, to the east, is between 700 and 5,350 feet wide; the lower section narrows to between 20 and 350 feet. All along its length, the cliffs rise and fall. The gorge's depth varies from 875 feet at one point to 2,500.

Vertiginous roads wind along both rims of the canyon, giving you the opportunity to pull over at any of several scenic belvederes. Among the best of these is the **Balcon de la Mescla,** the first stop traveling west from Trigance on the canyon's south side, where the sheer cliffs drop 900 feet to the river. A short distance away is **Falaise de**

Cavaliers (Horseman's Cliff), dropping 1,075 feet and signaling the beginning of the **Corniche Sublime,** where the gorge plunges to 1,425 feet along a stretch running west to Aiguines. In between these scenic stops, you can actually drive across the canyon on the dramatic **pont de l'Artuby,** a single-arched, 400-foot-long span 2,125 feet above the river.

Ancient villages cling to rocky outcroppings along the two rim roads. At **Aiguines,** a private castle, flanked by four turrets and covered in polished variegated tiles, dominates the skyline. On Route 19, 5½ miles north of the canyon on its western end, sits **Moustiers-Ste-Marie,** a medieval village of potters who sell their wares—but beware, prices here are celestial, especially in July and August when tourist dollars are easy to come by.

ESSENTIALS

GETTING THERE   From the Riviera, follow A85 for 52 miles northwest from Cannes to Castellane, then take Rte. 952 west to the intersection with Rte. 955 and proceed along 955 south to Trigance, about 12½ miles. From here, continue south to Rte. 71, 2 miles distant, and take a left to travel west along the southern edge of the canyon. At Les-Salles-sur-Verdon, on the banks of Lac St-Croix, turn right on D957 and drive north, crossing the Verdon where it flows into Lac St-Croix; then, just south of Moustiers-Ste-Marie, turn right again on Rte. 952 to trace the north side of the canyon back to the east.

VISITOR INFORMATION   Information about accommodations, activities, and events is available from the **Verdon Accueil,** 83630 Aiguines (☎ 04-94-70-21-64) or rue Nationale, 04120 Castellane (☎ **04-92-83-67-36**); the **Office de Tourisme de Castellane,** 04120 Castellane (☎ **04-92-83-61-14**); or the **Office de Tourisme d'Esparron,** 04800 Esparron (☎ **04-92-77-15-45**).

EXPLORING THE CANYON

Activities available in the canyon include guided hikes from the **Bureau des Guides,** 04120 La-Palud-sur-Verdon (☎ **04-92-77-32-02**), and the **Office de Tourisme d'Esparron,** 04800 Esparron (☎ **04-92-77-15-45**). Canoeing and kayaking are available through the **Aqua Vivae Est,** La Piscine, 04120 Castellane (☎ **04-92-83-75-74**), and the **Club Nautique,** 04800 Esparron (☎ **04-92-77-15-25**). Rafting trips are conducted by **Acti Raft,** 04120 Castellane (☎ **04-92-83-76-64**).

A deservedly popular walk in the area is a **2-hour round-trip trek** launched at the parking lot at Samson Corridor. The route is clearly marked as it bends its way to a tunnel after Point Sublime. Continue your trek to a footbridge spanning the Baou River. After crossing it, go straight ahead through another two tunnels until you reach a belvedere with a panoramic sweep of the Trescaïre Chaos. For the tunnels, carry along a flashlight.

A more strenuous **6- to 8-hour walk** starts at the Chalet de la Maline on the Crest Road and goes for about 9½ miles to Point Sublime. The footpath is marked with arrows. Again, you'll need a flashlight, but this trek is so long that food and water are also recommended. Before heading out, you can call ☎ **04-92-83-65-38,** 04-92-77-31-16, or 04-92-83-65-34 for a taxi company that will pick you up at a designated time when you reach Point Sublime.

WHERE TO STAY

Auberge Point-Sublime. 04120 Point Sublime, Rougon. ☎ **04-92-83-60-35.** Fax 04-92-83-74-31. 14 units. TEL. 279F ($47.45) per person, double occupancy, including half board. MC, V. Closed Nov 3–Mar. From Castellane, drive 12 miles north toward Moustiers-Ste-Marie; it's beside the road on the distant outskirts of Rougon.

Grand Canyon du Verdon

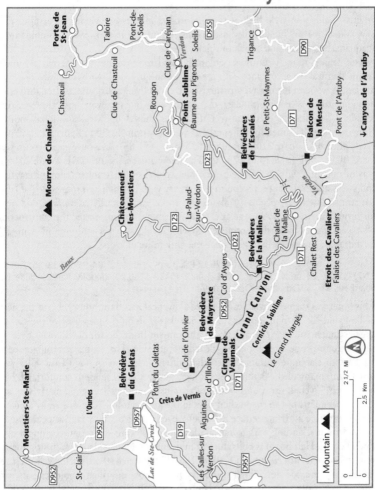

This hotel offers simple, unpretentious rooms, each with congenially battered, old-fashioned (but not antique) furniture. Bedrooms are small and without particular style, although each has a comfortable mattress, plus a somewhat cramped bathroom with a shower stall. You do get views over the gorge and a location that's a convenient, 1¼ miles south of the Couloir Samson, the point where many trekkers exit from hikes in the nearby gorge. The restaurant serves all-Provençal fixed-price meals priced at from 105F ($17.85) each. Specialties are civets of both rabbit and lamb, a truffle-studded omelet, and crayfish with truffles. Staff here is unusually bossy, insisting that residents consume at least one meal a day on-site.

✪ **Château de Trigance.** 83840 Trigance, Var. ☎ **04-94-76-91-18.** Fax 04-94-85-68-99. E-mail: trigance@relaischateaux.fr. 10 units. TV TEL. 600F–900F ($102–$153) double. AE, MC, V. Closed Nov 1–Mar 20. Free parking.

This Relais & Châteaux is the district's best hotel, rising on a rocky spur above a hamlet of fewer than 120 full-time inhabitants; it occupies the core of a 9th- and 10th-century fortress. There's no room for a garden, but there are views from virtually every window over the Provençal plain. The rooms contain strong hints of their medieval origins—baldaquin-style beds with comfortable mattresses. Modern amenities that were added in 1969 include tiled bathrooms equipped with shower/tub combinations, adequate shelf space, and a rack of thick towels.

The dining room is unusual; originally used to store weapons, it has a vaulted ceiling that was, in accordance with the era's techniques, built without groins or a central key. A wooden form was constructed and carefully chiseled stones fitted into position on top. When complete, the form was burnt away and the vaulting remained—somewhat precariously until it was shored up with additional mortar. Nonguests are welcomed for full meals, served daily from 12:30 to 2pm and 7 to 9pm. Fixed-price meals cost 210F to 305F ($35.70 to $51.85); à la carte main courses go for 110F to 150F ($18.70 to $25.50). The fare is intensely cultivated: "Marbled" foie gras of duckling with artichoke hearts; pressed leeks with smoked salmon, crayfish, and sweet-and-sour sauce; pigeon in puff pastry with polenta; and roasted leg of lamb "en surprise" with a "spaghetti" of zucchini and cream of garlic *en confit.* Good news for future guests: In 1999, at great expense, the hotel commissioned the construction of a parking lot near the entrance, thereby saving you the arduous hike up the medieval-looking steps that were once the only route of access.

Hôtel Les Gorges du Verdon. 04120 La-Palud-sur-Verdon. ☎ **04-92-77-38-26.** Fax 04-92-77-35-00. 28 units. TV TEL. 800F–1,060F ($136–$180.20) double. Rates include half board. AE, MC, V. Closed late Oct to late Apr. Free parking.

This hotel was inspired by an earth-toned Provençal *mas* (farmhouse). It's in the heart of La-Palud-sur-Verdon (pop. 250, alt. 3,000 ft.), about 4 miles west of the canyon edge. Though you won't be able to see the canyon from the windows, views over the rugged countryside stretch out on virtually every side. The rooms were upgraded in 1998, with elaborate curtains added that soften their modern angularity. Tiles were installed in many of the bathrooms, adding a glossy kind of modern comfort. All have hair dryers. Overall, the rooms aren't exactly plush, but they have good mattresses, and since most guests opt to spend their days in the great outdoors, no one really seems to care. Most have a private terrace or balcony overlooking a scenic landscape. Some are entered from a landing with a staircase leading down into the room, creating a mezzanine effect. Half board is obligatory in midsummer. Nonresidents often stop for set-price meals here, priced at from 120F to 180F ($20.40 to $30.60) each. Well-prepared menu items include duck thigh stuffed with mushrooms; grilled whole sea bass with anise-flavored butter; and Provençal lamb chops with tarragon-flavored butter sauce.

Hôtel Le Vieil Amandier. 83840 Trigance, Var. ☎ **04-94-76-92-92.** Fax 04-94-85-68-65. 12 units. TEL. 280F–350F ($47.60–$59.50) double. MC, V. Closed Nov 3–Apr 1. Free parking.

At the edge of town, this hotel offers clean, uncomplicated guest rooms and a dining room with straightforward but thoughtfully prepared cuisine. Half the rooms face the pool and get southern light; the remainder are just as comfortable but without views. The largest is the rustic and woodsy no. 6; nos. 3 and 4 are more Provençal, and the others are blandly international. About half contain TVs. Each comes with a good mattress and quality linen, plus a compact and tidily maintained private bathroom with a shower/tub combination and adequate shelf space. Your hosts are Cécile and Bernard Clap (Bernard is the hamlet's mayor). They maintain a pleasant, unpretentious restaurant where fixed-price lunch and dinner at 120F to 305F ($20.40 to $51.85) are served daily. Cuisine is artful and flavorful, featuring good value for the money. Menu items include profiteroles of goat cheese with chives and olive oil; duckling with myrtle leaves and garlic; and rack of lamb in puff pastry served with fine-textured ratatouille.

Inter Hôtel Grand Canyon de Verdon. Falaise des Cavaliers, 83630 Aiguines. ☎ **04-94-76-91-31.** Fax 04-94-76-92-29. 15 units. TV TEL. 700F–780F ($119–$132.60) double. Rates include half board. AE, DC, MC, V. Closed Oct–Apr.

This is the most charming and interesting hotel along the south bank of the Verdon canyon. It's on a rocky outcropping above the precipice, vertiginously close to the edge, and exists only because of the foresight of the grandfather of the present owner. In 1946, on holiday in Provence from his home in the foggy northern French province of Pas de Calais, he fell in love with the site, opened a brasserie, and secured permission to build a hotel here. In 1982 his charming grandson, Georges Fortini, erected the present two-story hotel. Rooms are simple, small, but comfortable, with light-grained wood and off-white walls. Each comes with a comfortable bed and firm mattress, plus a well-equipped tiled bathroom with a shower/tub combination, adequate shelf space, a hair dryer, and a rack of good-sized towels. Set on a 10-acre tract on the Corniche Sublime, it features a glassed-in restaurant overlooking a 1,075-foot drop to the canyon bottom. Meals are served daily from 11:30am to 9:30pm, with fixed-price menus at 85F to 250F ($14.45 to $42.50).

WHERE TO DINE

Many of the inns recommended under "Where to Stay," above, are also the finest places to dine—notably the **Château de Trigance.**

✪ **Les Santons.** Place de l'Eglise, 04360 Moustiers-Ste-Marie, Alpes-de-Haut-Provence. ☎ **04-92-74-66-48.** Reservations recommended. Main courses 90F–190F ($15.30–$32.30); fixed-price menus 230F–320F ($39.10–$54.40). AE, DC, MC, V. Mon noon–2pm, Wed–Sun noon–2pm and 7:30–9:30pm. Closed mid-Nov to mid-Dec and mid-Jan to mid-Feb. FRENCH/PROVENÇAL.

One of the region's most charming restaurants occupies a stone-sided 12th-century house adjacent to the village church. You'll find a cozy dining room filled with 19th-century paintings and antique pottery, reminders of Old Provence, and fewer than 20 seats. A terrace, lined with flowering plants, doubles the seating space during clement weather. André Abert is the sophisticated chef who makes as much use as possible of fresh local ingredients. These include truffles and honey. Examples are homemade noodles studded with truffles and chunks of foie gras, chicken roasted with lavender-scented honey and Provençal spices, and Sisteron lamb roasted with honey and spices and served with an herb-scented ratatouille and *gratin dauphinoise* (potatoes with grated cheese).

5

The Western Riviera: From St-Tropez to Cannes to Cap d'Antibes

The western part of the **Côte d'Azur** begins at glittering St-Tropez and ends at the even more elegant Cap d'Antibes. In between are mostly middle-class resort towns, like St-Raphaël, scattered along a coast that also features the wild and desolate landscape of the Massif de l'Estérel.

At the doorstep of St-Tropez, Port Grimaud contrasts with the antiquity of many communities, for it's a well-to-do pseudo fishing village that sprang from a swamp, fully developed, just 3 decades ago. Ste-Maxime and Fréjus offer some of the area's best budget accommodations, having been taken over by French families in search of a holiday getaway on the once-exclusive coast.

The area does, of course, embrace Cannes, the most famous resort in the region because of the glitz and glamour surrounding its film festival, which overflows into the upscale La Napoule-Plage, home of the Clews Museum.

Inland, the terrain climbs away from the coast to the hillside communities of Grasse, with its perfume distilleries, and Mougins, a charming old village and culinary center that makes for a romantic retreat. Food also lures gastronomes to Golfe-Juan, which features one of the region's best restaurants, Chez Tétou, a stop for a rich bowl of bouillabaisse.

Nightlife is the focus of neighboring Juan-les-Pins, attracting spirited adventurers to its all-night jazz clubs and discos. Nearby Vaullaris hosts Galerie Madoura, a pottery firm with exclusive rights to reproduce Picasso's earthenware designs. Antibes also profits from its association with Picasso by the museum dedicated to his life and work. This largely middle-class resort gives way to Cap d'Antibes, the peninsular resort that's as tony today as when F. Scott Fitzgerald used it as the setting for his novel *Tender Is the Night*.

EXPLORING THE REGION BY CAR

Here's how to link together the best of the region if you're driving a car.

Day 1   Begin at St-Tropez, where you can try to find your own bronzed god or goddess sunning or swimming in the surf that was famous even before Bardot made And God Created Woman. Take a room for the night, then enjoy a day on the beach and in the shops before spending an evening in the clubs.

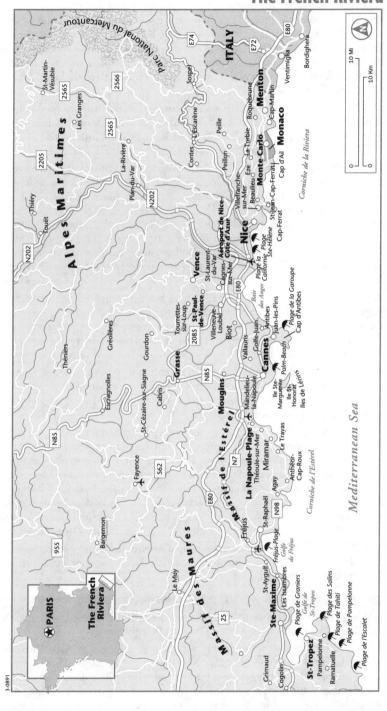

The French Riviera

ITALY

Parc National du Mercantour

Alpes Maritimes

Mediterranean Sea

3-0891

Day 2 Keep your hotel room in St-Tropez and make a day excursion. Drive 4 miles west, taking Rte. 98A to La Foux, then transfer to Rte. 98 and head northeast for the last half mile to arrive in **Port Grimaud,** the urban architect François Spoerry's vision of a coastal village. Stay on Rte. 98 headed northeast for another 4 miles to reach **Ste-Maxime,** which, like so many of the smaller resorts, is mainly about the beach. Return to St-Tropez for the night.

Day 3 Head northeast on Rte. 98 again, bypassing Port Grimaud and Ste-Maxime, then drive another 12½ miles to spend the morning in **Fréjus,** with its Roman ruins. From here, go 2 miles east on Rte. 98 to reach the beach at **St-Raphaël.** You can choose accommodations in whichever of the two resorts you like best.

Day 4 Drive northeast on Rte. 98 along the edge of the **Massif de l'Estérel** on your way to La Napoule-Plage, 18½ miles distant. You might turn inland along the way to view the surrounding landscape from the vantage point of Mont Vinaigre, 1,962 feet above sea level; Pic du Cap Roux, 1,438 feet above sea level; or Pic de l'Ours, 1,627 feet above the sea. You may also wish to see the panoramic view offered from St-Honorat's **Grotte de la Ste-Baume** or gaze into the depths of the **Gorge du Mal-Infernet.** Continue onward to **La Napoule-Plage,** which functions as a satellite community of Cannes, balancing that resort with its relatively low-key lifestyle. Overnight here.

Day 5 In the morning, follow Rte. 98 as it bends eastward around the Gulf of Napoule, driving 5 miles into **Cannes,** where you can stroll along the region's most famous beach, try your luck in the casinos, or expose yourself to a nightlife that's more sophisticated than any other offered along this stretch of coast. This is a day unto itself, so plan to stay at least a night.

Day 6 Briefly turning inland, follow Rte. 85 north for 10 miles to **Grasse,** with its perfume distilleries, then backtrack 6 miles along Rte. 85 to **Mougins,** an old stone village that contrasts with the modernity of much of the coast. For a change of pace, spend the night at this gastronomic citadel.

Day 7 Backtrack 4 miles into Cannes, then head northeast on Rte. 7, driving 3 miles into a cluster of communities that contrast middle-class values with the lifestyles of the rich and famous. Begin with **Golfe-Juan,** a middle ground to the exotica of Cannes or Cap d'Antibes. You may wish to take lunch here, dining on superb bouillabaisse, then continue on to Vallauris, standing at Golfe-Juan's inland edge. Here you'll definitely want to see Picasso's pottery. From **Vallauris,** get on Rte. 7 and follow the coastal road for 2 miles to **Juan-les-Pins,** on the Antibes peninsula, the primarily middle-class resort that sits in the midst of the grandeur that's the Côte d'Azur. Overnight here.

Day 8 On the same small peninsula lies **Cap d'Antibes,** an exclusive resort that contrasts with Juan-les-Pins. It borders **Antibes,** with its Picasso museum, a major attraction. Spend your final night here.

1 St-Tropez

543 miles (873.87km) S of Paris, 47 miles (75.64km) SW of Cannes

Sun-kissed lasciviousness is rampant in this carnival town, but the true Tropezian resents the fact that the port has such a bad reputation. "We can be classy too," one native has insisted. Creative people in the lively arts along with ordinary folk create a volatile mixture. One observer said that St-Tropez "has replaced Naples for those who accept the principle of dying after seeing it. It's a unique fate for a place to have made its reputation on the certainty of happiness."

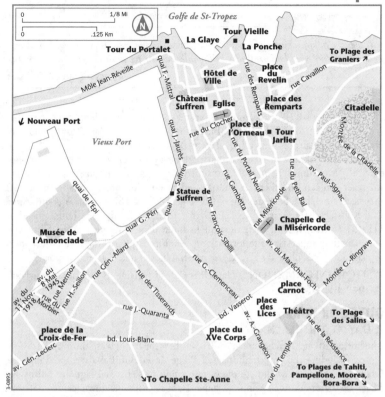

St-Tropez—this palimpsest of nostalgia—was popularized by sex-symbol Brigitte Bardot in *And God Created Woman,* but it had attracted the famous for a long time. Colette lived here for many years. Even the late diarist Anaïs Nin, confidante of Henry Miller, posed for a little cheesecake on the beach here in 1939 in a Dorothy Lamour-style bathing suit. Earlier, St-Tropez was visited by Matisse, Signac, and Bonnard, and even Maupassant before he died of syphilis.

Artists, composers, novelists, and the film colony come to St-Tropez in summer. Trailing them is a line of humanity unmatched anywhere else on the Riviera for sheer flamboyance. Chic people anchor their yachts here in summer, but disappear long before the dreaded mistral of winter.

In 1995, Bardot pronounced St-Trop dead—"squatted by a lot of no-goods, drugheads, and villains"—and swore she'd never go back, at least in summer. But 1997 saw her return, as headlines in France flashed the news that St-Tropez was "hot once again." Not only Bardot but other celebrities have been showing up, including Oprah Winfrey, Don Johnson, Quincy Jones, Barbra Streisand, Jack Nicholson, Robert DeNiro, and even Elton and Sly (not together!).

ESSENTIALS

GETTING THERE   The nearest rail station is in St-Raphaël. At the Vieux Port, four or five boats per day leave **Gare Maritime de St-Raphaël,** rue Pierre-Auble (☎ 04-94-95-17-46), for St-Tropez (trip time: 50 min.), costing 60F ($10.20) one-way. Some 15 Sodetrav buses per day leave from the **Gare Routière** in St-Raphaël

It was the happy mixture of old and young, wealthy and class. A person with no money could live like a millionaire and a millionaire could have fun living like a bohemian.

—Roger Vadim on St-Tropez

(☎ **04-94-95-24-82**) for St-Tropez (trip time: 1½ to 2¼ hours, depending on traffic). A one-way ticket costs 55F ($9.35). Buses run directly to St-Tropez from Toulon and Hyères, and the airport is at Toulon-Hyères 35 miles away.

If you drive, know in advance that parking in St-Tropez is extremely difficult, especially in summer. Be prepared to squeeze your car into impossibly small spaces wherever you can find them. A multistoried parking lot for 471 cars is underneath the place des Lices, **Parc des Lices** (☎ **04-94-97-34-46**). Entrance is on avenue Paul-Roussel; charges are 8F to 12F ($1.35 to $2.05) for the first hour, and 8F to 11F ($1.35 to $1.85)for each subsequent hour, depending on season. This is the most carefully supervised site for parking. Another large parking lot lies just south of place des Lices/place du XVe-Corps, several blocks inland from the port.

VISITOR INFORMATION   The **Office de Tourisme** is on quai Jean-Jaurès (☎ **04-94-97-45-21**).

OUTDOOR PURSUITS
A DAY AT THE BEACH

The hottest Riviera beaches are at St-Tropez. Best for families are those closest to the center, including the amusingly named **Plage de la Bouillabaisse** and **Plage des Graniers.** The more daring are the 6-mile sandy crescents at **Plage des Salins** and **Plage de Pampellone,** beginning some 2 miles from the town center and best reached by bike if you're not driving. Called "notoriously decadent," ✪ **Plage de Tahiti** occupies the north end of the 3½-mile-long Pampellone. Lined with concessions, cafes, and restaurants, it's a strip of golden sand that has long been favored by exhibitionists wearing next to nothing or truly nothing and cruising one another shamelessly. If you ever wanted to go topless or bottomless or wear a daring bikini, this is the place to do it.

STAYING ACTIVE

BICYCLING   The largest outfitter for bikes and motor scooters is **Louis Mas,** 5 rue Josef-Quaranta (☎ **04-94-97-00-60**). A deposit of 1,000F ($170) is required, payable with a credit card (AE, MC, or V) plus 48F ($8.15) per hour for a bike and 190F to 275F ($32.30 to $46.75) per hour for a motor scooter, depending on its size.

BOATING   The well-recommended **Suncap Company,** 15 quai de Suffren (☎ **04-94-97-11-23**), rents boats from 18 feet to 40 feet. The smallest can be rented to qualified sailors without a captain, but the larger ones come with a captain at the helm. Prices per day begin at 3,000F ($510).

GOLF   The nearest golf course, at the edge of Ste-Maxime, across the bay from St-Tropez, is the **Golf Club de Beauvallon,** boulevard des Collines (☎ **04-94-96-16-98**), a popular 18-hole course, known for a terrain that allows you to walk rather than rent a cart. Greens fees are 250F to 300F ($42.50 to $51) for 18 holes.

Sprawling over a rocky, vertiginous landscape that requires a golf cart and a lot of physical labor is the Don Harradine–designed **Golf de Ste-Maxime-Plaza,** route du Débarquement, Ste-Maxime (☎ **04-94-49-26-60**). Built in 1991 as part of the Plaza de Ste-Maxime, it welcomes nonguests; phone to reserve tee-off times. Greens fees for 18 holes are 280F ($47.60); cart rental for two golfers is 125F ($21.25) per 18 holes.

SCUBA DIVING   A team of dive enthusiasts—ready, willing, and able to show you the watery azure-colored depths off the coast of St-Tropez—operate from *Octopussy I* and *II,* two aluminum-sided, yellow-painted dive boats that are based year-round in St-Tropez's Nouveau Port. Experienced divers pay 230F ($39.10) for a one-tank *"exploration"* dive, and novices are charged 250F ($42.50) for a *baptème* that includes one-on-one supervision from a monitor and a descent to a depth of around 15 feet. For reservations and information, call or write *Les Octopussys,* Quartier de Berteau, Gassin, 83990 St-Tropez (☎ 04-94-56-53-10).

TENNIS   Anyone who phones in advance can use the eight courts (artificial grass and "Quick," a form of concrete) at the **Tennis-Club de St-Tropez,** route des Plages, in St-Tropez's industrial zone of St-Claude (☎ 04-94-97-15-52), about half a mile from the resort's center. Open throughout the year, the courts rent for 100F ($17) per hour to 5pm and 130F ($22.10) per hour after 5pm.

SEEING THE SIGHTS

In the Vieille Ville, the most interesting street is **rue de la Miséricorde.** At the corner of rue Gambetta is the **Chapelle de la Miséricorde,** with a blue, green, and gold tile roof.

Near the junction of quai Suffren and quai Jean-Jaurès stands the bronze **statue de Suffren,** paying tribute to Vice-Admiral Pierre André de Suffren. This St-Tropez hometown boy became one of the greatest sailors of 18th-century France, though he's largely forgotten today. The **Château Suffren** is east from the port at the top end of quai Jean-Jaurès. Now home to occasional art exhibits, it was built in 980 by Comte Guillame I of Provence.

Musée de l'Annonciade (Musée St-Tropez). Place Grammont. ☎ 04-94-97-04-01. Admission 30F ($5.10) adults, 15F ($2.55) children. June–Sept, 10am–noon and 3–7pm; Oct and Dec–May, Wed–Mon 10am–noon and 2–6pm; closed Nov.

Near the harbor, installed in the former chapel of the Annonciade, this museum is a legacy from the artists who loved St-Tropez. Opened in 1955, it is one of the finest modern art collections on the Riviera. The collection includes such works as Van Dongen's yellow-faced *Women of the Balustrade* and paintings and sculpture by Bonnard, Matisse, Braque, Dufy, Utrillo, Seurat, Derain, and Maillol. Many of the artists, including Paul Signac, depicted the port of St-Tropez.

SHOPPING

Among the touristy souvenirs, T-shirts, and sun-tan lotion are a few shops that are more interesting. Better stocked than the norm, **Choses,** quai Jean-Jaurès (☎ 04-94-97-03-44), is a women's clothing store typical of the hundreds of middle-bracket, whimsically nonchalant shops that thrive along the Riviera. Its specialty is clingy and often provocative T-shirt dresses. **Galeries Tropéziennes,** 56 rue Gambetta (☎ 04-94-97-02-21), crowds hundreds of unusual gift items—some worthwhile, some rather silly—and textiles into its rambling showrooms near place des Lices. The inspiration is Mediterranean, breezy and sophisticated.

Jacqueline Thienot, 12 rue Georges-Clemenceau (☎ 04-94-97-05-70), has an inventory of Provençal antiques prized by dealers from as far away as Paris. The three-room shop is in a late 18th-century building that shows the 18th- and 19th-century antiques to their best advantage. Also sold are antique examples of Provençal wrought iron and rustic farm and homemaker's implements.

WHERE TO STAY
VERY EXPENSIVE

✪ **Hôtel Byblos.** Av. Paul-Signac, 83990 St-Tropez. ☎ **800/223-6800** in the U.S., or 04-94-56-68-00. Fax 04-94-56-68-01. www.byblos.com. 102 units, 10 duplex suites. A/C MINIBAR TV TEL. 1,750F–3,260F ($297.50–$554.20) double; from 2,800F ($476) suite; from 4,300F ($731) duplex suite. AE, DC, MC, V. Closed Oct 15–Easter. Parking 140F ($23.80) in garage.

The builder said he created "an anti-hotel, a place like home." That's true if your home resembles a palace in Beirut with salons decorated with Phoenician gold statues from 3000 B.C. On a hill above the harbor, this deluxe complex has intimate patios and courtyards and seductive retreats filled with antiques and rare decorative objects, including polychrome carved woodwork on the walls and a Persian-rug ceiling. Every room is unique. A fireplace on a raised hearth or a bed recessed on a dais might be a feature. About 10 rooms are completely refurbished every season. Housekeeping standards are high here. Bedrooms range from medium in size to spacious, often with high ceilings and some with balconies overlooking an inner courtyard or opening onto a terrace of flowers. Each has a luxury mattress on an elegant French bed; some have four-posters with seductive furry spreads, or other antiques. Marble-clad baths are well equipped with robes, step-down tubs, fluffy towels, and deluxe toiletries; a few have sunken whirlpool baths. Le Hameau contains 10 duplex suites built around a small courtyard with an outdoor spa.

Dining/Diversions: You can dine by the pool at Les Arcades, enjoying Provençal food, or try an Italian restaurant offering an antipasti buffet, many pasta courses, and other typical fare from France's neighbor. Later in the evening, you can dance on a circular floor surrounded by bas-relief columns in the hotel's nightclub, Caves du Roy. There are also two bars.

Amenities: Room service (24 hours), same-day laundry/valet, beauty salon, high-fashion pool, sauna.

Résidence de la Pinède. Plage de la Bouillabaisse, 83990 St-Tropez. ☎ **04-94-55-91-00.** Fax 04-94-97-73-64. www.relaischateaux.fr/pinede. 43 units. A/C MINIBAR TV TEL. 1,260F–3,500F ($214.20–$595) double; 2,450–6,850F ($416.50–$1,164.50) suite. AE, DC, MC, V. Closed mid-Oct to Mar.

This four-star Relais & Châteaux hotel was built in the 1950s around a rustic stone-sided tower once used to store olives. Jean-Claude and Nicole Delion are the owners of this luxury place on the seaside. The airy, spacious rooms open onto balconies or terraces with a view over the bay of St-Tropez. The stylish but offhand staff seems constantly overburdened. The hotel is St-Tropez's only rival to the Byblos, and though as luxurious, it tends to have a more serious and staid clientele. Rooms are stylish and plush, with firm mattresses and thick towels. But overall, you're likely to be put off by the hysterically busy staff of whom, alas, there simply doesn't seem to be enough.

Dining/Diversions: Excellent food, especially seafood, is served in the dining room or on the terrace under the pine trees. In the past, mainly residents of the hotel dined here. However, the cuisine of Belgian-born Alois van Langenaucker has drawn many locals who want to sample his refined Provençal cuisine.

Amenities: Room service (24 hours), same-day laundry/valet, kidney-shaped pool, beach.

EXPENSIVE

Hôtel La Mandarine. Rte. de Tahiti, 83990 St-Tropez. ☎ **04-94-79-06-66.** Fax 04-94-97-33-67. E-mail: 101564.1050@compuserve.com. 42 units. A/C MINIBAR TV TEL. 990F–2,060F ($168.30–$350.20) double; from 2,290F ($389.30) suite. Rates include continental breakfast. AE, MC, V. Closed Oct 15–Mar 15. Take the road leading to Plage de Tahiti; it's just off the road, half a mile southeast of the center.

La Mandarine is built in the Provençal style with strong angles, thick stucco walls, a tile roof, and patios. Rooms are luxuriously furnished and open onto one or more terraces; some of the suites offer as many as three terraces. Quality mattresses, fine linens, and elegant fabrics grace the comfortable beds. Bathrooms are tiled and beautifully maintained with adequate shelf space, luxury toiletries, thick towels, and shower/tub combinations. You definitely get glamour here. The restaurant specializes in *cuisine moderne* using fish and shellfish. There's also a heated pool and a private beach.

Hôtel Le Yaca. 1 bd. d'Aumale, 83900 St-Tropez. ☎ **04-94-55-81-00.** Fax 04-94-97-58-50. www.nova.fr/yaca. 27 units. A/C MINIBAR TV TEL. 1,000F–2,400F ($170–$408) double; from 3,200–5,400F ($544–$918) suite. AE, DC, MC, V. Closed Oct–Easter. Parking 100F ($17).

Built in 1722 off a narrow street in the old part of town, this was the first hotel in St-Tropez. Colette lived here in 1927, and before that it was the home of pre-impressionists like Paul Signac. The high-ceilinged reception area boasts a view of an inner courtyard filled with flowers; many of the rooms also have views of this courtyard. Some are on the upper floor, with handmade terra-cotta floor tiles and massive ceiling timbers. Each has a comfortable bed, dignified and utilitarian furniture, a high ceiling, and a tile-sheathed bathroom with adequate numbers of acceptably thick towels. There's a swimming pool on the premises, and a restaurant that's open for dinner but not for lunch.

Hôtel Résidence des Lices. 135 av. Augustin-Grangeon, 83900 St-Tropez. ☎ **04-94-97-28-28.** Fax 04-94-97-59-52. www.nova.fr/lices. E-mail: lices@nova.fr. 41 units. A/C TV TEL. 400F–1,600F ($68–$272) double. AE, V. Closed Jan 4–Easter and Nov 11–Dec 23.

One consistently reliable bet for lodgings in St-Tropez is this modern hotel in its own small garden, close to place des Lices. The tastefully furnished rooms are tranquil, overlooking either the pool or the garden; their rates vary widely according to season, size, and view. Each unit is designed for comfort, from the quality mattresses to the well-appointed bathrooms with hair dryers, shower/tub combinations, and thick towels. Breakfast is the only meal served, though afternoon snacks are provided beside the pool.

✪ **La Bastide de St-Tropez.** Rte. des Carles, 83990 St-Tropez. ☎ **04-94-97-58-16.** Fax 04-94-97-21-71. www.bastidesaint-tropez.com. E-mail: bst@wanadoo.fr. 26 units. A/C MINIBAR TV TEL. 980F–2,200F ($166.60–$374) double; 1,480F–3,950F ($251.60–$671.50) suite. AE, DC, MC, V. Closed Jan.

Near the landmark place des Lices, this tile-roofed replica of a Provençal manor house looks deliberately severe, but the interior is far more opulent. It contains a monumental staircase leading from a sun-filled living room to the upper floors. The guest rooms are named according to their individual decor: "Rose of Bengal," "Fuschia," or "Tangerine Dawn." Each has a terrace or private garden, and some have Jacuzzis. Several, however, are quite small. The soft beds under fine quilting with matching draperies are among the most luxurious in St-Tropez. Well-appointed private baths have fluffy towels, shower/tub combinations, deluxe toiletries, and excellent plumbing. The hotel is noted for its restaurant, L'Olivier, with a star from Michelin.

MODERATE

Hôtel Ermitage. Av. Paul-Signac, 83990 St-Tropez. ☎ **04-94-97-52-33.** Fax 04-94-97-10-43. 26 units. TEL. 390F–990F ($66.30–$168.30) double. MC, V.

Attractively isolated amid the rocky heights of St-Tropez, this hotel was built in the 19th century as a private villa. Today its red-tile roof and green shutters shelter a plush hideaway. A walled garden is illuminated at night, and a cozy corner bar near a wood-burning fireplace takes the chill off blustery evenings. The guest rooms offer good value for St-Tropez. They are pleasantly but simply furnished, with quality mattresses and efficiently organized and well-maintained private baths. Breakfast is the only meal served.

Hôtel La Ponche. 3 rue des Remparts, 83990 St-Tropez. ☎ **04-94-97-02-53.** Fax 04-94-97-78-61. www.nova.fr/ponche. E-mail: laponche@nova.fr. 18 units. A/C MINIBAR TV TEL. 800F–1,900F ($136–$323) double. AE, MC, V. Closed Nov–Mar 15.

Overlooking the old fishing port, this has long been a cherished address, run by the same family for more than half a century. The hotel is filled with the original, airy paintings of Jacques Cordier, which add to the elegant atmosphere. Each room has been newly redecorated and is well equipped. There are two or three rooms per floor, all with sea views. Sun-colored walls with subtle lighting evoke a homelike feeling. Beds are elegantly appointed with beautiful linen and quality mattresses. Bathrooms are exceedingly well maintained and often come with shower/tub combinations; all have hair dryers. The hotel restaurant is big on Provençal charm and cuisine, and a sophisticated crowd can be found on its terrace almost any night in fair weather.

Hôtel La Tartane. Rte. des Salins, 83990 St-Tropez. ☎ **04-94-97-21-23.** Fax 04-94-97-09-16. www.hotellatartane.wanadoo.fr. 14 units. A/C MINIBAR TV TEL. 750–1,000F ($127.50–$170) double. AE, DC, V. Closed Oct–Mar.

This small-scale hotel is midway between the center of St-Tropez and the Plage des Salins, about a 3-minute drive from each. There's a stone-rimmed pool in the garden, attractive public rooms with terra-cotta floors, and an attentive management that works hard to keep everything pulled together. The guest rooms are well-furnished bungalows centered around the pool. They range from small to medium in size, but each comes with a fine mattress on a double bed or twins. Bathrooms are small and a bit cramped with minimum shelf space but with good maintenance. Amenities, like hair dryers, are lacking, however. Breakfasts are elaborate and attractive, lunch is offered between 1 and 3pm, and dinner is 7:30 to 9:30pm. Fresh grilled fish from the Mediterranean is the specialty. The cost of meals is from around 150F ($25.50).

Hôtel Le Levant. Rte. des Salins, 83990 St-Tropez. ☎ **04-94-97-33-33.** Fax 04-94-97-76-13. 28 units. MINIBAR TV TEL. 425F–895F ($72.25–$152.15) double. AE, DC, MC, V. Closed mid-Oct to Mar 15.

On the road leading from the old town of St-Tropez to the beach at Les Salins, this hotel stands behind a screen of cypresses and palmettos. Designed like a low-slung Provençal *mas* or farmhouse, it has thick stucco walls and a tile roof. The recently redecorated rooms, in Provençal motifs, have big windows and white walls as well as private entrances overlooking the garden and its pool. Each is fitted with a fine mattress on double or twin beds. Bathrooms are small but efficiently organized and tiled, each with a shower/tub combination.

Hôtel Lou Cagnard. Av. Paul-Roussel, 83990 St-Tropez. ☎ **04-94-97-04-24.** Fax 04-94-97-09-44. 19 units. TV TEL. 280F–510F ($47.60–$86.70) double. MC, V. Closed Nov 4–Dec 26.

This pleasant roadside inn, with a tile roof and green shutters, has quiet rooms in the rear overlooking the garden. M. and Mme Yvon have recently taken over and improved the hotel considerably, for it's fresher and more inviting than ever. They extend a warm welcome to their international guests. Although there is nothing grand about the bedrooms, they are comfortable with fine mattresses and well-maintained bathrooms. Although small, the bathrooms have shower/tub combinations or shower stalls and adequate shelf space. Continental breakfast is available. Of all the hotels in the center, Michelin gives this one the lowest rating, but at least it made the list—and it's a bargain in pricey St-Trop.

Hôtel Sube. 15 quai Suffren, 83900 St-Tropez. ☎ **04-94-97-30-04.** Fax 04-94-54-89-08. 30 units. A/C TV TEL. 390F–1,500F ($66.30–$255) double. AE, MC, V. Parking nearby 200F ($34).

If you want to be right on the port, this should be your first choice. A way station and hotel for the French postal services in the 1800s, it was renamed around 1900 for its then-owner. It's directly over the Café de Paris in the center of a shopping arcade. The two-story lounge has a beamed ceiling and a glass front, allowing a great view of the harbor activity. The lounge is furnished with a 10-foot-high fireplace, a wall torchère, and provincial chairs. The bedrooms are very small and decorated in a provincial style. Beds are soft, and the maids keep everything clean and tidy. Bathrooms are modest, with showers or shower/tub combinations.

WHERE TO DINE

The restaurant at the **Résidence de la Pinède** (see "Where to Stay," above) serves flavorful Provençal dishes.

EXPENSIVE

✪ **Bistrot des Lices.** 3 place des Lices. ☎ **04-94-55-82-82.** Reservations required in summer. Main courses 140F–180F ($–$30.60); fixed-price menus 99F ($16.85) at lunch, 150F–260F ($25.50–$44.20) at dinner. AE, MC, V. Daily noon–2pm and 7:30–11pm (to 2am July–Aug). PROVENÇAL.

Don't let the "bistrot" in the name fool you. This is a first-class restaurant, with the most celebrated cuisine in St-Tropez, a glamorous clientele, a world-class inventory of cigars, dessert wines, and after-dinner drinks, and an amused and bemused staff. There's a turn-of-the-century decor that subtly evokes the gaslight era, and tables are also set amid the manicured hedges and flowering shrubs of a garden in back. Chef Christophe Jourdren, who has worked in the kitchens of many stylish and expensive hotels of Provence, is known for his creative use of local produce at its most fresh— both vegetarians and meat-eaters are pleased by its originality. Examples include a risotto of fresh vegetables served with an essence of parsley; a salad of crayfish tails roasted with fresh thyme; codfish served in a basil-flavored crust, with essence of tomatoes and fresh garlic; leg of lamb *en confit* served with Provençal vegetables; and filets of young rabbit served with spice bread. Hearty appetites appreciate the filet of beef "Rossini," with foie gras and essence of truffles.

✪ **L'Echalotte.** 35 rue Allard. ☎ **04-94-54-83-26.** Reservations recommended in summer. Main courses 75F–140F ($12.75–$23.80); fixed-price menus 98F–160F ($16.65–$27.20). AE, MC, V. Thurs 8–11:30pm, Fri–Wed 12:30–2pm and 8–11:30pm. Closed Nov 15–Dec 15. FRENCH.

This charming restaurant, with a tiny garden and simple but clean dining room and tables on a veranda (weather permitting), serves consistently good food for moderate prices. Because of demand, reservations may be difficult to get, especially in peak summer weeks. The cuisine is solidly bourgeois, including grilled veal kidneys, crayfish with drawn-butter sauce, filet of turbot with truffles, and classic dishes of southwestern France such as three preparations of foie gras and magret of duckling. The menu includes several species of fish; daurade royale can be cooked in a salt crust.

Les Mouscardins. 1 rue Portalet. ☎ **04-94-97-01-53.** Reservations required. Main courses 150F–380F ($25.50–$64.60); fixed-price menus 320F–335F ($54.40–$56.95). AE, MC, V. Daily noon–2:30pm and 7:30–11:30pm. Closed 2 weeks in Nov, and for lunch mid-Nov to mid-Mar. FRENCH.

At the end of St-Tropez's harbor, this restaurant has won awards for culinary perfection. The dining room is in formal Provençal style with an adjoining sunroom under a canopy. The menu includes classic Mediterranean dishes; as an appetizer we recommend *moules* (mussels) *marinières*. The two celebrated fish stews of the Côte d'Azur are offered: bourride Provençale and bouillabaisse. The fish dishes are excellent, particularly the sauté of monkfish, wild mushrooms, and green beans. The dessert specialties are soufflés made with Grand Marnier or Cointreau.

MODERATE

Le Girelier. Quai Jean-Jaurès. ☎ **04-94-97-03-87.** Main courses 125F–500F ($21.25–$85); fixed-price menu 190F ($32.30). AE, DC, MC, V. Daily noon–2pm and 7–11pm. Closed Jan to mid-Feb and Nov 11–Dec 15. PROVENÇAL.

The Rouets own this portside restaurant whose blue-and-white color scheme has become its own kind of trademark. Filled with rattan furniture and boasting a large glassed-in veranda, it serves well-prepared grilled fish in many versions, as well as bouillabaisse, served for two only. Also available is brochette of monkfish, a kettle of mussels, and *pipérade* (a Basque omelet with pimentoes, garlic, and tomatoes).

MOSTLY GAY

Chez Joseph. Place de la Mairie. ☎ **04-94-97-01-66.** Reservations recommended. Main courses 90F–285F ($15.30–$48.45). AE, MC, V. May–Sept, daily 1–3pm and 8pm–midnight; Oct–Apr, Thurs–Tues 1–3pm and 8pm–midnight, closed Wed. FRENCH.

Chic, yet casual and friendly, this restaurant is a fixture on the St-Tropez restaurant scene. The cozy bar is outfitted with photos of the rich and famous (Elton John, George Michael, Michael Bolton); the crowd is heavily gay and fashionable. Glasses of champagne (65F/$11.05) are served to an animated crowd that seems to remain in place until 6am the next morning. Adjacent to the bar is a restaurant with about 35 tables, giving you lots of opportunities for people-gazing. Menu items are consciously artful: lobster salad, an adventurous tartare of salmon and lobster (advisable only for the strong and the brave), tournedos Rossini, grilled jumbo shrimp, and fricassée of scallops. Except for one or two costly seafood dishes, most prices are quite reasonable, generally costing no more than 140F ($23.80).

Chez Maggi. 7 rue Sibille. ☎ **04-94-97-16-12.** Reservations recommended. Fixed-price menu with wine 145F ($24.65). MC, V. Daily 8pm–3am. Closed Nov–Mar. PROVENÇAL/ITALIAN.

Across from Chez Joseph (above), this restaurant retained the name it was given by two women during its earlier incarnation as a lesbian bar. Since its acquisition by the present owners, it has emerged as St-Tropez's most flamboyant gay restaurant/bar. At least half its floor space is devoted to a very busy bar, where patrons tend to range from ages 25 to 35 and whose turf extends out onto the pavement in front. There are no tables and chairs in front, however, so cruising at Chez Maggi, in the words of loyal patrons, is "trés crazee" and seems to extend for blocks in every direction, spilling over into Chez Joseph.

Meals are served in an adjoining dining room. Menu items include chicken salad with ginger, *petits farcis Provençaux* (local vegetables stuffed with minced meat and herbs), brochettes of sea bass with lemon sauce, and a well-recommended chicken curry with coconut milk, capers, and cucumbers.

✪ **Le Bar à Vin.** 13 rue des Feniers. ☎ **04-94-97-46-10.** Reservations recommended. Main courses 100F–260F ($17–$44.20). MC, V. May–Sept, daily 7pm–1am; Oct–Apr, Wed–Mon 7pm–1am. Closed Jan. FRENCH/PROVENÇAL.

This appealing and reasonably priced bistro is close to place des Lices. In summer, the guests tend to be Europeans in their 20s and 30s on holiday. The crowd is mixed, though heavily gay. Things are calmer in winter, when the diners are usually locals. Managed by a bilingual entrepreneur, Bertrand Bertrand, it boasts a red-tile floor by the ceramic artist Alain Vagh. The menu items are designed to accompany a choice selection of wines, at 15F to 80F ($2.55 to $13.60) per glass. Provençal and Mediterranean flavors predominate: sardines *en escabèche* (grilled sardines marinated in olive oil, herbs, and vinegar and served cold); gratin of eggplant with goat cheese; and grilled beefsteak, veal, and lamb.

ST-TROPEZ AFTER DARK

On the lobby level of the Hôtel Byblos, **Les Caves du Roy,** avenue Paul-Signac (☎ 04-94-97-16-02), is the most self-consciously chic nightclub in St-Tropez. It's the kind of place where, if Aristotle Onassis were still alive and roving, he'd camp out with a cellular phone for late-night trysts. Entrance is free, but drink prices begin at a whopping 120F ($20.40).

Le Papagayo, in the Résidence du Nouveau-Port, rue Gambetta (☎ 04-94-97-07-56), is one of the largest nightclubs in town, with two floors, three bars, and lots of attractive women and men eager to pursue their bait. The decor was inspired by the psychedelic 1960s. Entrance is 110F ($18.70) and includes the first drink.

Located below the Hôtel Sube, the **Café de Paris,** sur le Port (☎ 04-94-97-00-56), is a consistently popular hangout. An attempt has been made to glorify a utilitarian room with turn-of-the-century globe lights, an occasional 19th-century bronze, masses of artificial flowers, and a long zinc bar. The crowd is irreverent and lively. Busy even in winter, after the yachting crowd departs, it's open daily.

Reporter Leslie Maitland once described the kind of crowd attracted to the **Café Sénéquier,** sur le Port (☎ 04-94-97-00-90), at cocktail hour: "What else can one do but gawk at a tall, well-dressed young woman who appears *comme il faut* at Sénéquier's with a large white rat perched upon her shoulder, with which she occasionally exchanges little kisses, while casually chatting with her friends?"

Le Pigeonnier, 13 rue de la Ponche (☎ 04-94-97-36-85), rocks, rolls, and welcomes a crowd from all over Europe, ages 20 to 50, that's 80% to 85% gay male. Most of the socializing goes on at the long, narrow bar. There's also a dance floor. Entrance is 70F ($11.90) and includes your first drink.

For other gay hot spots, check out the action at the bar of **Chez Maggi** or cruise over to **Chez Joseph** or **Le Bar à Vin** (see above).

2 Port Grimaud

4 miles (6.44km) W of St-Tropez, 17 miles (27.36km) S of Fréjus

Inspired by both Europe's ancient fishing villages and the wealthy dockside neighborhoods of St. Petersburg, Florida, this 247-acre marine village was created in a former swamp by the urban architect François Spoerry. Contractors broke ground in 1966, utilizing 4 miles of 13-foot-deep canals to drain the wetlands. Now 2,500 Provençal-style homes (including that of Joan Collins) line the fingerlike extensions of a 7½-mile basin capable of docking 3,000 boats. Sitting on an island of its own, the hamlet's **Eglise St-François-d'Assise** features stained glass by Victor Vasarély and a great view from its bell tower.

Port Grimaud was hailed as a great success on opening, one journalist calling the community "the most magnificent fake since Disneyland." In this miniature Provençal version of Venice, there are no roads or cars, and it's exceptionally clean and quiet, as mandated by the governing residents' association. However, it's an actual functioning village—the main square is lined with shops, cafes, banks, a post office, and a church. One point of interest: **Denise Spoerry Decoration,** rue de Ponant, Port Cogolin (☎ 04-94-56-16-63), an interior-decor shop, is owned by the wife of the village's creator, François Spoerry. It sells lamps and other items designed by the couple and their backup team. If you plan to eat or shop in Port Grimaud, be warned: This isn't a cheap town, and disproportionate prices reflect its status as a man-made tourist center.

A mile and a half inland, at a southeastern edge of the Massif des Maures, the authentically ancient village of **Grimaud** offers a counterpoint to its fraudulent namesake. Steep, narrow alleys run between restored Gothic homes that sit in shadows cast by the ruins of a multitowered **feudal castle,** once the stronghold of the Grimaldi family and a small army of Knights Templar. Their legacy is still evident, and you can follow the rue des Templiers to view the **Maison des Templiers,** which isn't open to the public, and the neighboring 12th-century **Eglise St-Michel.**

ESSENTIALS

GETTING THERE   The nearest train station is in St-Raphaël, a 30-minute drive east. A taxi to Port Grimaud costs about 50F ($8.50) each way. There are buses every 30 minutes from St-Raphaël in summer and about six a day in low season. For information on bus service, call **Sodetrav** (☎ 04-94-95-24-82). By car from St-Tropez, drive 3 miles west on A98 to Rte. 98, then 1 mile north to the Port Grimaud exit. From Fréjus, follow Rte. 98 south to the exit.

VISITOR INFORMATION   Information about accommodations and attractions is available at the **Offices de Tourisme:** at **St-Tropez,** quai Jean-Jaurès (☎ 04-94-97-45-21); at **Grimaud,** boulevard des Aliziers (☎ 04-94-43-26-98); at **Ste-Maxime,** promenade Simon-Lorière (☎ 04-94-96-19-24); and at **Fréjus,** rue Jean-Jaurès (☎ 04-94- 17-19-19).

WHERE TO STAY

Hôtel Giraglia. Place du 14-Juin, 83310 Port Grimaud, Var. ☎ **04-94-56-31-33.** Fax 04-94-56-33-77. 49 units. A/C MINIBAR TV TEL. 950F–1,600F ($161.50–$272) double; 1,600F–2,200F ($272–$374) suite. Half board 195F ($33.15) per person extra. AE, DC, MC, V. Closed Oct to mid-Apr.

Sitting on an extended dock between a canal and the beach, this hotel has the air of a rural Provençal inn (though it's fully modern). The illusion is carried over into rooms decorated in the style of bygone eras. Rooms range in size from small to medium, with quality mattresses; bathrooms, though small, are neatly organized with adequate shelf space. The hotel surrounds a pool and features a sandy private beach. The hotel's restaurant serves creative variations of traditional Provençal cuisine, with fixed-price menus costing 195F to 260F ($33.15 to $44.20) at dinner and 145F to 260F ($24.65 to $44.20) at lunch. The hotel overlooks the bay of St-Tropez and in summer allows dining on the pool terrace.

WHERE TO DINE

La Table du Mareyeur. 10–11 place des Artisans. ☎ **04-94-56-06-77.** Reservations recommended. Main courses 150F–200F ($25.50–$34); fixed-price menus 150F ($25.50) at lunch (with wine and coffee), 250F ($42.50) at dinner (without wine or coffee). AE, DC, MC, V. Daily noon–3:30pm and 7pm–midnight. Closed Mon Oct–May. SEAFOOD.

This is the resort's most engaging seafood restaurant, located near the entrance. It has a marine decor and terrace seating overlooking a flotilla of yachts and deep-sea fishing craft. Scotland-born Ewan Scutcher is the hardworking master of ceremonies. The seafood is fresh and flavorful and includes bouillabaisse perked up with lobster and crayfish; lobster prepared in half a dozen ways, including salads, chowders, as part of a flavorful tagliatelle, and even in a fricassée with cream-based port-wine sauce. There's also filet of beef flambéed with peppercorns, chicken, and sautéed foie gras served with a glass of sweet Muscat wine.

La Tartane. 8 rue de l'Octogone. ☎ **04-94-56-38-32.** Reservations recommended. Main courses 75F–240F ($12.75–$40.80); fixed-price menus 155F–220F ($26.35–$37.40). Daily noon–3pm and 7–11pm. Closed mid-Nov to Mar. FRENCH/SEAFOOD.

Across from the village church, this restaurant has a terrace that opens onto a view of boats and yachts, a nautical theme, and a cuisine with many reminders of Lyon (hometown of the chef). Lobsters and shellfish are kept in a bubbling aquarium, a focal point near the entrance. Consequently, you'll find lots of fresh shellfish, lobsters galore, and fresh grilled fish; other choices include Bresse chicken in champagne, filet of beef with green peppercorns, tournedos Rossini (beef layered with foie gras), and a flavorful beef cooked with marrow sauce.

3 Ste-Maxime

15 miles (24.14km) SW of St-Raphaël, 38 miles (61.16km) SW of Cannes

Ste-Maxime is just across the gulf from glitzy St-Tropez, but its atmosphere is much more sedate. Young families are the major vacationers here, though an occasional refugee from across the water will come over to escape the see-and-be-seen crowd. The town is surrounded by the red cliffs of the Massif des Maures, protecting it from harsh weather. However, the wide stretches of sand and the cafe-lined promenades lure travelers to spend their days basking in the sun. More active vacationers may want to try windsurfing or waterskiing in the calm waters, or even golfing. A 16th-century fort, built by the monks of Lérins (who also named the port), houses a museum. The best thing about Ste-Maxime is the price—though the town isn't as in vogue as St-Tropez, it's fun and affordable.

ESSENTIALS

GETTING THERE   The nearest train service is at St-Raphaël. Call **Sodetrav** buses (☎ **04-94-95-24-82**) for bus information from St-Raphael. Buses also travel to Ste-Maxime from St-Tropez for a fare of 31F ($5.25) each way. **Transports Maritimes MMG,** quai L.-Condroyer (☎ **04-94-96-51-00**), provides a boat service from St-Tropez to Ste-Maxime from April to October (trip time: 20 minutes). Tickets cost 32F ($5.45) one-way—only slightly more than bus fare, and for a much more pleasant ride.

GETTING AROUND   At 13 rue Magali, **Rent Bike** (☎ **04-94-43-98-07**) rents bikes and mopeds for exploring the town and countryside. Mountain bikes are 80F ($13.60) per day, with a 1,500F ($255) deposit; mopeds are 90F ($15.30), with a 2,500F ($425) deposit.

VISITOR INFORMATION   The **Office de Tourisme** is on promenade Simon-Lorière (☎ **04-94-96-19-24**).

A DAY AT THE BEACH

Beaches are the main attraction here. There are at least four nearby. Two are an easy walk from the town center: Across the road from the casino is **Plage du Casino**—we advise avoiding it because of the fumes from the nearby roadway, the narrow sands, and the hordes of sunbathers. A better bet is **Plage de la Croisette,** a wider, nominally less-congested expanse that's a 2-minute walk west of Plage du Casino. The most appealing are **Plage de la Nartelle** and the adjacent **Plage des Eléphants,** broad expanses of clean, fine-textured light-beige sand about 1¼ miles west of town. To reach them, follow signs along the coastal road pointing to St-Tropez. Here you can rent a mattress for sunbathing from any of several concessionaires, for around 70F to 80F ($11.90 to $13.60).

SEEING THE SIGHTS

Start with the 16th-century **Tour Carrée des Dames** (Dames Tower) at place des Aliziers. It was originally a defensive structure; today it's home to the **Musée des Traditions Locales,** place de l'église (☎ 04-94-96-70-30), with exhibits on the area's history and tradition. The museum is open Wednesday to Monday: April to October from 10am to noon and 3 to 6pm, and November to March from 3 to 6pm only. Admission is 15F ($2.55) for adults and 5F (85¢) for children.

Facing the tower is the **Eglise Ste-Maxime,** place des Niziers (☎ 04-94-55-74-60), with a green marble altar from the former Carthusian monastery of La Verne in the Massif des Maures. The choir stalls date from the 15th century.

St-Maxime hosts various markets, including a daily **flower-and-food market** on rue Fernand-Bessy Monday to Saturday 6am to 1pm and 4:30 to 8pm. On Thursday, a **crafts market** is held on and around place du Marché; on Friday vendors sell a variety of knickknacks on place Jean-Mermoz. In the pedestrian streets of the old town, an **arts-and-crafts fair** takes place daily in summer from 4 to 11pm.

Outside town are several worthy sights. About 6 miles north on the road to Muy is the **Musée du Phonographe et de la Musique Méchanique** (☎ 04-94-96-50-52). This extensive display of audio equipment is the result of one woman's 40-year obsession. Sometimes she gives personal tours. In the museum is one of Edison's original "talking machines," and an audiovisual pathegraphe used to teach foreign language in 1913. The museum is open Easter to October only, Wednesday to Sunday from 10am to noon and 2 to 6pm. Admission is 15F ($2.55) for adults and 7F ($1.20) for children 5 to 12 years.

If you're a nature lover, follow the signs along boulevard Bellevue for 1 mile north of town to the little town of **Sémaphore.** Here you'll find a panoramic view of the mountains and oceans from an altitude of 400 feet. There are also many hiking trails that wind along the coast or into the mountains. The tourist office has maps, or you can head for the **Sentier du Littoral** (Chemin des Douaniers), a trail that meanders along the coast toward St-Tropez and has access to the sea at almost all points along the way.

WHERE TO STAY

Although hotels are less expensive here than in the neighboring towns, you may find that you must pay for half board in July and August. Most places are closed in winter, but May, June, and September are good times to find a good deal.

MODERATE

Hôtel La Belle Aurore. 4 bd. Jean-Moulin, 83120 Ste-Maxime. ☎ **04-94-96-02-45.** Fax 04-94-96-63-87. 17 units. TV TEL. 600F–1,900F ($102–$323) double. AE, CB, DC, MC, V. Closed Jan 7–Feb, 2 weeks in Oct, and Nov–Dec.

La Belle Aurore is on its own private beach, and is, without argument, the finest address in Ste-Maxime; if it has a serious challenger, it's Les Santolines (see below). Though the well-furnished guest rooms aren't air-conditioned, each has a terrace overlooking the sea; the breezes keep the inside temperature comfortable. Ranging from small to medium, each bedroom has a good mattress, most often on a double or twin beds. Tiled bathrooms are small and tidy and tiled, mainly with a shower/tub combination. The large terrace dining area is the perfect place to enjoy a meal in the restaurant.

Hôtel La Croisette. 2 bd. des Romarins, 83120 Ste-Maxime. ☎ **04-94-96-17-75.** Fax 04-94-96-52-40. 17 units. MINIBAR TV TEL. 390F–980F ($66.30–$166.60) double. AE, CB, MC, V. Closed Nov–Mar.

This charming hotel is surrounded by its own lush garden. The hotel has an intimate aura. Room rates vary according to view—those with a balcony and sea view are most expensive; those that open onto the garden are less. Homelike and cozy, they are decorated in a charming, provincial southern style. Beds have quality mattresses; tiled bathrooms are tidy, mostly with shower/tub combinations. Maintenance here is high. In the pleasant outdoor dining area, the chef presents flavorful dishes prepared with fresh ingredients.

Hôtel Les Santolines. Quartier de la Croisette, 83120 Ste-Maxime. ☎ **04-94-96-31-34.** Fax 04-94-49-22-12. 13 units. TV TEL. 320F–790F ($54.40–$134.30) double. AE, CB, MC, V. Closed Jan 6–Mar 3.

This is a good choice for those who want to remove themselves from the madding crowds. Les Santolines is 10 minutes from the busy center area but still close to the beach. The building is arranged around a grassy courtyard that has a pool and the town's most inviting *jardin fleuri*. Rooms are comfortable and private; most have balconies. They are medium in size, each with a double or twin beds fitted with medium-sized mattresses. The look is very French provincial. Sometimes bathrooms are rather dramatically tiled in sea blue; all have double basins and shower/tub combinations, plus good-size towels. The hotel also has private tennis courts.

INEXPENSIVE

Hôtel de la Poste. 7 bd. Frédéric-Mistral, 83120 Ste-Maxime. ☎ **04-94-96-18-33.** Fax 04-94-96-41-68. 24 units. TEL. 300F–620F ($51–$105.40) double. AE, CB, DC, MC, V. Closed Oct 11–May 6.

This modern hotel's location in the town center, convenient to the beach and shopping, makes up for what it lacks in personality. The exterior is uninviting, but the inside is cool and comfortable, with a quiet lounge and a simple bar. Guest rooms aren't style setters—but they're clean, well maintained, and comfortably furnished. The range is from small to medium in size, all with fine mattresses on twin or double beds. Bathrooms are small but well maintained, for the most part with shower/tub combinations. There's a pool, and the staff will be happy to help you decide how to spend your day. There's no restaurant in the hotel, but you're not far from a wide selection.

Hôtel Le Chardon Bleu. 20 rue de Verdun, 83120 Ste-Maxime. ☎ **04-94-96-02-08.** Fax 04-94-43-90-89. 25 units. A/C TV TEL. 280F–470F ($47.60–$79.90) double. AE, CB, MC, V.

Situated 100 yards from the beach, Le Chardon Bleu is also close to the pedestrian area and the casino. The hotel has a garden where you can enjoy a meal amid the aroma of the flowers. The well-maintained rooms are comfortable and inviting, though the furnishings are standard; all have small balconies. Rooms range from small to medium, and each comes with a good mattress. Bathrooms are tiled and compact.

Hôtel Montfleuri. 4 av. Montfleuri, 83120 Ste-Maxime. ☎ **04-94-55-75-10.** Fax 04-94-49-25-07. 31 units. TV TEL. 290F–690F ($49.30–$117.30) double. CB, MC. Closed Oct 14–Mar 26.

This hotel on a hillside in a quiet residential neighborhood has a superb view of the Gulf of St-Tropez. The large guest rooms come with balconies. Each has a comfortable mattress and fine linen, twin or double beds, and small private bathrooms with adequate shelf space. The hotel restaurant serves "family cooking" Provençal style in a pleasant garden. There's also a pool.

WHERE TO DINE

Le Gruppi. 82 av. Charles-de-Gaulle. ☎ **04-94-96-03-61.** Reservations recommended. Main courses 120F–180F ($20.40–$30.60); fixed-price menus 128F–255F ($21.75–$43.35). AE, MC, V. Apr–Sept, daily noon–2:30pm and 7–10pm; Oct–Mar, Tues noon–2:30pm, Thurs–Mon noon–2:30pm and 7–10pm. Closed 2 weeks in Dec. FRENCH/PROVENÇAL.

Earthy and amusing, this restaurant has thrived on the promenade adjacent to the sea ever since the Lindermanns opened it in the 1960s. Bay windows illuminate dining rooms on two floors, decorated in bright green and salmon with rattan furnishings. The deluxe version of the establishment's savory bouillabaisse (230F/$39.10 per person) must be ordered a day in advance; otherwise, you get a simplified version, which the chefs refer to as a *soupe de poisson*. Other menu items are seafood platters; herbed and roasted lamb from Sisteron; and veal, chicken, and all the vegetarian bounty of Provence. If you opt for fish, a staff member will carry a basket filled with the best of the day's catch for your inspection and advise you on their respective merits. One particularly succulent example is braised sea wolf in champagne sauce.

Restaurant Sans Souci. 58 rue Paul-Bert. ☎ **04-94-96-18-26.** Reservations recommended. Main courses 68F–98F ($11.55–$16.65); fixed-price menus 98F–138F ($16.65–$23.45). CB, V. Feb–Oct, daily noon–2pm and 7–10:30pm. Closed Nov–Jan. FRENCH/PROVENÇAL.

Philippe Sibilia's Italian-born grandfather opened this place in 1953. In a turn-of-the-century building next to the church, it has a Provence-inspired decor with ceiling beams and old-time accessories. Menu items prepared by the good-humored owner are concocted from fresh ingredients and years of practice. Examples are pan-fried Provençal veal, sea wolf with fennel, octopus salad, filet of hake with basil, and one of our favorite dishes anywhere, noisettes of lamb with a tapenade of olives that's enhanced with pulverized anchovies and a hint of fresh cream.

4 Fréjus

2 miles (3.2km) W of St-Raphaël, 9 miles (14.4km) NE of St-Tropez

Fréjus was founded by Julius Caesar in 49 B.C. as Forum Julii; later, under Augustus's rule, it became a key naval base. The warships with which Augustus defeated Antony and Cleopatra at the battle at Actium were built here in 31 B.C. By the Middle Ages, however, the port had declined. It began to silt up from disuse and was eventually filled in. Today the port lies more than 2 miles inland.

The Vieille Ville still boasts remnants from Roman times, including parts of an arena and a theater. There's also an interesting section dating to medieval times called the **"Cité Episcopale."** The baptistery is one of France's oldest ecclesiastical buildings.

In more recent times, Fréjus has again expanded toward the water. The beach area, **Fréjus Plage,** tends to blend into St-Raphaël. The two towns are often considered a single holiday destination, though serious beachgoers often opt to stay in St-Raphaël, where the hotels are closer to the water and cheaper.

ESSENTIALS

GETTING THERE   From the main station at San Raphaël, several trains a day arrive at a small **train station** in Fréjus on rue Martin-Bidoure (☎ **08-36-35-35-35**). The beach is a shorter walk (about 15 minutes) from the St-Raphaël station than from the Fréjus station.

Estérel (☎ **04-94-53-78-46**) runs a bus service between the two towns every 30 minutes. Buses arrive at the Fréjus **Gare Routière**, place Paul-Vernet (☎ **04-94-82-16-88**), at the east end of the town center. One-way tickets cost 8F ($1.35). **Sodetrav** buses (☎ **04-94-95-24-82**) en route to St-Tropez from St-Raphaël stop along the coast in Fréjus.

GETTING AROUND   You can rent mopeds at **Location 2 Roues,** 83 Le Méditerranée-Nouveau Port (☎ **04-94-40-76-20**). Prices range from 150F to 300F ($25.50 to $51). Credit-card deposits are required. **Holiday Bikes,** 93 av. de Provence

(☎ 04-94-52-30-65), rents the pedal-powered version of two-wheeled transportation. Expect to pay 50F to 100F ($8.50 to $17), plus a security deposit.

For an overview of Fréjus's rich assortment of ancient and medieval monuments, take the municipally funded blue-and-white **Trains du Soleil** (also known as "le petit train"). Electrically powered and rubber wheeled, they operate hourly between 2:20 and 6:20pm, daily in July and August, and Tuesday to Saturday the rest of the year. Tickets cost 25F ($4.25) for adults, 15F ($2.55) for children 10 to 15, and 10F ($1.70) for children 2 to 9. Tours originate from parking lot Kennedy, midway between Fréjus and St-Raphaël adjacent to the Pont d'Arcole. Call ☎ 04-93-41-31-09 for more details.

VISITOR INFORMATION   The **Office de Tourisme** is at 325 rue Jean-Jaurès (☎ 04-94-51-83-83).

SPECIAL EVENTS   The **Fête des Plantes** is held annually in the park of the Villa Aurélienne (see below), during a 9-day period in late March and April (dates for 2000 will be March 26 to April 5). The biannual art exposition, **Art Tendence Sud,** a 4-day show of artists from southern France, is scheduled for sometime in May of 2000. For both events, call ☎ 04-94-52-90-41 or contact the local tourist office for information.

EXPLORING THE TOWN
THE TOP SIGHTS

The best way to see the Roman ruins is to hop on one of the town's sightseeing **Trains du Soleil** (see above).

The best preserved of the ruins is the **Amphithéâtre,** rue Henri-Vadon (☎ 04-94-51-34-31). In Roman times, it held up to 10,000 spectators. The upper levels of the galleries have been reconstructed with the same greenish stone used to create the original building. Today it's used as a venue for rock concerts and the city's two annual Spanish-style *corridas* (bullfights). Ask the tourist office for dates and details. It's open Wednesday to Monday: April to September from 9:30am to noon and 2 to 6:30pm, and October to March from 9am to noon and 2 to 4:30pm. Admission is free.

A quarter of a mile north of town on rue du Théâtre-Romain, the **Théâtre Romain** (☎ 04-94-51-34-31), not to be confused with the amphitheater, has been largely destroyed. However, one wall and a few of the lower sections remain and are used as a backdrop for occasional summer concerts. The site is open 24 hours, and visits, which aren't monitored, are free. Northwest of the theater you can see a few soaring arches as they follow the road leading to Cannes. These are the remaining pieces of the 25-mile-long **aqueduct** that once brought fresh water to Fréjus's water tower.

Cité Episcopale. Rue de Fleury. ☎ **04-94-51-26-30.** Admission includes entrance to all sites, the museum, and (optional) guided tour of cloister and baptistry: 25F ($4.25) adults, 15F ($2.55) students under 25 and children. Apr–Sept, daily 9am–7pm; Oct–Mar, 9am–noon and 2–7pm.

The town's most frequently visited site is its fortified cathedral in the heart of the Vieille Ville. At its center is the **Cathédrale St-Léonce,** completed in the 16th century after many generations of laborers had worked on it. It was begun in the 10th century, and parts of it date from the 12th and 13th centuries. Its most striking features are Renaissance—ornately carved walnut doors depicting scenes from the Virgin's life and tableaux inspired by Saracen invasions. The 5th-century **baptistry** is one of the oldest in France. Octagonal like many paleo-Christian baptisteries, it features eight black granite columns with white capitals. Most interesting are the two doors, which are different sizes. Catechumens would enter by the smaller of the two; inside, a bishop would wash their feet and baptize them in the center pool. The baptized would then leave through the larger door; this signified their enlarged spiritual stature.

The most beautiful of all the structures in the Episcopal quarter is the 12th-century **cloister.** The colonnade's two slender marble pillars are typical of the Provençal style. Inside, the wooden ceiling is divided into 1,200 small panels, decorated with animals, portraits, and grotesques by 15th-century artists. A bell tower rises above the cloister, its steeple covered with colored tiles. In the building is the **Musée Archéologique,** which features a collection of Roman finds from the area. Roman sculptures dominate, but the small Greek vases that Romans used during their travels are some of the most attractive pieces. Be sure to see the two-headed bust of Hermes; since its discovery in 1970, it has come to be the town's symbol.

MORE SIGHTS

The small, round **Chapelle Cocteau,** avenue Nicola (☎ **04-94-53-27-06**), was designed by the artist, film director, social gadfly, and *prince des poètes,* Jean Cocteau. It was built between 1961 and 1965, and decorated by Cocteau himself. Its octagonal shape, low-slung with small windows, might remind you of an African thatch-covered hut. It's open Wednesday to Monday: April to September from 2 to 6pm and October to March from 2 to 5pm. Admission is free.

Just outside Fréjus are two curiosities that reflect the cultural mixture of France's early 20th-century empire. The **Pagode Hong-Hien** (☎ **04-94-53-25-29**), still used as a Buddhist temple, is about 1¼ miles northeast on R.N. 7. It was built in 1919 by soldiers conscripted from Indochina as a shrine to their fallen comrades. It's open daily from 9am to noon and 3 to 6:30pm; admission is 5F (85¢). Off D4, leading to Bagnols, you can see the purple-red exterior of the **Mosquée Soudanaise** (no phone), built by Muslim soldiers conscripted from the French colony of Mali. It's controlled by the French Ministry of Defense and off-limits to casual visitors.

The grand neoclassical **Villa Aurélienne,** avenue du Général-d'Armée Calliès (☎ **04-94-52-90-41**), was originally a holiday home for an English industrialist in the 1880s. It's the venue of a widely varied series of temporary art exhibitions. Call for information. The 47-acre park surrounding the villa hosts occasional festivals (see "Special Events" above).

The **Parc Zoologique,** Le Capitou (☎ **04-94-40-70-65**), is off A8 about 3½ miles north of the center of Fréjus. The safari park is home to more than 250 species of animals and is open daily: May to September 9:30am to 6pm, and October to April 10am to 5pm. Admission is 55F ($9.35) for adults, 35F ($5.95) for children 3 to 10.

WHERE TO STAY

Hôtel L'Aréna. 145 rue du Général-de-Gaulle, 83615 Fréjus. ☎ **04-94-17-09-40.** Fax 04-94-52-01-52. 30 units. A/C MINIBAR TV TEL. 450F–650F ($76.50–$110.50) double. AE, MC, V. Closed Nov.

This hotel in the center of the Vieille Ville used to be a bank. Beautifully restored in bright Provençal colors, L'Aréna is an appropriately informal beachtown retreat. Each of the small but comfortable rooms opens onto a garden and pool area where tropical plants give the air a sweet smell. Furnishings and mattresses are comfortable and simple, but not at all plush. Likewise, bathrooms are small and tidy with minimal equipment. The sunny dining room is a pleasant place to stop for well-prepared seafood. The staff is friendly, and the hotel is a good value for the area.

WHERE TO DINE

Les Potiers. 135 rue des Potiers. ☎ **04-94-51-33-74.** Reservations required. Main courses 80F–98F ($13.60–$16.65); fixed-price menus 120F–165F ($20.40–$28.05). MC, V. Wed–Mon noon–1:20pm and 7–9:30pm. FRENCH/PROVENÇAL.

One of the town's smallest and most charming restaurants is midway between the town hall and the ancient arena. Staffed only by chef Hubert Guillard and his wife, Jeanne, it occupies a century-old stone house and has only 15 seats. Menu items change with the seasons but usually include rabbit à la Provençal; goat served with fruit salad and warm asparagus; filet of lamb marinated in thyme, olive oil, and garlic and served with a sauce miroir concocted from cream of Cassis and red Bandol wine; and filet of sea wolf with a rosemary-cream sauce. For dessert, how about a thin slice of apple tart with cinnamon-flavored ice cream?

5 St-Raphaël

2 miles (3.22km) E of Fréjus, 27 miles (43.45km) SW of Cannes

Between the red lava peaks of the Massif de l'Estérel and the densely forested hills of the Massif des Maures, St-Raphaël was first popular during Roman times, when rich families came to the large resort here. Barbaric hordes and Saracen invasions characterized the Middle Ages; it wasn't until 1799, when a proud Napoléon landed at the small harbor beach on his return from Egypt, that the city once again drew attention.

Fifteen years later, that same spot in the harbor was the point of embarkation for the fallen emperor's journey to exile on Elba. In 1864 Alphonse Karr, a journalist and ex-editor of *Le Figaro,* helped reintroduce St-Raphaël as a resort. Dumas, Maupassant, and Berlioz came here from Paris on his recommendation. Gounod also came; he composed *Romeo et Juliet* here in 1866. Unfortunately, most of the belle époque villas and grand hotels were destroyed during World War II when St-Raphaël served as a key landing point for Allied soldiers.

Today some of the mansions have been rebuilt and others have been replaced by modern resorts and buildings. The city boasts the wide beaches, good restaurants and hotels, and coastal ambience of other Côte d'Azur resorts—at a fraction of the price. This is why St-Raphaël, one of the richest towns on the coast, draws more families than couture-clad Parisians.

ESSENTIALS

GETTING THERE   Trains pull into the **Gare SNCF St-Raphaël–Valescure,** on the rue Valdeck–Rousseau in the center of town (☎ **08-36-35-35-35** for information and reservations). The town sits directly on the rail lines running parallel to the coast between Marseille and Ventimiglia in Italy, making direct transits at 40-minute intervals from such other resorts as Cannes (25-min. trip); and Nice (60-min. trip). From Paris, between 9 and 11 trains arrive a day (trip time: 8 to 9½ hours—St-Raphaël lies on the high-speed TGV lines from Paris, but parts of that line aren't yet fully developed).

The bus station behind the train station provides both local and regional service. **Estérel-Forum Autocars** (☎ **04-94-95-16-71**) links directly with Fréjus, charging around 7F ($1.20) each way for buses that run at 30-minute intervals, and around 38F ($6.45) for service from Nice, a 60-minute transit. **Sodetrav** (☎ **04-94-95-24-82**) links St-Raphaël with St-Tropez (trip time: 70 to 90 min.); fares are around 50F ($8.50) each way. Buses from Nice arrive every hour. Another option for local bus service into nearby hills and hamlets is provided by **Beltrame** (☎ **04-94-95-95-16**).

Between April and October, **Les Bateaux Bleus** (☎ **04-94-95-17-46**) provide waterborne transit—about a half-dozen per day—between a point near the railway station of St-Raphaël and St-Tropez for around 50F ($8.50) each way.

GETTING AROUND   Normally, **taxis** line up at the bus station; if you can't find one, call ☎ **04-94-95-04-25.** You can rent bikes and scooters from **Patrick Moto,**

260 av. du Général-Léclerc (☎ **04-94-53-87-11**). Bikes rent for 60F ($10.20), with an 800F ($136) deposit; mountain bikes rent for 95F ($16.15), with a 2,000F ($340) deposit; and scooters go for 185F ($31.45), with a 5,000F ($850) deposit. MasterCard and Visa can be used for the deposit.

VISITOR INFORMATION The **Office de Tourisme** faces the train station on rue Waldeck-Rousseau (☎ **04-94-19-52-52**).

SPECIAL EVENTS The **Competition Internationale de Jazz de New Orleans** is held during 3 days in early July, when Dixieland-style musicians from around the world congregate to display their talent. Call ☎ **04-94-19-88-47,** or contact the tourist office, for exact dates and musical venues. In mid-August, the **Festival St-Pierre des Pêcheurs** is conducted in and around the town center. Honoring the fishers who helped feed the town throughout most of its existence, it features a night of fireworks, a brief, medieval-style procession to and from the village church, music, dancing on platforms built beside the port, and a series of *jutes* (mock naval battles between competing boat teams) where everyone gets soaking wet.

A DAY AT THE BEACH

Of course, most visitors come here to have fun on the beaches. The best ones (some rock, some sand) are between the Vieux Port and Santa Lucia; stands rent equipment for water sports on each beach.

The closest to the town center is the **Plage du Veillat,** a long stretch of sand that's crowded and family friendly. Within a 5-minute walk east of the town center is **Plage Beau Rivage,** whose name is misleading because it's covered with a smooth and even coating of light-gray pebbles that might be uncomfortable to lie on without a towel. History buffs will enjoy a 4½-mile excursion east of town to the **Plage du Débarquement,** a partly pebble and partly sand stretch that was hurled into world headlines on August 15, 1945, when Allied forces overran the southern tier of occupied France, bringing World War II to a more rapid conclusion. Today expect relatively uncrowded conditions, except during the midsummer crush.

St-Raphaël's answer to the decadence of nearby St-Tropez is most visible in the municipality's official nude beach, the **Plage de St-Ayguls,** 6 miles west of the town center. Surrounded by thick screens of reeds that thrive along the marshy seafront, it's a short, clearly signposted walk from the heart of the simple fishing village of St-Ayguls.

SEEING THE SIGHTS

St-Raphaël is divided in half by railroad tracks. The historically interesting Vieille Ville (old city) lies inland from the tracks. Here you'll find St-Raphaël's only intact ancient structure, the **Eglise des Templiers,** place de la Vieille Eglise, Quartier des Templiers (☎ **04-94-19-25-75**). The 12th-century church is the third to stand on this site; two Carolingian churches underneath the current structure have been revealed during digs. A Templar watchtower sits atop one of the chapels, and at one time watchers were posted to look out over the sea for ships that might pose a threat. The church served as a fortress and refuge in case of pirate attack. In the courtyard are fragments of a Roman aqueduct that once brought water from Fréjus. Regrettably, at press time the church was closed because of an archaeological dig going on beneath its floors, with a completion anticipated for 2000 or 2001.

St-Raphaël's other major church, **Notre-Dame-de-la-Victoire,** boulevard Félix-Martin (☎ **04-94-19-81-29**), was completed in 1887, an ostentatious monument to the gilded age of commerce that helped finance its construction. May to September,

A Drive in the Hills

This drive is only 35 miles but it's across hilly, rough terrain, so allow about 3 hours, plus extra time for walks and views and perhaps a *pique-nique.* The roads aren't always surfaced, but the views are always dramatic.

Leave St-Raphaël on N98. Follow this route, the Estérel cliff road, as far as **Agay,** a little resort bordering a deep anchorage. The red porphyry slopes of Rastel d'Agay overlook a bay where Greeks and Romans traded centuries ago. After leaving Agay, follow the Valescure road, keeping right toward **Pic de l'Ours** (Ours Peak). After crossing the Agay River, follow the signposts to Ours Peak. The road leads around the north side of St-Pilon and Cap Roux. Eventually, the route comes to the Evêque Pass and then the Lentisques Pass, where only one-way traffic is permitted. At **Pic d'Aurelle,** one of the great panoramas on the Riviera unfolds at an elevation of 1,060 feet. The road continues from the Lentisques Pass to the Notre-Dame Pass, one of the most scenic rides in the Estérel.

At **Notre-Dame** another panorama unfolds, extending all the way to Cannes. Hairpin bends in the road lead to the summit of Pic de l'Ours at 1,627 feet. One of France's greatest views, a sweeping panorama of the coast, is the star here. Back at Notre-Dame Pass, continue for 3 miles, taking in the peaks of Petites Grues and Grosses Grues, until you come to the pass at **Cadière,** where you can stop for more views. At the next pass, Trois Termes, turn left and continue along a bad road to the **Suvières Pass.** The vegetation of cork oaks and evergreens is tough in this rugged terrain.

At Suvières, continue left in the direction of the Mistral Pass, where you connect with a tarred road. Keep left, moving toward the **Belle-Barbe Pass.** Here you can park and take a break, walking along a signposted trail that leads to a beauty spot, the lake of **Ecureuil.** Back at the Belle-Barbe Pass, continue left. At a lodge housing forest rangers, take a right and follow the signs back to St-Raphaël, going by way of **Velescure.** Passing vineyards, orchards, and eucalyptus trees, you reach Velescure, a pocket of posh surrounded by the villas of the wealthy. It has one of the finest climates in the south of France. After a look around, continue along D37 back to St-Raphaël.

it's open daily from 7:30am to 10pm; October to April, it's open daily from 7am to 8pm. Entrance is free.

Near the église des Templiers, the **Musée d'Archéologie Sous-Marine** (Museum of Underwater Archaeology), rue des Templiers (☎ 04-94-19-25-75), displays amphorae, ships' anchors, ancient diving equipment, and other interesting items recovered from the ocean's depths. At one time, rumors circulated about a "lost city" off the coast of St-Raphaël. Jacques Cousteau came to investigate; instead of a sunken city, he discovered a Roman ship that had sunk while carrying a full load of building supplies. From October to May, the museum is open Tuesday to Saturday from 9am to noon and 2 to 5:30pm. From June to September, it's open Tuesday to Saturday from 9am to noon and from 3 to 6:30pm. Admission costs 20F ($3.40) for adults, and 10F ($1.70) for students and children 17 and under.

You'll also find **flower and fruit markets** in the old city. Stall owners open every morning. On the second Saturday of each month, vendors selling a variety of odds and ends also appear. Also check out the **Marché Alimentaire de St-Raphaël,** where carloads of produce, fish, meat, wines, and cheeses are sold daily from 8am to 1pm at two sites—place Victor-Hugo and place de la République—a 5-minute walk apart.

The seafront's broad **promenades,** dotted with statues dedicated to Félix Martin (a 19th-century mayor and tireless promoter of the resort) and Alphonse Karr (a 19th-century artist and local luminary), wind between the beaches and hotels. Near the old port, a **pyramid** commemorating Napoléon's return to France from Egypt stands on avenue du Commandant-Guilbaud.

WHERE TO STAY

There are plenty of accommodations in St-Raphaël, but during summer even the less-than-desirable places fill up fast. Reserve well in advance.

Hôtel Bleu Marine. Noveau Port Santa Lucia, 83700 St-Raphaël. ☎ **04-94-95-31-31.** Fax 04-94-82-21-46. www.straphael.com/bleumarine. E-mail: bleumarine@var-provence.com. 100 units. A/C MINIBAR TV TEL. 450F–800F ($76.50–$136) double. AE, DC, V. Parking 40F ($6.80).

This three-star hotel overlooking the yacht basin harbor at Santa Lucia provides comfortable accommodations in a setting that's a bit removed from the crowded beaches. All the well-furnished rooms have private balconies and come with hair dryers and safes. Each is fitted with a good mattress on twin or double beds. Bathrooms are tidily organized and tiled, with shower/tub combinations or shower stalls, and adequate shelf space. The restaurant boasts well-prepared regional food, which can be served on a sunny terrace that looks down on the sailboats and yachts. Fixed-price menus are available at a cost of 115F to 195F ($19.55 to $33.15). The hotel also has an outdoor pool, a fitness room with a fitness instructor, and a sauna.

Hôtel Continental. 100 promenade du Président-René-Coty, 83700 St-Raphaël. ☎ **04-94-83-87-87.** Fax 04-94-19-20-24. E-mail: continental@infole.fr. 44 units. A/C MINIBAR TV TEL. 370F–1,120F ($62.90–$190.40) double. AE, V. Parking 55F ($9.35).

The Continental is a good choice for a cost-conscious beach vacation. A wide variety of room sizes and exposures ranges from compact (relatively cramped) to spacious, with rates charged according to view (seascape or urban). Some have balconies; all have comfortable mattresses and clean, tiled bathrooms with good-size towels and bathroom accessories. No meals are served other than breakfast, but many well-recommended restaurants lie within a short walk.

Hôtel Excelsior. 193 promenade du Président-René-Coty, 83700 St-Raphaël. ☎ **04-94-95-02-42.** Fax 04-94-95-33-82. www.excelsior-hotel.com. E-mail: info@excelsior.hotel.com. 40 units. A/C MINIBAR TV TEL. 500F–900F ($85–$153) double. AE, DC, MC, V.

This hotel, on the beachfront promenade, is a charming family-run place—the best address at St-Raphaël. The guest rooms are comfortably appointed; most have views of the ocean. Each is small to medium in size and is outfitted with a good mattress, plus a tidy and well-organized bathroom with adequate shelf space and shower/tub combinations. A sand beach is directly across the street. The restaurant, with its pretty outdoor eating area, is a popular choice.

WHERE TO DINE

L'Arbousier. 6 av. de Valescure. ☎ **04-94-95-25-00.** Reservations recommended. Main courses 145F–175F ($24.65–$29.75); set-price lunches 145F–310F ($24.65–$52.70); set-price dinners 185F–310F ($31.45–$52.70). AE, DC, MC, V. Tues–Sun noon–2:30pm and Tues–Sat 7:30–10:30pm. FRENCH/PROVENÇAL.

Thanks to the charm and humor of Christien Roncy, director of the dining room, and the cuisine of her husband, Philippe, this restaurant is a success story that deserves to be better known than it already is. In their own words, the architecture of the building "isn't particularly pretty," although lots of money was spent in 1998 making it cozier and more Provençal-looking. But there's something innately stylish and even fun about this place that keeps clients coming back again and again. Flavors are rich, sunny, and sometimes earthy; typical dishes are green asparagus and lobster served with lemon-flavored butter; cannelloni-shaped filets of red snapper and squid served with hearts of artichokes, chopped onions and peppers, and white wine; and a sophisticated version of roasted pigeon in a stewpot, accompanied by ravioli stuffed with the pigeon's by-products, served with sherry sauce and pepper. Hearty appetites usually appreciate the roasted rabbit with dried plums and garnished with foie gras of duckling. Dessert might be a delectable crystallized version of local strawberries served with a pepper-flavored mint sauce.

Restaurant Pastorel. 54 rue de la Liberté. ☎ **04-94-95-02-36.** Reservations recommended. Fixed-price menus 160F–210F ($27.20–$35.70). AE, MC, V. Tues–Sat noon–2pm and 7pm–10pm, Sun noon–2pm. FRENCH.

Across from the town hall, this restaurant has thrived since 1922, when it was founded by the mother (Mme Pastorel) of the present owner, Charles Floccia. In two dining rooms plus an outdoor terrace, you can enjoy traditional Provençal recipes such as bourride (a close approximation of the bouillabaisse served in Marseille), marinated sardines, rack of lamb with Provençal herbs and parsley, a medley of stuffed baby vegetables, and ragout of rabbit in red wine sauce. The signature dish is a succulent pot of stewed fish flavored with garlic and a medley of vegetables.

ST-RAPHAËL AFTER DARK

Because this is a family vacation spot, the after-dark scene is a little sparse. Of course, there's the **Grand Casino,** square de Grand (☎ **04-94-95-10-59**), with slot machines and gambling, plus a nightly dance party in summer featuring an upbeat orchestra. The slot machines are open daily from 11am to 4am; gambling begins at 8pm, and the dance club opens at 10pm. In summer, the entire place stays open to 4am.

One of our favorite bars is **Le Coco Club,** Port Santa Lucia (☎ **04-94-95-95-56**), where live music and stiff drinks contribute to a kind of gregarious, often flirtatious conviviality. Alternative choices include **La Réserve** (☎ **04-94-95-02-02**), a popular disco with a punk-rock crowd between 16 and 25. Another disco, with less emphasis on youth culture, is **Le Kilt,** rue Jules-Barbier (☎ **04-94-95-29-20**). A more formal venue is the piano bar in the casino, **Le Madison Club** (☎ **04-94-95-10-59**). It's the latest of the late-night watering holes of St-Raphaël, open in midsummer till 4am. Gay people, both men and women, tend to congregate at **Le Pipeline,** 16 rue Charabois (☎ **04-94-95-93-98**), where there's disco music and a long-standing reputation as a dance palace that can be animated and fun for everyone. For more information, contact the town's tourist office.

6 Massif de l'Estérel

2 miles (3.22km) NE of Fréjus, 5 miles (8.05km) SE of Cannes

Stretching for 24 miles of coast from La Napoule to St-Raphaël, this mass of twisted red volcanic rock is a surreal landscape of dramatic panoramas. Forest fires have devastated all but a small section of cork oak, adding barrenness to an already otherworldly place. This was once the stomping ground of a colorful 19th-century highwayman, Gaspard de Besse, who hid in the region's many caves and terrorized local travelers until, at age 25, he was hanged and then decapitated by military authorities in the main square at Aix-en-Provence.

Following the path of the ancient Roman Aurelian Way, N7 traces the area's northern edge, running through the Estérel Gap between Fréjus and Cannes. To get to the massif's summit, **Mont Vinaigre** (elevation 1,962 ft.), turn right at the

Testannier crossroads 7 miles northeast of Fréjus. A parking area allows you to leave your car and make the final 15 minutes of the ascent on foot, climbing to the observation deck of a watchtower for a view stretching from the Alps to the Massif des Maures. At La Napoule, turn around to follow the southwesterly trail of N98 back to Fréjus.

This route offers the massif's most stunning vistas, first turning inland just beyond Le Trayas at **Pointe de l'Observatoire,** where you can ascend to the **Grotte de la Ste-Baume** for the views that inspired the medieval hermit St. Honorat, who once dwelt in the cave. Farther along N98, at **Pointe de Baumette,** is a memorial to the French writer/aviator Antoine de St-Exupéry. At **Agay,** turn inland again to reach the rocky **Gorge du Mal-Infernet,** a twisted rut in the earth, offering a contrast to the surrounding peaks with their overview of the region. Continuing along this inland route leads you to **Pic du Cap-Roux,** at 1,438 feet, and **Pic de l'Ours,** at 1,627 feet, both offering sweeping views of land and sea. Although the park is administered by the **Office National des Forets** (☎ **04-94-44-16-45**), the local tourist offices noted within this chapter are much better sources of information about diversions within its borders.

ESSENTIALS

GETTING THERE   Both of the area's twisted boundary roads run from Cannes to Fréjus, with N7 tracing the northern boundary and the southerly N98 following a route along the coast.

VISITOR INFORMATION   You can get additional information on sights, routes, and accommodations at the **Offices de Tourisme** in **St-Raphaël,** rue Waldeck-Rousseau (☎ **04-94-19-52-52**); **Fréjus,** 325 rue Jean-Jaurès (☎ **04-94-51-83-83**); **Les-Adrets-de-l'Estérel,** place de la Mairie (☎ **04-94-40-93-57**); and **Agay,** boulevard de la Plage (☎ **04-94-82-01-85**).

WHERE TO STAY

Note that the **Auberge des Adrets** (see below) also rents rooms.

Hôtel Le Chrystalin. Place de l'église, chemin des Philippons, 83600 Les-Adrets-de-l'Estérel, Var. ☎ **04-94-40-97-56.** Fax 04-94-40-94-66. 14 units. TV TEL. 430F–500F ($73.10–$85) double; 750F ($127.50) suite for up to 4. DC, MC, V. Closed Nov–Feb.

Adjacent to the village church of a town with fewer than 1,000 full-time residents, this simple inn has rooms outfitted in a plain but cozy Provençal style. Each has a reasonably comfortable mattress plus a small bathroom with a shower stall. Your hosts are Hervé Pandelle and his charming mother, Christiane, who work hard at maintaining a family-style dining room that attracts its share of locals. Dinner is the only meal served, nightly from 7:30 to 9pm, with traditional fixed-price menus at 115F to 195F ($19.55 to $33.15).

WHERE TO DINE

Auberge des Adrets. R.N. 7, 83600 Fréjus. ☎ **04-94-40-36-24.** Fax 04-94-40-34-06. Main courses 130F–180F ($22.10–$30.60); fixed-price menu 158F ($26.85). AE, MC, V. Tues–Sat noon–2pm and 7:30–10pm, Sun noon–2pm (open daily July–Aug). Closed Nov. PROVENÇAL/FRENCH.

Despite an official mailing address that places this medieval inn in Fréjus, 11 miles away, it lies only 1½ miles east of Les-Adrets-de-l'Estérel. Records of its existence go back to 824, when troubadours sang and horses rested here after treks across a landscape even rougher and more arid than other points nearby. In 1653, the site was designated a Relais de Poste, where travelers and their horses could find lodging. Today it focuses on upscale versions of Provence's rural dishes, as interpreted by Cosima de Megvinet. She presides over an antiques-filled dining room that spills out onto a large terrace overlooking arid landscapes and the faraway Baie de Cannes. Menu items are likely to include warm foie gras sautéed with roughly textured bread, magret of duckling roasted with a honey-flavored sesame sauce, and aromatic rack of lamb with an olive tapenade. Dessert might be a hot soufflé with black chocolate.

The hotel offers 10 carefully decorated rooms, each with TV, phone, air-conditioning, some kind of ornate (usually baldaquin) bed, and views over a garden. Depending on the season, doubles cost from 600F to 880F ($102 to $149.60).

7 La Napoule-Plage

560 miles (901.23km) S of Paris, 5 miles (8.05km) W of Cannes

This secluded resort is on the sandy beaches of the Golfe de la Napoule. In 1919, the once-obscure fishing village was a paradise for the eccentric sculptor Henry Clews, son of a New York banker, and his wife, Marie, an architect. Clews fled America's "charlatans," whom he believed had profited from World War I. His house is now a museum.

✪ **Château de la Napoule/Musée Henry-Clews.** Bd. Henry-Clews. ☎ **04-93-49-95-05.** Admission 25F ($4.25) adults, 20F ($3.40) students ages 5–15. By guided tour only (both French and English): Mar–Oct, Wed–Mon 3 and 4pm; additional tour July–Aug at 5pm. Closed Nov–Feb.

An inscription over the entrance to this fairy-tale-like chateau reads: ONCE UPON A TIME. The château, a brooding, medieval-looking fortress whose foundations begin at the edge of the sea, was rebuilt from the ruins of a real medieval château. Clews covered the capitals and lintels with his own grotesque menagerie—scorpions, pelicans, gnomes, monkeys, lizards—the revelations of a tortured mind. Women and feminism are recurring themes in the sculptor's work; an example is the distorted suffragette depicted in his *Cat Woman*. The artist was preoccupied with old age in both men and women and admired chivalry and dignity in man as represented by Don Quixote—to whom he likened himself. Clews died in Switzerland in 1937, and his body was returned to La Napoule for burial. Marie Clews later opened the château to the public as a testimonial to the inspiration of her husband.

ESSENTIALS

GETTING THERE La Mandelieu Napoule-Plage lies on the bus and train routes between Cannes and St-Raphaël. For **information and schedules,** call ☎ **08-36-35-35-35.**

VISITOR INFORMATION The **Office de Tourisme** is at 274 bd. Henry-Clews (☎ **04-93-49-95-31**).

WHERE TO STAY

✪ **Ermitage du Riou.** Bd. Henry-Clews, 06210 La Napoule. ☎ **04-93-49-95-56.** Fax 04-92-97-69-05. www.ermitage-du-riou.fr. E-mail: hotel@ermitage-du-riou.fr. 43 units. A/C MINIBAR TV TEL. 735F–1,710F ($124.95–$290.70) double; from 2,020F ($343.40) suite. AE, DC, MC, V.

This old Provençal hotel is the most tranquil choice at the resort. It borders the Riou River and the Cannes-Mandelieu international golf club. The rooms are furnished in Provençal style with genuine furniture and ancient paintings. The most expensive rooms have private safes. Rooms range in size from medium to spacious, each fitted with an elegant bed with a quality mattress and fine linen. Bathrooms have toiletries,

Following La Route Napoléon

On March 1, 1815, having escaped from a Senate-imposed exile on Elba that began in April 1814, Napoléon, accompanied by a small band of followers, landed at Golfe-Juan. The deposed emperor was intent on marching northward to reclaim his throne as emperor.

Though the details of his journey have been obscured by time, there are two versions of a local legend about one of his first mainland encounters. The first version claims that shortly after landing at Golfe-Juan, Napoléon and his military escort were waylaid by highwaymen unimpressed by his credentials. The other turns the story around, claiming that Napoléon's men, attempting to build a supply of money and arms, waylaid the coach of the prince de Monaco, whose principality, stripped of independence during the Revolution, had just been restored by Louis XVIII. When the prince told Napoléon that he was on his way to reclaim his throne, the exiled emperor stated that they were in the same business and bid his men to let the coach pass unhindered.

Napoléon's return was far from triumphant. He was met by sullen rejection at the garrison in Antibes where he wished to spend the night. This lack of enthusiasm was echoed throughout the region; still fresh in the minds of the citizenry was a series of international blunders that had isolated France from the rest of Europe and alienated Napoléon's bourgeois followers. On being denied a bed at Antibes, he moved on to Cannes for the night. This cool reception didn't dampen his determination, but it was a key factor in his deciding that travel north should be along rough mule paths carved through the hinterlands, avoiding large population centers. It was a sound plan, and by March 19 he was back in the Tuileries in Paris. But there was little time to savor this victory—only 100 days later he met his defeat at the Battle of Waterloo. He was finally and

thick towels, hair dryers, and shower/tub combinations for the most part. Views are of either the sea or the golf course. The restaurant, boasting a wood ceiling with beams, features seafood, with meals beginning at 175F ($29.75). There's also a pool, solarium, garden, and sauna.

La Calanque. Bd. Henry-Clews, 06210 La Napoule. ☎ **04-93-49-95-11.** Fax 04-93-49-67-44. 17 units, 12 with bathroom. TEL. 195F ($33.15) double without bathroom, 300F–330F ($51–$56.10) double with bathroom. July–Aug 480F ($81.60) double without bathroom, 600F–630F ($102–$107.10) double with bathroom (these rates include half board). MC, V. Closed Nov–Mar.

The foundations of this charming hotel date from the Roman Empire. The present hotel, run by the same family since 1942, looks like a hacienda, with salmon-colored stucco walls and shutters. Register in the bar in the rear (through the dining room). Bedrooms range from small to medium, each with a comfortable mattress. Those who take the bathless units will find the corridor bathrooms adequate and well maintained. The hotel's restaurant spills onto a terrace and offers some of the cheapest fixed-price meals in La Napoule, at 95F to 135F ($16.15 to $22.95). Nonguests are welcome.

Royal Hôtel Casino. 605 av. du Général-de-Gaulle, 06212 Mandelieu La Napoule. ☎ **04-92-97-70-06.** Fax 04-92-97-70-49. www.royal-hotel-casino.com. 110 units. A/C MINIBAR TV TEL. 720F–1,710F ($122.40–$290.70) double; from 2,500F ($425) suite. AE, DC, MC, V. Parking 60F ($10.20).

absolutely banished to the isolated island of St. Helena, where he died on May 5, 1821.

In the 1930s, the French government recognized Napoléon's positive influence on internal affairs by building Rte. 85, **La Route Napoléon,** to roughly trace the steps of the exiled emperor in search of a throne. It stretches from Golfe-Juan to Grenoble, but the most scenic stretch is in Provence, between Grasse and Digne-les-Bains. The route is well marked with commemorative plaques sporting an eagle in flight, though the "action" documented south of Grenoble revolves around simple stops made for food and sleep along the way.

The **Office de Tourisme** at place du Tour, St-Vallier-de-Thiey (☎ **04-93-42-78-00**), can provide you with a detailed account of the trek, a map of the three campsites where Napoléon and his men slept, and a map indicating where the road deviates from Napoléon's actual route, now maintained as a hiking trail where you can follow in his footsteps. The office is open Monday to Friday from 9am to noon and 2:30 to 5:30pm, and Saturday from 10am to noon.

After embarking from Cannes on the morning of March 2, the group passed through Grasse and halted just beyond St-Vallier-de-Thiey, spending the night. From this point to our end destination at **Digne-les-Baines,** the route touches only a handful of small settlements; the most notable is Castellane and the village of Barrème, where an encampment was set up on the night of March 3. The next day, the group stopped for lunch in Digne-les-Bains before leaving the region to continue north toward the showdown at Grenoble. Although the relais where he dined is long gone, you can stop at **Bourgogne,** 3 av. Verdun (☎ **04-92-31-00-19**), our choice for dining in the town, where tasty fixed-price menus will cost 90F to 250F ($15.30 to $42.50).

This Las Vegas-style hotel owned by the Accor group is on the beach near a man-made harbor, about 5 miles from Cannes. This was the first French hotel to include a casino and the last (just before the building codes changed) to be allowed to have a casino directly on the beach. The interior is dramatically contemporary, with plush touches, warm shades, and lots of marble. About 80% of all bedrooms were completely renovated and upgraded in 1998, with the remainder scheduled for renovations by 2000. Each unit has a quality mattress and comes with a well-equipped bath with thick towels, a shower/tub combination, and a hair dryer. Most of the attractive modern rooms are angled toward a view of the sea. Those facing the street are likely to be noisy in spite of soundproofing. The restaurant, Le Féréol, is recommended under "Where to Dine," below. An informal cafe (Le Poker) serves both Tex-Mex and specialties of Provence, and a nightclub offers live music. The casino (open daily from 8pm to 4am) offers blackjack, craps, and roulette. Facilities include a pool, tennis courts, a sauna, a private beach, and easy access to an 18-hole golf course.

WHERE TO DINE

Note that the restaurant in **La Calanque** (see above) is open to nonguests.

Brocherie II. Au Port. ☎ **04-93-49-80-73.** Reservations recommended. Main courses 120F–300F ($20.40–$51); set-price menu 190F ($32.30). MC, V. Daily noon–2pm and 7:30–10pm. Closed Jan.

The way this restaurant curves along the shoreline gives the impression that you're riding out to sea on a floating houseboat. You'll enter its precincts by crossing a gangplank lined with flaming torches. Specialties include virtually every fish that can be found in local waters—the freshest and best are grilled and served as simply as possible. Your choices of sauce include a rich hollandaise or béarnaise, or an herb-flavored version of white wine, butter, or vinaigrette. There's also a heady version of bouillabaisse, priced at 250F ($42.50) per person, and a selection of (very expensive) lobsters from the establishment's bubbling holding tank. Meat dishes include succulent brochettes of Provençal lamb with rosemary and red wine.

Le Féréol. In the Royal Hôtel Casino, 605 av. du Général-de-Gaulle. ☎ **04-92-97-70-00.** Reservations recommended. Main courses 100F–185F ($17–$31.45); buffet lunch (June–Sept only) 215F ($36.55); fixed-price dinner 260F ($44.20). AE, DC, MC, V. Daily noon–2:30pm (to 3:30pm July–Aug) and 7–10:30pm (to 11pm July–Aug). FRENCH.

This well-designed restaurant services most of the culinary needs of the largest hotel (and the only casino) in town. Outfitted in a nautical style that includes some of the seagoing accessories of an upscale yacht, it offers one of the most impressive lunch buffets in the neighborhood. At night the place is candlelit and elegant, and the view through bay windows over the pool is soothing. Menu items include foie gras, scampi tails fried with ginger, zucchini flowers with mousseline of lobster, mignon of veal with Parma ham and tarragon sauce, sole braised with shrimp, and an émincé of duckling baked under puff pastry with cèpe mushrooms. The dessert buffet lays out a wide array of sophisticated pastries, some light and fruity summer dishes, others designed as irresistible temptations for chocoholics.

L'Oasis. Rue Honoré-Carle. ☎ **04-93-49-95-52.** Reservations required. Main courses 240F–270F ($40.80–$45.90); fixed-price lunch (with wine) 295F ($50.15); fixed-price lunch or dinner (without wine) 320F–680F ($54.40–$115.60). AE, DC, MC, V. Daily noon–2pm and 7:30–10pm. Closed Jan 1–Feb 7. FRENCH.

At the entrance to the harbor of La Napoule, in a 40-year-old house with a lovely garden and an unusual re-creation of a mock-medieval cloister, this restaurant became world-famous under the now-retired Louis Outhier. Today chef Stéphane Raimbault prepares the most sophisticated cuisine in La Napoule. Presumably, Raimbault has learned everything Outhier had to teach him and charts his own culinary course. Because Raimbault cooked in Japan for 9 years, many of his dishes are of the "East meets West" variety. In summer, meals are served in the shade of the plane trees in the garden. Menu choices might include roasted saddle of monkfish and risotto of squid with an ink sauce; medaillons of veal and duck in a muscat wine and grape sauce; and a roasted Dover sole with parsley scorzonera. The wine cellar houses one of the finest collections of Provençal wines anywhere. Regrettably, there can be rocky moments here thanks to a staff that's a lot less helpful than they could be.

8 Cannes

562 miles (905km) S of Paris, 101 miles (163.6km) E of Marseille, 16 miles (25.8km) SW of Nice

When Coco Chanel came here, got a suntan and returned to Paris bronzed, she startled the milk-white ladies of society. Today the bronzed bodies—in nearly nonexistent swimsuits—that line the sandy beaches of this chic resort continue the trend started by the late fashion designer.

Cannes is at its most frenzied during the **International Film Festival** at the Palais des Festivals on promenade de la Croisette. On the seafront boulevards, flashbulbs pop as the stars and wannabes emerge and pose and pose and pose. For wannabes (particularly female), *outrageous* is the key word. The festival's stellar activities are closed to most visitors, who are forced to line up in front of the Palais des Festivals. Known as "the bunker," this concrete structure is the venue for premières that draw some 5,000 spectators. With paparazzi shouting ("Bruce, Demi, over here!") and shooting away, and a guard of gendarmes holding back the fans, the guests parade along the red carpet into the building, perhaps stopping for a moment or two to strike a pose and chat with a journalist. *C'est la Cannes!*

International regattas, galas, *concours d'élégance,* and even a Mimosa Festival in February—something's always happening at Cannes, except in November, traditionally a dead month.

ESSENTIALS

GETTING THERE   Cannes is connected to each of the Mediterranean resorts, Paris, and the rest of France by rail and bus lines. Cannes lies on the major coastal rail line along the Riviera, with trains arriving frequently throughout the day. From Antibes to Cannes by train takes only 15 minutes, or 35 minutes from Nice. The TGV from Paris going via Marseille also services Cannes. (Transit from Paris to Cannes via TGV takes only about 3 breathless hours.) For **rail information** and schedules, call ☎ **08-36-35-35-35.** Buses pick up passengers at the Nice airport every 40 minutes during the day, delivering them in Cannes at the **Gare Routière,** place Bernard Cornut-Gentille (☎ **04-93-39-18-71**). Service to Cannes is also available from Antibes at the rate of one bus every half hour. The international airport at Nice lies a 20-minute drive northeast.

VISITOR INFORMATION   The largest of Cannes' **Office de Tourisme** is in the Palais des Festivals, boulevard de la Croisette (☎ 04-93-39-24-53). Another choice is the office at the **Gare SNCF** (☎ 04-93-99-19-77).

SPECIAL EVENTS   The world-famous **International Film Festival** is conducted every year during April or May. In the year 2000, scheduled dates are May 10 to 21, when the festival celebrates its 53rd anniversary.

SEEING THE SIGHTS

For many, Cannes consists of only one street, **promenade de la Croisette** (or just **La Croisette**), curving along the coast and split by islands of palms and flowers. It's said that Edward, Prince of Wales (before he became Edward VII) contributed to its original cost. But he was a Johnny-come-lately to Cannes. In 1834, Lord Brougham, a lord chancellor of England, set out for Nice and was turned away because of an outbreak of cholera. He landed at Cannes and liked it so much that he decided to build a villa here. Returning every winter until his death in 1868, he proselytized it in London, drawing a long line of British visitors. In the 1890s Cannes became popular with Russian grand dukes (it's said that more caviar was consumed here than in all of Moscow). One French writer claimed that when the Russians returned as refugees in the 1920s, they were given the garbage-collection franchise.

A port of call for cruise liners, the seafront of Cannes is lined with hotels, apartment houses, and chic boutiques. Many of the bigger hotels, some dating from the 19th century, claim part of the beach for the private use of their guests. But there are also public areas. Above the harbor, the old town of Cannes sits on Suquet Hill, where you'll see a 14th-century tower, the **Tour du Suquet,** which the English dubbed "the Lord's Tower."

Nearby is the **Musée de la Castre,** in the Château de la Castre, Le Suquet (☎ **04-93-38-55-26**), containing paintings, sculpture, examples of decorative arts, and a section on ethnography. The latter includes relics and objects from everywhere, from the

Cannes

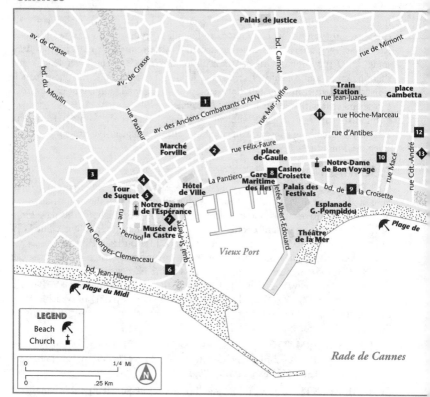

Pacific islands to Southeast Asia, to South American Peruvian and Mayan pottery. There's also a gallery devoted to relics of ancient Mediterranean civilizations. Five rooms are devoted to 19th-century paintings. The museum is open Wednesday to Monday: April to June from 10am to noon and 2 to 6pm, July to September from 10am to noon and 3 to 7pm, and October to March from 10am to noon and 2 to 5pm. Admission is 10F ($1.70), free for students and children.

Though nobody plans a trip to Cannes to see churches, the city does contain some worthy examples. The largest and most prominent is **Notre-Dame de Bon Voyage,** square Mérimée (☎ 04-93-39-16-22), near the Palais des Festivals; it was built in a *faux* Gothic style in the late 19th century. The most historic church, **Notre-Dame de l'Espérance,** place de la Castre (☎ 04-93-39-17-49), was built between 1521 and 1627 and combines both Gothic and Renaissance elements. The town's most unusual church is the **Eglise Orthodoxe Russe St-Michel Archange,** 36–40 bd. Alexandre-III (☎ 04-93-43-00-28), built in 1894 through the efforts of Alexandra Skripytzine, a Russian in exile; it's capped with a cerulean-blue onion dome and a gilded triple cross. Be warned that it's usually locked, except for services on Saturday at 5pm and Sunday between 9:30am and noon.

A DAY AT THE BEACH

Beachgoing in Cannes is more involved with exhibitionism and voyeurism than with actually enjoying the water or swimming (which might even be considered gauche). Here's a rundown on the resort's most user-friendly beaches:

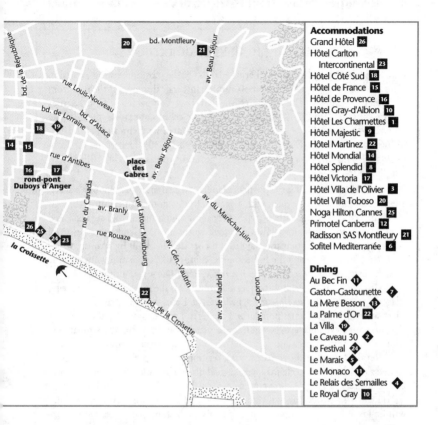

Accommodations

Grand Hôtel 26
Hôtel Carlton
    Intercontinental 23
Hôtel Côté Sud 18
Hôtel de France 15
Hôtel de Provence 16
Hôtel Gray-d'Albion 10
Hôtel Les Charmettes 1
Hôtel Majestic 9
Hôtel Martinez 22
Hôtel Mondial 14
Hôtel Splendid 8
Hôtel Victoria 17
Hôtel Villa de l'Olivier 3
Hôtel Villa Toboso 20
Noga Hilton Cannes 25
Primotel Canberra 12
Radisson SAS Montfleury 21
Sofitel Mediterranée 6

Dining

Au Bec Fin 11
Gaston-Gastounette 7
La Mère Besson 13
La Palme d'Or 22
La Villa 19
Le Caveau 30 2
Le Festival 24
Le Marais 5
Le Monaco 11
Le Relais des Semailles 4
Le Royal Gray 10

✪ **Plage de la Croisette** extends between the Vieux Port and the Port Canto. Though the beaches along this billion-dollar stretch of sand aren't in the strictest sense private, they're *payante,* meaning that you must pay between 90F and 100F ($15.30 and $17). You don't need to be a guest of the Noga Hilton, Martinez, Carlton, or Majestic to use the beaches associated with those hotels, though if you are, you'll usually get a reduction of around 50%. Each beach is separated from its neighbor by a wooden barricade that stops several feet from the sea, allowing easy transit from one to another.

Why should you pay a fee at all? Well, it includes a full day's use of a mattress, a chaise longue (the seafront isn't particularly sandy or even soft, covered as it is with pebbles and dark-gray shingle), and a parasol, as well as easy access to freshwater showers and kiosks selling beverages. Many beaches have outdoor restaurants where no one minds if you appear in a swimsuit. Every beach here is insouciant about topless bathing but absolutely adamant in outlawing bottomless sea- or sunbathing.

For nostalgia's sake, our preferred beach is the one associated with the Carlton—it was the first beach we ever went on as teenagers in Cannes. The relative merits of the 20 or so beaches along La Croisette vary daily depending on the crowd.

Looking for a free public beach where you'll have to survive without rentable chaises or parasols? Head for the **Plage du Midi,** sometimes called **Midi Plage,** just west of the Vieux Port (☎ **04-93-39-92-74**), or **Plage Gazagnaire** (☎ **04-93-90-39-09**), just east of the Port Canto (no phone). Here you'll find numbers of families with children and lots of caravan-type vehicles parked nearby.

Ferrying to the Iles de Lérins

Across the bay from Cannes, the Lérins Islands are the most interesting excursion from the port. Ferryboats depart at 30-minute intervals throughout the day, from 7:30am to sundown. The largest of the ferryboat companies is **Compagnies Estérel-Chanteclair** (☎ **04-93-39-11-82**), but other contenders include **Cie Horizon 4** (☎ **04-93-99-15-09**); **Compagnie Maritime Cannoise** (☎ **04-93-38-66-33**); and **Trans-Côte d'Azur** (☎ **04-92-98-71-30**). Departures are from the Gare Maritime des îles, 06400 Cannes. Round-trip passage costs 50F ($8.50) per person.

ILE STE-MARGUERITE   The first island is named after St. Honorat's sister, Ste. Marguerite, who lived here with a group of nuns in the 5th century. Today it is a youth center whose members (when they aren't sailing and diving) are dedicated to the restoration of the fort. From the dock where the boat lands, you can stroll along the island (signs point the way) to the **Fort de l'Ile**, built by Spanish troops from 1635 to 1637. Below the hill is the 1st-century B.C. Roman town where the unlucky man immortalized in *The Man in the Iron Mask* was imprisoned.

One of French history's most perplexing mysteries is the identity of the man who allegedly wore the *masque du fer,* a prisoner of Louis XIV who arrived at Ste-Marguerite in 1698. Dumas popularized the legend that he was a brother of Louis XIV, and it has even been suggested that the prisoner and a mysterious woman had a son who went to Corsica and "founded" the Bonaparte family. However, the most common theory is that the prisoner was a servant of the superintendent, Fouquet, named Eustache Dauger. He may have earned his fate by aiding Fouquet in embezzling the king's treasury. At any rate, he died in the Bastille in Paris in 1703.

You can visit his cell at Ste-Marguerite, where it seems that every visitor has written his or her name. As you stand listening to the sound of the sea, you realize what a forlorn outpost this was.

The **Musée de la Mer,** Fort Royal (☎ **04-93-38-55-26**), traces the history of the island, displaying artifacts of Ligurian, Roman, and Arab civilizations, plus paintings, mosaics, and ceramics discovered in excavations. The museum is open Wednesday to Monday, April to June, 10:30am to 12:15pm and 2:15 to 5:30pm; July to September, 10:30am to 12:15pm and 2:15 to 6:30pm; October to March, 10:30am to 12:15pm and 2:15 to 4:30pm. Admission is 10F ($1.70) for adults, free for children and students.

ILE ST-HONORAT   Only a mile long, but richer in history than any of its sibling islands, the île St-Honorat is the site of a working monastery whose origins go back to the 5th century. Today the **Abbaye de St-Honorat,** les Iles de Lérins, 06400 Cannes (☎ **04-92-99-54-00**), boasts a combination of medieval ruins and early 20th-century ecclesiastical buildings, inhabited by a permanent community of about 30 Cistercian monks. If space is available, outsiders can visit, for prayer and meditation only, and spend the night. However, most visitors come to wander through the pine forests on the island's western side, and sun themselves on its beaches.

OUTDOOR PURSUITS

BICYCLING & MOTOR-SCOOTERING   Despite the roaring traffic, the flat landscapes between Cannes and such satellite resorts as La Napoule are well suited for riding a bike or motor scooter. **Alliance Location de Cannes,** 9 rue des Frères

Pradignac (☎ **04-93-94-61-94**), rents pedal bikes for 62F ($10.55) per day and requires a 1,000F ($170) deposit (payable with American Express, MasterCard, or Visa). Motor scooters rent for 175F to 200F ($29.75 to $34) per day and require a deposit of 4,000F to 10,000F ($680 to $1,700) per day, depending on their value. None of the motor scooters rented here requires a driver's license or special permit.

BOATING   In an annex of the Hôtel Latitude, **New Boat,** rue de la Laiterie (☎ **04-93-93-12-34**), is in Mandelieu, 4 miles west of Cannes. With a good reputation and a hardworking staff, it maintains a flotilla of powerboats and small yachts ranging from 12 to 45 feet long. They rent, usually with a staff included for navigation and safety, from 3,500F ($595) per day.

GOLF   One of the region's most challenging and interesting courses, **Country-Club de Cannes-Mougins,** 175 Rte. d'Antibes, Mougins (☎ **04-93-75-79-13**), 4 miles north of Cannes, is a 1976 reconfiguration by Dye & Ellis of a course laid out in the 1920s. Noted for the olive trees and cypresses that adorn a relatively flat terrain, it has many water traps and a deceptively tricky layout loaded with technical challenges. It has a par of 72 and a much-envied role since 1981 as host to the Cannes-Mougins Open, an important stop on the PGA European Tour. The course is open to anyone with proof of his or her handicap willing to pay greens fees of 290 to 310F ($49.30 to $52.70), depending on the day of the week. An electric golf cart rents for 280F ($47.60), and golf clubs can be rented for 150F ($25.50) per set. Reservations are recommended.

SWIMMING   Most of the larger hotels in Cannes have their own pools. In addition, the **Complexe Sportif Montfleury,** 23 av. Beauséjour (☎ **04-93-38-75-78**), boasts a large modern pool that's about 100 feet long. Anyone who pays the entrance fee of 22F ($3.75) can spend the entire day lounging beside it.

TENNIS   Its 10 tennis courts are one of the highlights of the **Complexe Sportif Montfleury,** 23 av. Beauséjour (☎ **04-93-38-75-78**). You'll find 8 hard-surfaced courts, at 70F ($11.90) per hour, and 2 clay-surfaced courts, at 90F ($15.30) per hour.

SHOPPING

Cannes competes more successfully than many of its neighbors in a highly commercial blend of resort-style leisure, luxury glamour, and media glitz. So you're likely to find branch outlets of virtually every stylish Paris retailer.

There's every big-name designer you can think of (Saint Laurent, Rykiel, Hermès) as well as big-name designers you've never heard of (Claude Bonucci, Basile, and Durrani)—but, more important, there are real-people shops, resale shops for gently worn star-studded castoffs, two flea markets for fun junk, and a fruit, flower, and vegetable market.

ANTIQUES & *BROCANTE*   In the Casino Croisette (also called the Palm Beach Casino) on La Croisette, Cannes hosts one of France's most prestigious **antiques salons,** conducted biannually during week-long periods in mid-July and late December or early January. Its organizers absolutely refuse to include low- or even middle-bracket merchandise. This is serious—not for the gilt-free crowd—with lots of 18th- and early 19th-century stuff. Admission is 60F ($10.20) per person. Available at this event are services like crating and freighting and flying whatever you buy to wherever you want it sent. For dates and information, call or write the **Association des Antiquaires de Cannes,** 13 rue d'Oran, 06400 Cannes (☎ **04-93-38-13-64**).

Looking for top-notch antiques dealers whose merchandise will wow you? Two of the city's most noteworthy dealers are **Hubert Herpin,** 20 rue Macé (☎ **04-93-39-56-18**), and **Marc Franc,** 142 rue d'Antibes (☎ **04-93-43-86-43**). Also noteworthy is **Boglio Antiquité,** 21 rue St-Antoine (☎ **04-93-39-03-03**). In all these stores, you'll find a wide selection of bronze and marble statues, marquetry, and 18th- and 19th-century furniture.

Things are a lot less elevated at Cannes's two regular flea markets. Casual, dusty, and to an increasing degree filled with the castaways of various estate sales, the **Marché Forville,** conducted in the Marché Forville neighborhood near the Palais des Festivals, is a battered stucco structure with a roof and a few arches but no sides. Between Tuesday and Sunday, it functions as the fruit, vegetable, and flower market that supplies the raw materials for dozens of grand restaurants. But Monday is *brocante* day, when the market fills with off-handed, sometimes strident antiques dealers selling everything from grandmère's dishes to bone-handled carving knives.

Every Saturday, a somewhat disorganized and invariably busy **flea market** is held outdoors along the edges of the allée de la Liberté, across from the Palais des Festivals. Exact hours depend on the whims of the dealers, but they usually begin around 8am and run out of steam by around 4:30pm. Note that the vendors at the two flea markets may or may not be the same.

CHOCOLATE & JELLIED FRUITS   There are several famous chocolatiers in Cannes—try **Maiffret,** 31 rue d'Antibes (☎ **04-93-39-08-29**)—but the real local specialty is *fruits confits* (jellied fruits, also called crystallized fruits), which became the rage in the 1880s. Maiffret sells these, especially in summer, when the chocolates tend to melt. Pâtés and confits of fruit, some of which decorate cakes and tarts, are also sold. Look for the Provençal national confection, *calissons,* crafted from almonds, a confit of melon, and sugar. A block away is **Chez Bruno,** 50 rue d'Antibes (☎ **04-93-39-26-63**). Opened in 1929 and maintained today by a matriarchal descendant of its founder, the shop is famous throughout Provence for *fruits confits* as well as its recipe for glazed chestnuts *(marrons glacés),* made fresh daily.

DEPARTMENT STORES   Near the train station in the heart of Cannes, **Galeries Lafayette** has a small branch at 6 rue du Maréchal-Foch (☎ **04-93-39-27-55**). It's noted for self-consciously upscale fashion available in carefully arranged interiors. You'll save some francs and get an insight into the layout of a French-speaking five-and-dime by checking out its downscale sibling, **Monoprix,** across the street at no. 9 (☎ **04-93-39-35-01**). Monoprix contains a grocery store as well.

DESIGNER SHOPS   Most of the big names in designer fashion, for both men and women, line **La Croisette.** These stores are all in a row, stretching from the Hôtel Carlton almost to the Palais des Festivals, with the best names closest to the high-rise **Gray-d'Albion,** 17 La Croisette (☎ **04-92-99-79-79**), which is both a mall and a hotel (how convenient). The stores in the Gray-d'Albion mall include **Hermès** and **Souleiado.** The mall is broken down into two parts, so you go outdoors from the first part of the building and then enter again for the second part. It serves also as the shopper's secret cutaway from the expensive shopping street, La Croisette, to the less expensive shopping street, **rue d'Antibes.**

You'll find a few more designer shops inside the posh hotels lining La Croisette: **Alexandra,** rond-point duboys d'Angers (☎ **04-93-38-41-29**), is the fanciest boutique in town for a mixture of designers and for the kind of service demanded by stars and local ladies who lunch. In the words of the owners, *"pour la ville, le soir, et les céré-monies."* Here you'll find garments by Mori, Givenchy, Rochas, Lacroix, and Montana. Find it by ducking around to the back end of the Noga Hilton.

FOOD   A charmingly old-fashioned shop, **Cannolive,** 16–20 rue Vénizelos (☎ **04-93-39-08-19**), is owned by the Raynaud family, who founded the place in 1880. It sells Provençal olives and their by-products—purées *(tapenades)* that connoisseurs refer to as "Provençal caviar," black "olives de Nice," and green "olives de Provence," as well as three grades of olive oil from several regional producers. Oils and food products are dispensed from no. 16, but gift items (fabrics, porcelain, and Provençal souvenirs) are sold next door. *Note:* Of the many streets that will attract you with rustic and authentic Provençal allure, the most appealing, with the greatest number of old-fashioned emporiums selling wine, olives, herbs, and oils, is the **rue Meynadier.**

MARKETS   At the edge of the Quartier Suquet, the **Marché Forville** is the town's primary fruit, flower, and vegetable market. On Monday, it's a *brocante* market. See "Antiques & *Brocante,*" above.

PERFUME   The best shop is **Bouteille,** 59 rue d'Antibes (☎ **04-93-39-05-16**), but it's also the most expensive. Its prices are high because it has a wider selection, gives away many more free samples, and presents you with a tote bag. Other perfume shops dot rue d'Antibes. Any one of them may feature your favorite fragrance in a promotional deal (they rotate the deals). A final option for reasonably priced perfumes is the boutiques in the previously recommended Hôtel Gray-d'Albion (see above).

WHERE TO STAY
VERY EXPENSIVE

✪ **Hôtel Carlton Intercontinental.** 58 bd. de la Croisette, 06400 Cannes. ☎ **800/327-0200** in the U.S., or 04-93-06-40-06. Fax 04-93-06-40-25. www.cannes.intercontinental.com. 354 units. A/C MINIBAR TV TEL. 1,330F–3,975F ($226.10–$675.75) double; from 7,750F ($1,317.50) suite. AE, DC, MC, V. Parking 180F ($30.60).

Cynics say that one of the most amusing sights in Cannes is the view from under the vaguely art-deco grand gate of the Carlton. Here you'll see vehicles of every description pulling up to drop off huge amounts of baggage and vast numbers of oh-so-fashionable guests. The epitome of luxury, the hotel has become such a part of the city's heartbeat that to ignore it would be to miss the resort's spirit. The twin gray domes at either end of the facade are often the first things recognized by starlets planning their grand entrances in the hotel's public and private rooms.

Shortly after it was built in 1912, the Carlton attracted Europe's *haut monde,* including royalty. They were followed decades later by battalions of important screen stars. Today the hotel is more democratic, hosting conventions and motor-coach tour groups; however, in summer (especially during the film festival) the public rooms are still filled with all the voyeuristic and exhibitionistic fervor that seems so much a part of the Riviera. The guest rooms were renovated in 1990. Double-glazing, big combination bathrooms with hair dryers, and luxurious appointments such as deluxe mattresses are standard. The most spacious rooms are in the west wing, and many of the upper-floor rooms open onto balconies fronting the sea.

Dining/Diversions: The hotel contains four restaurants. La Belle Otéro, on the seventh floor, offers the most cultivated cuisine, followed by the elegant but less spectacular Restaurant du Casino and Restaurant de la Côte, which was renovated in 1997. A ground-floor Brasserie doles out less-expensive fare, and at the waterfront Restaurant de la Plage, virtually everyone seems to arrive in *maillots de bain.*

Facilities: Private beach, health club with spa facilities, glass-roofed indoor pool.

Hôtel Majestic. 14 bd. de la Croisette, 06400 Cannes. ☎ **04-92-98-77-00.** Fax 04-93-38-97-90. 263 units. A/C MINIBAR TV TEL. 1,940F–4,600F ($329.80–$782) double; from 4,600F ($782) suite. AE, DC, MC, V. Parking 150F ($25.50).

At the west end of La Croisette, the Majestic has stood for glamour since 1926 and, like the Carlton, is a favorite with celebs during the annual film festival. Constructed around an overscale front patio with a pool, the hotel opens directly onto the esplanade and the sea. Inside, the setting is one of marble, crystal chandeliers, Oriental carpets, Louis XV silk furniture, and potted palms. The guest rooms are furnished with antiques and reproductions, Oriental rugs, and marble tables. All rooms are fitted with safes, bedside controls, and luxury mattresses; the most special of the lot are 16 sea-view units with private terraces. The spacious, bright corner accommodations offer the best value. Bathrooms are sumptuous, with makeup mirrors, thick towels, robes, hair dryers, scales, and deluxe toiletries.

Dining/Diversions: There's a classic haute cuisine restaurant, and a grill with tables placed around the pool. There's also a restaurant and bar on the beach.

Amenities: Room service (24 hours), same-day laundry/valet service, hairdresser, pool.

✪ **Hôtel Martinez.** 73 bd. de la Croisette, 06400 Cannes. ☎ **04-92-98-73-00.** Fax 04-93-39-67-82. www.hotel-martinez.com. 430 units. A/C MINIBAR TV TEL. 1,250F–4,800F ($212.50–$816) double; from 2,750F ($467.50) suite. AE, DC, MC, V. Parking 160F ($27.20).

When this landmark art-deco hotel was built in the 1930s, it rivaled any along the coast in sheer size alone. Over the years, however, it has fallen into disrepair and closed and reopened several times. But in 1982, the Concorde chain returned the hotel and its restaurants to their former luster, and today it competes with the Carlton and Noga Hilton. Despite its grandeur, the hotel is a little too convention-oriented for our tastes, but the rooms remain in good shape. The aim of the decor was a Roaring Twenties style, and all units boast private safes, marble baths with thick towels, wood furnishings, tasteful carpets, quality mattresses, and pastel fabrics.

Dining/Diversions: La Palme d'Or, among the finest restaurants in Cannes, is recommended under "Where to Dine," below. The poolside restaurant, L'Orangerie, serves light, low-calorie meals in a decor of azure and white lattices.

Amenities: Room service (24 hours), same-day laundry/valet, private beach, water-skiing school, cabanas, octagonal pool, seven tennis courts.

Noga Hilton Cannes. 50 bd. de la Croisette, 06414 Cannes. ☎ **800-445-8667** in the U.S., or 04-92-99-70-00. Fax 04-92-99-70-11. www.hilton.com. 229 units. A/C MINIBAR TV TEL. 1,181F–3,990F ($200.75–$678.30) double; 2,190F–8,220F ($372.30–$1,397.40) suite. AE, DC, MC, V.

Opened in 1992, the Hilton was the first major palace hotel to open in Cannes since the 1930s. This six-story deluxe place, with massive amounts of exposed glass, boasts a contemporary design mimicking the best aspects of its older twin, the lakefront Noga Hilton in Geneva. You register in a soaring lobby sheathed in semitranslucent white marble. The guest rooms are stylish, with impeccable soundproofing and all the electronic accessories you'll ever need. Since all rooms are equivalent, the difference in rates is determined by exposure to the sea. Many of the appointments evoke a 1930s aura; all have private safes, balconies, bedside controls, and luxury mattresses. The Prestige Rooms have very large beds and elegant carpeting. Other units, less desirable, are called "city-view" and "garden-view" accommodations. There are six rooms for persons with disabilities, and 21 are reserved for nonsmokers. Marble bathrooms contain hair dryers, thick towels, and toiletries.

Dining/Diversions: The most expensive dining venue is La Scala, a smart restaurant with its own piano bar one floor above lobby level. It specializes in the cuisines of the Riviera—both French and Italian. Less grand is the Brasserie Le Grand Bleu. La Plage is an informal lunch restaurant on the beach. There are also a casino and an 825-seat theater for cabarets and conventions.

Amenities: Room service (24 hours), baby-sitting, health club with sauna, outdoor pool, shopping arcade with about 30 boutiques, waterfront pier for mooring yachts, business center, access to nearby golf course.

EXPENSIVE

Grand Hôtel. 45 bd. de la Croisette, 06400 Cannes. ☎ **04-93-38-15-45.** Fax 04-93-68-97-45. 77 units. A/C MINIBAR TV TEL. 660F–1,580F ($112.20–$268.60) double; 1,580F–2,600F ($268.60–$442) suite. AE, MC, V. Closed Nov to Dec 14. Parking 40F ($6.80).

This hotel is graced with a garden with tall date palms and a lawn sweeping down to the waterfront esplanade. A recently renovated structure of glass and marble, it's part of a complex of adjoining apartment-house wings and encircling boutiques. Eleven floors of rooms (with wall-to-wall picture windows) open onto tile terraces. Vibrant colors are used throughout: sea blue, olive, sunburst red, and banana. The bathrooms are lined with colored checkerboard tiles, and have matching towels and rows of decorative bottles, plus hair dryers. Those rooms with sea views are the most expensive.

Hôtel Gray-d'Albion. 38 rue des Serbes, 06400 Cannes. ☎ **04-92-99-79-79.** Fax 04-93-99-26-10. 186 units. A/C MINIBAR TV TEL. 900F–1,580F ($153–$268.60) double; from 3,250F–4,450F ($552.50–$756.50) suite. AE, DC, MC, V.

The smallest of the major hotels is not on La Croisette, but its pastel-colored rooms are outfitted with all the luxury a modern hotel can offer. Groups form a large part of its clientele, but it also caters to the individual guest. Rooms on the eighth and ninth floors have views of the Mediterranean. All bedrooms are fairly standardized and medium in size, blending both contemporary and traditional furnishings along with such amenities as private safes and bedside controls. Each room has a balcony, but the views aren't notable. Bathrooms are well equipped and clad in marble and granite, each with a set of deluxe toiletries, thick towels, hair dryers and make-up mirrors. Dining selections include Le Royal Gray, one of the best in Cannes (see below) and a beach-club restaurant.

Radisson SAS Montfleury. 25 av. Beauséjour, 06400 Cannes. ☎ **800/333-3333** in the U.S. and Canada, or 04-93-68-91-50. Fax 04-93-38-37-08. 181 units. A/C MINIBAR TV TEL. 550F–800F ($93.50–$136) double; from 1,500F ($255) suite. AE, DC, MC, V. From Cannes, follow the signs to Montfleury or the blue-and-white signs to the Radisson SAS Montfleury.

Few other hotels in Cannes have been through as many renovations and changes as this one, and at press time it was being radically upgraded into a four-star Radisson SAS. Although it seems distant from the crush of Cannes, it's actually only a short but winding drive away. The modern palace shares a 10-acre park with a sports complex. The magnificent curved pool has a sliding roof and is surrounded by palms. Other facilities include 11 tennis courts (many lit for night play), a volleyball court, a sauna, massage facilities, and a gymnasium, plus two restaurants. The guest rooms are stylishly filled with all the modern conveniences, including bedside controls, luxury mattresses, and thick towels and hair dryers in the well-appointed bathrooms.

Sofitel Mediterranée. 2 Bd. Jean-Hibert, 06400 Cannes. ☎ **800/221-4542** in the U.S., or 04-92-99-73-00. Fax 04-92-99-73-29. 149 units. A/C MINIBAR TV TEL. 1,095F–1,500F ($186.15–$255.85) double, from 2,360F ($401.20) suite. Rates include breakfast. AE, DC, MC, V. Parking 95F ($16.15). Bus: 1.

On the harborfront of Cannes, with views that extend over some of the most expensive private yachts in the Mediterranean, this seven-story chain hotel has surrounding balconies and an open-air swimming pool on its top floor. A remake of an older hotel, it has a well-designed, bright interior, offering a well-trained staff and contemporary-looking upscale bedrooms, some with views over the sea, and well-designed bathrooms with thick towels.

Dining/Diversions: The most formal of two restaurants is La Mediteranée, serving a gastronomic cuisine that specializes in fish and shellfish. Less expensive is Chez Panisse, a bistro that specializes in spit-cooked fish and meats.

Amenities: Roof swimming pool with its own bar.

MODERATE

Hôtel Splendid. Allée de la Liberté (4 and 6 rue Félix-Faure), 06400 Cannes. ☎ **04-93-99-53-11.** Fax 04-93-99-55-02. 64 units. A/C TV TEL. 612F–1,092F ($104.05–$185.65) double; 1,200F–1,500F ($204–$255) suite. Rates include continental breakfast. AE, DC, MC, V. Parking 40F ($6.80).

This is a good, conservative choice—a favorite of academicians, politicians, actors, and musicians. Opened in 1871, it's one of the oldest hotels at the resort. An ornate white building with sinuous wrought-iron accents and an old-fashioned staff, the Splendid looks out onto the sea, the old port, and a park. The rooms boast antique furniture and paintings as well as videos; about half of them have kitchenettes. The more expensive rooms have sea views. Each comes with a good mattress and a small but efficient bathroom with a shower/tub combination.

Hôtel Victoria. Rond-point Duboys-d'Angers, 06400 Cannes. ☎ **04-93-99-36-36.** Fax 04-93-38-03-91. E-mail: hotelvicto@aol.com. 25 units. A/C MINIBAR TV TEL. 410F–1,250F ($69.70–$212.50) double. AE, DC, MC, V. Closed Nov–Dec. Parking 70F ($11.90).

The Victoria is a stylish modern hotel in the heart of Cannes. Nearly half the rooms have balconies overlooking the small park and the hotel pool; the best rooms have terraces. Period reproductions, bedspreads of silk, and padded headboards with quality mattresses evoke a boudoir quality in the rooms. Those facing the park cost a little more but are well worth it. Rooms come with refrigerators, and bathrooms have shower/tub combinations and hair dryers. After a day on the beach, guests congregate in the paneled bar with its comfortable couches and armchairs.

Primotel Canberra. 120 rue d'Antibes, 06400 Cannes. ☎ **04-93-38-20-70.** Fax 04-92-98-03-47. 45 units. A/C MINIBAR TV TEL. 520F–850F ($88.40–$144.50) double. AE, DC, V. Parking 50F ($8.50).

This hotel has a marvelous location between the deluxe Carlton and the Palais des Festivals, but seems little known. It's often booked during the festival by independent producers hoping to hit the big time. The rooms are well maintained, a blend of traditional and modern; those with southern exposure are sunnier and cost more. Size ranges from small to medium, but each comes with a good mattress plus a standard bathroom, often with shower/tub combination. Hair dryers are available from the reception. Breakfast is the only meal served, and limited parking is available by the hotel's small garden.

INEXPENSIVE

Hôtel Côté Sud. 6 rue Lecerf, 06400 Cannes. ☎ **04-93-38-69-54.** Fax 04-92-98-68-30. E-mail: cotesudg@aol.com. 15 units. A/C MINIBAR TV TEL. 440F–640F ($74.80–$108.80) double; 700F–900F ($119–$153) suite. AE, DC, MC, V. Parking 30F ($5.10).

Set on a quiet commercial street about 4 blocks from the seafront, this small hotel occupies the 2nd floor of a four-story apartment building built in the 1970s. In 1998, it was radically renovated and upgraded by its new owner, Brice Guëlle, who lives on the premises, keeping a tight grip on things. Bedrooms are clean and unpretentious. Breakfast is the only meal served, though three neighborhood bistros offer inexpensive fixed-price meals to guests (50F/$8.50 at lunch and 100F/$17 at dinner). It's a good value in an otherwise relatively expensive neighborhood.

Hôtel Les Charmettes. 47 rue de Grasse, 06400 Cannes. ☎ **04-93-39-17-13.** Fax 04-93-68-08-41. 15 units. A/C TV TEL. 300F–410F ($51–$69.70) double. AE, DC, MC, V.

This is a modern, somewhat boxy hotel near the center of Cannes, with a laissez-faire attitude about who checks in with whom. With one of the most liberal images in a very liberal town, it welcomes many gays and lesbians. As they say at the reception desk, "What else would you expect in France, the world's centerpiece of human rights?" Each soundproofed room is individually decorated in a tasteful style. Rooms were newly renovated in 1998. Though small, bathrooms are neatly arranged with adequate shelf space and medium-sized towels. Breakfast is the only meal served, though you can get drinks in the lobby. Be warned that the hotel doesn't have any parking facilities.

✪ **Hôtel de France.** 85 rue d'Antibes, 06400 Cannes. ☎ **04-93-06-54-54.** Fax 04-93-68-53-43. www.cannes.hotels.com/de-france. E-mail: hotel-france.cannes@wanadoo.fr. 33 units. A/C TV TEL. 390F–640F ($66.30–$108.80) double July–Aug; 350F ($59.50) double rest of year. AE, DC, MC, V. Closed Nov 20–Dec 25. Parking 30F ($5.10).

This centrally located hotel is 2 blocks from the sea. The rooms are functional but well maintained and reasonably comfortable with good mattresses. Most bathrooms contain a shower/tub combination, and all have hair dryers. Even the Michelin inspectors view this as one of the best of the affordable hotels in Cannes. You can sunbathe on the rooftop.

Hôtel de Provence. 9 rue Molière, 06400 Cannes. ☎ **04-93-38-44-35.** Fax 04-93-39-63-14. 30 units. A/C MINIBAR TV TEL. 400F–520F ($68–$88.40) double. AE, MC, V. Parking 50F ($8.50).

Built in the 1930s and renovated into its present uncluttered format in 1992, this small-scale, unpretentious hotel is a distinct contrast to its intensely stylish, huge competitors. Most of the rooms have private balconies, and many overlook the carefully tended shrubs and palms of the hotel's walled garden. Bedrooms are showing their age but still offer fine comfort, and for Cannes the place is a remarkable bargain. Each unit comes with quality mattresses and good linen on twin or double beds, and a small bath with a shower stall, but few amenities. In warm weather, breakfast is served under the vines and flowers of an arbor.

Hôtel Mondial. 77 rue d'Antibes and 1 rue Teïsseire, 06400 Cannes. ☎ **04-93-68-70-00.** Fax 04-93-99-39-11. 56 units. A/C TV TEL. 580F–800F ($98.60–$136) double. AE, DC, MC, V.

This modern hotel on a commercial street, with stores on its lower floor, is about a 3-minute walk from the beach. Three-quarters of its rooms have views of the water, and the others overlook the mountains and a street. The soft Devonshire-cream facade has a few small balconies. The attractive rooms are the draw here, with matching fabrics for the comfortable beds and draperies, and sliding mirror doors on wardrobes. Bathrooms, though small, are neatly organized, with hair dryers and mainly shower/tub combinations.

Hôtel Villa de l'Olivier. 5 rue des Tambourinaires, 064000 Cannes. ☎ **04-93-39-53-28.** Fax 04-93-39-55-85. 24 units. A/C TV TEL. 465F–715F ($79.05–$121.55) double. AE, DC, MC, V. Free parking.

Small, charming, and personalized, with a low-key management by the Schildknecht family, this well-positioned hotel was once a private villa. In the 1960s, it was transformed into a hotel, and a six-unit annex was built in the garden. Today, you'll find structures with lots of glass that overlook a kidney-shaped swimming pool, and a decor that has aspects of the French colonial tropics, with lots of potted plants and a breezy indoor-outdoor motif that is appealing and relaxing. Bedrooms are outfitted with fabric-covered walls, in different colors and patterns, with lots of Provençal accessories. Each comes with a reasonably comfortable mattress, usually on a double or twin bed. Bathrooms are small but tidily maintained, with adequate shelf space.

Hôtel Villa Toboso. 7 allée des Olivers (bd. Montfleury), 06400 Cannes. ☎ **04-93-38-20-05.** Fax 04-93-68-09-32. 12 units. A/C MINIBAR TV TEL. 250F–700F ($42.50–$119) double. AE, DC, V.

Adjacent to the largest sports center in Cannes, this former private villa has been transformed into a small, homey hotel. (In a romantic outburst, the former owner named it after the city in Spain where Cervantes's Don Quixote is said to have met Dulcinea.) The main lounge has a concert piano, and dancers from the neighboring Rosella Hightower School often frequent the place. Most of the personalized rooms have windows facing the garden, and some have terraces and kitchens. Beds have comfortable mattresses, and bathrooms are well kept, with adequate shelf space and shower stalls. There's a pool in the garden.

WHERE TO DINE
EXPENSIVE

✪ **La Palme d'Or.** In the Hôtel Martinez, 73 bd. de la Croisette. ☎ **04-92-98-74-14.** Reservations required. Main courses 180F–480F ($30.60–$81.60); fixed-price menus 295F ($50.15) Mon–Sat (lunch only) and 350F–580F ($59.50–$98.60). AE, DC, MC, V. Wed–Sun 12:30–2pm and 7:30–10:30pm (also Tues 7:30–10:30pm mid-June to mid-Sept). Closed Nov 20–Dec 20. FRENCH.

When the Taittinger family (of champagne fame) renovated their hotel, one of their primary concerns was to establish a restaurant that could rival the tough competition in Cannes. And they've succeeded. The light-wood-paneled, art-deco marvel has bay windows, a winter garden theme, and outdoor and enclosed terraces overlooking the pool, the sea, and La Croisette. Your meal will be artfully handled by Vincent Rouard, maître d'hôtel, and the Alsatian-born chef Christian Willer. Menu items change with the seasons but are likely to include warm foie gras with fondue of rhubarb; filets of fried red mullet with a beignet of potatoes, zucchini, and an olive-cream sauce; or a medley of crayfish, clams, and squid marinated in peppered citrus sauce. A modernized version of a Niçois staple includes three parts of a rabbit with rosemary sauce, fresh vegetables, and chickpea rosettes. The most appealing dessert is wild strawberries from nearby Carros, with a Grand Marnier-flavored nage and a "cream sauce of frozen milk." The service is sensitive, sophisticated, and worldly, without being stiff.

Le Royal Gray. In the Hôtel Gray-d'Albion, 38 rue des Serbes. ☎ **04-92-99-79-60.** Reservations required. Main courses 175F–195F ($29.75–$33.15); fixed-price menus 235F–350F ($39.95–$59.50). AE, DC, MC, V. Daily noon–2pm and 8–10:30pm. FRENCH.

This restaurant manages to be both cozy and grand, replete with leather chairs, late-19th-century colors of brown and bordeaux, and warm lighting. Michel Bigot's cuisine is subtle and sometimes surprisingly simple, not aiming for the cutting-edge cerebrality of the place's more innovative competitors. Examples are terrines of foie gras; smoked salmon with a "bouquet" of shrimp and sweet-and-sour quenelles; fricassée of lobster with creamy tarragon sauce; a risotto of scallops with Provençal herbs; roasted filets of John Dory with olives and baby mushrooms; a sauté of monkfish with shrimp; and grilled filet of beef with béarnaise sauce.

MODERATE

Gaston-Gastounette. 7 quai St-Pierre. ☎ **04-93-39-49-44.** Reservations required. Main courses 78F–450F ($13.25–$76.50); fixed-price menus 170F ($28.90) at lunch, 205F ($34.85) at dinner. AE, DC, MC, V. Daily noon–2pm and 7–11pm. Closed Dec 1–20. FRENCH.

This restaurant has the best views of the marina from its location in the old port. It has a stucco exterior with oak moldings and big windows and a sidewalk terrace surrounded by flowers. You can choose from three different bouillabaisses: from full-blown authentic stewpots that are meals in their own right to an appetizer version. Other choices include baby turbot with hollandaise sauce; filets of John Dory with wild mushrooms; an unusual broth composed in a style reminiscent of Japan, flavored with monkfish, saltwater salmon, and chives; and a succulent platter of fried mixed fish served with basil-flavored butter sauce. Profiteroles with hot chocolate sauce make a memorable dessert.

✪ La Mère Besson. 13 rue des Frères-Pradignac. ☎ **04-93-39-59-24.** Reservations required. Main courses 70F–140F ($11.90–$23.80); fixed-price menus 140F–170F ($23.80–$28.90) at dinner. AE, DC, MC, V. Mon–Sat 12:15–2pm and 7:30–10:30pm. FRENCH.

The culinary traditions of the late Mère Besson, who opened her restaurant in the 1930s, are carried on in one of Cannes's favorite places. Dishes are served up in great steaming portions; all are prepared with respect for Provençal traditions and skill. Most delectable is *estouffade Provençal* (beef braised with red wine and rich stock flavored with garlic, onions, herbs, and mushrooms). You can also sample an old-fashioned platter with codfish, fresh vegetables, and dollops of the famous garlic mayonnaise (aïoli) that Provence produces by the tubful. Other specialties are fish soup, a *bourride Provençale* (a form of thick fish and vegetable stew), and shoulder of lamb with Provençal herbs and purée of garlic.

Le Festival. 55 bd. de la Croisette. ☎ **04-93-38-04-81.** Reservations required. Main courses 150F–300F ($25.50–$51); fixed-price from 195F ($33.15). AE, DC, V. Daily 11:30am–3pm and 7:30–10pm. Closed Nov 20–Dec 26. FRENCH.

Screen idols and sex symbols flood the front terrace of this place during the film festival. Almost every chair is emblazoned with the name of a movie star (whose bottoms may or may not have graced it), and tables here are among the most sought-after in town. You can choose from the Restaurant or the less formal Grill Room. Meals in the Restaurant may include bourride Provençale, *soupe des poissons* with rouille, simply grilled fresh fish (perhaps with aïoli), bouillabaisse with lobster, pepper steak, and sea bass flambéed with fennel. Items in the Grill are more in the style of an elegant brasserie, served a bit more rapidly and without as much fuss but at more or less the same prices. An appropriate finish in either section might be a smoothly textured peach Melba, invented by Escoffier.

Le Relais des Semailles. 9 rue St-Antoine. ☎ **04-93-39-22-32.** Reservations required. Main courses 160F–185F ($27.20–$31.45); fixed-price menus 180F–280F ($30.60–$47.60). AE, DC, MC, V. Daily 7:30–11:30pm. FRENCH.

This long-enduring favorite is reason enough to visit Le Suquet, Cannes's old town. The casual atmosphere is complemented by the food, based on available local ingredients. Stuffed pigeon and roasted slices of foie gras are typical dishes, and the vegetables are always beautifully prepared. Try, if featured, their salad of wild greens (mâche) with truffles—sublime. The grilled sea bass is perfectly fresh and aromatically seasoned with herbs. Depending on what looked good at the market that day, the chef might be inspired to, say, whip up a rabbit salad with tarragon *jus*. The setting is intimate, offering casual dining out on the terrace or in air-conditioned comfort.

INEXPENSIVE

Au Bec Fin. 12 rue du 24-Août. ☎ **04-93-38-35-86.** Reservations required. Main courses 45F–60F ($7.65–$10.20); fixed-price menus 90F–115F ($15.30–$19.55). AE, DC, MC, V. Tues–Sat noon–2:30pm and 6–10:30pm, Mon noon–2:30pm. Closed Dec 15–Jan 15. FRENCH.

On a street halfway between the train station and the beach, this 1880s bistro has little decor—sometimes red carnations are brought in from the fields to brighten the tables—but offers especially good food. A typical meal might include salade Niçoise, the house specialty; then *caneton* (duckling) with *cèpes* (flap mushrooms); and finally a choice of cheese and dessert.

La Villa. 7 rue Marceau. ☎ **04-93-38-79-73.** Reservations recommended. Main courses 95F–150F ($16.15–$25.50); set-price menus 180F–260F ($30.60–$44.20). AE, DC, MC, V. Daily 8pm–4am (till 5am during the Film Festival). FRENCH.

Sophisticated, urbane, and permissive, this restaurant also has a bar and a dance floor where patrons can dance and drink till long, long after the usual dinner hour, and even arrive for a meal long after everything else in Cannes is closed. The interior has trompe l'oeil and ornate plaster ceilings, and an outdoor terrace accented with decorative columns and the smell of night-flowering vines. The menu is not terribly long, but it's well-chosen and filled with the kind of food that stars, starlets, movie-industry wannabes, and the merely rich can nibble and never feel guilty about. Examples include a diet-conscious array of grilled fish; a platter with shrimp and scallops; and filets of beef garnished either with morels or foie gras. There's sometimes live music presented here, supplementing a regime of recorded music. If you opt to come in here just for a drink, expect to pay from around 50F ($8.50) for a beer, and from around 70F ($11.90) for a whiskey with soda.

Le Caveau 30. 45 rue Félix-Faure. ☎ **04-93-39-06-33.** Reservations required. Main courses 85F–350F ($14.45–$59.50); fixed-price menus 117F–168F ($19.90–$28.55). AE, DC, MC, V. Daily noon–2:15pm and 7–11pm. FRENCH/SEAFOOD.

The emphasis in this place, specializing in fine cuisine, is fresh seafood. Begin with a seafood platter and follow with one of the chef's classic dishes, pot-au-feu "from the sea" or shellfish paella. Bouillabaisse is the classic dish, of course, but you may prefer a *filet au poivre* (pepper steak) or even fresh pasta. The 1930s decor, air-conditioning, and terrace all make dining a pleasant experience.

Le Marais. 9 rue du Suquet. ☎ **04-93-38-39-19.** Reservations recommended. Main courses 80F–130F ($13.60–$22.10); fixed-price menu 125F ($21.25). CB, V. Tues–Sun 7:30–11pm. FRENCH.

The most successful gay restaurant in Cannes, this draws a crowd of mostly gay men dining as couples or groups, sometimes with an entourage from the world of fashion or entertainment. The setting is a warm and appealing mix of Parisian and Provençal, with paneled walls and a bustling terrace that in its way is one of the most sought-after outdoor venues in town. Menu items are conservative and not particularly experimental—ravioli of duck meat, a mixed fish platter, or jumbo shrimp fried with garlic.

✪ **Le Monaco.** 15 rue du 24-Août. ☎ **04-93-38-37-76.** Reservations required. Main courses 50F–90F ($8.50–$15.30); fixed-price menus 90F–115F ($15.30–$19.55). MC, V. Mon–Sat noon–2:30pm and 7–10:30pm. Closed Nov 10–Dec 10. FRENCH/ITALIAN.

Restaurant tabs on La Croisette often resemble the annual budget of an Ivory Coast country. But believe it or not, pricey Cannes has working people who have to eat, and they often go to Le Monaco, a blue-collar place with great food served bistro style. The likeable ambience features closely placed tables, clean napery, and a staff dressed in bistro-inspired uniforms. Menu choices include osso buco with sauerkraut, spaghetti bolognese, paella, couscous, roast rabbit with mustard sauce, mussels, trout with almonds, and minestrone with basil. Another specialty is grilled sardines, which many restaurants won't serve anymore, considering them too messy and old-fashioned.

CANNES AFTER DARK

On the eighth floor (seventh in France) of the Hôtel Carlton Intercontinental, 58 bd. de la Croisette, is **Le Carlton Casino Club** (☎ 04-93-68-00-33). Considerably smaller than its major competitor (the Casino Croisette), its modern decor nonetheless draws many devotees. Jackets are required for men, and a passport or government-issued identity card is required for admission. It's open daily from 7:30pm to 4am; however, access to the slot machines is from noon daily. Admission is 70F ($11.90).

The largest and most legendary casino in Cannes is the **Casino Croisette,** in the Palais des Festivals, 1 jetée Albert-Edouard, near promenade de la Croisette (☎ 04-93-38-12-11). Within its glittering confines, you'll find all the roulette and blackjack you'd expect. Entrance into the more glamorous gaming rooms incurs a fee of 70F ($11.90). Men are required to wear a jacket, and all guests must present their passport or identity card. The gaming room is open from 5pm till 4 or 5am. For a more casual spot of gambling, slot machines are also available from 11am until closing. Entrance is free and the dress code is far more relaxed. The casino also has one of the best nightclubs in town, **Jimmy's de Régine** (☎ 04-93-68-00-07). Jimmy's is open Wednesday to Sunday from 11pm to dawn. Admission is 100F ($17) and includes a drink.

Less formal discos include **Jane's Club,** in the cellar of the Hôtel Gray-d'Albion, 38 rue des Serbes (☎ 04-92-99-79-79), where male clients in a wide range of ages tend to wear jackets and ties. At this writing, the hippest and most consistently in demand is **Le Cat-Corner,** 22 rue Macé (☎ 04-93-39-31-31), where a multicultural blend of very hip night owls, most under 35, come to dance, drink, talk, and flirt.

Gays and lesbians will feel especially comfortable in **Le Vogue,** 20 rue du Suquet (☎ 04-93-39-99-18), a bar and gay disco that's open Tuesday to Sunday from around 9pm till 2:30am. Another option for gays is **Disco Le Sept,** 7 rue Rouguière (☎ 04-93-39-10-36), where a dance floor is available simultaneously with two drag shows, each lasting 2 hours, that begin every night at 11:30pm and 2am. Entrance is free, but drinks begin at 70F ($11.90) each. Attracting an older, somewhat more conservative crowd of mostly gay men, you'll find the **Zanzi-Bar Pub,** La Pantiéro, rue Félix Faure (no phone), opposite Vieux Port.

9 Grasse

563 miles (906.06km) S of Paris, 11 miles (17.70km) N of Cannes, 6 miles (9.66km) NW of Mougins

Grasse, a 20-minute drive from Cannes, is the most fragrant town on the Riviera, though it *looks* tacky modern. Surrounded by jasmine and roses, it has been the capital of the perfume industry since the days of the Renaissance. It was once a famous resort, attracting such royalty as Queen Victoria and Princess Pauline Borghese, Napoléon's promiscuous sister.

Today, some three-quarters of the world's essences are produced here from foliage that includes violets, daffodils, wild lavender, and jasmine. It takes 10,000 flowers to produce 2.2 pounds of jasmine petals; almost a ton of petals is needed to distill 1½ quarts of essence. These figures are important to keep in mind when looking at that high price tag on a bottle of perfume.

ESSENTIALS

GETTING THERE   Buses arrive from Cannes daily at 30- or 60-minute intervals (trip time: 45 min.); one-way fare is 20F ($3.40). About 30 buses a day arrive from Nice (trip time: 60 min.); one-way fares are around 38F ($6.45). Buses disembark at the **Gare Routière,** avenue Thiers (☎ **04-93-36-37-37**), a 10-minute walk north of the town center.

VISITOR INFORMATION   The **Office de Tourisme** is in the Palais des Congrès, 22 Cours Honoré Cresp (☎ **04-93-36-66-66**).

SEEING THE SIGHTS

A market for fruits and vegetables from the surrounding hills, **Marché aux Aires,** is conducted in the place aux Aires every Tuesday to Sunday from 8am to noon.

PERFUME FACTORIES

Parfumerie Fragonard. 20 bd. Fragonard. ☎ **04-93-36-44-65.** Free admission. Summer, daily (including holidays) 9am–6:30pm; off-season, Mon–Sat 9am–12:30pm and 2–6pm.

One of the best-known perfume factories, it's named after the famous 18th-century French painter. This factory is the best one to visit. An English-speaking guide will show you how "the soul of the flower" is extracted. After the tour, you can explore the museum of perfumery, which displays bottles and vases that trace the industry back to ancient times. Of course, if you're shopping for perfume and want to skip the tour, that's okay.

Parfumerie Molinard. 60 bd. Victor-Hugo. ☎ **04-93-36-01-62.** Free admission. May–Sept, daily 9am–6:30pm; Oct–Apr, 9am–12:30pm and 2–6pm.

Another popular place is this firm, well known in the United States; its products are sold at Saks, Neiman Marcus, and Bloomingdale's. In the factory, you can witness the extraction of the essence of the flowers, and the process of converting flowers into essential oils is explained in detail. You'll discover why turning flowers into perfume has been called a "work of art" and you can admire a collection of antique perfume-bottle labels as well as see a rare collection of perfume *flacons* (bottles) by Baccarat and Lalique.

MUSEUMS

Musée d'Art et d'Histoire de Provence. 2 rue Mirabeau. ☎ **04-93-36-01-61.** Admission 20F ($3.40) adults, 10F ($1.70) children 8 to 16, free for children 7 and under. June–Sept, daily 10am–7pm; Oct–May, Wed–Sun 10am–noon and 2–5pm.

This museum is in the Hôtel de Clapiers-Cabris, built in 1771 by Louise de Mirabeau, marquise de Cabris and sister of Mirabeau. The collection includes paintings, four-poster beds, marquetry, ceramics, brasses, kitchenware, pottery, urns, and archaeological finds.

Musée International de la Parfumerie. 8 place de Cours. ☎ **04-93-36-80-20.** Admission 12.50F ($2.15) adults, 10F ($1.70) students and children. Dec–Oct, daily 10am–noon and 2–5pm. Closed Nov.

This museum will teach you even more than you may want to know about perfume—for example, you learn that it takes a metric ton of flowers to make 1 gram of fragrance. You can also see interesting, often bizarre, exhibits relating to the perfume industry. One of the most fascinating on the second floor displays a 3,000-year-old mummy's perfumed hand and foot. Apparently, the flesh stayed preserved over the centuries because of the perfuming process. In the fourth floor greenery, you can smell some of the base elements that go into the creation of celebrated perfumes. Was that Elizabeth Taylor we saw whiffing and sniffing, perhaps trying to come up with some new exotic fragrance?

Villa Fragonard. 23 bd. Fragonard. ☎ **04-93-36-01-61.** Admission 20F ($3.40) adults, 10F ($1.70) children under 16; exhibitions 25F ($4.25) adults, 12.50F ($2.15) children under 16. June–Sept, daily 10am–7pm; Oct–May, Wed–Sun 10am–noon and 2–5pm. Closed holidays.

Jean-Honoré Fragonard was born in Grasse in 1732. The villa's collection includes his paintings as well as the paintings of other members of his family—his sister-in-law, Marguerite Gérard, his son, Alexandre, and his grandson, Théophile. The grand staircase was decorated by Alexandre.

WHERE TO STAY

Hôtel La Bellaudière. 78 Rte. de Nice, 06130 Grasse. ☎ **04-93-70-42-01.** 17 units. TEL. 200F–390F ($34–$66.30) double. AE, DC, MC, V. Closed Nov 15–Dec 28. Free parking.

This hotel is in a stone-sided farmhouse whose foundations go back 400 years, 2 miles north of the town center. The cost-conscious, completely unpretentious hotel is run by Fréderique and Phillippe Maure. Bedrooms are simple but severely dignified, outfitted with Provençal motifs and accessories. Each has a medium-quality but comfortable mattress, and tiled bathrooms with small, relatively thin towels. There's a view of the sea from many of the bedrooms, a garden terrace lined with flowering shrubs, and a sense of friendly cooperation from the hosts.

Hôtel Panorama. 2 place du Cours, 06130 Grasse. ☎ **04-93-36-80-80.** Fax 04-93-36-92-04. 36 units. MINIBAR TV TEL. 300F–480F ($51–$81.60) double. AE, MC, V. Parking 25F ($4.25).

Built in 1984 in the commercial center, this hotel has a facade in a sienna hue that its owners call "Garibaldi red." The more expensive rooms have balconies, southern exposures, and views of the sea; 20 have air-conditioning. Furnishings are basic and simple, although all the mattresses are reasonably comfortable. Bathrooms are small, tiled, and well kept. There's no bar or restaurant, but food is brought to your room on request, and the staff is cooperative and hardworking.

WHERE TO DINE

✪ **La Bastide St-Antoine (Restaurant Chibois).** 48 av. Henri-Dunant. ☎ **04-93-70-94-94.** Reservations recommended. Main courses 170F–280F ($28.90–$47.60); fixed-price menus 230F ($39.10; Mon–Sat lunch) and 550F–700F ($93.50–$119). AE, MC, V. Daily noon–2pm and 8–10:30pm. FRENCH/PROVENÇAL.

The renown that this restaurant has gained since it opened in 1996 is viewed with amazement and envy by every restaurateur in France. It occupies a 200-year-old Provençal farmhouse surrounded by 7 acres of stately trees and verdant shrubberies. What intrigued the French press was the elevation to superstardom of Jacques Chibois, formerly employed in the dining room of Cannes's Hôtel Gray-d'Albion. His fame came in 1997 with awards lavished on him by the controversial Gault-Millau group.

With a hardworking team directed by the maître d'hôtel Hervé Domenge, the restaurant serves a sophisticated array of dishes that aren't so much composed as "harmonized"—at least according to Domenge. To begin, you might try a salad of red snapper with parsley, Provençal vegetables, and olive oil; or a slice of braised foie gras with a "pyramid" of artichokes and a dollop of terrine of foie gras. Main courses to look for are butterflied crayfish with a chiffonnade of basil; a pan-fried medley of exotic mushrooms and truffles; red mullet with *chayote* (a confit of lemons and fresh thyme); and an exotic recipe for veal chops cooked in laurel leaves and flavored with sherry and a *pain perdu* of eggplant and dried flap mushrooms. Dessert might be sliced apples in puff pastry with a caramel sauce or frozen rhubarb flavored with oranges, wild strawberries, and rhubarb sorbet.

In 1998, the owners added eight rooms and three suites, outfitted in a whimsical and idiosyncratic Provençal style. Each has air-conditioning, minibar, TV, telephone, upscale furnishings, and exceptionally comfortable beds. Doubles cost from 1,000F to 1,200F ($170 to $204); suites from 1,600F to 1,800F ($272 to $306). Free parking is available.

Restaurant Amphitryon. 16 bd. Victor-Hugo. ☎ **04-93-36-58-73.** Reservations recommended. Main courses 95F–160F ($16.15–$27.20); fixed-price menus 127F–254F ($21.60–$43.20). AE, DC, MC, V. Mon–Sat noon–1:30pm and 7:30–9:30pm. Closed Aug 1–Sept 1 and Dec 23–31. FRENCH.

Many of the buildings that line this street, including the premises of this restaurant, were stables in the 19th century. Today, amid fabric-covered walls and soothing grays and off-whites, you can enjoy the flavorful cuisine of Michel André. The food is inspired by southwestern France, with plenty of foie gras and duckling as well as lamb roasted with thyme. A ragout of fish in red wine has in recent years become one of the chef's most popular dishes. Also recommendable are the Mediterranean fish soup with Provençal rouille and virtually any of the autumn dishes enhanced with seasonal fresh mushrooms.

10 Mougins

561 miles (902.84km) S of Paris, 7 miles (11.27km) S of Grasse, 5 miles (8.05km) N of Cannes

This once-fortified town on the crest of a hill provides an alternative for those who want to be near the excitement of Cannes but not in the midst of it. Picasso and other artists appreciated these rugged, sun-drenched hills covered with gnarled olive trees. Picasso arrived in 1936, and in time was followed by Jean Cocteau, Paul Eluard, and Man Ray. Picasso decided to move here permanently, choosing as his refuge an ideal site overlooking the Bay of Cannes near the Chapelle Notre-Dame de Vie, which Winston Churchill once painted. Here he continued to work and spent the latter part of his life with his wife, Jacqueline. Fernand Léger, René Clair, Isadora Duncan, and even Christian Dior have lived at Mougins.

Mougins is the perfect haven for those who feel that the Riviera is overrun, spoiled, and overbuilt. It preserves the quiet life very close to the international resort. The wealthy come from Cannes to golf here. Though Mougins looks serene and tranquil, it's actually part of the industrial park of Sophia Antipolis, a technological center where more than 1,000 national and international companies have offices.

ESSENTIALS

GETTING THERE   Mougins has a limited daily bus service on the route from Cannes to Grasse. It stops in Mougins at Val de Mougins, about a 10-minute walk from the center. Fares from Cannes are about 22F ($3.75) each way. For information about departure times and schedules, call **Rapides–Côte-d'Azur** (☎ 04-92-96-88-88), or call 04-93-39-31-37. The easier way to get here is just to pay about 125F ($21.25) for a taxi northward from Cannes.

VISITOR INFORMATION   The **Office de Tourisme** is at 15 av. Jean-Charles-Mallet (☎ **04-93-75-87-67**).

SEEING THE SIGHTS

For a preview of the history of the area, the **Musée Municipal,** place du Commandant Lamy (☎ **04-92-92-50-42**), is in the Sant Bernardin Chapel, built in 1618. It's open

Monday to Friday from 10am to noon and 2 to 6pm (closed November). Admission is free.

You can also visit the **Chapelle Notre-Dame de Vie,** Chemin de la Chapelle, a mile southeast of Mougins. The chapel, once painted by Churchill, is more famous for the priory next door where Picasso spent the last 12 years of his life. The chapel was built in the 12th century as a place where stillborn babies could be brought to be baptized. It was reconstructed in 1646. It's open only during Sunday mass between 9 and 10am. The priory is still a private home occupied intermittently by the Picasso heirs.

Musée de l'Automobiliste. Aire des Bréguières. ☎ **04-93-69-27-80.** Admission 40F ($6.80) adults, 25F ($4.25) children 11 and under. July–Aug, daily 10am–7pm; Sept–June, daily 10am–6pm. Closed Nov.

This museum is ranked seventh in the list of cultural sights on the Côte d'Azur. Founded in 1984 by Adrien Maeght, this ultramodern concrete-and-glass structure houses temporary exhibitions, but also owns one of Europe's most magnificent collections of original and prestigious automobiles—more than 100 vehicles from 1894 to the present.

WHERE TO STAY

Note that **Le Moulin de Mougins** (see "Where to Dine," below) offers charming rooms and suites.

Manoir de l'Etang. Aux Bois de Font-Merle, allée du Manoir, 06250 Mougins. ☎ **04-93-90-01-07.** Fax 04-92-92-20-70. 16 units. TV TEL. 600F–1,000F ($102–$170) double; 1,350F–1,600F ($229.50–$272) apt. AE, MC, V. Closed Nov–Feb.

Housed in a 19th-century Provençal building in the midst of olive trees and cypresses, this is a choice place to stay. It boasts all the romantic extras, including "love goddess" statuary in the garden and candlelit dinners around a pool, but it still charges reasonable rates. The rooms are bright and modern—you'll feel almost as if you're staying in a private home, which this place virtually is. Some rooms are extremely spacious. All have quality mattresses and fine linen, and bathrooms are well maintained, with shower/tub combinations and adequate shelf space. In winter, meals are served around a wood-burning fireplace. The chef bases his menu on the freshest ingredients available in any season. Set-price lunches, with wine included, cost from 150F to 170F ($25.50 to $28.90). Set-price dinners, without wine, cost from 150F to 190F ($25.50 to $32.30).

Mas Candille. Bd. Rebuffel, 06250 Mougins. ☎ **04-93-90-00-85.** Fax 04-92-92-85-56. www.oda.fr/aa/mas-candille. 24 units. A/C MINIBAR TV TEL. 980F–1,500F ($166.60–$255) double; from 1,800F ($306) suite. AE, DC, MC, V. Closed Nov to mid-Mar.

This 200-year-old Provençal farmhouse was skillfully converted. The public rooms contain many 19th-century furnishings, and some open onto the gardens. The renovated guest rooms are cozy and tranquil, with traditional Provençal furnishings. They usually range in size from small to medium, each with a fine mattress on a double or twins. Bathrooms, though compact, are tidily maintained. The family managers are always willing to provide you with whatever you need to make your room more comfortable.

The dining room has elegant stone detailing and a massive fireplace with a timbered mantelpiece. The food is exceptional, with menus costing 185F to 270F ($31.45 to $45.90). Typical dishes are *soupe de poissons,* stuffed zucchini flowers, and braised sweetbreads with mushrooms. Fresh salads and light meals are available throughout the day. In good weather, lunch is served on the terrace; dinner is served on the terrace in summer only.

WHERE TO DINE

Brasserie de la Méditerranée. Place de la Mairie. ☎ **04-93-90-03-47.** Reservations recommended. Main courses 80F–200F ($13.60–$34); set menus 165F–198F ($28.05–$33.65). AE, DC, MC, V. Daily noon–2:30pm and 7–10:30pm. FRENCH.

This outfit adds a much-needed informality to the restaurant scene of a town noted for hyper-upscale gastronomy. Set within a modern building overlooking the village's main square, and outfitted in tones of pink and salmon, it specializes in the kind of cuisine you'd expect in a bustling brasserie in Lyons, but with a Provençal accent. Menu items include scallops with a balsamic vinaigrette; superb lobster served with a *barigoule* of artichoke hearts; sliced turbot in a white butter sauce; and veal saltimbocca (with ham).

L'Amandier de Mougins Café-Restaurant. Place du Commandant-Lamy. ☎ **04-93-90-00-91.** Reservations recommended. Main courses 70F–120F ($11.90–$20.40), fixed-price menus 140F–180F ($23.80–$30.60). AE, DC, MC, V. Daily noon–2:15pm and 8–10pm. NIÇOIS/PROVENÇAL.

The illustrious founder of this relatively inexpensive bistro is the world-famous Roger Vergé, whose much more expensive Moulin de Mougins is described below. Conceived as a mass-market satellite to its exclusive neighbor, it serves relatively simple platters in an airy stone house. The specialties are usually based on traditional recipes and may include a terrine of the elusive Mediterranean hogfish with lemon; a tartare of fresh salmon and a céviche of tuna with hot spices; magret of grilled duckling with honey sauce and lemons, served with undercooked polenta; and filets of farm-raised sea bass on a Moroccan-inspired ragout of vegetables and saffron-flavored potatoes.

Le Feu Follet. Place de la Mairie. ☎ **04-93-90-15-78.** Reservations required. Main courses 140F–160F ($23.80–$27.20); fixed-price menu 168F ($28.55). AE, MC, V. Tues–Sat noon–2pm and 7:30–10pm, Sun noon–2pm. FRENCH.

Beside the square in the old village, this restaurant has two roughly plastered rooms that always seem cramped and overcrowded, but the quality of the cuisine (and the affordable prices) make it a worthy choice. Only top-quality ingredients, the best in the market, go into the cooking. One longtime habitué, describing the Provençal vegetables served here, claimed they were "filled with the sun." Fancy sauces and over-preparation of dishes are never a factor, and the fresh herbs of Provence are used effectively. Typical dishes are baked filet of beef in red wine and butter, crayfish in lemon juice, and snails in garlic cream.

✪ Le Moulin de Mougins. Notre-Dame de Vie, 06250 Mougins. ☎ **04-93-75-78-24.** Fax 04-93-90-18-55. Reservations required. Main courses 190F–450F ($32.30–$76.50); fixed-price menus 250F–740F ($42.50–$125.80) at lunch, 520F–740F ($88.40–$125.80) at dinner. AE, DC, MC, V. Tues–Sun noon–2:15pm and 8–10pm. Closed Feb 12–Mar 12. FRENCH.

This place is the kingdom of Roger Vergé, the *maître cuisinier de France,* and is among France's top 20 restaurants. It's 4 miles from Cannes. A 10-foot-wide stone oil vat, with a wooden turnscrew and a grinding wheel, sits near the entrance. M. Vergé's specialties include *filets de rougets* (red mullet) with artichokes; *noisettes d'agneau* (lamb) de Sisteron with an eggplant cake in thyme-flavored sauce and *poupeton* (zucchini flowers) stuffed with a mixture of truffles and pulverized mushrooms, served with truffle-flavored butter sauce; fricassée of lobster with sweet wine, cream sauce, and sweet peppers; and pepper steak "à la Mathurin," with grapes, pepper, and brandy. Dessert might be a lemon soufflé. His forté is fish from the Mediterranean, bought fresh each morning. Monsieur Vergé lists a lot of fantastic, even historic wines but also has a good selection of local vintages.

The old mill offers four beautiful suites and three rooms, with air-conditioning, minibars, TVs, phones, and fax machines, decorated with French antiques. These rent for 800F to 1,300F ($136 to $221).

11 Golfe-Juan & Vallauris

567 miles (912.50km) S of Paris, 4 miles (6.44km) E of Cannes.

Napoléon and 800 men landed at Golfe-Juan in 1815 to begin his Hundred Days. Protected by hills, Golfe-Juan was also the favored port for the American navy, though it's primarily a family resort known for its beaches. It contains one notable restaurant: Chez Tétou.

The 1¼-mile-long R.N. 135 leads inland from Golfe-Juan to Vallauris. Once merely a stopover along the Riviera, Vallauris (noted for its pottery) owes its reputation to Picasso, who "discovered" it. The master came to Vallauris after World War II and occupied a villa known as "The Woman from Wales."

ESSENTIALS

GETTING THERE   Trains headed for Golfe-Juan's sleepy railway station on avenue de la Gare require transfers through Cannes. Fares from Cannes are around 10F ($1.70) each way. Call ☎ **08-36-35-35-35** for railway information and schedules. **RCA (Rapides Côte-d'Azur)** operates frequent buses from Cannes (trip time: 20 mins.) that cost 10F ($1.70) each way; and from Nice (trip time: 60 mins.) that cost 25F ($4.25) each way. Call ☎ **04-93-39-11-39** for information.

VISITOR INFORMATION   There's an **Office de Tourisme** at 84 av. de la Liberté in Golfe-Juan (☎ **04-93-63-73-12**) and another on square 8-Mai 1945 in Vallauris (☎ **04-93-63-82-58**).

SEEING THE SIGHTS

Landlocked Vallauris depends on the sale of tourist items and ceramics. Merchants selling the colorful wares line both sides of avenue Georges-Clemenceau, which begins at a point adjacent to the Musée Picasso and slopes downhill and southward to the edge of town. Some of the pieces displayed in these shops are in poor taste. In recent years, the almost-universal emphasis on the traditional rich burgundy color has been replaced with a wider variety geared to modern tastes.

On the place du Marché in Vallauris, near the site where Aly Khan and Rita Hayworth were married, you'll see Picasso's **Homme et Mouton** (Man and Sheep). The town council of Vallauris had intended to ensconce this statue in a museum, but Picasso insisted that it remain on the square "where the children could climb over it and the dogs water it unhindered."

Bordering place de la Liberation is a chapel of rough-hewn stone, shaped like a Quonset hut, containing the **Musée Picasso La Guerre et La Paix** (☎ **04-93-64-16-05**), and also the entrance to the 16th-century **Château de Vallauris** (same phone). Inside the château is a two-in-one museum, **Musée Alberto Magnelli** and the **Musée de la Céramique Moderne.** This trio of museums developed after Picasso decorated the chapel with two paintings: *La Paix* (Peace) and *La Guerre* (War), offering contrasting images of love and peace on the one hand and violence and conflict on the other. In 1970, a house painter gained illegal entrance to the museum one night and after whitewashing a portion of the original, substituted one of his own designs. When the aging master inspected the damage, he said, "Not bad at all." In July 1996, the site was enhanced with a permanent exposition devoted to the works of the Florentine-born Alberto Magnelli, a pioneer of abstract art whose first successes were acclaimed in 1915, and who died in 1971, 2 years before Picasso. The third section showcases ceramics, both traditional and innovative, from potters throughout the region. All three museums are open Wednesday to Monday from 10am to noon and 2 to 6pm. During July and August, they're open from 9am to 12:30pm and from 2 to 6:30pm. Admission costs 17F ($2.90) for adults and 8.50F ($1.45) for students and children 15 and under.

A DAY AT THE BEACH

Because of its position beside the sea, Golfe-Juan developed long ago into a warm-weather resort. The town's twin strips of beach are **Plages du Soleil** (east of the Vieux Port and the newer Port Camille-Rayon) and **Plages du Midi** (west of those two). Each stretches half a mile and is free, with the exception of small areas administered by concessions that rent mattresses and chaises and offer access to kiosks dispensing snacks and cold drinks. Regardless of which concession you select (on Plage du Midi, they sport names like **Au Vieux Rocher, Palma Beach,** and **Corail Plage;** on Plage du Soleil, **Plage Nounou** and **Plage Tétou**), you'll pay around 75F ($12.75) for a day's use of a mattress. Plage Tétou is associated with the upscale Chez Tétou (see "Where to Dine," below). If you don't want to rent a mattress, you can cavort unhindered anywhere along the sands, moving freely from one area to another. Golfe-Juan indulges bathers who remove their bikini tops, but in theory forbids nude sunbathing. Consequently, local beaches (along with most of the others along the Côte d'Azur) usually witness midsummer hordes of women who sunbathe, topless, and clad only in a G-string, beside the sea.

SHOPPING IN VALLAURIS

The **Galerie Madoura,** avenue de Georges et Suzanne Ramié (☎ 04-93-64-66-39), is the only shop licensed to sell Picasso reproductions. The master knew and admired the work of the Ramie family, who founded Madoura. The shop is open Monday to Friday from 10am to 12:30pm and 2:30 to 7pm (to 6pm October to March). Some of the reproductions are limited to 25 to 500 copies.

Other galleries to seek out are **Galerie 52,** 52 av. Georges-Clemenceau (☎ 04-93-63-10-12); **Galerie Jean Marais,** avenue des Martyrs-de-la-Résistance (☎ 04-93-63-85-74); and **Galerie Sassi-Milici,** 65 bis av. Georges-Clemenceau (☎ 04-93-64-65-71), displaying works by contemporary artists.

Market day at Vallauris takes place every Tuesday to Sunday from 7am to 12:30pm at **place de l'Homme au Mouton,** with its flower stalls and local produce. For a souvenir, you may want to visit a farming cooperative, **Cooperative Nérolium,** 12 av. Georges-Clemenceau (☎ 04-93-64-27-54). The cooperative produces such foods as bitter orange marmalade and quince jam; and such scented products as orangeflower water and rosewater. Another unusual outlet for local products is **Parfumerie Bouis,** 50 av. Georges-Clemenceau (☎ 04-93-64-38-27). Local glass, blown by artisans in and around the town, is available from **Creations GR,** 69 av. Georges Clemenceau (☎ 04-93-63-19-20).

La Boutique de l'Olivier, 52 av. Georges-Clemenceau (☎ 04-93-64-32-70), is a specialist in wood objects made of olive wood. These include pepper mills, salad servers, cheese boards, free-form bowls, and slatted bread-slicing boxes. A final place, **Terres à Terre,** 58 av. Georges-Clemenceau (☎ 04-93-63-16-80), is known for its culinary pottery, made of local clay. This is an excellent outlet for picking up earthenware pottery made of terra-cotta. Gratin dishes and casseroles are big sellers here, and have been since antiquity in this town.

WHERE TO DINE

Auberge du Relais Imperial. 21 rue Louis Chabrier. ☎ **04-93-63-70-36.** Reservations recommended. Main courses 78F–218F ($13.25–$37.05); set-price menus 125F–178F ($21.25–$30.25). MC, V. Tues–Sun noon–2pm, Tues–Sat 7:30–10pm; during July and Aug, Tues–Sun noon–2pm and daily 7:30–10pm. Closed Nov to mid-Dec. FRENCH/PROVENÇAL.

On a narrow, antique-looking street running parallel to the harborfront, this is an all-Provençal, cheerful restaurant that's outfitted with old-fashioned paneling and a scattering of regional antiques. It's a well-managed alternative to the high prices and off-hand grandeur of the also-recommended **Chez Tétou.** Menu items are savory and well prepared, including foie gras "with five perfumes"; Breton lobster in an herb-flavored crust; minced shrimp fried with parsley and garlic; and a roster of fresh fish such as *rascasse* (hogfish), monkfish, and sea bass. Bouillabaisse can be prepared at a price of 480F ($81.60) for two—about half the price of its counterpart at Chez Tétou—if it's ordered a day in advance.

✪ **Chez Tétou.** Av. des Frères-Roustand, sur la Plage, Golfe-Juan. ☎ **04-93-63-71-16.** Reservations required. Fixed-price menus 500F–700F ($85–$119); bouillabaisse 400F–480F ($68–$81.60). No credit cards. Daily noon–2:30pm and 8–10pm. Closed Nov–Apr. SEAFOOD.

In its own amusing way, this is one of the Côte d'Azur's most famous restaurants, capitalizing on the glittering *beau monde* who frequented it during the 1950s and 1960s. Retaining its Provençal earthiness despite its incredibly high prices, it has thrived in a white-sided beach cottage for more than 65 years. It still serves a bouillabaisse often remembered years later by diners. Other items on the deliberately limited menu are grilled sea bass with tomatoes Provençal, sole meunière, and several preparations of lobster—the most famous of which is grilled and served with lemon-butter sauce, fresh parsley, and a bed of Basmati rice. Appetizers are limited to platters of charcuterie (cold cuts) or several almost-perfect slices of fresh melon since most diners order the house specialty, bouillabaisse. Your dessert might be a special powdered croissant with "grandmother's jams" (winter) or a homemade raspberry and strawberry tart (summer).

12 Juan-les-Pins

567 miles (912.50km) S of Paris, 6 miles (9.66km) S of Cannes

This suburb of Antibes is a resort that was developed in the 1920s by Frank Jay Gould. At that time, people flocked to "John of the Pines" to escape the "crassness" of nearby Cannes. In the 1930s, Juan-les-Pins drew a chic crowd during winter. Today it attracts young Europeans from many economic backgrounds, in pursuit of sex, sun, and sea, in that order.

Juan-les-Pins is often called a honky-tonk town or the "Coney Island of the Riviera," but anyone who calls it that hasn't seen Coney Island in a long time. One newspaper writer called it "a pop-art Monte Carlo, with burlesque shows and nude beaches"—a description much too provocative for such a middle-class resort. Another newspaper writer said that Juan-les-Pins is "for the young and noisy." Even F. Scott Fitzgerald decried it as a "constant carnival." If he could see it now, he'd know that he was a prophet.

ESSENTIALS

GETTING THERE Juan-les-Pins is connected by train and bus to most other Mediterranean coastal resorts. From Nice, frequent trains arrive throughout the day (trip time: 30 min.). For **rail information** and schedules, call ☎ **08-36-35-35-35.** The train station is on avenue l'Esterel. Buses arrive from Nice and its airport at 40-minute intervals throughout the day. A bus leaves from Antibes at place Guynemer (☎ **04-93-34-37-60**) every 20 minutes during the day (trip time: 10 min.); one-way fares are 7F ($1.20). Buses disembark at an open-air parking spot, **La Régence,** beside the boulevard Poincaré (☎ **04-93-34-37-60**).

VISITOR INFORMATION The **Office de Tourisme** is at 51 bd. Charles-Guillaumont (☎ **04-92-90-53-05**).

SPECIAL EVENTS The 10-day **Festival International de Jazz** at the end of July attracts international artists. For information, contact the Office de Tourisme.

A DAY AT THE BEACH

Part of the success of Juan-les-Pins as a beach resort is the fact that its beaches actually have sand. **Plage de Juan-les-Pins** is the town's most central beach. Its sub-divisions, all public, include **Plage de la Salis** and **Plage de la Garoupe.** Many people opt to tote their own blankets, chairs, and picnic hampers, but you can rent a chaise with a mattress at the concessions operated by the major beachfront hotels; they cost 65F to 75F ($11.05 to $12.75). The chicest area is maintained by the Hôtel des Belles-Rives. Competitors more or less in the same category are **La Jetée** and **La Voile Blanche,** both opposite the tourist information office. Topless sunbathing is permitted, but total nudity is not.

WATER SPORTS

If you're interested in **scuba diving,** check with your hotel concierge or one of these companies: the **Spondyle Club,** 62 av. des Pins-du-Cap (☎ **04-93-61-45-45**); **Club de la Mer,** Port Gallice (☎ **04-93-61-26-07**); or **EPAJ,** embarcadère Courbet (☎ **04-93-67-52-59**). **Waterskiing** is available at virtually every beach in Juan-les-Pins, including one outfit that's more or less permanently located on the beach of the Hôtel des Belles-Rives. Ask any beach attendant or bartender where to find the waterskiing representatives who station themselves on the sands. The cost for a 10-minute session is about 150F ($25.50).

WHERE TO STAY
EXPENSIVE

Belles-Rives. 33 bd. Baudoin, 06160 Juan-les-Pins. ☎ **04-93-61-02-79.** Fax 04-93-67-43-51. E-mail: bellerives@atsat.com. 45 units. A/C MINIBAR TV TEL. 700F–3,090F ($119–$525.30) double; 4,480F–5,880F ($761.60–$999.60) suite. Half board 390F ($66.30) per person extra. AE, MC, V. Closed Oct–Mar. Free parking.

This is one of the Riviera's fabled addresses, on a par with the equally famous Juana, though the Juana boasts a somewhat superior cuisine. Once it was a holiday villa occupied by Zelda and F. Scott Fitzgerald, so it was the scene of many a drunken brawl. In the following years, it hosted the illustrious—the duke and duchess of Windsor, Josephine Baker, and even Edith Piaf. A certain 1930s aura still lingers. A major restoration was concluded in 1990, with less comprehensive upgrades at 2-year intervals since. Double-glazing and a new air-conditioning system help a lot. As befits a hotel of this age, rooms come in a variety of shapes and sizes, ranging from small to spacious, but each is fitted with a luxurious mattress on a double or set of twins. All the tiled bathrooms are spotlessly maintained and have shower/tub combinations, plus hair dryers and deluxe toiletries. The lower terraces are devoted to garden dining rooms and a waterside aquatic club with a snack bar/lounge and a jetty extending into the water. Dinners are served in the romantic setting at "La Terrasse" with a panoramic bay view. Set menus cost from 280F ($47.60) each. Lunches are stylish but somewhat less formal and offered in a setting overlooking the beach. Also on the premises are a private beach and a landing dock.

✪ **Hôtel Juana.** La Pinède, av. Gallice, 06160 Juan-les-Pins. ☎ **04-93-61-08-70.** Fax 04-93-61-76-60. 50 units. A/C TV TEL. 950F–2,450F ($161.50–$416.50) double; 1,600F–3,500F ($272–$595) suite. MC, V. Closed Nov–Mar. Parking 50F ($8.50).

This balconied art-deco four-star hotel, owned by the Barache family since 1929, is separated from the sea by the park of pines that gave Juan-les-Pins its name and that was so beloved by F. Scott Fitzgerald. The hotel has a private swimming club where you can rent a "parasol and pad" on the sandy beach at reduced rates. Nearby is a park with umbrella tables and shady palms. The hotel is constantly being refurbished, as reflected in the attractive rooms, with mahogany pieces, well-chosen fabrics, tasteful carpets, and large bathrooms in marble or tile imported from Italy. The rooms also have such extras as safes and (in some) balconies. Each is fitted with a quality mattress, and each bathroom comes with a hair dryer and thick towels. (We discuss La Terrasse restaurant below.) There's a bar in the poolhouse. Also on the premises are a private beach club, a heated marble outdoor pool with a solarium, and a verdant garden.

MODERATE

Hôtel des Mimosas. Rue Pauline, 06160 Juan-les-Pins. ☎ **04-93-61-04-16.** Fax 04-92-93-06-46. 34 units. MINIBAR TEL. 470F–680F ($79.90–$115.60) double. AE, MC, V. Closed Sept 30–Apr 30. From the town center, drive ¹/₄ mile west, following N7 toward Cannes.

This elegant 1870s-style villa sprawls in a tropical garden on a hilltop. Michel and Raymonde Sauret redesigned the interior with the help of an architect who trained in the United States. The decor is a mix of high-tech and Italian-style comfort, with antique and modern furniture. Rooms range in size from small to medium, and each comes with a fine mattress plus a compact tiled bathroom, most often with a shower/tub combination. There's a bar but no restaurant. The rooms have balconies. A pool is set, California style, amid huge palm trees. The hotel is fully booked in summer, so reserve far in advance.

Hôtel Le Pré Catelan. 22 av. des Palmiers, 06160 Juan-les-Pins. ☎ **04-93-61-05-11.** Fax 04-93-67-83-11. 18 units. TEL. 450F–550F ($76.50–$93.50) double. AE, DC, MC, V. Closed Nov–Feb.

In a residential area near the town park, this circa-1900 Provençal villa has a garden with rock terraces, towering palms, lemon and orange trees, large pots of pink geraniums, trimmed hedges, and outdoor furniture. The atmosphere is casual, the setting uncomplicated and unstuffy. The more expensive rooms have terraces; furnishings are durable and rather basic. Nonetheless, there is fine comfort here with soft mattresses and bathrooms that are tidily maintained and equipped with tubs and showers. Despite the setting in the heart of town, the garden here manages to provide a sense of isolation. No meals are served other than breakfast, as the place closed its faltering restaurant in 1996.

INEXPENSIVE

Hôtel Cecil. Rue Jonnard, 06160 Juan-les-Pins. ☎ **04-93-61-05-12.** Fax 04-93-67-09-14. 21 units. TV TEL. 220F–400F ($37.40–$68) double. MC, V. Closed Oct 15–Jan 1. Parking 50F ($8.50).

Located 50 yards from the beach, this small, well-kept hotel is one of the best bargains in Juan-les-Pins. The owner/chef Michel Courtois provides a courteous welcome and good meals beginning at 80F ($13.60). The rooms are well worn, yet clean. Mattresses are still comfortable after much use, and bathrooms are small with shower stalls and rather thin towels. In summer, you can dine on a patio.

Hôtel Le Passy. 15 av. Louis-Gallet, 06160 Juan-les-Pins. ☎ **04-93-61-11-09.** Fax 04-93-67-91-78. 35 units. TV TEL. 340F–600F ($57.80–$102) double. AE, DC, MC, V. Parking 35F ($5.95).

Centrally located, Le Passy opens onto a wide flagstone terrace. The other side faces the sea and coastal boulevard. The furnishings are Nordic modern, and the newer rooms have little balconies. Those that overlook the sea carry the higher price tag. Most rooms are small but have comfortable beds; each bathroom is compact and tidily maintained, with a hair dryer and a rack of medium-sized towels. In high-priced Juan-les-Pins, this is considered one of the more affordable choices, even though it's a bit sterile.

WHERE TO DINE

La Romana. 21 av. Dautheville. ☎ **04-93-61-05-66.** Pizzas 35F–55F ($5.95–$9.35); main-course salads and platters 50F–100F ($8.50–$17). DC, V. Daily noon–2:30pm and 7pm–midnight. Winter noon–2:30pm only. FRENCH/INTERNATIONAL.

Behind the town's casino, this is an aggressively unpretentious restaurant that successfully caters its trade to the thousands of budget-conscious holiday makers who flood the town every season. Don't expect grande cuisine, as the venue is too simple, too informal. What you'll get—amid a generic 1930s-style decor accented with touches of wrought iron—is pizzas, meal-sized salads, fried fish and fried scampi, grilled steaks with French fries, and *plats du jour* whose composition change every day.

✪ **La Terrasse.** In the Hôtel Juana, La Pinède, av. Gallice. ☎ **04-93-61-20-37.** Reservations required. Main courses 265F–395F ($45.05–$67.15); fixed-price menus 280F–650F ($47.60–$110.50) at lunch, 480F–650F ($81.60–$110.50) at dinner. AE, MC, V. July–Aug, daily 12:30–2pm and 7:30–10:30pm; Apr–June and Sept–Oct, Thurs–Tues 12:30–2pm and 7:30–10:30pm. Closed Nov–Mar. FRENCH/MEDITERRANEAN.

Bill Cosby loves this gourmet restaurant so much that he's been known to fly chef Christian Morisset and his Dalí mustache to New York to prepare dinner for him. Morisset, who trained with Vergé and Lenôtre, cooks with a light, precise, and creative hand. His cuisine is the best in Juan-les-Pins. The setting is lively and sophisticated, with a conservatively modern decor overlooking the verdant garden, and a glassed-in terrace whose roof opens for midsummer ventilation and a view of the stars. Menu items are steeped in flavors of Provence, and are served in a setting that's airy, sun-flooded, and chic. Examples include giant ravioles (Morisset is very specific and refers to them as *ravioles* and not *raviolis*) stuffed with fresh crayfish and an olive-flavored essence of shellfish; and a rack of lamb from the salt marshes of Pauillac cooked in a clay pot from nearby Vallauris, served with stuffed zucchini flowers and Provençal herbs. Dessert might include a Napoléon *(mille feuille)* of wild strawberries with a mascarpone cream sauce.

✪ **Le Bijou.** Bd. Charles-Guillaumont. ☎ **04-93-61-36-07.** Reservations recommended. Main courses 170F–450F ($28.90–$76.50); fixed-price menus 165F–280F ($28.05–$47.60); shellfish platters 270F ($45.90); bouillabaisse 330F ($56.10). AE, DC, MC, V. Daily noon–2:30pm and 7:30–10:30pm (to 11:30pm June to mid-Sept). FRENCH/PROVENÇAL.

This upscale brasserie has flourished beside the seafront promenade for almost 80 years. The marine-style decor includes lots of varnished wood and bouquets of blue and white flowers in a mostly blue-and-white interior. Windows overlook a private beach with less crowded sands than the public beaches nearby. Menu items are succulent, sophisticated, and less expensive than you'd expect. Examples are a version of bouillabaisse that might make you clamor for more, platters of grilled sardines, steamed mussels with sauce poulette (frothy cream sauce with herbs and butter), grilled John Dory with a vinaigrette enriched with a tapenade of olives and fresh basil, and a supersize *plateau des coquillages et fruits de mer* (shellfish). Don't confuse this informally elegant place with its beachfront terrace below. The terrace offers a lunch buffet to diners in swimsuits, which are strictly forbidden in the main restaurant. The terrace is open only from April to September, daily from noon to 4pm; the cost of the buffet is 70F ($11.90).

Le Perroquet. Av. Georges-Gallice. ☎ **04-93-61-02-20.** Reservations recommended. Main courses 80F–165F ($13.60–$28.05); fixed-price menus 140F–170F ($23.80–$28.90). MC, V. Daily noon–2pm and 7–11pm. Closed Nov–Dec 26. PROVENÇAL.

The cuisine is well presented and prepared, and the restaurant's ambience is carefully synchronized to the resort's casual and carnival-like summer aura. It's across from the Parc de la Pinède, and it's decorated with depictions of every imaginable form of parakeet, the restaurant's namesake. Look for savory versions of fish, at its best when grilled simply, with olive oil and basil, and served with lemons. A worthwhile appetizer is the *assortiment Provençale,* which includes tapenade of olives, marinated peppers, grilled sardines, and stuffed and grilled vegetables. Steaks might be served with green peppercorns or béarnaise sauce, and desserts include three types of pastries on the same platter.

JUAN-LES-PINS AFTER DARK

In this Rivera nightlife hot spot, the action reaches its frenzied height during the annual jazz festival. The **Festival International de Jazz** transpires for 10 days at the end of July, attracting stellar jazz masters and their devoted fans. Concerts are presented in a temporary stadium in Le Parc de la Pinède, custom built for the event every summer, and dismantled at the end of the festival. Tickets range from 110F to 200F ($18.70 to $34) and can be purchased at the Office de Tourisme (see "Essentials," above).

For starters, visit the **Eden Casino,** boulevard Baudoin in the heart of Juan-les-Pins (☎ **04-92-93-71-71**), and try your luck at the roulette wheel or at one of the slot machines (there's no admission charge to play the slot machines). The casino is open every day from 10am to 5pm. *Les grands jeux* (blackjack, roulette, and chemin de fer) are open daily from 8pm to 5am; the entrance fee is 70F ($11.90) per person.

At **Le Pam Pam,** route Wilson (☎ **04-93-61-11-05**), you can sip rum drinks in an exotic ambience created and celebrated by live reggae, Brazilian, and African performances of music and dance.

If you prefer high-energy spots, check out the town's many discos. The best are **Whisky à Gogo,** boulevard de la Pinède (☎ **04-93-61-26-40**), with its young trendsetters and pounding rock beat; the richly dramatic **Le Bureau,** avenue Georges-Gallice (☎ **04-93-67-22-74**), keeping the fast and frenzied beat going with anything from Latin salsa to disco; and **Le Village,** 1 bd. de la Pinède (☎ **04-93-61-18-71**), which boasts an action-packed dance floor and hip DJs spinning the latest from the international music scene. The cover charge at these clubs is a stiff 100F ($17).

For a more relaxed evening, go to the British pub **Le Ten's Bar,** 25 av. du Dr.-Hochet (☎ **04-93-67-20-67**), where you'll find 56 brands of beer and a sociable crowd of young and old. You could even choose the tranquil piano bar **Le Cambridge,** 25 rue du Dr.-Hochet (☎ **04-93-67-49-89**), with its older, more sophisticated crowd, or **Le Madison,** 1 av. Alexandre-III (☎ **04-93-67-83-80**), with the town's best jazz and blues.

13   Antibes & Cap d'Antibes

567 miles (912.50km) S of Paris, 13 miles (20.92km) SW of Nice, 7 miles (11.27km) NE of Cannes

On the other side of the Baie des Anges (Bay of Angels), across from Nice, is the port of Antibes. This old Mediterranean town has a quiet charm unique on the Côte d'Azur. Its little harbor is filled with fishing boats and pleasure yachts, and in recent years it has emerged as a new "hot spot." The marketplaces are full of flowers, mostly roses and carnations. If you're in Antibes in the evening, you can watch fishers playing the traditional Riviera game of *boule*.

Spiritually, Antibes is totally divorced from Cap d'Antibes, which is a peninsula studded with the villas and pools of the super-rich. In *Tender Is the Night*, F. Scott Fitzgerald described it as a place where "old villas rotted like water lilies among the massed pines." Photos of film and rock stars lounging at the Eden Roc have appeared in countless magazines.

ESSENTIALS

GETTING THERE   The railway station is in the place Pierre Semard. Trains from Cannes (trip time: 10 min.) and Nice (trip time: 18 min.) arrive every 30 minutes. One-way fares from Cannes are around 16F ($2.70); from Nice, 22F ($3.75). There's also a bus station, **La Gare Routière,** on the place Guynemer (☎ **04-93-34-37-60**), that receives buses from throughout Provence.

VISITOR INFORMATION   The **Office de Tourisme** is at 11 place du Général-de-Gaulle (☎ **04-92-90-53-00**).

SEEING THE SIGHTS

Musée Picasso. Place du Château. ☎ **04-92-90-54-20** for recorded message, or 04-92-90-54-26 for an attendant. Admission 30F ($5.10) adults, 18F ($3.05) students and ages 15 to 24 and over 60, free for children 14 and under. July–Sept, 10–11:50am and 2–5:50pm; Oct–June, Tues–Sun 10–11:50am and 2–4:50pm.

Housed in the ancient Château Grimaldi on the ramparts above the port is one of the world's greatest Picasso collections. Picasso came here after his bitter war years in Paris and stayed in a small hotel at Golfe-Juan until the museum director at Antibes invited him to work and live at the museum in 1946. Picasso spent a year painting here. When he departed, he gave the museum all the work he had done—24 paintings, 80 ceramics, 44 drawings, 32 lithographs, 11 oils on paper, 2 sculptures, and 5 tapestries. There is also a gallery of other modern artists—Léger, Miró, Ernst, and Calder, among others. Be warned in advance that some of these works might be in storage when you visit, based on whether a temporary exhibition is being displayed.

Musée Naval et Napoléonien. Batterie du Grillon, boulevard J.-F.-Kennedy. ☎ **04-93-61-45-32.** Admission 30F ($5.10) adults, 20F ($3.40) students, children 14 and under free. Mon–Fri 9:30am–noon and 2:15–6pm, Sat 9:30am–noon.

Anyone interested in the meteoric career of Napoléon Bonaparte should be intrigued by this museum. Its interesting collection of Napoleonic memorabilia includes naval models, paintings, and mementos. A toy soldier collection depicts various uniforms, including one used by Napoléon in the Marengo campaign. A wall painting on wood shows Napoléon's entrance into Grenoble; another tableau shows him disembarking at Golfe-Juan on March 1, 1815. In contrast to the Greek-god image of Napoléon in the famous paintings by Canova in the Louvre, a miniature pendant by Barrault reveals the Corsican general as he really looked, with pudgy cheeks and a receding hairline. In the rear rotunda is one of the many hats worn by the emperor. The museum is in a 17th to 18th century stone-sided fort and tower; the view of the coast from the top of the tower is worth the admission price.

WHERE TO STAY

VERY EXPENSIVE

✪ **Hôtel du Cap–Eden Roc.** bd. J.-F.-Kennedy, 06160 Cap d'Antibes. ☎ **04-93-61-39-01.** Fax 04-93-67-76-04. www.edenroc-hotel.fr. 140 units. A/C TEL. 1,800F–6,500F

($306–$1,105) double; 5,000F–7,000F ($850–$1,190) suite. No credit cards. Closed mid-Oct to Mar. Bus: A2.

Legendary for the glamour of both its setting and its clientele, this Second Empire hotel, opened in 1870, is surrounded by 22 splendid acres of gardens. It's like a great country estate, with spacious public rooms, marble fireplaces, scenic paneling, chandeliers, and richly upholstered armchairs. Rooms are among the most sumptuous on the Riviera, each a statement of the deluxe tastes of another era. Some guest rooms and suites have regal period furnishings. Beds are lush and plush with deluxe mattresses and elegant appointments. Marble bathrooms are roomy, offer deluxe toiletries, and have every amenity. Know in advance that there is much emphasis on clothing and style here, especially in the evening, but even around the pool. (The pool, blasted out of the cliffside at enormous expense, is one of the most famous on the Azure Coast.) The staff is well rehearsed, but regardless of how important you are, they can always claim they've dealt with bigger and more famous names. The world-famous Pavillon Eden Roc, near a rock garden apart from the hotel, has a panoramic Mediterranean view. Venetian chandeliers, Louis XV chairs, and elegant draperies add to the drama. Lunch is served on an outer terrace, under umbrellas and an arbor. Dinner specialties include bouillabaisse, lobster Thermidor, and sea bass with fennel. Lunches cost from around 400F ($68) each; and dinners from around 500F ($85).

EXPENSIVE

○ **Hôtel Imperial Garoupe.** 770 Chemin de la Garoupe, 06600 Antibes. ☎ **800/ 525-4800** or 04-92-93-31-61. Fax 04-92-93-31-62. www.imperial-garoupe.com. 34 units. A/C MINIBAR TV TEL. 1,250F–2,200F ($212.50–$374) double; 2,200F–4,500F ($374–$765) suite. AE, DC, MC, V. Free parking. Bus: A2.

One of the Riviera's newest upscale hotels, it is run by Gilbert Irondelle (son of the director of Antibes' Hôtel du Cap), who transformed it into a low-key and very charming pocket of posh that's a bit less intimidating than the hyper-chic, hyper-expensive hotel run by his father. A one-story building designed around a landscaped patio, with architectural elements that evoke both Tudor England and the deserts of Morocco, the hotel offers luxurious and comfortable bedrooms filled with oversized contemporary furnishings and lots of padded upholsteries. Bedrooms are generous in size and fitted with luxury mattresses on the plush beds. Marble or tile bathrooms have plenty of amenities, and a deluxe set of toiletries. The hotel, set within 50 yards of the beach, is the centerpiece of a 3½-acre park whose rows of pines block some of the sea views.

Dining/Diversions: Drinks are served wherever you want one, but there is no bar per se. Room service is available 24 hours a day. The in-house restaurant serves a French and international cuisine.

Amenities: A concierge provides information about diversions within the region.

MODERATE

Auberge de la Gardiole. Chemin de la Garoupe, 06160 Cap d'Antibes. ☎ **04-93-61- 35-03.** Fax 04-93-67-61-87. 20 units. MINIBAR TV TEL. 425F–525F ($72.25–$89.25) per person. Rates include half board. AE, MC, V. Closed Nov–Feb. Bus: A2.

Monsieur and Mme Courtot run this country inn with a delightful personal touch. The large villa, surrounded by gardens, is in an area of private estates. The charming rooms are on the upper floors of the inn and in the little buildings in the garden. They come in a variety of shapes and sizes, each furnished with a certain charm and an eye to comfort. Fifteen are air-conditioned. Bathrooms are small and compact. The cheerful dining room has a fireplace and hanging pots and pans, and in good weather you can dine under a wisteria-covered trellis. The owners buy the food and supervise its preparation; the cuisine is French/Provençal with fixed-price menus at 150F ($25.50).

Castel Garoupe. 959 bd. de la Garoupe, 06160 Cap d'Antibes. ☎ **04-93-61-36-51.** Fax 04-93-67-74-88. www.oda.fr/aa/castelgaroupe. 27 units. MINIBAR TV TEL. 685F–995F ($116.45–$169.15) apt for 2. Rates include continental breakfast. MC, V. Closed Nov 15–Mar 7. Bus: A2.

We highly recommend this Mediterranean villa, on a private lane in the center of the cape, because it offers spacious, tastefully furnished rooms, some equipped with kitchenettes. Accommodations are exceedingly comfortable, with fine mattresses, quality linens, and well-maintained, compact bathrooms. The hotel has private balconies, shuttered windows, and a tranquil garden. Facilities include a freshwater pool and a tennis court.

Hôtel Beau Site. 141 bd. J.-F.-Kennedy, 06150 Cap d'Antibes. ☎ **04-93-61-53-43.** Fax 04-93-67-78-16. 30 units. TV TEL. 360F–650F ($61.20–$110.50) double. AE, DC, V. Bus: A2.

This white stucco villa with a tile roof and heavy shutters is surrounded by eucalyptus trees, pines, and palms. Located off the main road, a 7-minute walk from the beach, it has a low wall of flower urns and wrought-iron gates. The interior is like a country inn, with oak beams and antiques. The guest rooms are comfortable and well maintained. Each comes with a good mattress, most often on twin or double beds. Bathrooms are small, usually with shower/tub combinations.

Hôtel Royal. Bd. du Maréchal-Leclerc, 06600 Antibes. ☎ **04-93-34-03-09.** Fax 04-93-34-23-31. 38 units. TEL. 395F–495F ($67.15–$84.15) double. Rates include half board. DC, MC, V. Closed Nov 2–Dec 18. Parking 35F ($5.95). Bus: A2.

Built 86 years ago, this is the oldest hotel in Antibes. The famous guests of yesterday, like novelist Graham Greene, have long since checked out, and celebrities now go elsewhere. But the Royal has done a good job of staying abreast of changing times. All of its bedrooms have been modernized. The furniture is undistinguished but the good mattresses are firm. Bathrooms have a tub or shower stalls, and each is supplied generously with towels. The Royal has its own private beach, a cafe terrace in front, two restaurants, and an English bar just off the lobby. Even if you're not a guest at the hotel, you can enjoy a meal at **Le Dauphin** (open April to October, daily from noon to 2:30pm and 7 to 10pm). Fixed-price menus run 130F to 300F ($22.10 to $51).

La Baie Doré. 579 bd. de la Garoupe, 06160 Cap d'Antibes. ☎ **04-93-67-30-67.** Fax 04-92-93-76-39. www.hotel-french-riviera.com. 17 units. A/C MINIBAR TV TEL. 900F–1,750F ($153–$297.50) double; 1,800F–2,600F ($306–$442) suite or duplex. Extra bed 250F ($42.50). AE, MC, V. Closed Nov to mid-Dec.

Set between the sea and the coastal road, this hotel appears to rise from the water like a series of boxy, interlocked rectangles, each capped with a terra-cotta roof and ringed with strategically positioned balconies and terraces. From its base, a pier jutting out to sea allows clients to swim and boat, despite the lack of a sandy beach nearby. On one terrace is a swimming pool. Public areas are dignified modern spaces with high ceilings, rectilinear lines, simple, summery furnishings, and big windows that seem to flood the interior with views of the nearby sea, almost as if you were aboard a yacht. Each room has a private terrace, contains a safe for valuables, and has comfortable mattresses. The upper-tier rooms have Jacuzzis. There's a restaurant, open daily for lunch and dinner, and bar on the premises, both of which sprawl outward onto a terrace.

INEXPENSIVE

Le Cameo. Place Nationale, 06600 Antibes. ☎ **04-93-34-24-17.** Fax 04-93-34-35-80. 8 units, 3 with shower only, 5 with bath. TV TEL. 300F ($51) double with shower only, 380F ($64.60) double with bath. MC, V. Closed Jan–Feb. Parking 35F ($5.95). Bus: A2.

On a historic square, this 19th-century Provençal villa is in the center of town. The rooms are old-fashioned and admittedly not for everyone—perhaps they are typical of the kind of place where Picasso might have stayed when he first hit town. Mattresses are well worn but still have comfort in them; plumbing is at a minimum, and towels rather thin. Locals gather in the bar and often eat in the adjacent home-style dining room with its bouquets of flowers and crowded tables. Lunches are snack-style: Platters cost from 35F to 50F ($5.95 to $8.50). More elaborate dinners, with set-price menus, are priced at around 150F ($25.50) each. Look for a simple setting here, and a goodwilled welcome from the accommodating staff.

WHERE TO DINE

La Bonne Auberge. Quartier de Brague, Rte. N7. ☎ **04-93-33-36-65.** Reservations required. Main courses 120F–170F ($20.40–$28.90); fixed-price menu 200F ($34). MC, V. Tues–Sun noon–2pm and 7–10pm. Closed mid-Nov to mid-Dec. Take the coastal highway (N7) 2½ miles from Antibes. FRENCH.

For many years after it opened in 1975, this was one of the most famous restaurants on the French Riviera. In 1992, when its founder, Jo Rostang, died, his culinary heir, Philippe Rostang, limited its scope and transformed it into a worthwhile but less ambitious restaurant. The fixed-price menu offers a wide selection. Choices vary but may include a Basque-inspired *pipérade* with poached eggs, sea wolf with soya sauce, savory swordfish tart, chicken with vinegar and garlic, and perch-pike dumplings Jo Rostang. Dessert might be an enchanting peach soufflé.

La Taverne du Saffranier. Place du Saffranier. ☎ **04-93-34-80-50.** Reservations recommended. Main courses 50F–80F ($8.50–$13.60); set-price menu 60F ($10.20). No credit cards. Tues–Sun noon–12:30pm and 7–10:30pm. PROVENÇAL.

Earthy, irreverent, and firmly entrenched in a century-old building in the Provençal motif, this cost-conscious brasserie trots out a changing medley of local specialties for a local clientele. Portions are savory and generous, and locals find it replete with associations from their real or imagined Provençal childhood. Examples include a platter of stuffed vegetables *(petits farcis)*; céviche or cold raw fish in hot sauce (particularly refreshing on a hot day); a savory version of fish soup; and grilled fish with only a dash of fresh lemon. The kitchens can also prepare their own version of bouillabaisse, but they require a day's advance notice.

Les Vieux Murs. Promenade de l'Amiral-de-Grasse. ☎ **04-93-34-06-73.** Reservations recommended. Main courses 100F–200F ($17–$34); fixed-price menu 200F ($34). AE, MC, V. Daily noon–2pm and 7:30–10pm. Closed Mon Oct–Apr. Bus: A2. FRENCH/SEAFOOD.

This charming Provençal tavern has a raffish kind of chic. It occupies a room inside the 17th-century ramparts that used to fortify the old seaport, not far from the Picasso Museum (see above). The space contains soaring stone vaults and a simple white-painted decor, with a glassed-in front terrace that offers a pleasant view of the water. Menu specialties are a warm salad of mullet, sophisticated arrays of crudités that reflect the bounty of the local harvest; artichoke hearts with a confit of tomatoes; and fresh filets of daurade, hogfish, sole, salmon, and red mullet prepared dozens of ways. Especially appealing is the roast chapon, a local seafish, with a simple but ultra-fresh fricassée of fresh vegetables and olive oil. Suzanne and Georges Romano often have more hungry diners than tables, so try to book early. Their fixed-price menu is one of the best values on the coast.

✪ **Restaurant de Bacon.** Bd. de Bacon. ☎ **04-93-61-50-02.** Reservations required. Fixed-price menus 250F–450F ($42.50–$76.50). AE, DC, MC, V. Tues–Sun 12:30–2pm and 8–10pm (open Mon dinner July–Aug). Closed Nov–Jan.

In a posh area, set on a rocky peninsula, this restaurant has a panoramic coast view. Bouillabaisse aficionados claim that Bacon offers the best version in France of this fish stew, conceived centuries ago as a simple fisher's supper and translated into one of the world's great dishes. In its deluxe version, saltwater crayfish float atop the savory brew, but we prefer the simple version, where a waiter adds the finishing touches at your table. You can also try the fish soup with traditional garlic-laden rouille sauce, fish terrine, sea bass, John Dory, or one of the exotic collection of fish unknown in North America—these include sar, pageot, and denti, prepared several ways. Fish dishes are priced by the gram (like lobster in America): A guideline is that light lunches cost around 250F to 400F ($42.50 to $68); substantial dinners go for 550F to 800F ($93.50 to $136).

The Eastern Riviera: From Biot to Monaco to Menton

At Biot, the Riviera continues east through a string of upscale resorts that embody the glamour of the **Côte d'Azur.** Several have been home to the 20th century's great writers and artists. Biot is no exception, with its museum dedicated to the art and life of long-time resident Fernand Léger. Set back from the coast, nearby Villeneuve-Loubet pays tribute to another art in the haute cuisine of Auguste Escoffier, the greatest chef ever to man a kitchen in a nation with a rich culinary heritage.

Farther into the foothills, many artisans live and work in Tourrettes-sur-Loup, where they sell their wares in small shops. Nearby Vence boasts Matisse's Chapelle du Rosaire, adorned by the masterful painter in his twilight years. The great artist is represented side by side with his contemporaries in St-Paul-de-Vence's Fondation Maeght, a museum as modern as the art it houses. Along the coast, Cagnes-sur-Mer continues the region's list of who's who in the 20th century—it was once home to Simone de Beauvoir, and contains Les Collettes, Renoir's final home.

Nice, the Riviera's capital and largest city, is one of the few budget-oriented resorts on the coast, making it a good base for exploring the region. It features no less than five worthy museums and is filled with noteworthy architecture. Its residents have included Matisse, Stendhal, Nietzsche, George Sand, and Flaubert.

East of Nice is Villefranche-sur-Mer, a fishing village and naval port where small houses climb the hillside; these were once the residences of notables like Aldous Huxley, Katherine Mansfield, and Jean Cocteau. If you can't afford to stay at the ultrachic St-Jean-Cap-Ferrat, you can at least sample the lifestyle at the Musée île-de-France, former home of a Rothschild heir, Baronne Ephrussi. Beaulieu is another pocket of posh, featuring a replica of an ancient Greek residence. Eze attracts with its garden of exotic plants, and the Roman ruins at La Turbie ensure a never-ending stream of visitors. Peillon is a scenic foothill village, seated 1,000 feet above the nearby shore.

The tiny principality of Monaco is awash with rumors of royal romance and indiscretion, glamorous nightlife, and gambling. Just inland, northeast of Monaco, is the tranquil medieval mountain village of Roquebrune. Cap-Martin is another spot associated with the rich and famous ever since Empress Eugénie wintered here in the 19th century. And sleepy Menton, 5 miles east of Monaco, is more Italianate than French as it stands right at the border with Italy at the far eastern extremity of the Côte d'Azur.

EXPLORING THE REGION BY CAR

Here's how to link together the best of the region if you rent a car:

Day 1 Start at the Musée National Fernand-Léger in **Biot,** 5 miles north of Antibes off A8. Then drive north on A8 for 3 miles and turn west on Rte. 2085, going another mile to **Villeneuve-Loubet,** where you can visit a museum of memorabilia of Escoffier, France's greatest chef. From here, backtrack to A8 and take the first exit, no. 48 at Cagnes-sur-Mer, following Rte. 36 for 5½ miles to Vence; then turn west on Rte. 2210, driving 3 miles to **Tourrettes-sur-Loup,** where artisans sell their crafts. Backtrack and stop for the night in **St-Paul-de-Vence,** a lovely village of 16th-century homes occupied by great artists in the 1920s. The highlight is the Fondation Maeght's impressive collection of contemporary art.

Day 2 Start the day in **Vence,** spending the morning in Matisse's masterful Chapelle du Rosaire, then backtrack to **Cagnes-sur-Mer** for a visit to the Musée d'Art Moderne Méditerranéen and Renoir's Les Collettes. Spend the night here.

Day 3 Get on A7 and drive 8 miles northeast to **Nice,** where you'll spend the day and night. Visit the museums and architectural sights, then stroll along the coast of this former home of Matisse, Nietzsche, Flaubert, and Hugo.

Day 4 A little over 4 miles northeast of Nice on A7, small houses climb the hillside in **Villefranche-sur-Mer,** which was once home to Huxley, Mansfield, and Cocteau. Unwind here, spending the day and night in this scenic port.

Day 5 Two miles south of Villefranche-sur-Mer on the peninsula they share, **St-Jean-Cap-Ferrat** is an area of luxurious living, which is well illustrated in the Musée île-de-France, once home of Baronne Ephrussi. Spend a day and night here enjoying the coast.

Days 6–7 Still traveling on A7, head toward Monaco, 10 miles northeast, stopping along the way in **Beaulieu** at the replicated ancient Greek residence. Then admire the layout and architecture of the medieval hilltop towns **Eze** and **La Turbie.** From La Turbie, take D2204 inland to D21 and go 3 miles to **Peillon,** an unspoiled village 1,000 feet above the coast, where the architecture is the attraction. Backtrack and drive into **Monaco,** spending 2 nights so that you'll have time to visit the palace, museums, shops, beach, casinos, and nightclubs.

Day 8 Continue north on Rte. 7 for 5 miles to the mountain village of **Roquebrune** and its seaside companion community at **Cap-Martin.** Just 3½ miles farther along, **Menton** is your final stop. Be sure to include visits to the Musée Jean-Cocteau and Musée des Beaux-Arts.

1 Biot

570 miles (917.33km) S of Paris, 6 miles (9.66km) E of Cagnes-sur-Mer, 4 miles (6.44km) NW of Antibes

Biot has been famous for its pottery ever since merchants began to ship earthenware jars to Phoenicia and destinations throughout the Mediterranean. Biot was first settled by Gallo-Romans and has had a long war-torn history. The potters and other artists still work at their ancient crafts today. Biot is also the place Fernand Léger chose to paint until the day he died.

ESSENTIALS

GETTING THERE Biot's train station is 2 miles east of the town center, with frequent service from Nice and Antibes. For **rail information** and schedules, call ☎ 08-36-35-35-35. The bus from Antibes is even more convenient than the train. For **bus**

information and schedules, call ☎ **04-93-34-37-60** in Antibes. In Biot, buses pull into and depart from the place Guynemer.

VISITOR INFORMATION   The **Office de Tourisme** is on rue St-Sebastien (☎ **04-93-65-05-85**).

EXPLORING THE TOWN

To explore the village, begin at the much-photographed **place des Arcades,** where you can see the 16th-century gates and the remains of the town's former ramparts. The **Eglise de Biot,** place des Arcades (☎ **04-93-65-00-85**), dates from the 15th century, when it was built by Italian immigrants who arrived to resettle the town after its population was decimated by the "black death." The church is known for two stunning 15th-century retables: the red-and-gold *Retable du Rosaire* by Ludovico Bréa, and the recently restored *Christ aux Plaies* by Canavesio. The church is open daily from 8am to 7pm. Between May and October, usually but not always on Friday or Saturday at 9pm, it's the site of **Les Heures Musicales** wherein a series of classical concerts makes the ceiling vaults resonate with the sounds of classical music.

Musée d'Histoire Locale et de Céramique Biotoise. Place de la Chapelle. ☎ **04-93-65-11-79.** Admission 12F ($2.05) adults, 6F ($1) children 6–16. Thurs–Sun 2:30–6pm.

This museum displays the historical and contemporary work of local glassblowing artists, potters, ceramists, painters, and goldsmiths of the area.

✪ **Musée National Fernand-Léger.** Chemin du Val-de-Pome. ☎ 04-92-91-50-30. Admission (depending on special exhibits): 30F–38F ($5.10–$6.45) adults, 20F–28F ($3.40–$4.75) ages 18–24, free for those 17 and under. July–Sept, Wed–Mon 11am–6pm; Oct–June, Wed–Mon 10am–12:30pm and 2–6pm.

The greatest collection of Léger's work is in this museum, opened in 1960. It's on the eastern edge of town, beside the road leading to Biot's train station. The collection was assembled by the artist's widow, Nadia Léger, who donated its contents to the French government. The stone-and-marble facade is enhanced by Léger's mosaic-and-ceramic mural. On the grounds is a polychrome ceramic sculpture, *Le Jardin d'enfant.* The collection includes gouaches, paintings, ceramics, tapestries, and sculptures, showing the development of the artist from 1905 until his death. His geometrical forms in pure flat colors abound in cranes, acrobats, scaffolding, railroad signals, buxom nudes, casings, and crankshafts. From his first cubist paintings, Léger was dubbed a "Tubist." The most unusual work is *La Giaconde aux clés,* which depicts Mona Lisa contemplating a set of keys, a widemouthed fish dangling at an angle over her head.

SHOPPING

Glass, pottery, and other crafts are what to look for in Biot. In the late 1940s, glassmakers created a bubble-flecked glass known as *verre rustique.* It comes in brilliant colors like cobalt and emerald and is displayed in many store windows on the main shopping street, **Rue St-Sebastien.** Many interesting stores are also found in the pedestrian zone in Biot's historic center. Stroll along some of the oldest streets, like the **rue des Tines** and the **place des Arcades.** Most of the glassworks, and many shops selling glass, are at the lower (southern) side of town, beside the Rte. de la Mer.

The best place to watch the glassblowers and buy glass is ✪ **Verreries de Biot,** 5 chemin des Combes (☎ **04-93-65-03-00**), at the edge of town. Established in 1956, it was the first, and remains the largest, of the many glassblowing establishments. Have a look at one-of-a-kind collector pieces at the Galerie International du Verre, where the beautifully displayed glass is for sale, often at exorbitant prices. Hours are Monday to Saturday from 9am to 6:30pm. You can also visit the showroom on Sunday from 10:30am to 1pm and 2:30 to 6:30pm.

The namesake of the **Galerie Jean-Claude Novaro** (also known as **Galerie de la Patrimoine**), place des Arcades (☎ **04-93-65-60-23**), is known as the "Picasso of glass artists." His works are pretty and colorful, though sometimes lacking the diversity and intellectual flair of the artists displayed at the Galerie International du Verre.

La Poterie Provençale, 1689 Rte. de la Mer (☎ **04-93-65-63-30**), almost adjacent to the Musée Fernand-Léger about 2 miles southeast of town, is one of the last potteries in Provence to specialize in the tall, amphoralike containers known as *jarres.* The place refers to itself as *une jarrière* because of its emphasis on the containers.

WHERE TO DINE

✪ **Les Terraillers.** 11 rte. du Chemin-Neuf. ☎ **04-93-65-01-59.** Reservations required, as far in advance as possible. Main courses 170F–190F ($28.90–$32.30); fixed-price menus 180F–380F ($30.60–$64.60) at lunch, 250F–380F ($42.50–$64.60) at dinner. AE, MC, V. Thurs–Tues noon–2pm and 7–10pm. Closed lunchtime July–Aug and Nov. Take Rte. du Chemin-Neuf, following the signs to Antibes. MEDITERRANEAN.

Stone-sided and deeply evocative of Provence, this restaurant is about a half mile south of Biot, in what was once a 16th-century potter's studio. The cuisine is prepared by a young and effervescent staff, Chef Claude Jacques and his colleagues Chantal and Pierre, and it's more sophisticated and appetizing than many of its competitors. Roasted scallops come with a saffron and mussel-flavored cream sauce and a confit of leeks; a tart of artichoke hearts and tomatoes *en confit* arrive with a lobster salad; ravioli filled with pan-fried foie gras is served with essence of morels and a *duxelle* of mushrooms. Main courses include a combination of two distinctly different preparations of pigeon, served with a corn galette and the pigeon's own drippings; and a simply braised John Dory Provençal style with olive oil, and served with a fricassée of zucchini, artichokes, tomatoes, and olives.

2 Villeneuve-Loubet

568 miles (914.11km) SE of Paris, 10 miles (16.09km) W of Nice, 6 miles (9.66km) N of Antibes, 13 miles (20.92km) N of Cannes

This small fishing village dominated by a 12th-century castle was where French king François I and Spanish Charles V came to make peace in 1538 after their disputes over the duchies of Burgundy and Milan. However, it's much better known as the birthplace of Auguste Escoffier, "the king of chefs and the chef of kings."

Villeneuve-Loubet-Plage is home to the **Marina Baie des Anges,** at the center of the beachfront. This grouping of four concrete apartment buildings shaped like ziggurats and built by André Minanfoy in the 1970s caused an uproar among locals, who cried that they marred the beautiful coast. The buildings remain, however, and are referred to by some as the most fascinating and amazing properties on the Riviera. Whether you like the architecture or not, the marina is the place to go for water sports. There are 600 slips for docking boats, a public pool, and facilities for sailing, water-skiing, windsurfing, and deep-sea fishing.

ESSENTIALS

GETTING THERE   The small-scale railway station, behind the marina, has few trains, all requiring a transfer in either Nice (7½ miles away) or Antibes (3¾ miles away). For **railway information** call ☎ **08-36-35-35-35.** From Nice and Antibes, buses run at 20-minute intervals along RN7, stopping at place de la France d'Outre-Mer or beside a parking lot adjacent to RN7, about a quarter-mile from the center. For **bus information,** contact the Gare Routière in Nice at ☎ **04-93-85-61-81.**

VISITOR INFORMATION   The **Office de Tourisme** that services both Villeneuve-Loubet and Villeneuve-Loubet-Plage lies in Villeneuve-Loubet-Plage, at 16 av. de la Mer (☎ **04-93-20-49-14**).

WHERE THE KING OF CHEFS WAS BORN

Musée de l'Art Culinaire. 3 rue Escoffier. ☎ **04-93-20-80-51**. Admission 10F ($1.70) adults and students, free for children under 10. July–Aug, Tues–Sun 2–7pm; Sept–June, Tues–Sun 2–6pm.

The house where Escoffier was born in 1846 was made into a museum in 1956 by Joseph Donon, his former apprentice. Escoffier's career began in 1859 at the age of 13. In the 1890s, he became the world-famous chef of the Savoy in London. He worked until he retired from London's Carlton in 1920 and died in 1935 at Monte Carlo, at the age of 89. In the museum, a 19th-century Provençal kitchen is complete with every utensil imaginable—many of which Escoffier invented. His famous creations are featured, and displayed throughout is a collection of several thousand menus describing delicious dishes that would make cardiologists and their patients run for their lives today. There are also some elaborate sugar sculptures, like the one in the shape of a Japanese pagoda. A signed photo of opera singer Nellie Melba thanks the chef for naming his peach dessert for her.

WHERE TO STAY

Rooms are also available at the restaurant, **La Franc Comtoise** (see below).

Hamotel. Hameau du Soleil, Rte. de la Colle-sur-Loup, 06270 Villeneuve-Loubet. ☎ **04-93-20-86-60**. Fax 04-93-73-33-94. E-mail: hamotel@wanadoo.fr. 30 units. MINIBAR TV TEL. 350F–450F ($59.50–$76.50) double. AE, DC, MC, V.

Less than a mile from the center, this hotel was inspired by a sprawling Provençal *mas,* or farmhouse, complete with a tiled roof and a boxy earth-toned exterior. Rated three stars by the local municipality, it's a simple affair, with modern rooms that range from small to medium, each coming with a comfortable bed fitted with a quality mattress and a compact tiled bathroom. The pool is the focal point of social life and the staff is quite likeable. Breakfast is the only meal served.

WHERE TO DINE

La Franc Comtoise. Grange Rimade, Rte. de la Colle-St-Paul, 06270 Villeneuve-Loubet. ☎ **04-93-20-97-58**. Fax 04-92-02-74-76. Reservations not required. Main courses 55F–100F ($9.35–$17); fixed-price menus 120F–150F ($20.40–$25.50); bouillabaisse 300F ($51). MC, V. Daily noon–1:15pm and 7:30–8:30pm. Oct–May closed Sun dinner and Mon. PROVENÇAL.

In a hotel about half a mile from town (beside the highway leading to St-Paul-de-Vence), this restaurant has well-prepared food, but its drawback is the narrow range of hours. Menu items include a wonderful version of bouillabaisse, authentic paella, a Niçois version of *daube* (stew) of beef, and Niçois-style daurade.

The hotel contains 30 unpretentious and very clean rooms, each with TV and phone. A double is 415F ($70.55) without meals and 320F ($54.40) per person with half board and wine. A pool is adjacent to the hotel, and guests can use the parking garage for free.

3 Tourrettes-sur-Loup

577 miles (928.59km) SE of Paris, 18 miles (28.97km) W of Nice, 4 (6.44km) miles W of Vence, 13 miles (20.92km) NE of Grasse

Often called the "City of Violets" because of the small purple flowers cultivated in abundance beneath the olive trees, Tourrettes-sur-Loup sits atop a sheer cliff overlooking the Loup valley. Though violets are big business for the town (they're sent to the perfume factories in Grasse, made into candy, and celebrated during a festival held each March), you'll probably find the many shops lining the streets much more interesting. These small businesses are often owned by artisans who sell their own art—most notably hand-woven fabrics and unique pottery. Even if you're not interested in buying, walking through the old town is worth the trip up the hill.

The unusual city was built so that the walls of the outermost buildings form a rampart; three towers rising above the village give it its name. A rocky horseshoe-shaped path leads from the main square, then loops back again; follow it for a pleasant tour of the medieval village. Along the way, you'll pass the **Chapelle St-Jean,** with naïve frescoes that tell biblical stories, weaving in the traditions of local life. Also in the village is a **15th-century church** that has paintings by the school of Brea. Immediately adjacent is a ruined 1st-century **pagan shrine** in honor of the Roman god Mercury. Access to these monuments is erratic and whimsical, depending on a local representative of the nearby town hall (☎ **04-93-59-30-11;** at press time, it was an M. Wittersheim, although the situation is fluid and might have changed by the time you arrive). In theory, the sites can be visited Monday to Friday from 9am to 5pm.

ESSENTIALS

GETTING THERE   The nearest rail junction is at Cagnes-sur-Mer; buses run about every 45 minutes to Vence, where you must change to another bus (about six a day; trip time: 10 mins.). To go from Cagnes to Tourrettes takes about an hour—it's more convenient to take a taxi (☎ **04-93-24-18-87**) from Cagnes (they line up at the train station), around 125F ($21.25) each way.

VISITOR INFORMATION   The **Office de Tourisme** is at 5 Rte. de Vence, at the edge of place de la Libération (☎ **04-93-24-18-93**).

SHOPPING

Tourrettes-sur-Loup boasts more crafts studios than any other town its size in Provence. Nearly 30 artisans, including a handful of noted ones from as far away as Paris, have set up their studios and outlets, often in stone-sided buildings facing the town's main street, **Grand'Rue.** The best way to sample their offerings is to wander and window shop (the town's small size makes this feasible). Here's a list of recommendable artisans:

You'll find jewelry, in designs ranging from old-fashioned to contemporary, at **La Paësine,** 14 Grand'Rue (☎ **04-93-24-14-55**). Original clothing—sometimes in silk—for men and women, including vests, ponchos, shirts, blouses, and dresses, as well as draperies, bed linens, and tablecloths, usually in creative patterns, is available at the **Atelier Arachnée,** 8 Grand'Rue (☎ **04-93-24-11-42**). Ceramics crafted from local clay in patterns inspired by the many civilizations that have pillaged or prospered in Provence are sold at **Poterie Tournesol,** 7 Grand'Rue (☎ **04-93-59-35-62**). **Marie L'Amoureux Fonderie d'Art,** 73 Grand'Rue (☎ **04-93-24-11-74**), sells very unusual bronzes, some authorized by well-known masters of the modernist movement. For a view of canvases by painters inspired by the colors and traditions of Provence, head for **Comet Galerie,** 51 Grand'Rue (☎ **04-93-24-11-12**), where the featured artist and owner is someone named Macha, a situation which could easily change by the time of your visit. For an insight into the kinds of modern sculpture and ceramics being created in southern France, head for **Creations Olivia,** 25 Grand'Rue (☎ **04-93-59-39-50**).

Looking for a pick-me-up after a day of shopping? Head for one of the region's best candy shops, **Confiserie des Gorges du Loup,** rue Principale (☎ **04-93-59-32-91**), where age-old techniques are used to layer fresh fruit with sugar. The result is an ultra-chewy, ultrasweet confection that gradually melts as it explodes flavor into your mouth—the taste has been called "angelic." Sample chocolate-covered orange peel, rose-petal jam, and sugar-permeated sliced apricots, tangerines, plums, cherries, and grapes. Even the local violets are transformed into edible, sugary treats.

WHERE TO STAY

Auberge Belles Terrasses. 1315 Rte. de Vence, 06140 Tourrettes-sur-Loup. ☎ **04-93-59-30-03.** Fax 04-93-59-31-27. 15 units. TEL. 280F–330F ($47.60–$56.10) double. MC, V. From town, drive about half a mile, following the signs toward Vence.

This hotel has views of the faraway peninsula of Antibes and the sea beyond. Its boxy shape and terra-cotta roof were inspired by an architect's fantasy of an old Provençal manor house, and it was named after the terraces that are angled for maximum exposure to the view. The rooms are simple, traditional, and comfortable but not particularly stimulating. They range from small to medium, each with a comfortable Provençal bed fitted with a firm mattress. Bathrooms are small, with shower stalls. Much of the allure of this place is its restaurant, where fixed-price menus are 90F to 150F ($15.30 to $25.50). Menu items include civet of roast suckling pig, young hen with freshwater crayfish, roast wild hare with mustard sauce, Provençal frogs' legs with garlic-and-butter sauce, and assorted game dishes. The restaurant is closed every Monday to nonguests.

Résidence des Chevaliers. Rte. du Caire, 06140 Tourrettes-sur-Loup. ☎ **04-93-59-31-97.** Fax 04-93-59-27-97. 12 units. TEL. 450F–750F ($76.50–$127.50) double. MC, V. Closed Nov–Mar.

About 500 yards from the village's periphery, this place was built around 1900 as a *bastide Provençal* (manor house), and because the furnishings are relatively simple and the lines severe, the inn evokes a monastery. It has functioned as a hotel since the 1960s, when a pool was installed in the garden. Breakfast is the only meal served. The site has very simple comfort, reflected in the rather functionally furnished bedrooms that are a bit cramped, but comfortable, with middle-grade mattresses and a small bathroom with adequate shelf space and a shower stall.

WHERE TO DINE

The **Auberge Belles Terrasses** (see "Where to Stay," above) is also recommended for its cuisine, except on Monday when it's closed to nonguests.

If you're looking for a head-on view of everyday Provençal life, consider either a *plat du jour,* a glass of pastis, or *un petit café* at the most colorful and animated pub in town, **Le Café des Sports,** 1 Rte. de Vence/place de la Libération (☎ **04-93-59-30-26**). Its paneled interior is representative of old-fashioned Provence; it's open for drinks and coffee every day from 6:30am to 11pm, although their generous *plats du jour,* priced at 45F ($7.65; no credit cards), are trotted out only between noon and 2:45pm. There's recorded music every day after around 7pm, when it's everybody's favorite hangout for gossip, chitchat, and local scandal-mongering.

Le Petit Manoir. 21 Grande'Rue, Tourrettes-sur-Loup. ☎ **04-93-24-19-19.** Reservations recommended. Main courses 60F–130F ($10.20–$22.10); fixed-price menus 96F–245F ($16.30–$41.65). AE, MC, V. Thurs–Tues noon–2pm and 7:30–10pm (closed Sun night). Closed 2 weeks in Nov and 2 weeks in Feb. FRENCH.

There are only about 25 seats in the simple dining room of this 17th-century building in an all-pedestrian zone in the heart of town, and the cuisine is based on traditional

French recipes with an occasional modern twist. The food is flavorful and appetizing and includes old-fashioned staples like cured ham braised with herbs, foie gras of duckling with acacia-scented honey, roast rack of rabbit stuffed with basil, and a marmite of fish with aromatic herbs.

4 St-Paul-de-Vence

575 miles (925.37km) S of Paris, 14 miles (22.53km) E of Grasse, 17 miles (27.36km) E of Cannes, 19 miles (30.58km) N of Nice

Of all the perched villages of the Riviera, St-Paul-de-Vence is the best-known. It was popularized in the 1920s when many noted artists lived here, occupying the 16th-century houses flanking the narrow cobblestone streets. The feudal hamlet grew up on a bastion of rock, almost blending into it. Its ramparts (allow about 30 minutes to circle them) overlook a peaceful setting of flowers and olive and orange trees. They remain somewhat as they were when they were constructed from 1537 to 1547 by François I. From the ramparts to the north you can look out on Baou de St-Jeannet, a sphinx-shaped rock that was painted into the landscape of Poussin's *Polyphème.*

ESSENTIALS

GETTING THERE   The nearest railway station is in Cagnes-sur-Mer, from which buses depart every 45 minutes for St-Paul-de-Vence. Clients who arrive in Nice usually rent a car or opt for one of about 20 buses a day, departing from the Gare Routière, near the Nice railway station. For bus information, call **Cie SAP** (☎ **04-93-58-37-60**). Buses stop in St-Paul near the post office, on the Route de Vence, about a quarter mile from the town center.

VISITOR INFORMATION   The **Office de Tourisme** is at Maison de la Tour, 2 rue Grande (☎ **04-93-32-86-95**).

EXPLORING THE TOWN

Except for local residents and service-related deliveries (such as dropping your luggage off at your hotel), driving a car within the center of St-Paul's old town is prohibited. The pedestrian-only **rue Grande** is the most interesting street, running the entire length of St-Paul. Most of the stone houses along it are from the 16th and 17th centuries, many still bearing the coats-of-arms placed here by the original builders. Today most of them are antiques shops, art-and-crafts galleries, and souvenir and gift shops—some are still artists' studios.

Near the church is a minor museum in a 16th-century village house, the **Musée d'Histoire de St-Paul,** place de Castre (☎ **04-93-32-53-09**). It was restored and refurnished in a 1500s style, with many artifacts illustrating the history of the village. It's open daily from 10am to 5:30pm. Admission is 20F ($3.40) for adults, 12F ($2.05) for students and for children under 12.

La Collégiale de la Conversion de St-Paul. Place de l'Eglise. No phone. Free admission. Daily 9am–6pm (9am–7pm July–Aug).

The church was constructed in the 12th and 13th centuries though much altered over the years. The Romanesque choir is the oldest part, containing some remarkable stalls carved in walnut in the 17th century. The bell tower was built in 1740, but the vaulting was reconstructed in the 1800s. Although the facade today isn't alluring, the church is filled with art, notably a painting of Ste-Cathérine d'Alexandrie, attributed to Tintoretto and hanging to the left as you enter. The Trésor de l'Eglise is one of the most beautiful in the Alpes-Maritimes, with a spectacular ciborium. Look also for a low relief of the Martyrdom of St-Clément on the last altar on the right. In the baptismal chapter is a 15th-century alabaster Madonna.

○ **Fondation Maeght.** ☎ **04-93-32-81-63**). Admission (depending on season) 35F–45F ($5.95–$7.65) adults, 25F–35F ($4.25–$5.95) students and ages 10 to 18, free for children 9 and under. July–Sept, daily 10am–7pm; Oct–June, daily 10am–12:30pm and 2:30–6pm.

The most important attraction of St-Paul-de-Vence lies outside the walls. It is one of the most modern art museums in Europe. On a hill in pine-studded woods, the avant-garde building houses one of the finest collections of contemporary art along the Riviera. Nature and the creations of people blend harmoniously in this unique achievement of the architect José Luís Sert. Its white concrete arcs give the impression of a giant pagoda. A stark Calder rises like some futuristic monster on the grassy lawns. In a courtyard, the elongated bronze works of Giacometti form a surrealistic garden, creating a hallucinatory mood. Sculpture is also displayed inside, but it's at its best in a natural setting of surrounding terraces and gardens. The museum is built on several levels, its many glass walls providing an indoor-outdoor vista. The foundation, a gift "to the people" from Aimé and Marguerite Maeght, also provides a showcase for new talent. Exhibitions are always changing. Everywhere you look, you see 20th-century art: mosaics by Chagall and Braque, Miró ceramics in the "labyrinth," and Ubac and Braque stained glass in the chapel. Bonnard, Kandinsky, Léger, Matisse, Barbara Hepworth, and many other artists are well represented.

There are a library (open only to scholars and only by appointment), a cinema, and a cafeteria here. In one showroom, you can buy original lithographs by artists like Chagall and Giacometti and limited-edition prints.

WHERE TO STAY

La Colombe d'Or also rents deluxe rooms (see "Where to Dine," below).

VERY EXPENSIVE

Le Mas d'Artigny. Rte. de la Colle et des Hauts de St-Paul, 06570 St-Paul-de-Vence. ☎ **04-93-32-84-54.** Fax 04-93-32-95-36. E-mail: mas.artigny@wanadoo.fr. 83 units. A/C MINIBAR TV TEL. 975F–1,950F ($165.75–$331.50) double; 1,850F–2,850F ($314.50–$484.50) suite. AE, DC, MC, V. Parking 60F ($10.20) in a garage. From the town center, follow the signs west about 1¼ miles.

This hotel, one of the Riviera's grandest, evokes a sprawling Provençal homestead set in an acre of pine forests. In the lobby is a constantly changing exhibition of art. Each of the comfortably large rooms has its own terrace or balcony, and private suites with a private pool are on a slope below the blue-tile pool, with hedges for privacy. Mattresses are relatively new and supremely comfortable; towels and bath linens are plentiful and of high quality. For such an elegant Relais & Châteaux, the restaurant is a bit lackluster in decor and has a staff that isn't always too alert, but it does have great views of the garden. Chef Francis Scordel regales you with his flavors of Provence— everything tastes as if it were ripened in the sun. Only quality ingredients are used to shape this harmonious and rarely complicated cuisine. The wine cellar deserves a star for its vintage collection, but watch those prices!

EXPENSIVE

○ **Hôtel Le St-Paul.** 86 rue Grande, 06570 St-Paul-de-Vence. ☎ **04-93-32-65-25.** Fax 04-93-32-52-94. www/relaischateaux.fr. E-mail: Le.St.Paul@wanadoo.fr. 18 units. A/C MINIBAR TV TEL. 850F–1,600F ($144.50–$272) double; 1,400F–2,600F ($238–$442) suite. Half board 390F ($66.30) per person extra. AE, DC, MC, V.

Converted from a 16th-century Renaissance residence and retaining many original features, this four-star Relais & Châteaux is in the heart of the medieval village. The rooms, decorated in a sophisticated Provençal style, have safe-deposit boxes, satellite TVs, and many extras. Beds are quite sumptuous, with elegant fabrics, deluxe mattresses, and quality linen. Bathrooms are maintained in state-of-the-art condition with generous shelf space, robes, hair dryers, and plush towels. One woman wrote us that while sitting on the balcony of Room 30 she understood why Renoir, Léger, Matisse, and even Picasso were inspired by Provence. Many rooms enjoy a view of the valley with the Mediterranean in the distance. The restaurant has a flower-bedecked terrace sheltered by the 16th-century ramparts as well as a superb dining room with vaulted ceilings. Menus may include locally inspired dishes like cream of salt cod with a thin slice of grilled pancetta, risotto of crayfish and broadbeans, roast veal chop with morels and barley, and a delightful crème brûlée with a hint of rosemary.

MODERATE

Auberge Le Hameau. 528 Rte. de la Colle (D107), 06570 St-Paul-de-Vence. ☎ **04-93-32-80-24.** Fax 04-93-32-55-75. 17 units. A/C MINIBAR TEL. 430F–620F ($73.10–$105.40) double; from 750F ($127.50) suite. MC, V. Closed Jan 6–Feb 15 and Nov 16–Dec 22. From the town, take D107 about a half mile, following the signs south of town toward Colle.

This romantic Mediterranean villa is on a hilltop on the outskirts of St-Paul-de-Vence, on the road to Colle at Hauts-de-St-Paul. Originally built as a farmhouse in the 1920s, and enlarged and transformed into a hotel in 1967, it contains high-ceilinged, comfortable bedrooms, all with firm mattresses, tiled bathrooms, middle-grade towels, and conservatively modern furniture. You get a remarkable view of the surrounding hills and valleys, and most of the comfortable whitewashed rooms overlook a vineyard. There's also a sunny terrace with fruit trees, flowers, and a pool.

Les Orangers. Chemin des Fumerates, Rte. de la Colle (D107), 06570 St-Paul-de-Vence. ☎ **04-93-32-80-95.** Fax 04-93-32-00-32. 9 units. TEL. 650F–750F ($110.50–$127.50) double; 850F ($144.50) suite. Rates include breakfast. MC, V. Free parking. From the town center, follow the signs to Cagnes-sur-Mer for half a mile south.

M. Franklin has created a beautiful "living oasis" in his villa. The scents of roses, oranges, and lemons waft through the air. The main lounge is impeccably decorated with original oils and furnished in a provincial style. Mattresses are relatively comfortable; towels are acceptably thick. Expect to be treated like a guest in a private home. The rooms, with antiques and Oriental carpets, have panoramic views. On the sun terrace are banana trees and climbing geraniums.

INEXPENSIVE

Confort Hotel. 940 Rte. de la Colle, 06570 St-Paul-de-Vence. ☎ **04-93-32-94-24.** Fax 04-93-32-91-07. 19 units. TV TEL. 500F–600F ($85–$102) double. AE, DC, MC, V. Free parking. From the coast, the hotel is situated on the left side of the road, 800 meters before the village of St-Paul.

This complex of low-slung, tile-roofed town houses is at the end of a steep driveway. While reclining in a chair by a pool, you can survey the countryside. Each comfortably furnished room has its own small salon, balcony, or terrace. Rooms are a bit small but the comfort promised in the name of the hotel is evidenced by the firm mattresses on the excellent beds. Bathrooms are compact with middle-grade towels, shower/tub combos, and hair dryers.

Les Bastides St-Paul. 880 Rte. des Blaquières (Rte. Cagnes-Vence), 06570 St-Paul-de-Vence. ☎ **04-92-02-08-07.** Fax 04-93-20-50-41. E-mail: pr.Prestige@webstore.fr. 17 units. MINIBAR TV TEL. 450F–700F ($76.50–$119) double. AE, DC, MC, V. From the town center, follow the signs toward Cagnes-sur-Mer for 1 mile south.

This hotel is in the hills outside town, a mile south of St-Paul and 2½ miles south of Vence. Divided into three buildings, it offers clean and comfortably carpeted rooms, each accented with regional artifacts, and a terrace and garden. Bedrooms are small to medium in size, each with a fine mattress giving you a good night's sleep. Bathrooms have shower stalls and middle-grade towels, but if you want a hair dryer you have to request one from reception. On the premises is a pool shaped like a cloverleaf, a cozy breakfast area, and a sensitive management staff headed by the long-time hoteliers Marie José and Maurice Giraudet. Breakfast is served anytime you want it.

WHERE TO DINE

La Colombe d'Or. 1 place du Général-de-Gaulle, 06570 St-Paul-de-Vence. ☎ **04-93-32-80-02.** Fax 04-93-32-77-78. Reservations required. Main courses 100F–250F ($17–$42.50). AE, DC, MC, V. Daily noon–2pm and 7–10pm. Closed Nov to Dec 20. FRENCH.

"The Golden Dove" has for decades been St-Paul's most celebrated restaurant, famous for its remarkable art collection: You can dine amid Mirós, Picassos, Klees, Dufys, Utrillos, and Calders. In fair weather, everyone tries for a seat on the terrace to soak up the view. You won't find cutting-edge cuisine or wildly exotic experiments. Begin with smoked salmon or foie gras from Landes if you've recently won at the casino. Otherwise, you can count on a soup made with the fresh seasonal vegetables. The best fish dishes are poached sea bass with mousseline sauce and sea wolf baked with fennel. Tender beef comes with *gratin dauphinois* (potatoes), or you may prefer lamb from Sisteron. A classic finish to any meal is a soufflé flambé au Grand-Marnier.

The guest rooms (16 doubles, 10 suites) in this three-star hotel are scattered among three areas: the original 16th-century stone house, a more recent wing that stretches into the garden adjacent to the pool, and an even more modern annex, built in the 1950s and upgraded several times since. Some have exposed stone and heavy ceiling beams; all are very comfortable, with air-conditioning, minibars, TVs, and phones. Prices are 1,350F ($229.50) for a double and 1,550F ($263.50) for a suite.

5 Vence

575 miles (925.37km) S of Paris, 19 miles (30.58km) N of Cannes, 15 miles (24.14km) NW of Nice

Travel up into the hills northwest of Nice—across country studded with cypresses, olive trees, and pines, where carnations, roses, and oleanders grow in profusion—and Vence comes into view. Outside the town, along boulevard Paul-André, two olive presses carry on with their age-old duties. But the charm lies in the **Vieille Ville.** Visitors invariably have themselves photographed on place du Peyra in front of the urn-shaped **Vieille Fontaine,** a background shot in several motion pictures. The 15th-century square tower is also a curiosity.

ESSENTIALS

GETTING THERE   Frequent buses (no. 400 or 410) arrive from Nice (trip time: about an hour); cost is 22F ($3.75) each way. For bus information, contact **Compagnie SIP** (☎ **04-93-58-37-60**). The nearest railway station is in Cagnes-sur-Mer, about 4½ miles from Vence. From here, about 20 buses per day make the route into Vence. For railway information, call ☎ **08-36-35-35-35.**

VISITOR INFORMATION   The **Office de Tourisme** is on place Grand-Jardin (☎ **04-93-58-06-38**).

EXPLORING THE TOWN

If you're wearing the right kind of shoes, the narrow, steep streets of the Old Town are worth exploring. Dating from the 10th century, the **cathedral** on place Godeau is unremarkable except for some 15th-century Gothic choir stalls. But if it's the right day

Exploring the Gorges du Loup

After paying your respects to Matisse at the Chapelle du Rosaire in Vence, you can take D2210 through some of the Riviera's most luxuriant countryside. The 4-mile-long **Gorges du Loup** isn't as dramatic as the Grand Canyon du Verdon (see chapter 4) but still features a scenic 8-mile drive that loops along the eastern and western edges. This drive showcases waterfalls, most notably the **Cascades des Demoiselles,** with its partially fossilized plantlife, and the 130-foot **Cascade de Courmes.** There are also jagged glacial holes best exemplified by the **Saut du Loup** at the valley's northeastern end.

Gourdon, the only village along the gorge's western rim, with a year-round population of only 59 but a larger summer population, functions as a tourist trap. If you stop here, ignore the souvenir shops and visit the immense 13th-century **Château de Gourdon** (☎ **04-93-09-68-02**). It houses two museums: The **Musée Historique** features a Rembrandt self-portrait, Marie Antoinette's writing desk, and an assortment of armor, arms, and torture instruments; and the **Musée de Peinture Naïve** offers a small Rousseau portrait, among other works. The magnificent 17th-century formal garden is graced with topiaries often photographed by gardening magazines. The museums are open June to September, daily from 11am to 1pm and 2 to 7pm; October to May, Wednesday to Monday from 2 to 5pm. A combined ticket to the garden and the museums is 25F ($4.25). Tickets to one or the other aren't available.

On the southeastern edge of the gorge, at **Pont-du-Loup,** go to **La Confiserie des Gorges du Loup,** rue Principale (☎ **04-93-59-32-91**), where you can sample sweets while watching the confectioners sugarcoat tangerines or chocolate-dip orange peels. Less than a mile farther south, the 15th-century **Gothic church** at **Le Bar-sur-Loup** features a morbid *Danse Macabre,* a 15th-century painting of fallen and dancing humans whose souls are being wrested away by black demons, then weighed by St. Michael before being tossed into the pits of hell. Speculation links the anonymous work of art to the plague.

After taking in this sober vision, backtrack to Pont-du-Loup and travel 5 miles east to **Tourrettes-sur-Loup,** where you can find accommodations in an unspoiled medieval village on a rocky bluff high above a violet-filled valley (see earlier in this chapter).

If you're coming from Cannes, take A85 for 13 miles northwest to Grasse, then travel east for 3¾ miles on Rte. 2085, where you'll turn north at Magagnosc, following D3 for 5 miles north to Gourdon, at the edge of the gorge. To come from Nice, take E80 for 2 miles west to Rte. 2085, then drive 16 miles west to Magagnosc, to follow the same path north to Gourdon. Once in Gourdon, you can continue north on D3 along the western rim of the gorge, and after 4 miles turn right onto D6 to return south along its eastern lip. Turn east on D2210 at Pont-du-Loup for a 5-mile drive to Tourrettes-sur-Loup, or continue on to Vence, another 2 miles along, where you can turn south on Rte. 36 for a 5½-mile drive back to the coast.

For information, contact the **Office de Tourisme,** 22 cours Henri-Cresp, 06130 Grasse (☎ **04-93-36-03-56**); place Grand-Jardin, 06140 Vence (☎ **04-93-58-06-38**); or route de Vence, 06140 Tourrettes-sur-Loup (☎ **04-93-24-18-93**).

of the week, most visitors quickly pass through the narrow gates of this once-fortified walled town to where the sun shines more brightly.

✪ **Chapelle du Rosaire.** Av. Henri-Matisse. ☎ **04-93-58-03-26.** Admission 13F ($2.20), contributions welcomed. Tues–Thurs 10–11:30am and 2:30–5:30pm, or by special arrangement.

Just outside Vence, Matisse created this masterwork for the Dominican nuns of Monteils, partly as a gesture of thanks for Sister Jacques-Marie, a member of the order, who nursed him back to health after a debilitating illness. From the front, you might find it unremarkable and pass it by—until you spot a 40-foot crescent-adorned cross rising from a blue-tile roof.

It was a beautiful golden autumn along the Côte d'Azur, and the great Henri Matisse was 77 when, after a turbulent introspective time, he set out to design and decorate this "culmination of a whole life dedicated to the search for truth." Matisse wrote: "What I have done in the chapel is to create a religious space . . . in an enclosed area of very reduced proportions and to give it, solely by the play of colors and lines, the dimensions of infinity." The light picks up the subtle coloring in the simply rendered leaf forms and abstract patterns: sapphire blue, aquamarine, and lemon yellow. In black-and-white ceramic, St. Dominic is depicted in just a few lines. Most remarkable are the black-and-white tile Stations of the Cross, with Matisse's self-styled "tormented and passionate" figures. The bishop of Nice came to bless the chapel in the late spring of 1951 when the artist's work was completed. Matisse died 3 years later.

The price of admission includes entrance to **L'Espace Matisse,** a gallery that documents the way Matisse handled the design of the chapel during its construction (1949–51). It also shows lithographs and religious artifacts that concerned Matisse in one way or another.

WHERE TO STAY
VERY EXPENSIVE

✪ **Le Château du Domaine St-Martin.** Av. des Templiers BP102, 06142 Vence. ☎ **04-93-58-02-02.** Fax 04-93-24-08-91. www.chateau-st-martin.com. E-mail: st-martin@webstore.fr. 33 units, 5 cottages. A/C TV TEL. 2,500F–3,000F ($425–$510) double; 2,800F–4,500F ($476–$765) suite; 2,700F–3,200F ($459–$544) cottage. AE, DC, MC, V. Closed Nov–Mar. From the town center, follow the signs toward Coursegoules and Col-de-Vence for 1 mile north.

This château, in a 35-acre park, was built in 1936 on the grounds where the Golden Goat treasure, a legendary stash of gold, was reputedly buried. A complex of tile-roofed villas with suites was built in the terraced gardens. You can walk through the gardens on winding paths lined with tall cypresses, past the ruined chapel and olive trees. The guest rooms are furnished in elegant taste. Rooms are exceedingly spacious, with deluxe mattresses and state-of-the-art bathrooms with dual basins, plush towels, a shower/tub combination, and most-generous shelf space along with a set of luxury toiletries. The restaurant has a view of the coast and offers superb French cuisine. In summer, many guests prefer the poolside grill.

MODERATE

Le Florél. Av. Rhin-et-Danube, 06140 Vence. ☎ **04-93-58-64-40.** Fax 04-93-58-79-69. 43 units. A/C TV TEL. 440F–540F ($74.80–$91.80) double (prices increase over Christmas). AE, DC, MC, V. Free parking.

On the road to Grasse is this pleasant, comfortable hotel with a view of the mountains and a refreshing lack of pretension. Many of the well-furnished rooms look out on the large pool in the garden, where orange trees and mimosa add fragrance to the breezes. Most accommodations are medium-sized, and each is most comfortable with quality mattresses and fine linen. Bathrooms are compact and tiled and contain hair dryers and shower/tub combinations (for the most part). The hotel has air-conditioned lounges, a restaurant (Le Patio), and a bar.

✪ **Relais Cantemerle**. 258 chemin Cantemerle, 06140 Vence. ☎ **04-93-58-08-18**. Fax 04-93-58-32-89. 19 units. A/C MINIBAR TV TEL. 680F ($115.60); 1,030F ($175.10) 1-bedroom duplex for 2; 1,230F ($209.10) 1-bedroom duplex for 3. 200F ($34) additional bed for fourth occupant. 270F ($45.90) supplement for half board. AE, DC, MC, V. Closed mid-Oct to mid-Apr.

One of the most appealing places in Vence is this artfully designed cluster of accommodations that resembles an old-fashioned compound of Provençal buildings. It surrounds a verdant lawn dotted with old trees; a swimming pool is in the center. Public areas are stylishly outfitted with art-deco furniture and accessories; they include a richly paneled bar area and a flagstone terrace that's the site of sun-flooded meals. Accommodations aren't overly large, but contain unusual overscaled art deco armchairs, louvered wooden closet doors, and balcony-style sleeping lofts. Bathrooms are beautifully kept and come with shower/tub combinations. An on-site restaurant serves worthwhile versions of regional and mainstream French cuisine.

INEXPENSIVE

Auberge des Seigneurs (Inn of the Noblemen). Place du Friene, 06140 Vence. ☎ **04-93-58-04-24**. Fax 04-93-24-08-01. 6 units. TEL. 384F ($65.30) double. AE, DC, MC, V. Closed Nov 15–Mar 15.

This 400-year-old stone hotel gives you a historic taste of Provence. Inside is a long wooden dining table, in view of an open fireplace with a row of hanging copper pots and pans. The cuisine of François I is served in an antique atmosphere with wooden casks of flowers and an open spit for roasting and grilling. Fascinating decorative objects and antiques are everywhere. The restaurant offers fixed-price menus costing 165F to 240F ($28.05 to $40.80).

Guest rooms are well maintained, though management gives priority to the restaurant, which generates far more revenue. Bedrooms have lots of exposed paneling and beams. Twin or double beds are fitted with firm mattresses. The compact tiled bathrooms have adequate shelf space and most have shower stalls.

Hôtel Villa Roseraie. Av. Henri-Giraud, Rte. de Coursegoules, 06140 Vence. ☎ **04-93-58-02-20**. Fax 04-93-58-99-31. 14 units. TV TEL. 395F–730F ($67.15–$124.10) double. AE, MC, V. From the town center, drive for less than a quarter mile, following the signs toward Col-de-Vence.

This charming small hotel, a 5-minute walk from the historic center of Vence, lies in a totally renovated 19th-century manor house. Marc Chagall lived for many years on a hill across from the hotel. It's an easy walk from the Matisse Chapel. Monica and Maurice Garnier are among the most charming hosts at Vence, and they've furnished their home with old-fashioned pieces, often antiques. The garden offers perfect southern exposure, and contains a moon-shaped swimming pool. The "Rose Garden" (its English name) is studded with magnolias, yucca, eucalyptus, banana trees, palms, and, of course, roses. Rooms 4, 5, and 8 have balconies; nos. 12, 14, 15, and 16 have ground-floor patios. Mattresses were recently renewed, and bathrooms are decked in Provençal tiles from neighboring Salernes. There's no better way to start the day here than by sampling one of the fresh house-baked croissants.

WHERE TO DINE

The **Auberge des Seigneurs** (see above) is an excellent place to dine at reasonable prices.

La Farigoule. 15 rue Henri-Isnard. ☎ **04-93-58-01-27.** Reservations recommended. Main courses 90F–130F ($15.30–$22.10); set-price menus 130F–160F ($22.10–$27.20). Wed 7:30–10:30pm; Thurs–Mon noon–2:30pm and 7:30–10:30pm. PROVENÇAL.

In a century-old house that opens onto a rose garden, where tables are set out during summer, this restaurant specializes in Provençal cuisine prepared by skilled, English-speaking chef Patrick Bruot, formerly a resident of New York. Menu items include a conservative but flavorful array of dishes that feature a bourride Provençal; shoulder of roasted lamb with a ragout of fresh vegetables, served with fresh thyme; aïoli; and such fish dishes as dorado with a confit of lemons and fresh aromatic coriander.

6 Cagnes-sur-Mer/Le Haut-de-Cagnes

570 miles (917.33km) S of Paris, 13 miles (20.92km) NE of Cannes

Cagnes-sur-Mer, like the Roman god Janus, has two faces. Perched on a hill in the "hinterlands" of Nice, **Le Haut-de-Cagnes** is one of the most charming spots on the Riviera. Naomi Barry of the *New York Times* wrote that it "crowns the top of a blue-cypressed hill like a village in an Italian Renaissance painting." At the foot of the hill is an old fishing port and rapidly developing beach resort called **Cros-de-Cagnes,** between Nice and Antibes.

For years, Le Haut-de-Cagnes attracted the French literati, including Simone de Beauvoir, who wrote *Les Mandarins* here. A colony of painters also settled in—Renoir stated that the village was "the place where I want to paint until the last day of my life."

The racecourse is one of the finest in France.

ESSENTIALS

GETTING THERE   Buses from Nice and Cannes stop at Cagnes-Ville and at Béal/Les Collettes, within walking distance of Cros-de-Cagne. For **bus information,** call ☎ **04-93-39-18-71** in Cannes or ☎ **04-93-85-61-81** in Nice. The climb from Cagnes-Ville to Le Haut-de-Cagnes is very strenuous, so from June to September a minibus runs about every 30 minutes from place du Général-de-Gaulle in the center of Cagnes-Ville to Le Haut-de-Cagnes at a cost of 7F ($1.20) per person.

VISITOR INFORMATION   The **Office de Tourisme** is at 6 bd. du Maréchal-Juin, Cagnes-Ville (☎ **04-93-20-61-64**).

SPECIAL EVENTS   The **Festival International de la Peinture** is presented in cooperation with Cagne's Town Hall and the Musée d'Art Moderne Méditerranéen from mid-November to mid-January in the Château-Musée, 7 place Grimaldi. Painters from about 40 nations participate in the exposition and promotion of their works. For information, call ☎ **04-93-20-87-29.**

SEEING THE SIGHTS

The orange groves and fields of carnations of the upper village provide a beautiful setting for the narrow cobblestone streets and 17th- and 18th-century homes. Drive your car to the top, where you can enjoy the view from **place du Château** and have lunch or a drink at a sidewalk cafe.

While in Le Haut-de-Cagnes, visit the **fortress** on place Grimaldi. It was built in 1301 by Rainier Grimaldi I, a lord of Monaco and a French admiral (see the portrait inside). Charts reveal how the defenses were organized. In the early 17th century, the dank castle was converted into a more gracious Louis XIII–style château.

The château contains two interconnected museums, the **Musée de l'Olivier** (Museum of the Olive Tree) and the **Musée d'Art Moderne Méditerranéen** (Museum of Modern Mediterranean Art), 7 place Grimaldi (☎ **04-93-20-87-29**). The modern art gallery displays works by Kisling, Carzou, Dufy, Cocteau, and Seyssaud, among others, with temporary exhibitions. In one salon is an interesting trompe-l'oeil fresco, *La Chute de Phaeton.* From the tower, you get a panoramic view of the Côte d'Azur. The museums are open Wednesday to Monday: May to September from 10am to noon and 2 to 6pm, and October to April 10am to noon and 2 to 5pm. Admission to both museums is 20F ($3.40) for adults and 10F ($1.70) for students and children under 12. The International Festival of Painting (see above) takes place here.

A DAY AT THE BEACH

Cros-de-Cagnes is known for 2¼ miles of seafront evenly covered with light-gray pebbles (the French refer to it as *galet*) that've been worn smooth by centuries of wave action. These beaches are collectively identified as the **Plages de Cros-de-Cagnes.** The expanse is punctuated by five concessions that rent beach mattresses and chaises for around 85F ($14.45). The best, or at least the most centrally located, are **Tiercé Plage** (☎ **04-93-20-02-09**), **Le Cigalon** (☎ **04-93-07-74-82**), and **La Gougouline** (☎ **04-93-31-08-72**). As usual, toplessness is accepted but full nudity isn't.

A NEARBY ATTRACTION

Les Collettes. 19 chemin des Collettes. ☎ **04-93-20-61-07.** Admission 20F ($3.40) adults, 10F ($1.70) for children (ticket sales end 30 min. before the lunch and evening closing hour). May–Sept, Wed–Mon 10am–noon and 2–6pm; Oct–Apr, Wed–Mon 10am–noon and 2–5pm.

The house, built in 1907 in an olive and orange grove, has been restored to what it looked like when Renoir lived here from 1908 until his death in 1919. He continued to sculpt, even though he was crippled by arthritis and had to be helped in and out of a wheelchair. He also continued to paint, with a brush tied to his hand and with the help of assistants. One of his last paintings, *Rest After Bathing,* can be seen in the Louvre.

You can explore the drawing room and dining room on your own before going up to the artist's bedroom. In his atelier are his wheelchair, easel, and brushes. From the terrace of Mme Renoir's bedroom is a stunning view of Cap d'Antibes and Le Haut-de-Cagnes. Although Renoir is best remembered for his paintings, it was in Cagnes that he began experimenting with sculpture. The museum has 20 portrait busts and portrait medallions, most of which depict his wife and children. A bust of Mme Renoir is in the entrance room. The curators say they represent the largest collection of Renoir sculpture in the world. On a wall hangs a photograph of one of Renoir's sons, Pierre, as he appeared in the 1932 film *Madame Bovary.*

WHERE TO STAY
IN CAGNES-SUR-MER

Hôtel Le Chantilly. Chemin de la Minoerie, 06800 Cagnes-sur-Mer. ☎ **04-93-20-25-50.** Fax 04-92-02-82-63. 20 units. MINIBAR TV TEL. 320F ($54.40) double. MC, V. Free parking.

This is the best bargain for those who prefer to stay at a hotel near the beach instead of an inn in the hills. It won't win any architectural awards, but the owners have landscaped the property and made the interior as homelike and inviting as possible, using Oriental rugs and potted plants, including dwarf palms, as grace notes. Everything was freshly painted and upgraded in 1999, including the firm mattresses. Bathrooms are compact and tiled, well organized with shower stalls, good plumbing, and adequate shelf space. In fair weather you can enjoy breakfast, the only meal served, on an outdoor terrace. The rooms, for the most part, are small but cozily furnished and well kept, often opening onto balconies. The owners, Monique and Jean-Claude Barran, will direct you to nearby restaurants.

IN LE HAUT-DE-CAGNES

Note that **Le Grimaldi** (see "Where to Dine," below) also rents rooms.

✪ **Le Cagnard.** Rue du Pontis-Long, Le Haut-de-Cagnes, 06800 Cagnes-sur-Mer. ☎ **04-93-20-73-21.** Fax 04-93-22-06-39. www.i-france.com/riviera. 25 units. A/C MINIBAR TV TEL. 800F–1,100F ($136–$187) double; 1,200F–2,400F ($204–$408) suite. AE, DC, MC, V. Parking 50F ($8.50).

Several village houses have been joined to form this handsome hostelry owned by Félix Barel. The dining room is covered with frescoes, and there's a vine-draped terrace. The rooms and salons are furnished with family antiques—Provençal chests, armoires, and Louis XV chairs. Each room has its own style: Some are duplexes, others have terraces and views of the countryside. Beds offer grand comfort with deluxe mattresses, elegant fabrics, and quality linen. Bathrooms have shower/tub combinations, generous shelf space, plush towels, and hair dryers. The cuisine of chef Jean-Yves Johany is reason enough to make the trip here. Fresh ingredients are used in the delectable dishes placed on one of the finest tables set in Provence. This talented chef features Sisteron lamb (*carré d'agneau*) spit-roasted with Provençal herbs for two, as well as tender *côte de boeuf.* The *pièce de résistance* dessert is the extravagant mousseline of ice cream.

IN CROS-DE-CAGNES

Hôtel Le Minaret. 3 Av. Serre, 06800 Cros-de-Cagnes. ☎ **04-93-20-16-52.** Fax 04-92-13-05-56. 20 units. TV TEL. 200F–350F ($34–$59.50) double. MC, V. Free parking.

This two-star hotel has a courtyard with tables in the front and a hardworking staff. It once sported a decorative minaret in the Provençal style; though it was removed in a restoration, the name has remained. Fifty yards from the beach, Le Minaret also has a shaded garden filled with mimosa, orange trees, and palms. Rooms in both offer a terrace or balcony and comfortable mattresses. Each has a kitchenette with minimum cooking utensils and appliances; the decor is simple but clean with serviceable furniture. Bathrooms are boxy and cramped with minimal plumbing, shower stalls, and rather thin towels. There's a bar on the premises, but no restaurant. Several dining places are within walking distance.

WHERE TO DINE
IN LE HAUT-DE-CAGNES

Josy-Jo. 8 place du Planastel. ☎ **04-93-20-68-76.** Reservations required. Main courses 135F–198F ($22.95–$33.65). AE, MC, V. Mon–Fri noon–2pm and 7:30–10pm, Sat 7:30–10pm. Closed Aug 1–15. FRENCH.

Sheltered behind a 200-year-old facade covered with vines and flowers, this restaurant on the main road to the château used to be the home and studio of Modigliani and Soutine, when they borrowed it from a friend during their hungriest years. Today it functions as a cheerful and often bustling dining enclave. Everything is kept running smoothly by the good-natured Bandecchi family. Their cuisine is simple, fresh, and excellent, featuring grilled meats and a roster of fish. You can enjoy brochette of gigot of lamb with kidneys, four succulent varieties of steak, calves' liver, a homemade terrine of foie gras of duckling, and an array of salads.

Le Grimaldi. 6 place du Château. ☎ **04-93-20-60-24.** Reservations recommended. Main courses 60F–130F ($10.20–$22.10); fixed-price menus 110F–160F ($18.70–$27.20). AE, DC, MC, V. Daily noon–3pm and 7:30–11pm. Closed Jan 15–Feb 15. FRENCH.

Here you can dine under bright umbrellas on the town's main square or in a dining room built during the Middle Ages. Run by the same hardworking family since 1963, the restaurant serves specialties like salade Niçoise, *lapin* (rabbit) *chasseur,* a savory version of bouillabaisse, mussels Provençal, and trout with almonds. A noteworthy specialty is escalope of veal "Grimaldi" that's prepared with cheese, crème fraîche, and port.

The hotel also offers six simply furnished rooms, usually with original, roughly hewn ceiling beams, a wash basin, and a bidet. The price is 200F ($34) for a single or double, plus 50F ($8.50) for overnight parking. None has a toilet or shower, although shared facilities are accessible via the upstairs corridors.

✪ **Restaurant des Peintres.** 71 montée de la Bourgade. ☎ **04-93-20-83-08.** Reservations required. Main courses 140F–300F ($23.80–$51); fixed-price menus 200F–420F ($34–$71.40). AE, DC, MC, V. Mon 7:30–10:30pm, Tues noon–2pm, Thurs–Sun noon–2pm and 7:30–10:30pm. Closed Nov 10–30. FRENCH.

About half a mile north of the town center, on the rocky hillside above the center of Cagnes, this 200-year-old building contains an undeniable sense of Provençal authenticity, and Philippe Guerin presents a well-choreographed cuisine. Menu items include foie gras, vegetarian risotto, filets of fried red mullet with eggplant caviar, and stuffed pigeon en cocotte.

IN CROS-DE-CAGNES

✪ **Loulou (La Réserve).** 91 bd. de la Plage. ☎ **04-93-31-00-17.** Reservations recommended. Main courses 150F–325F ($25.50–$55.25); fixed-price menu 220F ($37.40). AE, DC, MC, V. Mon–Fri noon–2:30pm and 7–9:45pm, Sat 7–9:45pm. Closed for lunch July 14–Aug 31. FRENCH.

Run by the Campo family, this place is named for a famous long-departed chef. Brothers Eric and Joseph Campo prepare dishes that include spectacular versions of calamari and octopus salad; fish soup; shrimp steamed and then served with fresh ginger and cinnamon; and grilled, very fresh versions of what local suppliers have brought in that day. These are served as simply as possible, usually with just a drizzling of olive oil and balsamic vinegar. Meat dishes include a flavorful version of veal kidneys with port sauce, usually featured in autumn and winter, and delectable grilled steaks, chops, and cutlets. Everything here is solid, intelligent, and reliable, with a staff that isn't afraid to be gutsy and creative, and flavors that are inherent in virtually every dish. In front is a glassed-in veranda that's a prime spot for people-watching.

7 Nice

577 miles (928.59km) S of Paris, 20 miles (32.19km) NE of Cannes

The Victorian upper classes and tsarist aristocrats loved Nice in the 19th century, but it's solidly middle class today, and far less glamorous and expensive than Cannes—the least expensive of any resort. It's also the best excursion center on the Riviera, especially if you're dependent on public transportation. For example, you can go to San Remo, "the queen of the Italian Riviera," and return to Nice by nightfall. From the Nice airport, the second largest in France, you can travel by bus along the entire coast to resorts like Juan-les-Pins and Cannes.

Nice is the capital of the Riviera, the largest city between Genoa and Marseille. It's also one of the most ancient, having been founded by the Greeks, who called it "Nike," or Victory. Because of its brilliant sunshine and relaxed living, it has attracted artists and writers. Among them were Dumas, Nietzsche, Apollinaire, Flaubert, Victor Hugo, George Sand, Stendhal, Chateaubriand, and Mistral. Henri Matisse, who made his home in Nice, said, "Though the light is intense, it's also soft and tender." The city has, on the average, 300 days of sunshine a year.

ESSENTIALS

GETTING THERE   Trains arrive at **Gare Nice-Ville,** avenue Thiers (☎ **08-36-35-35-35**). From here, you can take frequent trains to Cannes, Monaco, and Antibes, with easy connections to virtually anywhere else along the Mediterranean coast. A small-scale branch of the tourist information office at the station is open Monday to Saturday from 8am to 6:30pm and Sunday from 8am to noon and 2 to 5:30pm. If you face a delay, you can take showers at the station and eat at the cafeteria.

Visitors who arrive at **Aéroport Nice–Côte d'Azur** (☎ **04-93-21-30-30**) can board a yellow-sided bus, the *navette Nice-Aéroport,* which travels several times a day between the railway station and the airport for 21F ($3.55) each way. They operate every day from 6am to 10:30pm, and the last departure of the day meets the last incoming flight. There is also a slower, less comfortable silver-sided municipal bus (including no. 400), but routes stop at 8am every night. A taxi from the airport into the city center will cost at least 140F ($23.80) each way.

VISITOR INFORMATION   The **Office de Tourisme** is at 5 promenade des Anglais (☎ **04-92-14-48-00**), near place Masséna. This office will make a hotel reservation without charging a fee if you show up in person. Be warned in advance that this is a hysterically overworked tourist office, without enough staff members—they are intent on hustling you in and out as fast as possible.

GETTING AROUND   Most of the local buses in Nice connect with one another at their central hub, the **Station Central,** 10 av. Félix-Faure (☎ **04-93-16-52-10**), a very short walk from the place Masséna. Municipal buses each charge 8.50F ($1.45) within Greater Nice. To save money, consider the purchase of a five-ticket *carnet* for 55F ($9.35). If you plan on doing a lot of transits through the city's municipal buses, consider the purchase of a **Carte-Passe Niçoise,** available from the local tourist office, which allows unlimited transit on any city bus during a fixed period. Passes cost 22F ($3.75) for 1 day, 85F ($14.45) for 5 days, and 110F ($18.70) for 1 week. Buses no. 2 and 12 make frequent trips to the beach. Long-distance buses making the trek, say, between Nice and Monaco, Cannes, St-Tropez, and other parts of France and Europe depart from the **Gare Routière,** 5 bd. Jean-Jaurès (☎ **04-93-85-61-81**).

You can rent bicycles and mopeds at **Nicea Rent,** 9 av. Thiers (☎ **04-93-82-42-71**), near the Station Centrale. March to October, it's open daily from 9am to noon and 2 to 6pm (closed Sunday November to April). The cost begins at 120F ($20.40) per day, plus a 1,500F ($255) deposit. Credit cards are accepted.

SPECIAL EVENTS   The **Nice Carnaval** draws visitors from all over Europe and North America to this ancient spectacle. The Riviera's Mardi Gras begins sometime in February, usually 12 days before Shrove Tuesday, with parades, floats *(corsi),* masked balls *(veglioni),* confetti, and battles in which young women toss flowers (and only the most wicked throw rotten eggs instead of carnations). Climaxing the event is a fireworks display on Shrove Tuesday, lighting up the Baie des Anges (Bay of Angels). King Carnaval goes up in flames on his pyre but rises from the ashes the following spring.

The **Nice Festival du Jazz,** from July 10 to 17, takes place in the ancient Arène de Cimiez. For information and tickets, contact the Comité des Fêtes, Mairie (town hall) de Nice, 5 rue de l'Hôtel-de-Ville, 06000 Nice (☎ **04-97-13-20-00**).

EXPLORING THE CITY

In 1822, the orange crop at Nice was bad and the workers faced a lean time, so the English residents put them to work building the **promenade des Anglais,** a wide boulevard fronting the bay. Split by "islands" of palms and flowers, it stretches for about 4 miles. Fronting the beach are rows of grand cafes, the Musée Masséna, villas, and hotels—some good, others decaying.

In the east, the promenade becomes **quai des Etats-Unis,** the original boulevard, lined with some of the best restaurants in Nice, all specializing in bouillabaisse. Rising sharply on a rock is the site known as **Le Château,** the spot where the ducs de Savoie built their castle, which was torn down in 1706. All that remains are two or three stones—even the foundations have disappeared in the wake of Louis XIV's deliberate destruction of what was viewed at the time as a bulwark of Provençal resistance to his regime. The steep hill has been turned into a garden of pines and exotic flowers. To reach the panoramic site, you can take an elevator. The park is open daily from 8am to dusk.

At the north end of Le Château is the famous old **graveyard** of Nice, visited primarily for its lavishly sculpted monuments that make their own enduring art statement. It's the largest in France and the fourth largest in Europe. To reach it, you can take a small canopied **Train Touristique de Nice** (☎ 04-93-92-45-59), which departs from the Jardin Albert-1er. Rolling on rubber wheels, it makes a 40-minute sightseeing transit past many of Nice's sites—place Masséna, promenade des Anglais, and quai des Etats-Unis. The train operates daily, with departures every 30 to 60 minutes. June to August, it operates from 10am to 7pm; April to May and in September, from 10am to 6pm; and October to March, from 10am to 5pm. There's no service between mid-November and mid-December, and during most of January. Train rides last about 45 minutes each. The price is 35F ($5.95) per person.

In the Tour Bellanda is the **Musée de la Marine/Musée Naval,** Parc du Château (☎ 04-93-80-47-61), sitting on "The Rock." The tower stands on a precariously perched belvedere overlooking the beach, the bay, the old town, and even the terraces of some of the nearby villas. Of the museum's old battle prints, one depicts the exploits of Caterina Segurana, the Joan of Arc of the Niçois. During the 1543 siege by Barbarossa, she ran along the ramparts, raising her skirt to show her shapely bottom to the Turks as a sign of contempt, though the soldiers were reported to have been more excited than insulted. The museum is open June to September, Wednesday to Sunday from 10am to noon and 2 to 7pm. Admission is 15F ($2.55) for adults and free for students and children under 16.

Continuing east from "The Rock," you reach **the harbor,** where the restaurants are even cheaper and the bouillabaisse is just as good. While sitting here lingering over an apéritif at a sidewalk cafe, you can watch the boats depart for Corsica (perhaps take one yourself). The port was excavated between 1750 and 1830. Since then, an outer harbor—protected by two jetties—has also been created.

The "authentic" Niçois live in **Vieille Ville,** the old town, beginning at the foot of "The Rock" and stretching out from place Masséna. Sheltered by sienna-tiled roofs, many of the Italianate facades suggest 17th-century Genoese palaces. The old town is a maze of narrow streets, many of them teeming with local life. Some, including the rue Masséna, the rue Droite, and the rue Pairolière, are reserved exclusively for pedestrians. On these narrow streets, you'll find some of the least expensive restaurants in Nice. Buy an onion pizza *(la pissaladière)* from one of the local vendors. Many of the old buildings are painted a faded Roman gold, and their banners are multicolored laundry flapping in the sea breezes.

While here, try to visit the **Marché aux Fleurs,** the flower market at cours Saleya. The vendors start setting up their stalls Tuesday to Sunday from 8am to 6pm in summer, and from 8am till between 2 and 4pm in winter. A flamboyant array of carnations, violets, jonquils, roses, and birds of paradise is hauled in by vans or trucks, then displayed in the most fragrant market in town.

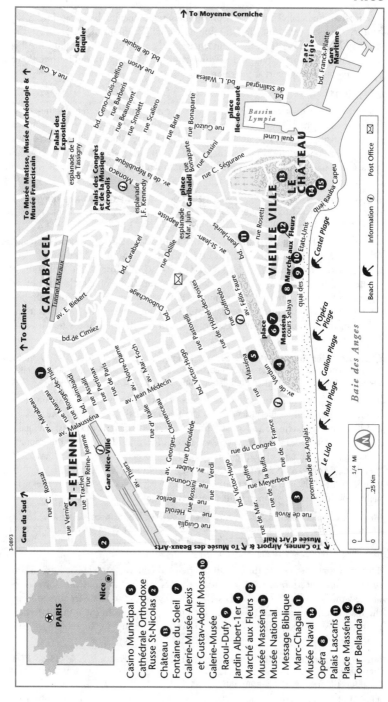

Nice

To Moyenne Corniche ↑

To Cimiez ↑

To Musée Matisse, Musée Archéologie & Musée Franciscain ←

Gare du Sud ↑

Gare Riquier

Parc Vigier

Gare Franck-Pilatte / Gare Maritime

CARABACEL

ST-ETIENNE

Gare Nice-Ville

VIEILLE VILLE

LE CHATEAU

Palais des Expositions

Palais des Congrès et de la Musique Acropolis

place Île-de-Beauté

Bassin Lympia

place Garibaldi

place Masséna

Baie des Anges

Castel Plage

l'Opéra Plage

Galion Plage

Ruhl Plage

Le Lido

Tunnel Malraux

esplanade de L. de Tassigny
esplanade J.F. Kennedy
esplanade Mar. Juin

rue A. Gal
rue Arson
bd. de Riquier
bd. Geno-Louis-Delfino
rue Barberis
rue Beaumont
rue Smollett
rue Scaliero
rue Barla
rue Guizol
rue Cassini
rue C. Ségurane
rue Bonaparte
av. de la République
av. de Verdun
rue Delille
bd. Carabacel
bd. de Cimiez
av. E. Biekert
bd. Dubouchage
rue de l'Hôtel-des-Postes
rue Pastorelli
rue Gioffredo
rue Félix Faure
av. Félix Faure
cours Saleya
bd. Jean-Jaures
rue St-Jean
rue Rossetti
bd. Barla Bonaparte
rue Lunel
quai Lunel
bd. de Stalingrad
bd. L. Walesa
quai Rauba Capeu
quai des Etats-Unis
promenade des Anglais
rue de France
rue du Congrès
rue Meyerbeer
rue de la Buffa
bd. Victor-Hugo
av. Georges-Clemenceau
av. Jean Médecin
rue d'Italie
rue de Paris
rue Pertinax
rue Assalit
bd. Raimbaldi
rue Rouge-de-Lisle
rue Mirabeau
av. Malaussèna
av. Thiers
rue Reine-Jeanne
rue Trachel
rue Vernier
rue C. Roassal
rue Guiglia
rue de Rivoli
rue de Mar.
rue Hérold
rue Berlioz
rue Gounod
rue Rossini
rue Verdi
av. Auber
Joffre
av. Mar. Foch
rue Notre-Dame
rue Déroulède
av. Victor-Hugo
rue Masséna
rue de Mar.

To Cannes, Airport & ↑ To Musée des Beaux-Arts
Musée d'Art Naïf

Beach ↙   Information ⓘ   Post Office ✉

1/4 Mi
.25 Km

N

PARIS ✴   Nice ◉

Casino Municipal ⑤
Cathédrale Orthodoxe Russe St-Nicolas ②
Château ⑬
Fontaine du Soleil ⑦
Galerie-Musée Alexis et Gustav-Adolf Mossa ⑩
Galerie-Musée
Raoul-Dufy ⑨
Jardin Albert-1er ④
Marché aux Fleurs ⑫
Musée Masséna ③
Musée National Message Biblique Marc-Chagall ①
Musée Naval ⑭
Opéra ⑧
Palais Lascaris ⑪
Place Masséna ⑥
Tour Bellanda ⑮

3-0893

287

Nice's commercial centerpiece is **place Masséna,** with pink buildings in the 17th-century Genoese style and the **Fontaine du Soleil** (Fountain of the Sun) by Janoit, from 1956. Stretching from the main square to the promenade is the **Jardin Albert-1er,** with an open-air terrace and a Triton Fountain. With palms and exotic flowers, it's the most relaxing oasis at the resort.

MUSEUMS

There are more museums in Nice than in many comparable French cities. If you decide to forgo the pleasures of the pebbly beach and devote your time to visiting some of the best-respected museums in the south of France, you can buy a **Carte Passe-Musée** from the local tourist office for 70F ($11.90) for a 3-day pass or 140F ($23.80) for a 4-day pass. There are no reductions for students or children. It will allow you admission into seven of the city's largest museums.

Galerie-Musée Raoul-Dufy. 77 quai des Etats-Unis. ☎ **04-93-62-31-24.** Admission 15F ($2.55) adults, 9F ($1.55) children (25F/$4.25 adults, 15F/$2.55 children to include Musée des Beaux-Arts; see below). Tues–Sat 10am–noon and 2–6pm, Sun 3–6pm. Bus: 8.

La Galerie des Ponchettes, inaugurated in 1950 by Matisse, in 1990 became an annex of the Musée des Beaux-Arts under its new name. It presents one of the most beautiful collections by the artist from Le Havre (1877–1953). Most of the collection was bequeathed to the museum by his widow. The diversified works include 28 oils, 15 watercolors, 88 drawings, three ceramics, a tapestry, and 15 proposals for fabric designs commissioned by the legendary couturier Paul Poiret. Dufy himself is immortalized in the new setting that faces the waters of the Baie des Anges that his works helped immortalize.

✪ **Musée des Beaux-Arts.** 33 av. des Baumettes. ☎ **04-92-15-28-28.** Admission (includes entry to the Galerie-Musée Raoul-Dufy) 25F ($4.25) adults, 15F ($2.55) children under 16. Tues–Sun 10am–noon and 2–6pm. Bus: 3,9, 12, 22, 23, or 38.

The collection is housed in the former residence of the Ukrainian Princess Kotchubey. There's an important gallery devoted to the masters of the Second Empire and belle époque, with an extensive collection of the 19th-century French experts. The gallery of sculptures includes works by J. B. Carpeaux, Rude, and Rodin. Note the important collection by a dynasty of painters, the Dutch Vanloo family. One of its best-known members, Carle Vanloo, born in Nice in 1705, was Louis XV's premier *peintre.* A fine collection of 19th- and 20th-century art is displayed, including works by Ziem, Raffaelli, Boudin, Renoir, Monet, Guillaumin, and Sisley.

Musée International d'Art Naïf Anatole-Jakovsky (Museum of Naïve Art). Av. Val-Marie. ☎ **04-93-71-78-33.** Admission 25F ($4.25) adults, 15F ($2.55) students and seniors, free for children 17 and under. Wed–Mon 10am–noon and 2–6pm. Bus: 9, 10, or 12; the walk from the bus stop takes 10 min.

This museum is housed in the beautifully restored Château Ste-Hélène in the Fabron district. The collection was once owned by the namesake of the museum, for years one of the world's leading art critics. His 600 drawings and canvases were turned over to the institution and made accessible to the public. Artists from more than two-dozen countries are represented here—from primitive painting to contemporary 20th-century works.

Musée d'Art et d'Histoire Palais Masséna. 65 rue de France. ☎ **04-93-88-11-34.** Admission 25F ($4.25) adults, 15F ($2.55) children; free for everyone 1 Sun per month. Tues–Sun 10am–noon and 2–6pm. Bus: 3, 7, 8, 9, 10, 12, 14, or 22.

The fabulous villa housing this collection was built in 1900 in the style of the First Empire as a residence for Victor Masséna, the prince of Essling and grandson of

Napoléon's marshal. The city of Nice has converted the villa, next door to the Hôtel Négresco, into a museum of local history and decorative art. A remarkable First Empire drawing room furnished in the opulent taste of that era, with mahogany-veneer pieces and ormolu mounts, is on the ground floor. Of course, there's the representation of Napoléon as a Roman Caesar and a bust by Canova of Maréchal Masséna. The large first-floor gallery exhibits a collection of Niçoise primitives and also has a display of 14th- and 15th-century painters, as well as a collection of 16th- to 19th-century masterpieces of plates and jewelry decorated with enamel (Limoges). There are art galleries devoted to the history of Nice and the memories of Masséna and Garibaldi. Yet another gallery is reserved for a display of views of Nice during the 18th and 19th centuries. *Warning:* Check with the tourist office before going here, as the museum will be closed for part of 2000 for renovations.

More Sights

✪ **Cathédrale Orthodoxe Russe St-Nicolas à Nice.** Av. Nicolas-II (off bd. du Tzaréwitch). ☎ **04-93-96-88-02.** Admission 12F ($2.05). May–Sept daily 9am–noon and 2:30–6pm; Oct–Apr daily 9:30am–noon and 2:30–8pm. From the central rail station, head west along av. Thiers to bd. Gambetta; then go north to av. Nicolas-II.

Ordered built by none other than Tsar Nicholas II, this is the most beautiful religious edifice of the Orthodoxy outside Russia and is the perfect expression of Russian religious art abroad. It dates from the belle époque, when some of the Romanovs and their entourage turned the Riviera into a stomping ground (everyone from grand dukes to ballerinas walked the promenade). The cathedral is richly ornamented and decorated with lots of icons. You'll easily spot the building from afar because of its collection of ornate onion-shaped domes. Church services are held on Sunday morning.

Palais Lascaris. 15 rue Droite. ☎ **04-93-62-05-54.** Admission 25F ($4.25) adults, 15F ($2.55) ages 81–18, free for children under 8. Tues–Sun 10am–noon and 2–6pm. Bus: 1, 2, 3, 5, 6, 14, 16, or 17.

The baroque Palais Lascaris in the city's historic core is intimately linked to the Lascaris-Vintimille family, whose recorded history predates 1261. Built in the 17th century, it contains elaborately detailed ornaments. An intensive restoration undertaken by the city of Nice in 1946 brought back its original beauty, and the palace is now classified a historic monument. The most elaborate floor is the *étage noble,* retaining many of its 18th-century panels and plaster embellishments. A circa-1738 pharmacy, complete with many of the original Delftware accessories, is on the premises. Every Wednesday between 2 and 4pm, the museum focuses attention on children of any age: Various craftspeople are invited to show the details of how they accomplish their art forms through live demonstrations.

Nearby Sights in Cimiez

In the once-aristocratic hilltop quarter of **Cimiez,** Queen Victoria wintered at the Hôtel Excelsior and brought half the English court with her. Founded by the Romans, who called it Cemenelum, Cimiez was the capital of the Maritime Alps province. Recent excavations have uncovered the ruins of a Roman town, and you can wander among the diggings. The arena was big enough to hold at least 5,000 spectators, who watched contests between gladiators and wild beasts shipped in from Africa. To reach this suburb, take bus no. 15 or 17 from place Masséna.

Monastère de Cimiez (Cimiez Convent). Place du Monastère. ☎ **04-93-81-00-04.** Free admission. Museum Mon–Sat 10am–noon and 3–6pm; church daily 8:30am–12:30pm and 2–7pm.

The convent embraces a church that owns three of the most important works from the primitive painting school of Nice by the Bréa brothers. See the carved and gilded wooden main altarpiece. In a restored part of the convent where some Franciscan friars still live, the **Musée Franciscain** is decorated with 17th-century frescoes. Some 350 documents and works of art from the 15th to the 18th century are displayed, and a monk's cell has been re-created in all its severe simplicity. See also the 17th-century chapel. In the gardens, you can get a panoramic view of Nice and the Baie des Anges. Matisse and Dufy are buried in the cemetery.

Musée Matisse. In the Villa des Arènes-de-Cimiez, 164 av. des Arènes-de-Cimiez. ☎ **04-93-81-08-08.** Admission 25F ($4.25) adults, free for ages 17 and under. Wed–Mon 10am–6pm (closes at 5pm off-season).

This museum honors the great artist who spent the last years of his life in Nice; he died here in 1954. Seeing his nude sketches today, you'll wonder how early critics could have denounced them as "the female animal in all her shame and horror." The museum has several permanent collections, most painted in Nice and many donated by Matisse and his heirs. These include *Nude in an Armchair with a Green Plant* (1937), *Nymph in the Forest* (1935/1942), and a chronologically arranged series of paintings from 1890 to 1919. The most famous of these is *Portrait of Madame Matisse* (1905), usually displayed near a portrait of the artist's wife by Marquet, painted in 1900. There's also an ensemble of drawings and designs *(Flowers and Fruits)* he prepared as practice sketches for the Matisse Chapel at Vence. The most famous are *The Créole Dancer* (1951), *Blue Nude IV* (1952), and around 50 dance-related sketches he did between 1930 and 1931.

✪ **Musée National Message Biblique Marc-Chagall.** Av. du Dr.-Ménard. ☎ **04-93-53-87-20.** Admission 30F ($5.10) adults, 20F ($3.40) ages 18-24, free for children 17 and under. Fees may be higher for special exhibits. July–Sept, Wed–Mon 10am–6pm; Oct–June, Wed–Mon 10am–5pm.

In the hills of Cimiez above Nice, this handsome museum, surrounded by shallow pools and a garden planted with thyme, lavender, and olive trees, is devoted to Marc Chagall's treatment of biblical themes. Born in Russia in 1887, Chagall became a French citizen in 1937. The artist and his wife donated the works—the most important collection of Chagall ever assembled—to France in 1966 and 1972. Displayed are 450 of his oils, gouaches, drawings, pastels, lithographs, sculptures, and ceramics; a mosaic; three stained-glass windows; and a tapestry. A splendid concert room was especially decorated by Chagall with brilliantly hued stained-glass windows. Temporary exhibitions are organized each summer featuring great periods and artists of all times.

TWO COUNTRYSIDE DRIVES

FROM NICE TO MONT CHAUVE   This scenic 33-mile tour circles through the much-eroded rocky foothills north of Nice, where vertiginous cliffs add to the drama. Leave Nice by heading north on avenue du Ray. Take a sharp right on avenue de Gairaut, marked with signs to get you to D14, heading toward Aspremont. Pass under the motorway (about 1¼ miles), then follow the D14 signs, first bearing right and then turning left. The first sight, after four switchbacks just north of town, is the **Cascade de Gairaut** (Gairaut waterfall), to your left, where the water of the Vesubie Canal makes two descents into a basin that supplies water to Nice.

The next 3 miles include views to the left of Nice and Cap d'Antibes before climbing to **Aspremont,** where the panorama expands to include the Baous, the Var Valley, and the Alps. Aspremont is known for its Gothic church and the ruins of a hilltop castle from whose terrace you have a commanding view of the villages and hills.

Leave on D719, which follows the Aspremont Pass between two hills to **Tourrette-Levens.** The sights here include an 18th-century church and a partially restored castle from which you can enjoy another great view.

Leave by turning left onto D19, the new name for D719 south of town, and drive down into the Gabre Valley. On the right, you'll pass the **Gorges du Gabres** (Gabre Gorge), with its sheer walls of limestone, and will shortly come to an intersection with D114, where you'll bear right toward **Falicon,** with its buildings clustered on a rocky outcropping in the midst of olive groves. In the village, the Bellevue Inn pays tribute to the author Jules Romains and offers a splendid view from its terrace. Continue along D114, turning left out of the village. At the Chapelle St-Sebastien, turn right onto D214, a narrow curving road that ends at the foot of **Mount Chauve.** A half-hour hike will take you to the summit, where an abandoned fort overlooks the Alps, the Nice foothills, and the coast.

Backtrack past Falicon and make a sharp right on D19, heading toward Nice. On the way, you'll see the **Benedictine Abbaye St-Pontius,** dating from the reign of Charlemagne and rebuilt early in the 18th century, recognizable looming above the horizon with its Genoese bell tower and tall baroque facade. Its elliptical floor plan includes a semicircular choir loft and side chapels, the latter separated from the main sanctuary by immense columns. After viewing the abbey, continue south on D19 for about 2½ miles to return to Nice.

FROM NICE TO LEVENS   Levens is an attractive residential town guarding the Vallée de la Vésubie. Fifteen miles from Nice on D19, it's at an altitude of 1,800 feet. Here you'll find some of the most beautiful spots in the mountains. We recommend taking a trip to **Saut des Français** (Frenchmen's Leap), at the exit from the village of Duranus. In 1793, French Republican soldiers were tossed over this belvedere by guerrilla bands from Nice, called Barbets. The fall—without a parachute—was some 1,200 feet down to the Vésubie. Fifteen miles farther, **La Madone d'Utelle,** at 3,900 feet, offers a panoramic view of the Maritime Alps.

If you want to overnight here, try the **Hôtel Malaussena,** 9 place de la République, Levens, 06670 St-Martin-du-Var (☎ **04-93-79-70-06;** fax 04-93-79-85-89). This centrally located hotel offers 14 clean, comfortable units, some with first-rate plumbing. Though the inn is fairly simple, the welcome is first-class. The rates are 230F ($39.10) for a double (American Express, MasterCard, and Visa accepted). The food is excellent but not recommended for dieters, and two fixed-price menus from 80 to 195F ($13.60 to $33.15) are offered. Dinner is served at 7:30pm. The restaurant is closed to nonguests, except in July and August when the public is welcome, with reservations. The hotel is closed in November and December.

OUTDOOR PURSUITS

THE BEACH   On the beach, wearing the briefest of bikinis or thongs, are some of the world's most attractive bronzed bodies. The pebbles of the shingled beach—"on the rocks," as it's called here—are tough on tender feet and one of the least attractive (and least publicized) aspects of the cosmopolitan resort city. Many bathhouses provide mattresses for a charge.

GOLF   The oldest golf course on the Riviera is about 10 miles from Nice: **Golf Bastide du Roi** (also known as the Golf de Biot), avenue Jules-Grec, Biot (☎ **04-93-65-08-48**). Open daily throughout the year, this is a flat, not particularly challenging sea-fronting course. (Regrettably, it's necessary to cross over a highway midway through the course to complete the full 18 holes.) Tee-off times are 8am to 6pm, with the understanding that players then continue their rounds as long as the daylight allows. Reservations aren't necessary, though on weekends you should probably expect a delay. Greens fees are 240F ($40.80) for 18 holes, and clubs can be rented for 50F ($8.50).

HORSEBACK RIDING   Club Hippique de Nice, 368 Rte. de Grenoble (☎ 04-93-71-24-34), rents 13 of its horses. About 3 miles from Nice, near the airport, it's hemmed in on virtually every side by busy roads and highways and conducts all activities in a series of riding rinks. Riding sessions should be reserved in advance; they last about an hour, and cost 80F ($13.60).

SCUBA DIVING   The best outfit is the **Centre International de Plongée de Nice,** 2 ruelle des Moulins (☎ 04-93-55-59-50). Adjacent to the city's old port, midway between quai des Docks and boulevard Stalingrad, it's maintained by the Champagne-born Raymond Lefevre, whose dive boat, *René-Madeleine,* is an amalgam of the names of his parents. A *baptême* (initiatory dive for first-timers) costs 150F ($25.50) and a one-tank dive for experienced divers, with all equipment included, is 190F ($32.30).

TENNIS   The oldest tennis club in Nice is the **Nice Lawn Tennis Club,** Parc Impérial, 5 av. Suzanne-Lenglen (☎ 04-92-15-58-00), near the train station. It's open daily from 8:30am to 9pm and charges 120F ($20.40) per person for 2 hours of court time, or a reduced rate of 300F ($51) per person for unlimited access to the courts for 1 week. The club contains a cooperative staff, a loyal clientele, 13 clay courts, and 6 hard-surfaced courts. Reservations should be made the evening before.

SHOPPING

You might want to begin with a stroll through the streets and alleys of Nice's historic core. The densest concentrations of boutiques are along **rue Masséna, place Magenta, l'avenue Jean-Médecin, rue de Verdun,** and the **rue Paradis,** as well as on the streets funneling into and around them. Individual shops of note include **Gigi,** 7 rue de la Liberté (☎ 04-93-87-81-78) and **Carroll,** 9 rue de la Liberté (☎ 04-93-16-15-25), both of which sell sophisticated-looking clothing for women, and **Trabaud,** 10 rue de la Liberté (☎ 04-93-87-53-96), an emporium for menswear. Timeless and endlessly alluring, despite the passage of time, are the products sold at **Yves Saint-Laurent Rive Gauche,** 4 av. de Suéde (☎ 04-93-87-70-79), where the most upscale of the ready-to-wear St-Laurent line is sold, as well as the less expensive garments from the company's cost-conscious Variations line.

Opened in 1949 by Joseph Fuchs, the grandfather of the present English-speaking owners, the **Confiserie Florian du Vieux-Nice,** 14 quai Papacino (☎ 04-93-55-43-50), is near the Old Port. The specialty here is glazed fruits crystallized in sugar or made into chocolates. Look for exotic jams (rose-petal preserves or mandarin marmalade) and the free recipe leaflet as well as candied violets, verbena leaves, and rosebuds. Prices for the sugary confections range from 150F to 215F ($25.50 to $36.55) per kilo, depending on the fruits you select.

Façonnable, 7–9 rue Paradis (☎ 04-93-87-88-80), is the site that sparked the creation of what is today several hundred Façonnable menswear stores around the world. This is one of the largest Façonnable stores in the world, with a wide range of men's suits, raincoats, overcoats, sportswear, and jeans. The look is youthful and conservatively stylish.

If you're thinking of indulging in a Provençale *pique-nique,* **Nicola Alziari,** 14 rue St-François-de-Paule (☎ 04-93-85-77-98), will provide everything you'll need: from olives, anchovies, and pistous to aïolis and tapenades. It's one of Nice's oldest purveyors of olive oil, with a house brand that comes in two strengths—a light version that aficionados claim is vaguely perfumed with Provence, and a stronger version suited to the earthy flavors and robust ingredients of a Provençal winter. Also look for a range of objects crafted from olive wood.

Other shopping recommendations include **La Couquetou,** 8 rue St-François-de-Paule (☎ **04-93-80-90-30**), selling *santons,* the traditional Provençal figurines. The best selection of Provençal fabrics is found at **Le Chandelier,** 7 rue de la Boucherie (☎ **04-93-85-85-19**), where the designs of two of the region's best-known producers of cloth, Les Olivades and Valdromme, are modelled on the burnt yellows and cerulean tones of Provence.

Nice is also known for its colorful street markets. The flower market, **Marché aux Fleurs,** cours Saleya, is open from 6am to 5:30pm except Monday and Sunday afternoon. The main Nice flea market, **Marché à la Brocante,** also at cours Saleya, takes place every Monday from 8am to 5pm. There's another flea market on the port, **Les Puces de Nice,** place Robilante, open Tuesday to Saturday from 9am to 6pm.

WHERE TO STAY
VERY EXPENSIVE

✪ **Hôtel Négresco.** 37 promenade des Anglais, 06007 Nice CEDEX. ☎ **04-93-16-64-00.** Fax 04-93-88-35-68. E-mail: negresco@nicematin.fr. 150 units. A/C MINIBAR TV TEL. 1,350F–2,550F ($229.50–$433.50) double; from 3,400F–8,150F ($578–$1,385.50) suite. AE, DC, MC, V. Parking 160F ($27.20) in the garage. Bus: 9, 10, or 11.

The Négresco is one of the Riviera's many super-glamorous hotels, though it's not sited for tranquillity—the Négresco stands in the heart of noisy Nice. Jeanne Augier has taken over the place and has triumphed. This Victorian wedding-cake hotel is named after its founder, Henry Négresco, a Romanian who died franc-less in Paris in 1920. It was built on the seafront, in the French château style, with a mansard roof and domed tower; its interior decorators scoured Europe to gather antiques, tapestries, paintings, and art. Some of the guest rooms are outfitted in homage to the personalities who stayed at the hotel during its long and illustrious history: The Coco Chanel Room, for example. Others are fancifully modeled after literary or musical themes, like La Traviata. Each was renovated sometime during the mid-to-late 1990s, and in 1998, most of the bathrooms were upgraded into well-engineered, state-of-the art affairs, usually with pink or white marble, all with plush towels and hair dryers. Suites and public areas are even grander, as is the case with the Louis XIV salon, reminiscent of the Sun King himself, or the Napoléon III suite, where swagged walls, a leopard-skin carpet, and a half-crowned canopy in pink create an undeniable sense of majesty. The most expensive rooms with balconies face the Mediterranean. All rooms are equipped with sumptuous beds containing luxury mattresses. The staff wears 18th-century costumes. Reasonably priced meals are served in La Rotonde, but the featured restaurant—one of the Riviera's greatest—is Chantecler (see "Where to Dine," below).

✪ **Palais Maeterlinck.** Basse Corniche, 06300 Nice. ☎ **04-92-00-72-00.** Fax 04-92-04-18-10. www.webstore.fr/Maeterlinck. 40 units. A/C MINIBAR TV TEL. 1,450F–2,800F ($246.50–$476) double; 2,500F–10,000F ($425–$1,700) suite. AE, DC, MC, V. Closed Jan 4 to mid-Mar. Drive 4 miles east of Nice along the Basse Corniche.

On 9 landscaped acres east of Nice, this deluxe hotel—"the jewel of the Côte d'Azur"—occupies a fin-de-siècle villa that was inhabited between the world wars by the Belgian-born writer Maurice Maeterlinck, winner of the Nobel Prize for Literature. Many visitors find the setting sumptuous, though, frankly, the service and experience of the staff simply do not match that of similarly priced palace hotels. Calmer and more tranquil than the hotels in the center, it enjoys the added allure of verdant terraces and a large outdoor pool set amid banana trees, gnarled olive trees, and soaring cypresses. A funicular will carry you down to the rock-strewn beach and nearby marina. Each of the elegant guest rooms is outfitted in a different monochromatic color scheme and neoclassical Florentine styling, and each has a terrace opening onto views of such chic enclaves as Cap d'Antibes and Cap-Ferrat. Mattresses are very comfortable; bathrooms are plush with fluffy towels.

The hotel's two restaurant include Mélisande, a gastronomic hideaway whose neo-Renaissance decor was upgraded in 1998. Set-price meals there cost 240F ($40.80). Less formal, and slightly less expensive, is the Club Nautique, a brasserie with a nautical theme and a series of Provençal and international specialties.

EXPENSIVE

✪ Château des Ollières. 39 av. des Baumettes, 06000 Nice. ☎ **04-92-15-77-99.** Fax 04-92-15-77-98. 6 units. A/C MINIBAR TV TEL. 800F–2,000F ($136–$340) double; 1,900F–3,000F ($323–$510) suite. AE, MC, V. Bus: 38.

The most appealing and unusual place to open in Nice in many years made its debut as a hotel in 1996, and as a French restaurant a year later. The setting is a 5-minute walk from the Négresco and the Promenade des Anglais, in a 20-acre park loaded with exotic trees and shrubs. Its centerpiece is a Beaux-Arts villa built in the 1870s by a Russian prince. Inside, you'll find a noteworthy collection of oil paintings and "neo-Napoléonienne" and Empire-inspired antiques, including a set custom-made for the dining room at the time of the villa's construction. Bedrooms are outfitted in the same high-ceilinged, ornate style as the public areas. Bathrooms are elegant, with every amenity, including bidets, plush towels, robes, and deluxe toiletries.

Hôtel Beau Rivage. 24 rue St-François-de-Paule, 06300 Nice. ☎ **04-93-80-80-70.** Fax 04-93-80-55-77. www.newhotel.com. 118 units. A/C MINIBAR TV TEL. 700F–1,100F ($119–$187) double; 1,900F ($323) suite. AE, DC, MC, V. Bus: 1, 2, 5, or 12.

This hotel is famous for having housed both Matisse and Chekhov during its heyday around the turn of the century. It was radically renovated in the early 1980s, and today the interior has a bland but tasteful modern decor and a staff that seems to make a point of appearing overworked regardless of how few guests there may be. The sound-proof rooms are vaguely art deco and rather small, with contemporary baths and firm mattresses. For dining, Le Bistrot du Rivage is relatively formal and very appealing. Its specialties are meats and fish prepared on a large grill. Between May and September, tables are set on a terrace.

Hôtel Elysée Palace. 59 promenade des Anglais, 06000 Nice. ☎ **04-93-86-06-06.** Fax 04-93-44-50-40. 143 units. A/C MINIBAR TV TEL. 850F–1,000F ($144.50–$170) double; from 1,250–1,850F ($212.50–$314.50) suite. AE, DC, MC, V. Parking 75F ($12.75). Bus: 9, 10, or 12.

Views sweep out over the sea from most of the rooms of this hotel. Decor is conservative and contemporary, and the amenities in the rooms are typical, including comfortable beds with firm mattresses and bedside controls. The seafront rooms, of course, are the more desirable. Rooms on the fifth, sixth, and seventh floors overlook the Mediterranean. Bathrooms are clad in marble with bidets, phones, thick towels, and shower/tub combinations, but you have to request robes and hair dryers from reception. The hotel has its own private beach a short walk from its premises as well as a rooftop pool. The well-managed restaurant, Le Caprice, serves French cuisine.

Hôtel Méridien. 1 promenade des Anglais, 06000 Nice. ☎ **04-93-82-25-25.** Fax 04-93-16-08-90. www.meridien.nice.fr. 314 units. A/C MINIBAR TV TEL. 1,050F–1,800F ($178.50–$306) double; from 2,800F–3,200F ($476–$544) suite. Discounts of around 15% during selected dates Oct–Apr. AE, DC, MC, V. Bus: 8, 9, 10, or 3.

One of Nice's largest hotels, this one rises five floors above the junction of the promenade des Anglais and a small formal park, the Jardin Albert-1er. Built in the 1960s by Air France in an angular design with lots of shiny metal and glass, it was later acquired by Britain's Forte group and hosts many organized tours from Britain and northern

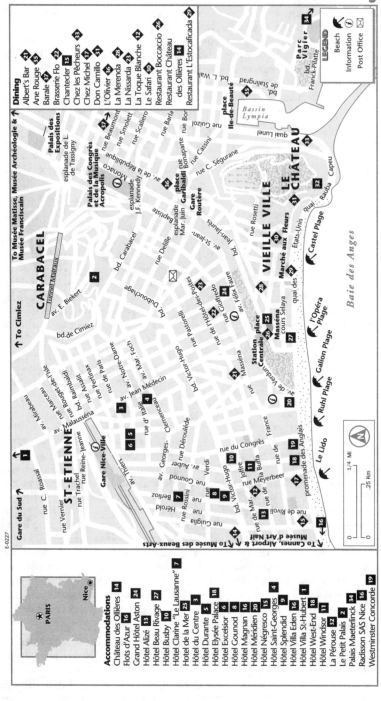

Nice Accommodations & Dining

Dining
Albert's Bar 21
Ane Rouge 35
Barale 37
Brasserie Flo 15
Chantecler 17
Chez les Pêcheurs 31
Chez Michel 28
Don Camillo 23
L'Olivier 6
La Merenda 24
La Nissarda 12
La Toque Blanche 14
Le Safari 29
Restaurant Boccaccio
Restaurant Château des Ollières
Restaurant L'Estocaficada 29

Accommodations
Château des Ollières 14
Flots d'Azur 16
Grand Hôtel Aston 24
Hôtel Alizé 13
Hôtel Beau Rivage 27
Hôtel Busby 10
Hôtel Clarine "Le Lausanne" 7
Hotel de la Mer 25
Hôtel du Centre 3
Hôtel Durante 5
Hôtel Elysée Palace 18
Hôtel Excelsior 6
Hôtel Gounod 8
Hôtel Magnan 16
Hôtel Méridien 20
Hôtel Négresco 15
Hôtel Saint-Georges 4
Hôtel Splendid 9
Hôtel Villa Eden 16
Hôtel Villa St-Hubert 18
Hôtel West-End 1
Hôtel Windsor 11
La Pérouse 32
Le Petit Palais 2
Palais Maeterlinck 34
Radisson SAS Nice 16
Westminster Concorde 19

LEGEND
Beach
Information
Post Office

PARIS

Nice

Baie des Anges

Bassin Lympia

CARABACEL

ST-ETIENNE

VIEILLE VILLE

LE CHÂTEAU

To Cimiez

To Musée Mattisse, Musée Archéologie & Musée Franciscain

E-0227

295

Europe. Two escalators carry you up through a soaring, impersonal atrium to the reception area. Guest rooms are modern and standardized, many with sea views; they sport new mattresses, carpets, and paint. The seafront rooms, though desirable for the view, are actually the smallest in the hotel; space has been sacrificed to make way for terraces or balconies. Bathrooms are well equipped. Amenities include trouser presses, plush towels, and hair dryers. There's a piano bar, and a zesty restaurant, Le Colonia Café, that celebrates the late-19th-century overseas conquests of France and England—the emphasis is on spicy, sometimes curried, international cuisine. On the roof of the hotel are a large swimming pool and a sun deck.

Hôtel Splendid. 50 bd. Victor-Hugo, 06048 Nice. ☎ **04-93-16-41-00.** Fax 04-93-87-02-46. www.cote-dazur.com/splendid. 130 units. A/C MINIBAR TV TEL. 690F–950F ($117.30– $161.50) double; from 1,000F ($170) suite. AE, DC, MC, V. Parking 75F ($12.75). Bus: 9 or 10.

This is one of Nice's best modern hotels, on the corner of a wide boulevard lined with shade trees, 4 blocks from the beach. Built on the site of the circa-1881 Hôtel Splendid, it was heralded as a new era in French hotels. Frequent renovations have kept the place fresh. The rooms usually have terraces or balconies, and several floors are reserved for nonsmokers. Accommodations come in various shapes and sizes, but have the same amenities: private safes, electronic locks, and soundproofing. Beds are a bit narrow but the mattresses are first-class. Bathrooms are tiled and well equipped with hair dryers, scales, deluxe toiletries, and plush towels. Le Concerto features classic French cooking, with a three-course lunch or dinner at 145F ($24.65). Adjacent to the rooftop pool, the Topsail Bar offers a salad buffet and views over the city and sea. Facilities include an open-air solar-heated pool and a wading pool for kids.

Radisson SAS Nice. Promenade des Anglais 328, 06200 Nice. ☎ **04-93-37-17-17.** Fax 04-93-71-21-71. www.radisson.com. 328 units. A/C MINIBAR TV TEL. 890F–1,500F ($151.30–$255) double; from 2,900F ($493) suite. AE, DC, MC, V. Parking 110F ($18.70). Bus: 8.

Set alongside the major beachside thoroughfare of Nice, this streamlined and tastefully contemporary hotel has undergone more name and ownership changes than any other major hotel in town. In 1998, it was acquired by the Radisson chain, which inaugurated renovations to the public areas and bedrooms. Today, it features a sun-floored, elegantly simple lobby and attractive bedrooms with conservatively modern furniture. Many business travelers come here. Standardized accommodations come with built-in furniture, double glazing, and comfortable beds with two sets of lamps. They are equipped with a tile and marble bathroom with adequate shelf space and a shower/tub combination. Overall, there's a sense of bustle, with an alert staff that's hip to the goings-on in Nice and along the Côte d'Azur—a feel of Paris-on-the-beach. Visitors enjoy soft piano music in the sophisticated piano bar in the lobby. Les Mosaiques offers a gastronomic French cuisine. At lunchtime, between June and September, one of the most sumptuous buffets in Nice is served beside the pool at 195F ($33.15) per person. Amenities include a 24-hour concierge, same-day laundry and valet service, a rooftop pool with bar, boutiques, a beauty salon, a sauna, a fitness center, and an underground garage.

Westminster Concorde. 27 promenade des Anglais, 06000 Nice. ☎ **04-92-14-86-86.** Fax 04-93-82-45-35. 120 units. A/C MINIBAR TV TEL. 750F–1,300F ($127.50–$221) double; from 1,500F ($255) junior suite. AE, DC, MC, V. Parking 100F ($17). Bus: 9, 10, or 11.

This 1860 hotel stands prominently along the famous promenade. Its elaborate facade was restored in 1986 to its former grandeur, and many renovations were made, including the installation of air-conditioning. The contemporary rooms have soundproof windows; a few open onto balconies. Accommodations range in size from medium to spacious, running the gamut from period styling to contemporary. Often they have high ceilings, antique mirrors, French windows, and brass beds. All are fitted with quality linen and deluxe mattresses. Bathrooms are tiled or marble, each with shower/tub combination and generous shelf space. The dining and drinking facilities include plant-ringed terraces with a view of the water and a simple in-house restaurant.

MODERATE

Grand Hôtel Aston. 12 av. Félix-Faure, 06000 Nice. ☎ **04-92-17-53-00.** Fax 04-93-80-40-02. 156 units. 650F–1,300F ($110.50–$221) double. AE, DC, MC, V. Parking 100F ($17). Bus: 12.

One of the most alluring in its price bracket, this elegantly detailed 19th-century hotel has been radically renovated. Bedrooms are outfitted in monochromatic color schemes, with comfortable mattresses. Price scales vary according to view: the street, the splashing fountains of the place Masséna, or the panorama of the coastline from the top floor. Bathrooms are medium in size with shower/tub combinations and hair dryers. On summer evenings, an outdoor, garden-style bar, sometimes with dance music, provides diversions from a spot on the hotel's uppermost floor. The hotel is associated with Holland's Golden Tulip chain.

Hôtel Busby. 36–38 rue du Maréchal-Joffre, 06000 Nice. ☎ **04-93-88-19-41.** Fax 04-93-87-73-53. 80 units. A/C TV TEL. 500F–700F ($85–$119) double. AE, DC, MC, V. Closed Nov 15–Dec 20. Bus: 9, 10, 12, or 22.

This place should please you if you want a nostalgic hotel of faded early 20th-century grandeur. The Busby-family owners refer to its ornate facade as "style Garibaldi" and have retained the balconies and the shutters at the tall windows. Renovated at regular intervals, yet looking a bit tired, the guest rooms are dignified; some contain mahogany twin beds and white-and-gold wardrobes. Mattresses are a bit worn but there is still comfort here, along with tiled bathrooms that are a bit cramped, with adequate shelf space and shower stalls. There's a cozy bar on the premises but no restaurant.

Hotel Clarine "Le Lausanne." 36 rue Rossini, 06000 Nice. ☎ **04-93-88-85-94.** Fax 04-93-88-15-88. 35 units. A/C TV TEL. 370F–440F ($62.90–$74.80) double. AE, DC, MC, V. Parking 40F ($6.80). Bus: 8.

This is a solid, middle-bracket hotel with a central location in a commercial neighborhood in the heart of Nice. It was radically renovated in the mid-1990s, and does not retain very much of its original architectural embellishments. Views from the windows look out over the street, and its efficient bedroom furnishings are standard for the well-respected Clarine chain. Rooms have comfortable mattresses, tiled bathrooms, adequate numbers of good-sized towels, and color schemes of blue or green. Overall, this is a reliable, although not particularly exciting, hotel choice. No meals are served other than breakfast.

Hôtel Excelsior. 190 av. Durante, 06000 Nice. ☎ **04-93-88-18-05.** Fax 04-93-88-38-69. 45 units. TV TEL. 337F–497F ($57.30–$84.50) double. AE, MC, V. Parking 65F ($11.05). Bus: 1, 2, 5, 12, 18, 23, or 24.

Its ornate corbels and chiseled stone pediments rise grandly a few steps from the railway station. This 19th-century, much renovated, and altered hotel has a pleasantly modern decor with durable rooms that have seen a lot of wear but are still serviceable. Mattresses are middle grade, on twin or double beds. Furnishings, for the most part, are functional and conservative; units were last renovated in 1998. Bathrooms are small and tiled. The beach is a 20-minute walk through the residential and commercial heart of Nice.

✪ **Hôtel Gounod.** 3 rue Gounod, 06000 Nice. ☎ **04-93-88-26-20.** Fax 04-93-88-23-84. www.cote-dazur.com/gounod. 46 units. A/C MINIBAR TV TEL. 420F–650F ($71.40–$110.50) double; 550F–890F ($93.50–$151.30) suite. AE, DC, MC, V. Closed Nov 20–Dec 20. Parking 60F ($10.20). Bus: 8.

This is our favorite three-star hotel in Nice, built around 1910 in a neighborhood where the street names honor composers. The Gounod *(un petit Négresco)* boasts ornate balconies, a domed roof, and an elaborate canopy of wrought iron and glass. The attractive lobby and adjoining lounge are festive and stylish, with old prints, copper pots with flowers, and antiques. The high-ceilinged guest rooms are quiet and usually overlook the gardens of private homes on both sides. Other than comfortable mattresses and adequate numbers of good-sized towels, there are few amenities, but you have free unlimited use of the facilities at the Hotel Splendid next door, especially the pool, cafe-bar, and heated Jacuzzi.

Hôtel West-End. 31 promenade des Anglais, 06000 Nice. ☎ **800/528-1234** in the U.S., or 04-92-14-44-00. Fax 04-93-88-85-07. 135 units. A/C MINIBAR TV TEL. 750F–1,450F ($127.50–$246.50) double; 1,800–2,000F ($306–$340) suite. AE, DC, MC, V. Parking 120F ($20.40). Bus: 8.

A belle époque monument whose flowering terrace overlooks the sea, this Best Western is named after London's theater district. Though the ornate facade and the stately lobby were retained in honor of the original construction, the guest rooms were streamlined during several modernizations, yet are comfortable and well furnished. The best units are found on the fifth and sixth floors and are called "Elite." Rooms labeled "Business" and "Tradition" are more standardized and commercial, often filled with business travelers. All come with comfortable mattresses, most often on twin or double beds. Most have a compact tiled bathroom with a shower/tub combo, adequate shelf space, and a hair dryer. Many offer sea views. You can enjoy drinks on the terrace near a restaurant serving French and international cuisine. There's also a private beach. Because of the hotel's relatively large size, the staff can often appear a bit overworked, but overall it's a worthy choice.

✪ **Hotel Windsor.** 11 rue Dalpozzo, 06000 Nice. ☎ **04-93-88-59-35.** Fax 04-93-88-94-57. E-mail: windsor@webstore.fr. 420F–700F ($71.40–$119) double. AE, DC, MC, V. Parking 60F ($10.20). Bus: 8.

One of the most arts-conscious hotels in Provence, it's in a *maison bourgeoise,* built by disciples of Gustav Eiffel in 1895, near the Hotel Négresco and the Promenade des Anglais. A one-of-a-kind series of frescoes adorns each of the bedrooms. The heir of the long-time owners, the Redolfi family, is responsible for commissioning these paint-ings, based on his mystical visions after he had extensively traveled in Africa and South America. About 40 of the rooms were frescoed by the since-deceased Antoine Bodoin, who was a talented decorator rather than an artist. The rest of the paintings were arranged for by Christian Bernard, a museum curator in Belgium who sent a series of well-known artists here on long-term residencies, including American Richard Barry, British Glenn Baxter, and French-born François Morellet. These artists have left an enduring creative legacy on the walls of the rooms you might inhabit. Bedrooms are small to medium in size, with good mattresses and small bathrooms that are tidily maintained. Amid the public areas that have a kind of Zen-inspired feeling of well-being are more mythical frescoes. An unusual and complicated fifth-floor superstruc-ture is today the site of a health club, steamroom, and sauna. The dining room is open only to residents of the hotel. The garden contains scores of tropical and exotic plants, and the recorded sounds of birds singing in the jungles of the Amazon. There's also a swimming pool, and a deeply rooted sense of total immersion into the priorities and politics of southern France's world of contemporary gallery-goers. Whether it's wonderful or *de trop* will depend on you.

La Pérouse. 11 quai Rauba-Capéu, 06300 Nice. ☎ **04-93-62-34-63.** Fax 04-93-62-59-41. 66 units. A/C MINIBAR TV TEL. 745-1,490F ($126.65–$253.30) double; 1,870F–2,520F ($317.90–$428.40) suite. AE, DC, MC, V. Parking 60F ($10.20).

Once a prison, La Pérouse has been reconstructed and is now a unique Riviera hotel. Set on a cliff, it overlooks the sea and is entered through a lower-level lobby, where an elevator takes you up to the gardens and a pool. There's no hotel in Nice with a better view over both the old city and the Baie des Anges. Many people stay here for the view alone. In fact, La Pérouse is built right into the gardens of an ancient château-fort. Inside, the hotel is like an old Provençal home, with low ceilings, white walls, and antiques. Most of the lovely rooms have loggias overlooking the bay. Medium-sized guest rooms are fairly standardized but evoke the tropics in their use of rattan and bamboo along with floral fabrics. Some of the pieces are in a cheap veneer, but the mattresses are first-rate, and added features include spacious closets and often balconies. Baths are tiled and nicely equipped with hair dryers, adequate shelf space, and middle-grade towels. The restaurant, with a different menu every day, specializes in a Niçois cuisine and is open only for dinner in summer (in winter, guests rely on room service).

INEXPENSIVE

Flots d'Azur. 101 promenade des Anglais, 06000 Nice. ☎ **04-93-86-51-25.** Fax 04-93-97-22-07. 21 units. A/C TEL. 270F–500F ($45.90–$85) double. MC, V. Bus: 8.

This three-story villa-hotel is next to the sea, a short walk from the more elaborate and costlier promenade hotels. While the rooms vary in size and decor, all have good views and sea breezes, and 12 contain TVs and minibars. Double-glazed windows were recently added to cut down on the noise. Each room is fitted with a firm mattress on twin or double beds. Bathrooms are tiled and compact with shower stalls. There's a small sitting room and sun terrace in front, where a continental breakfast is served.

Hotel Alizé. 65 rue Buffa, 06000 Nice. ☎ and fax **04-93-88-99-46.** 10 units. A/C TEL. 290F–360F ($49.30–$61.20) double. AE, MC, V. Parking 69F ($11.75). Bus: 8.

Right on the promenade des Anglais and boulevard Gambetta, this modest hotel, near the chic and pricey Négresco, is a real bargain. Breakfast is the only meal served, but there are many restaurants nearby. Each of the small to medium-sized bedrooms comes with a good mattress; the decor often features bright, inviting colors. There were extensive renovations in 1998 and 1999, and the accommodations are much improved, as are the baths with shower stalls. About half of the rooms also contain a TV.

Hôtel de la Mer. 4 place Masséna, 06000 Nice. ☎ **04-93-92-09-10.** Fax 04-93-85-00-64. 12 units. TV TEL. 250F–380F ($42.50–$64.60) double. AE, MC, V. Parking 100F ($17) in a nearby covered garage. Bus: 1, 2, 5, 15, or 17.

In the center of Old Nice, this place was built around 1910. Though it was renovated in 1993, it manages to keep its prices low. Ms. Feri Forouzan, the owner, welcomes you with personalized charm. Most guest rooms are of good size and have such items as a minibar and TV, not often found in inexpensive hotels. Mattresses are firm and well chosen, dating from 1994. Bathroom amenities and towels are of good overall quality. From the hotel, it's a 2-minute walk to promenade des Anglais and the seafront. Breakfast is served in one of the public salons or your room.

Hôtel du Centre. 2 rue de Suisse, 06000 Nice. ☎ **04-93-88-83-85.** 28 units. TV TEL. 257F–297F ($43.70–$50.50) double. AE, MC, V. Parking 8F ($1.35). Bus: 23.

Near the train station, this simple but clean hotel welcomes a clientele that is about 100% gay. The uncomplicated rooms are very close to the attractions of downtown Nice. Mattresses are well worn but still comfortable. Bathrooms are small and standardized with shower stalls and rather thin towels. The staff is a useful source of inside information for whatever you might be seeking.

Hôtel Durante. 16 av. Durante, 06000 Nice. ☎ **04-93-88-84-40.** Fax 04-93-87-77-76. 26 units. TV TEL. 380F–500F ($64.60–$85) double. MC, V. Closed Nov 8–Feb 8.

A comfortable and much-modified building dating from around the turn of the century, this hotel is very popular with producers, actors, and directors during the nearby Cannes Film Festival. Many rooms face a quiet courtyard, and all have a kitchenette and refrigerator. The furnishings have known a better day, but the beds are still quite comfortable. Bathrooms are compact with shower stalls, hair dryers, and rather thin towels. The owner, Mme Dufaure de Citres, dispenses both charm and information about local cinematic events. There's also a private garden.

Hôtel Magnan. Square du Général-Ferrié, 06200 Nice. ☎ **04-93-86-76-00.** Fax 04-93-44-48-31. 25 units. TV TEL. 280F–380F ($47.60–$64.60) double. AE, MC, V. Parking 35F ($5.95). Bus: 12, 23, or 24.

This well-run modern hotel was built around 1945 and has been renovated frequently during its long and busy life. It's a 10-minute bus ride from the heart of town but only a minute or so from promenade des Anglais and the bay. Many of the simply furnished rooms have balconies facing the sea, and some contain minibars. The look is a bit functional but for Nice this is a good price considering how comfortable the beds are. Don't expect much from the bathrooms other than a shower stall and a rack of middle-grade towels. The owner, Daniel Thérouin, occupies the apartment on the top floor, guaranteeing close supervision. Breakfast can be served in your room.

Hotel Saint-Georges. 7 av. Georges Clemenceau, 06000 Nice. ☎ **04-93-88-79-21.** 35 units. A/C TV TEL. 295F–320F ($50.15–$54.40) double. AE, MC, V. Bus: 1.

Originally built during the grand days of Niçois tourism, this hotel dates from around 1900, and still retains a few of its original architectural grace notes. A verdant patio and garden are the site of clusters of iron chairs and tables, where breakfast is served, and which many clients select as a site for afternoon reading. Inside, the motif is less nostalgic—angular and contemporary, it has mirrored, sometimes stark walls, and efficient modern furnishings. Most bedrooms have high ceilings, and casement doors that open onto tiny porches hemmed in with wrought-iron railings. Bedrooms don't have a lot of space, but each comes with a firm mattress, usually on a double bed. Bathrooms are compact and tiled, each with a shower stall and a hair dryer.

✪ **Hôtel Villa Eden.** 99 bis promenade des Anglais, 06000 Nice. ☎ **04-93-86-53-70.** Fax 04-93-97-67-97. 15 units. A/C TV TEL. 200F–390F ($34–$66.30) double. AE, DC, MC, V. Bus: 3, 9, 10, 22, 23, or 24 from the center, or 12 from the train station.

In 1925, an exiled Russian countess built this art-deco villa on the seafront, surrounded it with a wall, and planted a tiny garden. The pastel-pink villa still remains, despite the construction of much-taller modern buildings on both sides. You can enjoy the ivy and roses in the garden and stay in old-fashioned, partly modernized rooms whose sizes vary greatly. Bathrooms are also old-fashioned but still functioning smoothly, with shower stalls but few amenities. The owner has a wry sense of humor and greets you at breakfast, the only meal served.

Hotel Villa St.-Hubert. 26 rue Michel-Ange, 06100 Nice. ☎ **04-93-84-66-51.** Fax 04-93-84-70-96. TV TEL. 270F–340F ($45.90–$57.80). AE, DC, MC, V. Parking 40F ($6.80).

Set 5 blocks inland from the seacoast and the beach, this hotel consists of an interconnected pair of early–20th century townhouses. Today, they're the property of the Chevalier family, who maintain clean, well-appointed bedrooms, each with a different color scheme. Some of the rooms have air-conditioning; a few come with little kitchenettes. Bedrooms are medium in size with firm mattresses and well-maintained bathrooms with shower stalls. One of the hotel's most appealing corners is the ivy-covered, geranium-filled courtyard, site of morning breakfast and afternoon teas. No meals are served other than breakfast, but in light of the many nearby restaurants, no one seems to care.

Le Petit Palais. 10 av. Emile-Bieckert, 06000 Nice. ☎ **04-93-62-19-11.** Fax 04-93-62-53-60. E-mail: petitpalais@provence.riviera.com. 25 units. TV TEL. 430F–780F ($73.10–$132.60) double. AE, DC, MC, V. Parking 50F ($8.50).

This whimsical hotel occupies a mansion built around 1890; in the 1970s, it was the home of the actor/writer Sacha Guitry, a name that's instantly recognized in millions of French households. It lies about a 10-minute drive from the city center in the Carabacel residential district. Much of its architectural grace remains, as evoked by the Florentine moldings and friezes and the art-deco/Italianate furnishings. The preferred rooms, and the most expensive, have balconies for sea views during the day and sunset watching at dusk. Accommodations are generally small to medium, each with a firm mattress and a neatly organized bathroom with a shower stall or shower/tub combo, plus a hair dryer, and adequate shelf space. You can order light food from room service until midnight, and breakfast is served in a small but pretty salon.

WHERE TO DINE
VERY EXPENSIVE

✪ **Chantecler.** In the Hôtel Négresco, 37 promenade des Anglais. ☎ **04-93-16-64-00.** Reservations required. Main courses 210F–350F ($35.70–$59.50); fixed-price menus 415F–590F ($70.55–$100.30) at lunch, 395F–560F ($67.15–$95.20) at dinner. AE, DC, MC, V. Daily 12:30–2:30pm and 7:30–10:30pm. Closed mid-Nov to mid-Dec. Bus: 9, 10, or 11. FRENCH.

This is Nice's most prestigious restaurant. In 1989, a massive redecoration sheathed its walls with panels removed from a château in Puilly-Fussé, a Regency-style salon was installed for before- or after-dinner drinks, and a collection of 16th-century paintings, executed on leather backgrounds in the Belgian town of Malines, was imported. A much-respected chef, Alain Llorca, revised the menu to include the most sophisticated and creative dishes in Nice. Dishes change almost weekly but may include filet of turbot served with a purée of broad beans, sun-dried tomatoes, and fresh asparagus; roasted suckling lamb served with beignets of fresh vegetables and ricotta-stuffed ravioli; and a melt-in-your-mouth fantasy of marbled hot chocolate drenched in an almond-flavored cream sauce.

EXPENSIVE

Barale. 39 rue Beaumont. ☎ **04-93-89-17-94.** Reservations required. Meals 250F–300F ($42.50–$51). No credit cards. Tues–Sun 8:15–9pm. Closed Aug. FRENCH/ITALIAN.

This is the hearty domain of Chatherine-Hélène Barale, the grand mère of Nissarda cuisine, a unique blend of Italian and French cookery. For decades, it has reigned as the most offbeat choice in Nice. Everything depends on the whim of Madame Barale, who may or may not take a liking to you. If she doesn't like you, she might show you to the door. Yet in spite of her eccentricities, even her refusal to define precise prices on her menu, this remains an enduring favorite, at least for some; others may feel that one dinner here is enough. It's certainly not a conventional restaurant. Filled with antiques, it is usually crowded with diners who seek old-time flavors that have largely disappeared from many menus. Madame Barale was born here, and she has learned the family secrets well. Her menu is listed on a blackboard hung with garlic pigtails, and it depends on her shopping that day. However, she almost always sells squares of the Nice pizza called pissaladière, and, of course, the classic salade Niçoise. For a second course, try gnocchi or green lasagne. Main courses often include *pieche*—poached veal stuffed with fresh Swiss chard, cheese, ham, eggs, and rice—which is superb. We recommend the fresh fruit tart for dessert.

Restaurant Château des Ollières. In the Château des Ollières hotel, 39 av. des Baumettes. ☎ **04-92-15-77-99.** Reservations recommended. Set-price lunch 220F ($37.40); set-price dinners 250F ($42.50). AE, MC, V. Daily noon–1:30pm and 8–9:30pm. FRENCH.

Few other restaurants in Nice provide such an opportunity for insights into the belle époque life of grandeur and ease. You might find yourself coming here as much for the beauty of the setting as for the food. It was built in the 1870s by a Russian prince for the French woman whose marriage he ended. The restaurant is in a new wing architecture matching the original, added in the late 1990s. At this writing, the only dining option is a set-price menu that consists of "amuses-gueules" of the chef: a starter; a fish (sea bass or turbot) or meat (rack of lamb is an excellent choice); and a dessert. Know in advance that although the food is delicate and very well-prepared, the real allure of this restaurant is its beauty, its collection of antiques, and its many references to yesteryear.

MODERATE

Ane Rouge. 7 quai des Deux-Emmanuels. ☎ **04-93-89-49-63.** Reservations required. Main courses 95F–138F ($16.15–$23.45); fixed-price menus 158F–258F ($26.85–$43.85); bouill-abaisse 265F ($45.05). AE, DC, MC, V. Thurs–Tues noon–2pm and 7:30–10:30pm. Closed 2 weeks in Jan. Bus: 30. PROVENÇAL.

Facing the old port and occupying an antique building with its original ceiling beams and stone walls, is one of the city's best-known seafood restaurants. In one of the pair of cozy modern dining rooms, you can enjoy traditional and time-tested specialties like bouillabaisse; bourrides; filet of John Dory with roulades of stuffed lettuce leaves; mussels stuffed with chopped parsley, bread crumbs, and herbs; and salmon in wine sauce with spinach. Service is correct and commendable.

Chez les Pêcheurs. 18 quai des Docks. ☎ **04-93-89-59-61.** Reservations recommended. Main courses 95F–160F ($16.15–$27.20); fixed-price menu 155F ($26.35); bouillabaisse 430F ($73.10) for two. AE, MC, V. May–Oct, Thurs 7–10pm, Fri–Tues noon–2pm and 7–10pm; mid-Dec to Apr, Tues 7–10pm, Thurs–Mon noon–2pm and 7–10pm. Closed Nov to mid-Dec. Bus: 1, 2, or 7. FRENCH.

This likable, well-managed tavern is directly on the old harbor at the end of a long string of less-desirable restaurants, with a view of the city's ruined castle and the sailboats and fishing craft bobbing at anchor. The decor is inspired by the interior of a yacht, complete with touches of polished brass and varnished hardwood. You can enjoy bouillabaisse (more reasonably priced here than at some nearby competitors), bourride, grilled lobster, or sea bass flavored with tarragon. Some of the best dishes are also the simplest, including carefully grilled fish seasoned with herbs, olive oil, and lemon.

Chez Michel (Le Grand Pavois). 11 rue Meyerbeer. ☎ **04-93-88-77-42.** Reservations required. Main courses 125F–210F ($21.25–$35.70); bouillabaisse 320F–450F

($54.40–$76.50); fixed-price menus 185F–300F ($31.45–$51). AE, DC, MC, V. Daily noon–2:30pm and 7–11pm. Bus: 8. SEAFOOD.

This seafood brasserie was established by members of the family that owns Chez Tétou, the fabulously stylish seafood restaurant in Golfe Juan that's beloved by movie stars, glitterati, and the merely rich. Jacques Marquise, one of the patriarchs of the Chez Tétou success story, and manager of the place during the glory years of *La Dolce Vita*, is the creative force here, and he's committed to maintaining prices that are between 30% and 40% less than those charged by Chez Tétou. Bouillabaisse is the specialty here, priced at 320F ($54.40) for a succulent and authentic version of which any bona fide Provençal would be proud, and at 450F ($76.50) for a version garnished with lobster and crayfish. Other delectable choices include sea bass in white wine, herbs, and lemon sauce; and fish (snapper, hogfish, sea bass, and John Dory) that's grilled and then flambéed with a combination of fennel and fennel-flavored brandy. The wine list has a number of reasonably priced bottles.

Don Camillo. 5 rue des Ponchettes. ☎ **04-93-85-67-95.** Reservations recommended. Main courses 65F–138F ($11.05–$23.45); fixed-price menus 165F ($28.05). AE, MC, V. Mon 8–9:30pm, Tues–Sat noon–1:30pm and 8–9:30pm. Bus: 8. PROVENÇAL.

Named in the 1950s after its founder, Camille, a Niçois patriot (who preferred the Italian version of his name), this nine-table restaurant promises (and delivers) some of Nice's most authentic Provençal food. The dining room is adorned with the modern paintings of the Niçois painter Laurent Gerbert, and Franck Cerutti, assisted by his wife, Véronique, applies the gilded training he learned during stints at some of the grand restaurants of the Côte d'Azur. Staples of the menu are fava beans, Swiss chard, goat cheese, stockfish, cuttlefish, and a medley of herbs produced on the region's dry hillsides. Every dish bears the mark of a master chef who's almost guaranteed to become much better known among Provence's gastronomes. At the end of your meal, do your best to sample the selections from the cheese tray. Each derives from a small local farm, with goodly numbers fermented from sheep's or goat's milk.

✪ **La Merenda.** 4 rue Terrasse. No phone. Reservations required. Fixed-price menus 150F–210F ($25.50–$35.70). No credit cards. Mon–Fri noon–2pm and 7–9:30pm. Closed Aug 4–18, Dec 24–Jan 4, and Feb 16–22. Bus: 8. NIÇOIS.

Since there's no phone, you have to go by this place twice: once to make a reservation and once to dine. However, it's worth the extra effort—this is the best bistro in Nice. Forsaking his two-star chef crown at the renowned Chantecler (above), Dominique Le Stanc opened up this tiny bistro serving a sublime cuisine. "A no-star hole in the wall," the press screamed. But that's what Le Stanc wanted. Born in Alsace, his heart and soul belong to the Mediterranean, the land of black truffles, seasonal wild morels, fat sea bass, and plump asparagus. His food is rightly called a lullaby of gastronomic unity, with texture, crunch, richness, and balance. "I've known my days of glory in the gastronomic world. Now I'm doing family cooking, which is what I always like to eat." Le Stanc never knows what he's going to serve until he goes to the market. Look for his specials on a chalkboard. Perhaps you'll find stuffed cabbage, fried zucchini flowers, or oxtail flavored with fresh oranges. Lamb from the Sisteron is cooked until it practically falls from the bone. Raw artichokes are paired with a salad of *mâche*. Service is discreet and personable. We wish we could dine here every day.

La Toque Blanche. 40 rue de la Buffa. ☎ **04-93-88-38-18.** Reservations not required. Main courses 120F–220F ($20.40–$37.40); fixed-price menus 145F–160F ($24.65–$27.20). MC, V. Tues–Sat 12:30–2pm and 7–9:30pm, Sun 12:30–2pm. Bus: 8. FRENCH.

La Toque Blanche has only about a dozen tables amid its winter-garden decor. The owners, Denise and Alain Sandelion, pay particular attention to their shopping and buy only very fresh ingredients. The cuisine is skillfully prepared—try the sea bass roasted with citrus juice, sautéed sweetbreads with crayfish, or salmon prepared with fresh shrimp. The fixed-price menus are a particularly good value.

Restaurant Boccaccio. 7 rue Masséna. ☎ **04-93-87-71-76.** Reservations recommended. Main courses 85F–210F ($14.45–$35.70); fixed-price menu 200F ($34); bouillabaisse 340F ($57.80) per person. AE, DC, MC, V. Daily noon–2:30pm and 7–11pm. Bus: 4, 5, or 22. MEDITERRANEAN.

Adjacent to place Masséna, in a pedestrian zone that enhances the desirability of its streetfront terrace, this restaurant boasts worthy cuisine and a devoted local following. Bouillabaisse is reasonably priced here, and the range of fresh fish (grilled with lemon-butter or baked in a salt crust) is broad and well prepared. The paella might remind you of Spain, and desserts like cappuccino tiramisú and crêpes Suzettes round out meals nicely. There's a large dining room upstairs, inspired by the interior of a yacht, if the outdoor terrace doesn't appeal to you.

INEXPENSIVE

Albert's Bar. 1 rue Maurice-Jaubert. ☎ **04-93-87-30-20.** Reservations recommended. Main course pastas and risottos 95F–180F ($16.15–$30.60); main course meats and fish 105F–250F ($17.85–$42.50). AE, DC, MC, V. Mon–Sat noon–2:30pm and 7–9:30pm. Bus: 7, 9, or 22. FRENCH.

Despite its name, this mahogany-paneled restaurant is much more than just a bar. In fact, casual bar patrons who don't plan on dining here are not particularly welcome, as the actual bar facilities are rather limited. Instead, you'll find a serious restaurant with vaguely British antecedents (its long-ago founder, Albert, was a Brit) and a reputation for well-prepared, not terribly expensive food. You might be tempted to define any of the pastas or risottos as a main course here, perhaps teaming it with a salad, and if you do, no one will mind. A worthy example is risotto with saffron and fresh mussels. Otherwise, delectable menu items might include scallops garnished with warm foie gras; escalope of veal with artichoke hearts; filet of beef with marrow sauce; and swordfish steak served with a very light and tangy lemon sauce.

Brasserie Flo. 2–4 rue Sacha-Guitry. ☎ **04-93-13-38-38.** Reservations recommended. Main courses 80F–120F ($13.60–$20.40); fixed-price menus 119F ($20.25) at lunch, 159F ($27.05) all day, and 119F ($20.25) after 10pm. AE, DC, MC, V. Daily noon–3pm and 7pm–12:30am. Bus: 1, 2, or 5. FRENCH.

In 1991, a France-based restaurant chain (the Jean-Paul Bucher group) noted for its skill at restoring historic brasseries bought the premises of a faded turn-of-the-century restaurant near place Masséna and injected it with new life. Its high ceilings covered with their original frescoes, the place is brisk, stylish, reasonably priced, and fun. Menu items include an array of grilled fish, *choucroute* (sauerkraut) Alsatian style, steak with brandied pepper sauce, and fresh oysters and shellfish. (Flo isn't associated with Le Florian, above, though they are frequently confused.)

La Nissarda. 17 rue Gubernatis. ☎ **04-93-85-26-29.** Reservations recommended. Main courses 70F–120F ($11.90–$20.40). MC, V. Mon–Sat noon–2pm and 7–10pm. Closed Aug. NIÇOIS.

Set in the heart of town, about a 10-minute walk from place Masséna, this restaurant is maintained by a Normandy-born family (the Adam Pruniers) who work hard to maintain the aura and (some of) the culinary traditions of Nice. In an intimate (40-seat) setting lined with old engravings and photographs of the city, the place serves local versions of ravioli, spaghetti, carbonara, lasagne, and fresh-grilled salmon with herbs. A handful of Norman-based specialties also manage to creep into the menu, much to the appreciation of diners lonely for northern France, including escalopes of veal with cream sauce and apples. Ceiling fans spin overhead as you dine.

✪ Le Safari. 1 cours Saleya. ☎ **04-93-80-18-44.** Reservations recommended. Main courses 80F–130F ($13.60–$22.10); fixed-price menu 150F ($25.50). AE, DC, MC, V. Daily noon–2:30pm and 7–11:30pm. (Closed Mon Nov–Mar). Bus: 1. PROVENÇAL/NIÇOIS.

The decor couldn't be simpler: a black ceiling, white walls, and an old-fashioned terra-cotta floor. The youthful staff is relaxed, sometimes in jeans, and always alert to the waves of fashion. Look for mobs here, many of whom prefer the outdoor terrace over-looking the Marché aux Fleurs and all of whom appreciate the earthy, reasonably priced meals that appear in generous portions. Menu items include a pungent *bagna cauda*, where vegetables are immersed in a sizzling brew of hot oil and anchovy paste; grilled peppers bathed in olive oil; *daube* (stew) of beef; fresh pasta with basil; an omelet with *blettes* (tough but flavorful greens); and the unfortunately named *merda de can* (dogshit), which, as a gnocchi stuffed with spinach, is a lot more appetizing than it sounds.

L'Olivier. 3 place Garibaldi. ☎ **04-93-26-89-09.** Reservations recommended. Main courses 55F–85F ($9.35–$14.45). AE, DC, MC, V. Daily noon–2:30pm, Thurs–Tues 7:45–10pm. Closed 1 week in Aug. PROVENÇAL/SICILIAN.

Established in 1989, this charming restaurant lies beneath the arcades of place Garibaldi, in the heart of Old Nice, just in back of the Museum of Modern Art. Named in honor of the premises' former occupant (an old-style shop selling olives, olive oil, and anchovies), the restaurant serves an original and sometimes unique cui-sine based on modern versions of local culinary traditions. Flavorful and well-prepared items include smoked slices of foie gras, deboned sea bass stuffed with shellfish and herbs and served with a crabmeat sauce, lasagne made with a *daube joues de boeuf*, and a Sicilian-inspired medley of eggplant, olives, olive oil, and herbs combined into a southern Italian ratatouille. Dessert might be a gratin of frozen and caramelized lemons, or black-chocolate truffles.

Restaurant L'Estocaficada. 2 rue de l'Hôtel-de-Ville. ☎ **04-93-80-21-64.** Reservations recommended. Main courses 50F–95F ($8.50–$16.15); fixed-price menus 58F–82F ($9.85–$13.95); pizzas 30F–45F ($5.10–$7.65). AE, MC, V. Tues–Sun noon–2pm and 7–9:30pm. Bus: 1, 2, or 5. NIÇOIS.

Estocaficada is the Provençal word for stockfish, the ugliest fish in Europe. You can see one for yourself—there might be a dried-out, balloon-shaped version on display in the cozy dining room. Brigitte Autier is the owner/chef, and her busy kitchens are visible from everywhere in the dining room. Descended from a matriarchal line (since 1958) of mother-daughter teams who have managed this place, she's devoted to the preser-vation of recipes prepared by her Niçois grandmother. Examples are gnocchis, beignets, several types of *farcies* (tomatoes, peppers, or onions stuffed with herbed fill-ings), grilled sardines, or bouillabaisse served as a main course or in a mini-version. As a concession to popular demand, the place also serves pizzas and pastas.

NICE AFTER DARK

Nice has some of the most active nightlife along the Riviera, with evenings usually beginning at a cafe. You can pick up a copy of *La Semaine des Spectacles,* available at kiosks around town, that outlines the week's diversions.

The major cultural center along the Riviera is the **Opéra de Nice,** 4 rue St-François-de-Paule (☎ **04-92-17-40-44**). The opera house was built in 1885 by Charles Gar-nier, fabled architect of the Paris Opera. A full repertoire is presented, with special emphasis on serious, often large-scale operas. In one season you might see *Tosca,*

Tristan und Isolde, Verdi's *Macbeth,* Beethoven's *Fidelio,* and *Carmen,* as well as a *saison symphonique,* dominated by the Orchestre Philharmonique de Nice. The opera house is also the major venue for concerts and recitals. The box office is open Tuesday to Saturday from 10am to 5:30pm. Tickets cost from 40F ($6.80) for a high-altitude, low-visibility seat to 380F ($64.60) for front-and-center seats.

Near the Hotel Ambassador, **L'Ambassade,** 18 rue des Congrès (☎ 04-93-88-88-87), is designed in a mock-Gothic style and has two bars and a dance floor. Its clients come in all physical types and age ranges. The cover is 100F ($17), including the first drink. **Piano Bar Louis XV/Disco Inferno,** 10 rue Cité-du-Parc (☎ 04-93-80-49-84), is a double-tiered nightclub with a piano bar in its 200-year-old vaulted cellar and a modern disco on its street level. There's a cover of 80F ($13.60), including the first drink. Newer contenders include **Disco Butterfly,** 67 que des Etats-Unis (☎ 04-93-92-27-31), a site where hip recorded music (including house, garage, techno, and whatever strikes the fancy of the DJ) attracts a high-energy, highly sociable crowd under 35 to dance the night away. An alternative is **Club Nautique,** 20 quai Lunel (☎ 04-93-89-68-00), beside the Vieux Port, where an ambience that's midway between a rustic waterside pub and a big-city singles bar attracts the prosperous and the restless.

Le Cabaret du Casino Ruhl, in the Casino Ruhl, 1 promenade des Anglais (☎ 04-93-87-95-87), is Nice's answer to the cabaret glitter that appears in a more ostentatious form in Monte Carlo and Las Vegas. It includes just enough flesh to titillate; lots of spangles, feathers, and sequins; a medley of cross-cultural jokes and nostalgia for the good old days of French *chanson;* and an acrobat or juggler. The cover of 100F ($17) includes the first drink; dinner and the show, complete with a bottle of wine per person, cost 300F ($51). Shows are presented every Friday and Saturday at 10pm.

The **casino** has an area devoted exclusively to slot machines (open daily from noon to 4 or 5am, entrance free). A more formal gaming room, replete with blackjack, baccarat, chemin de fer, and 21 tables, has an entrance fee of 75F ($12.75) per person; it's open nightly, Monday to Friday from 8pm to 4 or 5pm, Saturday and Sunday from 5pm to 5am.

Le Relais American Bar, in the Hotel Négresco, 37 promenade des Anglais (☎ 04-93-16- 64-00), is the most beautiful bar in Nice, filled with white columns, an oxblood-red ceiling, Oriental carpets, English paneling, Italianate chairs, and tapestries. It was once a haunt of the actress Lillie Langtry. With its piano music and white-jacketed waiters, the bar still attracts a chic crowd.

Increasingly, Nice continues as the gay centerpiece of southern France. Near the Hôtel Négresco and promenade des Anglais, **Le Blue Boy,** 9 rue Spinetta (☎ 04-93-44-68-24), is the oldest gay disco on the Riviera. With two bars and two floors, it's a vital nocturnal stopover for passengers from the dozens of all-gay cruises that make regular calls at Nice and such nearby ports as Villefranche. The cover varies from free to 60F ($10.20) depending on the night.

L'Ascenseur, 18 bis rue Emmanuel Philibert (☎ 04-93-26-35-30), is one of the most popular of the new crop of gay bars. This is a bustling, friendly gay bar that's loaded with wood paneling, billiard tables, metallic accents, and some of the more appealing gay men in Provence and the rest of Europe. It's open Tuesday through Saturday from 9pm till at least 3am. There's no dance floor, but disco music plays as gay men and (to a lesser degree) women, laugh, converse, and flirt.

You can make a night of it (or several nights of it) at the following establishments: **Le Santiago,** 28 rue Lepante (☎ 04-93-13-83-01), with its hotel bar and restaurant; **Latinos,** 6 rue Chauvain (☎ 04-93-85-01-10), for "gay tapas"; **La Table Coquine,** 44 av. de la République (☎ 04-93-55-39-99), a gay restaurant; **Café Chris,** 3 rue

Smolett (☎ **04-93-26-75-85**), a gay café; and **Le C.D. Restaurant and Salad Bar,** 22 rue Benoit-Bunico (☎ **04-93-92-47-65**), where you can cruise while you munch.

8 Villefranche-sur-Mer

581 miles (935.03km) S of Paris, 4 miles (6.44km) E of Nice

According to legend, Hercules opened his arms and Villefranche was born. It sits on a big blue bay that looks like a gigantic bowl, large enough to accommodate U.S. Sixth Fleet cruisers and destroyers. Quietly slumbering otherwise, Villefranche takes on the appearance of an exciting Mediterranean port when the fleet's in.

Once popular with such writers as Katherine Mansfield and Aldous Huxley, it's still a haven for artists, many of whom take over the little houses—reached by narrow alleyways—that climb the hillside. Two of the more recent arrivals who've bought homes in the area are Tina Turner and Bono.

ESSENTIALS

GETTING THERE   Trains arrive from most towns on the Côte d'Azur; from Nice, every 30 minutes. For **rail information** and schedules, call ☎ **08-36-35-35-35.** There's no formal bus station—buses merely stop at a point along the avenue Foch opposite the tourist office. For bus information, contact the **Gare Routière** in Nice (☎ **04-93-85-61-81**). Visitors who drive come via the Corniche Inférieure (Lower Corniche).

VISITOR INFORMATION   The **Office de Tourisme** is on Jardin François-Binon (☎ **04-93-01-73-68**).

EXPLORING THE TOWN

Rue Obscure is one of the strangest streets in France. It lies beneath a vaulted ceiling dating from 1295. In spirit it belongs more to a North African casbah. People live in tiny houses on this street, protected from the elements. Occasionally, however, there's an open space, allowing for a tiny courtyard. To get to it, take rue de l'église.

One of the artists who came to Villefranche left a memorial behind. Jean Cocteau, the legendary filmmaker, writer, painter, and dilettante, spent a year (1956–57) painting frescoes on the 14th-century walls of the Romanesque **Chapelle St-Pierre,** quai de la Douane/rue des Marinières (☎ **04-93-76-90-70**). He eventually presented it to "the fishermen of Villefranche in homage to the Prince of Apostles, the patron of fishermen." One panel pays homage to the gypsies of the Stes-Maries-de-la-Mer. In the apse is a depiction of the miracle of St. Peter walking on the water, not knowing that he's supported by an angel. On the left side of the narthex, Cocteau honored Villefranche's young women in their regional costumes. The chapel, which charges 12F ($2.05) admission, is open Tuesday to Sunday: July to September from 10am to noon and 4 to 8:30pm, April to June from 9:30am to noon and 2:30 to 7:30pm, and October to March from 9:30am to noon and 2 to 5pm (closed mid-November to mid-December).

WHERE TO STAY

Hôtel Versailles. Av. Princesse-Grace-de-Monaco, 06230 Villefranche-sur-Mer. ☎ **04-93-01-89-56.** Fax 04-93-01-97-48. www.hotelversailles.com. 49 units. A/C TV TEL. 500F ($85) double; 1,000F ($170) suite. AE, DC, MC, V. Closed late Oct to late Dec. Free parking.

Several blocks from the harbor and outside the main part of town, this three-story hotel gives you a perspective of the entire coast. The hotel offers comfortably furnished rooms and suites (suitable for up to three) with big windows and panoramas. Guests can order breakfast or lunch under an umbrella on the roof terrace. The hotel's pool also has a terrace and is surrounded by palms and bright flowers. Rooms are clean and bright, with comfortable mattresses and tiled bathrooms.

Hôtel Welcome. 1 quai Courbet, 06230 Villefranche-sur-Mer. ☎ **04-93-76-27-62.** Fax 04-93-76-27-66. www.riviera.fr/hotels/welcome.htm. E-mail: welcome@riviera.fr. 32 units. A/C MINIBAR TV TEL. 504F–950F ($85.70–$161.50) double. Rates include breakfast. Half board 155F ($26.35) per person extra. AE, DC, MC, V. Closed Nov 15–Dec 20.

The Welcome was a favorite of Jean Cocteau, who'd probably still check in if he were still around, as it's the best hotel at the port. In this six-floor villa, with shutters and balconies, everything has recently been modernized and extensively renovated. Bedrooms are mostly medium in size, each comfortably appointed with a firm mattress resting on a twin or double. Bathrooms are tiled and small, each with a shower stall and adequate shelf space. Try for a fifth-floor room overlooking the water. The sidewalk cafe is the focal point of town life. The lounge and the restaurant, St-Pierre, have open fireplaces and fruitwood furniture.

WHERE TO DINE

Chez Michel's. Place Amélie Pollonais. ☎ **04-93-76-73-24.** Reservations recommended. Main courses 80F–150F ($13.60–$25.50). AE, MC, V. Wed–Mon 12:30–3:30pm and 5:30–11:30pm. FRENCH.

This bustling and animated brasserie is owned and managed by a husband-and-wife team (Michel and Michelle). The setting is a cozily unpretentious dining room lined with Provençal landscapes. Well-prepared menu items made with fresh ingredients include dishes such as a filet of beef Rossini (layered with foie gras); grilled sea bass with a tapenade of olives; rack of lamb with Provençal herbs, and a roster of fresh, char-grilled fish of the day that is usually served either with a basil-flavored vinaigrette or with lemon-flavored butter sauce.

La Mère Germaine. Quai Courbet. ☎ **04-93-01-71-39.** Reservations recommended. Main courses 140F–460F ($23.80–$78.20); fixed-price menu 195F ($33.15). AE, MC, V. Daily noon–2:30pm and 7–10pm. Closed Nov 20–Dec 20. FRENCH/SEAFOOD.

Plan to relax here over lunch while watching fishers repair their nets—this is the very best of a string of restaurants on the port. The cuisine is prepared by the grandson (the likable Thierry Blouin) of the matriarch, Mère Germaine, who opened the place in the 1930s. It's popular with U.S. Navy officers, who've discovered the bouillabaisse made with tasty morsels of freshly caught fish and mixed in a cauldron with savory spices. We recommend the grilled loup (sea bass) with fennel, salade Niçoise, sole Tante Marie (stuffed with mushroom purée), and beef filet with three peppers. The perfectly roasted *carré d'agneau* (lamb) is for two.

✪ **La Trinquette.** Port de la Darse. ☎ **04-93-01-71-41.** Reservations recommended. Main courses 50F–140F ($8.50–$23.80); bouillabaisse 220F ($37.40); fixed-price menus 105F–190F ($17.85–$32.30). No credit cards. Thurs–Tues noon–2:15pm and 7–10pm. Closed Dec–Jan. PROVENÇAL/SEAFOOD.

Charming and traditional, in a pre-Napoleonic building a few steps from the harborfront, this restaurant prides itself on the excellence of its fish and bouillabaisse. The fish is brought out from a back room if anyone is skeptical enough to ask to see the actual fish before it's cooked. You can choose from among 15 to 20 kinds, prepared any way you specify, with a wide variety of well-flavored sauces. Bouillabaisse is an enduring favorite—much cheaper here than at many other places. There's even a roasted version of *chapon de mer,* served with a Provençal sauce. How do the hardworking owners, Paul and Monique Osiel, recommend their fresh John Dory? Roasted as simply as possible, served only with a hint of beurre blanc. Alternatives for this or any of the other offerings include aïoli, the region's garlic-enriched mayonnaise.

9 St-Jean-Cap-Ferrat

583 miles (938.25km) S of Paris, 6 miles (9.66km) E of Nice

This place has been called "Paradise Found"—of all the oases along the Côte d'Azur, none has quite the snob appeal of Cap-Ferrat. It's a 9-mile promontory sprinkled with luxurious villas, outlined by sheltered bays, beaches, and coves. The vegetation is lush. In the port of St-Jean, the harbor accommodates yachts and fishing boats.

ESSENTIALS

GETTING THERE   Most visitors drive or take the hourly bus or a taxi from the rail station at nearby Beaulieu. There's also bus service from Nice. For **bus information** and schedules, call ☎ **04-93-85-61-81.**

VISITOR INFORMATION   The **Office de Tourisme** is on avenue Denis-Séméria (☎ **04-93-01-02-21**).

SEEING THE SIGHTS

Though there are few **public paths** where you can enjoy the scenery, a path from Plage de Paloma takes you to Pointe St-Hospice, where a panoramic view of the Riviera landscape unfolds.

   St-Jean is a colorful fishing village with bars, bistros, and simple inns. The **beaches,** though popular, are all shingled; the best one belongs to the Grand Hôtel du Cap-Ferrat (see "Where to Stay," below) but is open to anyone willing to pay 100F ($17) to rent a mattress and beach umbrella.

   Everyone tries to visit the **Villa Mauresque,** avenue Somerset-Maugham, but it's closed to the public. This villa near the cape is where Maugham spent his final years, avoiding tourists; to visitors he would loudly proclaim that he wasn't one of the local sights. One man did manage to crash through the gate. When he encountered the author, Maugham snarled, "What do you think I am, a monkey in a cage?"

   The **Villa Les Cèdres,** directly west of the port of St-Jean, was once the property of Leopold II, king of Belgium. Although it is in private hands and can't be visited, you can go to the nearby **Parc Zoologique,** boulevard du Général-de-Gaulle, northwest of the peninsula (☎ 04-93-76-04-98). It's open daily: April to October from 9:30am to 7pm, to 5:30pm in winter. Admission is 50F ($8.50). This private zoo is set in the basin of a drained lake and was Leopold's private domain. You'll find a wide variety of reptiles, birds, and animals in outdoor cages. Six times a day there's a chimps' tea party, which explains Maugham's remark.

✪ **Musée Ile-de-France.** Av. Denis-Séméria ☎ **04-93-01-33-09.** Admission 45F ($7.65) adults, 33F ($5.60) ages 9–24, free for children 8 and under. Daily 10am–6pm (July–Aug to 7pm).

The museum offers a chance to visit one of the Côte d'Azur's most legendary villas, an Italianate villa built by Baronne Ephrussi de Rothschild. She died in 1934, leaving the stately building and its magnificent gardens to the Institut de France on behalf of the Académie des Beaux-Arts. The wealth of her collection is preserved: 18th-century furniture; Tiepolo ceilings; Savonnerie carpets; screens and panels from the Far East; tapestries from Gobelins, Aubusson, and Beauvais; original drawings by Fragonard; canvases by Boucher; rare Sèvres porcelain; and more. Covering 12 acres, the gardens contain fragments of statuary from churches, monasteries, and torn-down palaces. One entire section is planted with cacti.

WHERE TO STAY
VERY EXPENSIVE

✪ **Grand Hôtel du Cap-Ferrat.** Bd. du Général-de-Gaulle, 06230 St-Jean-Cap-Ferrat. ☎ **04-93-76-50-50.** Fax 04-93-76-04-52. www.grand.hotel.cap.ferrat.com. E-mail: marketin@ grand.hotel-cap-ferrat.com. 55 units. A/C MINIBAR TV TEL. 950F–6,900F ($161.50–$1,173) double; 3,600F–13,000F ($612–$2,210) suite. AE, DC, MC, V.

One of the best features of this turn-of-the-century palace is its location at the tip of the peninsula in the midst of a 14-acre garden of semitropical trees and manicured lawns. It has been the retreat of the international elite since 1908, and occupies the same celestial status as the Réserve and Métropole in Beaulieu. Its cuisine even equals the Métropole's. The building has open loggias and big arched windows, and a terrace over the sea where you can enjoy the views. Guest rooms are conservatively modern, with dressing rooms. For the most part, they look as if the late Princess Grace might settle in comfortably at any minute. They are generally spacious and open to sea views, with deluxe beds and mattresses, private safes, thick carpets, and elegant fabric wall coverings. Bathrooms are state-of-the-art, with hair dryers, robes, bidets, power showerheads, and plush towels. Rates include admission to the pool, Club Dauphin. The beach is accessible via funicular from the main building. The hotel is open year-round.

Dining/Diversions: The hotel's indoor/outdoor restaurant serves *cuisine du marché*, which might include salad of warm foie gras and chanterelle mushrooms, nage of crayfish and lobster, or breast of duckling with honey and cider vinegar. The dining room is one of the last of the great belle époque palaces on the Côte d'Azur. The meals and service are flawless but come at a very high price. The American-style bar opens onto the garden.

Services: Room service (24 hours), same-day laundry.

Facilities: Olympic-sized heated pool, tennis courts, hotel bicycles.

✪ **Hotel Royal Riviera.** 3 av. Jean Monnet, 06230 Saint-Jean-Cap-Ferrat. ☎ **04-93-76-31-00.** Fax 04-93-01-23-07. 77 units. A/C MINIBAR TV TEL. 1,600F–3,950F ($272–$671.50) double; 3,600F–6,500F ($612–$1,105) suite. Rates include half board. AE, DC, MC, V.

Rising five graceful stories above the thin line that separates the quietly prestigious towns of St.-Jean and Beaulieu, this turn-of-the-century hotel evokes the Riviera's gilded age—it might remind you of a scene from a novel by F. Scott Fitzgerald. It occupies a 1-acre tract with a beach of its own, to which tons of sand are added at regular intervals. There's also a rectangular swimming pool. Bedrooms are posh and plush, with big windows, private balconies, deep sofas, and fruitwood armoires. The largest and most appealing are the corner units (any room ending in -16). Regardless, each is charming, elegant, chic and modern. All have private safes and large, supremely comfortable beds with deluxe mattresses; closet space is ample. Bathrooms are fairly routine but well equipped with hair dryers, robes, and plush towels.

Dining/Diversions: The main restaurant and bar have beautiful views of the Mediterranean, and the hotel always employs top chefs, making the half-board arrangement here a joy. The regional fare of southern France is superb, and the desserts are some of the finest along the coast.

Amenities: Huge pool, room service, concierge, and a beach where the sand has to be replenished at frequent intervals.

✪ **La Voile d'Or.** 31 av. Jean-Mermoz, St-Jean-Cap-Ferrat, 06230 Villefranche-sur-Mer. ☎ **04-93-01-13-13.** Fax 04-93-76-11-17. E-mail: voiledor@calva.net. 45 units. A/C MINIBAR TV TEL. 1,100F–3,200F ($187–$544) double; 2,600F–3,700F ($442–$629) suite. Rates include continental breakfast. AE, MC, V. Closed Nov–mid Mar. Parking 100F ($17).

The "Golden Sail" is a brilliant tour de force offering intimate luxury in a converted villa. As a deluxe hotel, it's absolutely equal to the Grand Hôtel, though its cuisine isn't quite as superb. It's owned by an antiques collector turned hôtelier, Jean R. Lorenzi, and stands at the edge of the little fishing port and yacht harbor, with a panoramic view of the coast. The guest rooms, lounges, and restaurant open onto terraces. Rooms are individually decorated with hand-painted reproductions, carved gilt headboards, baroque paneled doors, parquet floors, antique clocks, and paintings. Each has comfortable beds, thick towels, and a sense of intimacy you'd expect in a private home.

Dining/Diversions: Lunch is served on the canopied outer terrace, and dinner in a stately room with Spanish armchairs and white wrought-iron chandeliers. The sophisticated menu offers regional specialties and international dishes, as well as classic French cuisine. Set menus cost from 320F to 480F ($54.40 to $81.60). The drawing room is richly decorated. Most intimate is a little bar, with Wedgwood-blue paneling and antique mirroring.

Facilities: Two pools, private beach.

MODERATE

Hôtel Brise Marine. Av. Jean-Mermoz, St-Jean-Cap-Ferrat, 06230 Villefranche-sur-Mer. ☎ **04-93-76-04-36.** Fax 04-93-76-11-49. 16 units. A/C TV TEL. 670F–730F ($113.90–$124.10) double. AE, MC, V. Closed Nov–Jan.

This circa-1878 villa with a front and rear terrace is on a hillside. A long rose arbor, beds of subtropical flowers, palms, and pines provide an attractive setting. The atmosphere is casual and informal, and the rooms are comfortably but simply furnished. Each comes with a good bed with a firm mattress, plus a small tiled bathroom. You can have breakfast in the beamed lounge or under the rose trellis. The little corner bar is for afternoon drinks.

✪ **Hôtel Clair Logis.** 12 av. Centrale, 06230 St-Jean-Cap-Ferrat. ☎ **04-93-76-04-57.** Fax 04-93-76-11-85. 18 units. TEL. 400F–680F ($68–$115.60) double. AE, DC, MC, V. Closed Nov to mid-Mar.

A rare find here, this hotel is in a 19th-century villa surrounded by 2 acres of semi-tropical gardens. The pleasant rooms are scattered over three buildings. The hotel's most famous guest was de Gaulle, who lived in a room called *Strelitzias* ("Bird of Paradise") during many of his retreats from Paris. Each room is named after a flower. The most romantic and spacious accommodations are in the main building; the seven rooms in the annex are the most modern but have the least character, and tend to be smaller and cheaper. Rooms were renovated in 1998, and each has a comfortable mattress and adequate numbers of good-sized towels.

Hôtel Panoramic. 3 av. Albert-1er, 06230 St-Jean-Cap-Ferrat. ☎ **04-93-76-00-37.** Fax 04-93-76-15-78. 20 units. TV TEL. 580F–720F ($98.60–$122.40) double. AE, DC, MC, V. Closed Nov 4–Dec 20.

This hotel was built in 1958 with a red-tile roof and much style and glamour. It's one of the more affordable choices here. You'll reach the hotel by passing over a raised bridge lined with colorful pansies. The well-furnished rooms have a sweeping view of the water and the forest leading down to it. Accommodations are a bit small, but each is fitted with fine linen and a good mattress, plus a compact tiled bathroom, mainly with shower/tub combinations. Breakfast is the only meal served.

WHERE TO DINE

✪ **Le Provençal.** 2 av. Denis-Séméria. ☎ **04-93-76-03-97.** Reservations required. Main courses 220F–280F ($37.40–$47.60); fixed-price menus 300F–350F ($51–$59.50). AE, MC, V.

Mid-May to mid-Oct, Fri–Sun noon–2:30pm and daily 7:30pm–midnight; Nov–Apr, Fri–Sun noon–2:30pm and 7:30–midnight. FRENCH.

With the possible exception of the Grand Hôtel's dining room, this is the grandest restaurant of this very grand resort. Near the top of the resort's highest peak, it has a panoramic view, with sightlines that on good days sweep as far away as Menton and the Italian border. Many of the menu items are credited directly to the inspiration of "the Provençal" in the kitchen—in this case the well-trained Jean-Jacques Jouteux. No stranger to the fine art of catering to an upscale clientele, he's assisted by an attractive staff. Menu items include marinated artichoke hearts presented beside half a lobster, a tarte fine of potatoes with undercooked foie gras, rack of lamb with local herbs and tarragon sauce, and crayfish asparagus and black-olive tapenade. The best way to appreciate the desserts is to order the house sampler, *"les cinq desserts du Provençal"*—a potpourri of five petits desserts that usually includes macaroons with chocolate and crème brûlée. With the passage of years here, the cooking seems more inspired than ever.

Le Sloop. Au Nouveau Port. ☎ **04-93-01-48-63.** Reservations recommended. Main courses 138F–155F ($23.45–$26.35); fixed-price menu 155F ($26.35). AE, MC, V. June–Sept, Wed 7–9:30pm, Thurs–Tues noon–2pm and 7–11pm; Oct–Nov 15 and Dec 15–May, Thurs–Tues noon–2pm and 7–11pm. Closed Nov 15–Dec 15. FRENCH.

The most popular and most reasonably priced bistro in this very expensive area, it sits directly at the edge of the port, outfitted in blue and white inside and out. The best of regional produce is handled deftly. A meal here might begin with a salad of flap mushrooms steeped *"en cappuccino"* with liquefied foie gras; or perhaps a sautéed panful of flap mushrooms served with grated parmesan cheese. This might be followed with a filet of deboned sea bass served with a red ("Bandols") wine sauce or a mixed fish fry of three kinds of Mediterranean fish, bound together with olive oil, oils, and truffles. Dessert might include a custom-baked *("à la minute")* tarte with red plums, or any of about seven other desserts, each based on "the red fruits of the region." The regional wines are reasonably priced.

10 Beaulieu

583 miles (938.25km) S of Paris, 6 miles (9.66km) E of Nice, 7 miles (11.27km) W of Monte Carlo

Protected from the cold north winds blowing down from the Alps, Beaulieu-sur-Mer is often referred to as "La Petite Afrique" (Little Africa). Like Menton, it has the mildest climate along the Côte d'Azur and is especially popular with wintering wealthy. Originally, English visitors staked it out. Beaulieu is graced with lush vegetation, including oranges, lemons, and bananas, as well as palms.

ESSENTIALS

GETTING THERE   Train service connects Beaulieu with Nice, Monaco, and the rest of the Côte. For **rail information** and schedules, call ☎ **08-36-35-35-35.** Buses arrive at a point under the railway bridge near the junction of the bd. Maréchal Leclerc and the avenue Joffre. For bus information and schedules, call ☎ **04-93-85-61-81.** Most visitors drive from Nice via the Moyenne Corniche or the coastal highway.

VISITOR INFORMATION   The **Office de Tourisme** is on place Georges-Clemenceau (☎ **04-93-01-02-21**).

EXPLORING THE TOWN

The ✪ **Villa Kérylos,** rue Gustave-Eiffel (☎ **04-93-01-01-44**), is a replica of an ancient Greek residence, painstakingly designed and built by the archaeologist Theodore Reinach. Inside, the cabinets are filled with a collection of Greek figurines and ceramics. But most interesting is the reconstructed Greek furniture, much of which would be fashionable today. One curious mosaic depicts the slaying of the minotaur and provides its own labyrinth (if you try to trace the path, expect to stay for weeks). It's open daily from 10:30am to 6pm. Admission is 40F ($6.80) for adults and 20F ($3.40) for children and seniors.

The **Casino de Beaulieu,** avenue Fernand-Dunan (☎ **04-93-76-48-00**), built in the art-nouveau style in 1903, was revitalized with new management in 1997. The main part of the casino where the blackjack, roulette, and chemin de fer tables are housed is open every night from 8pm to dawn. The ambience is glamorous and men are required to wear jacket and tie. Entrance is 70F ($11.90). For a more casual spot of gambling, the casino has a separate area reserved for slot machines only. Entrance is free and there is no dress code. This area is open every day from 11am to dawn. There are also a bar and a disco on the premises.

The town boasts an important church, the late 19th-century **Eglise de Sacré-Coeur,** a quasi-Byzantine, quasi-Gothic mishmash at 13 bd. du Maréchal-Leclerc (☎ **04-93-01-18-24**). With the same address and phone is the 12th-century Romanesque chapel of **Santa Maria de Olivo,** used mostly for temporary exhibits of painting, sculpture, and civic lore. Both sites are open daily from 8am to 7pm.

As you walk along the seafront promenade, you can see many stately belle époque villas that evoke the days when Beaulieu was the very height of fashion. Although you can't go inside, you'll see signs indicating **Villa Namouna,** which once belonged to Gordon Bennett, the owner of the *New York Herald,* who sent Stanley to Africa to find Livingstone; and **Villa Léonine,** former home of the marquess of Salisbury.

MEMORABLE STROLLS

For a memorable **90-minute walk,** start directly north of boulevard Edouard-VII, where a path leads up the Riviera escarpment to Sentier du Plateau St-Michel. A belvedere here offers panoramic views from Cap d'Ail to the Estérel. A **1-hour alternative** is the stroll along promenade Maurice-Rouvier, beginning at a point adjacent to the sea and the Royal Riviera hotel. The promenade runs parallel to the water, and stretches between Beaulieu and the old port of St-Jean de Cap Ferrat. Expect a walk of about 30 minutes each way, although you might opt to prolong the experience with a *café* or drink in Cap Ferrat once you get there. As you walk, you'll see some of the region's most elegant mansions, set within manicured gardens overlooking the blue sea and the curving shoreline of the French Riviera.

A DAY AT THE BEACH

Don't expect soft sands. Some seasons might have more sand than others, depending on tides and storms, but usually the surfaces are covered with light-gray gravel that has a finer texture than beaches at other resorts nearby. The longer of the town's two beaches is **Petite Afrique,** adjacent to the yacht basin; the shorter is **Baie des Fourmis,** whose main bathing spot is **Plage des Calanques** (☎ **04-93-01-45-00**), adjacent to the town's landmark Villa Kerylos. Access to both of them is free. If you want to rent a mattress for the day and have easy access to a beachfront kiosk selling snacks and drinks, the two most visible purveyors of comfort on the sands are on Petite Afrique: **Africa Plage** (☎ **04-93-01-11-00**) and **Beaulieu Plage** (☎ **04-93-01-14-36**). Mattresses rent for 90F ($15.30).

WHERE TO STAY
VERY EXPENSIVE

✪ **La Réserve de Beaulieu.** 5 bd. du Maréchal-Leclerc, 06310 Beaulieu-sur-Mer. ☎ **04-93-01-00-01.** Fax 04-93-01-28-99. 37 units. A/C MINIBAR TV TEL. 900F–4,250F

($153–$722.50) double; 3,100F–8,150F ($527–$1,385.50) suite. AE, DC, MC, V. Closed Nov 20–Dec 20 and Jan 10–Feb. Parking 100F ($17).

One of the Riviera's most famous hotels, this pink-and-white fin-de-siècle palace is on the Mediterranean. Here you can sit having an apéritif watching the sun set over the Riviera while a pianist treats you to Mozart. A number of the public lounges open onto a courtyard with bamboo chairs, grass borders, and urns of flowers. Social life centers around the main drawing room, much like the grand living room of a country estate. The hotel has been rebuilt in stages, so the rooms range widely in size and design; however, all are deluxe and individually decorated, with beautiful views of mountains or sea. The rooms are constantly being upgraded and improved. Accommodations are sumptuous—read that gorgeous. They come with private safes, generous closets, rich carpeting, elegant fabrics, and deluxe mattresses. Most of them overlook the Mediterranean, and some even have their own private balconies. Luminous tile baths come with plush towels, hair dryers, deluxe toiletries, and dual basins. In 1998, the hotel joined the ranks of Europe's Relais & Châteaux.

Dining/Diversions: The dining room has a coved frescoed ceiling, parquet floors, crystal chandeliers, and picture windows facing the Mediterranean. Specialties are sea bass with thin slices of potatoes in savory tomato sauce, sea bream stuffed with local vegetables, and roast rack of lamb.

Facilities: Private harbor for yachts, submarine fishing gear, sauna, thalassotherapy, seawater pool.

✪ **Le Métropole.** 15 bd. du Maréchal-Leclerc, 06310 Beaulieu-sur-Mer. ☎ **04-93-01-00-08.** Fax 04-93-01-18-51. www.webstore.fr/metropole. E-mail: metropole@relais-chateaux.fr. 40 units. A/C MINIBAR TV TEL. 1,200F–3,000F ($204–$510) double; 2,300F–5,500F ($391–$935) suite. Rates include half board. AE, DC, MC, V. Closed Oct 20–Dec 20.

This Italianate villa offers some of the most luxurious accommodations along the Côte d'Azur and as a hotel is on equal rank with the fabled Réserve. It's a Relais & Châteaux and set on 2 acres of grounds, discreetly shut off from the resort's traffic. You'll enter a world of polished French elegance: balconies opening onto sea views, marble, Oriental carpets, and polite staff members. Guest rooms are furnished in tasteful fabrics and flowery wallpapers, each coming with a deluxe mattress and quality linen on comfortable beds. Baths are elegantly spacious, most often tiled, and have double sinks, hair dryers, and fluffy towels.

Dining/Diversions: Though the in-house restaurant recently lost a star from the Michelin judges, the food is nonetheless superb. The restaurant has a seaside terrace/bar, which elegantly retreats inside when the weather turns chilly.

Services: Room service (24 hours).

Facilities: Concrete jetty for sunning, heated pool; tennis and golf nearby.

EXPENSIVE

Hôtel Carlton. 7 av. Edith-Cavell, 06310 Beaulieu-sur-Mer. ☎ **04-93-01-14-70.** Fax 04-93-01-29-62. 30 units. A/C TV TEL. 900F–1,120F ($153–$190.40) double. AE, DC, MC, V. Closed Nov–Mar.

This contemporary four-star hotel rises from a desirable position within 200 yards of the beach and a 3-minute walk from the public tennis courts. Immaculate and painted a rosy tone of beige, it's a solid, reliable choice. Rooms are sunny, conservatively modern, and tasteful, many offering views of the garden or the sea. Every year the rooms are spruced up, and they contain excellent period furnishings, all with standardized but fine mattresses and crisp linen. Bathrooms are rather cramped although most of them have a shower/tub combo. The restaurant is open daily for lunch and dinner but closed when the hotel closes.

Don't confuse this hotel with the less expensive, less desirable **Hôtel Carlton Résidence,** avenue Albert-1er (☎ **04-93-01-06-02**). The 30 simple rooms there (with phones) are available here only when the main hotel has more business than it can handle; this tends to be only from late June to early September, but at press time the joint management hadn't yet solidified its plans. The rates are 800F to 900F ($136 to $153) for a double.

MODERATE

Hôtel Frisia. Bd. Eugéne-Gauthier, 06310 Beaulieu-sur-Mer. ☎ **04-93-01-01-04.** Fax 04-93-01-31-92. 32 units. A/C MINIBAR TV TEL. 520F–740F ($88.40–$125.80) double. AE, MC, V. Closed Nov 14–Dec 12.

In the mid-1990s, this hotel was renovated; a bath and air-conditioning were added to each room. Rooms are decorated in a modern style, most often open to views of the harbor, with sea-views the most expensive. They range from small to medium in size, each fitted with a quality mattress and crisp linen. Bathrooms are compact and tiled, and contain adequate shelf space and shower stalls for the most part. English is spoken, and the American ownership makes foreign guests feel especially welcome. The hotel has a sunny garden and inviting lounges. Breakfast is the only meal served, but many reasonably priced dining places are nearby.

INEXPENSIVE

Hôtel Le Havre Bleu. 29 bd. du Maréchal-Joffre, 06310 Beaulieu-sur-Mer. ☎ **04-93-01-01-40.** Fax 04-93-01-29-92. 22 units. TEL. 280F–320F ($47.60–$54.40) double. AE, DC, MC, V.

In what used to be a private Victorian villa, the hotel has one of the prettiest facades of any inexpensive hotel in town, with arched, ornate windows and a front garden dotted with flowering urns. Guest rooms are functional and, as befits a house of this age, vary in shape and size; all come with comfortable mattresses and tiled baths. Breakfast is the only meal served.

Hôtel Marcellin. 18 av. Albert-1er, 06310 Beaulieu-sur-Mer. ☎ **04-93-01-01-69.** Fax 04-93-01-37-43. 37 units. TEL. 160F–180F ($27.20–$30.60) double without bath, 250F–300F ($42.50–$51) double with bath; 500F–700F ($85–$119) suite. MC, V. Closed Nov–Dec 15.

A good budget selection in an otherwise high-priced resort, the turn-of-the-century Marcellin rents restored rooms with homelike amenities, all with a southern exposure. It has been run by the same family since 1938. Ranging from small to medium, rooms have first-rate mattresses. Bathrooms are a bit cramped and have shower stalls for the most part. The hotel stands amid the town's congestion, near its western periphery, a 5-minute walk to the beach. Its only breathing space consists of a small outdoor terrace. Despite that, it's a pleasant, well-maintained place to stay. The government has given the Marcellin a well-deserved two stars. Breakfast is the only meal served, but many restaurants are nearby.

WHERE TO DINE

La Pignatelle. 10 rue de Quincenet. ☎ **04-93-01-03-37.** Reservations recommended. Main courses 55F–150F ($9.35–$25.50); fixed-price menus 80F–188F ($13.60–$31.95). AE, MC, V. Thurs–Tues 12:15–1:30pm and 7–9:30pm. Closed mid-Nov to mid-Dec. FRENCH.

Even in this super-expensive resort, you can find an excellent and affordable Provençal bistro. Despite its relatively low prices, La Pignatelle prides itself on the fact that all the products that go into its robust cuisine are fresh. As a result, it's usually crowded. Specialties are salade Niçoise, a succulent version of *soupe de poissons* where someone has labored to remove the bones, cassolette of mussels, monkfish steak garnished only with olive oil and herbs, scampi Provençal, tripe Niçoise, scallops, and a *"petite friture du pays"* that incorporates very small fish with Provençal traditions that are many hundreds of years old.

✪ **Les Agaves.** 4 av. Maréchal Foch. ☎ **04-93-01-13-12.** Reservations recommended. Main courses 75F–190F ($12.75–$32.30); set-price menu 165F ($28.05). AE, MC, V. Tues–Sun noon–3pm and Tues–Sat 7:15–10:30pm. Closed Nov. FRENCH.

One of the most stylish restaurants in Beaulieu is housed within a turn-of-the-century villa across the street from the railway station. Inside, within an ambience of richly grained paneling and high ceilings, you'll enjoy the kind of food that such U.S.-based publications as *Bon Appetit* have praised as delectable. Of particular note is curry-enhanced scallops served with garlic-flavored tomatoes and parsley; lobster salad with mango; chopped shrimp with Provençal herbs, and several different preparations of foie gras. Filet of sea bass with truffles and champagne sauce is particularly delectable. Bouillabaisse, a full meal in its own right, is the most visible exception to the range of prices of main courses printed above, priced at 250F ($42.50) per person.

The African Queen. Port de Plaisance. ☎ **04-93-01-10-85.** Reservations recommended. Main courses 78F–150F ($13.25–$25.50); pizzas 48F–62F ($8.15–$10.55). MC, V. Daily noon–midnight. INTERNATIONAL.

Named by its movie-loving founders after the Hollywood classic, this hip and popular restaurant is filled with posters of Hepburn and Bogie and has a jungle-inspired decor. Much influenced by the U.S. (its sophisticated maître d' lived in Miami for 6 years), it has welcomed stars like Jack Nicholson, Raymond Burr, Robert Wagner, and Diana Ross during the nearby Cannes Film Festival. Menu specialties are a *dégustation de bouillabaisse,* African curry of lamb or beef and served like a rijstaffel with about a dozen condiments, or any of an array of steaks, fish, or shellfish. Less expensive are the seven or eight kinds of pizza, which even visiting Italians claim are very good. No one will mind if you stop in for only a strawberry daiquiri or piña colada. The check is presented in a videocassette case labeled—what else?—*The African Queen.*

11 Eze & La Turbie

585 miles (941.47km) S of Paris, 7 miles (11.27km) NE of Nice

The hamlets of Eze and La Turbie, though 4 miles apart, have so many similarities that most of France's tourist officials speak of them as if they were one. Both boast fortified feudal centers high in the hills overlooking the Provençal coast, built during the early Middle Ages to stave off raids from corsairs. Clinging to the rocky hillsides around these hamlets are upscale villas, many of which were built since the 1950s by retirees. Closely linked, culturally and fiscally, to nearby Monaco, Eze and La Turbie each have full-time populations of fewer than 3,000.

ESSENTIALS

GETTING THERE   Eze (also known as Eze-Village) is accessible via the Moyenne (Middle) Corniche road, La Turbie via the Grande (Upper) Corniche. Signs are positioned along the coastal road indicating the direction motorists should take to reach either of the hamlets.

VISITOR INFORMATION   The **Office de Tourisme** is on place du Général-de-Gaulle, Eze-Village (☎ **04-93-41-26-00**).

EXPLORING THE TOWNS

The medieval cores of both towns contain art galleries, boutiques, and artisans' shops that have been restored. Two art galleries of particular note within Eze-Village are

Galerie Sevek, rue du Barri (☎ **04-93-41-06-22**), and **Galerie Doussot,** rue Princi-pale (☎ **04-93-41-01-62**).

The leading attraction in **Eze** is the **Jardin Exotique,** boulevard du Jardin-Exotique (☎ **04-93-41-10-30**), a lushly landscaped showcase of exotic plants at the pinnacle of the town's highest hill. Entrance is 12F ($2.05), free for children 11 and under. In July and August, it's open from 8:30am to 8pm; the rest of the year, it opens between 8:30 and 9am and closes between 5 and 7:30pm, depending on the time of sunset.

La Turbie boasts a ruined monument erected by the ancient Roman emperor Augustus in 6 B.C., the **Trophée des Alps** (also called by locals, "La Trophée d'Au-guste"). It rises near a rock formation known as La Tête de Chien, at the highest point along the Grand Corniche, 1,500 feet above sea level. The monument, restored with funds donated by Edward Tuck, was erected by the Roman Senate to celebrate the sub-jugation of the people of the French Alps by the Roman armies. A short distance from the monument is the **Musée du Trophée des Alps,** rue Albert-1er, La Turbie (☎ **04-93-41-20-84**), a mini-museum containing finds from archaeological digs nearby and information about the monument's restoration. It's open daily: April to June from 9am to 6pm, July to September from 9am to 7pm, and October to March from 9:30am to 5pm. Entrance is 25F ($4.25) for adults, 15F ($2.55) for students and youths 12 to 25, and free for children 11 and under. Closed January 1, May 1, November 1, and December 25.

WHERE TO STAY & DINE

Auberge Eric Rivot. 44 av. de la Liberté, 06360 Eze-Bord-de-Mer. ☎ **04-93-01-51-46.** Fax 04-93-01-58-40. 10 units. TV TEL. 300F ($51) double. Half board 330F ($56.10) per person extra. AE, DC, MC, V. Closed mid-Nov to Dec 1.

This straw-yellow stucco villa is a few steps from the Basse Corniche. It has a quiet rear terrace, and the decor features rattan chairs, exposed brick, and lots of brass. The simply furnished doubles draw mainly a summer crowd, though the inn is open most of the year. Bedrooms are small but decently furnished with beds containing middle-grade mattresses. Bathrooms are tiled and compact, and have hair dryers. Half board is a good deal here—the meals are satisfying and wine is included.

✪ **Hostellerie du Château de la Chèvre d'Or.** Rue du Barri, 06360 Eze-Village. ☎ **04-92-10-66-66.** Fax 04-93-41-06-72. 33 units. A/C MINIBAR TV TEL. 1,500F–2,950F ($255–$501.50) double; 3,100F–15,000F ($527–$2,550) suite. AE, MC, DC, V. Closed mid-Nov to Feb.

This is a miniature village retreat built in the 1920s in neo-Gothic style, but without a beach. On the side of a stone village off the Moyenne Corniche, this Relais & Châteaux is a complex of village houses, all with views of the coastline. The owner has had the interior of the "Golden Goat" flawlessly decorated to maintain its old char-acter while adding modern comfort. Great care is taken to maintain comfortable mat-tresses and lots of fluffy towels. Even if you don't stop in for a meal or a room, try to visit for a drink in the lounge, which has a panoramic view.

Dining/Diversions: This hotel maintains three restaurants. The most expensive and prestigious is the Restaurant de la Chèvre d'Or. It charges from 280F to 390F ($47.60 to $66.30) for a fixed-price lunch, and 590F ($100.30) for a fixed-price dinner. The middle-bracket choice is an Italian trattoria, Olivetto, and the least expen-sive choice is Le Grill du Château. All three enterprises are open daily, except during the hotel's annual closing noted above, for both lunch and dinner.

Le Cap Estel. 06380 Eze-Bord-de-Mer. ☎ **04-93-01-50-44.** Fax 04-93-01-55-20. www. web-store.fr/capestel. 40 units. A/C MINIBAR TV TEL. 1,310F–2,540F ($222.70–$431.80) double; 1,890F–3,440F ($321.30–$584.80) suite. AE, DC, MC, V. Closed Oct–Mar. Free parking.

At one of the most dramatic points along the Côte between Nice and Monte Carlo, this hotel is a successful reincarnation of a turn-of-the-century villa built for a princess. It's on a rocky promontory jutting into the sea, 2 miles east of Beaulieu, reached along the Lower Corniche. Below the coast road, Le Cap Estel sits in 5 acres of terraced, landscaped gardens. Exotic birds are kept in cages and the reflection pool has a spray fountain and is lit by colored lights at night. Because of the hotel's location, all the rooms overlook the sea, and each is near a terrace. Bedrooms are elegantly appointed and beautifully furnished, with excellent mattresses on the deluxe beds. Bathrooms contain bidets, shower/tub combinations, hair dryers, and plush towels. You can dine inside, on an open-air terrace, or at umbrella-shaded tables under the trees. Occasional barbecues and chicken-on-the-spit dinners are featured. Set-price lunches and dinners cost from around 300F ($51) each. There's a saltwater outdoor pool in the garden and a heated indoor pool, which projects out over the waves like the bow of a ship.

12 Peillon

12 miles (19.31km) NW of Nice

This fortified medieval town is the most spectacular "perched village" along the Côte d'Azur. At 1,000 feet above the sea, it's also unspoiled, unlike so many other perched villages that are filled with day-trippers and souvenir shops.

The main incentive to visit Peillon is the town itself, with its semifortified architecture, which makes you feel that even today it could lock its doors, bar its windows, and keep any intruder at bay. Specific sites of interest include the town's severely dignified parish church, the **Eglise St-Sauveur** (open daily from 8am to around 6pm). Built in a simple country-baroque style, it's the site of many marriages, baptisms, and wedding ceremonies. Another site of interest is the 15th-century **Chapelle des Pénitents Blancs,** on place August-Arnuls. It's usually locked, so visits require that you first drop by the town hall (La Mairie; place de la Mairie; ☎ 04-93-79-91-04), where an employee—if it's convenient and if he or she isn't otherwise occupied—will accompany you with a key and wait for you while you admire the interior. The service is free, but a gratuity is appreciated. If you plunk 2F (35¢) into a machine near the gate, lights will illuminate the interior's noteworthy frescoes. Painted in 1491 by Jean Cannavesio, they represent the eight stages of the passion of Christ.

The narrow streets radiate outward from the town's "foyer," **place Auguste-Arnuls,** which is shaded by rows of plantain trees centered around a fountain that has splashed water from its basin since 1800. Some of the streets are enclosed with vaulting and accented with potted geraniums and strands of ivy.

If you're in the mood for walking, consider a 2-hour, 7½-mile northward hike across the dry and rocky landscape to Peillon's remote twin, **Peille,** a smaller version of Peillon.

ESSENTIALS

GETTING THERE   Few other towns in Provence are as easy to reach by car and as inconvenient to reach by public transportation. Peillon is an easy 20-minute drive (depending on traffic) northeast from Nice; take D2204 to D21.

Only two trains a day stop near Peillon, at St-Techle, an antiquated station connecting Nice with Coni, a town across the border in Italy. For **rail information** and schedules, call ☎ 08-36-35-35-35. You'll find lots of dilapidated local color at the railway station of St-Techle. There are no taxis waiting, and no bus service to carry you on to Peillon. If you can find a phone in St-Techle, the phone number of the best local **cab service** is ☎ 04-93-27-00-83. You can also contact the company's cell phone by dialing ☎ **06-13-43-89-29.** Transit from the railway station at St-Techle to Peillon costs about 50F ($8.50) each way. Most backpackers continue into Peillon by hitch-hiking.

The **Santa Azur** bus line operates four buses a day from Nice, with multiple stops en route (trip time: around 25 minutes). Don't expect it to be convenient—you'll be dropped off about 2 miles from Peillon's center, at a tiny crossroads known as Le Moulin. Many hardy souls opt to continue on to the center by foot, as there's no transport into Peillon. For **bus information,** call ☎ **04-93-85-61-81.**

VISITOR INFORMATION   The **Tourist Office** in Nice (☎ **04-93-79-92-04**) is responsible for supplying information about Peillon. But a more likely bet for on-the-spot tourist information is to chat with the staff at Auberge de la Madone (see below), or to informally contact anyone at Peillon's Town Hall (☎ **04-93-79-91-04**).

WHERE TO STAY & DINE

✪ **Auberge de la Madone.** 06440 Peillon. ☎ **04-93-79-91-17.** Fax 04-93-79-99-36. 20 units. TEL. Main building: 450F–840F ($76.50–$142.80) double; 920F ($156.40) suite. Annex: 210F–380F ($35.70–$64.60) double. DC, MC, V. Closed Jan 7–24 and Oct 20–Dec 20; restaurant closed Wed. Free parking.

This hotel, with its well-recommended restaurant, has thrived here since the 1930s. The oldest section of the stone-sided complex of buildings dates from the 12th century. Evocative of a sprawling *mas Provençal,* it gives you a real glimpse of Provence long ago. It's capped with terra-cotta tiles and draped with a small version of the hanging gardens of Babylon. On the opposite side of place Auguste-Arnuls from the rest of the village, it boasts a wide terrace offering a great view of the town's vertical, angular architecture. The guest rooms are comfortable and rustic, outfitted with Provençal themes and fabrics. In 1998, the hotel built an annex, within a 5-minute walk, with seven additional rooms—the annex's accommodations are much simpler than those in the main building; rates depend on the plumbing and views. All bedrooms have excellent mattresses and crisp linen. Bathrooms are generally small, with shower stalls for the most part.

The hotel restaurant is by far the most formal in town, serving lunch and dinner every day except Wednesday and during the annual closing noted above. Menu items are based on cuisine that developed over the centuries and include unusual dishes like *tourton des pénitents,* a salty tart enriched with 17 herbs, almonds, eggs, and cream; suckling lamb with garlic mashed potatoes and a tapenade of olives; farm-raised guinea fowl with a confit of pears; and a pot au feu, a savory kettle of seafood served with aïoli. A recipe that was specifically praised early in 1999 by the American edition of *Bon Appetit* for its originality and subtle flavors was a white beet tart capped with a "petal" of foie gras.

13 Monaco

593 miles (954.34km) S of Paris, 11 miles (17.70km) E of Nice

The outspoken Katharine Hepburn once called Monaco "a pimple on the chin of the south of France." She wasn't referring to the principality's lack of beauty but rather to the preposterous idea of having a little country, a feudal anomaly, taking up some of the choicest coastline along the Riviera. Hemmed in by France on three sides and facing the Mediterranean, tiny Monaco staunchly maintains its independence. Even Charles de Gaulle couldn't force Prince Rainier to do away with his tax-free policy. As almost everybody in an overburdened world knows by now, the Monégasques do not pay taxes. Nearly all their country's revenue comes from tourism and gambling.

Monaco—or rather its capital of Monte Carlo—has for a century been a symbol of glamour. Its legend was further enhanced by the 1956 marriage of the man who was at that time the world's most eligible bachelor, Prince Rainier III, to the American actress Grace Kelly. She had met the prince when she was in Cannes for the film festival to promote *To Catch a Thief,* the Hitchcock movie she made with Cary Grant. A journalist friend arranged a *Paris Match* photo shoot with the prince—and the rest is history. The Monégasques welcomed the birth of daughter Caroline in 1957, but went wild at the birth of Albert, a male heir, in 1958. According to a 1918 treaty, Monaco will become an autonomous state under French protection should the ruling dynasty become extinct. However, the fact that Albert is still a bachelor has the entire principality concerned. The third royal daughter, Stephanie, was born in 1965.

Though not always happy in her role, Princess Grace soon won the respect and adoration of her people. In 1982, a sports car she was driving, with her daughter Stephanie as a passenger (not as the driver, as was viciously rumored), plunged over a cliff, killing Grace but only injuring Stephanie. The Monégasques still mourn her death.

Monaco became a property of the Grimaldi clan, a Genoese family, as early as 1297. With shifting loyalties, it has maintained something resembling independence ever since. In a fit of impatience the French annexed it in 1793, but the ruling family recovered it in 1814; however, the prince at that time couldn't bear to tear himself away from the pleasures of Paris for "dreary old Monaco."

ESSENTIALS

GETTING THERE   Monaco has rail, bus, and highway connections from other coastal cities. Trains arrive every 30 minutes from Cannes, Nice, Menton, and Antibes. For **rail information** and schedules, call ☎ **93-10-60-01.** Monaco's railway station **(Gare SNCF)** is on the avenue Prince Pierre. There are no border formalities for anyone entering Monaco from mainland France. Buses arrive hourly from Nice. From Nice, motorists can continue east along N98 or N7.

VISITOR INFORMATION   The **Direction du Tourisme** office is at 2A bd. des Moulins (☎ **92-16-61-16**).

SPECIAL EVENTS   Important **car-racing events** are held in January (Le Rallye) and May (the Grand Prix). Mid-April witnesses one of the Riviera's most famous **tennis tournaments,** the corporate-sponsored Le Open International de Tennis de Monte Carlo, which takes place in the spring at the Monte Carlo Country Club (☎ **04-93-41-30-15** for information). Every February, Monte Carlo is home to a week-long convention that attracts media moguls from virtually everywhere: **Le Fes-**

Number, Please: Monaco's Telephone System

Since 1996, Monaco's phone system has been independent of France.

To call Monaco from within France, dial 00 (access code for international long-distance calls placed from mainland France), followed by Monaco's country code, 377, and then the eight-digit local phone number. To call Monaco from North America, dial the international access code, 011, followed by Monaco's country code, 377, plus the local eight-digit Monaco number.

If you're calling France from within Monaco, dial 00 (the international access code), 33 (the country code for France), 4 (the area code, without the zero), and the eight-digit number. To call locally within Monaco, dial all eight digits of the phone number.

Monaco

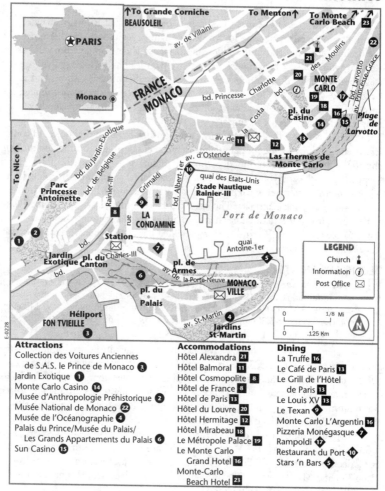

↑To Grande Corniche
BEAUSOLEIL

To Menton↑

To Monte
Carlo Beach 23

★PARIS

Monaco ⊙

FRANCE MONACO

To Nice ↑

av. de Villaini

MONTE
CARLO 22

21

des Moulins

20

bd. Larvotto
av. Princesse-Grace

bd. Princesse- Charlotte

bd.

ℹ

19

18

17

pl. du
Casino

16

15

14

Plage
de
Larvotto

av. de la Costa

11 ✉

12

13

av. d'Ostende

Las Thermes de
Monte Carlo

bd. du Jardin-Exotique

bd. de Belgique

Rainier-III

Grimaldi

bd. Albert-1er

10

quai des Etats-Unis

Stade Nautique
Rainier-III

Port de Monaco

9

✝

8

LA
CONDAMINE

rue

Station ✉

7

quai
Antoine-1er

Jardin
Exotique

pl. du
Canton

Charles-III

bd.

pl. de
Armes

av. de la Porte-Neuve

5

1 2

Parc
Princesse
Antoinette

6

pl. du
Palais

MONACO-
VILLE

✉

LEGEND	
Church	✝
Information	ℹ
Post Office	✉

Héliport
FON TVIEILLE

3

av. St-Martin

4

Jardins
St-Martin

0	1/8 Mi
0	.125 Km

Ⓝ

E-0228

Attractions

Collection des Voitures Anciennes
de S.A.S. le Prince de Monaco ⧫3

Jardin Exotique ⬡1

Monte Carlo Casino ⬡14

Musée d'Anthropologie Préhistorique ⬡2

Musée National de Monaco ⬡22

Musée de l'Océanographie ⧫4

Palais du Prince/Musée du Palais/
Les Grands Appartements du Palais ⬡6

Sun Casino ⬡15

Accommodations

Hôtel Alexandra 21

Hôtel Balmoral 11

Hôtel Cosmopolite 8

Hôtel de France 8

Hôtel de Paris 13

Hôtel du Louvre 20

Hôtel Hermitage 12

Hôtel Mirabeau 18

Le Métropole Palace 19

Le Monte Carlo
Grand Hotel 16

Monte-Carlo
Beach Hotel 23

Dining

La Truffe 16

Le Café de Paris 13

Le Grill de l'Hôtel
de Paris 13

Le Louis XV 13

Le Texan ⧫9

Monte Carlo L'Argentin 16

Pizzeria Monégasque ⧫7

Rampoldi ⬡17

Restaurant du Port ⧫10

Stars 'n Bars ⧫5

---

tival International de la Télévision, when the winning shows from all over the world are broadcast and judged on their individual merits. For information and further details, write or call Festival International de la Télévision, 4 bd. des Jardins Exotiques (☎ 93-10-40-60).

EXPLORING THE PRINCIPALITY

The second-smallest state in Europe (Vatican City is the tiniest), Monaco consists of four parts. The old town, **Monaco-Ville,** on a promontory, "The Rock," 200 feet high, is the seat of the royal palace and the government building, as well as the Oceanographic Museum. To the west of the bay, **La Condamine,** the home of the Monégasques, is at the foot of the old town, forming its harbor and port sector. Up from the port (walking is steep in Monaco) is **Monte Carlo,** once the playground of European royalty and still the center for wintering wealthily, the setting for the casino and its gardens and the deluxe hotels. The fourth part, **Fontvieille,** is a neat industrial suburb.

Ironically, **Monte-Carlo Beach,** at the far frontier, is on French soil. It attracts a chic crowd, including movie stars in scanty bikinis and thongs. The resort has a freshwater pool, an artificial beach, and a sea-bathing establishment.

No one used to go to Monaco in summer, but now that has totally changed—in fact, July and August tend to be so crowded it's hard to get a room. Furthermore, with the decline of royalty and multimillionaires, Monaco is developing a broader base of tourism (you can stay here moderately—but it's misleading to suggest that you can stay cheaply). The Monégasques very frankly court the affluent visitor. And at the casinos here you can also lose your shirt. "Suicide Terrace" at the casino, though not used as frequently as in the old days, is still a real temptation to many who have foolishly gambled away family fortunes.

Life still focuses on the **Monte Carlo Casino,** which has been the subject of countless legends and the setting for many films (remember poor Lucy Ricardo and the chip she found lying on the casino floor?). High drama is played to the fullest here. Depending on the era, you might have seen Mata Hari shooting a tsarist colonel with a jewel-encrusted revolver when he tried to slip his hand inside her bra to discover her secrets—military, not mammary. The late King Farouk, known as "The Swine," used to devour as many as 8 roast guinea hens and 50 oysters before losing thousands at the table. *Chacun à son goût.* Richard Burton presented Elizabeth Taylor with the obscenely huge Koh-i-noor diamond here.

SEEING THE SIGHTS

Les Grands Appartements du Palais. Place du Palais. ☎ **93-25-18-31.** Combination ticket 40F ($6.80) adults, 20F ($3.40) children 8–14, free for children 7 and under. Palace, June–Sept daily 9:30am–6:30pm; Oct daily 10am–5pm. Closed Nov–May. Museum, June–Sept daily 9:30am–6:30pm; Oct–Nov 11 daily 10am–5pm; Dec 17–May Tues–Sun 10:30am–12:30pm and 2–5pm. Closed Nov 12–Dec 16.

The Italianate home of Monaco's royal family, the Palais du Prince, dominates the principality from "the Rock." When touring Les Grands Appartements, you're shown the Throne Room and allowed to see some of the art collection, including works by Brueghel and Holbein, as well as Princesse Grace's stunning state portrait. The palace was built in the 13th century, and part dates from the Renaissance. You're also shown the chamber where England's George III died. The ideal time to arrive is 11:55am to watch the 10-minute **Relève de la Garde** (changing of the guard).

In a wing of the palace, the **Musée du Palais du Prince (Souvenirs Napoléoniens et Collection d'Archives)** (☎ **93-25-18-31**), contains a collection of mementos of Napoléon and Monaco itself. When the royal residence is closed, this museum is the only part of the palace the public can visit.

Jardin Exotique. Bd. du Jardin-Exotique. ☎ **93-15-29-80.** Admission to museum 39.50F ($6.70) adults, 18.50F ($3.15) children 6–18, free for children 5 and under. June–Sept daily 9am–7pm; Oct–May daily 9am–6pm.

Built on the side of a rock, the gardens are known for their cactus collection. They were begun by Prince Albert I, who was a naturalist and a scientist. He spotted some succulents growing in the palace gardens, and knowing that these plants were normally found only in Central America or Africa, he created the garden from them. You can also explore the grottoes here, as well as the **Musée d'Anthropologie Préhistorique** (☎ **93-15-80-06**). The view of the principality is splendid.

Musée de l'Océanographie. Av. St-Martin. ☎ **93-15-36-00.** Admission 60F ($10.20) adults, 30F ($5.10) children 6–18, free for children 5 and under. July–Aug daily 9am–8pm; Apr–June and Sept daily 9am–7pm; Mar and Oct daily 9:30am–7pm; Nov–Feb daily 10am–6pm.

This museum was founded in 1910 by Albert I, great-grandfather of the present prince. In the main rotunda is a statue of Albert in his favorite costume—that of a sea captain. Displayed are specimens he collected during 30 years of expeditions aboard his oceanographic ships. The aquarium—one of the finest in Europe—contains more than 90 tanks.

Prince Albert's collection is exhibited in the zoology room. Some of the exotic creatures here were unknown before he captured them. You'll see models of the oceanographic ships aboard which he directed his scientific cruises from 1885 to 1914. The most important part of its laboratory has been preserved and reconstituted as closely as possible. The cupboards contain all the equipment and documentation necessary for a scientific expedition. Skeletons of specimens are on the main floor, including a giant whale that drifted ashore at Pietra Ligure in 1896—it's believed to be the same one the prince harpooned earlier that year. The skeleton is remarkable for its healed fractures sustained when a vessel struck the animal as it was drifting asleep on the surface. An exhibition devoted to the discovery of the ocean is in the physical-oceanography room on the first floor. Underwater movies are shown continuously in the lecture room.

Collection des Voitures Anciennes de S.A.S. le Prince de Monaco. Les Terrasses de Fontvieille. ☎ **92-05-28-56.** Admission 30F ($5.10) adults, 15F ($2.55) students and children 8–14, free for children 7 and under. Daily 10am–6pm (closed in Nov).

Prince Rainier III has opened a showcase of his private collection of more than 100 exquisitely restored vintage autos, including the 1956 Rolls-Royce Silver Cloud that carried the prince and princess on their wedding day. It was given to the royal couple by Monaco shopkeepers as a wedding present. A 1952 Austin Taxi on display was once used as the royal "family car." Other exhibits are a Woodie, a 1937 Ford station wagon once used by Prince Louis II when on hunting trips, and a 1925 Bugatti 35B, winner of the Monaco Grand Prix in 1929. Other outstanding autos are a 1903 De Dion Bouton and a 1986 Lamborghini Countach.

Musée National de Monaco. 17 av. Princesse-Grace. ☎ **93-30-91-26.** Admission 30F ($5.10) adults, 20F ($3.40) children 6–14, free for children 5 and under. Easter–Sept daily 10am–6:30pm; Oct–Easter daily 10am–12:15pm and 2:30–6:30pm.

In a villa designed by Charles Garnier (architect of Paris's Opéra Garnier), this museum houses one of the world's greatest collections of mechanical toys and dolls. See especially the 18th-century Neapolitan crib, which contains some 200 figures. This collection, assembled by Mme de Galea, was presented to the principality in 1972; it stemmed from the 18th- and 19th-century trend of displaying new fashions on doll models.

OUTDOOR PURSUITS
A DAY AT THE BEACH

Just outside the border, on French (not Monacan) soil, the ✪ **Monte-Carlo Beach** adjoins the Monte-Carlo Beach Hotel, 22 av. Princesse-Grace (☎ **04-93-28-66-66**). Permeated with intricate social rituals that might not be immediately visible to first-timers, the beach club has thrived for years as an integral part of Monaco's social life. You'll find a beach whose sand is replenished at regular intervals, two large pools (one for children), beach cabanas, a restaurant, a cafe, a bar, and memories of Princess Grace, who used to come here in flowery swimsuits, greeting her friends and subjects with humor and style. As the Celsius reading lowers in late August, expect the beach to close for the winter. The admission charge, depending on the season, varies from 150F to 200F ($25.50 to $34) for the day, which grants you access to the public changing rooms, toilets, the restaurants, and the bar. A day's use of a private cubicle, which you'll use to change and to lock up your street clothes, costs an additional 65F ($11.05). And a full day's rental of a mattress for sunbathing costs 75F ($12.75). As usual, topless is acceptable for both genders, but bottomless isn't.

The Shaky House of Grimaldi

Monaco, according to Somerset Maugham, is 370 sunny acres peopled with shady characters. According to a 1918 treaty, Monaco must maintain an ongoing stream of male heirs to retain its independence from France. The tax-free principality is the oddest fiscal and social anomaly in Europe, a blend of Las Vegas hype and aristocratic glitter whose luster has been sorely tarnished since the demise of Princess Grace ("a snow-covered volcano," said Alfred Hitchcock).

Ah, those young Grimaldis—Albert, Stephanie, and Caroline. Beneficiaries of an empire based on medieval precedent, gambling, and showmanship, they're descended from Genoese merchants on their father's side and a curious blend of Philadelphia conservatism and Hollywood flash on their mother's. Before the advent of Prince Charles and the late Princess Di, they were the product of the most unhappy royal marriage in Europe.

The marriage of the world's most eligible bachelor and the Hollywood golden goddess dominated headlines in April 1956. However, omens were ripe for marital disaster. All six of Grace's bridesmaids ended at least one of their marriages in divorce, and the much-photographed mother of the bride frequently managed to confuse Monaco and Morocco as the site of her famous daughter's love nest.

Like Grace and Rainier themselves, the marriage did not age gracefully. Rainier's snide public assessments of his celebrity wife's accomplishments showed an unpleasant rivalry. Even though the Monégasques reacted in horror when, a few years into the marriage, Grace contemplated returning to Hollywood to star in Hitchcock's *Marnie* (she backed out because of the furor), they soon embraced her again, as well as her many cultural projects, like the establishment of the Monaco Arts Festival and the Princess Grace Foundation.

"How can I bring up my daughters not to have an affair with a married man," Grace once asked, "when I was having affairs with married men all the time?" Clark Gable, Ray Milland, and William Holden come to mind. The admired and envied fairy-tale princess was, beneath it all, a lonely and frustrated woman with a strong sense of loyalty to her friends, a gift for promoting her kingdom by the sea, an obsession with appearances, and a predilection for romances with younger men as she matured. When she was young, the men had been older. But as she reached middle age, the men became younger. For example, she was 46 (in 1976) when she met one of her long-standing lovers, the 30-year-old film director Robert Dornhelm.

The children of this ill-fated union have rebelled against the strictures imposed on them by their less-than-noble parents. More at home in the watering holes of big-city Paris than in the claustrophobic and judgmental homeland, they take turns in being the one most likely to shock the multinational residents of their tax-free domain.

The most obviously disaffected is Stephanie, whose tantrums as a 13-year-old were duly noted by scads of journalists and whose sexual insouciance has contributed, according to local wits, to the ill health of her not particularly serene father. Her affairs have included the sons of both Jean-Paul Belmondo and Alain Delon, also children of second-generation fame. For a time, she moved to Los Angeles, where she tried to build a show-business career. Promising beginnings in Stephanie's fertile roster of career options were stymied by maneuvering from the Grimaldi fortress. Her ambitions have mostly collapsed, as well as her attempts to become a model or pop singer. In 1995, Stephanie married a former palace guard, Alain Ducruet, by whom she had borne two children; however, a year later she divorced him because he had been caught cavorting naked with Miss Bare Breasts of Belgium. In 1998, Stephanie continued to make headlines by staying mum about her new baby's dad—Camille Marie Kelly was Stephanie's third child born out of wedlock. One palace guard summed up Stephanie's affairs and babies: "In these times, it's not a question of morals. A princess can do what she likes." She still makes public appearances and lives around the corner from her father and brother.

Everyone in his prospective kingdom constantly urges Albert, now in his early 40s, to take a bride and produce the male heir necessary to preserve the principality's independence. He has publicly denied rumors of homosexuality and has cavorted with an assortment of famous faces, from Brooke Shields to Donna Rice to Claudia Schiffer. As a local commentator has said, "It's one thing for him to marry a bimbo; it's another to marry someone like his mother." At the moment (subject to change at any minute), Albert continues to play the field, finding no replacement to fill the shoes of Princess Grace.

Caroline, mother of three, has done her royal part. She would if she could, according to observers, force a power struggle with Albert for the right of succession. Her first husband, the much older businessman/*boulevardier* Philippe Junot, was the sort of man every mother hopes her daughter will *not* marry—which is probably why Caroline did. After she announced that she was divorcing womanizing Junot, the Vatican was called in to annul the marriage (which it *finally* did in 1992). Within a year of her mother's death, Caroline met and fell deeply in love with 27-year-old Stefano Casiraghi, son of an Italian industrialist. She was 4 months pregnant when they married in 1984, and she and Stefano had two more children (who remained "illegitimate" until 3 years after their father's death). In 1989, Stefano died in a speedboating accident and Caroline went into severe mourning, chopping off her hair and withdrawing from her duties. Eventually, she and her children moved to France and she returned to her position as "First Lady of Monaco." On January 23, 1999, her 42nd birthday, Caroline took a new husband, Prince Ernst of Hanover, who had been married to her best friend. Oddly, by marrying Ernst, she fulfilled the wishes of her late mother, who always wanted her to marry him. The couple will not be poor: Ernst is reportedly worth $800 million.

On May 31, 1997, the prince and his family marked the 700th anniversary of Grimaldi rule—6,600 Monégasques showed up for an open-air ceremony at place du Palais. With all their troubles and scandals, the clan has come a long way since January 8, 1297—that's when a political refugee from Genoa, Francesco Grimaldi, accompanied by some cronies in monks' clothing, persuaded the defenders of the local castle to give him shelter. Once he and his men penetrated the defenses, they ripped off their hoods and took the castle by force. The Principality of Monaco was born, and it's been in Grimaldi hands ever since.

One Monégasque summed up the Grimaldi situation well: "I go to church every morning to pray for the Prince and his family. I pray God will keep them safe and sane. Because that is my security. Without the Grimaldis, we would be merely hors d'oeuvres for France."

Monaco, in its role as the quintessential kingdom by the sea, also offers sea bathing at its most popular beach, the **Plage de Larvetto,** off avenue Princesse-Grace (☎ 93-30-63-84). There's no charge for bathing on this strip of beach, whose sands are frequently replenished with sand hauled in by barge. The beach is open to public access at all hours.

OTHER OUTDOOR ACTIVITIES

GOLF   The **Monte Carlo Golf Club,** route N7, La Turbie (☎ 04-93-41-09-11), on French soil, is a par-72 golf course with ample amounts of prestige, scenic panoramas, and local history. Certain perks (including use of electric golf buggies) are reserved for members. Before they're allowed to play, nonmembers will be asked to show proof of membership in another golf club and provide evidence of their handicap ratings. Greens fees for 18 holes are 350F ($59.50) Monday to Friday and 450F ($76.50) Saturday and Sunday. Clubs can be rented for 120F ($20.40). The course is open daily from 8am to sunset.

SPA TREATMENTS   In 1908, the Société des Bains de Mer launched a seawater (thalassotherapy) spa in Monte Carlo. It was inaugurated by Prince Albert I himself. However, in World War II it was bombed and only reopened in 1996. **Les Thermes Marins de Monte-Carlo,** 2 av. de Monte-Carlo (☎ 92-16-40-40), is one of the largest spas in Europe and the only one in Monaco. Spread over four floors are a gigantic pool, a Turkish haman, a diet restaurant, a juice bar, two tanning booths, a fitness center, a beauty center, and private treatment rooms.

SWIMMING   The stupendous **Stade Nautique Rainier-III,** quai Albert-1er, at La Condamine (☎ 93-15-28-75), an outdoor pool that overlooks the yacht-clogged harbor, was a gift from the prince to his loyal subjects. It's open in July and August, daily from 9am to midnight; and March to June and September to November, daily from 9am to 6pm (closed December to February). Admission is 25F ($4.25).

An indoor pool open year-round, the **Piscine du Prince Héréditaire Albert,** lies in the Stade Louis II, at 7 av. de Castellane (☎ 92-05-42-13). It's open Monday, Tuesday, Thursday, and Friday from 7:30am to 2:30pm; Saturday from 2 to 6pm; and Sunday from 9am to 1pm. Admission is 15F ($2.55).

TENNIS & SQUASH   The **Monte Carlo Country Club,** in France on avenue Princesse-Grace, Roquebrune-St-Roman (☎ 04-93-41-30-15), has 23 tennis courts (21 clay and two concrete). Payment of the 215F ($36.55) entrance fee will provide access to a restaurant, a health club with Jacuzzi and sauna, a putting green, a beach, and squash courts as well as the well-maintained tennis courts. Plan to spend at least half a day, ending a round of tennis with use of any of the other facilities. It's open daily from 8am to 8 or 9pm, depending on the season.

SHOPPING

Rising costs and an increase in crime have changed women's tastes in jewelry, perhaps forever. **Bijoux Cassio,** 10 bd. des Moulins (☎ 93-25-55-10), sells only imitation gemstones. They're rather shamelessly copied from the real McCoy sold by Cartier and Van Cleef & Arpels. Made in Italy of gold-plated silver, the fake jewelry costs between 200F and 2,000F ($34 and $340) per piece, many thousands of francs less than the authentic gems.

The **Boutique du Rocher,** 1 av. de la Madone (☎ 93-30-91-17), is the largest of two roughly equivalent boutiques opened in 1966 by Princess Grace as the official retail outlets of her charitable foundation. The organization merchandizes Monégasque and Provençal handcrafts—carved frames for pictures or mirrors; housewares;

gift items crafted from porcelain, textiles, and wood; toys and dolls. On the premises are workshops where local artisans produce the goods for sale. It's a short walk from place du Casino; a second branch is at 25 rue Emile de Loth, in Monaco-Ville (☎ 93-30-33-99).

Brett Merrill, 17 bd. des Moulins (☎ 93-50-33-85), is a menswear store aiming at the solid middle-bracket man who simply wants to dress appropriately and look good. You can pick up a swimsuit, shorts, slacks, a blazer, and a pair of socks to replace the ones you ruined by too many walking tours, at prices that won't require that you remortgage your house.

You don't have to be Princess Caroline to be able to afford to shop in Monaco, especially now that **FNAC** (☎ 93-10-81-81), a member of the big French chain that sells records, CDs, tapes, and books, has opened in the heart of town at the **Centre Commercial Le Métropole,** 17 av. des Spélugues in the Jardins du Casino, alongside the Hôtel Métropole and across from the casino.

If you insist on ultrafancy stores, you'll find them cheek by jowl with the Hôtel de Paris and the casino, and lining the streets leading to the Hôtel Hermitage or across from the gardens at the mini-mall Park Palace. Look for the Belgian handbag maker deluxe, **Delvaux,** in the Park Palace, 27 av. de la Costa (☎ 93-25-11-80); **D. Porthault,** the luxury French linen maker, at 26 av. de la Costa (☎ 93-50-16-28); **Chanel,** on place de la Casino at allée Serge-Diaghilev (☎ 93-50-55-55). Allée Serge-Diaghilev is just that, an alley, but a very tiny one filled with designer shops.

However, to get a better perspective on upper-middle-class shopping, visit the **Galaxie de Metropole,** 17 av. des Spélugues. It has a few specialty shops worth visiting (especially if you aren't going into France). Check out **Geneviève Lethu** (☎ 93-50-09-41) for colorful and country tabletop design; or **Manufacture de Monaco** (☎ 93-50-64-63) for glorious bone china and elegant tabletop design. If the prices send you to bed, two doors away is a branch of the chic but often affordable French linen house **Yves Delorme** (☎ 93-50-08-70).

Royal Food (☎ 93-15-05-04) is a tiny gourmet grocery store down a set of curving stairs hidden in the side entrance of the mall; here you can buy food items from France, Lebanon, and the U.S.A., or stock up for *le pique-nique* or for your day trips. This market is open Monday to Saturday from 9am to 8pm.

For real-people shopping, stroll **rue Grimaldi,** the principality's most commercially minded street, near the fruit, flower, and food market (below), and **boulevard des Moulins,** closer to the casino, where glamorous boutiques specialize in international chic. There's also an all-pedestrian thoroughfare with shops less forbiddingly chic: **rue Princesse-Caroline** is loaded with bakeries, flower shops, and the closest thing you'll find to funkiness in Monaco. Also check out the **Formule 1** shop, 15 rue Grimaldi (☎ 93-15-92-44), where everything from racing helmets to specialty key chains and T-shirts celebrates the roar of high-octane—and outside the racetrack, utterly impractical—racing machines.

Should you be looking for the heart and soul of the real Monaco, get away from the glitz and head to place des Armes for the **fruit, flower, and food market** held daily from 9am to noon. It has an indoor and an outdoor market complete with a fountain, cafes, and hand-painted vegetable tiles set beneath your feet. While the outdoor market packs up promptly at noon, some dealers at the indoor market stay open to 2pm. If you prefer bric-a-brac, there's a small but very funky (especially for Monaco) flea market, **Les Puces de Fontvieille,** held Saturday from 10am to 5pm at the Espace Fontvieille, a panoramic open-air site near the heliport in Monaco's Fontvieille district.

WHERE TO STAY
VERY EXPENSIVE

✪ **Hôtel de Paris.** Place du Casino, 98000 Monaco. ☎ **92-16-30-00.** Fax 93-16-38-50. www.montecarloresort.com. E-mail: hp@sdm.mc. 200 units. A/C MINIBAR TV TEL. 2,100F–3,400F ($357–$578) double; from 6,000F ($1,020) suite. AE, DC, MC, V. Parking 130F ($22.10).

On the resort's ornate main plaza, opposite the casino, this is one of the world's most famous hotels and most spectacular beaux-arts monuments. Linked with the sybaritic, high-spending image of Monte Carlo, it's the principality's choice address, more famous and legendary even than the Hermitage. At least two-dozen movie companies have used its lobby as a background. The ornate facade has marble pillars, and the impressive lounge has an art-nouveau rose window at the peak of the dome. The hotel is furnished with a dazzling decor that includes marble pillars, statues, crystal chandeliers, sumptuous carpets, Louis XVI chairs, and a wall-sized fin-de-siècle mural. The guest rooms are fashionable and, in many cases, sumptuous. The rooms opening onto the sea aren't as spacious as those in the rear. Rooms come in a variety of styles, with elaborate period decor or a fashionably contemporary one. Some of the rooms are so large that if Edward VII were still alive, he would no doubt find plenty of living space for his corpulent body. Elegant tasteful fabrics, rich carpeting, and classic accessories make this a continuing favorite among the world's discerning guests who go to sleep at night in some of the most luxurious beds on the Riviera. Bathrooms are commodious, clad in marble with all the amenities—hair dryers, plenty of room for your stuff, dual basins, fluffy towels, robes, and deluxe toiletries.

Dining/Diversions: The evening usually begins in the bar. The hotel's most famous dining options are Le Louis XV and Le Grill (see "Where to Dine," below). Both restaurants benefit from a collection of rare fine wines kept in a dungeon chiseled out of the rock. The less formal Restaurant Côté Jardin offers a daily lunch buffet whose food is inspired by the culinary traditions of the Mediterranean.

Facilities: Thermes Marins spa, directly connected to both the Hôtel de Paris and the Hôtel Hermitage, offers complete courses of thalassotherapy under medical supervision, (including "antismoking," "anticellulite thighs," and "postnatal" cures); a large indoor pool; two saunas; fitness center; beauty center.

✪ **Hôtel Hermitage.** Square Beaumarchais, 98005 Monaco CEDEX. ☎ **92-16-40-00.** Fax 92-16-38-52. www.montecarloresort.com. E-mail: HH@SBM.MC. 247 units. A/C MINIBAR TV TEL. 1,650F–2,950F ($280.50–$501.50) double; from 4,300F ($731) suite. AE, MC, V. Parking 120F ($20.40).

Picture yourself sitting in a wicker armchair, being served drinks under an ornate stained-glass dome with an encircling wrought-iron balcony. The clifftop Hermitage, with its "wedding cake" façade, was the creation of Jean Marquet (who invented marquetry). Large brass beds anchor every room, and decoratively framed doors open onto balconies. Even the smallest rooms are medium in size. Large mirrors, spacious lighted closets, private safes, elegant fabrics and upholstery, and sumptuous beds with luxurious mattresses make living here idyllic. The newest rooms are in the Coasta and Excelsior wings. They lack tradition, but they equal the accommodations in the main building, which many guests still prefer because of its old-fashioned French decor and street-front exposure. Clad in marble, bathrooms are roomy and well appointed with plenty of shelf space, robes, deluxe toiletries, dual basins, hair dryers, and plenty of fluffy towels. High-season rates are charged during Christmas, New Year's, Easter, and July and August. The stylish dining room has Corinthian columns and chandeliers and serves a refined modern cuisine. The Bar Terrasse is a chic rendezvous that at night is a piano bar.

EXPENSIVE

Hôtel Mirabeau. 1 av. Princesse-Grace, 98000 Monaco. ☎ **92-16-65-65.** Fax 93-50-84-85. 103 units. A/C MINIBAR TV TEL. 1,400F–2,450F ($238–$416.50) double; from 2,250F ($382.50) suite. AE, DC, MC, V. Parking 125F ($21.25).

Only the five lowest floors of this 30-story skyscraper are devoted to a hotel—the remainder houses upscale private apartments. Set in the heart of Monte Carlo next to the casino, and known for its La Coupole restaurant, it's a sophisticated hybrid with many functions. Each of the rooms boasts conservatively modern, rather elegant furnishings, and many contain terraces with a romantic view overlooking the pool and Mediterranean seascape. The rooms facing the sea are the most sought after, but units facing traffic are soundproof. Bedrooms are well appointed with walk-in closets and two large beds fitted with luxury mattresses. Bathrooms are spacious and contain hair dryers, deluxe toiletries, and plush towels. **La Coupole,** which earned a Michelin star, is highly praised for its inventive yet classical cooking (closed August). Between May and September, the poolside Café Mirabeau provides an attractive setting for relaxed breakfasts, casual buffet lunches, and upscale dinners.

Le Métropole Palace. B.P. 19, 4 av. de la Madone, 98007 Monaco. ☎ **93-15-15-15.** Fax 93-25-24-44. www.metropole.mc. E-mail: metropole@metropole.mc. 158 units. A/C MINIBAR TV TEL. 1,350F–2,000F ($229.50–$340) double; from 2,100F ($357) suite. AE, DC, MC, V. Parking 120F ($20.40).

In the heart of Monaco, this hotel was rebuilt on the site of the original Métropole, on Monte Carlo's "golden square." The hotel is superb in every way and has an array of handsomely furnished and beautifully decorated rooms. Each includes a radio, hypoallergenic pillows, a hair dryer, and a full line of toiletries. Spaces are generous, furnishings classical, including occasional antiques; all come with quality mattresses and fine linen, plus double glazing and soothing pastel color schemes. Marble bathrooms have robes and plush towels, and often a whirlpool tub. The upscale **Le Jardin** serves splendid French and international cuisine. Services include 24-hour room service, same-day and overnight laundry, valet service, and baby-sitting. There's also a heated seawater pool.

Le Monte Carlo Grand Hotel. 12 av. des Spélugues, 98007 Monaco CEDEX. ☎ **93-50-65-00.** Fax 93-30-01-57. www.monaco.mc. E-mail: grandhotel@monaco.mc. 619 units. A/C MINIBAR TV TEL. 1,650F–2,400F ($280.50–$408) double; 2,000–8,400F ($340–$1,428) suite. AE, DC, MC, V. Parking 120F ($20.40).

Originally conceived and built by the Loews Corporation, this glittering modern palace hotel was bought and renamed late in 1998 by local investors. It hugs the seacoast from a position below the terraces that support the famous casino—on one of the most valuable pieces of real estate along the Côte d'Azur. Architecturally daring when it was completed in 1975 (some of its foundations were sunk directly into the seabed, and some of the principality's busiest highways roar beneath it) the resort is now viewed as an integral part of Monégasque life. It contains Monaco's highest concentration of restaurants, bars, and nightclubs—it's somewhat like Las Vegas with a Gallic accent. Many celebrities have been attracted here, including Walter Cronkite and Peter Ustinov. Guest rooms are tastefully, even conservatively, furnished in a style somewhere between Los Angeles and Miami, and are flooded with light from big windows, with views over the town or the sea. Each has a summery, pastel-colored decor, comfortable mattresses, well-designed bathrooms with lots of plush towels, and a sense of well-upholstered modern comfort. Touches of glitter and flash are consistent with its status as the site of one of the principality's casinos.

Dining/Diversions: There's a sprawling lobby bar festooned with potted palms. L'Argentin serves South American–style grilled meats and succulent, very fresh fish. The nautically decorated Café de la Mer is open for breakfast. Near the rooftop, Le Pistou re-creates the flavors of Provence. There's also the cavernous Sun Casino in the lobby, combining aspects of Atlantic City with *la belle France*, and a separate area with slot machines on the hotel's seventh floor. Le Café Viennois is a site for elaborate pastries, teas, snacks, and coffee. A gastronomic, upper-tier restaurant, La Truffe, is open only for dinner.

Amenities: Easy access to tennis, golf, deep-sea fishing, sailing, scuba diving, and a radically upgraded, state-of-the-arts fitness center that was redesigned and reconfigured in 1999.

Monte-Carlo Beach Hotel. Av. Princesse-Grace, Monte-Carlo Beach, 06190 Roquebrune/Cap-Martin. ☎ **04-93-28-66-66.** Fax 04-93-78-14-18. 45 units. A/C MINIBAR TV TEL. 1,450F–2,700F ($246.50–$459) double; 2,400F–4,200F ($408–$714) suite. AE, DC, MC, V. Closed Jan–Feb. Free parking.

Despite its name, this hotel is in France, not Monaco. Built in 1928, it was known for years as the "Old Beach Hotel" until the Société des Bains de Mer decided that was too unglamorous a title for such a luxury retreat. Tons of money later, it emerged with a new name and vastly improved rooms and facilities. The most pampered guest always asks for the most beautiful accommodation in the house, the spacious circular unit above the lobby. Eva Peron stayed here in 1947 during her infamous Rainbow Tour of Europe, and Princess Grace came here almost every day in summer to paddle around the pool, a rendezvous for the rich and beautiful. Though Roquebrune/Cap-Martin is its postal address in France, the hotel is located not there but at the border of Monaco. All of the rooms are identical, each having a sea view. The hotel's last major renovation occurred in 1995, when virtually everything—furniture, mattresses, carpets—was replaced with conservative-looking modern furnishings. Throughout, standards are high, mattresses are comfortable, and towels are thick and plentiful.

Dining/Diversions: The greatest choice of dining venues here occurs between June and September, when "Le Restaurant," the hotel's best, serves gourmet meals at both lunch and dinner; Le Rivage offers brasserie-style lunches and dinners from a point near the pool; Le Potinière features gastronomic lunches (closed for dinner); and La Vigie, a short walk from the hotel—accessible to several piers where yacht-owners can tie up their boats—presents a series of buffets inspired by the cuisine of Provence. Throughout most of the year, however, from October to May, only Le Rivage is open.

MODERATE

Hôtel Alexandra. 33 bd. Princesse-Charlotte, 98000 Monaco. ☎ **93-50-63-13.** Fax 92-16-06-48. 56 units. A/C TV TEL. 615F–850F ($104.55–$144.50) double. AE, DC, MC, V. Parking 40F ($6.80).

This hotel is in the center of the business district, on a busy and often-noisy street corner. Its comfortably furnished guest rooms don't generate much excitement, but they're reliable and respectable. Rooms are small to medium in size, each quite comfortable with a firm mattress and fine linen. Bathrooms are tidily organized with shower stalls (or shower/tub combos) and adequate shelf space. The Alexandra knows it can't compete with the giants of Monaco and doesn't even try. But it attracts those who'd like to visit the principality without spending a fortune.

Hôtel Balmoral. 12 av. de la Costa, 98006 Monaco. ☎ **93-50-62-37.** Fax 04-93-15-08-69. E-mail: balmoral@cyber-monaco.mc. 65 units. TV TEL. 570F–1,050F ($96.90–$178.50) double; 1,260F–1,600F ($214.20–$272) suite. AE, DC, MC, V. Parking 60F ($10.20).

This hotel was built in 1898 by the grandfather of the present owner, Jacques Ferrey-rolles. On a cliff halfway between the casino and the Palais du Prince, it boasts eight floors of rooms and lounges with sea views. The rooms, of which 50 are air-conditioned, are like the public rooms—homelike, immaculate, and quiet. You get comfort here but not necessarily a lot of space to spread out. Mattresses are firm, and white crisp linen is used. Bathrooms are small and tiled, with shower stalls. The Balmoral is so inviting that guests often extend their stays.

Hôtel du Louvre. 16 bd. des Moulins, 98000 Monaco. ☎ **93-50-65-25.** Fax 04-93-30-23-68. 33 units. A/C MINIBAR TV TEL. 780F–880F ($132.60–$149.60) double. AE, DC, MC, V. Parking 50F ($8.50).

Built like a traditional century-old mansion, this hotel is filled with antique furniture. The guest rooms are comfortable, carpeted, and come in a variety of shapes and sizes, each with a good mattress on twins or a double bed. Bathrooms are small with shower stalls and middle-grade towels. Expect to pay higher prices for rooms facing the sea. Breakfast is the only meal served.

INEXPENSIVE

Hôtel Cosmopolite. 4 rue de la Turbie, 98000 Monaco. ☎ **93-30-16-95.** Fax 93-30-23-05. 24 units, none with toilet, all with sink, some with shower. 228F ($38.75) double without shower or toilet, 314F–369F ($53.40–$62.75) with shower but without toilet. No credit cards. Free parking on street.

When it was built in the 1930s, this hotel was sited in the then-fashionable neighborhood a few steps downhill from the railway station. Today it's an appealingly dowdy art-deco monument with three floors, no elevator, and comfortable but anonymous-looking rooms. Madame Gay Angèle, the English-speaking owner, is proud of her "Old Monaco" establishment. Her more expensive rooms have showers, but the cheapest way to stay here is to request a room without a shower—there are adequate facilities in the hallway. Mattresses ands towels are a bit thin, but there is still reasonable comfort, especially at these prices.

Hôtel de France. 6 rue de la Turbie, 98000 Monaco. ☎ **93-30-24-64.** Fax 92-16-13-34. E-mail: hotel-france@monte-carlo.mc. 26 units. TV TEL. 380F ($64.60) double; 450F ($76.50) triple. MC, V. Parking 40F ($6.80).

Not all Monégasques are rich, as a stroll along this street will convince you. Here you'll find some of the cheapest living and eating places in this high-priced principality. This 19th-century hotel, 3 minutes from the rail station, has modest furnishings but is clean and comfortable. Bedrooms are small but well-organized with firm mattresses, plus tiny tiled bathrooms with shower stalls and hair dryers.

WHERE TO DINE
VERY EXPENSIVE

Le Grill de l'Hôtel de Paris. In the Hôtel de Paris, place du Casino. ☎ **92-16-29-66.** Reservations required. Main courses 195F–850F ($33.15–$144.50). AE, DC, MC, V. Daily noon–2:15pm and 8–10:15pm. Closed Jan 6–31 and at lunch in summer. FRENCH.

In the flood of publicity awarded to this hotel's street-level restaurant, Le Louis XV (see below), it's been easy to overlook the equally elegant contender on the rooftop. The view alone is worth the expense, with the turrets of the fabled casino on one side and the yacht-clogged harbor of Old Monaco on the other. The decor is gracefully modern, the ambience somewhat less intense than that in the self-consciously cutting-edge Ducasse citadel downstairs. Despite that, the place is undeniably elegant, with a two-fisted approach to cuisine that includes every imaginable sort of grilled fish (sea wolf, monkfish, sole, salmon, mullet, cod, or turbot) and meat such as Charolais beef and lamb from the foothills of the nearby Alps. In fair weather and in summer, the ceiling opens to reveal the starry sky. The fine cuisine is backed up by one of the Riviera's finest wine lists, with some 20,000 bottles; the wine cellar is carved out of the rock below. Service is faultless but never intimidating or off-putting.

✪ **Le Louis XV.** In the Hôtel de Paris, place du Casino. ☎ **92-16-30-01.** Reservations recommended. Jacket and tie required for men. Main courses 310F–590F ($52.70–$100.30); fixed-price menus 840F–950F ($142.80–$161.50). AE, DC, MC, V. July–Aug, Wed 8–10pm, Thurs–Mon noon–2pm and 8–10pm; Sept–June, Thurs–Mon noon–2pm and 8–10pm. Closed Feb 2–17. FRENCH/ITALIAN.

On the lobby level of the five-star Hôtel de Paris, the three-star Louis XV offers what one critic called "down-home Riviera cooking within a Fabergé egg." Despite the place's regal trappings (or as a reaction against them?), the culinary star chef/namesake Alain Ducasse creates a refined but not overly adorned cuisine, which is served by the best staff in Monaco. Everything is light, attuned to the seasons, with an intelligent and modern interpretation of both Provençal and northern Italian dishes. He commands the finest ingredients in Europe, and his menu is ever changing to take advantage of what is best in any season. The service is superb. Ducasse is now dividing his time between this glittering enclave and his restaurant in Paris.

EXPENSIVE

La Truffe. In the Monte Carlo Grand Hotel, 12 av. des Spélugues. ☎ **93-50-65-00.** Reservations recommended. Main courses 90F–170F ($15.30–$28.90). Set-price menus 380F ($64.60). AE, MC, V. Daily 7:30–11:30pm. FRENCH.

This is the showcase restaurant within one of Monte Carlo's most unusual modern hotels. The decor is based on English Regency models, complete with big crystal chandeliers, rich paneling, deep armchairs, and accessories inspired by the world of horse breeding and horse racing. The food is superbly produced. Thanks to the restaurant's name, menu items include a higher-than-usual percentage of dishes made from truffles, including artichoke hearts on bread smeared with bone marrow, black truffles and olive oil; winter root vegetables served with essence from a pot-au-feu and garnished with truffles; foie gras cooked the old-fashioned way *"en torchon"*; a piccata of Tuscan-style veal prepared with sage and truffles; a superb version of rack of lamb with thyme served with an *estouffade* of truffled potatoes; and free-range cock stuffed with foie gras and truffles.

Le Café de Paris. Place du Casino. ☎ **92-16-20-20.** Reservations recommended. Main courses 100F–200F ($17–$34). AE, DC, MC, V. Daily 8am–4am. FRENCH.

Its *plats du jour* are well-prepared, and its location encourages a front-seat view of the comings and goings on Monte Carlo's nerve center—the plaza adjacent to the casino and the Hotel de Paris. But to our tastes, this circa-1985 re-creation of old-timey Monaco is a bit too theme-ish, too enraptured with the devil-may-care glamour of turn-of-the-century Monte Carlo, and a bit too claustrophobic to be really comfortable. Despite that, the Café de Paris continues to draw an active crowd of patrons who appreciate the materialistic razzmatazz and upscale format the French refer to as a *brasserie de luxe.* Menu items change frequently, and platters, especially at lunchtime, are popular with local office workers because they can be served and consumed relatively quickly. Adjacent to the restaurant, you'll find (and hear) a jangling collection of slot machines and a cliché-riddled cluster of boutiques selling expensively casual resort wear and souvenirs.

Monte Carlo L'Argentin. In the Grand Hotel, 12 av. des Spélugues. ☎ **93-50-65-00.** Reservations recommended. Main courses 140F–260F ($23.80–$44.20); fixed-price menu 350F ($59.50). AE, DC, MC, V. Daily 7:30pm–4am. STEAKS/GRILLS.

Conceived with panache, L'Argentin is a generous, stylish, international restaurant. It's one of the largest in town, banked with windows facing the sea, and has the most impressive grill set-up. Uniformed chefs tend three blazing fires, from which diners are protected by a thick sheet of glass. The decor was inspired by the Argentinian pampas and has gaucho accessories, like cowskin-draped banquettes. All the beef served here is imported from the American Midwest; menu choices include a mixed grill called parillada Argentine, Mexican-style flank steak, many kinds of grilled fish, and a perennial favorite, standing rib of American beef grilled over a wood-burning fire. The restaurant remains open, albeit with a limited menu, from 1 to 4am, mimicking the hours of the roulette wheels in the hotel's nearby casino.

Rampoldi. 3 av. des Spélugues. ☎ **93-30-70-65.** Reservations required. Main courses 120F–310F ($20.40–$52.70). AE, MC, V. Daily 12:15–2:30pm and 7:30–11:30pm. FRENCH/ITALIAN.

Rampoldi is closely linked to the charming but somewhat dated interpretation of *La Dolce Vita*. Established in the 1950s, and staffed with a complementary mix of old and new, it has a spirit more Italian than French. It also serves some of the best cuisine in Monte Carlo from an agreeable location at the edge of the Casino Gardens. Menu items include a succulent array of pastas like tortelloni with cream and white truffle sauce; sea bass roasted in a salt crust; ravioli stuffed with crayfish; chateaubriand with béarnaise sauce; and veal kidneys in Madeira sauce. Crêpes Suzette make a spectacular finish.

Restaurant du Port. Quai Albert-ler. ☎ **93-50-77-21.** Reservations recommended. Main courses 98F–220F ($16.65–$37.40); set lunch 150F ($25.50); set dinner 180F ($30.60). Daily noon–2:30pm and 8–10:30pm. Closed Nov. ITALIAN/FRENCH.

Set in a big-windowed restaurant directly on one of the quays overlooking the old port, this is a seafood restaurant that's a bit tough but glamorous, with a sometimes hysterically busy staff that might remind you of the dockyards of Genoa. The venue is very much macho Italian. Menu items might include a selection of elegant pastas (tagliatelle with smoked salmon and spaghetti with lobster), antipasti, and meat dishes like filet of beef aux délices, mignon of veal in orange sauce, rack of lamb with Mediterranean herbs, and a full array of Italian and French wines. Other excellent courses from across-the-border Italy include spaghetti with seafood and a superb filet of veal with porcini mushrooms. The very fresh fish of the day is grilled to perfection. Dessert? Why not a cassata siciliana? In summer, the restaurant expands onto an outdoor terrace overlooking the yachts of the harbor.

INEXPENSIVE

Le Texan. 4 rue Suffren-Reymond. ☎ **93-30-34-54.** Reservations recommended. Main courses 110F–140F ($18.70–$23.80); pizzas 50F–65F ($8.50–$11.05). AE, DC, MC, V. Daily noon–midnight. TEX-MEX.

These Tex-Mex specialties have entertained even the most discriminating French taste buds. There's a handful of outdoor tables, a long bar, a roughly plastered dining room draped with the flag of the Lone Star State, and a scattering of Mexican artifacts. You'll find Le Texan on a sloping residential street leading down to the old harbor—a world away from the glittering casinos and nightlife of the upper reaches. Menu items include T-bone steak, barbecued ribs, pizzas, nachos, tacos, a Dallasburger (with guacamole), and the best margaritas in town.

Pizzeria Monégasque. 4 rue Terrazzani. ☎ **93-30-16-38.** Pizzas 40F–60F ($6.80–$10.20); main courses 90F–105F ($15.30–$17.85); fixed-price menu 130F ($22.10). AE, MC, V. Daily noon–2:30pm and 7:30–11pm (till midnight Fri–Sat). Closed Dec 25–Jan 1. FRENCH/ITALIAN.

This *pizzeria de luxe* offers four dining rooms and an outdoor terrace. Almost anyone might arrive—in a limousine or on a bicycle, in all kinds of garb that could quickly convince you that Monaco is actually a rather small and gossipy town. The owner has grown accustomed to seeing all the follies and vanities of this town pass through his door; he serves pizzas, fish, and grilled meats to whoever shows up. Specialties are magret du canard (duckling), grilled steaks, carpaccio, and beef tartare. Of the 10 kinds of pizza, the most popular are pizza Terrazzini (it includes cheese and pistou) and the "special" version that's served with Tunisian-style *merguez*.

Stars 'n Bars. 6 quai Antoine-1er. ☎ **93-50-95-95.** Reservations recommended. Dinner salads and platters 64F–135F ($10.90–$22.95); sandwiches 50F–76F ($8.50–$12.90). AE, DC, MC, V. Tues–Sun 11am–midnight. AMERICAN.

This place revels in the cross-cultural differences that have contributed so much to Monaco's recent history. Modeled on the sports bars popular in the States, it features two distinct dining and drinking areas devoted to American-style food, and a third-floor space, The Club—a sports bar with memorabilia donated by athletes of note. There is even a disco after 10:30pm (sometimes with live performances). No one will mind if you drop in just for a drink—they cost 45F to 90F ($7.65 to $15.30)—but if you're hungry, menu items read like an homage to the macho American experience. Try an Indy 500 or a Triathlon salad, a Wimbledon or a Slam Dunk sandwich, or a Breakfast of Champions (eggs and bacon and all the fixings). If your children happen to be in tow and are feeling nostalgic about the ballpark back home, order a Little Leaguer's platter (for those under 12). Unless an artist of international note appears, there's never a cover charge.

MONACO AFTER DARK

The **Sun Casino,** in the Monte Carlo Grand Hotel, 12 av. des Spélugues (☎ **93-50-65-00**), is a huge room filled with one-armed bandits. It also features blackjack, craps, and American roulette. Additional slot machines are available on the roof starting at 11am—for those who want to gamble with a wider view of the sea. It's open daily from 4pm to 4am (to 5am for slot machines). Admission is free.

A speculator, François Blanc, developed the ✪ **Monte Carlo Casino,** place du Casino (☎ **92-16-21-21**), into the most famous in the world, attracting the exiled aristocracy of Russia, Sarah Bernhardt, Mata Hari, King Farouk, and Aly Khan (Onassis used to own a part interest). The architect of Paris's Opéra Garnier, Charles Garnier, built the oldest part of the casino, and it remains an extravagant example of the 19th century's most opulent architecture. It's rather schizophrenically divided into areas—one devoted to the casino and others for different kinds of nighttime entertainment, including a theater (see below) presenting opera and ballet.

Unlike the jaded roués whose presence here became a cliché during the belle époque, the new grand dukes are likely to include fast-moving international business-people on short-term vacations and a crowd that's more varied than in days of yore. Baccarat, roulette, and chemin-de-fer are the most popular games, though you can play *le craps* and blackjack as well.

The Salle Américaine, containing only Las Vegas–style slot machines, opens at noon, as do doors for roulette and *trente-quarante*. A section for roulette and chemin-de-fer opens at 3pm. Most of the facilities inside are operational by 4pm, when additional rooms open with more roulette, craps, and blackjack. The gambling continues until very late/early—the closing depending on the crowd. To enter the casino, you must carry a passport, be at least 21, and pay an admission of between 50F and 100F ($8.50 and $17), depending on where you want to go. In lieu of a passport, an identity card or driver's license will suffice. After 9pm, the staff will insist that gentlemen wear jackets and neckties for entrance into the private rooms.

The premises also contain a **Cabaret** in the Casino Gardens. An orchestra plays before the show. A sexy cabaret featuring lots of feathers, glitter, jazz dance, ballet, and Riviera-style semi-nudity is presented at 10pm Tuesday to Sunday from mid-September to the end of June. If you want dinner as part of the show, service begins at 9pm and, with the show included, costs 450F ($76.50) per person. If you want to see just the show, your drinks will cost from 150F ($25.50) each. For reservations, call ☎ **92-16-36-36.**

In the casino's **Salle Garnier,** where lots of gilt and belle époque accents evoke the 19th-century opera house of Paris, concerts are held periodically. For information, contact the tourist office (☎ **04-93-41-26-00**) or the Atrium du Casino (see below). The music is usually classical, featuring the Orchestre Philharmonique de Monte Carlo.

The casino also contains the **Opéra de Monte-Carlo,** whose patron is Prince Rainier. This world-famous house, opened in 1879 by Sarah Bernhardt, presents a winter and spring opera repertoire that traditionally includes Puccini, Mozart, and Verdi. It was here that the legendary Les Ballets Russes de Monte-Carlo was first introduced 1918 by Serge Diaghilev, starring Karsavina and the immortal Nijinsky, and choreographer Michel Fokine. The national orchestra and Les Ballets de Monte Carlo appear here. Tickets may be hard to come by; your best bet is to ask your hotel concierge. You can make inquiries about tickets on your own at the **Atrium du Casino** (☎ **92-16-22-99**), open Tuesday to Sunday from 10am to 7pm. Standard tickets are 100F to 600F ($17 to $102).

CLUBS & BARS

Tiffany, avenue des Spélugues (☎ **93-50-53-13**), is a favorite of the 25- to 40-year-old crowd who like a glamorous modern setting. On Sunday, a bevy of showgirls is featured. **Le Symbole,** rue du Portier (☎ **93-25-09-25**), is a hot spot for those over 30. The decor glitters with a high-tech gloss, and the music is disco.

More high-energy and hip than any of the entries posted above is **Le Box,** 39 Av. Princesse Grace (☎ **93-30-15-22**), where the young, the restless, the beautiful, and Princess Stephanie wannabes dance, drink, flirt, and carouse until the wee hours. It's open nightly from 11pm till dawn. The entrance fee of 90F ($15.30) includes the first drink.

Les Folies Russes, in the Grand Hotel, 12 av. des Spélugues (☎ **93-50-65-00**), is a dinner-dance cabaret. Many viewers like its shows much more than those staged at the cabaret in the Monte Carlo casino. Vaudeville acts are thrown in to ease the "monotony" of all those nude dancers. There's a dinner dance on Friday and Saturday with food served from 8:30 to 9:30pm, and a floor show, *La Folie Russe,* is presented Tuesday to Sunday at 11pm. Jackets for men are mandatory. The show with dinner is 550F ($93.50); 250F ($42.50) gets you only the show.

14 Roquebrune & Cap-Martin

592 miles (952.73km) S of Paris, 3 miles (4.83km) W of Menton

Roquebrune, along the Grande Corniche, is a charming mountain village with vaulted streets. It has been restored, though some critics have found the restoration "artificial." Today, its rue Moncollet is lined with artists' workshops and boutiques with inflatedly priced merchandise.

Three miles west of Menton and 1½ miles west of Roquebrune, **Cap-Martin** is a satellite of the larger resort, associated with the rich and famous since Empress Eugénie wintered here in the 19th century. In time the resort was honored by the presence of Sir Winston Churchill, who came here often in his final years. Two famous men died here—William Butler Yeats in 1939 and Le Corbusier, who drowned while swimming off the cape in 1965. Don't think you'll find a wide sandy beach—you'll encounter plenty of rocks, against a backdrop of pine and olive trees.

ESSENTIALS

GETTING THERE Cap-Martin has train and bus connections from Nice, Menton, and other coastal cities. To reach **Roquebrune,** you'll have to take a taxi or bus from the small train station in the Carnoles district of Cap-Martin. From Cap-Martin or Carnoles, buses to Roquebrune, marked DIRECTION MENTON, travel at 15-minute intervals along R.N. 7. Buses stop in Roquebrune at designated spots along the highway. If you arrive by TGV from France, you'll be routed through Menton. Buses to Roquebrune from the train station at Menton are marked DIRECTION NICE. For more **railway information and schedules,** call ☎ **08-36-35-35-35.** For more information about bus routes, contact the **Gare Routière** in Menton (☎ **04-93-85-64-44**).

VISITOR INFORMATION The **Office de Tourisme** is at 218 av. Aristode-Briand in Roquebrune (☎ **04-93-35-62-87**).

EXPLORING ROQUEBRUNE

It will take you about an hour to explore Roquebrune. You can stroll through its colorful covered streets, which still retain their authentic look even though the buildings are now devoted to handcrafts, gift and souvenir shops, or art galleries. From the parking lot at place de la République, you can head for place des Deux-Frères, turning left into rue Grimaldi. Then head left to **rue Moncollet,** the town's most interesting street dating back to the 10th century. This long, narrow street is covered with stepped passageways and filled with houses that date from the Middle Ages, most often with barred windows.

Rue Moncollet leads into **rue du Château,** where you may want to take time to explore the **Château de Roquebrune** (☎ **04-93-35-07-22**). The only one of its kind, the château was originally a 10th-century Carolingian castle—the present structure dates in part from the 13th century. It houses a historic museum. The castle is dominated by two square towers; from the towers there's a panoramic view along the coast to Monaco. The castle gates are open daily from 10am to noon and 2 to 6pm (closed Friday off-season); admission is 20F ($3.40) for adults, 15F ($2.55) for students, and 10F ($1.70) for children 11 and under. From February through May, it's open Saturday to Thursday from 10am to 12:30pm and 2 to 6pm; from June through September, 10am to 12:30pm and 3 to 7:30pm; and October through January, 10am to 12:30pm and 2 to 5pm.

Rue du Château leads to place William-Ingram. After crossing this square, you reach rue de la Fontaine. Take a left. This will lead you to the **Olivier Millénaire** (millennary olive tree). This olive tree is said to be one of the oldest in the world, having survived for at least 1,000 years.

Back on rue du Château, you can reach the **Eglise Ste-Marguerite** (no phone), which hides behind a relatively ordinary baroque facade that masks a church from the 12th century. The interior is of polychrome plaster. Look for two paintings by a 17th-century local artist, Marc-Antoine Otto—a Crucifixion (the second altar) and a Pietà (above the entrance door). The church is open every afternoon from 3 to 6pm, and for religious services on Sunday morning from around 9am till noon.

EXPLORING CAP-MARTIN

Cap-Martin is a rich town. At the center of the cape is a feudal tower, used today as a telecommunications relay station. At its base you can still see the ruins of the **Basilique St-Martin,** the only remains of a priory constructed here by the monks of the Lérins Islands in the 11th century. After repeated pirate raids in the 15th century, it was destroyed and abandoned. If you follow the road (by car) along the eastern shoreline of the cape, you'll be rewarded with a view of Menton set against a backdrop of mountains. In the far distance looms the coastline of the Italian Riviera, and you can see as far as the resort of Bordighera.

You can take one of the most interesting walks along the Riviera here, but be aware that it's a 3-hour trek. If you have a car, you can leave it in the parking lot at avenue Winston-Churchill. The coastal path, called **Sentier Touristique,** leads from Cap-Martin to Monte Carlo Beach. The path is marked by a sign labeled PROMENADE LE CORBUSIER. As you go along you can take in a view of Monaco set in a natural amphitheater. In the far distance, you'll see Cap-Ferrat and even Roquebrune with its château. The scenic path comes to an end at Monte Carlo Beach.

You can also take a scenic 6-mile **drive** that takes about an hour. Leave by D23, following the signs to Gorbio, a perched village standing on a hill. Along the way on the narrow, winding road, you'll pass homes of the wealthy in a verdant setting of pines and silvery olives. The site of the village is wild and rocky, the buildings having been constructed as a safe haven from pirate attacks. The most interesting street is rue Garibaldi, which leads past an old church to a panoramic belvedere.

WHERE TO STAY

Hôtel Victoria. 7 promenade du Cap, 06190 Roquebrune/Cap-Martin. ☎ **04-93-35-65-90.** Fax 04-93-28-27-02. 32 units. A/C MINIBAR TV TEL. 418F–588F ($71.05–$99.95) double. Rates include breakfast. AE, DC, MC, V. Closed Jan 5–31. Parking 30F ($5.10).

This rectangular low-rise building is set behind a garden in front of the beach. Built in the 1970s, it was renovated in the mid-1990s in a neoclassical style that weds tradition and modernity. It's the "second choice" in town for those who can't afford the lofty prices of the more spectacular Vista Palace. Bedrooms are medium in size and well appointed with firm mattresses on comfortable beds. Rooms open onto balconies fronting the sea. Bathrooms are small but well organized, mainly with tub and shower combos, each with a hair dryer. The casual bar/lounge near the entrance sets a stylishly relaxed tone. Breakfast is the only meal served.

✪ **Hôtel Vista Palace.** Grande Corniche, 06190 Roquebrune/Cap-Martin. ☎ **800/447-7452** in the U.S., or 04-92-10-40-00. Fax 04-93-35-18-94. www.webstore.fr/vistapalace. E-mail: vistapalace@webstore.fr. 70 units. A/C MINIBAR TV TEL. 1,200F–2,300F ($204–$391) double; 2,300F–7,000F ($391–$1,190) suite. AE, DC, MC, V. Parking 130F ($22.10) in garage.

This extraordinary hotel/restaurant stands on the outer ridge of the mountains running parallel to the coast, giving a spectacular "airplane view" of Monaco. And the design of the Vista Palace is just as fantastic: Three levels are cantilevered out into space so every room seems to float. Nearly all have balconies facing the Mediterranean. Bedrooms are spacious and elegantly appointed with deluxe mattresses, plus a good-sized bathroom in marble or tile, each with a shower/tub combo, a hair dryer, luxury toiletries, and plush towels. If you don't want to stay here, at least consider stopping by for a meal—it's expensive but worth it. **Le Vistaero** is open daily from 12:15 to 2:15pm and 8 to 10pm; three fixed-price menus are available featuring Mediterranean cuisine envied by the region's other restaurateurs. Facilities include a pool, a sauna, a masseuse, an indoor squash court, a fitness center, a boutique, a helipad, and a 9-acre landscaped Mediterranean garden.

WHERE TO DINE

Au Grand Inquisiteur. 18 rue du Château. ☎ **04-93-35-05-37.** Reservations required. Main courses 77F–140F ($13.10–$23.80); fixed-price menus 147F and 218F ($25 and $37.05). MC, V. Wed–Sun noon–1:30pm and Tues–Sun 7:30–10pm. Closed Nov–Dec 25. FRENCH.

This culinary find is a miniature restaurant in a two-room cellar near the top of the medieval mountaintop village of Roquebrune. On the steep, winding road to the château, this climate-controlled building is made of rough-cut stone, with large oak beams. The cuisine, though not the area's most distinguished, is quite good; try the chef's duck special or scallops meunière. Most diners opt for one of the fresh-fish choices. The wine list is exceptional—some 150 selections, most at reasonable prices.

Hippocampe. 44 av. Winston-Churchill. ☎ **04-93-35-81-91.** Reservations required. Main courses 75F–280F ($12.75–$47.60); fixed-price menus 155F–235F ($26.35–$39.95). AE, MC, V. Tues–Wed and Fri–Sat noon–1:45pm and 7:30–9:30pm, Thurs and Sun noon–1:45pm. Closed Oct 18–Nov 18, 10 days in Jan, and 10 days in May. FRENCH.

Opened in 1963, this fine restaurant along the seafront has a full view of the bay and even the Italian coastline. Made safe by a thick stone wall, its terrace is shaded by five crooked pines. The "Sea Horse" is a stone-and-glass garden house with a tile roof and scarlet and pink potted geraniums. Specialties include filets de sole en brioche, coq au vin (chicken cooked in wine), terrine of salmon in basil sauce, and duck with peaches.

'Idee-Fixe. 1 rue de la Fontaine. ☎ **04-93-28-97-25.** Reservations recommended. Main courses 80F–125F ($13.60–$21.25). Set-price menu 140F ($23.80). MC, V. Wed–Mon 7–10:30pm. FRENCH.

This well-managed unpretentious restaurant with a hardworking staff is in an antique building in the heart of the old town. Food is well prepared; you can order an *omelette soufflé* garnished with crabmeat, and a tart but savory appetizer of fried St-Marcellin cheese served with slices of golden apples, or a tartare of salmon. Pastas include gnocchi and tagliatelle with either Roquefort cheese or salmon. Main courses feature such delights as filets of red snapper with a lemon-flavored mousse; sea bass with Provençal herbs, and filet of beef sandwiched between slices of foie gras and flambéed in cognac. There's both a terrace and a small balcony for outdoor dining.

15 Menton

596 miles (959.17km) S of Paris, 39 miles (62.76km) NE of Cannes, 5 miles (8.05km) E of Monaco

Menton is more Italianate than French. Right at the border of Italy, Menton marks the eastern frontier of the Côte d'Azur. Its climate is the warmest on the Mediterranean coast, and in winter it attracts a large, rather elderly British colony. The impact of these senior citizens on the population of 130,000 has earned Menton the sobriquet "the Fort Lauderdale of France."

According to a local legend, Eve was the first to experience Menton's glorious climate. When she and Adam were expelled from the Garden of Eden, she tucked a lemon in her bosom, planting it at Menton because it reminded her of her former stamping grounds. Lemons still grow in profusion here, and the fruit is given a position of honor at the **Lemon Festival** held over a 2-week period in February. Actually, the oldest Menton visitor may have arrived 30,000 years ago. He's still around—or at least his skull is—in the Musée de Préhistoire Régionale (see below).

Don't be misled by all those "palace-hotels" studding the hills. They are no longer hotels—they've been divided up and sold as private apartments. Many of these turn-of-the-century structures were erected to accommodate elderly Europeans, English and German, who arrived carrying a book written by one Dr. Bennett in which he extolled the joys of living at Menton.

ESSENTIALS

GETTING THERE   Two trains per hour arrive from Nice (trip time: 35 min.), and two per hour from Monte Carlo (trip time: 10 min.). For **rail information** and schedules, call ☎ **08-36-35-35-35.** Two local bus companies, **Autocars Broch** (☎ **04-93-31-10-52**) and **Autocars Breuleux** (☎ **04-93-35-73-51**), run buses between Nice, Monte Carlo, and Menton, usually around one per hour; a one-way ticket costs 45F ($7.65) from Nice and around 28F ($4.75) from Monaco. Many visitors arrive by car along one of the corniche roads.

VISITOR INFORMATION   The **Office de Tourisme** is in the Palais de l'Europe, 8 av. Boyer (☎ **04-92-41-73-73**).

SEEING THE SIGHTS

Menton is situated on the Golfe de la Paix (Gulf of Peace), on a rocky promontory that divides the bay in two. The fishing town, the older part with its narrow streets, is in the east; the tourist zone and residential belt are in the west.

The filmmaker, writer, and artist Jean Cocteau liked this resort, and in the **Musée Jean-Cocteau,** Bastion du Port, quai Napoléon-III (☎ **04-93-57-72-30**), you can see his death portrait, sketched by MacAvoy. Some of the artist's memorabilia is here—stunning charcoals and watercolors, brightly colored pastels, ceramics, and signed letters. The museum is open Wednesday to Monday from 10am to noon and 2 to 6pm. Admission is free.

At **La Salle des Mariages,** in the Hôtel de Ville (town hall), rue de la République (☎ **04-92-10-50-00**), Cocteau painted frescoes depicting the legend of Orpheus and Eurydice, also the subject of his film, *Orphée*. A tape in English helps explain them. The room, with its red-leather seats and leopard-skin rugs, is used for civil marriage ceremonies. It's open Monday to Friday from 8:30am to 12:30pm and 1:30 to 5pm. Admission is 5F (85¢). Advance reservations are necessary.

The **Musée de Préhistoire Régionale,** rue Lorédan-Larchey (☎ **04-93-35-84-64**), presents human evolution on the Côte d'Azur for the past million years. It contains the 25,000-year-old head of the *Nouvel Homme de Menton* (sometimes known as "Grimaldi Man"), found in 1884 in the Baousse-Rousse caves. Audiovisual aids, dioramas, and videocassettes enhance the exhibition. The museum is open Wednesday to Monday from 10am to noon and 2 to 6pm. Admission is free.

The **Musée des Beaux-Arts,** Palais Carnoles, 3 av. de la Madone (☎ **04-93-35-49-71**), contains 14th-, 16th-, and 17th-century paintings from Italy, Flanders, Holland, and the French schools, as well as modern paintings by Dufy, Valadon, Derain, and Leprin—all acquired by a British subject, Wakefield-Mori. The museum is open Wednesday to Monday from 10am to noon and 2 to 6pm. Admission is free.

A DAY AT THE BEACH

Menton's beaches stretch for 2 miles between the Italian border and the city limits of Roquebrune and are interrupted only by the town's old and new ports. Collectively, they're known as **La Plage de la Promenade du Soleil** and with rare exceptions are public and free. Don't expect soft sands or even any sand at all, as the beaches are narrow, covered with gravel (or more charitably, big pebbles), and notoriously uncomfortable to lie on. Don't expect big waves or tides either. Who goes there? In the words of one nonswimming resident, mostly Parisians or residents of northern France, who are grateful for any escape from their urban milieux. Topless bathing is widespread, but complete nudity is forbidden.

Unlike Cannes, where thousands of chaises pepper the beaches, there are few options in Menton for renting mattresses and parasols (most people bring their own). Two exceptions are **Le Splendid Plage** (☎ 04-93-35-60-97) and **Les Sablettes** (☎ 04-93-35-44-77), both charging around 85F ($14.45) for use of a mattress. They're immediately to the east of the Vieux Port.

WHERE TO STAY

Hôtel Aiglon. 7 av. de la Madone, 06500 Menton. ☎ **04-93-57-55-55.** Fax 04-93-35-92-39. www.oda.fr/aa/hotel-Aiglon. E-mail: Aiglon.hotel@wanadoo.fr. 30 units. A/C MINIBAR TV TEL. 430F–780F ($73.10–$132.60) double; 750F–1,010F ($127.50–$171.70) suite. Half board 395F–685F ($67.15–$116.45) per person extra. AE, DC, MC, V. Closed Nov 4–Dec 20. Free parking.

A nugget along the coast, this three-star hotel was converted from a stately Riviera villa. In a large park filled with Mediterranean vegetation, it offers an intimate and homelike environment. Rooms come in various shapes and sizes, tastefully furnished and containing quality mattresses on the elegant beds. Bathrooms are small and tiled, with adequate shelf space and hair dryers. The magnet of the hotel is a heated pool around which is a 1900s veranda. The garden setting is beautifully maintained. Other facilities include a solarium and a children's game area. An excellent Provençal and international cuisine is offered, with view windows opening onto the pool and garden.

Hôtel Chambord. 6 av. Boyer, 06500 Menton. ☎ **04-93-35-94-19.** Fax 04-93-41-30-55. 40 units. A/C MINIBAR TV TEL. 530F–580F ($90.10–$98.60) double. AE, V. Parking 50F ($8.50).

Located on the main square next to the casino, this is a well-maintained hotel with rows of balconies and awnings. The guest rooms have generous space and are neatly organized with streamlined modern furniture, including quality mattresses and fine linen. Bathrooms are well maintained, each with a hair dryer, middle-grade towels, and a shower/tub combo. Breakfast is the only meal served.

Hôtel Le Dauphin. 28 av. du Général-de-Gaulle, 06500 Menton. ☎ **04-93-35-76-37.** Fax 04-93-35-31-74. www.french-riviera.fr/hotels/m/mentondauphin.html. 30 units. TV TEL. 350F–520F ($59.50–$88.40) double; 620F ($105.40) triple. Rates include continental breakfast. AE, DC, MC, V. Closed Oct 20–Dec 20.

This affable hotel lies just off the beach. The double-insulated rooms are bright and uncluttered, each with a balcony opening onto the mountain range or the sea. Small to medium in size, they are well organized and tidily maintained. Small tiled bathrooms have adequate shelf space and hair dryers. The multilingual owner/director Jacques Ridés is a classical-music buff who has created an unusual hotel feature: two acoustically inviting practice studios—the Apollo, with a grand piano, and the Dionysos, with a baby grand, for round-the-clock rehearsal. The attentive staff is welcoming. Three meals per day are served, featuring many specialties of Provence. In the afternoon, the restaurant becomes a tea salon.

Hôtel Méditerranée. 5 rue de la République, 06500 Menton. ☎ **04-93-28-25-25.** Fax 04-93-57-88-38. 90 units. A/C MINIBAR TV TEL. 335F–545F ($56.95–$92.65) double. Children 4 and under stay free in parents' room. AE, DC, MC, V. Free parking.

This white-and-salmon hotel is 3 short blocks from the sea. A raised terrace with a view of the water, chaises longues, and potted plants are on the premises. The rooms are attractively decorated and include private balconies opening onto the sea. Most are spacious with quality mattresses on the beds (usually twins). Bathrooms are fully equipped with generous shelf space, middle-grade towels, a hair dryer, and a tub and shower combo. The hotel also has a restaurant offering veranda dining in fair weather.

Hôtel Napoléon. 29 Porte de France, 06503 Menton. ☎ **04-93-35-89-50.** Fax 04-93-35-49-22. 40 units. A/C MINIBAR TV TEL. 460F–730F ($78.20–$124.10) double. Rates include breakfast. AE, DC, MC, V. Closed Nov 10–Dec 18. Free parking.

On a palm tree–shaded avenue, this recently renovated hotel has a pool set in a small garden and stone terrace. The main lounge and bar, furnished with 18th-century English and Italian pieces, is really like a large living room. The guest rooms, decorated in vivid colors, have mahogany furniture, comfortable beds, thick towels, and balconies overlooking the sea and the old town. There are a rooftop terrace and an air-conditioned restaurant with great views. Nonguests are welcome to visit for lunch or dinner. The hotel has a private beachfront, and a swimming pool with a separate restaurant that overlooks it. The staff here is particularly attentive and helpful.

Hôtel Princesse et Richmond. 617 promenade du Soleil, 06500 Menton. ☎ **04-93-35-80-20.** Fax 04-93-57-40-20. 46 units. A/C MINIBAR TV TEL. 335F–585F ($56.95–$99.45) double; 610F–810F ($103.70–$137.70) suite. AE, DC, MC, V. Parking 40F ($6.80). Closed Nov 5–Dec 17.

At the edge of the sea near the commercial district, this hotel boasts a facade of warm Mediterranean colors, with a sunny garden terrace. The owner rents comfortable soundproof rooms with modern and French traditional furnishings and balconies. They range from small to medium in size, each with a good mattress on a comfortable bed. Bathrooms are tiled and contain hair dryers and adequate shelf space. Drinks are served on the roof terrace, where you can enjoy a view of the curving shoreline. There's an open-air Jacuzzi, plus a small fitness room in the solarium. The staff organizes sightseeing excursions. A restaurant in the garden of the nearby Hôtel Aiglon, under the same ownership, offers lunch and dinner, and you may use the heated pool there.

Hotel Riva. 600 promenade du Soleil, 06500 Menton. ☎ **04-92-10-92-10.** Fax 04-93-28-87-87. E-mail: hotelriva@pcse.fr. 40 units. A/C MINIBAR TV TEL. 420F–620F ($71.40–$105.40) double. AE, MC, V. Parking 40F ($6.80).

This hotel is adjacent to a verdant park, a few steps from the beach. Its design is conservative and angular-looking. It has many of the amenities and much of the feeling of a hotel you would find along the coast of Southern Florida. Its modern design includes lots of balconies and multileveled terraces for sunbathing and cocktail-drinking. Bedrooms are small to medium in size, but elegantly furnished with quality mattresses and fine linen. Bathrooms are tiled and have all the necessary equipment: shower/tub combinations, adequate shelf space, hair dryers, and plush towels. High-quality materials such as marble and granite are used throughout, complementing dignified beechwood furniture. There's a solarium on the building's top floor, and a sauna and Jacuzzi. Other than breakfast and brunch, no meals are served, but considering the proximity of many restaurants, no one seems to mind.

WHERE TO DINE

✪ **La Calanque.** 13 square Victoria. ☎ **04-93-35-83-15.** Main courses 68F–115F ($11.55–$19.55); fixed-price menus 100F–148F ($17–$25.15). AE, DC, MC, V. Tues–Sun noon–2pm and 7:15–9:30pm. FRENCH/SEAFOOD.

Informal and earthy in a charming, rustic Provençal way, this restaurant provides a waterside view and well-prepared food. In fair weather, tables are set under shade trees in full view of the harbor. We recommend the spaghetti napolitaine, tripe Niçoise, *soupe de poissons* (fish soup), and fresh sardines (grilled over charcoal and very savory), with the focus on locally harvested seafood. Two specialties are bouillabaisse and *barba giuan*, small biscuits cooked in olive oil after having been stuffed with a variety of local greens.

L'Albatros. 31 quai Bonaparte. ☎ **04-93-35-94-64.** Reservations recommended. Main courses 50F–200F ($8.50–$34). Fixed-price menu 130F ($22.10). MC, V. Tues–Sun noon–3pm and 7pm–midnight. FRENCH/PROVENÇAL.

This charming little bistro along the port specializes in fish dishes from the Mediterranean. On the second floor and on the terrace you can enjoy a view over the old harbor and bay while sampling fresh fish purchased directly from Menton fishers. Menu items are conservative but savory, with lots of emphasis on Provençal interpretations of fish and seafood. Examples include a succulent bouillabaisse, prepared for a minimum of two diners, and priced at 200F ($34) per person. There's also a *cassoulet des pêcheurs*, a stewpot brimming with herbs, saffron, and fish; and a thick and juicy charolais of beef with béarnaise sauce. Everything here is fresh, unpretentious, and low-key.

Petit Port. 1 place Fontana. ☎ **04-93-35-82-62.** Reservations recommended. Main courses 120F–150F ($20.40–$25.50); fixed-price menus 85F–180F ($14.45–$30.60). AE, MC, V. Thurs–Tues noon–3pm and 7pm–midnight. FRENCH.

Small and charming, employing many members of an extended family, this restaurant serves well-prepared fresh fish in a century-old house near the medieval port. Everything is homemade, even the bread. Specialties are grilled sardines (increasingly difficult to find), fish soup, several kinds of grilled meats and fish, and (in honor of the northern France origins of its owner) tripe in the style of Caen. The place prides itself on its location—less than a mile from the Italian border.

Rocamadour. 1 square Victoria. ☎ **04-93-35-76-04.** Reservations recommended. Main courses 45F–145F ($7.65–$24.65); fixed-price menu 85F–160F ($14.45–$27.20). AE, MC, V. Thurs–Tues noon–2:30pm and 7:30–10pm. FRENCH.

This pleasant restaurant overlooks the port. You dine at tables set under a canopy where colored lights are turned on at night. Some specialties offered by the chef are from the Périgord region, including foie gras. *Magret de canard* (duckling) is another specialty. But basically the cookery is grounded in the rich tradition of the Côte d'Azur, with an emphasis on very fresh fish. The restaurant was founded almost a century ago by a chef from Rocamadour, and the name of that town has stayed with the place.

Appendix:
The South of France
in Depth

Though **Provence** is hardly the region Edith Wharton and others discovered long ago, this legendary area today has more museums and attractions than ever before, better hotels, and a great increase in the number of chefs earning Michelin stars. So it hasn't been irretrievably spoiled. It's true that its overpopularity and overbuilding, together with the summer hordes descending on such cities as Avignon and on the French Riviera, have made parts of the province undesirable—especially if you're caught driving behind a mile-long line of cars in summer heat. The once-sweet disposition of its citizens is a bit taxed, too, by endless tourist pressure. But there's the vast hilly hinterland to explore, where you'll find old traditions intact, where old men play a leisurely game of *boule* on a hot afternoon, preferably under shade trees.

One of the major joys of visiting Provence is seeking out the scenery and locations depicted in the canvases of Cézanne and van Gogh, and other painters. A trail of modern artists attracted to the brilliant light of the Côte d'Azur have left a rich heritage: Matisse's chapel at Vence, Cocteau at Menton and Villefranche, Picasso at Antibes, Léger at Biot, Renoir at Cagnes, and Bonnard at Le Cannet.

Every habitué has a favorite oasis along the **Riviera** and will try to convince you of its merits: Some say "Nice is passé." Others maintain that "Cannes is queen." Others shun both in favor of Juan-les-Pins, and still others would winter only at St-Jean-Cap-Ferrat. If you have a large bankroll you may prefer Cap d'Antibes, but if money is short you can try the old port of Villefranche. Each resort on the Côte d'Azur offers its own special flavor and special merits. Glitterati and eccentrics have always been attracted to this narrow strip of fabled real estate only 125 miles long, between the Mediterranean and the mountain ranges.

The corniches of the Riviera stretch from Nice to Menton. The Alps here drop into the Mediterranean, and roads were carved along the way. The lower road, about 20 miles long, is the Corniche Inférieure. Along this road are the ports of Villefranche, Cap-Ferrat, Beaulieu, and Cap-Martin. The Moyenne Corniche (Middle Road), 19 miles long, also runs from Nice to Menton, winding spectacularly in and out of tunnels and through the mountains. We can thank Napoléon for the panoramic Grande Corniche that he ordered built in 1806—La Turbie and Le Vistaero are the principal towns along the 20-mile stretch, which reaches more than 1,600 feet in elevation at Col d'Eze.

The landscape, cuisine, lifestyle, history, and architecture of **Languedoc** is similar to that of its neighbor, Provence. The mighty

Everything is full-blooded. The food is full of strong earthy flavors. There is nothing bland about Provence.

—Peter Mayle, *A Year in Provence*

I'd like to live and die on the French Riviera.

—F. Scott Fitzgerald

Rhône marks the dividing line between the region of Provence and the Côte d'Azur and that of Languedoc-Roussillon. The city of Nîmes, for example, seems very Provençal in character, though officially it's in Languedoc. You'll find Languedoc both less touristed than Provence and more affordable. You'll find outstanding museums like the Toulouse-Lautrec museum at Albi and the Goya museum at Castres, and unique landscapes like the Carmague. The ancient city of Toulouse, with its medieval monuments, is today an important center of France's high-tech industry.

PROVENCE & THE MILLENNIUM   What is Provence and the Riviera doing to prepare for the millennium? "Not much," said one official. "The Brits are going hysterical over their Millennium Dome at Greenwich, Rome is practically being rebuilt, but our attractions remain the same. There may be some observances here and there, with more going on in Avignon than anywhere else in the south of France."

Indeed that is true—Avignon, even as we write, is planning numerous events between May and November during the year 2000. Named one of 10 European Cultural Cities of the Year (2000), Avignon is bracing itself for a number of events. The Avignon Festival of Theater will perform 15 plays by artists from eastern European countries. A vast exhibit on "Beauty" will be presented (details to be announced at the beginning of 2000), drawing upon the contributions of landscape artists, artists, architects and designers, writers, fashion designers, choreographers, filmmakers, and others. Many other cultural events will be announced as the years 2000 and 2001 unfold.

Another millennial concern is the advent of the euro, already a currency, that will replace the French franc in 2001. The people of the south of France are preparing to welcome the greatest horde of visitors in their history, and they plan to wine, dine, and house them well—admittedly all at a rather steep price.

1 History 101: A Few Thousand Years in Provence

THE GREEKS ARRIVE

During the Bronze Age, Provence was inhabited by primitive tribes whose artistic legacy, in the form of etched pottery, dates from around 6000 B.C. (see "Art & Architecture from Paleolithic to Postmodern," later in this chapter). By around 700 B.C. traders from Greek-speaking areas around the Aegean established colonies at Antipolis (Antibes), Nikaia (Nice), and Massilia (Marseille). Mediterranean wines, grains, and ceramics were exchanged for pewter and livestock from west-central France.

The Greeks even sailed up the Rhône, trading with the Celtic and Ligurian tribes and influencing them with their sophisticated ways. They introduced the grape and the olive—both were to play vital roles in the Provençal economy for millennia to come.

In 600 B.C. Protis, captain of a group of Greek traders, was guest of honor at a Provençal celebration in honor of Gyptis, daughter of a local tribal leader. So charmed was she by her father's guest, she selected Protis as her husband. Her dowry included the harborfront of what is now Marseille, the gateway through which massive amounts of matériel, ancient warriors, and weapons later poured.

Around the same time, waves of migration from the Celtic north added to the non-Mediterranean population. The Celts intermarried easily with the native Ligurians and eventually formed a fierce force that opposed the expansionist efforts of the Greeks. In 218 B.C. some tribes supported Hannibal in his advance on Rome across the Alps, an alliance that Rome would severely punish several generations later. As the local forces faced off against the Greeks in the south, tensions grew to the point where the Greeks called on the rapidly emerging Roman state to subdue the threat to their colonial power. The resulting genocide helped define the future racial and cultural makeup of Provence.

THE ROMANS TAKE OVER

Because of the need for a buffer between Rome and the "savages" of Gaul—and also because of the area's fertility—the Romans considered the Mediterranean coastline one of its most treasured provinces. They named their new possession Provincia Transalpina—later it was bastardized into "Provence." Gallia Narbonensis (Narbonne) was the administrative center. By 55 B.C. Julius Caesar had conquered all of Gaul and even invaded Britain, an act that suddenly diminished Provence's importance in the context of the Roman Empire.

Few Roman regions received such a concentrated dose of Romanization as did this area. Evidence remains in the ruins of grandiose construction: amphitheaters, bath houses, temples, and stadiums at Arles, Orange, Nîmes, Glanum (near St-Rémy), Fréjus, and Cimiez. The pont du Gard—a masterpiece of civil engineering and one of France's most frequently photographed sites—was completed in 19 B.C. Marseille, whose pedigree predated that of virtually every other site in Provence, was bypassed during this explosion of Roman building because of its alliance with the losing side in the civil war between Pompey and Caesar.

Later, as the scope of the empire diminished and its far reaches became frayed and tattered, Provincia Narbonensis remained staunchly Roman. Even after the empire's East-West schism and long after Paris and the Rhône valley became centerpieces for Frankish resistance, Provence remained a beneficiary of the empire.

ROME COLLAPSES

The conversion of the emperor Constantine to Christianity marked the beginning of the end for Rome. Although Constantine's attention was mainly directed to the Middle East and he ruled from Constantinople rather than Rome, he declared Arles his favorite city in the western empire and built a palace there—ironically, faced with the pressures of his position, he rarely visited it. In A.D. 400 the short-lived emperor Honorius gave Arles a fleeting role as the capital of the Three Gauls (Britain, Spain, and France). Meanwhile, the spread of the inflammatory new religion, Christianity, reached Provence. You can see some of the earliest evidence of this in Marseille in the oft-repaired Basilique St-Victor.

Arles's brief preeminence served it poorly after the empire's collapse. In A.D. 471 it was sacked by the Visigoths, and a few years later, along with other important Provence settlements, it was sacked by other tribes. From A.D. 600 to 800 the area was devastated by the Saracens (Moors) and by Charles Martel himself, one of the patriarchs of modern France. Between 736 and 740, he led his Frankish troops in orgies of appalling brutality. The only relief came with the brief ascendency of the Merovingians around A.D. 500.

Charlemagne passed through Provence en route to Rome, where he was crowned Emperor of the West by the pope. After Charlemagne's death, his empire was split among three feuding grandsons; Provence was bequeathed to Lothair, the eldest. Lothair placed his own son, Charles, on the throne of Provence, designating it a kingdom in its own right. By 879, Provence was ruled jointly with Burgundy by the medieval ruler Boson, brother-in-law of Charles the Bald.

CULTURAL FLOWERING

In 1032, with its capital at Aix-en-Provence, the eastern half of Provence joined the Holy Roman Empire, a loose configuration of duchies and kingdoms unified mainly by fear and loathing of the Moors. The area west of the Rhône came under the control of the comtes de Toulouse. During a period of almost 300 years, architecture, poetry, and music flourished. This cultural high point was marked by the songs and poetry of the troubadours, who traveled from castle to castle, and the beginnings of literature and popular entertainment as we know them today.

By around 1125, the comtes de Toulouse and the comtes de Barcelona controlled Provence. For a time it appeared that they might have united their kingdoms against their enemy, the French. By 1246, however, control of Provence tipped in favor of the French kings, thanks to marriages among the family of Louis IX (St. Louis) and the rulers of Barcelona. Today the village of Barcelonette derives its medieval name from the influence of these counts.

The Paris-based kings understood Provence's strategic importance as a starting point for conquests of other Mediterranean kingdoms. St. Louis ordered the construction of one of the most remarkable sites in southern France, the fortified town of Aigues-Mortes, as a bulwark against the Moors. In 1248, he set sail with his army on the Seventh Crusade, only to die en route in Tunis.

POPES & PLAGUES

In 1307, the French-born pope Clement V fled Rome, causing one of the most bizarre political imbroglios in European history. Fearful of the instability in Rome, he decided to move the official seat of the papacy to Avignon. And surrounded by an army of courtiers, priests, soldiers, and purveyors of luxury goods, the papacy remained for 70 years under the protection of the kings of France and the comtes de Provence. At one point there were actually two popes, one in Rome and one in Avignon. During this period, Avignon became a vibrant and prosperous city, a center of wealth and culture. Eventually, after much contention, the papacy was returned to Rome, and Avignon's importance collapsed.

Plagues decimated the population of Provence in 1348 and 1375. At the same time, extortion, plundering, and highway robbery by small-time feudal despots, especially the rulers of the much-dreaded Les Baux, added to a general sense of confusion, unrest, and despair.

By 1409, however, things were looking up. The University of Aix was founded as southern France's answer to the thriving Sorbonne in Paris, and in 1434, René d'Anjou was designated count of an independent Provence. He fostered economic development and supported the arts. Shortly after René's death, his nephew and heir signed a pact with the wily French king Louis XI, who immediately used it to annex Provence.

WARS OF RELIGION

Provence's first religious war was a result of a heresy that spread rapidly over Europe in the 13th century. The Cathars, or the "Pure Ones," also known as Albigenses, were a highly ascetic sect who believed the material world was the incarnation of evil, and should be rejected in favor of a mystical union with Christ. Most Cathari strongholds were in Languedoc, but many adherents lived in Provence. The heresy was an excuse for the French monarchs and the Church to attack and seize the area. The rallying cry of the French forces as they slaughtered the Cathars—"Kill them all, and God will decide who is guilty"—lives in infamy even today. The Albigensian Crusade, begun in 1208, not only violently obliterated the heresy but destroyed medieval Provençal culture as well, and assured the ascendance of French as spoken in the northern part of the country over the French of Provence.

The second religious war began in the 1500s, when the Reformation changed Europe forever. Influenced by the thriving community of Protestants under John Calvin, whose stronghold lay in Geneva, Huguenots (Protestants) in Provence grew in number and power. One of the most extreme of these sects was the Vaudois. Founded in the 1200s by a wealthy merchant, Valdès or Vaudès, from Lyon, the sect rejected the idea of an ecclesiastical hierarchy, preached the virtues of poverty, and denied the authenticity of the sacraments. Memories of the Cathari may have fueled this movement, which was greeted with horror by the church. When in 1545 the Vaudois responded to their persecutors by attacking several Catholic churches near their stronghold in the Luberon hills, the armies of François I massacred more than 3,000 of them over a 4-day period, and sent 600 into the French navy as slaves.

However, Protestantism continued to flourish in Orange, Uzès, and especially Nîmes. For 40 years beginning in 1560, religious battles occurred regularly. Chief of state Richelieu, whose obsession was the unification of all aspects of French society into a form approved by Paris, eventually suppressed or destroyed Huguenot communities throughout France. The bloodiest of these skirmishes was in the Atlantic coast port of La Rochelle, but also destroyed were the Provençal strongholds at Uzès and Les Baux.

REVOLUTIONARY TIMES

In 1720, a devastating plague was imported through the harbor of Marseille, killing what is conservatively estimated at 100,000 people. Despite this and other setbacks, Provence had become one of France's wealthier regions. An aesthetic had developed that was distinct to the region and is imitated today around the world. Majestic town houses were built in the towns, and *mas,* estates in the country.

As revolutionary fervor swept over France in 1789, Provence made its contribution. One of the most articulate and inflammatory members of Paris's Etats-Généraux—the radical committee that controlled the Revolution in its early stages—was the comte de Mirabeau, elected as representative by Aix-en-Provence. In 1792, a corps of volunteers from Marseille, singing a call to arms written by Rouget de Lisle, marched through the streets of Paris toward the Tuileries. The song's original name was "L'Hymn de Bataille de l'Armée du Rhin" ("Battle Hymn of the Army of the Rhine") but that was later changed to "La Marseillaise."

It was at Golfe-Juan, a minor seaport near Cannes, that Napoléon Bonaparte began his Hundred Days, his last bid for power. The enthusiasm that welcomed his armies in Provence set a pattern for his reception along the route of his march to Paris. The route he followed—now Route N85 through Dignes and Sisteron—has been known ever since as "La Route Napoléon."

In 1790, an act of the Revolutionary government had a permanent impact on Provence. France was divided into a labyrinth of political districts (*départements*) that shattered both the country's medieval boundaries and political networks. In the process, the once-autonomous region of Provence was carved into three, and later five, subdivisions.

THE 19TH CENTURY

Partly because of its strategic dominance of more than half of France's Mediterranean ports, Provence gained enormous prosperity during the 19th century.

In 1864, a railway line linked Provence with the rest of France, encouraging increased travel. The 1869 opening of the Suez Canal and the expansion of French influence into Morocco, Algeria, Tunisia, and Egypt thrust Provence's ports into international prominence and helped develop Marseille into one of the greatest seaports in the world.

The development of Nice and the Riviera into international resorts was largely a result of the unemployment caused by the phylloxera epidemic in Provençal vineyards and the collapse of the silkworm industry. Tourism was a logical answer to the economic deprivation. In 1822 the expatriate British colony in Nice helped finance their namesake promenade. In 1830, Lord Brougham bought an estate in Cannes and promoted Cannes in Britain as a suitably hedonistic place for the upper classes to escape from the fog, the cold, and the Victorian repressions of England. In 1860, the region around Nice, whose administration by the House of Savoy represented an anachronistic holdover from the feudal age, was fully integrated into France. Then, a few years later, the ruler of one of western Europe's least prosperous territories, Monaco, built the most opulent casino in the world. Thanks to the patronage granted to the site by the haut monde, profits came pouring in.

In the mid-19th century, a group of cultural luminaries, fearing a total demise of Provençal language and culture, founded Félibrige, an organization devoted to the restoration of Provence's medieval literary forms. Five years later the artistic patriarch Frédéric Mistral published his Provençal poem *Mirèio*, which was met with widespread acclaim.

WORLD WARS & POSTWAR

Fortunately for Provence, most of the destruction of World War I occurred in other areas of France. During World War II, Provence and Languedoc were part of the territory controlled by the collaborationist Vichy government, which initially meant some protection from the Nazi rule in the rest of France. In 1940, after Nazi-dominated North Africa fell to the Allied forces, the Nazis retracted their pledge not to occupy the zones controlled by Vichy and moved into Provence with heavy artillery. Two years later, when they moved to confiscate the French navy's warships, French saboteurs sank most of the Mediterranean fleet in the harbor at Toulon.

On August 15, 1944, Allied forces landed successfully on the Provençal coast between St-Raphaël and St-Tropez, and within 14 days, all Provence was liberated.

Few other regions of the world have zoomed into the international consciousness the way Provence has since 1945. In 1947, Cannes began its role as Europe's film capital with its first film festival, grown since to almost mythic proportions. Farming and industry were modernized, tourism took a giant leap forward. Celebrity watching seemed to go hand-in-hand with voyeurism and exhibitionism, as the Riviera's topless beaches caused a stir as far away as Chicago and as stars like Brigitte Bardot elevated St-Tropez to its role as sybaritic capital of the most sybaritic country.

In 1953, the socialist Gaston Defferre, a pivotal figure in the region's politics, was elected mayor of Marseille, a post he held for 33 years. His ardent appeals for the semiautonomy of Provence finally came to fruition in 1981 with Mitterrand's approval of a limited form of self-government.

In 1962, the collapse of the French government in Algeria introduced a new element—a flood of newly impoverished, newly homeless French citizens who arrived by the thousands. Mainlanders contemptuously called them *pieds-noirs* (blackfeet). The wave of anti-immigrant sentiment was to have repercussions for years to come, and move the traditional leftist political scene sharply to the right.

In 1970, the opening of the A6/A7 high-speed autoroute between the French capital and Marseille made access to the region much easier. Between 1970 and 1977, two major national parks (Parc Naturel Régional de la Camargue and Parc Naturel Régional de Lubéron) were created for the preservation of Provence's native ecology. And in 1981, the high-speed Train à Grande Vitesse (TGV) was launched between Paris and Marseille, reducing transit time to less than 4 hours.

However, anti-immigrant sentiment has been growing, and in 1985 voters supported Jean-Marie Le Pen's anti-immigration platform, Le Front National. In some French minds, North Africans were unwelcome, regardless of their French citizenship. The event that brought about a more generous attitude was France's win in the World Cup in 1998. Zinedine Zidane, who scored the winning goals, is the son of Algerian immigrants. President Chirac pinned Legion of Honor ribbons on Zidane and his teammates. But expecting Zidane to lead France into its multicultural future is a bit much to ask, even for a World Cup hero. Anti-immigrant fever still remains a social problem in France, especially in Provence.

The creation of a Euro-Mediterranean free-trade zone by the year 2010, announced in 1995 in Barcelona, together with a vast financial aid program funded by European Union loans, bodes well for Marseille and other ports of Provence just when it seemed that decay was inevitable. This massive development should have enormous impact on the region.

2 Art & Architecture from Paleolithic to Postmodern

ANCIENT ORIGINS

The sense of timelessness that permeates Provençal architecture goes back to ancient times. Excavations like Terra Amata, above the old port in Nice, have unearthed remnants of circular huts *(bories)* from around 6000 B.C., each with a central fire pit, and tombs from the late Paleolithic age have revealed skeletons covered in sea shells strung into necklaces. Many sociologists believe that the later development of the rural farmhouse *(mas)* was based on these bories, erected from flat stones laid on top of one another without mortar. Dating from around the same time are a series of mysterious standing stones or *dolmens,* and scattered rock carvings, poised on their ends in a vertical position for reasons that no one really understands.

For about 400 years, beginning in the 4th century B.C., Celtic tribes migrated into Provence, bringing with them the skill of carving rock with iron tools. Their greatest legacy is a network of fortified *oppidi* (fortresses on hilltops). (The best remaining example is Oppidum de Nages, at Nages-et-Solorgues, 6 miles southeast of Nîmes. Another example is the Plateau d'Entrement, 1½ miles from the center of Aix-en-Provence.) The trading links that mariners from the Greek-speaking eastern Mediterranean developed around 600 B.C. was with this new breed of Celts, who had by that time intermarried with the local Ligurians. The Greeks established the ports of Antibes, St-Tropez, La Ciotat, Nice, and Hyères, but very little of the Greek era survives in Provence today.

Because of Provence's status as a buffer zone between Italy and savage Gaul, the Romans lavished it with a comprehensive assortment of public buildings. Examples are the arenas at Nîmes and Arles; the triumphal arches at St-Rémy-de-Provence, La Turbie (La Trophée des Alpes), and Orange; and aqueducts like pont du Gard, which were some of the finest examples of civil engineering in the ancient world. You can still see remains of ruined villas at Vaison-la-Romaine. Maison Carré in Nîmes is the most often copied monument, after the Parthenon in Athens and the Pantheon in Rome. The Romans passed on their knowledge of the arch, the barrel vault (a masonry technique in which individual stones were so carefully cut that mortar was unnecessary), and a primitive form of concrete. Since Provence, because of its proximity to Rome, was Christianized before virtually any of the other regions of Gaul, it has one of the oldest Christian basilicas in France, the Basilique St-Victor in Marseille. Inaugurated in the 400s and enlarged and modified many times since, it's unique in France for its associations with the early Christian church.

After Rome's collapse, Provence experienced a rapidly changing parade of feudal anarchies, and few buildings survive from the period. A handful of octagonal baptisteries that combine aspects of classical Roman design with Frankish motifs from northeastern France still exist in Fréjus, Aix-en-Provence, and the hamlet of Venasque.

PROVENÇAL ROMANESQUE & GOTHIC

Beginning around 1100, a revitalized interest in building, usually by monks, began to enrich Provence. Church floor plans were usually laid out in a cross shape, with soaring pillars and barrel vaulting, small severe-looking windows, and facades (especially western-facing facades) that were sculpted with allegorical scenes of punishment, salvation, and redemption, or other religious themes. The best examples of Provençal Romanesque are Aix's Cathédrale St-Sauveur (interior), Arles's Eglise St-Trophime, and St-Rémy's and Montmajour's village churches.

As Provence was pulled more tightly into France's orbit, it began to depend more on artistic and architectural inspiration from areas like Normandy. Gothic style was adopted, with its sophisticated use of pointed arches, ribbed vaulting, and flying buttresses (the means of counterbalancing the outward thrust of heavy roofs) that allowed for larger windows and more elaborate decoration. The soaring, vertical Gothic was in direct contrast to the more horizontal and rounded lines of Romanesque architecture. You can best see Provençal Gothic in the newer part of Avignon's Palais des Papes, St-Maximin's basilica, Béziers's cathedral, and Fréjus's cloisters. The best examples of Flamboyant Gothic—the final and most ornate phase of the movement—are the Eglise St-Siffrein in the village of Carpentras and the facade of the Cathédrale St-Sauveur in Aix.

THE ART OF FORTIFICATION

But perhaps the most original aspect of Provence's architecture is its fortified towns and villages. Testimonials to the frequency of raids, sieges, and other incursions, they are perched atop jagged hills or cliffs, meticulously crafted from chiseled blocks of stone and punctuated with crenellated battlements. Many have openings through which boiling oil or molten lead could be poured on attackers; some are surrounded by moats. Many of these fortified places—like Les Baux, Sisteron, and Tarascon—developed spontaneously over decades, the result of improvisation and brutish labor. A handful of others, like the rigidly symmetrical quadrangle of Aigues-Mortes, were commissioned and designed before the first stone was laid. Carcassonne, another example, is less rigidly symmetrical but even more impregnable.

So great was the fear of attack from assorted enemies that many Provençal churches also incorporated fortification into their design. In the event of attack, the church could provide physical as well as spiritual shelter. Early medieval prelates used this lure as a means of eliciting cheap or free labor from the faithful who built the churches. Examples are the village church in Les Stes-Maries and the redbrick Cathédrale Ste-Cécile in Albi.

The development of large-scale cannons in the 1400s made many of these fortifications obsolete, but by that time defensive warfare had changed so drastically that the fortress-style churches and towns were bypassed and left intact.

THE RENAISSANCE & THE RISE OF SECULAR ART

Although the Renaissance had far less impact in Provence than in neighboring Italy, it left two distinct legacies in Nice and Avignon. In Nice, beginning in the late 1400s, a school of design spearheaded by Louis Bréa produced a great number of painted altarpieces. These can be seen around Nice, notably in the village church at Lucéram.

An equivalent school flourished in Avignon, fueled by the need to adorn the network of churches constructed during the "Babylonian exile" of the papacy. The leading artist was Enguerrand Charenton, also known as Quarton. His *Coronation of the Virgin,* in Villeneuve, is the era's best-known painting. A worthy colleague was Nicolas Froment, painter to the court of King René. His most famous work is *The Burning Bush,* in Aix's Cathédrale St-Sauveur. Other members of the Avignon school, founded by Charenton and Froment, were Nicolas Mignard and members of the Parrocel family, whose works you can see in museums and churches throughout Provence. The school survived until the 1800s.

Beginning around 1650, artists began to abandon religious subjects. The works of Pierre Puget (1620–94), a native-born Marseillais and Provence's greatest sculptor, evoke the exalted drama of Bernini. The best places to see his works are Paris, Toulon, and Marseille. The Dutch-born Van Loos painted in Aix and Nice during the 17th century; some of his best works are displayed in Nice's Musée Cheret. And though he more or less abandoned Provence at an early age for the court in Paris, Jean-Honoré Fragonard (1732–1806)—painter of the frivolity of life during the *ancien régime*—was born in Grasse.

Neoclassicism had a limited impact in Provence, but you can see 17th- and 18th-century examples of the style's appeal in the many private mansions in Montpellier, Aix-en-Provence, and Avignon.

INDUSTRIALIZATION & IMPRESSIONISM

The wealth produced by Europe's increasing industrialization in the 19th century was frequently displayed in the form of architectural showcases. Public buildings and private villas were erected in styles that ranged from classical revival to mock-feudal to neo-Byzantine. Provençal examples of the latter are Marseille's Cathédrale de la Major and Basilique Notre-Dame de la Garde. The casino—designed by Charles Garnier, quintessential architect of the belle époque—and the Hôtel de Paris in Monte Carlo were lavished with gilded stucco and extravagant ornamentation. A few years later the Hôtel Négresco in Nice captured the essence of the Gilded Age with its elaborate beaux arts style. Around 1910, the lavish construction boom continued in the form of the Hôtel Carlton at Cannes.

At the same time a new aesthetic influenced the way the world interpreted light and color. Paul Cézanne (1839–1906) was born in Aix and spent a large part of his career depicting the area's terra-cotta roofs and verdant cypresses. One of his repeated subjects was Mont-St-Victoire. Vincent van Gogh (1853–90) painted the fiercely vibrant landscapes around Arles. Ironically, very little of the work of Cézanne or van Gogh is exhibited in Provence's museums. By around 1900, Paul Signac (1863–1935), a neo-impressionist, retreated to St-Tropez and established a mania for "Le Trop" that has existed ever since, attracting both Matisse and Bonnard for "paint fests."

Auguste Renoir (1841–1919) spent his final years near Cagnes-sur-Mer, painting and sculpting despite bouts of agonizing arthritis. Henri Matisse (1869–1954) lived at Cimiez, near Nice, and at Vence beginning in 1917, where he created his marvelous *Chapelle du Rosiare.* Pablo Picasso (1881–1973) came to Antibes in 1945 and there spent two of the most prolific and pivotal years of his career. Later he was instrumental in reviving the pottery traditions of Vallauris, whose output of ceramics is among France's most prolific. Marc Chagall (1887–1985), master of the dreamlike power of artistic free association, moved to the Riviera and created his world-acclaimed *Biblical Message,* now displayed in his namesake museum in Nice. Others to flock here were Dufy, Braque, Vlaminck, Léger (who has a namesake museum in Biot), and Vaserély (whose works are exhibited in Gordes and Aix). Even Jean Cocteau (1889–1963), known for frivolity in his earlier years, reached a more intense level of spirituality during his final years in Provence, as shown by his frescoes in Villefranche's Chapelle St-Pierre.

THE PROVENÇAL *MAS*

No review of Provençal art and architecture would be complete without mention of the region's utilitarian rural architecture. Farmhouses *(mas)* built as late as 1910 were directly influenced by fortified buildings of the Middle Ages, and construction techniques—walls made of coarsely chiseled stone, often sheathed with stucco or plaster—was roughly equivalent to what had been developed 2,000 years before by the Romans. The mas were designed for protection from the local climate, with thick masonry walls, undersize windows, and solid stocky doors. North-facing walls were often designed with curved sides and without windows as a means of deflecting the harsh mistral, and roofs were pitched at low angles to reduce the possibility of tiles breaking loose and sliding off. Hinged shutters could be opened or closed as protection against heat, wind, and sun; chimneys never rose high enough to risk being demolished by windstorms. Evergreen cypresses were usually planted as windbreaks on a farmhouse's north side, and deciduous broad-leaved trees like sycamores provided midsummer shade to the south but let in the warming sunshine in winter. Virtually every farmhouse and outbuilding in Provence was capped with rounded terra-cotta roof tiles *(tuiles romaines)* named for and used by the Roman conquest.

Though ignored or even scorned by aristocratic 19th-century newcomers, the primal appeal of the mas and their age-old stonework has since entered the mainstream. Today the boxy-looking old farmhouses, along with the olives, vines, and cypresses that traditionally surround them, are prized and they fetch awesome sums. Of the thousands of technically sophisticated buildings erected in Provence since the end of World War II, an enormous percentage were designed along lines inspired by the timeless allure of the mas.

THE POSTWAR BOOM

Since World War II a building boom has transformed many of the suburbs of such cities as Aix-en-Provence, Avignon, and Arles into banal urbanized landscapes. The need for holiday villas and housing for service personnel has resulted in vast blocks of apartment houses. Only a handful, including Le Corbusier's 1952 design for a massive apartment block in Marseille (L'Unité d'Habitation) and J. L. Sert's design for the Fondation Maeght at St-Paul-de-Vence, are praised for their intelligent application of age-old styles in bold new ways.

3 The Rise & Fall of Provençal

In the Middle Ages, Provençal was an evocative tongue in its own right. This part of the very identity of Provence was deliberately suppressed by the French. Today only a handful of Provençaux, most of them professional scholars, are familiar with the language. However, hints of old speech patterns persist: for example, *maintenant* is pronounced "mangtenang," *demain* "demang," and *vin* "vang."

THE LATIN INFLUENCE

During the Roman occupation of what is now France, the Celtic, Ligurian, and Teutonic dialects were gradually replaced by a form of Latin that later gave rise to the Romance languages—Catalán, the Italian dialects, Portuguese, Romanian, Spanish, and French. In France, two distinctly different languages developed: the *langue d'oïl* in the north where Frankish and Teutonic influences were strong, and the *langue d'oc* in the south, where Roman influence was deeply entrenched. Both the words *oïl* and *oc* later developed into the modern French *oui,* or "yes." The Mediterranean coastline west of the Rhône derives its name (Languedoc) from the medieval language of the south.

By around A.D. 700 the differences between the dialects of the north and the Occitanian or Provençal of the south were in full bloom. By around 1000 it was in the more sophisticated south, a wide belt that stretched from Bordeaux along the Atlantic coast to Nice, that literature and poetry flowered.

THE TROUBADOURS & ORAL TRADITION

As feudalism developed, power was concentrated in a network of fortified castles, where life was tenuous and anxiety-ridden. Banquets were the main form of amusement, and every banquet needed some kind of entertainment. Troubadours (the term comes from the Provençal verb *trobar,* "to seek and find") filled the need for popular entertainment. The best composed their own sonnets and poems; others drew on a repertoire that grew rapidly into an impressive body of music and literature in the *langue d'oc*. Accompanying themselves on a harp, nomadic minstrels unified popular tastes and perceptions; only the Catholic church had greater influence. Members of a community all their own, they migrated freely across political frontiers between northern Italy and the Pyrénées. In some cases they collected valuable strategic information for one or more patrons, sometimes selling the information to whomever paid the highest price. Often they became entangled in romantic imbroglios and had to flee for their lives. The troubadour embodied the courtly aspects of chivalry—in occasional cases, they were of noble birth themselves. Their poems, delivered in melodic patterns whose nuances can only be imagined today, were divided into stanzas, often with sophisticated rhythms and rhymes. Famous names from the era include Peire Vidal de Toulouse, Bertran de Born, Joffroy Rudel, Raimbaut d'Orange, Raimbaut de Vaqueiras, Folquet de Marseille, Jaufré de Blaise, and Bernard de Ventadour. A limited number of poems even survive from a female poet, the comtesse de Die.

Recurrent themes involved the medieval interpretation of courtly love—the ardor of a knight or minstrel for a lady would eventually win over her reservations. This artistic reinforcement of the hierarchical systems of court life continued as an influence in France until the late 1700s at Versailles, with its elaborate court rituals.

PROVENÇAL'S PEAK

The genocidal crusade to stamp out the Albigensian heresy led to the decline of the troubadour tradition around 1280. Despite that, the Provençal language continued for a time. Other than Latin, it was the only written administrative language in Europe. It was the everyday tongue of the papal court at Avignon during the 70 years of the Catholic church's "Babylonian exile," and it's believed that Dante (1265–1321) came very close to selecting it as the language for his *Divine Comedy*. Later on, Petrarch (1304–74) occasionally deviated from his use of Latin and Italian to compose sonnets in Provençal. His *Canzonière* was composed in Provençal after the death of his beloved, Laura de Noves, in 1348.

By around 1300 separate dialects of the *langue d'oc*, some of them appearing in written form, had developed; examples include the Nissard dialect of Nice, the Dauphinoise dialect of the French Alps, the Rhodanien Provençal of the Rhône valley, the Languedocien dialect of the region around Toulouse, the Gascon dialect used around Bordeaux, the Auvergnat used around Clermont-Ferrand, and the North Occitanian dialect, used around Limoges, that mingled aspects of the *langue d'oc* with the northerly *langue d'oïl*. Even today, despite the homogenization of modern-day French, occasional words from these medieval dialects still crop up in popular slang along with the names of some food items.

ONE GOVERNMENT, ONE LANGUAGE

As Paris increasingly became the center of power, the *langue d'oïl* (the precursor of modern standardized French) began to replace the widespread use of *langue d'oc*. The beginning of the end for Provençal and other French dialects came in 1539 through a Parisian edict, Villers Cotterèts, that has stood ever since as an early proof of Paris's cultural imperialism. Impressed with the difficulty of governing a linguistically fragmented nation, the decree made the official administrative language of France the language as it was used in Paris and the Ile de France. Later on, thanks to the efforts of a chauvinistic corps of government—sanctioned academics, the Académie Française—France emerged one of the most linguistically consistent countries in the world.

Despite these setbacks, the *langue d'oc* continued to be respected and admired. A soldier-poet who helped revive literary interest in the tongue was

Bellaud de la Bellaudière, born in 1534 in Grasse. An ardent opponent of Protestantism, he composed 160 personalized and subjective sonnets, *Oeuvres et Rimes,* while in prison. Writers who emulated his style around the same time included Raynier de Briançon, François de Bègue, and Claude Bruey. In the 1600s Nicolas Saboly composed a group of simple poems called *Noëls* in Provençal.

In 1661 Racine complained that during a trip through the south of France, no one in Uzès understood him, as the entire town spoke only Provençal. Mme de Sévigné, the quintessential arbiter of 18th-century French taste and gossip, was surrounded by a mostly Provençal-speaking staff during her sojourns in Grignan. Even the Catholic church, with Latin as its official language, often conducted masses in Provence and parts of the Midi in Provençal up until the end of the 19th century.

The Revolution, with its thousands of edicts composed in standardized French, contributed to a whittling away of the Provençal language. Later the military campaigns of Napoléon and the conscriptions of the Franco-Prussian War and World World I drew many men of the Midi into military life where administrative communications were conducted in mainstream French. In modern times the centralized French state and the intrusion of radio and television into even the most isolated of communities has all but obliterated the use of Provençal.

PROVENÇAL REVIVED

The first in the series of attempts to revive Provençal as a literary language was in 1795 with the publication of Abbot Favre's satirical poem *Siège de Caderousse* (critiqued by some as derivative of Rabelais). In 1847, as Europe experienced a rebirth of interest in the national cultures, Joseph Roumanille (1818–91) published *Lie Margarideto,* an epic poem in Provençal. Although it wasn't widely distributed outside his hometown of Avignon, it inspired the linguistic nationalism of Provençal's greatest modern-day patriarch, Frédéric Mistral (1830–1914), who began composition of the 12 cantos of his Provençal epic *Miréiro* in 1851.

In 1854 Mistral, along with half a dozen other Provençal writers, founded Le Félibrige, a group of cultural nationalists whose goal involved the restoration of the Provençal language and the codification of its grammar and spelling. In 1859 *Miréiro* was published to wild acclaim by critics like Lamartine. Composer Charles Gounod transformed it into an opera. Between 1878 and 1886, Mistral painstakingly compiled the world's first Provençal dictionary, *Lou Trésor du Félibrige,* and welcomed an impressive roster of important French writers, including Rostand, Zola, Daudet, and Alcard, into membership in Félibrige. In 1904, he was awarded the Nobel Prize for literature for at least a half-dozen major works, all written in Provençal.

While professional academics appreciate the resonance and lyricism of the medieval Provençal sonnets, and the idealistic blend of cultural nationalism and literary skill shown by the 19th-century revivalists, Provençal has all but disappeared as a spoken language. However, the sense of regional identity in Provence is strong. Directions throughout the south of France are being signposted both in mainstream French and Provençal, and the ancient language is now included as an elective in the curricula of some schools. But faced with the practicality of English as an international second language, it's doubtful that Provençal will ever be revived as France's second language. It remains today an esoteric oddity in scholastic circles.

4 A Taste of Provence

LA CUISINE DU SOLEIL

Pungent and earthy, Provençal cuisine is generally high in vitamins and fiber and low in saturated fat. The flavors of southern France incorporate the liberal use of olive oil; herbs like basil, garlic, rosemary, and sage; and a sophisticated blend of products from the mountain areas, such as lamb from the Alpilles, and the bounty of the Mediterranean. This is *la cuisine du soleil*, infused with warmth and sunshine, based on a wealth of produce and raw ingredients that spring from soil whose richness is belied by its parched, often stony surface.

THE BOUNTY OF PROVENCE

As much of the allure of Provençal cuisine derives from its raw ingredients, menus are likely to state the source of what you're about to consume. To see this wealth firsthand, head for any of the open-air markets where vast amounts of meat, cheese, produce, wine, and herbs with evocative names like purple hyssop and *sarriette* (summer savory) are sold from simple kiosks.

FRUITS & VEGETABLES   Strawberries from the village of Carpentras or the district of Bouches-du-Rhône have a special cachet. Melons, especially ogen melons, from the town of Cavaillon were so famous that in 1864 civic leaders opted to present a dozen perfect melons each year to the French novelist Alexandre Dumas *père* as a sign of their ongoing respect. He later wrote that he hoped that the readers of Cavaillon would always find his books as charming as he found their melons. Apricots are delicious anywhere, but if they're from the slopes of the Roussillon, your menu will usually let you know. *Mousserons,* one of many varieties of wild mushrooms you'll see in local markets, evoke *frissons* among gastronomes when they're from the Ardèche, west of the Rhône. Lots of species of onions are for sale; one of the most intriguing is the banana-shaped *échalotes-bananes.*

OLIVES   Along with bread and wine, olives were practically the staff of life for many centuries in Provence. Look for varieties like *olives cassées* from Les Baux and fennel-flavored *picholines du Gard.* Any resident of Nice might rebel at the idea of making a *salade Niçoise* with anything other than nut-brown *olives de Nyons.*

CHEESE   Sophisticated gastronomes consider a well-selected cheese tray to be one of the symbols of civilization, and in the south of France you could spend hours choosing among the varieties of *chèvre* alone. A Provençal folk saying likens goats to "the poor man's cow," but over the centuries, goat-milk cheese has attained gourmet status. Merchants who deal in the creamy delicacies are proud of the variety and will provide details about any cheese's origin. Looking for something esoteric? Ask for a rare tomme de Camargue, a firm but creamy cheese that combines milk from both goats and sheep and whose disclike surface is embedded with sprigs of rosemary. There's also *Banon vrai,* a goat-milk cheese made in the hamlet of Banon in northern Provence. During its fermentation, it's marinated in *eaux de vie,* aged in clay pots on dried chestnut leaves, and wrapped with raffia string. Equally delicious is *lou pevre,* a goat cheese whose pungency is enhanced by a black-pepper coating.

BREAD   Almost as varied as the cheeses are the shapes and ingredients of the bread. You can buy it as long, thin *ficelles,* marvelously crusty, and as *gibassiers,* baked with a dollop of olive oil for flavor. These aren't to be confused with *pain d'olives,* with the flesh of the olive in the dough; *pain de raisins,* flavored with dried raisins; *pain à l'anis,* aniseed bread; and earthy *pain au levain,* sourdough bread. In Aix you'll find a regional recipe for *pain d'Aix,* a double-mounded staple that resembles women's breasts. The most democratic of Provençal breads is *pain d'égalité,* developed in response to an edict during the Revolution declaring that only one kind of bread, composed of one part rye flour and three parts wheat, could be consumed in an egalitarian society. Today this is scorned as something akin to generic supermarket bread, but it's still occasionally available in Provençal markets. Beware of Provençal witches, who, according to legend, will come to dance on any loaf of bread that's turned upside down.

PASTRIES & SWEETS   As far as pastries go, southern France is expert at turning out *calissons,* rectangular sweets concocted from almond paste; they invariably taste best when baked in Aix-en-Provence. There are more recipes for *nougat,* honey-sweetened chewy candy flavored with either almonds or pistachios, than anyone could possibly document—nougat from the industrial-looking town of Montelimar seems to have a slight edge. A variety of almond-and-honey cookies, *croque moines* (crusty monks), were named for the monks who baked them to raise money for their causes. *Une galette Provençale,* a tartlet filled with pralines, almond cream, and grated orange zest, is a perennial childhood favorite in Arles and St-Rémy.

A MENU OF CHOICES

CASSOULET & BOUILLABAISSE   What dish should you especially look for in the southwest? The magic word is cassoulet, not to be confused with a *cassolette,* a fancy word for a small stewpot and whatever ingredients someone might be tempted to throw into it. *Cassoulet* is to Toulouse what bouillabaisse is to Marseille, a succulent mixture of slow-cooked white beans flavored with an herbed combination of roasted lamb, mutton, goose, sausages, duck, and various forms of pork.

Bouillabaisse is Provence's most famous dish. Traditionally, it combines a trio of fish: rascasse, grondin, and congre (the spiny red hogfish, gurnet, and conger eel). The original recipe from Marseillaise kitchens actually called for a dozen kinds of fish, including fielan, rouquier, and sard. Increasingly, mussels are added, or, to make it elegant, spiny lobsters. The kettle of fish is cooked rapidly in bouillon and flavored with olive oil and various seasonings (bay leaf, saffron, onion, and fennel). We always toss in some cognac or white wine. A paste of Spanish peppers, called a rouille, sharpens the sauce, giving it an extra reddish color. The cooking time is 10 minutes.

VEGETARIAN DISHES   Provence has a delightful emphasis on vegetarian dishes, which seem to have a transcendent earthiness from deep within the soil. Examples are succulent grilled eggplant with basil-tomato sauce, and grilled vegetables garnished with zucchini flowers (stuffed with a purée of zucchini and herbs, coated with batter, and deep-fried). No one denies the international appeal of room-temperature *ratatouille,* the soothing combination of eggplant, onions, peppers, and herbs slowly stewed in olive oil.

The perfect accompaniment for any of these dishes is *aïoli,* the garlic-laced mayonnaise that's the appropriate foil for fish, grilled vegetables, and plain or toasted bread. Incidentally, *aïoli* can also refer to an entire meal composed of poached salt cod, boiled vegetables, and (in some cases) roasted snails; the garlic mayonnaise binds the disparate ingredients together.

Also look for specialties like *pissaladière,* a doughy form of onion pizza; *mesclun,* assorted wild greens that make divine salads; and *pistou,* a rich basil-infused soup similar to minestrone.

The Pleasure of Pastis

The proper start to a Provençal meal is a glass or two of the unpretentious local apéritif, a translucent yellow liqueur, *pastis,* that becomes cloudy when you add water or ice. Although it's usually associated with truck drivers and dockyard laborers in Marseille, you might really appreciate it once you develop a taste for it. It's scented with anise, fennel, mint, and licorice, but in the case of France's most popular brand name (Ricard, beneficiary of millions of francs' worth of ad campaigns, or its sweeter rival, Pernod), it contains some additional secret ingredients as well.

GOOSE & DUCK Southwestern France is the world's headquarters of dishes boasting fattened goose and duck. The appreciation of *foie gras* from either bird has been elevated to something approaching a cult, and many dishes gain a noteworthy unctuousness when fried in *graisse d'oie* (goose fat). Thighs of both species are cooked in large quantities of their own ample fat to create tender *confits,* and the breast of ducks *(magrets)* are often grilled over charcoal or oak fires. *Aiguillettes* (long, thin strips carved from the duck's back) are prepared according to a varied repertoire of techniques. Pâtés made from the by-products of duck, and sometimes studded with truffles, figure high on everyone's favorite appetizer list. Goose, at least in Gascony, might be flambéed in Armagnac, then slowly braised with wine and vegetables for the classic *daube d'oie.*

HEARTY STEWS A specialty remembered (sometimes fondly, sometimes not) from many Provençaux childhoods is *pieds et paquets,* a combination of mutton or lamb tripe and lambs' feet cooked with cured, unsmoked pork, garlic, wine, and tomatoes. This classic is much appreciated by adventurous gastronomes. An equally prized variation is a *gratin de pieds de porc aux truffes* (gratin of pigs' feet with truffles). *Civet de lapin* is wild rabbit stewed with herbs and red wine, with rabbit blood added to the stew at the last minute as a thickener. *Daube de boeuf à la provençale* is an unusual combination of stewed beef marinated in garlic purée with red wine. *Bourride,* a succulent fish stew, is Languedoc's answer to the world-famous bouillabaisse of Provence. *Baudroie* is a simple but flavorful mix of monkfish, thin-sliced potatoes, garlic, onions, herbs, and an unexpected ingredient—the zest of navel oranges.

GAME If you're planning a trip to the deep south in autumn, you'll discover many game dishes at your disposal. These include *perdreau* (partridge), *sanglier* (wild boar), *chevreuil* (venison), *faison* (pheasant), and *lièvre* (wild hare). Often the meat will be marinated in herbs and wine, roasted with acute care by experts, and served with vibrant red wine from grapes grown in the Rhône Valley.

BULL Throughout the south, but especially in the flat wetlands and bull-raising terrain of the Camargue, look for *gardiane de taureau.* Concocted from tough and somewhat fibrous bull flesh and flavored with olives and red wine, it's invariably served with *riz de Camargue*—rice from the lowlands of the delta of the Rhône.

LES VINS DE PROVENCE

For wine-making purposes, Provence is defined as the area between Cannes, not far from the Italian border, and the eastern banks of the Rhône. Although

*An optimistic description of Provence wines always mentions the sun-baked
pines, thyme, and lavender, and claims that the wine takes its character from
them. This is true of some of the best of them. . . . Others get by on a pretty
colour and a good deal of alcohol. 'Tarpaulin edged with lace' is a realistic
summing up of one of the better ones.*

—Hugh Johnson, *World Atlas of Wine*

Avignon, Châteauneuf-du-Pape, and Orange are historically and culturally a
part of Provence, their wines fall into a distinctly separate district, the Côtes-
du-Rhône, which begins at Avignon and extends about 140 miles northward
up the valley of the Rhône to just south of Lyon, near Côte Rotie. Wine produced west of the Rhône, within an area that extends about 40 miles north of
the Mediterranean coast all the way to the Spanish border, belongs to a still
different entity, Languedoc-Roussillon.

Most of the wines from these three districts are red and tend to be strong,
solid, and flavorful, usually with a potent level of alcohol (a by-product of the
high sugar content of the grape varieties that thrive in the heat and constant
sunlight).

The pleasure of Provence's wine is undeniable. However, the threat of inad-
equate rainfall in a region known for its droughts keeps local vintners peren-
nially insecure. Consequently, vintners have traditionally relied on a
complicated blending of grapes. Strains of this grape, since the phylloxera epidemic of the late 19th century, have included varietals from Italy and Spain.
The result, according to many connoisseurs, enamored with the more aristocratic vintages of Burgundy and Bordeaux, is an occasional inconsistency in
the way the wines might age.

In 1923, a distinguished Provençal landowner, Baron Le Roy de Boiseaumarie, inaugurated a series of quality controls from his lands near
Châteauneuf-du-Pape. His efforts were instrumental in imposing standards on
vintners and helped launch what later evolved into the national Appellations
d'Origine Contrôllées (A.O.C.).

Despite the appeal of southern French wines as an accompaniment for
strongly flavored foods like anchovies, sardines, and bouillabaisse, the region
has a lower percentage of wines that oenophiles call "great" than do more
temperate regions. So pride is taken by vintners with lands in designated
A.O.C. districts, and massive investments in recent years have helped elevate
many of the region's vintages to international repute. While no guarantee of
quality, looking for A.O.C. labels is a beginning point for newcomers who
want to distinguish prestigious vintages from ordinary *vin de table*. Many
A.O.C. designations are relatively new—upstarts compared to the more venerable designations in Burgundy and Bordeaux. Côtes du Provence, producer
of more than 100 million bottles annually, was designated A.O.C. as recently
as 1977.

The two best Provençal whites are produced near Aix, most notably the delicate Cassis and the more forthright Palette. Bellet, a relatively small wine-
growing district in the hills above Nice, produces fashionable reds, whites, and
rosés.

Particularly strong reds are Gigondas and Vacqueras, whose alcohol content
sometimes exceeds 13%. Names to look for on a wine list are Côtes de
Provence (Pierrefeu and Château Minuty are two important producers) from

the dry hills north of Toulon, Côtes du Rhône Villages, Côtes du Vivarais, and Châteauneuf-du-Pape, the only wine in the world that's allowed to bear the crest of the long-ago popes of Avignon. Any bottle of this last wine, because of the vagaries of rainfall and the growing season, may be composed of more than a dozen grapes from around the district. A memorable sweet wine from the Côtes du Rhône, favored by pastry chefs as a foil for their concoctions, is Baumes de Venise.

The two most famous rosés of the south are Tavel, a name that's been used by several novelists as the wine of choice of their dashing heroes; and Bandol, a worthy producer of which is Château Simone. A recent contender rapidly growing in repute is Listel, a cloudy rosé produced on the sun-baked plains of the Camargue.

The vineyards of Languedoc-Roussillon represent more than a third of France's total acreage devoted to grapes. The fields around Nîmes, Béziers, and Narbonne produce rivers of ordinary table wine, which, thanks to newfangled methods of cultivation and harvesting, have of late been more favorably regarded by wine scholars. Aristocratic vintages from Languedoc include unusual sweet wines like Banyuls and Muscat de Rivesaltes and the reds from towns on the eastern foothills of the Pyrénées, Côtes de Roussillon.

SAMPLING THE VINTAGES

A cost-effective means of trying ordinary table wines is bringing your own container (usually a plastic jug sold on the premises or in hardware stores) to a large-scale producer. At bargain-basement prices, they'll use a gas pump–inspired nozzle to pump wine from enormous vats directly into your container. In a restaurant such a vintage would be sold in a glass carafe or ceramic *pichet* at a low price. If you're driving through the vineyards and see one of the many signs announcing *vente au détail*, it means that you'll be able to buy estate-bottled wine by the bottle, invariably at lower prices than in retail wine shops.

If you opt to visit some of Provence's vineyards, don't be disappointed by the overuse of the word *château*. Only in rare instances will you discover baronial homes or showcase architecture. In unpretentious rural Provence, most of the wine is produced by small or medium-sized farms on plots family-owned for many generations. In fact, nearly half the wine of southern France is produced by cooperative wineries. However, most of the places described in "The Best Vineyards" in chapter 1 just happen to have an impressive château associated with their land.

Index

See also Accommodations and Restaurants indexes, below.

ACCOMMODATIONS

RESTAURANTS

FROMMER'S® DOLLAR-A-DAY GUIDES

Australia from $50 a Day
California from $60 a Day
Caribbean from $70 a Day
England from $70 a Day
Europe from $60 a Day
Florida from $60 a Day

Hawaii from $70 a Day
Ireland from $50 a Day
Israel from $45 a Day
Italy from $70 a Day
London from $85 a Day
New York from $80 a Day

New Zealand from $50 a Day
Paris from $85 a Day
San Francisco from $60 a Day
Washington, D.C.,
  from $60 a Day

FROMMER'S® PORTABLE GUIDES

Acapulco, Ixtapa &
  Zihuatanejo
Alaska Cruises & Ports of Call
Bahamas
Baja & Los Cabos
Berlin
California Wine Country
Charleston & Savannah
Chicago

Dublin
Hawaii: The Big Island
Las Vegas
London
Maine Coast
Maui
New Orleans
New York City
Paris

Puerto Vallarta, Manzanillo
  & Guadalajara
San Diego
San Francisco
Sydney
Tampa & St. Petersburg
Venice
Washington, D.C.

FROMMER'S® NATIONAL PARK GUIDES

Family Vacations in the
  National Parks
Grand Canyon

National Parks of the
  American West
Rocky Mountain

Yellowstone & Grand Teton
Yosemite & Sequoia/
  Kings Canyon
Zion & Bryce Canyon

FROMMER'S® GREAT OUTDOOR GUIDES

New England
Northern California

Southern California & Baja
Washington & Oregon

FROMMER'S® MEMORABLE WALKS

Chicago
London

New York
Paris

San Francisco
Washington D.C.

FROMMER'S® IRREVERENT GUIDES

Amsterdam
Boston
Chicago
Las Vegas

London
Los Angeles
Manhattan

New Orleans
Paris
San Francisco

Seattle & Portland
Vancouver
Walt Disney World
Washington, D.C.

FROMMER'S® BEST-LOVED DRIVING TOURS

America
Britain
California

Florida
France
Germany

Ireland
Italy
New England

Scotland
Spain
Western Europe

THE UNOFFICIAL GUIDES®

Bed & Breakfast in
  New England
Bed & Breakfast in
  the Northwest
Beyond Disney
Branson, Missouri
California with Kids
Chicago

Cruises
Disneyland
Florida with Kids
The Great Smoky &
  Blue Ridge
  Mountains
Inside Disney
Las Vegas

London
Miami & the Keys
Mini Las Vegas
Mini-Mickey
New Orleans
New York City
Paris
San Francisco

Skiing in the West
Walt Disney World
Walt Disney World
  for Grown-ups
Walt Disney World
  for Kids
Washington, D.C.

SPECIAL-INTEREST TITLES

Born to Shop: France
Born to Shop: Hong Kong
Born to Shop: Italy
Born to Shop: New York
Born to Shop: Paris
Frommer's Britain's Best Bike Rides
The Civil War Trust's Official Guide
  to the Civil War Discovery Trail
Frommer's Caribbean Hideaways
Frommer's Europe's Greatest Driving Tours
Frommer's Food Lover's Companion to France
Frommer's Food Lover's Companion to Italy
Frommer's Gay & Lesbian Europe
Israel Past & Present
Monks' Guide to California

Monks' Guide to New York City
The Moon
New York City with Kids
Unforgettable Weekends
Outside Magazine's Guide
  to Family Vacations
Places Rated Almanac
Retirement Places Rated
Road Atlas Britain
Road Atlas Europe
Washington, D.C., with Kids
Wonderful Weekends from Boston
Wonderful Weekends from New York City
Wonderful Weekends from San Francisco
Wonderful Weekends from Los Angeles

WHEREVER YOU TRAVEL, *H*ELP IS NEVER FAR AWAY.

From planning your trip to providing travel assistance along the way, American Express® Travel Service Offices are always there to help you do more.

Provence & the Riviera

AIX-EN-PROVENCE
L'Agence (R)
15 Cours Mirabeau
(33) (4) 42269393

CANNES
American Express Travel Service
8 Rue Des Belges
(33) (4) 93381587

MARSEILLE
Canebiere Voyages (R)
39 La Canebiere
(33) (4) 91137121

NICE
American Express Travel Service
11 Promenade Des Anglais
(33) (4) 93165348

Travel
www.americanexpress.com/travel

American Express Travel Service Offices are found in central locations throughout Provence and the Riviera.